Grammar and Writing

Student Edition

First Edition

Christie Curtis

Mary Hake

Houghton Mifflin Harcourt Publishers, Inc.

Grammar and Writing 8

First Edition

Student Edition

ISBN-13: 978-1-4190-9858-1
ISBN-10: 1-4190-9858-6

©2010 Houghton Mifflin Harcourt Publishers, Inc.

All rights reserved. No part of this publication may be reproduced or transmitted in any form or by any means, electronic or mechanical, including photocopying, recording, taping, or any information storage and retrieval system, without permission in writing from the Publisher.

Houghton Mifflin Harcourt Publishers, Inc.
181 Ballardvale Street
Wilmington, MA 01887

http://saxonhomeschool.com

Printed in the United States of America.

3 4 5 6 7 8 0982 16 15 14

4500462579

Contents

	Introduction	1
Lesson 1	Four Types of Sentences • Simple Subjects and Simple Predicates	2
Lesson 2	Complete Sentences, Sentence Fragments, and Run-on Sentences	9
Lesson 3	Action Verbs • Diagramming the Simple Subject and Simple Predicate	16
Lesson 4	Nouns: Proper, Concrete, Abstract, and Collective	22
Lesson 5	Present and Past Tense of Regular Verbs	29
Lesson 6	Helping Verbs	36
Lesson 7	Singular, Plural, Compound, and Possessive Nouns • Noun Gender	40
Lesson 8	Future Tense	45
Lesson 9	Capitalization: The Pronoun *I*, Poetry, Titles, Outlines Quotations	51
Lesson 10	Irregular Plural Nouns, Part 1	58
Lesson 11	Irregular Plural Nouns, Part 2	63
Lesson 12	Irregular Verbs, Part 1: Be, Have, Do	70
Lesson 13	Four Principal Parts of Verbs	75
Lesson 14	Prepositions	80
Lesson 15	The Perfect Tenses	88

Lesson 16	Verbals: The Gerund as a Subject	93
Lesson 17	The Progressive Verb Forms	99
Lesson 18	Linking Verbs	106
Lesson 19	The Infinitive as a Subject	112
Lesson 20	Phrases and Clauses	117
Lesson 21	The Direct Object • Diagramming a Direct Object	123
Lesson 22	Capitalization: People Titles, Family Words, and School Subjects	129
Lesson 23	Descriptive Adjectives • Proper Adjectives	134
Lesson 24	The Limiting Adjective • Diagramming Adjectives	140
Lesson 25	Capitalization: Areas, Religions, Greetings • No Capital Letter	146
Lesson 26	Transitive and Intransitive Verbs	153
Lesson 27	Active or Passive Voice	158
Lesson 28	Object of the Preposition • The Prepositional Phrase	164
Lesson 29	The Prepositional Phrase as an Adjective • Diagramming	170
Lesson 30	Indirect Objects	176
Lesson 31	The Period • Abbreviations	182
Lesson 32	Proofreading Symbols, Part 1	190
Lesson 33	Coordinating Conjunctions	196
Lesson 34	Compound Subjects and Predicates • Diagramming Compounds	201
Lesson 35	Correlative Conjunctions	207
Lesson 36	Diagramming Predicate Nominatives	212
Lesson 37	Noun Case	219

Lesson 38	Diagramming Predicate Adjectives	226
Lesson 39	Comparison Adjectives	231
Lesson 40	Irregular Comparison Adjectives	238
Lesson 41	The Comma, Part 1: Dates, Addresses, Series	244
Lesson 42	Appositives	251
Lesson 43	The Comma, Part 2: Direct Address, Appositives, Academic Degrees	256
Lesson 44	Overused Adjectives • Unnecessary Articles	263
Lesson 45	Verbals as Adjectives: Infinitives and Participles	269
Lesson 46	Pronouns and Antecedents	276
Lesson 47	The Comma, Part 3: Greetings, Closings, Last Name First, Introductory/Interrupting Elements, Afterthoughts, Clarity	283
Lesson 48	Personal Pronouns	291
Lesson 49	Irregular Verbs, Part 2	298
Lesson 50	Nominative Pronoun Case	304
Lesson 51	Objective Pronoun Case	310
Lesson 52	Personal Pronoun Case Forms	317
Lesson 53	Possessive Pronouns and Possessive Adjectives • Diagramming Pronouns	323
Lesson 54	Dependent and Independent Clauses • Subordinating Conjunctions	330
Lesson 55	Gerunds Versus Participles and Verbs • Gerund Phrases	336
Lesson 56	Participle Phrases • Diagramming Participle and Gerund Phrases	343
Lesson 57	Reflexive and Intensive Personal Pronouns	349

Lesson 58	The Comma, Part 4: Descriptive Adjectives, Dependent Clauses	356
Lesson 59	Compound Sentences • Coordinating Conjunctions	362
Lesson 60	The Comma, Part 5: Compound Sentences, Direct Quotations	369
Lesson 61	Relative Pronouns • Diagramming the Dependent Clause	375
Lesson 62	The Comma, Part 6: Nonessential Parts • *That* or *Which*	384
Lesson 63	Pronoun Usage: Appositions and Comparisons	391
Lesson 64	Interrogative Pronouns	397
Lesson 65	Quotation Marks, Part 1	405
Lesson 66	Quotation Marks, Part 2	410
Lesson 67	Demonstrative Pronouns	416
Lesson 68	Indefinite Pronouns	421
Lesson 69	Italics or Underline	428
Lesson 70	Irregular Verbs, Part 3	434
Lesson 71	Irregular Verbs, Part 4	439
Lesson 72	Irregular Verbs, Part 5	444
Lesson 73	The Exclamation Mark • The Question Mark • The Dash	449
Lesson 74	Subject-Verb Agreement, Part 1	456
Lesson 75	Subject-Verb Agreement, Part 2	462
Lesson 76	Subject-Verb Agreement, Part 3	468
Lesson 77	Subject-Verb Agreement, Part 4	475
Lesson 78	Negatives • Double Negatives	481

Lesson 79	The Hyphen: Compound Nouns, Numbers	488
Lesson 80	Adverbs that Tell "How"	494
Lesson 81	Using the Adverb *Well*	500
Lesson 82	The Hyphen: Compound Adjectives	506
Lesson 83	Adverbs that Tell "Where"	513
Lesson 84	Word Division	518
Lesson 85	Adverbs that Tell "When"	524
Lesson 86	Adverbs that Tell "How Much"	529
Lesson 87	Comparison Adverbs	536
Lesson 88	The Semicolon	543
Lesson 89	Descriptive Adverbs • Adverb Usage	549
Lesson 90	The Colon	556
Lesson 91	Proofreading Symbols, Part 2	562
Lesson 92	The Prepositional Phrase as an Adverb • Diagramming	568
Lesson 93	Preposition or Adverb? • Preposition Usage	574
Lesson 94	The Infinitive as an Adverb • The Infinitive Phrase • Diagramming	580
Lesson 95	The Apostrophe: Possessives	587
Lesson 96	The Apostrophe: Contractions, Omitting Digits and Letters	593
Lesson 97	The Adjective Clause • The Adverb Clause • The Noun Clause	599
Lesson 98	Diagramming the Noun Clause	604
Lesson 99	The Complex Sentence • The Compound-complex Sentence • Diagramming the Adverb Clause	610

Lesson 100	Parallel Structure	617
Lesson 101	Sentence Conciseness	625
Lesson 102	Dangling or Misplaced Modifiers	632
Lesson 103	Parentheses • Brackets	639
Lesson 104	Interjections	645
Lesson 105	Dictionary Information about a Word	651
Lesson 106	The Subjunctive Mood	657
Lesson 107	Spelling Rules: Silent Letters *k, g, w, t, d,* and *c*	663
Lesson 108	Spelling Rules: Silent Letters *p, b, l, u, h, n* and *gh*	668
Lesson 109	Spelling Rules: Suffixes, Part 1	673
Lesson 110	Spelling Rules: Suffixes, Part 2	680
Lesson 111	Spelling Rules: *ie* or *ei*	685
	Appendix	691
	Index	709

Introduction

Welcome to a language arts program designed for easy reading and instruction. Behind this program is a team of dedicated teachers who care about your success and desire to present incremental teaching material in a simple format.

This program consists of a series of **daily lessons**, **review sets**, and **tests** that are carefully sequenced to develop a variety of skills and concepts. We include lessons on capitalization, punctuation, parts of speech, sentence structure, spelling rules, and correct word usage, all with a focus on improving your writing.

To increase your understanding, you will learn to diagram sentences. Diagramming a sentence, like doing a puzzle, exercises your brain and helps you to see the structure of the sentence and the function of its parts. Knowing how to diagram an English sentence will make your future study of foreign languages much easier. It will also help you with correct word usage and punctuation as you write.

Because of the incremental nature of this program, **it is essential that the lessons be taught in order, that all review sets are completed, and that no lessons are skipped.**

In addition to the daily lessons, the program includes a series of **writing lessons**. These are designed to guide you through the process of composing a complete essay. Also included are weekly **dictations** for practice in spelling and punctuation. You will also be asked to keep a journal; the program contains suggested **journal topics**.

Before you start your lesson, you need not wait for teacher instruction because you know how to begin each day:

MONDAY—Find your weekly dictation in the appendix and copy it to practice for your Friday test.

TUESDAY, WEDNESDAY, THURSDAY—Find your journal topic in the appendix and begin writing.

FRIDAY—Look over your dictation to prepare for your dictation test.

The team is especially excited about this book, for it honors our great nation—the United States of America. Many of the lessons include examples from our history, our constitution, and our heroes. We wish to arouse spirits of gratitude and patriotism as we present the material.

No matter what your goals may be, mastery of the English language is one of the most valuable tools you can possess. It is our hope that this program provides you with a strong foundation not only for future language arts studies but for a lifetime of satisfying and successful writing.

Best wishes!

LESSON 1

Four Types of Sentences • Simple Subjects and Simple Predicates

> **Dictation or Journal Entry**
>
> **Vocabulary:** In this book, we will learn the definitions of many words related to government. Do you know the difference between a *direct democracy* and an *indirect democracy*?
>
> In a *direct democracy*, the people govern themselves. For example, the Congregational church denomination determines church policy by *direct democracy*, for the members themselves, rather than representatives, make all necessary decisions.
>
> In an *indirect democracy*, the citizens do not directly handle the affairs of the government. The United States has an *indirect democracy*; the people elect representatives (persons who speak and act for others) to make known their desires in government.

A group of words that expresses a complete thought is called a sentence. There are **four types of sentences.**

Declarative A **declarative sentence** makes a statement and ends with a period.

The Constitution of the United States of America became the supreme law of the nation on March 4, 1789.

The United States has the oldest continuous constitutional government in the world, directed by a written constitution.

Interrogative An **interrogative sentence** asks a question and ends with a question mark:

Why do we not have a direct democracy?

When was the Constitution written?

Imperative An **imperative sentence** expresses a command or a request and ends with a period, or an exclamation mark if the command indicates strong feeling:

Give the historical background of the Constitution.

Please become familiar with the supreme law of the nation.

Help me!

Exclamatory An **exclamatory sentence** shows excitement or strong feeling and ends with an exclamation point:

Wow, March 4, 1789, was an important date!

I passed the history test!

Example 1 Tell whether the following sentences are declarative, interrogative, imperative, or exclamatory.

(a) What are the Articles of the Confederation and Perpetual Union?

(b) Don't let the American flag touch the ground.

(c) We call the United States government a central government, federal government, or national government.

(d) Yippee! The Fourth of July is almost here!

Solution (a) This is an **interrogative** sentence because it asks a question and ends with a question mark.

(b) This sentence commands you to do something, and it ends with a period. Therefore, it is **imperative.**

(c) This **declarative** sentence makes a statement and ends with a period.

(d) These **exclamatory** sentences show strong feeling and end with an exclamation point.

A sentence has two main parts: (1) the subject and (2) the predicate. The subject is the part that tells who or what the sentence is about. The predicate is the part that tells something about the subject. The sentences below have been divided into their two main parts—subjects and predicates.

COMPLETE SUBJECT	COMPLETE PREDICATE
Loud, happy crowds	gather.
The American flag.....	is leading the band.
Kids in red vests........	sell peanuts and popcorn.
I..................................	love a Fourth of July parade!

The complete (whole) subject or predicate may consist of a single word or of many words. However, a subject or predicate consisting of many words always has an essential part that we call the *simple subject* or *simple predicate.*

Simple Subject	Simple Predicate
crowds	gather
flag	is leading
Kids	sell
I	love

Simple Subject The main word or words in a sentence that tell *who* or *what* is doing or being something, or *who* or *what* the sentence is about, is called the **simple subject.** In the sentences below, we have italicized the simple subjects.

In 1776, the thirteen *colonies* were disenchanted with British rule.

Delegates from the colonies gathered in Philadelphia, Pennsylvania.

Understood Subject In an imperative sentence, the subject, you, is understood:

(You) Study the Great Compromise.

(You) Please research the Declaration of Independence.

Example 2 Write the simple subject of each sentence.

(a) The colonists fought for their independence.

(b) Remember the fervency of the patriots.

Solution (a) Who or what fought for their independence? The colonists did, so **colonists** is the simple subject.

(b) This is an imperative sentence. Therefore, the subject, **you,** is understood.

Simple Predicate The **simple predicate** is the verb. A verb expresses action or being. We have underlined the simple predicates of the sentences below.

BEING VERB: The *colonies* <u>became</u> independent states.

ACTION VERB: The *Continental Congress* <u>created</u> a

feeble confederation in 1781.

Notice that sometimes the simple predicate contains more than one word as in the sentences below. We call this the *verb phrase*.

The *Articles of Confederation* <u>had dissatisfied</u> the young nation.

We <u>have been studying</u> the history of our country.

Reversed Order Sometimes the order of the subject and predicate is reversed as in these sentences:

From our founding fathers <u>came</u> a brilliant *constitution*.

Here <u>comes</u> the *parade!*

<u>Were</u> there many *trumpeters* in the band?

Split Predicate In interrogative sentences, we usually find parts of the predicate split by the subject as in these sentences:

<u>Did</u> *you* <u>hear</u> about the Great Compromise?

<u>Shall</u> *we* <u>discuss</u> the problems of the confederation?

<u>Will</u> the *delegate* from New Jersey <u>speak</u> first?

Example 3 Write the simple predicate of each sentence.
(a) The delegates had been arguing for hours.

(b) Into the meeting hall walked George Washington.

(c) What compromises did the delegates make?

Solution (a) *Delegates* is the subject. **Had been arguing** is the simple predicate because it describes the action of the delegates.

(b) *George Washington* is the subject. **Walked** is the simple predicate because it tell what George Washington did.

(c) The subject is *delegates*. **Did make** is the simple predicate because it tells what the delegates did.

Practice For a–d, write whether the sentence is declarative, imperative, interrogative, or exclamatory.

a. James Madison, Gouverneur Morris, Benjamin Franklin, Alexander Hamilton, and George Washington were geniuses!

b. The legislative, executive, and judicial branches comprise the federal government.

c. Please explain the function of each branch of government.

d. Have you memorized the Preamble?

For e–g, write the simple subject of the sentence. Then write and underline the simple predicate.

e. Does the legislative branch make the laws of the land?

f. The judicial branch must explain the laws.

g. From the executive branch comes law enforcement.

Replace each blank with the correct vocabulary word.

h. In a(n) _____ _____, people vote for a state assembly person to represent them.

i. Each person in the _____ _____ has an opportunity to vote on every issue.

More Practice See Master Worksheets.

Review Set 1 Choose the correct word to complete sentences 1–10.

1. In a(n) (direct, indirect) democracy the citizens govern themselves; they are not represented by others.

2. A(n) (declarative, interrogative) sentence makes a statement and ends with a period.

3. A(n) (declarative, interrogative) sentence ends with a question mark.

4. A(n) (interrogative, imperative) sentence expresses a command or a request.

5. A(n) (exclamatory, declarative) sentence shows strong feeling.

6. The simple (subject, predicate) tells *who* or *what* is doing or being something.

7. The simple (subject, predicate) is the verb.

8. In an imperative sentence, the (subject, predicate) "you" may be understood and not stated.

9. A (subject, verb) expresses action or being.

10. The simple predicate is the (subject, verb).

Replace each blank with the correct word to complete sentences 11–15.

11. A sentence begins with a _____ letter.

12. A(n) _____ sentence ends with an exclamation point.

13. A(n) _____ sentence ends with a question mark.

14. Declarative sentences end with a _____.

15. A sentence expresses a _____ thought.

For 16–19, write whether each sentence is declarative, interrogative, exclamatory, or imperative.

16. Have you ever read *Johnny Tremain*?

17. John Newbery was a famous publisher and seller of children's books in England.

18. List the Newbery Medal and Newbery Honor books that you have read.

19. The novel *Johnny Tremain* won the Newbery medal!

For 20–28, write the simple subject and simple predicate of each sentence. Then underline the simple predicate.

20. In 1943, *Johnny Tremain* was awarded the John Newbery Medal.

21. Describe the character of Johnny Tremain.

22. From the author Esther Forbes comes an exciting and dangerous story.

23. Was life turbulent before the Revolutionary War?

24. There goes James Otis!

25. Johnny Tremain is a young apprentice silversmith.

26. Here comes John Adams!

27. Does Johnny participate in the Boston Tea Party?

28. Will Johnny fight in the Battle of Lexington?

29. Unscramble these words to make a declarative sentence:
    attic   the   sleep   the   in   apprentices

30. Unscramble these words to make an imperative sentence: up   wake   now

LESSON 2

Complete Sentences, Sentence Fragments, and Run-on Sentences

> **Dictation or Journal Entry**
>
> **Vocabulary:** Notice the difference between the two similar words, *advert* and *avert*.
>
> *Advert* means to call attention to something. When writing the Constitution, the founding fathers *adverted* to the flaws in the Articles of Confederation.
>
> *Avert* means to turn away. The founding fathers *averted* complaints from the small states by providing equal representation in the Senate.

Complete Sentences A **complete sentence** expresses a complete thought. It has both a subject and a predicate. The following are **complete sentences**. Simple subjects are italicized, and simple predicates are underlined.

Citizens <u>belonged</u> to the state in which they lived.

States <u>vied</u> for power.

<u>Did</u> the *people* <u>call</u> themselves Americans?

<u>Explain</u> the flaws in the Articles of Confederation.

Notice that the sentence above, "Explain the flaws in the Articles of Confederation," does not appear to have a subject. It is an imperative sentence, a command. The subject, *you*, is understood.

(*You*) <u>Explain</u> the flaws in the Articles of Confederation.

Sentence Fragments A **fragment** is a piece of a sentence that lacks a subject or a verb or both. When a sentence fragment fails to tell us who or what is doing the action, it is missing the subject:

Will handle all governmental affairs. (who or what?)

If we identify the subject, and we do not know what it is doing, the expression is missing a verb:

The people in a direct democracy. (do what?)

Other errors that result in fragments are leaving out punctuation marks or using the *to* form and *ing* form of the verb as in this sentence:

The citizens electing representatives. (*ing* form of verb)

Officials to represent the people. (*to* form of verb)

We can correct these sentence fragments by adding subjects and/or verbs.

Example 1 Make a complete sentence from each sentence fragment.

(a) Handle all governmental affairs.

(b) The people in a direct democracy.

(c) The citizens electing representatives.

Solution (a) We add a subject to tell who or what "handle all governmental affairs." There is more than one correct answer.

Elected *officials* handle all governmental affairs.

(b) We might add an action verb telling what "the people in a direct democracy" do.

The people in a direct democracy <u>govern</u> themselves.

We might also add a being verb to tell who "the people in a direct democracy" are.

The people in a direct democracy <u>are</u> the governing body.

(c) Without a helping verb, the *ing* verb form, *electing*, creates a sentence fragment. So, we add a helping verb, <u>are</u>.

The citizens <u>are electing</u> representatives.

Run-on Sentences A sentence is complete only if it expresses a complete thought. Two complete thoughts written or spoken as one sentence without proper punctuation or connecting words is called a **run-on sentence**.

RUN-ON SENTENCE:
There were no presidents or courts under the Articles of Confederation each state had one vote in Congress.

TWO COMPLETE SENTENCES:
There were no presidents or courts under the Articles of Confederation. Each state had one vote in Congress.

If we use a comma instead of a period, or if we omit the joining words or punctuation between sentences, we have a run-on sentence.

> RUN-ON SENTENCE:
> Congress could not tax the people, they asked the states for financial support.

> ONE COMPLETE SENTENCE:
> Congress could not tax the people, so they asked the states for financial support.

We correct run-on sentences by inserting punctuation and/or connecting words.

Example 2 Correct this run-on sentence:

> Congress could print or coin money the states could print or coin money as well.

Solution We add a comma and a connecting word to make this a complete sentence.

> **Congress could print or coin money, but the states could print or coin money as well.**

Solution We can also correct this run-on sentence by adding a period and a capital letter to make two complete sentences.

> **Congress could print or coin money. The states could print or coin money as well.**

Practice For a–c, tell whether each expression is a sentence fragment, run-on sentence, or complete sentence.

a. A big mix-up over money under the Articles of Confederation.

b. Congress could not control foreign trade the states quarreled about it.

c. The states could break the treaties that Congress made with other countries.

d. Rewrite and correct this run-on sentence. There is more than one answer.

Congress could ask for an army it could not make men join.

e. Rewrite and correct this sentence fragment. There is more than one answer.

A great need for a stronger central government.

Vocabulary: Replace each blank with the correct word.

f. History books _____ to the role James Madison played in writing the Constitution.

g. Through compromise, George Washington and his fellow delegates tried to _____ chaos and discontent among the states.

More Practice

For 1–12, write whether the expression is a complete sentence, sentence fragment, or run-on sentence.

1. Larger states with higher populations.

2. People argued.

3. It wasn't fair, big states wanted more votes.

4. Would have more votes?

5. Each state has two representatives in the Senate.

6. Larger states insisting, "Not fair!"

7. The Senate provided equal representation, the House of Representatives provided representation by population.

8. This was the Great Compromise, it succeeded.

9. Vote now.

10. Students to understand their government.

11. Against regulating the slave trade, taxing exports, and ratifying treaties with foreign governments without a two-thirds vote of the Senate.

12. The Commercial Compromise addressed slave trade, exports, and treaties.

Rewrite 13–15, making a complete sentence from each sentence fragment. Answers may vary.

13. Finally agreed to ratify the Constitution.

14. The framers of our Constitution.

15. Any powers not named in the Constitution belonging to states and people.

Rewrite 16–18, correcting each run-on sentence. Answers will vary.

16. The Federalists favored strong central government the Antifederalists favored strong state government.

17. Ten states ratified the Constitution it was adopted.

18. Many states wanted a "Bill of Rights" these personal liberties were added to the Constitution in 1791.

Review Set 2

*Numbers in parentheses indicate the lesson in which the concept was introduced.

Choose the correct word to complete sentences 1–10.

1. The United States has a(n) (direct, indirect) democracy; citizens elect representatives to govern.
(1)

2. (Avert, Admit, Advert) means "to call attention to something."
(2)

3. When a group of words fails to tell who or what is doing the action, it is missing a (subject, predicate).
(2)

4. A (declarative, run-on) sentence contains two or more complete thoughts written or spoken as one without proper punctuation.
(1, 2)

5. A sentence (subject, predicate) expresses action or being.
(1)

6. A (complete, run-on) sentence contains both a subject and a predicate and has proper punctuation.
(2)

7. We can correct run-on sentences by adding punctuation and/or (descriptive, connecting) words.
(2)

8. If a sentence fragment fails to tell us what the subject is doing or being, it is missing a (subject, verb).
(2)

9. The simple (subject, predicate) is the verb.
(2)

10. A(n) (imperative, interrogative, exclamatory) sentence asks a question.
(1)

11. Which sentence is imperative? Choose A or B.
(1)
  A. Fetch some drinking water.
  B. Johnny asked Dove and Dusty to fetch some water.

12. Unscramble these words to make an interrogative sentence:

will   when   marry   Johnny

13. Unscramble these words to make a declarative sentence:

be   will   bride   his   Cilla

For 14–16, write whether the expression is a complete sentence or a sentence fragment.

14. Reading verses from the Bible.

15. Mr. Lapham warned Johnny about his pride.

16. The immediate effect on Johnny.

For 17 and 18, write whether each sentence is a complete sentence or a run-on sentence.

17. Cilla and Isannah Lapham taunt Johnny his ears turn red.

18. Both Dorcas and Madge Lapham were older than Johnny.

Write the simple subject of sentences 19–22.

19. Hurry.

20. John Hancock orders a sugar basin.

21. There walks the richest man in town.

22. Does Johnny recognize little Jehu?

Write the simple predicate in sentences 23–26.

23. Little Jehu holds John Hancock's horse by the bridle.

24. Keep that horse away from the flowers.

25. Can you finish the basin by Monday?

26. Into the shop hurries the apprentice.

27. Rewrite and correct this run-on sentence. There is more than one answer.

Johnny expresses his surprise Mr. Lapham has fashioned the original sugar and creamer set.

28. Rewrite and correct this sentence fragment. There is more
(2) than one answer.

Marco returning from Washington D. C.

29. Rewrite and correct this sentence fragment. There is more
(2) than one answer.

Spent all his money on souvenirs.

30. Write the simple subject of this sentence:
(1) There go the loud, long-necked geese.

LESSON 3

Action Verbs • Diagramming the Simple Subject and Simple Predicate

> **Dictation or Journal Entry**
>
> **Vocabulary:** The Latin root *bell-* means "war," as in the familiar word *belligerent.*
>
> *Bellicose* means warlike, aggressive, and quarrelsome. The *bellicose* colonists demanded a stronger central government after the Articles of Confederation failed.
>
> *Antebellum* refers to times before a war, especially the American Civil War. Some Southern plantation owners pined for the *antebellum* society of the past.

Action Verbs We remember that a complete sentence contains a subject and a verb. The verb tells what the subject is or does. An **action verb** describes what the subject does, did, or will do. In the sentence below, *ratified* is the action verb telling what the states did.

Every state <u>ratified</u> the Constitution by 1790.

Sometimes a sentence contains more than one action verb. In the sentence below, *discussed* and *accepted* are two action verbs telling what the states did.

Each state <u>discussed</u> and <u>accepted</u> the terms of the document.

Example 1 Identify each action verb in these sentences.

(a) The Preamble proclaims the purpose of the Constitution.

(b) The people desire a better form of government.

Solution (a) The action verb, **proclaims,** tells what the Preamble does.

(b) The action verb, **desire,** tells what the people do.

Improving Our Writing We can make our writing more vivid and accurate by using descriptive and precise action verbs. Consider these two sentences:

Voters <u>went</u> to the polls.

Voters <u>hurried</u> to the polls.

We notice that the verb *hurried* gives a clearer picture of how the voters went to the polls. *Walked, drove, sauntered, dashed,* and *rushed* are also descriptive action verbs. We select the action verb that most precisely depicts the behavior or action being described.

Example 2 Replace the action verb in this sentence with one that might be more precise or descriptive. Consider the different possibilities.

A politician <u>talks</u> for ten minutes.

Solution Our answers will vary. Here are some possibilities:

A politician **argues** for ten minutes.

A politician **shouts** for ten minutes.

A politician **whispers** for ten minutes.

Diagramming Simple Subjects and Simple Predicates

In Lesson 2, we identified simple subjects and simple predicates. Now, we will learn to **diagram** the simple subject and simple predicate of a sentence according to this pattern:

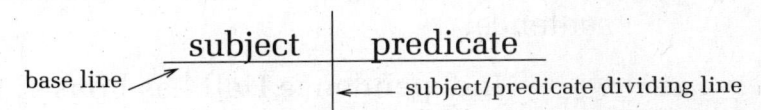

```
            subject  |  predicate
base line  ↗         ↑
                     ← subject/predicate dividing line
```

Subject and predicate sit on a horizontal "base line" and are divided by a vertical line that passes through the base line.

Below, we diagram the simple subject and simple predicate of this sentence: Citizens want peace and fairness.

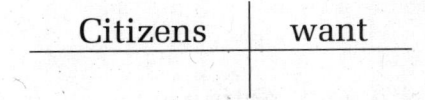

```
Citizens  |  want
```

We place the simple subject on the left and the simple predicate on the right. We separate the subject and predicate with a vertical line.

If the subject is understood, as in an imperative sentence, we place *you* in parentheses on the left like this:

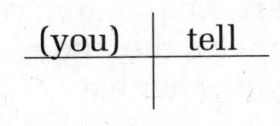

```
(you)  |  tell
```

Tell the truth.

Example 3   Diagram the simple subject and simple predicate of this sentence: The Liberty Bell pealed the news of national independence in 1776.

Solution   The "who or what" (subject) of the sentence is *Liberty Bell*, so we place it on the left. "Pealed" tells what the Liberty Bell did; it is the simple predicate, so we place it on the right.

| **Liberty Bell** | **pealed** |

We remember that a simple predicate is not always an action verb. It can also show "being."

The Liberty Bell <u>is</u> a symbol of our independence.

Some simple predicates consist of more than one word.

The *bell* <u>had been cast</u> in London.

Example 4   Diagram the simple subject and simple predicate of this sentence:

Independence Hall has housed the Liberty Bell.

Solution   The simple predicate of this sentence is "has housed." We ask ourselves, "*What* has housed?" The answer is the subject, *Independence Hall*. Our diagram looks like this:

| **Independence Hall** | has housed |

Practice   Write each action verb in sentences a and b.

  a. The Constitution protects the rights of United States citizens for all time.

  b. The founding fathers created and established two houses of legislature.

  c. Write an action verb that might be more descriptive to replace the underlined verb in this sentence: Miss Molly <u>drinks</u> her tea.

Diagram the simple subject and simple predicate of sentences d and e.

  d. The people elect four hundred thirty-five members to the House of Representatives.

e. Members of the House of Representatives must be at least twenty-five years of age.

For f–h, replace each blank with the correct vocabulary word.

f. The Latin root meaning "war" is _____.

g. The British monarch viewed the colonists as _____ and rebellious.

h. The word _____ means "before the war."

More Practice Write each action verb in sentences 1–5.

1. Members of the House of Representatives must have resided in the United States as citizens for at least seven years.

2. Each state discusses and determines the residential requirements of its representatives.

3. Vote today for your representative.

4. Voters replace the entire House of Representatives every two years.

5. Members of the House serve two-year terms.

Diagram the simple subject and simple predicate of sentences 6–12.

6. The population of the state determines the number of representatives.

7. Have you ever run for a political office?

8. Run for office, please.

9. Did James Wu win his election?

10. George Washington was nominated as the country's first President.

11. Now, each member of the House of Representatives represents approximately 620,000 people.

12. Give the President your support.

Review set 3 Choose the correct word to complete sentences 1–5.

1. Representatives speak and act for others in a(n) (direct, indirect) democracy.
(1)

2. (Avert, Alert, Advert) means "to turn away."
(2)

3. (Antebellum, Bellicose, Avert) means warlike, or aggressive.
(3)

4. An action verb tells what the subject (does, is, wants).
(3)

5. The simple predicate is the (subject, verb).
(1)

Write each action verb in sentences 6–9.

6. Loryn prepared for a quiz on *Johnny Tremain*.
(3)

7. John Hancock inherited his wealth from his uncle.
(3)

8. Did John Hancock give the apprentices any money?
(3)

9. From the kitchen came rye bread, dried apples, and cold meat pie.
(3)

For 10–12, replace the action verb in each sentence with one that might be more accurate or descriptive. There are many possibilities.

10. Cilla and Johnny go to the end of the wharf.
(3)

11. They talk along the way.
(3)

12. An artist made a picture of the wharf.
(3)

For 13–15, make a complete sentence from each sentence fragment. Answers will vary.

13. Matthew Cheng describing Johnny's mother.
(2)

14. Contributed by Lauren Chumen.
(2)

15. When Estee entered the classroom.
(2)

For 16–18, correct each run-on sentence. Answers may vary.

16. Johnny's mother gave him a Lyte cup this proved his relationship to Merchant.
(2)

(2) **17.** The cup had the Lyte motto this was "Let there be Lyte."

18. Johnny lets Mr. Lapham sleep he wakes him after an hour.
(2)

For 19–21, write whether the expression is a sentence fragment, a run-on sentence, or a complete sentence.

19. Completing the chapter titled "The Pride of Your Power."
(2)

20. Mr. Lapham fashions a beautiful sugar basin for John Hancock.
(2)

21. Johnny dislikes his own work he visits the silversmith Paul Revere for advice.
(2)

For 22–25, write whether each sentence is declarative, interrogative, imperative, or exclamatory.

22. Does Johnny accept Paul Revere's offer?
(1)

23. Johnny owes much to the Lytes.
(1)

24. You want me to work for you!
(1)

25. Please fetch more coal for the furnace.
(1)

Diagram the simple subject and simple predicate of sentences 26–30.

26. Can we avert this disaster?
(3)

27. Mr. Lapham warns Johnny about pride.
(3)

28. From heaven would come punishment.
(3)

29. Stop!
(3)

30. Must we rest on Sundays?
(3)

LESSON 4 Nouns: Proper, Concrete, Abstract, and Collective

> **Dictation or Journal Entry**
> **Vocabulary:**
>
> *Bicameral* is a government term meaning, "having two branches, chambers, or houses." The legislature of the United States is a *bicameral* system consisting of the House of Representatives and the Senate.
>
> *Impeachment* is the process of bringing formal charges against a public official. The sole power of *impeachment* is given to the House of Representatives.

Proper Nouns   We remember that a noun is a person, place, or thing. A noun may be common or proper. A *common noun* does not name a specific person, place, or thing. A **proper noun** does name a specific person, place, or thing and requires a capital letter.

Common Noun	Proper Noun
legislature	House of Representatives
senator	Senator Brown
sea	Salton Sea
holiday	Independence Day
document	U. S. Constitution
month	March

Common Nouns Within Proper Nouns   When a common noun such as "avenue," "college," "mountain," "family," or "lake" is a part of a proper noun, we capitalize it as in the examples below.

Common Noun	Proper Noun
avenue	First Avenue
college	Boston College
channel	English Channel
family	Cheung Family
lake	Lake Erie
mountains	Sierra Nevada Mountains
hemisphere	Eastern Hemisphere

Small Words Within Proper Nouns   When the following small words are parts of a proper noun, we do not capitalize them unless they are the initial or final word:

a, an, and, at, but, by, for, from,

if, in, into, of, on, the, to, with

Notice the examples below.

>*All Quiet on the Western Front*
>City of Hope
>Straits of Magellan
>House of Lords
>Speaker of the House
>"Stars and Stripes Forever"

Example 1 Capitalize proper nouns in these sentences as needed.

(a) Yes, gouverneur morris wrote the u. s. constitution in its final form.

(b) Have you read *the federalist papers?*

(c) The adams family served the government of the united states in several different capacities.

(d) The jews celebrate yom kippur.

Solution (a) We capitalize **Gouverneur Morris** because he is a specific person. We capitalize **U. S. Constitution** because it is a specific document.

(b) *The Federalist Papers* is a proper noun, for it is the title of a group of writings by Alexander Hamilton and others.

(c) **Adams Family** is a specific family and needs capital letters. Also, **United States** is a specific country.

(d) **Jews** is capitalized because it is a group of people with a distinctive religion. **Yom Kippur** is a specific holiday.

Concrete Nouns A **concrete noun** names a person, place, or thing. It may be either common or proper.

CONCRETE COMMON	CONCRETE PROPER
ship	Titanic
mayor	Mayor Quigley
ocean	Atlantic Ocean

Abstract Nouns An **abstract noun** names something that cannot be seen or touched. It names something that you can think about. An abstract noun can be common or proper as well.

ABSTRACT COMMON NOUNS	ABSTRACT PROPER NOUNS
day	Tuesday
religion	Judaism
holiday	Thanksgiving Day

nationality	Turkish
language	Arabic
social theory	Marxism

Example 2 For sentences a–c, write each noun and label it *C* for concrete or *A* for abstract.

(a) Priests of Catholicism practice celibacy, availability, and godliness.

(b) With courage and determination, supporters of the Constitution brought the document before the states.

(c) Did Gouverneur Morris study Latin as well as English?

Solution (a) **Priests—C; Catholicism—A; celibacy—A; availability—A; godliness—A**

(b) **courage—A; determination—A; Constitution—C; document—C; states—C**

(c) **Gouverneur Morris—C; Latin—A; English—A**

Collective Nouns A **collective noun** names a collection of persons, places, animals, or things. We list a few examples below.

PERSONS: club, Congress, jury, panel, staff, committee

ANIMALS: swarm, herd, flock, litter, gaggle, pack

PLACES: United Kingdom, South America, Southeast Asia

THINGS: collection, assortment, batch, bunch, selection

Example 3 Write each collective noun from these sentences.

(a) Congress consists of two bodies—the House of Representatives and the Senate.

(b) An interested crowd waited outside the Capitol Building to hear the final vote of the Senate.

(c) North America includes Canada and the United States.

(d) The gaggle of geese flew in formation.

Solution (a) **Congress, House of Representatives, Senate**

(b) **crowd, Senate**

(c) **North America, Canada, United States**

(d) **gaggle**

Practice For sentences a and b, write and capitalize each proper noun.

a. During the american revolution, the colonists referred to british soldiers as redcoats.

b. The bellicose boston colonists threw tea into boston harbor to protest british taxes on tea.

For sentences c–e, write each noun and label it *C* for concrete or *A* for abstract.

c. With dignity, the judge announced the verdict of the jury.

d. Patriotism reflects the loyalty of citizens.

e. Mr. Gomez treats his iguana with affection.

Write each collective noun that you find in sentences f–h.

f. The Senate appointed a committee to examine each issue.

g. A swarm of journalists camp out in front of the White House to report the latest news.

h. Did you see that bunch of hooligans at the Boston Tea Party?

For i and j, replace each blank with the correct vocabulary word.

i. In an indirect democracy, the representatives determine whether a government official's offense necessitates his or her _____.

j. The House of Commons and the House of Lords form the _____ Parliament in England.

More Practice See Master Worksheets for more practice capitalizing proper nouns.

For 1–8, tell whether each noun is abstract or concrete.

1. freedom   2. patriot   3. independence   4. person

5. briefcase **6.** rebellion **7.** democracy **8.** tea

For sentences 9–12, write each noun and label it *C* for concrete or *A* for abstract.

9. Old Ben Franklin and young Alexander Hamilton supported the Constitution with vim and vigor.

10. With logic and patience, the representatives discussed the proposal.

11. Gouverneur Morris Of New York wrote with precision and clarity.

12. George Washington spoke with elegance.

Write each collective noun that you find in sentences 13–15.

13. The Washington Family included George and Martha.

14. The council will sponsor a team to explore the new territory.

15. Miss Casey donated to the historical society a batch of old documents from her collection.

Review Set 4 Choose the correct word to complete sentences 1–10.

1. Citizens directly handle the affairs of the government in
(1) a(n) (direct, indirect) democracy.

2. In my letter to the power company, I will (avert, advert)
(2) to our many troublesome power failures.

3. (Antebellum, Bellicose, Advert) means "before the war."
(3)

4. (Antebellum, Bellicose, Bicameral) means "having two
(4) branches, chambers, or houses."

5. A (predicate, verb, noun) is a person, place, or thing.
(4)

6. A(n) (concrete, abstract) noun cannot be seen or touched.
(4)

7. A (common, proper) noun requires a capital letter.
(4)

8. *Procrastination* is a(n) (concrete, abstract) noun.
(4)

9. *Team* and *flock* are (bellicose, collective) nouns.
(4)

10. *Glockenspiel* is a (concrete, abstract) noun.

Write and capitalize each proper noun in sentences 11–15.

11. The tallest boy in this class is jordan davis.

12. The author, esther forbes, uses metaphors to describe boston.

13. The lapham family lived on fish street.

14. It was illegal to work on sunday.

15. Did mrs. lapham send for gran' hopper, the midwife, to treat johnny's burnt hand?

For 16 and 17, replace the action verb with one that might be more precise or descriptive.

16. Elle will <u>get</u> some blueberries for the pie.

17. With a scarred hand, Johnny cannot <u>do</u> anything.

For 18–21, write whether the sentence is declarative, interrogative, exclamatory, or imperative.

18. Does Dove plan to give Johnny a cracked crucible?

19. Mr. Lapham reveals Dove's prank.

20. Forgive him.

21. I'm going to get him for that!

For 22–24, write whether the expression is a sentence fragment, run-on sentence, or complete sentence.

22. Waving a tattered white flag from a balcony on the third floor.

23. The tailor's work was done he left.

24. Appearance is not worth much in a winter snow storm.

25. Make a complete sentence from this sentence fragment:

Does not want to lose an illiterate patron.

For 26 and 27, rewrite and correct each run-on sentence.

26. Johnny enters the butcher shop the thought of
(2) slaughtering animals sickens him.

27. Johnny daydreams of Cilla he hopes to accomplish great
(2) things for her.

Diagram the simple subject and simple predicate of sentences 28–30.

28. Out of the woods dashed the bandit.
(3)

29. Sometimes Johnny's stomach growls with hunger.
(3)

30. Did someone put food in his pockets?
(3)

LESSON 5

Present and Past Tense of Regular Verbs

> **Dictation or Journal Entry**
>
> **Vocabulary:** The words *affection* and *affectation* look similar but have different meanings.
>
> *Affection* means fondness or devotion. My dog, Penny, shows her *affection* for me by sitting on my feet.
>
> *Affectation* means phoniness, pretension, and artificiality. Mr. Buffoon's *affectation* of interest in art was apparent when he could not identify a well-known painting by Picasso.

Tense means time. Verbs tell us not only what action is occurring but also when it is occurring. The form of a verb, or the verb tense, changes in order to show when the action takes place. Three simple verb tenses are present, past, and future. In this lesson, we will talk about the present and past tense of regular verbs. Later, we will review the many irregular verbs.

Present Tense The **present tense** refers to action that is happening now. We add an *s* when the subject is singular, except for when the pronoun is *I* or *you*.

PLURAL SUBJECTS AND PRONOUNS *I* AND *YOU*	SINGULAR SUBJECTS
Roosters crow.	The rooster crows.
I pack.	He packs.
We vote.	She votes.
They cheer.	The sister cheers.
You whistle.	Yumi whistles.
Jasper and he crawl.	The baby crawls.

When a verb ends in *s, x, z, ch,* or *sh*, we add *es* when the subject is singular.

PLURAL SUBJECTS AND PRONOUNS *I* AND *YOU*	SINGULAR SUBJECTS
We clash.	The militia clashes.
Bees buzz.	A bee buzzes.
Seamstresses patch.	A seamstress patches.
Cannon balls miss.	A cannon ball misses.
Arbitrators coax.	The arbitrator coaxes.

When a verb ends in a consonant and a *y*, we change the *y* to *i* and add *es* for the singular form.

PLURAL SUBJECTS AND PRONOUNS *I* AND *YOU*	SINGULAR SUBJECTS
Spies <u>pry</u>.	A spy <u>pries</u>.
The states <u>comply</u>.	A state <u>complies</u>.

Example 1 Replace each blank with the singular present tense form of the verb.

(a) You <u>reply</u>. He _____.

(b) Lonely puppies <u>cry</u>. A lonely puppy _____.

(c) Leaders <u>delay</u>. The leader _____.

(d) We <u>floss</u> our teeth. She _____ her teeth.

(e) Rulers <u>squelch</u> rebellion. A ruler _____ rebellion.

Solution (a) **replies** (Since the verb ends in a consonant and a *y*, we change the *y* to *i* and add *es*.)

(b) **cries** (Since the verb ends in a consonant and a *y*, we change the *y* to *i* and add *es*.)

(c) **delays** (We add an *s* when the subject is singular.)

(d) **flosses** (The verb ends in *s*, so we add *es*.)

(e) **squelches** (The verb ends in *ch*, so we add *es*.)

Past Tense The **past tense** shows action that has already occurred. To form the past tense of regular verbs, we add *ed*.

gawk—gawked

toss—tossed

When a one-syllable verb ends in a consonant, we double the consonant and add *ed*.

slip—slipped

hop—hopped

When a verb ends in *e*, we drop the *e* and add *ed*.

regulate—regulated

tithe—tithed

When the verb ends in *y*, we change the *y* to *i* and add *ed*.

supply—supplied

party—partied

Example 2 Write the past tense form of each verb.

(a) wrap (b) shave (c) reply

(d) pit (e) muddy (f) promote

Solution (a) **wrapped** (Since this is a short verb ending in a consonant, we double the consonant and add *ed*.)

(b) **shaved** (The verb ends in *e*, so we drop the *e* and add *ed*.)

(c) **replied** (The verb ends in *y*, so we change the *y* to *i* and add *ed*.)

(d) **pitted** (Since this is a short verb ending in a consonant, we double the consonant and add *ed*.)

(e) **muddied** (The verb ends in *y*, so we change the *y* to *i* and add *ed*.)

(f) **promoted** (The verb ends in *e*, so we drop the *e* and add *ed*.)

Errors to Avoid Do not use the present tense form for the past tense.

NO: Last week, they <u>elect</u> officers.
YES: Last week, they <u>elected</u> officers.

NO: Yesterday, we <u>drop</u> off the ballots.
YES: Yesterday, we <u>dropped</u> off the ballots.

NO: The judges <u>reply</u> earlier this morning.
YES: The judges <u>replied</u> earlier this morning.

Do not shift from past to present in the same phrase.

NO: He <u>stepped</u> out and <u>slips</u> on a banana peel.
YES: He <u>stepped</u> out and <u>slipped</u> on a banana peel.

NO: The House <u>impeached</u> and <u>removes</u> the offending public official.

YES: The House <u>impeached</u> and <u>removed</u> the offending public official.

Example 3 Choose the correct form of the verb to complete each sentence.

(a) James drew a picture of the Capitol and (paints, painted) it white.

(b) While discussing politics, we (sip, sipped) our tea and ate our cookies.

Solution (a) James drew a picture of the Capitol and **painted** it white.

(b) While discussing politics, we **sipped** our tea and ate our cookies.

Practice For a–d, replace each blank with the singular present tense form of the underlined verb.

a. Patriots <u>preach</u> zealously. That patriot _____ zealously.

b. Delegates <u>talk</u> about compromise. The delegate _____ about compromise.

c. Clerks <u>box</u> old meeting agendas. The clerk _____ old meeting agendas.

d. Reporters <u>try</u> to obtain the truth. A reporter _____ to obtain the truth.

For e–l, write the past tense form of each verb.

e. prop   f. sully   g. knot   h. raise

i. amplify   j. brake   k. drip   l. trot

For m and n, choose the correct verb form.

m. A few days ago, my dog (chews, chewed) a hole in the sofa.

n. One of our state's representatives (serves, served) as clerk of the House last term.

For o and p, replace each blank with the correct vocabulary word.

o. The candidate's opponent made an _____ of interest in the environment.

p. Did Martha Washington show much _____ for her husband?

Review set 5 Choose the correct word to complete sentences 1–5.

1. Citizens themselves make all decisions in a(n) (direct,
(1) indirect) democracy.

2. Does your paper on the Constitutional Convention (avert,
(2) alert, advert) to Benjamin Franklin's contributions?

3. The Latin root *bell-* means (before, after, war).
(3)

4. The United States has a (bellicose, bicameral,
(4) antebellum) government consisting of the House of Representatives and the Senate.

5. (Affection, Impeachment, Affectation) is fondness or
(5) devotion.

For 6–9, replace each blank with the singular present tense form of the verb.

6. Peacocks <u>cry</u>. The peacock _____.
(5)

7. Boys <u>brag</u>. Johnny Tremain _____.
(5)

8. Girls <u>comb</u> their hair. Natalie _____ her hair.
(5)

9. Students <u>study</u> hard. Tristan _____ hard.
(5)

For 10–14, replace each blank with the past tense form of the verb.

10. Benjamin Franklin (*supply*) _____ us with many
(5) wise sayings.

11. A thirsty hiker (*cup*) _____ her hands and drank
(5) from the swiftly-flowing stream.

12. Mr. Lapham (*believe*) _____ that the *Boston*
(5) *Observer* was wicked.

13. Rab (*listen*) _____ carefully to Johnny's story.
(5)

14. Long ago, people (*rely*) _____ on horses for transportation.
(5)

For 15–17, write and capitalize each proper noun.

15. What nickname did johnny tremain give to mr. tweedie?
(4)

16. Searching for employment, he wandered along fish street, dock square, and long wharf.
(4)

17. Did a great ship from sugar isles arrive at hancock's wharf on monday?
(4)

Replace each blank with the correct verb form for sentences 18 and 19.

18. Last weekend, Lavinia Lyte (*attract*) _____ attention when she arrived in Boston.
(5)

19. My friend David (present tense of *play*) _____ basketball every Saturday.
(5)

20. Make a complete sentence from this sentence fragment:
(2) Only one flaw in Lavinia's marble beauty.

21. Rewrite and correct this run-on sentence:
(2) Lavinia has black hair and dead white skin her features are clear cut.

For 22–24, write whether each expression is a sentence fragment, run-on sentence, or complete sentence.

22. The clerk asks Johnny if he can read and write Johnny says he can.
(2)

23. John Hancock refuses to hire Johnny.
(2)

24. Sends Johnny money by way of Jehu, his servant.
(2)

For 25–27, write whether the sentence is declarative, interrogative, imperative, or exclamatory.

25. Why does Johnny gorge himself with food?
(1)

26. Show me your money.
(1)

27. I don't like spiders in my soup!
(1)

Diagram the simple subject and simple predicate of sentences 28–30.

28. Drink plenty of water.
(3)

29. Does Johnny buy shoes with Hancock's money?
(3)

30. Within this book lies the secret.
(3)

LESSON 6   Helping Verbs

> **Dictation or Journal Entry**
>
> **Vocabulary:** The Latin root *plac-* means "appease," and the Latin root *pac-* means "peace" or "agree."
>
> *Placate* means to calm or satisfy. By promising a "Bill of Rights," the writers of the Constitution *placated* those who were concerned about personal liberties.
>
> A *pacifist* is a person who opposes war or violence. On moral grounds Quaker *pacifists* refused to fight against the British.

Helping Verbs   The main verb in a sentence may have one or more **helping verbs.** The main verb shows the action; the helping verbs show do not show action, but they help to form the verb tense.

> You <u>might have wondered</u> about the qualifications for a United States Senator.

In the sentence above, "wondered" is the main verb, and "might" and "have" are helping verbs. "Might have wondered" is the entire verb phrase.

Please memorize these common helping verbs:

> *is, am, are, was, were, be, being, been,*
> *has, have, had, may, might, must,*
> *can, could, do, does, did,*
> *shall, will, should, would*

Example   Write the entire verb phrase and underline each helping verb in these sentences.

(a) The Senate is composed of one hundred members.

(b) Two Senators will represent each state.

(c) Each state must have wanted equal representation.

(d) Could that Senator have cast his vote against women's suffrage?

Solution   (a) <u>is</u> composed ("Is" is a helping verb for the main verb "composed.")

(b) <u>will</u> represent

(c) <u>must</u> <u>have</u> wanted

(d) <u>Could</u> <u>have</u> cast

Practice a. Memorize the helping verbs listed in this lesson. Practice saying them *in order* (perhaps to a teacher or friend). Then write as many as you can from memory.

For sentences b–e, write the entire verb phrase and underline the helping verbs.

b. One-third of the Senators have begun a new term in the Senate.

c. Shall I list the qualifications for Senator?

d. That representative might have been hoping for two terms in Congress.

e. His defeat in the election for a second term must have disappointed him.

For f–h, replace each blank with the correct vocabulary word.

f. To _____ the small states, the Senate was created to provide equal representation.

g. The _____ refused to serve in the infantry but agreed to serve in another capacity.

h. The Latin root meaning "peace" is _____; the root meaning "appease" is _____.

More Practice See Master Worksheets.

Review set 6 Choose the correct word to complete sentences 1–5.

1. Perhaps we can (avert, alert, advert) a flood with better
(2) storm drains.

2. The Latin root meaning "war" is (*bell-, plac-, pac-*).
(3)

3. (Impeachment, Government, Democracy) is the process of
(4) bringing formal charges against a public official.

4. (Affection, Impeachment, Affectation) is phoniness, or
(5) pretension.

5. A (concrete, abstract) noun can be seen or touched.
(4)

6. Write from memory the common helping verbs listed in
(6) this lesson. Check your list by referring to the lesson.

For 7–11, write the entire verb phrase and underline each helping verb.

7. Johnny has purchased gifts for Cilla and Isannah.
(6)

8. The girl's response might have broken his heart.
(6)

9. He had been sobbing on his mother's grave.
(6)

10. Does Johnny visit Merchant Lyte?
(6)

11. Should we read the next chapter?
(6)

For 12–13, write and capitalize each proper noun.

12. At christ's church, mr. lapham reads from the bible.
(4)

13. The lapham family practices christianity.
(4)

For 14–16, write whether the expression is a complete sentence, a sentence fragment, or a run-on sentence.

14. Merchant Lyte treats Johnny like a beggar then Johnny
(2) mentions the Lyte cup.

15. Rab labels Merchant Lyte "crooked."
(2)

16. With Rab's shirt, jacket, and taffeta tie.
(2)

For 17 and 18, replace each blank with the singular present tense form of the verb.

17. We <u>hurry</u>. He _____.
(5)

18. You <u>miss</u> the flight. Stefan _____ the flight.
(5)

For 19 and 20, replace each blank with the past tense form of the verb.

19. The printer (ship) _____ the books yesterday.
(5)

20. Last night my dog (bury) _____ his bone.
(5)

For 21–24, write whether the noun is concrete or abstract.

21. patriotism
(4)

22. apprentice
(4)

23. Catholicism
(4)

24. broom
(4)

25. Replace the blank with the correct verb form for this sentence:
(5)

Johnny (present tense of *cry*) _____ on his mother's grave.

26. Rewrite and correct this run-on sentence:
(2)

Johnny is arrested as a thief he goes to jail.

27. Write the collective noun from this sentence: One cup was missing from the set.
(4)

28. Write whether the following sentence is declarative, exclamatory, imperative, or interrogatory: Why did Merchant Lyte accuse Johnny of stealing his coat?
(1)

Diagram the simple subject and simple predicate of sentences 29 and 30.

29. Around Rab's neck hangs a medal.
(3)

30. I might have misunderstood you.
(3)

LESSON 7

Singular, Plural, Compound, and Possessive Nouns • Noun Gender

> **Dictation or Journal Entry**
> **Vocabulary:**
> The Latin term *pro tempore* means "for the time being" or "for a little while." The Constitution provides for a president *pro tempore* to preside over the Senate in the absence of the vice president.
>
> A *writ of habeas corpus* (Latin) is a legal term meaning that a prisoner has the right to know why he or she is in jail and to be brought before a judge. The Constitution guarantees us the privilege of the *writ of habeas corpus*.

Singular or Plural Nouns are either singular or plural. A **singular noun** names only one person, place, or thing. A **plural noun** names more than one person, place, or thing.

SINGULAR NOUNS	PLURAL NOUNS
tax	taxes
war	wars
veto	vetoes
tiff	tiffs

Example 1 Tell whether each noun is singular or plural.

(a) security (b) clashes (c) parties

Solution (a) **singular** (b) **plural** (c) **plural**

Compound A noun made up of two or more words is a **compound noun**. Sometimes we write a compound noun as one word:

thumbtack, eyebrow, pigpen

Often we write compound nouns as two words:

post office, rabble rouser, house mouse

Other compound nouns are hyphenated:

daughter-in-law, merry-go-round, forget-me-nots

There is no pattern for determining whether to spell a compound noun as one word, two separate words, or one hyphenated word. We must use the dictionary.

Example 2 Write each compound noun from this list:

vice president   naturalization   attorney general
great-uncle   milestone   responsibility

Solution The compound nouns from the list above are **vice president, attorney general, great-uncle,** and **milestone.**

Possessive A **possessive noun** tells "who" or "what" owns something. Possessive nouns can be either singular or plural. The possessive form of nouns have an apostrophe and an *s* added to them:

a *Senator's* vote	the *people's* choice
the *Chief Justice's* opinion	the *computer's* monitor
somebody's absence	a *fax's* message
the *boss's* mood	*Doris's* briefcase

Usually only an apostrophe is added to *plural* nouns when they end with the letter *s*:

the *Joneses'* duplex	those *hostesses'* uniforms
those *crocodiles'* mouths	these *lawyers'* credentials
some *churches'* hymn books	the *classes'* schedules

Example 3 Write the possessive noun from each sentence.

(a) One of the Senators' requirements is that they live in the state that they represent.

(b) The term's length is six years for a Senator.

(c) The Senator responded promptly to the children's letters.

(d) Before the Seventeenth Amendment of 1913, the states' legislatures chose their Senators.

Solution (a) **Senators'** (b) **term's** (c) **children's** (d) **states'**

Noun Gender We also group nouns according to gender. In English there are four **genders**: masculine, feminine, indefinite (either sex), and neuter (no sex). Below are examples of each gender of nouns.

MASCULINE	FEMININE	INDEFINITE	NEUTER
grandfather	grandmother	grandparent	pizza
brother	sister	sibling	shoe
stallion	mare	horse	bicycle
rooster	hen	chicken	nest

Example 4 Tell whether each noun is masculine, feminine, indefinite, or neuter.

(a) teacup   (b) bull   (c) child   (d) doe

Solution (a) **neuter** (b) **masculine** (c) **indefinite** (d) **feminine**

Practice For a–d, tell whether each noun is singular or plural.
   a. mice
   b. goose
   c. Congress
   d. wharves

   e. Write each compound noun from this list:
   birthright   attorneys-at-law
   sleepyhead   encyclopedia

Write each possessive noun from sentences f–i.
   f. A mother-in-law is the mother of one's husband or wife.

   g. Neither Louis's harassment nor Geraldine's criticism kept Raiko from running for office.

   h. The hosts' coats and the hostesses' aprons were white with black trim.

   i. The Congressperson's dinner included the President's favorite—chocolate mousse.

For j–m, tell whether each noun is masculine, feminine, indefinite, or neuter.
   j. debt   k. ram   l. receptionist   m. mare

Replace each blank with the correct vocabulary word(s) to complete sentences n and o.

   n. The _____ can be suspended for prisoners in times of rebellion, invasion, or terrorist attack.

   o. During the twentieth century, the Senate began electing the senior member of the majority party as president _____, to preside over the Senate.

Review Set 7 Choose the correct word to complete sentences 1–5.
   1. By conserving water, we might (avert, alert, advert) a
   (2) serious water shortage.

   (3) 2. *Antebellum* means "before the (parade, test, war)."

3. The United States government has two branches. Therefore, it is (bellicose, bicameral, antebellum).
(4)

4. We show our (affectation, affection, impeachment) for people we love.
(5)

5. The Latin root (*pro-, plac-, bell-*) means "appease."
(6)

6. Write from memory the common helping verbs listed in Lesson 6.
(6)

7. Write each plural noun from this list: juries, tankard, boss, impostors, debts, trial, lawyer
(7)

8. Write each compound noun from this list: egg slicer, afterthought, pandemonium, landmark, contentment, rabble rouser
(7)

9. Write each possessive noun from this list: Boston's, apprentices, thieves', mother's, plans
(7)

10. Write and capitalize each proper noun in this sentence: The catskill mountains form part of the appalachian mountains, near the hudson river.
(4)

For 11–14, write whether the noun is masculine, feminine, indefinite, or neuter.

11. lawyer   **12.** wig   **13.** seamstress   **14.** father
(7)   (7)   (7)   (7)

For 15 and 16, write the entire verb phrase, underlining each helping verb.

15. A mouse must have chewed through the wall!
(6)

16. May I help you?
(6)

For 17–19, write whether the expression is a complete sentence, a sentence fragment, or a run-on sentence.

17. While eating a peanut butter and jelly sandwich with lettuce and tomato on it.
(2)

18. Johnny almost cried when Isannah kissed his burnt hand.
(2)

19. Johnny needs money he tries to sell his cup to Merchant Lyte.
(2)

20. Make a complete sentence from this sentence
(2) fragment: to make interesting sandwiches

21. Rewrite and correct this run-on sentence: Johnny rides a
(2) wild horse named Goblin soon the horse and the boy become well known around Boston.

For 22–24, tell whether the noun is concrete or abstract.

22. beliefs   **23.** Goblin   **24.** treason
(4)   (4)   (4)

25. Write each collective noun from this list: club, member,
(4) staff, committee, soldier, militia

26. Write whether the following sentence is declarative,
(1) imperative, interrogative or exclamatory: Wow, that horse is spirited!

For 27 and 28, replace each blank with the singular present tense form of the verb.

27. Chickens <u>scratch</u>. This chicken _____.
(5)

28. Several boys <u>bully</u> Goblin. Dove _____ Goblin.
(5)

29. Replace the blank with the past tense form of the
(5) verb: Yesterday afternoon I (nap) _____ for three hours.

30. Diagram the simple subject and simple predicate of this
(3) sentence: Does Johnny write with his left hand?

LESSON 8 — Future Tense

> **Dictation or Journal Entry**
> **Vocabulary:** Notice the similar meanings of common and mutual.
> *Common* means "shared." The Federalists and the Antifederalists had a *common* goal of improving the Articles of Confederation.
> *Mutual* means "reciprocal." *Mutual* respect existed between Alexander Hamilton and Ben Franklin.

The **future tense** refers to action that has not yet occurred. The future tense is usually formed with the helping verbs *shall* or *will*. With the pronouns *I* and *we*, the use of *shall* is preferable in formal writing.

He *will* serve.	We *shall* serve.
They *will* vote.	I *shall* vote.
You *will* smile.	We *shall* smile.
The President *will* preside.	She and I *shall* preside.
Keiva *will* attend.	We *shall* attend.
Leo and Kai *will* speak.	I *shall* speak.

Example 1 Complete the future tense verb form by replacing each blank with *will* or *shall*, as you would do in formal writing.

(a) From now on, I _____ remember that the Vice President of the United States is the leader of the Senate.

(b) In the Senate chamber tomorrow, the Vice President _____ vote only if there is a tie.

(c) The O'Rourke Family _____ visit Washington, D.C. this spring.

(d) Next, we _____ research the orangutan of Indonesia.

Solution

(a) From now on, I **shall** remember that the Vice President of the United States is the leader of the Senate.

(b) In the Senate chamber tomorrow, the Vice President **will** vote only if there is a tie.

(c) The O'Rourke Family **will** visit Washington, D.C. this spring.

(d) Next, we **shall** research the orangutan of Indonesia.

In informal writing, the helping verb *shall* is sometimes used with pronouns other than *I* and *we* in order to show strong emotion or to imply a threat or command.

You <u>shall</u> wear your seat belt in the car.

She <u>shall</u> pay back every cent!

Michael <u>shall</u> finish his homework before playing!

Errors to Avoid Do not use the present for the future tense.

NO: Next week, I <u>give</u> my campaign speech.
YES: Next week, I <u>shall give</u> my campaign speech.

NO: The Senate <u>decides</u> the outcome next month.
YES: The Senate <u>will decide</u> the outcome next month.

NO: Later, they <u>announce</u> the winners of the election.
YES: Later, they <u>will announce</u> the winners of the election.

Example 2 Write the verb phrase in each sentence and label it present, past, or future tense.

(a) Each House keeps record of its day-to-day activities in the *Congressional Record*.

(b) Last year, neither House adjourned for more than three days.

(d) Will you investigate the privileges of Congress members?

Solution (a) **keeps—present tense**

(b) **adjourned—past tense**

(c) **Will investigate—future tense**

Example 3 Write the correct form of the verb.

(a) A Congressperson (present of *receive*) office space, postage, printing of speeches, allowances, and pensions.

(b) Yesterday, the police (past of *issue*) her a parking ticket.

(c) The President (future of *discuss*) foreign policy tomorrow.

(d) We (future of *expect*) our Congresswoman to speak the truth at her next political rally.

Solution (a) A Congressperson **receives** office space, postage, printing of speeches, allowances, and pensions.

(b) Yesterday, the police **issued** her a parking ticket.

(c) The President **will discuss** foreign policy tomorrow.

(d) We **shall expect** our Congresswoman to speak the truth at her next political rally.

Practice For sentences a–c, write the verb phrase and label it present, past, or future tense.

   a. Shall we read Section 7 of Article I later today?

   b. The House of Representatives passed a new tax bill.

   c. The Senate only amends tax bills.

For d–f, write the correct form of the verb.

   d. The vetoed tax bill (past of *need*) the approval of two-thirds of both Houses.

   e. Someday, I (future of *vie*) for the office of U.S. Senator.

   f. The President (present of *examine*) every Congressional order and resolution.

For g–i, replace each blank with *will* or *shall*, as you would do in formal writing, in order to complete the future tense form of the verb.

   g. The President _____ veto that bill.

   h. I _____ write a letter in support of the measure.

   i. _____ we vote by absentee ballot?

For j and k, replace each blank with the correct vocabulary word.

   j. The House of Representatives and the Senate have many _____ responsibilities.

   k. My aunt and uncle have _____ admiration for one another.

More Practice See "Hysterical Fiction #1" with Master Worksheets.

Review Set 8 Choose the correct word to complete sentences 1–5.

1. To (avert, advert) to the mustard on his tie might
(2) embarrass him.

2. We might call quarrelsome people (bellicose, antebellum,
(3) bicameral).

3. An elected official's immoral activity might lead to
(4) (democracy, impeachment, legislature).

4. An (affection, affectation, article) is artificial, or phony.
(5)

5. The Latin root (*pro-*, *bell-*, *pac-*) means "peace."
(6)

For 6–8, write the verb phrase and label it past, present, or future tense.

6. I shall conquer my sarcastic tongue.
(5, 8)

7. Cilla carries water on her shoulders.
(5, 8)

8. Johnny loved Rabbit very much.
(5, 8)

For 9–11, write the correct form of the italicized verb.

9. Congress (future of *convene*) next week.
(8)

10. Aunt Anabel (past of *sip*) her green tea.
(5)

11. Rab (present of *enjoy*) dancing immensely.
(5)

For 12 and 13, replace each blank with *will* or *shall* to complete the future tense form of the verb.

12. Twice Johnny _____ witness Rab's loss of reserve.
(8)

13. We _____ remember always the fight at the
(8) butcher shop.

For sentences 14 and 15, write each noun and label it singular or plural.

14. England addressed the grievances of the colonists and
(7) made adjustments.

15. At the stable, there was no groom to help Miss Lavinia
(7) dismount.

For 16–18, write each noun and label it feminine, masculine, indefinite, or neuter.

16. Violet wore a violet dress to the prom.
(7)

17. The stallion gave the rider a scare.
(7)

18. A boy and his puppy romped in the meadow.
(7)

19. Write the possessive noun in this sentence: Did you
(7) notice Dr. Warren's interest in Johnny's hand?

20. Write the compound noun in this sentence: The King's
(7) warships entered Boston Harbor.

21. From memory, write the twenty-three helping verbs from
(6) lesson 6.

22. Write the entire verb phrase from this sentence, and
(6) underline each helping verb.
The first of the tea ships had been sighted.

23. Replace the blank with the correct verb form for this
(5) sentence: Johnny (present tense of *change*) _____ his mind about showing his burnt hand to Dr. Warren.

24. Write whether this expression is a sentence fragment,
(2) run-on sentence, or complete sentence: After his rudeness to Dr. Warren.

25. Rewrite and correct this run-on sentence: We shall board
(2) the *Dartmouth,* the *Eleanor,* and the *Beaver* then we shall dump the tea into Boston Harbor!

For sentences 26 and 27, write each noun and label it concrete or abstract.

26. Public opinion favored the Sons of Liberty.
(4)

27. The colonists detested tyranny and treasured liberty.
(4)

28. Write and capitalize each proper noun from this
(4) sentence: In the office of the *boston observer*, the conspirators gathered to plan a tea party.

Diagram the simple subject and simple predicate of sentences 29 and 30.

29. Did the boys dress like Indians?
(3)

30. Dove secretly scooped tea into his breeches.
(3)

LESSON 9 Capitalization: Pronoun *I*, Poetry, Titles, Outlines, Quotations

> **Dictation or Journal Entry**
>
> **Vocabulary:** Many English words are derived from the Latin word *hospes*, meaning "guest." A familiar word is <u>hospital</u>.
>
> *Inhospitable* means "unfriendly," "uninviting," or "unwelcome." The war-torn country was *inhospitable* to democracy.
>
> A *hospice* is a place or program in which pilgrims, strangers, or the terminally ill find shelter, rest, or treatment. Local residents suggested that the weary soldiers take refuge in the nearby *hospice*.

The reasons for capitalizing words are many. Since proper nouns name a specific person, place, or thing, we capitalize them. We also remember that a common noun linked with a proper noun requires a capital letter. Therefore, the word "boulevard" is capitalized in "Hollywood Boulevard."

However, little words such as *a*, *of*, *the*, *an*, and *in* are not capitalized when they are part of a proper noun (as in the United States of America). Of course, the **first word of every sentence** requires a capital letter.

Now we will review more about capitalization.

The pronoun *I* The pronoun *I* is always capitalized, no matter where it is placed in the sentence.

> You and I have much in common!
> Shall I invite our mutual friend for pumpkin pie?
> No one likes dessert as much as I.

First word in a line of poetry The **first words of each line in most poetry** are usually capitalized. For example, Emily Dickinson writes the following:

> If my bark sink
> 'Tis to another sea.
> Mortality's ground floor
> Is immortality.

However, some poets, for effect, purposely do not capitalize the first words of every line of their poetry. For example, Robert Creeley writes:

> All night the sound had
> come back again,
> and again falls
> this quiet persistent rain.

51

Example 1   Write each word that should be capitalized in a and b.

(a) this article, i recall, addresses the powers of Congress.

(b) Ogden Nash capitalized the first word of each line in his poem "Edouard":

> a bugler named Dougal MacDougal
> found ingenious ways to be frugal.
> he learned how to sneeze
> in various keys,
> thus saving the price of a bugle.

Solution   (a) **This** article, **I** recall, addresses the powers of Congress. We capitalize the first word of a sentence and the pronoun *I*.

(b) We capitalize the first word of each line of the poem:

> **A** bugler named Dougal MacDougal
> **Found** ingenious ways to be frugal.
> **He** learned how to sneeze
> **In** various keys,
> **Thus** saving the price of a bugle.

Titles   **Titles** require special capitalization. In titles, we capitalize the following:

1. The first and last words of a title

2. All verbs (action or being words)

3. All other words in the title except certain short words

4. A preposition with five or more letters (such as outside, underneath, between, etc.)

Notice the examples below. (We will review the use of quotation marks and italics in a later lesson.)

David Copperfield

"The Tables Turned"

"When I Have Fears"

Unless located first or last in the title, words like *a, an, and, the, but, or, for, nor*, and prepositions with four letters or fewer do not need a capital letter. Here are some examples of properly capitalized titles:

Life on the Mississippi

My Utmost for his Highest

"Stopping by Woods on a Snowy Evening"

"A Matter of Principle"

Outlines We learn to organize written material by outlining. **Outlines** require capital letters for the Roman numerals and for the letters of the first major topics. We also capitalize the first letter of the first word in the outline.

    I. The House of Representatives
       A. Representation by population
       B. Members serve two-year terms
    II. The Senate
       A. Equal representation
       B. Members serve six-year terms

Quotations We capitalize the first word of a dialog **quotation,** as shown below.

    Freddy asked, "Have you underestimated the ability of the fourth man in Nebuchadnezzar's furnace?"

    Beth answered, "I believe I have. Thanks for the reminder!"

If a quoted sentence is interrupted, the second half of the quotation is not always capitalized.

    "That fourth man," said Freddy, "has frequently rescued me in times of need."

Example 2 Provide capital letters as needed in titles, outlines, and quotations.

(a) *america is worth saving*

(b) "on being brought from africa to america"

(c) i. qualifications for the Senate
       a. must be at least thirty years old
       b. must live in the state he or she represents
       c. must have been a U.S. citizen for nine years

(d) the old man exclaimed, "perhaps you will be the next mayor of our town!"

(e) "I think," said the old man, "that you are well qualified."

Solution (a) ***America Is Worth Saving*** (We capitalize first and last words in this title plus all verbs and important words.

(b) **"On Being Brought from Africa to America"** (In this title, we capitalize the first and last words, all verbs and other words except for the short prepositions "from" and "to."

(c) **I. Q**ualifications for the Senate
   A. Must be at least thirty years old
   B. Must live in the state he or she represents
   C. Must have been a U.S. citizen for nine years

(d) **The** old man exclaimed, "**Perhaps** you will be the next mayor of our town!"

(e) "I think," said the old man, "that you are well qualified." (No additional capitals are needed here. Since the quoted sentence is interrupted, the second part of the quotation, a continuation of the sentence, is not capitalized.)

Practice For a and b, write each word that should be capitalized.

a. How can i become a citizen?

b. Ezra Pound follows traditional capitalization rules in his poem "Taking Leave of a Friend":

   blue mountains to the north of the walls,
   white river winding about them;
   here we must make separation
   and go out through a thousand miles of dead grass

Rewrite c–e, using correct capitalization for outlines, titles, and quotations.

c. i. reasons to travel
      a. see new places
      b. meet new people
   ii. reasons to stay home
      a. relax
      b. enjoy family

d. *facts about the presidents* (title)

e. patrick henry said, "something must be done to preserve your liberty and mine."

For f–h, replace each blank with the correct vocabulary word.

f. The United States refused to trade with the _____ nation.

g. Those who worked in the _____ program comforted the terminally ill patient and his family.

h. The Latin word *hospes* means _____.

More Practice See Master Worksheets.

Review set 9 Choose the correct word to complete sentences 1–6.

1. (Common, Bellicose, Bicameral) means "shared."
(8)

2. The Latin term (*pro tempore, writ of habeas corpus*) means "for a little while."
(7)

3. (Avert, Advert, Placate) means to calm or satisfy.
(6)

4. My (affection, affectation, impeachment) of nobility caused people to believe I was a princess.
(5)

5. Bringing formal charges against a public official is called (nomination, impeachment, election).
(4)

6. Tomorrow we (shall, will) seize each opportunity.
(8)

For 7–9, write each word that should be capitalized.

7. Emily Dickinson capitalized the first word in each line of verse. Here are some familiar lines from "J. 49":
(4, 9)

    i never lost as much but twice,
    and that was in the sod.
    twice have I stood a beggar
    before the throne of God!

8. ms. cheung said, "notice that boston is bordered by the charles river, boston harbor, and the fort point channel."
(4, 9)

9. my friend alba wrote a poem called "ode to an ugly duckling."
(4, 9)

For 10–12, write the verb phrase and name its tense as present, past, or future.

10. The fox rummages through the actor's belongings.
_(5, 8)

11. Finally, he encountered the mask of a human head.
_(5, 8)

12. Will the fox appear wise with this mask on his face?
_(5, 8)

For 13–15, write the correct form of the verb.

13. Polly (present of *wish*) she were a princess.
₍₅₎

14. We (future of *demand*) no taxation without representation.
₍₈₎

15. Rab (present of *want*) a musket more than anything.
₍₅₎

For 16 and 17, write each noun and label it singular or plural.

16. Sophia enjoys plays and skits.
₍₇₎

17. Ancient flintlocks were not as good as modern muskets.
₍₇₎

For 18 and 19, write each noun and label it masculine, feminine, neuter, or indefinite.

18. A girl named Sophia traveled to a remote island in
₍₇₎ another country.

19. The singers are watching their director closely.
₍₇₎

For 20 and 21, replace each blank with the singular present tense form of the verb.

20. Students <u>pass</u> their tests. Josh Lim _____ his test.
₍₅₎

21. Shepherds <u>tend</u> their flocks. Ava _____ her flock.
₍₅₎

22. Write the compound noun from this list: sergeant,
₍₇₎ grandsire, musket, yokel, soldier

23. Write the possessive noun from this sentence: The
₍₇₎ Minute Men believed that it was God's will to resist tyranny.

24. From memory, write the twenty-three helping verbs from
₍₆₎ Lesson 6.

25. Write the entire verb phrase and underline each helping verb in this sentence: Rab and Cilla had been enjoying themselves.

26. Make a complete sentence from this sentence fragment: Unconsciously and unreasonably jealous.

27. In this sentence, write each noun and label it concrete or abstract: Sometimes jealousy affects our behavior.

28. Unscramble these words to make an imperative sentence: attention   give   your   me

Diagram the simple subject and simple predicate of sentences 29 and 30.

29. Cilla has changed so much!

30. Does Rab walk Cilla home?

LESSON 10

Irregular Plural Nouns, Part 1

> **Dictation or Journal Entry**
>
> **Vocabulary:**
>
> *Quorum* is the number of persons needed at a meeting in order for business to take place. Each house of Congress needs a *quorum* in order to accomplish any of its tasks.
>
> A *caucus* is a meeting organized to further the special interests of the group. In U.S. politics, the majority party organizes a caucus to choose its candidates for the officers in the Senate.

Plural Nouns We never form a plural with an apostrophe. In most cases, we make a singular noun plural by adding an *s*.

SINGULAR	PLURAL
republic	republics
federation	federations
candidate	candidates
term	terms

Irregular Forms Some nouns have irregular plural forms. We must learn these. We add *es* to a singular noun ending in the following letters: *s, sh, ch, x, z*.

SINGULAR	PLURAL
ditch	ditches
caucus	caucuses
Charles	Charleses
Dominguez	Dominguezes
fax	faxes
flash	flashes
Yepiz	Yepizes

We add an *s* when a singular noun ends with *ay, ey, oy,* or *uy*.

SINGULAR	PLURAL
fray	frays
lackey	lackeys
ploy	ploys
buy	buys

We change *y* to *i* and add *es* when a singular noun ends in a consonant and a *y*, *unless it is someone's name.

SINGULAR	PLURAL
judiciary	judiciaries
supply	supplies
tyranny	tyrannies
majority	majorities
*Danny	*Dannys (I know two Dannys)

Example For a–p, write the plural form of each singular noun.

(a) petition (b) lunch (c) fox (d) stray

(e) mess (f) legislature (g) minority (h) swish

(i) valley (j) toy (k) buzz (l) ruckus

(m) guy (n) lobby (o) loss (p) Sherry

Solution (a) **petitions** (regular) (b) **lunches** (ends in *ch*)

(c) **foxes** (ends in *x*) (d) **strays** (ends in *ay*)

(e) **messes** (ends in *ss*) (f) **legislatures** (regular)

(g) **minorities** (ends in consonant plus *y*)

(h) **swishes** (ends in *sh*) (i) **valleys** (ends in *ey*)

(j) **toys** (ends in *oy*) (k) **buzzes** (ends in *z*)

(l) **ruckuses** (ends in *s*) (m) **guys** (ends in *uy*)

(n) **lobbies** (ends in consonant plus *y*)

(o) **losses** (ends in *ss*) (p) **Sherrys** (someone's name)

Practice For a and b, replace each blank with the correct vocabulary word.

a. The students in Miss Ngo's class held a _____ to discuss emergency preparedness.

b. The school board adjourned its meeting, for a _____ of its members was not present.

For c–r, write the plural form of each singular noun.

c. play **d.** senate **e.** turnkey **f.** splash

g. decoy **h.** glass **i.** barnacle **j.** sentry

k. branch **l.** wax **m.** secretary **n.** hoax

o. penalty **p.** vacancy **q.** Barry **r.** Morty

More Practice Write the plural of each singular noun.

1. swatch 2. fray 3. assembly 4. pinch
5. holiday 6. belly 7. perch 8. replay
9. democracy 10. box 11. birthday 12. Mandy
13. clutch 14. relay 15. Betty 16. bench
17. turkey 18. Alan 19. brass 20. Tabby
21. blue jay 22. ax 23. finch 24. penny
25. Sammy 26. kiss 27. armory 28. suffix
29. prefix 30. journey 31. aviary 32. shoo fly

Review set 10 Choose the correct word to complete sentences 1–6.

1. The Latin term (*habeas corpus, hospes, bell*) means "guest."
(9)

2. (Antebellum, Mutual, Bicameral) means "reciprocal."
(8)

3. The president (pro tempore, habeas corpus) presides for the time being.
(7)

4. A (representative, pacifist, delegate) opposes war or violence.
(6)

5. Sometimes people demonstrate their (affection, affectation, impeachment) for others by sending flowers.
(5)

6. (Shall, Will) Dan build another spacecraft next year?
(8)

For 7–10, write the plural of each singular noun.

7. key 8. Eddy 9. porch 10. pencil
(7,10) (7,10) (7,10) (7,10)

11. Write each concrete noun from this list: spurs, boots, kindness, hat, envy
(4)

For 12 and 13, replace each blank with the singular present tense form of the verb.

12. I <u>fax</u> documents. Fong _____ documents.
(5)

13. Miss Meng and Mr. Ortiz <u>sit</u> here. Mr. Lim _____ there.
(5)

For 14–16, write the past tense of each verb.

14. trip   **15.** smash   **16.** pry
(5)   (5)   (5)

17. Write each possessive noun from this list: Ortizes, Ortiz's, friends, friend's, friends'
(7)

18. Write whether the following sentence is a complete sentence, run-on sentence, or sentence fragment: Mrs. Bessie, that enormous and fine woman cooking for the Lytes.
(2)

19. Write each word that should be capitalized in this sentence:
(4, 9)

Last month i read a poem by edward lear titled "there was an old man with a beard."

For 20 and 21, write the verb phrase labeling it present, past, or future tense.

20. Mrs. Bessie, the Lytes' cook, secretly helped Sam Adams.
(5, 8)

21. Next I shall describe Lavinia Lyte's indulgence of Isannah.
(5, 8)

For 22 and 23, write the correct form of the verb.

22. Isannah (future of *refuse*) to recognize Johnny.
(8)

23. The men (past of *clap*) in response to Lavinia's costume.
(5)

24. Write the collective noun from this sentence: The barracks housed many soldiers.
(4)

25. Write the noun from this sentence that is neuter in gender: Grandpa's goats, sheep, and chickens all sleep in the barn.
(7)

26. Write the compound noun from this sentence: How does a coachman assist Lavinia?
(7)

27. From memory, write the twenty-three helping verbs from Lesson 6.
(6)

28. Rewrite the following run-on sentence, using a period and a capital letter to correct it: Johnny discovers the truth Merchant Lyte is his grand uncle.
(2)

29. Write the abstract noun from this sentence: The tenderness of Johnny's mother haunts him.
(4)

30. Diagram the simple subject and simple predicate of this sentence: Will Joe be picking strawberries this afternoon?
(3)

LESSON 11 — Irregular Plural Nouns, Part 2

> **Dictation or Journal Entry**
> **Vocabulary:** Let us examine the similar words *ambiguous* and *ambivalent*.
> *Ambiguous* means having a double meaning; unclear; uncertain. The writers tried to avoid *ambiguous* statements.
> *Ambivalent* means having conflicting feelings or attitudes about something. Some colonists expressed *ambivalent* feelings about the Constitution.

We continue our study of plural nouns.

Irregular Forms Some singular nouns change completely in their plural forms.

SINGULAR	PLURAL
tooth	teeth
mouse	mice
ox	oxen
alga	algae
man	men
woman	women

Other nouns are the same in their singular and plural forms.

SINGULAR	PLURAL
offspring	offspring
deer	deer
cod	cod

Dictionary When we are uncertain, it is very important that we use a dictionary to check plural forms. If the plural form of the noun is regular (only add *s* to the singular noun), then the dictionary will not list it. Sometimes the dictionary will list two plural forms for a noun. The first one listed is the preferred one. (Example: fungus *n.*, *pl.* fungi, funguses)

Example 1 Write the plural form of each of the following singular nouns. Use a dictionary if you are in doubt.

    (a) child   (b) louse   (c) barracks   (d) vertebra

Solution (a) **children** (irregular form)   (b) **lice** (irregular form)

    (c) We check the dictionary and find that **barracks** is both the singular and plural form.

    (d) We check the dictionary and find that the preferable plural for vertebra is **vertebrae.**

Nouns Ending in *f, ff, fe* For most nouns ending in *f, ff,* and *fe,* we add *s* to form the plural.

SINGULAR	PLURAL
foodstuff	foodstuffs
chief	chiefs
safe	safes

However, for some nouns ending in *f,* and *fe,* we change the *f* to *v* and add *es.*

SINGULAR	PLURAL
self	selves
wife	wives
thief	thieves

Nouns Ending in *o* We usually add *s* to form the plurals of nouns ending in *o,* especially if they are musical terms.

SINGULAR	PLURAL
piano	pianos
alto	altos
studio	studios
video	videos
radio	radios
photo	photos

However, the following illustrate the rule that nouns ending in *-o* preceded by a consonent add *-es* to form the plural:

SINGULAR	PLURAL
embargo	embargoes
mosquito	mosquitoes
cargo	cargoes
tomato	tomatoes
mango	mangoes
veto	vetoes
echo	echoes

...and many more!

Example 2 Write the plural form of each singular noun. Use the dictionary if you are unsure.

(a) roof (b) potato (c) sheaf (d) virtuoso

Solution (a) **roofs** (word ending in *f*)

(b) **potatoes** (We check the dictionary and find that the plural of potato is *potatoes*.)

(c) We check the dictionary and find that the plural of sheaf is **sheaves.**

(d) **virtuosos** (musical term)

Compound Nouns We make the main element plural in a compound noun.

SINGULAR	PLURAL
commander-in-chief	commanders-in-chief
mother-in-law	mothers-in-law
zookeeper	zookeepers
footman	footmen
power of attorney	powers of attorney
justice of the peace	justices of the peace
Prince of Wales	Princes of Wales
songbird	songbirds

Nouns Ending in *ful* We form the plurals of nouns ending in *ful* by adding an *s* at the end of the word.

    SINGULAR   PLURAL

    cupful   cupfuls

    mouthful   mouthfuls

Example 3 Write the plural form of each of the following singular nouns. Use a dictionary if you are in doubt.

  (a) tablespoonful   (b) lady-in-waiting

Solution (a) **tablespoonfuls** (word ending in *ful*)

  (b) **ladies-in-waiting** (compound noun)

Practice For a–l, write the plural form of each singular noun. Use the dictionary if you are in doubt.

  a. plateful   **b.** father-in-law   **c.** scarf

  d. hoof   **e.** vermin   **f.** ox

  g. moose   **h.** goose   **i.** piccolo

  j. torpedo   **k.** loaf   **l.** knife

For m and n, replace each blank with the correct vocabulary word.

  m. An _____ Congressman vocalized both pros and cons of the bill.

  n. The _____ wording of the bill required clarification by its originator.

More Practice Write the plural of each noun.

  1. cliff   **2.** life   **3.** elf   **4.** leaf

  5. half   **6.** tooth   **7.** terminus   **8.** mouse

  9. species   **10.** woman   **11.** handful   **12.** man

  13. child   **14.** louse   **15.** goose   **16.** armful

  17. calf   **18.** shelf   **19.** soprano   **20.** mango

  21. sister-in-law   **22.** serviceman

Review set 11 Choose the correct word to complete sentences 1–5.

1. A (caucus, quorum, hospice) is a meeting organized to further a special interest.

2. The words inhospitable and (common, appease, hospice) come from a Latin word meaning "guest."

3. Two enemies might have (mutual, bicameral, phony) hatred for one another.

4. A (pro tempore, writ of habeas corpus) gives one the right to know why he or she is in jail.

5. (Participants, Pacifists, Presbyterians) refused to fight against the British.

For 6–9, write the plural form for each singular noun.

6. leaf

7. attorney-at-law

8. video

9. handful

For 10–12, tell whether each noun is feminine, masculine, indefinite, or neuter.

10. baroness

11. bayonet

12. cook

13. Write each concrete noun from this list: gratitude, emerald, pilgrim, eloquence, gopher, harmony, kitchen

For 14 and 15, replace the blank with the singular present tense form of the verb.

14. Parrots <u>screech</u>. My parrot _____.

15. Tim and Tom <u>fry</u> zucchini. Opal _____ zucchini.

16. Write the past tense of the verb *sip*.

17. Write each possessive noun from this list: pacifist's, pacifists, caucuses, caucuses', brothers-in-laws, brothers-in-law's, lobbies, lobby's

18. Write each word that should be capitalized in the sentence below.
_(4, 9)

in boston i made my way up copp's hill from the old north church where the lanterns were hung for paul revere.

For 19–21, write the correct form of the verb.

19. Patricia (present of *drink*) lemonade on hot summer afternoons.
₍₅₎

20. Soon we (future of *discover*) the truth about Johnny's lineage.
₍₈₎

21. Cilla (past of *hurry*) back to the Lytes for the silver.
₍₅₎

22. Write the entire verb phrase from this sentence labeling it past, present, or future tense: Rab attempted to buy a gun from a farmer.
_(5, 8)

23. Replace the verb in this sentence with one that is more descriptive: The police got the criminal.
₍₃₎

24. Write each collective noun from this list: meetinghouse, committee, bodyguard, humane society, vagabond
₍₄₎

25. Write each compound noun from this list: descendants, grandsons, pigtail, pandemonium, dog food, ambivalent
₍₇₎

26. Write whether this sentence is declarative, interrogative, imperative, or exclamatory: Why does Colonel Nesbit free Rab?
₍₁₎

27. Write the verb phrase from this sentence underlining each helping verb: Mrs. Lapham has married Mr. Tweedie.
₍₆₎

28. Write whether this expression is a sentence fragment, run-on sentence, or complete sentence: Johnny analyzes Cilla's face he discovers her beauty.
₍₂₎

Diagram the simple subject and simple predicate of sentences 29 and 30.

29. Does Cilla like the name Cilla Tremain?
(3)

30. James Otis might have been defining the acceptable
(3) reason for civil war.

LESSON 12

Irregular Verbs, Part 1: *Be, Have, Do*

> **Dictation or Journal Entry**
>
> **Vocabulary:** The Latin word *amare*, meaning "to love," forms the base of many English words.
>
> *Amiable* means "affable, pleasant, and good-natured." The *amiable* dog wagged its tail whenever anyone entered the yard.
>
> *Amicable*, not as personal, means "showing goodwill and formal friendliness." An *amicable* divorce is one in which the parties treat one another with respect and courtesy.

Be, have, and *do* are three of the most frequently used verbs in the English language. The tenses of these verbs are irregular; they do not fit the pattern of the regular verbs. Therefore, we must memorize them now if we have not done so already.

Points of View Verb forms often change according to three points of view: First person (*I* or *we*), second person (*you*), and third person (*he, she, it, they,* and singular or plural nouns). Below are charts showing the verb forms of *be*, *have*, and *do*.

Be   PRESENT   PAST

	SINGULAR	PLURAL	SINGULAR	PLURAL
1ST PERSON	I am	we are	I was	we were
2ND PERSON	you are	you are	you were	you were
3RD PERSON	he is	they are	he was	they were

Have   PRESENT   PAST

	SINGULAR	PLURAL	SINGULAR	PLURAL
1ST PERSON	I have	we have	I had	we had
2ND PERSON	you have	you have	you had	you had
3RD PERSON	he has	they have	he had	they had

Do   PRESENT   PAST

	SINGULAR	PLURAL	SINGULAR	PLURAL
1ST PERSON	I do	we do	I did	we did
2ND PERSON	you do	you do	you did	you did
3RD PERSON	he does	they do	he did	they did

Example   Complete each sentence with the correct form of the verb.

(a) Long ago, the writers of the Constitution (past of *be*) aware of the limitations of Congress.

(b) Congress (present of *have*) an "elastic clause" for any situation not covered by the Constitution.

(c) I (present of *be*) learning about the powers denied Congress.

(d) We (past of *have*) understood the writ of *habeas corpus*.

(e) How (present of *do*) one define a "bill of attainder"?

(f) The argumentative delegates (past of *do*) not seem amiable in the slightest.

Solution   (a) Long ago, the writers of the Constitution **were** aware of the limitations of Congress.

(b) Congress **has** an "elastic clause" for any situation not covered by the Constitution.

(c) I **am** learning about the powers denied Congress.

(d) We **had** understood the writ of *habeas corpus*.

(e) How **does** one define a "bill of attainder"?

(f) The argumentative delegates **did** not seem amiable in the slightest.

Practice   Write the correct verb form to complete sentences a–f.

a. A "bill of attainder" (present of *be*) an act by legislature to punish a person without a trial.

b. England (past of *have*) allowed "bills of attainder" to punish innocent people and to unfairly take property.

c. (Past of *be*) "bills of attainder" allowed during colonial times in America?

d. An *ex-post facto* bill (past of *be*) not legal.

e. The *ex-post facto* bill (present of *have*) unfairly punished crimes.

f. (present of *Do*) Congress have the power to tax a person a flat sum?

For g–i, replace each blank with the correct vocabulary word.

g. The Latin word _____ means "to love."

h. The _____ relationship between Canada and the United States makes it possible to share the same minimally guarded border.

i. _____ politicians attempt to please their constituents.

More Practice Choose the correct verb form for each sentence.

1. (Do, Does) the Constitution protect citizens from unfair legal action?

2. Congress (present of *have*) no right to tax articles exported from any state.

3. "Bills of attainder" (past of *be*) prohibited.

4. (Do, Does) amiable candidates always win elections?

5. The writers of the Constitution (was, were) concerned that some states might receive preferential treatment.

6. We (was, were) informed about the budget.

7. The Senate (was, were) discussing the new bill.

8. Titles of nobility (is, are) forbidden by the Constitution.

9. (Was, Were) you aware that an elected official may accept no special privileges from any king, prince, or foreign state?

10. States also (have, has) power limitations.

11. (Do, Does) a state have the right to enter into treaties or alliances?

12. A state (is, are) prohibited from coining or printing its own money.

Review set 12

Choose the correct word to complete sentences 1–5.

1. (Ambiguous, Ambivalent, Antebellum) means having more than one meaning, unclear.
(3, 11)

2. In order to conduct business, the Senate needs a (hospice, representative, quorum).
(9, 10)

3. The Latin word *hospes* means (war, agree, guest).
(9)

4. Sean-Carlos and I might have a (bicameral, common, habeas corpus) friend since we attend the same school.
(7, 8)

5. The Constitution guarantees us the privilege of the (pro tempore, writ of habeas corpus).
(7)

For 6–9, write the plural form for each singular noun.

6. sheriff (11)

7. brother-in-law (11)

8. studio (11)

9. fistful (11)

For 10 and 11, tell whether each noun is feminine, masculine, indefinite, or neuter.

10. lord (7)

11. horse (7)

12. Write each abstract noun from this list: persistence, persimmons, pandemonium, democracy, Democrat
(4)

For 13–15, choose the correct form of the verb.

13. Emiko and Carla (is, am, are) reading *David Copperfield*.
(12)

14. Jacob (have, has) spent the weekend dirt-biking.
(12)

15. Brittney (do, does) well on her assignments.
(12)

16. Write the past tense of the verb *worry*.
(5)

17. Write each possessive noun from this list: soldiers, soldier's, soldiers', uniform, uniform's
(7)

18. Write each word that should be capitalized in the sentence below.
_(4, 9)

christina rossetti wrote a poem called "who has seen the wind?"

For 19–21, write the correct form of the verb.

19. Kristin (present of *be*) kind and thoughtful.
₍₁₂₎

20. Jeff (future of *have*) tremendous success.
_(8, 12)

21. Johnny (past of *do*) all that he was told.
_(5, 12)

22. Write the entire verb phrase from this sentence labeling it past, present, or future tense: Perhaps next week I shall plant turnips in the side yard.
_(5, 8)

23. Replace the verb in this sentence with one that is more descriptive: The colonists <u>talk</u> about unfair taxes.
₍₃₎

24. Write each collective noun from this list: Central America, herd, orphan, company
₍₄₎

25. Write each compound noun from this list: checklist, property, rebel, sickroom, cash flow
₍₇₎

26. Write whether this sentence is declarative, interrogative, imperative, or exclamatory: Johnny feels pity for Dove.
₍₁₎

27. From memory, write the twenty-three common helping verbs listed in Lesson 6.
₍₆₎

28. Rewrite the following run-on sentence using a period and a capital letter to correct it: Fully mature adults respect others they treat people with kindness and compassion.
₍₂₎

Diagram the simple subject and simple predicate of sentences 29 and 30.

29. Does Pumpkin trade his musket for farmers' clothes?
₍₃₎

30. The British might have shot the deserter.
₍₃₎

LESSON 13

Four Principal Parts of Verbs

> **Dictation or Journal Entry**
>
> **Vocabulary:**
> A *lobby* is a special group that tries to influence legislation. The tobacco *lobby* attempted to block the passage of a bill raising cigarette taxes. *Lobby* can also be a verb meaning "to try to influence legislation." The tobacco industry *lobbied* against sales tax on cigarettes.
>
> A *census* is an official count of people in any given place. The book of *Numbers* in the *Old Testament* records a *census* of the Israelites.

Four Principal Parts Every verb has **four** basic forms, or **principal parts.** In order to form all the tenses of each verb, we need to learn these principal parts: (1) the verb, (2) the present participle, (3) the past tense, and (4) the past participle.

Present Tense The first principal part is the singular verb in its **present tense** form, which is used to express *present time*, something that is *true at all times*, and *future time*:

    lobby   appease   advert

Present Participle The second principal part, used to form the progressive tenses (continuing action), is preceded by a form of the *be* helping verb. The **present participle** is formed by adding *ing* to the singular verb:

    (is) lobbying   (are) appeasing   (is) adverting

Past Tense The third principal part of a verb, used to express *past time*, is the **past tense,** which we form by adding *ed* to most verbs.

    lobbied   appeased   adverted

Past Participle The fourth principal part of a verb, used to form the *perfect* tenses, is the **past participle.** It is preceded by a form of the *have* helping verb. For regular verbs, the past and the past participle are the same.

PAST	PAST PARTICIPLE
lobbied	(have) lobbied
appeased	(has) appeased
adverted	(have) adverted

Example Complete the chart by writing the second, third, and fourth principal parts (present participle, past tense, and past participle) of each verb.

Verb	Present Participle	Past Tense	Past Participle
avert	(is) averting	averted	(has) averted
(a) petition			
(b) ratify			
(c) tax			
(d) revise			
(e) expel			

Solution

Verb	Present Participle	Past Tense	Past Participle
(a) petition	**(is) petitioning**	**petitioned**	**(has) petitioned**
(b) ratify	**(is) ratifying**	**ratified**	**(has) ratified**
(c) tax	**(is) taxing**	**taxed**	**(has) taxed**
(d) revise	**(is) revising**	**revised**	**(has) revised**
(e) expel	**(is) expelling**	**expelled**	**(has) expelled**

Practice For a–e, complete the chart by writing the second, third, and fourth principal parts (present participle, past tense, and past participle) of each verb.

Verb	Present Participle	Past Tense	Past Participle
a. vote			
b. register			
c. impeach			
d. qualify			
e. rebel			

For f–h, replace each blank with the correct vocabulary word.

f. In the past, the American Cancer Society _____ Congress to mandate health warnings on packages of cigarettes.

g. The _____ of the year 2000 revealed minimal population growth in some areas.

h. The _____ for farming sought to convince Congress that financial assistance was needed in times of drought, flood, or other disaster.

More Practice Write the present participle, past tense, and past participle of each verb.

1. proceed
2. represent
3. constitute
4. legislate
5. export
6. justify
7. apportion
8. appoint
9. slander
10. pass

Review Set 13 Choose the correct word to complete sentences 1–6.

1. The Latin word (*hospes, amare, bell*) means "to love."
(9, 12)

2. (Ambiguous, Ambivalent, Antebellum) means having conflicting feelings or attitudes.
(3, 11)

3. The city council held a (quorum, caucus, habeus corpus) to determine how to help the homeless.
(7, 10)

4. (Common, Antebellum, Inhospitable) means "unfriendly."
(8, 9)

5. We like each other. Our admiration is (antebellum, mutual, bellicose).
(3, 8)

6. Every verb has (two, three, four) basic forms, or principal parts.
(13)

For 7 and 8, write the present participle, past tense, and past participle for each verb.

7. avert
(13)

8. skip
(13)

For 9–11, choose the correct form of the verb.

9. I (is, am, are) now reading Esther Forbes's *Johnny Tremain*.
(12)

10. Johnny (is, am, are) a young apprentice silversmith in Boston.
(12)

11. Dove and Dusty (is, am, are) likely to quarrel.
(12)

12. Write the entire verb phrase underlining each helping verb in this sentence: Have you been lobbying for less homework and more vacation time?
(6)

For 13 and 14, write the correct form of the verb.

13. The British army (future of *march*) soon.
(8)

14. General Gage's spies (past of *dress*) as Yankee men looking for work.
(5)

15. From this sentence, write each noun labeling it concrete or abstract: Overwhelmed with grief, Johnny watches Rab prepare to leave.
(4)

For 16–19, write the plural of each singular noun.

16. potato
(10, 11)

17. Martinez
(10, 11)

18. Queen of England
(10, 11)

19. goose
(10, 11)

Write each word that should be capitalized in sentences 20 and 21.

20. aunt christie said, "a magnanimous player wins without gloating and loses without complaining."
(9)

21. next october i shall explore the countryside of new england and boston's historic streets.
(4, 9)

22. Replace the action verb in this sentence with one that is more descriptive: Sam <u>made</u> a tent and slept in it.
(3)

23. Rewrite the following sentence fragment making a complete sentence: Renewing a delightful old friendship.
(2)

24. Write each possessive noun in this list: woman's, women, bosses, boss's
(7)

25. Write whether this expression is a complete sentence, run-on sentence, or sentence fragment: Please don't go I'll miss you.
(2)

26. Write each compound noun from this list: envelope, eyewitness, double header, boulevard
(7)

27. From the sentence below, write each noun, labeling it masculine, feminine, neuter, or indefinite.
(7)

Did the countess entertain a king in her parlor?

28. Write whether this sentence is declarative, interrogative, exclamatory, or imperative: God will be with you!
(1)

Diagram the simple subject and simple predicate of sentences 29 and 30.

29. Johnny should have said good-bye.
(3)

30. Hurry to Lexington!
(3)

LESSON 14

Prepositions

Dictation or Journal Entry

Vocabulary: Let us review the proper formal usage of the helping verbs *can* and *may*.

Can means "to be able to." The athlete *can* run a mile in five minutes.

May means "to be permitted to." The athlete *may* leave early with the coach's permission.

Informal usage allows *can* to be used for permission: *Can* I see you tomorrow? However, in formal speech and writing, we use *may* for permission: *May* I see you tomorrow?

Prepositions are words belonging to the part of speech that shows the relationship between a noun or pronoun and another word. Notice how a preposition (italicized) shows the relationship between a bug and the straw:

Bug #1 is *on* the straw. Bug #2 is *under* the straw. Bug #3 is *inside* the straw. Bug #4 is jumping *over* the straw. Bug #5 is walking *around* the straw.

Besides defining spatial relationships, prepositions also define temporal and other abstract relationships. Below is a list of common prepositions.

aboard	because of	excepting	off	since
about	before	for	on	through
above	behind	from	on account of	throughout
according to	below	from among	on behalf of	till
across	beneath	from between	on top of	to
across from	beside	from under	onto	toward
after	besides	in	opposite	under
against	between	in addition to	out	underneath
along	beyond	in behalf of	out of	until
alongside	but	in front of	outside	unto
alongside of	by	in place of	outside of	up
along with	by means of	in regard to	over	up to
amid	concerning	in spite of	over to	upon
among	considering	inside	owing to	via
apart from	despite	inside of	past	with
around	down	into	prior to	within
aside from	down from	like	regarding	without
at	during	near	round	
away from	except	near to	round about	
back of	except for	of	save	

Simple Prepositions Notice that some prepositions in the list above are single words while others are groups of words. We list single word prepositions, **simple prepositions,** below. To help you remember these, we list them in four columns.

1	2	3	4
aboard	*beside*	*inside*	*since*
about	*besides*	*into*	*through*
above	*between*	*like*	*throughout*
across	*beyond*	*near*	*till*
after	*but*	*of*	*to*
against	*by*	*off*	*toward*
along	*concerning*	*on*	*under*
alongside	*considering*	*onto*	*underneath*
amid	*despite*	*opposite*	*until*
among	*down*	*out*	*unto*
around	*during*	*outside*	*up*
at	*except*	*over*	*upon*
before	*excepting*	*past*	*via*
behind	*for*	*regarding*	*with*
below	*from*	*round*	*within*
beneath	*in*	*save*	*without*

Simple prepositions are underlined in the sentences below. Notice how they show the relationship between "protects" and "dictator."

Our Constitution protects us <u>against</u> a dictator.

Our Constitution protects us <u>from</u> a dictator.

A person, place, or thing always follows a preposition. We call this word the object of the preposition. In the first sentence, we see that *dictator* is the object of the preposition *against*. In the second sentence, *dictator* is the object of the preposition *from*. We will practice this concept more in a later lesson.

Example 1 Underline each preposition in sentences a and b.

(a) The Third Amendment prohibits the quartering of soldiers in homes.

(b) After the American Revolution, people worried about this issue.

Solution (a) The Third Amendment prohibits the quartering <u>**of**</u> soldiers <u>**in**</u> homes.

(b) <u>**After**</u> the American Revolution, people worried <u>**about**</u> this issue.

Complex Prepositions Here, we list **complex prepositions,** which contain more than one word. Let us become familiar with the following:

according to	in behalf of
across from	in front of
alongside of	in place of
along with	in regard to
apart from	in spite of
aside from	inside of
away from	next to
because of	on account of
by means of	on behalf of
down from	on top of
except for	outside of
from among	over to
from between	owing to
from under	prior to
in addition to	round about

Example 2 Underline each simple and complex preposition in sentences a and b.

(a) According to Article II of the Constitution, and prior to the Twenty-second Amendment, the President had no term limits.

(b) The Electoral College elects the President on behalf of the American people.

Solution (a) **According to** Article II **of** the Constitution, and **prior to** the Twenty-second Amendment, the President had no term limits.

(b) The Electoral College elects the President **on behalf of** the American people.

Practice a. Review the lists of prepositions from this lesson. Then have a "Preposition Contest" with a friend to see how many prepositions, both simple and complex, you can write or say in one minute.

List each simple or complex preposition that you find in sentences b–e.

b. In addition to being at least thirty-five years old, the President must be a natural born citizen and a resident of the United States for fourteen years.

c. If the President cannot stay in office because of death, impeachment, resignation, or some other reason, the Vice President becomes President.

d. By means of a ceremony called an Inauguration, the President is sworn into the Presidency.

e. The Inauguration takes place on January 20, after the presidential election in November and in front of the American people.

For f–i, replace each blank with *can* or *may*.

f. _____ you rescue that stranded cat on your roof?

g. _____ I address this issue, please?

h. Clarence _____ represent our class in the speech meet if the teacher approves.

i. Clarence _____ speak with clarity and conviction.

More Practice Write each preposition that you find in these sentences.

1. Before the fall of mankind, Adam and Eve walked with God in the Garden Eden.

2. Amid the confusion at the tower of Babel, people no longer spoke the same language.

3. Walking among the flames, Shadrach, Meshach, and Abednego survived inside of the furnace because of a fourth man.

4. What happened to Daniel in the lion's den?

5. The Babylonian king Belshazzar saw the handwriting on the wall.

6. Despite his brothers' jealousy, Joseph received a coat of many colors from his father, Jacob.

7. With an army of musicians, Joshua fought the battle of Jericho.

8. Jonah spent three days and nights inside the belly of a whale.

9. During his adult years, John the Baptist lived in the desert and feasted on locusts and wild honey.

10. Before the events at Calvary, Judas Iscariot betrayed Jesus with a kiss.

11. After the Resurrection, doubting Thomas would not believe without proof.

12. In addition to a caucus for human rights, Mario witnessed a lobby for free trade during his visit to Washington, D. C.

13. Considering the ambiguous wording of the bill, most of the voters felt ambivalent regarding its value to the community.

14. Apart from her affectation of injury since the auto accident, Aunt Emiko usually acts fairly normal in front of the jury.

15. Throughout his terminal illness, Nam felt comforted by means of many friends along with an amiable hospice worker.

16. Round about the nation's Capitol, pacifists gathered in protest of war.

17. Without a quorum, the school board could not vote on the issues at hand.

18. Besides mutual affection for one another, the two friends had many common interests owing to their similar backgrounds.

Review Set 14 Choose the correct word to complete sentences 1–5.

1. A (lobby, census, quorum) is a special group that tries to influence legislation.
^(10, 13)

2. The Latin word *amare* means "to (love, war, avert)."
⁽¹²⁾

3. Ambiguous means having (unclear meaning, conflicting feelings).
⁽¹¹⁾

4. A (caucus, hospice, quorum) is a certain number of persons present at a meeting.
^(9, 10)

5. Travelers or strangers might find shelter in a (direct democracy, habeas corpus, hospice).
^(7, 9)

For 6 and 7, replace each blank with the missing preposition from your alphabetical list of simple prepositions.

6. since, through, _____, till, _____, toward, under, _____, until, unto, _____ upon, via, with, _____, without
⁽¹⁴⁾

7. inside, _____, like, near, _____, off, _____, onto, opposite, out, _____, _____, past, regarding, round, save
⁽¹⁴⁾

For 8 and 9, replace each blank with the missing preposition from your alphabetical list of complex prepositions.

8. according to, _____, alongside of, _____, apart from, _____, away from, _____, by means of, _____, except for, from among
⁽¹⁴⁾

9. in behalf of, _____, in place of, _____, in spite of, _____, next to, _____, on behalf of, _____, outside of, over to
⁽¹⁴⁾

10. Write whether this expression is a complete sentence, run-on sentence, or sentence fragment: Dove shines the campaign saddle it is used for battle.
⁽²⁾

11. Write the present participle, past tense, and past participle of the verb *slip*.

12. For a–d, choose the correct past tense form of the verb.
  (a) They (was, were)   (b) It (have, had)
  (c) He (was, were)   (d) She (do, did)

Write the correct verb form for sentences 13–15.

13. Johnny (present of *trick*) Dove into revealing British plans.

14. Last night I (past of *mop*) the kitchen floor.

15. Colonel Smith (future of *leave*) at eight p.m. this evening.

For 16–19, write the plural of each noun.

16. tempo   **17.** shelf

18. bluff   **19.** fax

20. Write each word that should be capitalized in this sentence: the *somerset*, a battleship, moves into the mouth of the charles river.

21. Rewrite this outline placing capital letters where they are needed:

  i. literature
    a. poetry
    b. short stories
    c. tall tales
    d. myths

22. Write each abstract noun from this list: peninsula, freedom, overcoat, contentment, snapdragons, laziness

23. From this sentence, write each noun and label it masculine, feminine, neuter, or indefinite: Three rebels are lurking in the shadows.

24. Write each collective noun from this list: company, swindlers, audience, mannequins, family

25. Rewrite and correct this run-on sentence: Bill Dawes dresses like a drunk he smells like rum.
(2)

26. From memory, write the twenty-three common helping verbs listed in Lesson 6.
(6)

For 27–30, refer to this sentence:
Along with the other investigators, has Horace P. Corndog stumbled onto a clue?

27. Write the verb phrase, underlining the helping verb and circling the past participle.
(6, 13)

28. Write each preposition in the sentence.
(14)

29. Write whether the sentence is declarative, interrogative, imperative, or exclamatory.
(1)

30. Diagram the simple subject and simple predicate of the sentence.
(3)

LESSON 15

The Perfect Tenses

> **Dictation or Journal Entry**
>
> **Vocabulary:** The similar words *contemptible* and *contemptuous* both connote "scorn" but have different meanings.
>
> *Contemptible* means deserving scorn; despicable. Society views animal abuse as *contemptible*.
>
> *Contemptuous* means showing scorn; scornful. Her *contemptuous* remark sparked strife within the group.

We have reviewed the present, past, and future verb tenses. In this lesson, we will review the three **perfect tenses**—present perfect, past perfect, and future perfect. The perfect tenses show that an action has been completed or "perfected." To form these tenses, we add a form of the helping verb *have* to the past participle.

Present Perfect The present perfect tense describes an action that occurred in the past and is complete or continuing in the present. We add the present forms of the verb *have* to the past participle.

PRESENT PERFECT TENSE = HAVE OR HAS + PAST PARTICIPLE

The President has selected the members of his cabinet.

The Electors have voted for the appropriate presidential candidate.

Past Perfect The past perfect tense describes past action completed before another past action. We use the helping verb *had* before the past participle.

PAST PERFECT TENSE = HAD + PAST PARTICIPLE

The President had received his salary of $200,000 in 1999.

He had agreed to freeze his salary for his entire term.

Future Perfect The future perfect tense describes future action to be completed before another future action. We add the future form of the helping verb *have* to the past participle.

FUTURE PERFECT TENSE = WILL HAVE OR SHALL HAVE + PAST PARTICIPLE

By the end of this book, we shall have discussed the entire Constitution.

Before Monday, he will have chosen his replacement.

Congress will have voted on the issue by next week.

Example For sentences a–d, write the verb phrase, and tell whether it is present perfect, past perfect, or future perfect.

(a) Had the Speaker of the House accepted the Congressperson's contemptuous comments?

(b) Before the vote, all the lobbyists will have spoken to me.

(c) Has the President appointed any new ambassadors?

(d) By tomorrow, I shall have researched the various Cabinet positions.

Solution (a) **Had accepted**—We notice the past tense (had) form of the helping verb *have*, so we know that the tense is **past perfect.**

(b) **will have spoken**—We see the future tense form of *have* (will have), so we know that the tense is **future perfect.**

(c) **Has appointed**—The present tense form of *have* (has) is used, so the know that the tense is **present perfect.**

(d) **shall have researched**—The helping verb *have* is in future tense (shall have), so we know that the tense is **future perfect.**

Practice For a–c, write the verb phrase, and tell whether it is present perfect, past perfect, or future perfect.

a. The Constitution has provided for the President's housing, medical care, and transportation.

b. Had the judge desired a salary increase?

c. I shall have studied both sides of each issue before election day.

For d and e, replace each blank with the correct vocabulary word.

d. Blanca tried to forget the _____ atrocities of war in her country.

e. The angry candidate gave a _____ speech concerning his opponent's loose morals.

More Practice Diagram the simple subject and simple predicate of each sentence.

1. The managers have received the same salary since 1999.

2. The President had pronounced his oath on January 21.

3. By next year, some Senators will have completed their terms.

4. We shall have increased the President's salary several times since the adoption of the Constitution.

5. Had your great grandfather served in the military?

6. Has the Senate approved the new treaty?

Review Set 15 Choose the correct word to complete sentences 1–7.

1. (Can, May) means "to be able to."
(14)

2. To (avert, advert, lobby) is to try to influence legislation.
(2, 13)

3. (Amiable, Bellicose, Inhospitable) means "pleasant, friendly, or good-natured."
(9, 12)

4. Ambivalent means having (unclear meaning, conflicting feelings).
(11)

5. A caucus is a (meeting, representative, argument).
(10)

6. To form the perfect tenses, we add a form of the helping verb (be, have, do) to the past participle.
(15)

7. To form the perfect tenses, we add a form of the helping verb *have* to the (present, past) participle.
(15)

For 8–10, write the entire verb phrase and label its tense present perfect, past perfect, or future perfect.

8. Mrs. Dawes had performed well.
(15)

9. Johnny has gained insight into the Dawes Family.
(15)

10. Before Paul Revere's departure, Robert Newman will have hung the lanterns.
(15)

Write each preposition that you find in sentences 11–13.

11. Dr. Warren carried his black bag of instruments and medicine to Lexington.
(14)

12. The young man knows the seriousness for his country of the first shot at Lexington.
(14)

13. According to Dr. Warren, Boston has no knowledge of the fighting.
(14)

14. For a–d, choose the correct present tense form of the verb.
(12)
(a) They (am, are, is) (b) She (am, are, is)
(c) He (have, has) (d) It (do, does)

15. Write whether this expression is a complete sentence, sentence fragment, or run-on sentence: An article in the newspaper concerning Minute Men on the march.
(2)

16. Rewrite and correct this run-on sentence: Everybody knows something is happening no one knows what.
(2)

17. Write the present participle, past tense, and past participle of the verb *giggle*.
(13)

For 18–21, write the plural for each noun.

18. belief
(10, 11)

19. ego
(10, 11)

20. policy
(10, 11)

21. sketch
(10, 11)

22. Emily Dickinson capitalized the first word of each line in her poem below. Write each word that needs a capital letter in the following:
(9)

    success is counted sweetest
    by those who ne-er succeed.
    to comprehend a nectar
    requires sorest need.

23. Write each noun from this sentence and label it abstract or concrete: Has Lavinia mentioned the discontent of the colonists?
(4)

24. Write each possessive noun from this list: pilgrims, pilgrims', Madge's, sluggards, sluggard's, descendants, descendants'
(7)

For 25 and 26, write the verb phrase and name its tense.

25. Finally, news of the fighting has reached Boston.
(15)

26. The British loyalists had desired peace.
(15)

Write the correct verb form to complete sentences 27 and 28.

27. By the end of the week, we (future perfect of *completed*)
(15) *Johnny Tremain*.

28. Johnny almost (present of *salute*) the British flag.
(5)

Diagram the simple subject and simple predicate of sentences 29 and 30.

29. Have the Lytes fled to London?
(3)

30. Lavinia must have discovered the truth.
(3)

LESSON 16 — Verbals: The Gerund as a Subject

> **Dictation or Journal Entry**
> **Vocabulary:** The Latin root *crim-* means "fault, crime, or accusation."
> To *incriminate* is to show evidence of involvement in a crime. The witness's account of the robbery *incriminated* the defendant.
> A *recrimination* is a counter accusation. Sadly, the child custody battle involved *recriminations* between the father and the mother.

Verbals A **verbal** is a verb form that does not function as a verb. Rather, a verbal may function as a noun, an adjective, or an adverb. There are three kinds of verbals: the gerund, the infinitive, and the participle. In this lesson, we shall study the gerund.

The Gerund A **gerund** ends in *-ing* and functions as a noun. A noun can function as the subject of a sentence, a direct object, an object of a preposition, or a predicate noun. In this lesson, we shall see how the gerund can be used as the subject of a sentence.

To determine if a verb ending in *-ing* is a gerund, we must see how it is used in the sentence. We follow these steps:

1. Find the simple predicate.
2. Find the simple subject.

If the *-ing* form of the verb is the simple subject, then the subject of the sentence is a **gerund**. Gerunds used as sentence subjects are italicized below. Notice that we diagram the gerund on a "stair-step" line above the base line on "stilts."

Speech *writing* proved challenging.

Conscientious *voting* requires understanding of issues.

Her *campaigning* turned the election in her favor.

Example 1 Underline each gerund used as a subject in sentences a–c.

(a) Managing foreign relations is the primary responsibility of the Department of State.

(b) The President's vetoing certain bills angered some legislators.

(c) Residing in the White House remains a privilege of the President.

Solution (a) **Managing** foreign relations is the primary responsibility of the Department of State.

(b) The President's **vetoing** certain bills angered some legislators.

(c) **Residing** in the White House remains a privilege of the President.

The gerund has two tenses: present and perfect.

PRESENT: enduring, seeing, writing

PERFECT: having endured, having seen, having written

Perfect tense gerunds are italicized in these sentences:

Three years of *having endured* warfare toughened the soldiers.

Having seen action in the Revolutionary War was good experience for George Washington.

Having written the Constitution in only a few months left the Founding Fathers tired but happy.

Example 2 Diagram the simple subject and simple predicate of this sentence: Smiling improved his appearance.

Solution We diagram the gerund, *smiling,* on a stair-step line above the base line on stilts in the location of the sentence subject.

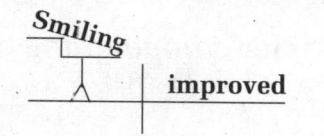

Example 3 For sentences a and b, tell whether the italicized gerund is present or perfect tense.

(a) *Having found* his cat yesterday brought him joy.

(b) *Studying* increases my test scores.

Solution (a) We notice the helping verb *have*, so we recognize that the gerund *having found* is **perfect tense.**

(b) Since there is no helping verb *have*, we know that the gerund *studying* is **present tense.**

Practice Write the gerund used as a subject in sentences a–c.

  a. Conserving energy saves money.

  b. Referring to the President's wife as the First Lady shows respect for her position.

  c. Our touring the Capitol Building enlightened us about government.

For d–g, write the gerund and label it present or perfect tense.

  d. Having appointed all the ambassadors gave the President and the Senators a sense of relief.

  e. Executing the laws weighs heavily upon the President.

  f. The nominating of judges to the Supreme Court by the President requires wisdom and knowledge.

  g. Having stood by his principles for four years showed that John Adams possessed integrity.

For h–j, replace each blank with the correct vocabulary word.

  h. The suspect's shoes may _____ her, for identical sole prints exist at the scene of the crime.

  i. The defendant issued a _____ concerning the person who had accused him.

  j. The Latin root _____ means "fault, crime, or accusation."

  k. Diagram the simple subject and simple predicate of this sentence: Walking will improve your fitness.

More Practice Diagram the simple subject and simple predicate of each sentence.

1. Does cooking interest you?

2. Waiting requires patience.

3. Lobbying may affect legislators.

4. Did gardening provide relaxation?

5. Might singing lift your spirits?

6. Has sharing encouraged him?

7. Having bicycled all day gave him great pleasure.

Review Set 16 Choose the correct word to complete sentences 1–10.

1. The word (contemptuous, amiable, amicable) means
(12, 15) scornful.

2. (Can, May) means "to be permitted to."
(14)

3. Environmentalists might (appease, impeach, lobby) for
(13) laws prohibiting the removal of trees.

4. Amiable means (grouchy, pleasant, impatient).
(12)

5. We did not know how to proceed, for the instructions
(11) were (ambivalent, ambiguous, bicameral).

6. A gerund ends in (-ing, -at, -ion) and functions as a noun.
(16)

7. A gerund functions as a(n) (adjective, verb, noun).
(16)

8. Next week we (will, shall) write poetry.
(8)

9. Dusty and Dove (was, were) asleep in the attic.
(12)

10. (Do, Does) Mrs. Lapham have four daughters?
(12)

11. Write whether this sentence is declarative, interrogative,
(1) imperative, or exclamatory: Lavinia Lyte takes Isannah with her to London.

12. Write whether this expression is a sentence fragment, a
(2) run-on sentence, or a complete sentence: A sixteen-year-old is a boy in time of peace and a man in time of war.

13. Rewrite this sentence fragment, making it a complete sentence: A falcon sitting on a fence post.

14. Write the gerund in this sentence: Does strutting make little people feel bigger?

15. Write each noun in this sentence and label it abstract or concrete: Does the act of strutting lift his spirits?

16. From memory, write the twenty-three common helping verbs listed in Lesson 6.

17. Write each compound from this list: goodwill, stand-in, bayonet, check mark, Minute Men

18. Write the possessive noun from this sentence: Thinking about Rab's welfare frightens Johnny.

19. Write each word that should be capitalized in this sentence: miss trang warned, "your perfectionism may become a nemesis causing you much grief."

20. Rewrite this book title, adding capital letters as needed: the light in the forest

For 21–24, write the plural of each noun.

21. hero   **22.** half

23. business   **24.** basketful

25. Write the present participle, past tense, and past participle of the verb *pacify*.

For 26 and 27, write the entire verb phrase labeling its tense.

26. By the end of this chapter, the British will have wounded Rab.

27. The British had failed to stop the Minute Men.

28. Write each preposition in this sentence: Johnny sits next to Rab's chair on the floor and puts his hands over Rab's thin ones.

Diagram the simple subject and simple predicate of sentences 29 and 30.

29. Sadly, Rab has died at the hands of the British.
(3, 6)

30. Does crying relieve grief?
(3, 16)

LESSON 17 — The Progressive Verb Forms

> **Dictation or Journal Entry**
>
> **Vocabulary:**
>
> A *consul* is an official appointed by a government to look after the welfare and commercial interests of its citizens in foreign countries. The President sent a *consul* to Brazil to watch over U. S. commercial interests.
>
> The *state of the union message* is a speech given by the President to Congress at the beginning of each session to recommend ways to improve the condition of the nation. President Bush suggested strong anti-terror measures in his *state of the union message*.

We have learned the six main verb tenses:

1. present ⟶ *incriminate(s)*
2. past ⟶ *incriminated*
3. future ⟶ *will/shall incriminate*
4. present perfect ⟶ *has/have incriminated*
5. past perfect ⟶ *had incriminated*
6. future perfect ⟶ *will/shall have incriminated*

All six of these main verb tenses also have a **progressive form.** A progressive verb phrase shows action in "progress," or continuing action.

PRESENT PROGRESSIVE TENSE	=	action still in progress at the time of speaking
PAST PROGRESSIVE	=	action in progress throughout a specific time in the past
FUTURE PROGRESSIVE	=	action that will be in progress in the future
PRESENT PERFECT PROGRESSIVE	=	action begun in the past and still continuing in the present
PAST PERFECT PROGRESSIVE	=	past action begun, continued, and terminated in the past
FUTURE PERFECT PROGRESSIVE	=	continuous future action completed at some time in the future

Progressive verb forms are expressed with some form of the verb *to be* and the present participle ("ing" added to the main verb).

Present Progressive The present progressive form consists of the appropriate present tense of *to be* (am/is/are) plus the present participle (verb + *ing*).

> PRESENT PROGRESSIVE = AM, IS, OR ARE + PRESENT PARTICIPLE

The Senate is expelling the senator by a two-thirds vote of its members.

Shh, I am listening to the state of the union message.

The people are voting for the electors.

Past Progressive The past progressive form consists of a past form of *to be* (was/were) plus the present participle.

> PAST PROGRESSIVE = WAS OR WERE + PRESENT PARTICIPLE

The amiable police officer was averting a riot among the bellicose protesters.

Several officers were averting chaos in the streets.

Future Progressive We form the future progressive by adding the present participle to the future of the *to be* verb (shall be/will be).

> FUTURE PROGRESSIVE = SHALL BE OR WILL BE + PRESENT PARTICIPLE

I shall be reviewing how a bill becomes a law.

Congress will be introducing some new bills later.

Present Perfect Progressive We form the present perfect progressive by using *has* or *have*, *been*, and the present participle.

> PRESENT PERFECT PROGRESSIVE = HAS BEEN OR HAVE BEEN + PRESENT PARTICIPLE

The originators of the bill have been proposing this idea to the appropriate committee.

This bill has been proceeding through the House and the Senate.

Past Perfect Progressive The past perfect progressive consists of *had*, *been*, and the present participle.

> PAST PERFECT PROGRESSIVE = HAD BEEN + PRESENT PARTICIPLE

The committee realized it had been reviewing the wrong bill.

Before his secretary interrupted him last Tuesday, the President had been signing bills all day.

Future Perfect Progressive We form the future perfect progressive with *will* or *shall have been*, and the present participle.

<u>FUTURE PERFECT PROGRESSIVE</u> = <u>WILL/SHALL HAVE BEEN</u> + <u>PRESENT PARTICIPLE</u>

At the end of this term, Mrs. Ishigaki <u>will have been representing</u> her community on the school board for sixteen years.

The consul <u>will have been pleading</u> with foreign diplomats for twelve hours by the end of the session.

Example For sentences a–f, write the verb phrase, and tell whether the progressive verb form is present, past, future, present perfect, past perfect, or future perfect.

(a) This June, we shall have been studying the Constitution for ten months.

(b) The House of Representatives was discussing the bill.

(c) Next, the Senate will be evaluating the bill.

(d) The House of Representatives and the Senate had been altering the bill.

(e) Now the senators are voting on the corrected bill.

(f) The President has been observing the progress of this bill.

Solution (a) **shall have been studying**—The verb phrase "shall have been" is a future perfect form, so the entire phrase is **future perfect progressive.**

(b) **was discussing**—We notice that "was" is the past tense form of *to be*, so we know that "was discussing" is the **past progressive.**

(c) **will be evaluating**—"Will be" is the future form of *to be*, so the verb phrase is **future progressive.**

(d) **had been altering**—"Had been" is the past perfect form, so the verb phrase is **past perfect progressive.**

(e) **are voting**—"Are" is a present form of *to be*, so the verb phrase is **present progressive.**

(f) **has been observing**—The verb phrase "has been" indicates the present perfect tense, so the entire verb phrase is **present perfect progressive.**

Practice For sentences a–f, write the verb phrase and name its tense.

  a. The bill was passing by a majority in the Senate.

  b. I shall be watching the President's response.

  c. The President is signing the bill into law.

  d. During that time, the President had been vetoing every law before him.

  e. In January, Kelly will have been working in the White House for two years.

  f. The President has been holding the law for seven days.

Choose the correct word to complete sentences g and h.

  g. The (progressive, perfect) tense shows action that is continuing.

  h. To make the progressive tense, we use some form of the verb *to be* plus the (present, past) participle, which ends in *ing*.

For i and j, replace each blank with the correct vocabulary word(s).

  i. The _____ to France assured the United States that the price of caviar would not increase.

  j. The President outlines his goals for the nation in his _____.

  k. Diagram the simple subject and simple predicate of this sentence: Bobby Ling had been lobbying all day.

More Practice Diagram the simple subject and simple predicate of each sentence. Then name the verb tense.

  1. By Monday, the President will have been stalling the bill for ten days.

  2. Congress had been hoping for the President's signature.

3. We have been waiting for this new law for years.

4. Has Dad been reading the newspaper?

Review Set 17

Choose the correct word to complete sentences 1–10.

1. To (avert, advert, incriminate) is to show evidence of involvement in a crime.
   _(2, 16)

2. The word (amicable, amiable, contemptible) means despicable, or deserving scorn.
   _(12, 15)

3. (Can, May) I borrow a pencil?
   ₍₁₄₎

4. A (census, hospice, lobby) might try to influence lawmakers.
   _(9, 13)

5. (Amicable, Ambiguous, Ambivalent) means "showing goodwill and formal friendliness."
   _(11, 12)

6. A (preposition, helping verb, gerund) is a verbal that functions as a noun.
   ₍₁₆₎

7. The (progressive, perfect) verb tenses show action that has been completed or "perfected."
   ₍₁₅₎

8. The (progressive, perfect) verb tenses show action in progress, or continuing action.
   ₍₁₇₎

9. The perfect verb forms are expressed with some form of the helping verb (be, have, do) plus the past participle.
   ₍₁₅₎

10. The progressive verb forms are expressed with some form of the helping verb (be, have, do) plus the present participle.
    ₍₁₇₎

11. Write whether this sentence is declarative, interrogative, imperative, or exclamatory: Have you read Conrad Richter's *The Light in the Forest*?
    ₍₁₎

12. Write whether this expression is a sentence fragment, a run-on sentence, or a complete sentence: Captured by the Lenni Lenape Indians at the age of four.
    ₍₂₎

13. Rewrite and correct this run-on sentence: In a little frontier town, True Son was born John Butler he was captured by Indians.
(2)

14. Write the gerund in this sentence: Hating became a way of life for True Son.
(16)

15. Write each collective noun in this sentence: True Son's tribe was the Lenni Lenape.
(4)

16. Write the entire verb phrase in this sentence and underline each helping verb: Has True Son been adopted by the Lenni Lenape?
(6)

17. Write each noun from this sentence and label its gender masculine, feminine, indefinite, or neuter: His father, Cuyloga, makes a treaty returning all white captives to their own people.
(7)

18. Write each possessive noun from this list: sons, son's, ladies, lady's, ladies', kidnappers, kidnapper's
(7)

19. Write each word that should be capitalized in this sentence: on boston's beacon hill, acorn street was built to be just wide enough for two cows to pass and is still paved with cobblestones.
(9)

20. Rewrite this song title, adding capital letters as needed:
(9)
"the battle hymn of the republic"

For 21–24, write the plural of each noun.

21. echo   **22.** life
(10, 11)   (10, 11)

23. workman **24.** sister-in-law
(10, 11)   (10, 11)

25. Write the present participle, past tense, and past participle of the verb *advert*.
(13)

For 26 and 27, write the entire verb phrase, labeling its tense.

26. Mrs. Butler is praying for the return of her son John.
(17)

27. Cuyloga has been rearing True Son to think, feel, and fight like an Indian.
(17)

28. Write each preposition in this sentence: By means of
(14) adoption, True Son takes the place of Cuyloga's dead son.

Diagram the simple subject and simple predicate of sentences 29 and 30.

29. Will loathing overcome True Son?
(3, 16)

30. Could Del be laughing at True Son's tears?
(3, 6)

LESSON 18 — Linking Verbs

> **Dictation or Journal Entry**
>
> **Vocabulary:** The words *censor* and *censure* appear similar but differ in meaning.
>
> To *censor* is to edit, bowdlerize, expurgate, or remove something considered objectionable. In 1818, Dr. Thomas Bowdler published a *censored* version of Shakespeare's plays suitable, from his point of view, for the family.
>
> To *censure* is to condemn or blame. In regard to the Constitution's adoption, the Federalists *censured* the Antifederalists.

Linking Verbs   A **linking verb** "links" the subject of a sentence to the rest of the predicate. It does not show action, and it is not "helping" the action verb. Its purpose is to connect a name or description to the subject.

    Daniel Webster <u>was</u> a Senator.

In the sentence above, *was* links "Daniel Webster" with "Senator." The word *Senator* renames Daniel Webster.

    Daniel Webster <u>was</u> respectable.

In the sentence above, *was* links "Daniel Webster" with "respectable." The word *respectable* describes Daniel Webster.

Action or Linking?   We must carefully examine our sentences. Some verbs can be used as either linking or action verbs, as shown in the two sentences below.

    The President <u>appears</u> healthy. (*Appears* is a linking verb. It links "President" with "healthy.")

    The President <u>appears</u> before the Senate to discuss the bill. (*Appears* is an action verb, not a linking verb. The President is doing something—appearing before the Senate.)

Common Linking Verbs   Common linking verbs include all the following forms of the verb "to be":

    is, am, are, was, were, be, being, been

The following are also common linking verbs. Memorize these:

look, feel, taste, smell, sound

seem, appear, grow, become

remain, stay

Identifying Linking Verbs To determine whether a verb is a linking verb, we replace it with a form of the verb "to be"—*is, am, are, was, were, be, being, been*, as in the example below.

The Senator *feels* exuberant.

We replace *feels* with *is*:

The Senator *is* exuberant.

Since the sentence still makes sense, we know that *feels* is a linking verb in this sentence. Now let us examine the word *feels* in the sentence below.

The Senator *feels* the tension in the room.

We replace *feels* with *is*:

The Senator *is* the tension in the room.

The sentence no longer makes sense, so we know that *feels* is not a linking verb in this sentence.

Example Identify and write the linking verb, if any, in each sentence.

(a) A filibuster is a long-winded speech.

(b) The Constitution became a highly respected document.

(c) Ben Franklin looked closely at the details of the Constitution.

(d) Alexander Hamilton appeared indefatigable in his defense of the Constitution.

(e) The writer felt numbness in her hand.

Solution (a) The linking verb **is** links "filibuster" to "speech."

(b) The verb **became** links "Constitution" to "document."

(c) We replace the verb *looked* with *was*: Ben Franklin *was* closely at the details of the Constitution. The sentence no longer makes sense, so we know that the word *looked* is not a linking verb in this sentence. It is an action verb. There are **no linking verbs** in this sentence.

(d) The verb **appeared** links "Alexander Hamilton" to "indefatigable."

(e) We replace the verb *felt* with *was*: The writer *was* numbness in her hand. The sentence no longer makes sense, so we know that the word *felt* is not a linking verb in this sentence. There are **no linking verbs** in this sentence.

Practice **a.** Review the linking verbs (including the "to be" verbs) listed in this lesson. Then say as many as you can to your teacher or to a friend.

Write the linking verbs, if any, from sentences b–h.

b. Lobbyists appear unscrupulous at times.

c. President Kennedy appeared before a joint session of Congress.

d. Alexander Hamilton remains famous for his authorship of *The Federalist Papers*.

e. The filibuster sounded irrelevant and verbose.

f. The President seemed determined to pocket veto the bill.

g. We smelled freshly popped popcorn.

h. The popcorn smelled delicious.

For i–m, replace each blank with the correct vocabulary word.

i. The organization will _____ their leader for accepting bribes.

j. The elementary school may _____ certain inappropriate books that are in the children's library.

k. To _____ means to edit or remove something objectionable.

l. To _____ means to condemn or blame.

m. Expurgate and bowdlerize mean the same as _____.

More Practice Write each linking verb from sentences 1–12.

1. Yes, the senator seemed apprehensive about the final vote.

2. Of course, the bill remains "alive" for ten days after passage in both houses.

3. With Congress in session, the President feels pressured to make a decision abut the bill.

4. Among politicians, selfish interests remain a hindrance to objectivity.

5. After many long hours of debate and discussion, the legislator grew impatient.

6. The representatives stayed loyal to their parties.

7. Last week, the bill finally became law.

8. The senator's voice sounded hoarse after his long filibuster.

9. The Vice President looks distinguished tonight.

10. England is our most loyal ally.

11. The lobbyists were ruthless in their efforts to pass the bill.

12. This outdated milk tastes sour.

For 13–16, write the verb phrase and label it action or linking.

13. Has Senator Hamilton tasted the coffee?

14. To me, the coffee tastes fresh.

15. That red switch sounds the fire alarm.

16. Does the alarm sound loud and disturbing?

Review Set 18 Choose the correct word to complete sentences 1–10.

1. The *state of the union message* is a (movie, newspaper, speech).
(17)

2. A (census, recrimination, caucus) is a counter accusation.
(13, 16)

3. A contemptuous person is (friendly, pleasant, scornful).
(15)

4. (Can, May) we leave class a few minutes early today?
(14)

5. A (caucus, census, lobby) is an official count of people.
(10, 13)

6. A gerund is a verbal that functions as a (linking verb, preposition, noun).
(16)

7. The perfect verb forms show (completed, continuing) action.
(15)

8. The progressive verb forms show (completed, continuing) action.
(17)

9. A (helping, linking) verb links the subject of a sentence to the rest of the predicate.
(18)

10. *Look, feel, taste,* and *smell* are often used as (linking, helping) verbs.
(18)

11. Write whether this expression is a sentence fragment, a run-on sentence, or a complete sentence: Although she's ninety-six, Grandma insists she's not a relic.
(2)

12. Rewrite and correct this run-on sentence: The white prisoners are ungrateful to their rescuers they want to remain with the Indians.
(2)

13. Write the gerund in this sentence: The Indians' crying shocks the soldiers.
(16)

14. Write the abstract noun in this sentence: True Son's rebelliousness shines in his eyes.
(4)

15. From memory, write the twenty-three common helping verbs listed in Lesson 6.
(6)

16. Write all the *to be* verbs and the eleven other linking verbs listed in this lesson.
(18)

17. Write each word that should be capitalized in the following sentence: tim said, "on pinckney street in boston, i saw author louisa may alcott's girlhood home."
(9)

19. In this sentence, write the verb and label it an action verb or a linking verb: After her exercise class, Elle felt invigorated.
(18)

19. Write each word that should be capitalized in this sentence: petunia schnutz said, "this wind is ruining my hairdo!"
(9)

20. Rewrite this outline, adding capital letters as needed:
(9)
    i. the light in the forest
      a. plot
      b. characters
      c. point of view

For 21–24, write the plural of each noun.

21. cello   **22.** thief
(10, 11)   (10, 11)

23. tooth   **24.** toothbrush
(10, 11)   (10, 11)

25. Write the present participle, past tense, and past participle of the verb *censor*.
(13)

For 26 and 27, write the entire verb phrase, labeling its tense.

26. True Son had been scheming his escape.
(17)

27. Make Daylight had eaten the May apple.
(15)

28. Write each preposition in this sentence: Little Crane and Half Arrow hop over logs, run through the deep woods, climb up hills, and trudge by the edge of the Tuscarawas.
(14)

Diagram the simple subject and simple predicate of sentences 29 and 30.

29. Hiking remains Allison's favorite sport.
(3, 16)

30. Has Little Crane been laughing at white men?
(3, 6)

LESSON 19

The Infinitive as a Subject

> **Dictation or Journal Entry**
>
> **Vocabulary:** The Latin root *prob-* means "upright, honorable" and suggests honesty or integrity. In the Middle Ages, it acquired the meaning "proof."
>
> *Approbation* is praise or commendation. The President underscored his *approbation* of the new bill by quickly signing it.
>
> *Probity* is integrity, honesty, and uprightness. The American people expect their elected leaders to have unquestioned *probity*.

The Infinitive The **infinitive,** like the gerund, is a verbal—a word that is formed from a verb but does not function like one. The infinitive is the basic form of the verb, usually preceded by the preposition "to."

    to censor   to incriminate

    to lobby   to appease

The infinitive may function as a noun, an adjective, or an adverb. In this lesson, we will identify infinitives used as nouns and as sentence subjects. Notice that we diagram the infinitive on "stilts" above the base line.

  To censor inappropriate material is the editor's job.

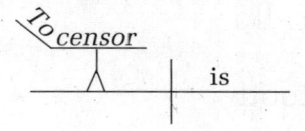

  To appease the angry crowd proved difficult.

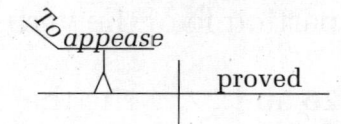

Example 1 Write the infinitive from each sentence.
(a) To delay was the President's intention.

(b) To hold a bill for ten days will veto the bill.

Solution (a) **To delay** is an infinitive used as the subject of the sentence.

(b) **To hold** is an infinitive used as the subject of the sentence.

Example 2 Diagram the simple subject and simple predicate of this sentence: To win seemed impossible.

Solution We diagram the infinitive, *to win*, above the base line on stilts in the location of the sentence subject.

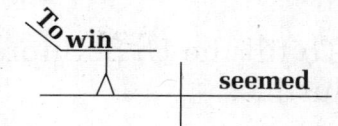

```
   To  win
   ╲  ╱
    ╳     |  seemed
   ╱  ╲___|_____
```

Like the gerund, the infinitive has two tense forms: present and perfect.

PRESENT: *to advert, to impeach, to veto*

PERFECT: *to have adverted, to have impeached, to have vetoed*

Present tense infinitives are italicized here:

To impeach an elected official requires clear evidence of wrongdoing.

To veto a bill demands sufficient reasons.

Perfect tense infinitives are italicized here:

To have adverted to the upcoming lawsuit demonstrated poor taste on the part of the lawyer.

To have appeased the terrorists would have been cowardly.

Example 3 For sentences a and b, write the infinitive and label its tense present or perfect.

(a) To have incriminated the thief gave the detective satisfaction.

(b) To avert more robberies was the detective's goal.

Solution (a) **To have incriminated**—The action is completed, so we know that it is **perfect tense.**

(b) **To avert**—The action is **present tense.**

Practice For a–d, write each infinitive used as a subject and label its tense present or perfect.

a. To recommend an outstanding Supreme Court justice challenged the President.

b. To have overthrown the lower court's verdict might have caused public outrage.

c. To have censured careless employees would have saved the employer's reputation.

d. To fill the U. S. Supreme Court completely requires nine justices.

For e–g, replace each blank with the correct vocabulary word.

e. His _____ won him the nomination for justice of the Supreme Court.

f. The Chief Justice's _____ of the Supreme Court's decision reassured the public.

g. The Latin root _____ means "upright, honorable" or "proof."

h. Diagram the simple subject and simple predicate of this sentence: To exercise regularly will make you fitter.

More Practice

Diagram the simple subject and simple predicate of each sentence.

1. To have snacked would have ruined my appetite for the feast.

2. To campaign requires a gregarious spirit.

3. To have reviewed might have raised my test score.

4. Fortunately, to cook is a pleasure for Aunt Steph.

5. Unfortunately, to sneeze could reveal my hiding place.

6. To have left would have been rude.

Review Set 19

Choose the best word to complete sentences 1–10.

1. To (censor, censure, avert) is to edit, or remove
(2, 18) something objectionable.

2. The (President, Governor, Secretary) gives the state of the
(17) union message.

3. The Latin root *crim-* means (agree, fault, peace).
(16)

4. Contemptible means (hospitable, despicable, honorable).
(15)

5. *Can* means "to be (able, permitted) to."
(14)

6. A(n) (infinitive, gerund) ends in *-ing* and functions as a noun.

7. A(n) (infinitive, gerund) is the basic form of the verb, usually preceded by the preposition "to."

8. A (perfect, progressive) tense verb shows completed action.

9. (Have, Has) Woolie entered the pigtail contest?

10. (Do, Does) she expect to win?

11. Write whether this sentence is declarative, interrogative, imperative, or exclamatory: Steven, your eyes are so blue!

12. Tell whether this group of words is a fragment, run-on, or complete sentence: To have been affected by the Great Depression.

13. From the following sentence, write each noun and label it abstract or concrete: With determination and perfection, Stephanie excels in school.

For 14 and 15, write the plural of each noun.

14. batch   **15.** fiasco

Write each word that should be capitalized in sentences 16 and 17.

16. homer, a little mouse living inside miss curtis's desk drawer, wrote an essay titled "what a mouse can learn in first grade."

17. on the way to fort pitt, little crane explains how the white people learned right from wrong.

18. Replace the blank with the singular present tense form of the verb: Rabbits <u>munch</u> alfalfa. A rabbit _____ alfalfa.

19. Write each preposition in this sentence: According to Little Crane, white men cannot hear; they stand next to him and talk loudly.

20. Write the present participle, past tense, and past participle of the verb *reach*.

For 21–23, write the verb phrase and name its tense.

21. Little Crane is explaining white man's idiosyncrasies.

22. Indians had lived longer in this land.

23. Half Arrow and Little Crane had been following the white captives to Fort Pitt.

24. For a and b, write the verb and label it action or linking.
(a) I smelled smoke in the basement.
(b) The smoke in the basement smelled sulphurous.

For 25 and 26, write the gerund and label its tense present or perfect.

25. Swaggering characterized the white-skinned legion.

26. Having swum two miles before breakfast left Ms. Williams famished.

Write the infinitive in sentences 27 and 28, and label its tense present or perfect.

27. To shake hands is an unfamiliar custom for True Son.

28. To have swum so far before breakfast was a great accomplishment for Ms. Williams.

Diagram the simple subject and simple predicate of sentences 29 and 30.

29. To have sneezed would have attracted attention to my whereabouts.

30. Could sneezing have caused my downfall?

LESSON 20 — Phrases and Clauses

> **Dictation or Journal Entry**
>
> **Vocabulary:** We will understand the U. S. Constitution better if we learn terms such as *pocket veto* and *ex post facto*.
>
> A *pocket veto* occurs when the President holds a bill unsigned until Congress is no longer in session. The bill is vetoed, for the President cannot send it back to Congress for revisions. Because the bill sat on the President's desk without his signature for ten days and Congress had adjourned, it received a *pocket veto*.
>
> *Ex post facto* means "made or done after something has occurred but having retroactive effect." An *ex post facto* law is one that allows punishment for a crime that was not illegal at the time it was committed. Because the Constitution declares *ex post facto* laws illegal, cars purchased before smog equipment was required are exempt from smog checks.

Phrases   A **phrase** is a group of words used as a single part of speech in a sentence. A phrase may contain nouns and verbs, but it does not have both a subject and a predicate. Phrases are italicized below.

PREPOSITIONAL PHRASES:

of nine justices

with the approval of Congress

for Supreme Court Justices

VERB PHRASES:

should have been committed

would have approved

might have selected

GERUND PHRASES:

averting disaster

censoring inappropriate material

campaigning effectively

INFINITIVE PHRASES:

to involve innocent bystanders

to make a complete court

to serve your country

Clauses   A **clause** is a group of words with a subject and a predicate. In the clauses below, we have italicized the simple subjects and underlined the simple predicates.

as the *judge* <u>tapped</u> the gavel

since these *courts* <u>are dealing</u> with federal cases

but only one *justice* <u>serves</u> as Chief Justice

(*you*) <u>Watch</u> the court proceedings.

Example 1 Tell whether each group of words is a phrase or a clause.

(a) to appoint Supreme Court Justices

(b) in the United States

(c) after the President nominates the justices

(d) qualifying for service on the highest court

(e) if Congress had passed the law

Solution (a) This group of words is an infinitive **phrase.** It does not have a subject or predicate.

(b) This word group is a prepositional **phrase.** It does not have a subject or predicate.

(c) This word group is a **clause.** Its subject is *President*; its predicate is <u>nominates</u>.

(d) This is a gerund **phrase.** It does not have a subject or predicate.

(e) This word group is a **clause.** Its subject is *Congress*; its predicate is <u>had passed</u>.

Every complete sentence has at least one clause. Some sentences have more than one clause. We have italicized the simple subjects and underlined the simple predicates in each clause of the sentence below. Notice that it contains four clauses (four subject and predicate combinations).

After the *court* <u>studied</u> the case, but before the *justices* <u>voted</u>, one *judge* <u>admitted</u> that *she* <u>felt</u> ambivalent.

Below, we have diagrammed the simple subjects and simple predicates of each clause from the sentence above.

1. After the court studied the case,   court | studied

2. but before the justices voted,   justices | voted

3. one judge admitted   judge | admitted

4. that she felt ambivalent.   she | felt

Example 2 Diagram the simple subject and simple predicate of each clause in this sentence:

After *Marbury vs. Madison* was decided, the Supreme Court determined if a law was within the bounds of the Constitution.

Solution We examine the sentence and find that there are three clauses:

1. After *Marbury vs. Madison* was decided,   M vs. M | was decided

2. the *Supreme Court* determined   S. Court | determined

3. if a *law* was within the bounds of the Constitution.   law | was

Practice For a–d, tell whether the group of words is a phrase or a clause.

a. because the Supreme Court will review the law

b. in the landmark case of a school in Topeka, Kansas

c. if segregation of schools proved unconstitutional

d. for fairness in the South

e. Diagram the simple subject and simple predicate of each clause in this sentence: Until the Supreme Court settled the *Brown vs. Board of Education* case, the South had schools in which black and white students were segregated.

For f and g, replace each blank with the correct vocabulary word(s).

f. Because _____ laws are unconstitutional, segregated schools received no fines or punishment for their practices.

g. A _____ is one way a President can stop a bill from becoming law when Congress is not in session.

More Practice Write whether each word group is a phrase or a clause.

1. after the court settled the case

2. with knowledge of the defendant's rights

3. since an accused person must be informed of his rights

4. so the police give the accused the Miranda warning

5. as an owner of personal property

6. depriving an owner of personal property without due process of the law

7. because the *Dred Scott vs. Sanford* case was overturned twice

8. about freeing a slave

9. for the Bill of Rights protects us

10. one of the greatest cases in history

Review Set 20 Choose the best word or root to complete sentences 1–9.

1. The Latin root (*crim-, plac-, prob-*) suggests honesty and integrity.
(19)

2. To (censor, censure, advert) is to condemn or blame.
(18)

3. The President gives the state of the union message to (Russia, Congress, Canada).
(17)

4. The Latin root (*plac-, bell-, crim-*) means "fault, or accusation."
(6, 16)

5. A cruel tyrant is (amicable, contemptible, bicameral).
(15)

6. A (phrase, clause) has both a subject and a predicate.
(20)

7. *Affection* and *affectation* are (concrete, abstract, collective) nouns.
(4)

8. A (perfect, progressive) tense verb shows continuing action.
(17)

9. (Have, Has) Mario and Abby ironed out their differences?
(12)

10. Write whether this expression is a phrase or a clause: for the Susquehanna River belongs to the Indian people
(20)

11. Write whether this sentence is declarative, interrogative, imperative, or exclamatory: True Son exhibits fear of the stairs and bannister rail.
(1)

12. Write whether this group of words is a sentence fragment, run-on sentence, or complete sentence: Gordie is born while True Son lives with the Indians.
(2)

13. Write the verb from this sentence and label it action or linking: Gordie appears pleased with his older brother.
(18)

For 14 and 15, write the plural of each noun.

14. photo
(10, 11)

15. ox
(10, 11)

16. Write each preposition in this sentence: The name of the girl next to Graham is Lauren.
(14)

17. Write each word that should be capitalized in this sentence: graham loves football and old automobiles like fords and chevys.
(9)

18. Replace the blank with the singular present tense form of the verb: They <u>teach</u> violin. She _____ violin.
(5)

19. Write the infinitive in this sentence and label its tense present or perfect: To have eaten so many pancakes was foolish.
(19)

20. Write the present participle, past tense, and past participle of the verb *tap*.
(13)

For sentences 21–23, write the verb phrase and name its tense.

21. In June, Ms. Finch will have been excelling in academics for nine years.
(17)

22. Had Aunt Kate recognized True Son?
(15)

23. To his white mother, True Son looks like an Indian.
(5)

24. Write the gerund in this sentence and label its tense present or perfect: Dressing differently is difficult for True Son.
(16)

For 25 and 26, write the correct verb form to complete each sentence.

25. Next winter we (future of *avert*) flooding with sand bags.
(8)

26. The new storm drains (present progressive of *avert*) flood problems downtown.
(17)

Diagram the simple subject and simple predicate of each clause in sentences 27 and 28.

27. True Son is given new clothing, but he refuses it.
(3, 20)

28. Gordie understands why True Son is angry.
(3, 20)

Diagram the simple subject and simple predicate of sentences 29 and 30.

29. Reading may give you great pleasure.
(3, 16)

30. To quit might indicate laziness.
(3, 19)

LESSON 21

The Direct Object • Diagramming a Direct Object

> **Dictation or Journal Entry**
>
> **Vocabulary:** In informal writing, we find the two Latin abbreviations *i.e.* and *e.g.*
>
> From the Latin *exempli gratia*, *e.g.* means "for example," indicating that some examples are being cited, but more exist. The novel featured many colorful characters, *e.g.*, the knight, the squire, the yeoman, and the prioress.
>
> From the Latin *id est*, *i.e.* means "that is to say," indicating equivalent terms. The class will study the document that governs the United States, *i.e.*, the Constitution.
>
> In formal writing we do not use these abbreviations. We use "for example" instead of *e.g.*, and we use "that is" instead of *i.e.*

Finding the Direct Object

A **direct object** follows an *action verb* and tells who or what receives the action.

The President selected the ambassador.

              ↑   ↑

      action verb   direct object

We can answer these three questions to find the direct object of a sentence:

1. What is the verb in the sentence?

2. Is it an *action verb*?

3. Who or what receives the action? (direct object)

We will follow the steps above to find the direct object of this sentence:

The ambassador earned an appointment.

QUESTION 1:   What is the verb?
ANSWER: The verb is "earned."

QUESTION 2:   Is it an *action verb*?
ANSWER: Yes.

QUESTION 3:   Who or what receives the action?
ANSWER: The *appointment* is "earned."

Therefore, "appointment" is the direct object.

Example 1   Follow the procedure above to find the direct object of this sentence:

   The Supreme Court may reverse a lower court's decision.

Solution   We answer the questions as follows:

   QUESTION 1:   What is the verb?
   ANSWER: The verb is "may reverse."

   QUESTION 2:   Is it an *action verb*?
   ANSWER: Yes.

   QUESTION 3:   Who or what receives the action?
   ANSWER: *decision* may be reversed.

   Therefore, **decision** is the direct object.

Example 2   Answer the three questions above to find the direct object of this sentence:

   Treason is a crime against the United States.

Solution   We answer the questions as follows:

   QUESTION 1:   What is the verb?
   ANSWER: The verb is "is."

   QUESTION 2:   Is it an *action verb*?
   ANSWER: No. "Is" is a linking verb.

   Therefore, this sentence has **no direct object.**

Diagramming the Direct Object   Below is a diagram of the simple subject, simple predicate, and direct object of this sentence:

   Juries weigh the evidence.

   Juries | weigh | evidence
   (subject) | (verb) | (direct object)

   Vertical line indicating direct object does not cross through base line.

Following the action verb, a vertical line indicates a direct object.

We remember that a gerund functions as a noun. The direct object in the sentence below is a gerund.

   Do the jurors enjoy deliberating?

   jurors | Do enjoy | deliberating
   (subject) | (verb) | (direct object)

An infinitive can function as a noun as well. The direct object in the following sentence is an infinitive.

Would you like **to speak**?

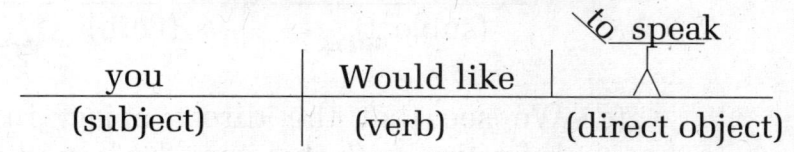

you	Would like	to speak
(subject)	(verb)	(direct object)

Notice that sometimes the word *to* is omitted from the infinitive:

Stephen will help **clean.**

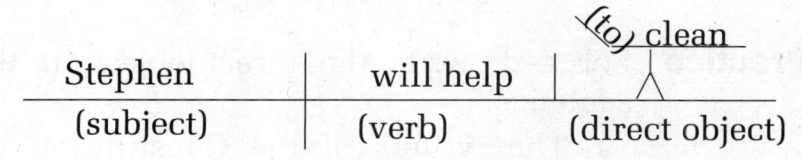

Stephen	will help	(to) clean
(subject)	(verb)	(direct object)

Can you help **vacuum**?

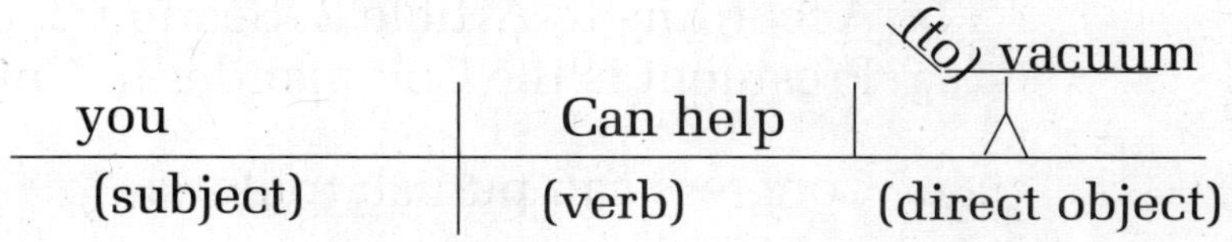

you	Can help	(to) vacuum
(subject)	(verb)	(direct object)

Example 3 Diagram the simple subject, simple predicate, and direct object of each sentence:

(a) Two witnesses may incriminate a traitor.

(b) Now the defendant desires to confess.

(c) Have you begun packing?

(d) On the camping trip, I shall help cook.

Solution (a) The vertical line after the verb, may incriminate, indicates the direct object, traitor.

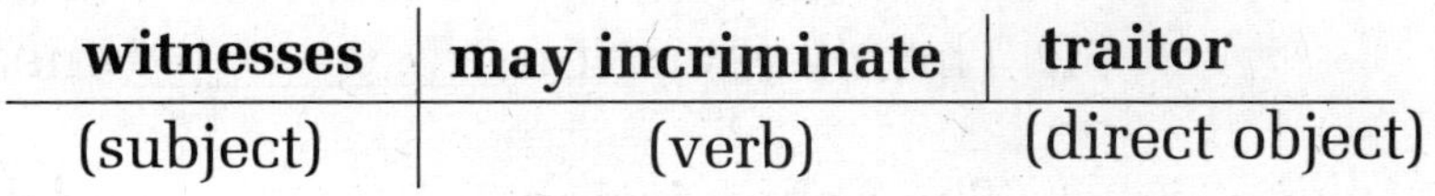

witnesses	**may incriminate**	**traitor**
(subject)	(verb)	(direct object)

(b) We see that the direct object in this sentence is an infinitive.

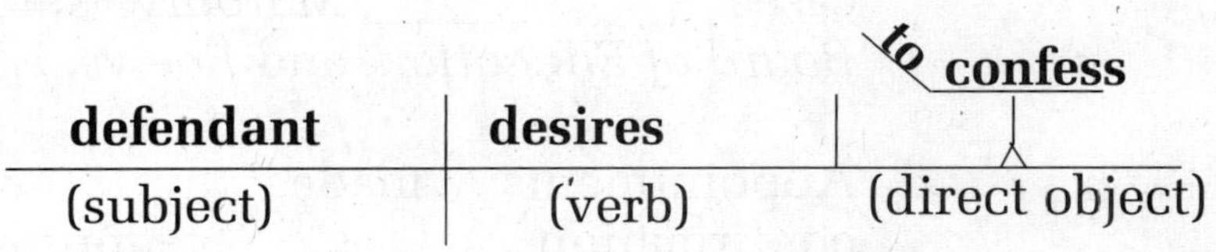

defendant	**desires**	to **confess**
(subject)	(verb)	(direct object)

(c) The direct object is a gerund.

```
  you     |  Have begun  |  packing
(subject)    (verb)         (direct object)
```

(d) We see that the direct object in this sentence is an infinitive with the word "to" omitted.

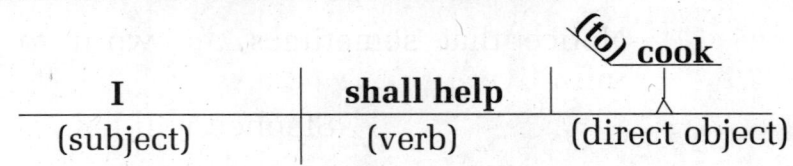

```
   I      |  shall help  |  (to) cook
(subject)    (verb)         (direct object)
```

Practice For a–d, write the direct object, if there is one, in each sentence.

a. The writers of the Constitution wanted a balance of power.

b. According to Article 2, Section 2, of the Constitution, the President is the Commander in Chief of the armed forces.

c. Congress can punish traitors.

d. Our President negotiates treaties with other countries.

Diagram the simple subject, simple predicate, and direct object of sentences e–h.

e. May the President veto bills?

f. Susan B. Anthony led a protest parade.

g. In 1913, women demanded to vote.

h. Woman suffragists began picketing.

For i–l, replace each blank with the correct vocabulary word.

i. The abbreviation _____ means "for example."

j. The abbreviation _____ means "that is."

k. The U. S. Supreme Court has heard many landmark cases, _____, *Marbury vs. Madison*, *Brown vs. The Board of Education*, and *Roe vs. Wade*.

l. Appointments made by the President require confirmation, _____, approval, by the Senate.

Review Set 21

Choose the correct word or root to complete sentences 1–7.

1. A (quorum, pocket veto, census) occurs when the President holds a bill for more than ten days when Congress is not in session.

2. The Latin root *prob-* suggests (fault, war, honesty).

3. The word *censor* means (agree, edit, avert).

4. A (census, caucus, consul) is a government official working in a foreign country.

5. This evidence may (appease, incriminate, advert) the thief.

6. The perfect tense shows (completed, continuing) action.

7. Robert (do, does) his math homework every day.

8. Unscramble the following words to make an imperative sentence: wise   listen   words   to

9. Write whether the following word group is a sentence fragment, a run-on sentence, or a complete sentence: True Son accuses Uncle Wilse of being one of the Paxton Boys the Paxton Boys massacre unsuspecting Indians.

10. Write each abstract noun from this list: pilgrim, grace, pacifist, pacifism, communism, communist

11. Rewrite this book title adding capital letters as needed: paul revere and the world he lived in

12. Write each possessive noun from this list: kings, king's, queens', bosses', boss's, bosses, James's, Jameses

For 13–15, write the plural of each noun.

13. embargo   14. proof   15. knife

16. Write the present participle, past tense, and past participle of the verb *appease*.

17. Write each preposition in the following sentence: In front of Del and Gordie, Aunt Kate talks about bathing and dressing True Son in his jacket and pantaloons.

For sentences 18–20, write the verb phrase and label its tense.

18. True Son detested Uncle Wilse.
(5)

19. Uncle Wilse had slapped True Son for his accusations.
(15)

20. Next month, Mrs. Butler will have been waiting for her son's return for twelve years.
(17)

21. From memory, write all the *to be* verbs and the eleven other linking verbs listed in Lesson 18.
(18)

22. From memory, write the twenty-three common helping verbs listed in Lesson 6.
(6)

23. Write the infinitive in this sentence and label its tense present or perfect: I would like to have won.
(19)

24. Write the gerund in this sentence and label its tense present or perfect: Does Maggie like shopping?
(16)

For 25 and 26, write whether the expression is a phrase or a clause.

25. while his eyes burned with black, consuming hatred
(20)

26. taking his Indian garb and two pairs of moccasins
(20)

27. Diagram the simple subject and simple predicate of each clause in this sentence: If I finish my homework, I shall read a magazine before I go to bed.
(3, 20)

Diagram the simple subject, simple predicate, and the direct object, of sentences 28–30.

28. I shall slice the watermelon.
(3, 21)

29. You may help to serve.
(19, 21)

30. Have they finished eating?
(16, 21)

LESSON 22

Capitalization: People Titles, Family Words, School Subjects

> **Dictation or Journal Entry**
> **Vocabulary:** The terms *judicial* and *jurisdiction* relate to courts of law.
> *Judicial* means having to do with a court of law or the administration of justice. The *judicial* branch of government interprets the law.
> *Jurisdiction* is the range or extent of authority; power. The Supreme Court has original *jurisdiction* over ambassadors, public ministers, and consuls.
> *Judicious* means having or exercising good judgment; wise; sensible. Fortunately, the general was a *judicious* commander of troops.

We remember that proper nouns require capital letters and that common nouns are capitalized when they are a part of a proper noun. We also capitalize parts of an outline, the first word of a sentence, the first word of every line of poetry, the pronoun *I*, the first word in a direct quotation, and the important words in titles. Now we will review additional capitalization rules.

Titles Used with Names of People

Titles used with names of people require a capital letter. Often, these are abbreviations. We capitalize initials when they stand for a proper name.

> M. E. Bradford
> Dr. Stanley Livingston
> Mr. and Mrs. George Washington
> General Robert E. Lee
> Reverend Samuel Johnson
> Senator Douglas
> King Henry VIII
> Aunt Ila Mae

Family Words

When **family words** such as *father, mother, grandmother,* or *grandfather* are used instead of a person's name, these words are capitalized. However, they are not capitalized when words such as *my, your, his, our,* or *their* are used before them.

> Hey, *Dad*, did you watch the news this morning?
> I asked *my dad* if he watched the news this morning.
>
> Zane gave *Grandmother* a new biscuit recipe.
> Zane gave *her grandmother* a new biscuit recipe.

School Subjects When the name of a school subject comes from a proper noun, it is capitalized. Otherwise it is not. See the examples below.

    Hebrew   government
    Greek   biology
    Mandarin   computer programming

Example Correct the following sentences by adding capital letters where they are needed.

(a) What do you know about king louis xiv?

(b) I'm going to ask uncle to take me to the library.

(c) My brother needs one more spanish class and two math classes in order to graduate.

Solution (a) We capitalize **King** because it is a title used with the name of a person. We capitalize **Louis** XIV because it is a proper noun.

(b) **Uncle** requires a capital because it is used instead of a person's name.

(c) **Spanish** comes from a proper noun, so we capitalize it. We do not capitalize brother, for it is preceded by "my." We do not capitalize math, for it does not come from a proper noun.

Practice Write each word that should be capitalized in a–d.

a. Many of our english words trace back to latin roots.

b. Oh, dad, will you help me study for my social studies test?

c. Did mary j. davison marry pastor hugh williamson?

d. His father, colonel lopez, fried the eggplant.

For e–g, replace each blank with the correct vocabulary word.

e. The U. S. Supreme Court has _____ to overturn decisions by lower courts.

f. Please do not interrupt the _____ proceedings while the court is in session.

g. I admire your _____ plan to study before watching a movie.

More Practice See Master Worksheets.

Review Set 22 Choose the correct word to complete sentences 1–7.

1. The Latin abbreviation (e.g., etc., i.e.) means "for
(21) example, indicating that some examples are cited, but more exist.

2. (*Habeas corpus, Ex post facto*) means "made or done after
(7, 20) something but having a retroactive effect."

3. (Approbation, recrimination, affectation) is praise, or
(16, 19) commendation.

4. The word *censure* means (advert, appease, blame).
(6, 18)

5. Matilda, a poor sport and a bitter loser, made several
(12, 15) (amiable, pacifist, contemptuous) comments to her opponent.

6. A progressive verb form shows (completed, continuing)
(17) action.

7. Lucy (have, has) curly hair.
(12)

8. Unscramble these words to make a declarative sentence:
(1)
rename   Indians   Butler   John   the

9. Write whether the following word group is a sentence
(2) fragment, a run-on sentence, or a complete sentence: When Del returns to his regiment, True Son actually misses him.

10. In this sentence, write each noun, labeling it masculine,
(7) feminine, neuter, or indefinite: A young doe watches eagles soaring high above the treetops.

11. Write each concrete noun from this list: language,
(4) stream, nephew, customs, basket

For 12 and 13, write each word that should be capitalized.

12. my mother said, "next semester, uncle robert will take
(9) biology and spanish at the university."

13. my grandfather read me a story called "the race for the
(9) south pole."

14. Write each possessive noun from this list: witness's,
(7) witnesses, signatures, judge's, judges

For 15–17, write the plural of each noun.

15. ratio   **16.** goose   **17.** cherry
(10, 11)   (10, 11)   (10, 11)

18. Write the present participle, past tense, and past
(13) participle of the verb *clap*.

19. Write each preposition in this sentence: In spite of the
(14) thunderstorm, we continued our trek through the forest, alongside the rushing river.

20. In this sentence, write the verb phrase and label its tense:
(17) True Son's anger has been brewing for several days.

For sentences 21 and 22, write the verb phrase and label it action or linking.

21. Bejance, the basket weaver, appears wise and
(18) compassionate.

22. Does Corn Blade, an old Indian, appear in Chapter Five?
(18)

23. In this sentence, write the infinitive and label its tense
(19) present or perfect: Mr. Turkey wanted to fly.

24. In this sentence, write the gerund and label its tense
(16) present or perfect: Having studied gave me confidence for the test.

For 25 and 26, write whether the expression is a phrase or a clause.

25. if everyone is a slave to his culture
(20)

26. like the brown furry back of an immense beast
(20)

27. Diagram the simple subject and simple predicate (not
(3, 20) including the direct object) of each clause in this
sentence: When Len was fourteen, he learned to play the
banjo.

Diagram the simple subject and simple predicate, including
the direct object, of sentences 28–30.

28. Pat needs to apologize.
(3, 21)

29. Have you tried surfing?
(3, 21)

30. Remember to smile.
(3, 21)

LESSON 23

Descriptive Adjectives
• Proper Adjectives

> **Dictation or Journal Entry**
> **Vocabulary:** Let us examine additional terms that we find in the Constitution.
> *Appellate* is "having to do with an appeal, or call for help." When people feel that they did not receive fair treatment in a lower court, they appeal to a higher court, an *appellate* court.
> To *apportion* is to give out parts or portions. "Representatives shall be *apportioned* among the states" means that each state will get its fair share of representatives.
> An *appropriation* is something, usually money, set aside for some specific purpose. Some people felt that Congress's *appropriation* for the army was not enough.

An adjective describes a person, place, or thing. There are many different kinds of adjectives. There are **limiting adjectives** such as *a*, *an*, and *the* (also called "articles"); **demonstrative adjectives** such as *this*, *that*, *those*, and *these*; and **possessive adjectives** such as *his, her, their, our, its, your,* and *my*.

Descriptive Adjectives

In this lesson we will concentrate on **descriptive adjectives**, which describe a person, place, or thing. Sometimes they answer the question, "What kind?" Descriptive adjectives are italicized below.

democratic government
world leader
intelligent, influential official

Often descriptive adjectives come before the person, place, or thing as in this sentence:

Did that *powerful, sensible* speech appeal to the *needy* citizens as well as to the *wealthy* citizens?

Sometimes descriptive adjectives come after the noun or pronoun as in this example:

The writers of the Constitution, *brilliant* and *cooperative,* created a document that has stood the test of time.

Some descriptive adjectives end in suffixes like these:

—able   amiable, amicable, suitable, unbelievable
—al   mutual, historical, congressional, trial, medical
—ful   peaceful, soulful, joyful, helpful, hopeful
—ible   contemptible, incredible, edible, divisible

—ic	stoic, autocratic, heroic, terrific, magnetic
—ive	legislative, submissive, inactive, attractive
—less	lawless, penniless, fearless, painless, ceaseless
—ous	ambiguous, famous, contemptuous, judicious
—y	hilly, shiny, crazy, snooty, sunny, greedy

Example 1 Write each descriptive adjective in sentences a–c.

(a) Senators and Representatives need not take religious tests.

(b) The Constitution is the supreme law of the land.

(c) Federal law supersedes state law.

Solution (a) **Religious** describes "tests".

(b) **Supreme** describes "law".

(c) **Federal** and **state** describe "law."

Improving Our Writing Descriptive adjectives help us to draw pictures using words. They make our writing more precise and more interesting. For example, hair can be *greasy, stringy, blonde, brunette, coarse, fine, thick, thin, curly, straight, wavy, poofy, matted, shiny,* or *dull*. When we write, we can use descriptive adjectives to create more detailed pictures.

Example 2 Replace each blank with a descriptive adjective to add more detail to the word "President" in this sentence:

The _____, _____ President remained extremely popular with the American people.

Solution Our answers will vary. Here are some possibilities: **astute, intelligent, receptive, gregarious, compassionate, hospitable, optimistic, fair, competent, brilliant, honest, trustworthy, courageous, moral, upright,** and **honorable.**

Proper Adjectives An adjective can be common or proper. Common adjectives are formed from common nouns and are not capitalized:

COMMON NOUN	COMMON ADJECTIVE
democracy	democratic
republic	republican
month	monthly

strength   strong

Proper adjectives are formed from proper nouns and are always capitalized:

PROPER NOUN	PROPER ADJECTIVE
New Jersey	New Jersey (turnpike)
Lincoln	Lincoln (penny)
Easter	Easter (basket)
Chrysler	Chrysler (convertible)

Sometimes the form of the proper adjective changes as in the examples below.

PROPER NOUN	PROPER ADJECTIVE
France	French (restaurant)
Spain	Spanish (hacienda)
Canada	Canadian (goose)
Alaska	Alaskan (glacier)

Example 3 For sentences a–d, write and capitalize each proper adjective. Then write the noun it describes.

(a) Modern buildings still reflect the influence of roman architecture.

(b) The american way of life appeals to many throughout the world.

(c) We enjoy authentic thai food in many local restaurants.

(d) Not all of the founding fathers agreed with the jeffersonian philosophy.

Solution (a) **Roman architecture**   (b) **American way**

(c) **Thai food**   (d) **Jeffersonian philosophy**

Practice Write each descriptive and proper adjective in sentences a–d.

a. Article VI, responsible and comprehensive, states that debts will be paid.

b. The British, French, and American governments have much in common.

c. All national laws must recognize the absolute authority of the Constitution.

d. The Veterans Day celebration honored all who had fought in the wars.

For e and f, write two descriptive adjectives to describe each noun. Answers will vary.

e. judge **f.** candidate

For g and h, write a noun that might be described by the proper adjective. Answers will vary.

g. African **h.** Thanksgiving

For i–k, replace each blank with the correct vocabulary word.

i. Max did not _____ the pizza fairly, for his slice was larger than the rest.

j. _____ courts have the power to rule on legal appeals.

k. Each government _____ results from an act of legislature.

More Practice See "Hysterical Fiction #2" in Master Worksheets.

Review Set 23 Choose the correct word to complete sentences 1–6.

1. The words judicial and jurisdiction relate to courts of
(22) (milk, tennis, law).

2. The Latin abbreviation (e.g., etc., i.e.) means "that is to
(21) say," indicating equivalent terms.

3. Congress declares (*habeas corpus, ex post facto,* tax) laws
(7, 20) illegal.

4. (Approbation, Probity, Recrimination) is integrity, or
(16, 19) uprightness.

5. *May* means "to be (able, permitted) to."
(14)

6. To make the (perfect, progressive) verb form, we use
(17) some form of the verb *to be* plus the present participle, which ends in *ing*.

7. Write whether this sentence is declarative, interrogative, imperative, or exclamatory: Change your clothes before dinner.
(1)

8. Write whether this word group is a sentence fragment, a run-on sentence, or a complete sentence: Is February the month when the first frog croaks?
(2)

9. From this sentence, write each noun and label it concrete or abstract: Have the Indians made a treaty with the white man?
(4)

For 10–12, write the plural of each noun.

10. branch   **11.** attorney-at-law   **12.** Monday
(10, 11)   (10, 11)   (10, 11)

Write each word that should be capitalized in 13 and 14.

13. my orthodontist, dr. richard curtis, has an office on green street in pasadena.
(9)

14. when i was a child, i ate scottish shortbread every christmas eve as grandma read a poem called "a lonely little tree in the forest."
(9)

15. Write two linking verbs that refer to our senses.
(18)

16. Write the present participle, past tense, and past participle of the verb *drop*.
(13)

For sentences 17 and 18, write the verb phrase and label its tense.

17. True Son hungered for the sight of an Indian face again.
(5)

18. Gordie and True Son had planned to visit Corn Blade.
(15)

For sentences 19 and 20, write the verb phrase and label it action or linking.

19. Uncle Wilse looked everywhere for True Son.
(18)

20. Gordie looked very unhappy.
(18)

For 21 and 22, write whether the expression is a phrase or a clause.

21. when Myra Butler learns of True Son's disappearance
(20)

22. across mountains and rivers through a dangerous land
(20)

23. Write each preposition from this sentence: According to
(14) Parson Elder, Myra Butler needs patience with Johnny.

Write each descriptive or proper adjective from sentences 24–26.

24. Grandma likes Danish cookies with strong black coffee.
(23)

25. In 1964, Stephen suffered incessant hiccups and high
(23) fevers from Hong Kong flu.

26. Relaxing on Mediterranean beaches, Juan enjoyed blue
(23) skies and warm temperatures.

Diagram the simple subject and simple predicate, including the direct object, of sentences 27–30.

27. Did Mr. Turkey try flying?
(16, 21)

28. To have flown would have revealed panic.
(19, 21)

29. Does diagramming help you?
(16, 21)

30. Has Harold learned to cook?
(19, 21)

LESSON 24

The Limiting Adjectives • Diagramming Adjectives

> **Dictation or Journal Entry**
>
> **Vocabulary:** The Latin root *lev-* means to lighten or to raise.
>
> *Alleviate* means to relieve, diminish, or lighten. Providing equal representation in the Senate *alleviated* the fears of the smaller states of being overpowered by the larger states.
>
> *Levity* is frivolity, giddiness, and lack of appropriate seriousness. The usher's *levity* during the funeral seemed disrespectful to those who were grieving.

Limiting Adjectives help to define, or "limit," a noun or pronoun. They tell "which one," "what kind," "how many," or "whose." There are six categories of limiting adjectives. They include articles, demonstrative adjectives, numbers, possessive adjectives (both pronouns and nouns), and indefinites.

Articles Articles are the most commonly used adjectives, and they are also the shortest—*a, an, the*.

a law	*the* branch
a statute	*the* jurisdiction
an appropriation	*the* recrimination
an amendment	*the* caucus

We use *a* before words beginning with a consonant sound, and *an* before words beginning with a vowel sound. It is the sound and not the spelling that determines whether we use *a* or *an*:

an honor	*a* habeas corpus
an urbanization	*a* uniform
an R-rating	*a* regulation
an x-axis	*a* xylophone

Demonstrative WHICH ONE?

this hospice	*that* levity
those pacifists	*these* lobbyists

Numbers HOW MANY?

two Senators	*nine* justices
seven articles	*ten* amendments

Possessive Adjectives Both pronouns and nouns commonly function as adjectives. They answer the question, WHOSE?

Pronouns WHOSE?

his opinion   *her* suggestion
their argument   *our* democracy
its longevity   *your* allegiance
my patriotism

Nouns WHOSE?

Hamilton's beliefs   *Franklin's* wisdom
Washington's leadership   *Morris's* articulation
Langdon's signature   *Sherman's* prestige

Indefinites HOW MANY?

some dissenters   *few* militants
many representatives   *several* consuls
no traitors   *any* solution

Example 1 Write each limiting adjective that you find in these sentences.

(a) Does your state legislature govern its constituents wisely?

(b) A candidate will need many supporters to win this election.

(c) One senator voted for the bill.

(d) These elected officials have few enemies.

(e) Those senators opposed the bill.

(f) John Adams's son became our sixth President.

Solution
(a) **your, its**   (b) **A, many, this**

(c) **One, the**   (d) **These, few**

(e) **Those, the**   (e) **John Adams's, our, sixth**

Diagramming Adjectives

We diagram adjectives by placing them on a slanted line beneath the noun or pronoun they describe, modify, or "limit."

America's (possessive adjective) *first* (limiting adjective) President united *the* (article) *many* (indefinite adjective) senators.

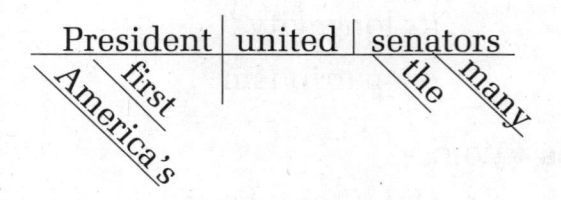

```
President | united | senators
 \  \              /   \
America's first         the many
```

In the sentence above, *America's* tells "whose," and *first* tells "which one" of the Presidents. *The*, an article, and *many*, an indefinite adjective modify the noun "senators."

Example 2 Diagram this sentence:

James Madison's hard work produced a practical constitution.

Solution We see that the adjectives *James Madison's* and *hard* describe, or modify, "work," and *a* and *practical* modify "constitution," so we diagram the sentence like this:

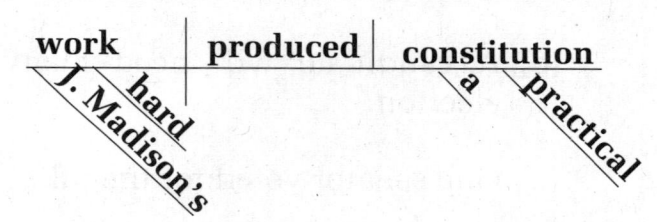

```
work      | produced | constitution
 \  \                    \   \
J. Madison's hard         a   practical
```

Practice For a and b, replace each blank with the correct vocabulary word.

a. Ms. Gleep's _____, evidenced by her snickering and joking, seemed inappropriate during the solemn ceremony.

b. Rest and relaxation _____ stress and frustration.

Write each limiting adjective that you find in sentences c–f.

c. The Constitution's ratification demonstrated the politicians' ability to compromise.

d. His name appears among many witnesses.

e. Article VII lists those nine states ratifying the Constitution.

f. These first ten amendments, or the Bill of Rights, protect our rights.

g. Diagram this sentence: Their persistent demands produced the Constitution's Bill of Rights.

More Practice See Master Worksheets

Review set 24 Choose the correct word to complete sentences 1–6.

1. (Judicial, Appellate, Ambiguous) means having to do
(23) with an appeal, or call for help.

2. (Ambiguous, Judicial, Ambivalent) means having to do
(11, 22) with a court of law or the administration of justice.

3. The Latin term *exempli gratia*, abbreviated *e. g.*, means
(21) ("that is to say," "for example," "to love").

4. We use the helping verb (can, may) when we are
(14) requesting permission.

5. A census is an official (group, carload, count) of people.
(13)

6. (Do, Does) Maxine tell the truth?
(12)

7. Write whether this sentence is declarative, interrogative,
(1) imperative, or exclamatory:

Take the road less traveled.

8. Write whether the following word group is a sentence
(2) fragment, run-on sentence, or complete sentence:

Alarmed by Johnny's illness, Aunt Kate returns to him his moccasins and Indian clothing.

9. Write the collective noun from this sentence: The flock
(4) has moved on to greener pastures.

10. Write the plural form of *handful*.
(10, 11)

Write each word that should be capitalized in sentences 11 and 12.

11. in college, jon is taking statistics, biology, japanese history, and latin.
(9, 22)

12. my great grandfather knew general patton.
(9, 22)

13. Write each preposition from this sentence: Owing to Becca, our class won the prize for the most correct answers in the geography section of the contest.
(14)

14. Write the word from this list that is *not* a linking verb: is, am, are, was, were, be, being, been, this, look, feel, taste, smell, sound, seem, appear, grow, become, remain, stay
(18)

For sentences 15 and 16, write the verb phrase and name its tense.

15. Had someone killed an Indian in the farmer's pasture?
(15)

16. For the last two days, Mr. Butler has been questioning Uncle Wilse.
(17)

For 17 and 18, write the verb phrase and label it action or linking.

17. Bugles will sound at sunrise.
(18)

18. The bugles sounded mournful at sunset.
(18)

For 19 and 20, write whether the word group is a phrase or a clause.

19. condemned to wear a bright red "A"
(20)

20. although Arthur Dimmesdale could not make the confession himself
(20)

21. Write the infinitive in this sentence and label its tense present or perfect: To have revealed the sinner would have satisfied the accusers.
(19)

22. Write the present participle, past tense, and past participle of the verb *censor*.
(13)

Write each limiting adjective in sentences 23 and 24.

23. Hester Prynne's punishment is a scarlet *A*.
(24)

24. One child results from this transgression.
(24)

25. Write each article in this sentence: A physician appears in town to harass the young woman.
(24)

26. Write the indefinite adjective in this sentence: Some people do not understand the importance of good nutrition and exercise.
(24)

Diagram each word of sentences 27–30.

27. Exercising will increase your endurance.
(16, 21)

28. Make judicious decisions.
(21, 24)

29. The witness desires to speak.
(21, 24)

30. Will the witness's words affect the jury's decision?
(21, 24)

LESSON 25   **Capitalization: Areas, Religions, Greetings • No Capital Letter**

> **Dictation or Journal Entry**
>
> **Vocabulary:** The words *amendment* and *suffrage* appear in the U. S. Constitution.
>
> The broad definition of *amendment* is the act of changing by correction, deletion, or addition. A Constitutional *amendment* is a change made after the Constitution was ratified. The first ten *amendments* to the Constitution are known as the Bill or Rights.
>
> *Suffrage* is the right to vote. Initially, *suffrage* belonged only to the male population in the United States.

We have reviewed capitalizing proper nouns, parts of an outline, the first word of a sentence, the first word in a line of poetry, the pronoun *I,* the first word in a direct quotation, important words in titles, people titles, family words when used as names, and the names of school subjects that come from a country. Let us review more capitalization rules.

Areas of the Country   We capitalize North, South, East, West, Midwest, Northeast, etc. when they refer to **certain areas of the country.**

    The writers of the Constitution lived in the *East*.

    The *West* followed the *Southeast* in becoming part of the United States.

    During the Civil War, the *North* battled the *South*.

However, we do not capitalize these words when they indicate a direction.

    The state of Washington lies *south* of British Columbia.

    The Atlantic Ocean is *east* of New Jersey.

    Washington, D.C. is *south* of Baltimore, Maryland, and *north* of Richmond, Virginia.

Religions, Deity, Bible   We capitalize **religions**, denominations, the **Bible** and its parts, and the **Deity**.

    The *Jewish* and *Christian* religions share the *Old Testament* part of the *Bible*.

    Puritanism influenced our nation's founders.

    The *Quakers* appreciated religious freedom and settled their own colony.

Greeting and Closing of a Letter We capitalize the first words in the **greeting and closing of a letter.** (Examples: Dear Alexander, My generous guardian, With love, Sincerely, Warmly, etc.)

Example 1 Write each word, if any, that should be capitalized in these sentences.

(a) Florida, Alabama, and Georgia lie east of the Mississippi River.

(b) Most of the fighting in the American Revolution occurred in the northeast.

(c) The catholic and anglican religions are not considered protestant.

(d) The citizen wrote, "dear Senator Hamilton," and ended the letter with "respectfully, Pauline Schori."

Solution (a) No correction is needed.

(b) We capitalize **Northeast** because it is a specific section of the country.

(c) We capitalize **Catholic** and **Anglican** and **Protestant** because they refer to religions.

(d) We capitalize **Dear** because it is the first word of a letter's greeting. **Respectfully** requires a capital because it is the first word of the closing.

No Capital Letter Here we will discuss when **not** to capitalize words.

Common Nouns Animals, plants, diseases, foods, trees, musical instruments, and non-trademarked games are **not** capitalized unless a proper adjective appears with them such as in "Hong Kong flu," "Australian shepherd," and "Scottish kilt." Here we only capitalize the proper adjectives and **not** the **common nouns.** We do not capitalize nouns such as the following:

COMMON NOUN	COMMON NOUN WITH PROPER ADJECTIVE
beagle	German shepherd
willow tree	Australian willow
peanut	Spanish peanut
apple	Rome Beauty apple
tonsillitis	Alzheimer's disease
card game	Monopoly (trademark) game

Example 2 Write each word that should be capitalized in these sentences.

(a) The antique dealer specializes in georgian furniture.

(b) Have you tried maine lobster?

(c) Did George Washington play checkers and chess?

(d) The soldiers marched to fifes and drums.

(e) In the early years of our nation, many people died of diphtheria, polio, and scarlet fever.

(f) Melody enjoys playing hopscotch and checkers.

Solution (a) We capitalize **Georgian,** a proper adjective. However, furniture is not capitalized because it is a common noun.

(b) We capitalize **Maine,** a proper adjective. However, lobster is not capitalized because it is a common noun.

(c) **No capital letter;** games are common nouns.

(d) **No capital letter.** Musical instruments are not capitalized unless part of their name is a proper noun as in French horn.

(e) Diseases are common nouns; they require **no capital letters.**

(f) **No capital letter.** The games of hopscotch and checkers are not trademarked, so we do not capitalize them.

Seasons of the Year We do **not** capitalize **seasons of the year**—fall, winter, spring, and summer.

During the cold *winter* of the East, tourism flourishes in the Southwest.

Hyphenated Words We treat a **hyphenated word** as if it were a single word. If it is a proper noun or the first word of a sentence, we capitalize only the first word, and **not** all the parts of the hyphenated word. See the examples below.

In *mid-October* we enjoy the fall colors.

Fifty-six years ago, Izzy left Asbury Park, New Jersey.

Example 3 Add capital letters where needed in this sentence:

Yes, sister-in-law esther will carry white roses in the wedding next summer.

Solution Yes, Sister-in-law Esther will carry white roses in the wedding next summer.

We capitalize **Sister** because it is a part of a person's name. However, we do not capitalize the other parts of the hyphenated word (-in-law). We capitalize **Esther** because it is a person's name. However, we do not capitalize "summer;" it is a season of the year.

Practice For a–j, write each word that should be capitalized.

a. the southeast is known for creole food like jambalaya and etouffee.

b. the calvinistic preacher stressed predestination, the sovereignty of god, and the authenticity of the bible.

c. the smithsonian institute attracts many visitors to the east.

d. dear doctor franklin,
   you certainly have many talents.
      fondly,
      miss sue

e. in the summer, father-in-law dale hops in his truck and heads for the nearest fishing pond.

f. the piano, clavichord, and organ are keyboard instruments.

g. the greek sandwich consisted of pita bread filled with roasted pork and topped with sliced onions.

h. the winner of the ping pong tournament treated everyone to dinner at a chinese restaurant.

i. cottonwoods, california oaks, australian willows, crepe myrtles, ornamental plums, and brazilian pepper trees grow magnificently in this neighborhood.

j. did candice and juliana participate in the chess tournament?

For k and l, replace each blank with the correct vocabulary word.

k. In 1920, the Nineteenth Amendment provided for women's _____, so that women could influence elections.

l. Three-fourths of the states must ratify any _____ to the Constitution.

Review set 25 Choose the correct word or root to complete sentences 1–6.

1. The Latin root (*grav-, crim-, lev-*) means to lighten or to raise.
(24)

2. Appellate means having to do with an (apple, appeal, aristocrat).
(23)

3. The (gravid, bellicose, judicial) branch of government interprets the law.
(22)

4. The Latin term *id est*, abbreviated *i.e.*, means ("that is to say," "for example, "to love").
(21)

5. Amicable means showing (hatred, affectation, goodwill).
(12)

6. *A, an* and *the* are common adjectives called (infinitives, articles, gerunds).
(24)

7. Write the three articles, which function as adjectives in a sentence.
(24)

8. Write the gerund in this sentence and label its tense present or perfect: Is reading your favorite pastime?
(16)

9. Rewrite the following chapter title from *The Scarlet Letter*, adding capital letters as needed: "hester and the physician"
(9)

10. Write whether this sentence is declarative, interrogative, imperative, or exclamatory: Were you surprised that Arthur Dimmesdale finally admitted his guilt?
(1)

11. Write whether this word group is a sentence fragment, run-on sentence, or complete sentence:
(2)
The Scarlet Letter is a romance it also reveals the truth of the human heart.

12. From this sentence, write each noun and label it concrete or abstract: With his confession, the emotional anguish of Arthur Dimmesdale finally ceases.
(4)

13. For a and b, write the plural of each noun.
(10, 11)   (a) logo   (b) stimulus

Write each word that should be capitalized in sentences 14–17.

14. matty's academic program includes greek, hebrew, art history, and math.
(22)

15. the grandson asked his grandfather if they could visit pearl harbor.
(9, 22)

16. hey, dad, may i go fishing with you?
(9, 22)

17. would you rather live in the east or in the west?
(25)

18. Write each preposition from this sentence: In addition to *Paradise Lost*, John Milton wrote *Paradise Regained*, about the redemption of mankind.
(14)

19. For a–c, choose the correct form of the irregular verb *be*.
(12)   (a) You (was, were)   (b) I (am, are, is)   (c) We (am, are, is)

For sentences 20 and 21, write the verb phrase and name its tense.

20. In the opening lines of *Paradise Lost*, Satan has fallen from Heaven.
(15)

21. This May, Mr. Fealko will have been working on his thesis for two years.
(17)

For 22 and 23, write the verb phrase and label it action or linking.

22. Satan appears shocked to find himself in Hell.
(18)

23. Does Satan appear in the first chapter of the book?
(18)

For 24 and 25, write whether the expression is a phrase or a clause.

24. Satan, the once radiant Lucifer, and his angels
(20)

25. after Satan perused his new home with horror
(20)

26. Write the present participle, past tense, and past
(13) participle of the verb *skip*.

Write each adjective in sentences 27 and 28.

27. The arrogant Satan and his many followers refuse to seek
(23, 24) forgiveness from a gracious and merciful God.

28. Those evil and vengeful beings seek to destroy the new
(23, 24) race called man.

Diagram sentences 29 and 30.

29. Studying has improved Matty's academic performance.
(16, 24)

30. Matty's two classmates chose to loaf.
(21, 24)

LESSON 26 — Transitive and Intransitive Verbs

> **Dictation or Journal Entry**
>
> **Vocabulary:** Let us see how the similar words *delusion*, *illusion*, and *allusion* differ in meaning.
>
> A *delusion* is a persistent false belief, which is usually pathological. Having the *delusion* that he is Tarzan, the man attempts to swing on branches from tree to tree.
>
> An *illusion* is a false belief produced by misinterpretation of things that actually exist. A mirage gave the thirsty hiker the *illusion* that water was nearby.
>
> An *allusion* is a casual or indirect mention of something. In his phone message concerning next month's meeting, my friend made *allusions* to my past forgetfulness.

Transitive Verbs A **transitive verb** is an action verb that has a direct object. The sentences below have transitive verbs.

Amendment I <u>protects</u> our freedom of religion.
↑ action verb   ↑ direct object

We <u>may have</u> peaceful assemblies.
↑ action verb   ↑ direct object

Intransitive Verbs An **intransitive verb** has no direct object. The sentences below have intransitive verbs.

Civil liberties <u>are</u> individual freedoms.
↑ linking verb — no direct object

The protesters <u>were gathering</u> quietly.
↑ action verb — no direct object

The same verb can be transitive in one sentence and intransitive in another.

Thomas Jefferson <u>wrote</u> political theories. (transitive)
↑ action verb   ↑ direct object

Thomas Jefferson <u>wrote</u> convincingly. (intransitive)
↑ action verb — no direct object

www.saxonhomeschool.com
©Houghton Mifflin Harcourt Publishers, Inc.

GRAMMAR AND WRITING 8
Student Edition, 9781419098581

Some action verbs are *always* intransitive. See examples below.

Max <u>sleeps</u> in class!
Congress <u>sits</u> in an orderly fashion.
We <u>rise</u> for the flag salute.

Example In the following sentences, underline the verb phrase and star the direct object if there is one. Then write whether the verb is transitive or intransitive.

(a) We will abide by the Constitution.

(b) Does the First Amendment guarantee free press?

Solution (a) **We <u>will abide</u> by the Constitution.** The verb "will abide" is **intransitive,** for it has no direct object.

(b) **<u>Does</u> the First Amendment <u>guarantee</u> free press?** The verb is **transitive,** for it has a direct object, "free press."

Practice For a–d, write the verb phrase and label it transitive or intransitive. Then write the direct object if there is one.

  a. According to the Second Amendment, citizens may possess guns.

  b. According to the Third Amendment, no soldiers will be housed in civilian homes during times of peace.

  c. According to the Fourth Amendment, no one may search a person without reasonable cause.

  d. Have you been reading about the candidates for governor?

For e–g, replace each blank with the correct vocabulary word.

  e. Suffering from the _____ that she was President of the United States, the young woman expected everyone to address her as Ms. President.

  f. The President's _____ to the Constitution reveals his familiarity with its provision for separation of power.

  g. Due to an optical _____, the figure on the sheet of paper looked three-dimensional.

More Practice Write the verb phrase and label it transitive or intransitive. Then write the direct object if there is one.

1. During his twenties, Thomas Jefferson read about philosophy, history, politics, and law.

2. In 1776, he drafted the Declaration of Independence.

3. Jefferson participated in criminal code reform.

4. This reform eliminated barbarous practices such as public whippings, dunkings, and bills of attainder.

5. From 1784 to 1789, Jefferson was a minister to France.

6. In the presidential election of 1800, Thomas Jefferson and Aaron Burr received an equal number of electoral votes.

7. Jefferson was elected by the House of Representatives.

8. As President, he faced opposition from the Federalists.

9. He appointed strong nationalists to the Supreme Court.

10. Jefferson died on the fiftieth anniversary of the signing of the Declaration of Independence.

Review Set 26 Choose the correct word or root to complete sentences 1–9.

1. (Jurisdiction, Amendment, Pocket Veto) is the act of changing by correction, deletion, or addition.
(25)

2. The Latin root *lev-* means (serious, lighten, proof).
(24)

3. To (appease, lobby, apportion) is to give out parts.
(13, 23)

4. (Approbation, Jurisdiction, Recrimination) is the range or extent of authority; power.
(19, 22)

5. We did not know how to proceed, for the instructions were (ambivalent, ambiguous, bicameral).
(4, 11)

6. A(n) (transitive, intransitive) verb has a direct object.
(26)

7. The progressive tense shows action that is (continuing, completed).
(17)

8. To make the progressive tense, we use some form of the verb *to be* plus the (present, past) participle.
(17)

9. The (present, past) participle ends in *ing*.
(13)

10. Write whether the following sentence is declarative,
(1) interrogative, imperative, or exclamatory:

Don't believe the serpent!

11. Write whether the following is a sentence fragment, run-
(2) on sentence, or complete sentence:

Despite Raphael's warnings, Eve succumbs to temptation Adam chooses to partake with her.

12. Write each concrete noun from this sentence and name
(7) its gender:

Ashley, a doctoral student in marine biology, takes an underwater census of the fish.

13. From this sentence, write each noun and circle each one
(7) that is possessive:

Mortality, pain in childbirth, and a world of toil represent God's punishment for Adam and Eve's disobedience.

14. For a–c, write the plural of each noun.
(10, 11)
(a) wife (b) safe (c) finch

Write each word that should be capitalized in sentences 15 and 16.

15. in milton's *paradise lost*, satan's victory turns to defeat.
(9, 22)

16. did uncle bob win his game of chinese checkers on
(22, 25) tuesday?

17. Write whether this word group is a phrase or a
(20) clause: long, formal speeches by the main characters

18. Write each preposition in this sentence: In addition to its
(14) high formal style, the unusual word order of *Paradise Lost* is difficult for modern readers.

For sentences 19 and 20, write the verb phrase and label it action or linking.

19. *Paradise Lost* sounds musical in its retelling of the
(18) Genesis account.

20. John Milton writes like Virgil and other epic poets.
(18)

Write the correct verb form to complete sentences 21 and 22.

21. Fleshy and alluring, Satan (past progressive tense of
(17) *flatter*) Eve.

22. A bee (present tense of *buzz*) around the yellow blossom.
(5)

23. For a–c, choose the correct form of the irregular verb
(12) *have*.

(a) I (has, have) (b) They (has, have) (c) He (has, have)

24. Write the four principal parts (present tense, present
(13) participle, past tense, past participle) of the verb
apportion.

25. Write each descriptive adjective from this
(23) sentence: Have you noticed Satan's eerie ability to sway
intelligent people away from moral convictions?

26. Write each article from this sentence: John Milton
(24) arouses sympathy in the unsuspecting reader for the
fallen devil in order to underscore Satan's uncanny
ability to make evil seem good.

27. From this sentence, write the proper adjective followed
(23) by the noun it describes: The English class featured such
works as *Beowulf* and *Paradise Lost*.

28. Write each gerund from this sentence and label its tense
(16) present or perfect: Having rested prepared me for the
hard work ahead.

Diagram sentences 29 and 30.

29. Six weary travelers were trying to sleep.
(21, 24)

30. Did the crows' cawing wake them?
(16, 24)

LESSON 27

Active or Passive Voice

> **Dictation or Journal Entry**
> **Vocabulary:** The Latin root *grav-* means "weighty, serious, or heavy."
> *Gravid* means "enlarged with something, or pregnant." The black cloud was *gravid* with rain. The inventor was *gravid* with ideas for new gadgets.
> *Gravity*, which is what holds us to the earth, can also mean "weighty importance or seriousness." The carefree cyclists suddenly realized the *gravity* of their situation when they saw the funnel cloud approaching swiftly.
> To *gravitate* is to be drawn toward something. Artistic people *gravitate* toward others with the same creative bent.

A transitive verb can be used in either the **active voice** or the **passive voice.** When the subject acts, the verb is in the **active voice.**

Benedict Arnold <u>took</u> a bribe.

When the subject is acted upon, the verb is in the **passive voice.**

A *bribe* <u>was taken</u> by Benedict Arnold.

Verbs that are in the passive voice contain a form of "to be." Often the sentence contains a prepositional phrase beginning with "by." The subject *receives* the action; it does not *do* the action.

                                                  "to be" verb

PASSIVE: *America* <u>was betrayed</u> (by Benedict Arnold)

                                                        prepositional phrase

(The subject, America, does not act; it is acted upon.)

ACTIVE: *Benedict Arnold* <u>betrayed</u> America.

(The subject, Benedict Arnold, acts.)

Active Voice Writing is more exciting and powerful in the active voice. We try to use the active voice as much as possible.

> WEAK PASSIVE:
> *Virginia* was raided by Benedict Arnold.
>
> STRONG ACTIVE:
> *Benedict Arnold* raided Virginia.
>
> WORDY PASSIVE:
> The traitor's *opponents* were browbeaten by him in his arrogance.
>
> CONCISE ACTIVE:
> The *traitor* browbeat his opponents in his arrogance.
>
> INDIRECT PASSIVE:
> This *story* was read to the class by Mr. Cruz.
>
> DIRECT ACTIVE:
> *Mr. Cruz* read the story to the class.

Passive Voice We see that the passive voice can be wordy and indirect. It can confuse the reader and tends to be dull. However, the passive voice does have a purpose. We use the passive voice in order to leave something unsaid. When the doer is unimportant or unknown, or when we want to emphasize the receiver of the action, we use the passive voice:

> The *Articles of Confederation* were rejected.
>
> The *Bill of Rights* was added to the Constitution.
>
> The national *anthem* had been sung.
>
> The *disaster* had been averted. (doer unknown)

Example Write the verb in each sentence and label it active or passive voice.

(a) The state was treating all citizens equally.

(b) All citizens were being treated equally by the state.

(c) One citizen was denied by the state the right to vote.

(d) The state denied one citizen the right to vote.

Solution (a) The verb, **was treating,** is **active voice.** The subject (state) acts.

(b) The verb, **were being treated,** is **passive voice.** The subject (citizens) is acted upon.

(c) The verb, **was denied,** is **passive voice.** The subject (citizen) is acted upon.

(d) The verb, **denied,** is **active voice.** The subject (state) acts.

Practice For sentences a–d, write the verb and label it active or passive voice.

    a. The criminal was incarcerated.

    b. The criminal had fled the scene of the crime.

    c. The defendant was incriminated by two witnesses.

    d. Two witnesses incriminated the defendant.

Vocabulary: For e–h, replace each blank with the correct vocabulary word.

    e. People _____ toward other people with similar beliefs and convictions.

    f. The root _____ means "weighty, serious, or heavy."

    g. The _____ cat was so large she could barely squeeze under the fence.

    h. My foolish neighbor was not aware of the _____ of the problem.

More Practice Write whether the verb in each sentence is active or passive voice.

    1. A republican form of government was created by the Constitution.

    2. The Constitution created a republican form of government.

    3. Article V provided for amendments to the Constitution.

    4. Amendments were provided for by Article V.

    5. Twelve amendments were proposed in September of 1789.

6. In 1789, Congress proposed twelve amendments.

7. The amendment was approved by two-thirds of both houses.

8. Three-fourths of the states ratified twenty-seven amendments.

Review Set 27

Choose the correct word to complete sentences 1–8.

1. A(n) (delusion, illusion, allusion) is a persistent false belief, which is usually pathological.
(26)

2. Amendment is the act of (speaking, stealing, changing).
(25)

3. (Apportion, Censure, Alleviate) means "to relieve, diminish, or lighten."
(24)

4. Mieko both loves and hates her job. She is (ambiguous, ambivalent, inhospitable).
(9, 11)

5. A (quorum, caucus, hospice) is the number of persons needed at a meeting for business to take place.
(9, 10)

6. A(n) (transitive, intransitive) verb has no direct object.
(26)

7. When the subject acts, the verb is (active, passive) voice.
(27)

8. When the subject is acted upon, the verb is (active, passive) voice.
(27)

In sentences 9 and 10, write the verb phrase and label it transitive or intransitive.

9. Were Bosco and Al hiding presents from the children?
(26)

10. Were Bosco and Al hiding behind the piano?
(26)

In sentences 11 and 12, write the verb phrase and label it active or passive voice.

11. A census is taken every ten years.
(27)

12. The government took a census in the year 2000.
(27)

13. Write the infinitive in this sentence and label its tense present or perfect: I know that to succeed will require hard work.
(19)

14. Rewrite this song title adding capital letters as needed: "i heard the bells on christmas day"

15. Write whether this sentence is declarative, interrogative, imperative, or exclamatory: Vitamins form cells, regulate the nervous system, and build strong bones.

16. Write whether this word group is a complete sentence, a sentence fragment, or a run-on sentence: Stored inside the fat tissue of the body for a long time.

Write each word that should be capitalized in sentences 17 and 18.

17. i asked my mom, "did you take all your vitamins, mother?"

18. "a primer on vitamins" in the *star news* offers many helpful hints.

19. Write each preposition from this sentence: According to the news article, one type of vitamin is fat soluble.

For sentences 20 and 21, write the verb phrase and name its tense.

20. Some people have been ingesting too many fat-soluble vitamins—*A, D, E,* and *K.*

21. The patient's body had excreted the excess water-soluble vitamins—*B* and *C.*

For sentences 22 and 23, write the verb phrase and label it action or linking.

22. Vitamin *A* promotes eye health, growth of immune cells, and healthy respiratory and gastrointestinal tracts.

23. Seven hundred micrograms seems reasonable as a daily dose for women.

For 24 and 25, write whether the expression is a phrase or a clause.

24. because it helps the body to metabolize amino acids and carbohydrates

25. in the production of digestive enzymes and the formation of antibodies
(20)

Write each adjective in sentences 26 and 27.

26. Do you know the eight essential *B* vitamins?
(23, 24)

27. We find the *B* vitamin folate in beans and peas, leafy greens, and whole grains.
(23, 24)

28. Write the present participle, past tense, and past participle of the verb *snap*.
(13)

Diagram sentences 29 and 30.

29. Has the classical pianist begun to play?
(21, 24)

30. Try smiling.
(16, 21)

LESSON 28

Object of the Preposition • The Prepositional Phrase

> **Dictation or Journal Entry**
>
> **Vocabulary:** Some words trace their roots to mythology and history. *Cicerone* and *hector* are two such words.
>
> Cicero was a Roman statesman and orator known for his long-windedness and eloquent style. A *cicerone* is one who guides sightseers through a museum or other interesting landmark. We asked the highly-recommended *cicerone* to show us the sights in Rome, Italy.
>
> Hector, the leader of the Trojan forces in the *Iliad,* killed several great Greek warriors. Now, to *hector* means "to bully, intimidate, or torment." Older students were asked not to *hector* the younger students on the playground.

Object of the Preposition

We have learned to recognize common prepositions—connecting words that link a noun or pronoun to the rest of the sentence. In this lesson, we will identify the **object of the preposition,** which is the noun or pronoun that follows the preposition. Every preposition must have an object. Otherwise, it is not a preposition. We italicize prepositions and star their objects in the phrases below.

aboard the *plane	*according to* the *law
within the *framework	*across from* our *home
during this *session	*in addition to* *Sylvester
despite the *opposition	*in regard to* a *complaint
over the *clouds	*by means of* *impeachment
except *Uncle Sam	*round about* the *Capitol
via *pony express	*owing to* your hard *work

Prepositions may have compound objects:

They settled the argument *by means of* *discussion and *compromise.

Opposite *Ben Franklin and *Alexander Hamilton sat John Adams.

Example 1 Underline each preposition and star the object or objects of each preposition in these sentences.

(a) In addition to the freedoms of speech and press, Amendment I guarantees the freedom of religion.

(b) Without Amendment V, people would testify against themselves.

Solution (a) <u>In addition to</u> the *freedoms <u>of</u> *speech and *press, Amendment I guarantees the freedom <u>of</u> *religion.

(b) <u>Without</u> *Amendment V, people would testify <u>against</u> *themselves.

Prepositional Phrase A prepositional phrase begins with a preposition and contains a noun and its modifiers. We italicize prepositional phrases below.

Amendment V provides protection *for any citizen* accused *of a crime* punishable *by death*.

The accused person must go *before a Grand Jury*.

Notice that there can be more than one prepositional phrase in a sentence:

An accused person found not guilty *by trial* (1) cannot be tried again *for the same crime* (2).

After our lunch (1), let's talk *about the reasons* (2) *for the amendments* (3) *to the Constitution* (4).

Example 2 For each sentence, write each prepositional phrase starring the object(s) of each preposition.

(a) Must I testify against myself in a court of law?

(b) All people have the right to life, liberty, and property.

Solution (a) **against *myself/ in a *court/ of *law**

(b) **to *life, *liberty, and *property**

Practice For sentences a–d, write each prepositional phrase and star the object of the preposition.

a. An accused person has the right to a speedy trial by an unbiased jury in the state and district of the crime.

b. The accused may have an attorney in addition to a fair trial.

c. I read the amendment concerning bails, fines, and punishments.

d. On account of this amendment, punishments must be fair.

For e and f, replace each blank with the correct vocabulary word.

e. Please do not _____ your younger siblings.

f. The _____ gave an entertaining and informative tour of the White House.

More Practice Write each prepositional phrase starring the object(s) of each preposition in these sentences.

1. Owing to the tyranny of George III, Americans wanted independence from Britain.

2. In the Declaration of Independence, Americans listed twenty-seven grievances against the king.

3. Americans had made appeals over the head of the tyrant to the English people.

4. In spite of their desperate petitions, they were ignored by most people in Britain.

5. After many attempts at reconciliation, America took steps toward independence.

6. Americans dissolved all political connection between themselves and Great Britain by means of a Declaration.

7. On behalf of the American people, and with reliance on Divine Providence, the writers of the Declaration pledged their lives and honor.

8. Americans had inherited a love for liberty because of their history of English traditions.

9. Despite King George's tyranny over America, English people had long respected political and religious freedom in their country.

10. In addition to John Locke, William Blackstone influenced America's thinkers concerning freedom and independence.

Review Set 28 Choose the correct word or root to complete sentences 1–6.

1. Travelers or strangers might find shelter in a (direct democracy, *habeas corpus*, hospice).
(9)

2. The Latin root (*grav-, prob-, crim-*) means "weighty, serious, or heavy."
(27)

3. A(n) (delusion, illusion, allusion) is a false belief produced by the misinterpretation of things that actually exist.
(26)

4. The first ten (lines, paragraphs, amendments) of the Constitution are known as the Bill of Rights.
(25)

5. A pacifist prefers (war, peace, solitude).
(6)

6. Every preposition has a(n) (gerund, object, subject).
(28)

For sentences 7 and 8, write the verb phrase and label it transitive or intransitive.

7. That flight attendant speaks four languages.
(26)

8. Will the flight attendant speak to the passengers?
(26)

For sentences 9 and 10, write the verb phrase and label it active or passive voice.

9. Another census will be taken in 2010.
(27)

10. Will the government take a census in the year 2020?
(27)

For sentences 11 and 12, write each prepositional phrase, starring the object(s) of each preposition.

11. According to weather forecasters, fog will remain along the coast until noon.
(28)

12. In spite of the storm, temperatures rose to a high of seventy in the valley.
(28)

13. Unscramble these words to make an imperative sentence: nutritious   eat   please   foods
(1)

14. Write whether the following word group is a sentence fragment, a run-on sentence, or a complete sentence: We find biotin in yeast, corn, soybeans, egg yolks, liver, cauliflower, peanut butter, and mushrooms.
(2)

15. From this sentence, write each noun, labeling it abstract of concrete: Most people strive for good health.
(4)

16. Write each possessive noun from this list: hero's, heroes, heroes', man's, men, men's
(7)

17. Write the plural of each noun.
(10, 11)   (a) alumnus   (b) alga   (c) larva

18. Write the present participle, past tense, and past
(13)   participle of the verb *cry*.

For 19 and 20, write the verb phrase and label its tense.

19. Scientists have discovered niacin in meat, poultry, fish,
(15)   milk, eggs, and enriched cereals and breads.

20. Ian will be taking niacin for heart health.
(17)

21. Write the infinitive in this sentence and label its tense
(19)   present or perfect: As she waved good-bye, Risa promised
       to return.

22. Write the gerund in this sentence and label its tense
(16)   present or perfect. Does Roger regret having relocated?

For 23 and 24, write whether the expression is a phrase or a clause.

23. converting carbohydrates into energy
(20)

24. if one ingests enough riboflavin
(20)

25. In this sentence, write each concrete noun labeling it
(7)   masculine, feminine, neuter, or indefinite: With
       enthusiasm, Kimberly studies vitamins and their
       benefits.

For 26 and 27, replace each blank with the singular present tense form of the verb.

26. Two planes *taxi* on the runway. A plane _____ on
(5)   the runway.

27. Many planes *fly* into Denver. A plane _____ into
(5)   Denver.

28. Diagram the simple subject and simple predicate of each
(3, 20) clause in this sentence: While Jonathan washed the
       family car, Lucy vacuumed the entire house, and Nate fed
       the chickens, sheep, and goats.

Diagram sentences 29 and 30.

29. Two ambivalent senators refused to vote.
(21, 24)

30. Diagramming increases understanding.
(16, 21)

LESSON 29

The Prepositional Phrase as an Adjective • Diagramming

> **Dictation or Journal Entry**
>
> **Vocabulary:** When studying the three branches of the United States government, we find the terms *hung jury* and *filibuster*.
>
> A *hung jury* cannot agree on the verdict of a person accused of a crime. The *hung jury* provided an avenue for the prosecutor to retry the scientist accused of selling national secrets to other countries.
>
> A *filibuster* is a method of delaying or stopping action on a legislative issue by the use of long speeches or prolonged debate. *Filibuster* is also a verb meaning "to obstruct legislative action by long speeches or debate." The Senator's *filibuster* angered many of his fellow legislators, for it stalled any action on the bill.

Adjective Phrases   We remember that a phrase is a group of words that functions as a single word. Prepositional phrases function as a single word, and some modify a noun or pronoun, so we call them **adjective phrases.** This type of prepositional phrase answers an adjective question—"Which one?" "What kind?" or "How many?" Here are some examples:

   The term *of a Senator* is six years. (modifies the noun "term," and tells "what kind")

   John Adams was the President *between Washington and Jefferson.* (modifies the noun "President," and tells "which one")

   The chamber had seats *for twelve people.* (modifies the noun "seats," and tells "how many")

Example 1   Write each adjective phrase and tell which noun or pronoun it modifies.

   (a) Susan B. Anthony was an American reformer on behalf of anti-slavery and women's suffrage.

   (b) She organized those rallies concerning women's suffrage.

   (c) The Nineteenth Amendment guarantees ballots for all citizens.

Solution   (a) The phrase **on behalf of anti-slavery and women's suffrage** modifies **reformer.** It tells "what kind" of reformer.

   (b) The phrase **concerning women's suffrage** modifies **rallies.** It tells "which ones."

(c) The phrase **for all citizens** modifies **ballots.** It tells "how many."

Diagramming the Prepositional Phrase

To diagram a prepositional phrase, we place the preposition on a slanted line attached to the word that the phrase modifies. We place the object of the preposition on a horizontal line at the bottom of the slanted preposition line:

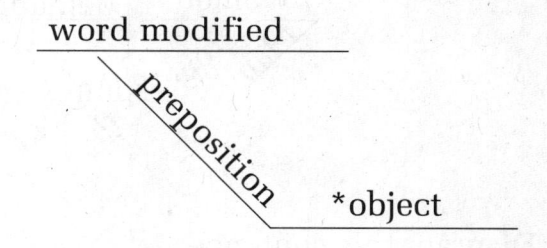

```
        word modified
            \preposition
                    \____*object
```

Let us diagram this sentence:

The Vice President took the place of the President.

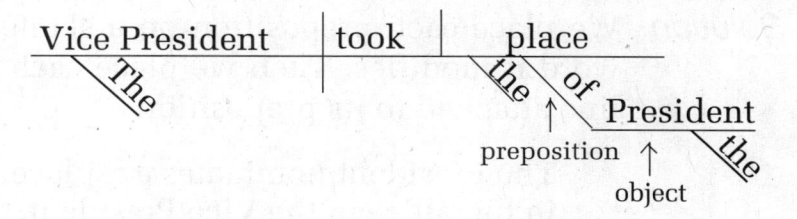

```
 Vice President | took | place
      \The            \the  \of
                          President
                    preposition  \the
                              object
```

Example 2 Diagram this sentence:

All citizens regardless of gender may vote.

Solution The prepositional phrase **regardless of gender** modifies the subject of the sentence, **citizens.** We place the preposition **regardless of** on a slanted line connected to **citizens.** Then we place the object, **gender,** on the horizontal line:

All citizens regardless of gender may vote.

```
    citizens    |  may vote
     \All \regardless
              \of  gender
```

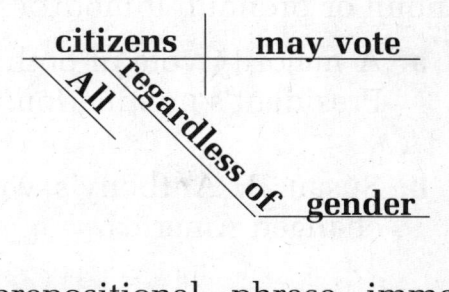

Sometimes a prepositional phrase immediately follows another one, as in the sentence below.

Many women from the state of New York demanded their rights.

171

In the sentence above, the first prepositional phrase, "from the state," modifies the subject "women." The second prepositional phrase, "of New York," modifies the noun "state." We show this by diagramming the sentence:

Many women from the state of New York demanded their rights.

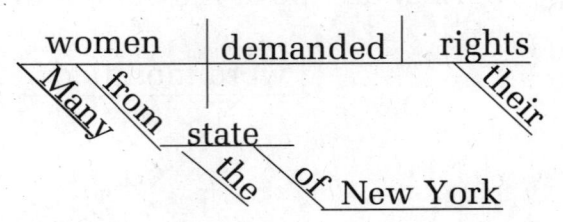

```
   women   |  demanded  |  rights
  /  \                          \
Many  from                       their
       \
        state
       /    \
     the    of New York
```

Example 3 Diagram this sentence:

The President nominates a replacement for a vacant office of Vice President.

Solution We place each preposition on a slanted line underneath the word it modifies. Then we place each object on a horizontal line attached to its preposition.

The President nominates a replacement for a vacancy in the office of the Vice President.

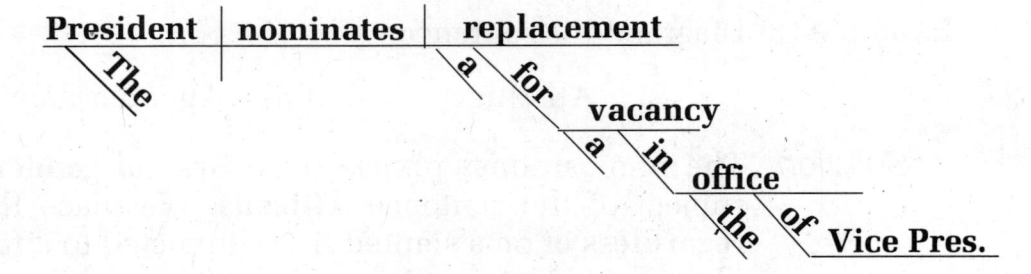

```
President | nominates | replacement
   \                    /      \
    The                a        for
                                 \
                                  vacancy
                                 /    \
                                a     in
                                       \
                                        office
                                       /    \
                                     the    of Vice Pres.
```

Practice For a–d, write each prepositional phrase followed by the noun or pronoun it modifies.

   a. A majority vote of both houses of Congress confirms the President's nomination.

   b. Susan B. Anthony's work in regard to women's rights changed America.

   c. The colonists demanded freedom from the constraints of the British empire.

   d. Elected officials may receive increases in their salaries.

Diagram sentences e and f.

e. Do you know the meaning of monarchy?

f. Taxation without representation disturbed the colonists.

For g and h, replace each blank with the correct vocabulary word(s).

g. The _____ could not agree whether or not the colonist was guilty of treason.

h. The legislator's _____ prevented a vote on the bill increasing income taxes.

Review Set 29

Choose the correct word or root to complete sentences 1–5.

1. (Cicero, Filibuster, Hector) was a Roman statesman and orator known for his eloquence and long-windedness.
(28)

2. The Latin root *grav-* means (accusation, proof, weighty).
(27)

3. A(n) (delusion, illusion, allusion) is a casual or indirect mention of something.
(26)

4. (Levity, Suffrage, Probity) is the right to vote.
(24, 25)

5. A (*pro tempore*, quorum, hospice) might offer treatment for the terminally ill.
(9, 10)

6. Write whether the following sentence is declarative, interrogative, exclamatory, or imperative: It's a home run!
(1)

7. Write whether the following is a sentence fragment, run-on sentence, or complete sentence: For the development of healthy brain and nerve cells.
(2)

8. In this sentence, write each noun and circle the one that is collective: The company lists thiamine in lean pork, whole grains, dried beans, nuts, seeds, fish, and enriched breads and cereals.
(4)

9. Write each possessive noun from this list: Does Mr. VanderLaan's article emphasize the benefits of good nutrition?
(7)

10. For a–c, write the plural for each noun.
(10, 11) (a) minuteman   (b) fiasco   (c) wrench

Write each word that should be capitalized in sentences 11 and 12.

11. in my biology class at plunket university, in riverside county, i studied the effect of thiamine on the immune system.
(9, 22)

12. i asked grandpa if he had read uncle ian's favorite book, *a tale of two cities*.
(9, 22)

13. Write whether the following is a phrase or a clause: telltale chocolate chip cookie crumbs underneath the kitchen table
(20)

For sentences 14 and 15, write each prepositional phrase, and star each object of the preposition.

14. On account of construction, the bridge will be closed throughout the summer.
(28)

15. Flights were delayed owing to dense fog at the airport.
(28)

For sentences 16 and 17, write the verb phrase and name its tense.

16. The physician has prescribed vitamin *C* to prevent cell damage and to encourage a healthy immune system.
(15)

17. Sunlight will provide vitamin *D* for strong bones and teeth.
(8)

18. Write the gerund from this sentence and label its tense present or perfect: I increased my endurance by cycling.
(16, 28)

19. Write the infinitive from this sentence and label its tense present or perfect: To have promoted heart health gave the nutritionist a sense of worth.
(19)

For sentences 20 and 21, write the verb phrase and label it action or linking.

20. Sadly, all the green and yellow vegetables remained on Stevie's plate.
(18)

21. Vitamin *K* remains critical for blood clotting and building strong bones.
(18)

For 22 and 23, write the verb phrase and label it transitive or intransitive.

22. Did the jet land in Memphis, Tennessee?
(26)

23. Captain Airborne has been flying jets for twenty years.
(26)

Write each adjective in sentences 24 and 25.

24. Green vegetables provide adequate vitamin *K*.
(23, 24)

25. Moe's friend served fresh, tender zucchini with red onions.
(23, 24)

26. From the following sentence, write the proper adjective followed by the noun it describes: Another prominent American novelist is William Faulkner.
(23)

For sentences 27 and 28, write the verb phrase and label it active or passive voice.

27. Our jet was flown by Captain Airborne.
(27)

28. Does Captain Airborne fly commercial jets into Denver, Colorado?
(27)

Diagram sentences 29 and 30.

29. The German woman with the noisy miniature dachshund needs to leave.
(24, 29)

30. Did that dog in her lap continue barking?
(24, 29)

LESSON 30

Indirect Objects

> **Dictation or Journal Entry:**
>
> **Vocabulary:** Let us examine the homophones *faze* and *phase*.
>
> *Faze* means "to perturb, disturb, or fluster." The prosecutor's incriminating comments did not *faze* Esther, for she knew she was innocent.
>
> *Phase*, as a noun, means a period or stage. Toddlers often have a *phase* of tantrums. *Phase*, as a verb, means "to introduce in stages." The school will gradually *phase* in a new grammar program.

Indirect Object We have learned that a transitive verb is an action verb with a direct object. A transitive verb may have two kinds of objects. The direct object receives the action. The **indirect object** receives the action indirectly. It tells *to whom* or *for whom* the action was done. In the sentences below, we have starred the direct objects and placed parentheses around the indirect objects.

> *M. E. Bradford* gives (us) the *background information.
>
> The *British* charged (the colonists) unfair *taxes.
>
> This *taxation* caused (them) great *resentment.
>
> Did the *colonists* give (the British) a *tea party?

In order to have an indirect object, a sentence must have a direct object. The indirect object usually follows the verb and precedes the direct object. One test of an indirect object is that it can be expressed alternately by a prepositional phrase introduced by *to* or *for*:

> M. E. Bradford gives *to* us the background information.
>
> The British charged *to* the colonists unfair taxes.
>
> This taxation caused *for* them great resentment.
>
> Did the colonists give *to* the British a tea party?

Indirect objects can be compound:

> The *Boston Tea Party* gave (the British) and (the King) the colonists' *message of disapproval.

Example 1 Identify the indirect object(s), if any, in each sentence.

(a) The response of the British government left the colonists no choice but to fight.

(b) The American Revolution continued for eight years.

(c) The Declaration of Independence gave the colonies freedom from British rule.

(d) George Washington and Alexander Hamilton told the delegates their views on the Articles of Confederation.

Solution (a) The response of the British government left *to* the colonists no choice but to fight. Therefore, **colonists** is the indirect object.

(b) This sentence has **no indirect object.**

(c) The Declaration of Independence gave *to* the colonies freedom from British rule. Therefore, **colonies** is the indirect object.

(d) George Washington and Alexander Hamilton told *to* the delegates their views. Therefore, **delegates** is the indirect object.

Diagramming Below is a diagram showing the simple subject, simple predicate, direct object, and indirect object of this sentence:

Thomas Jefferson drafted Congress the first Constitution of the United States.

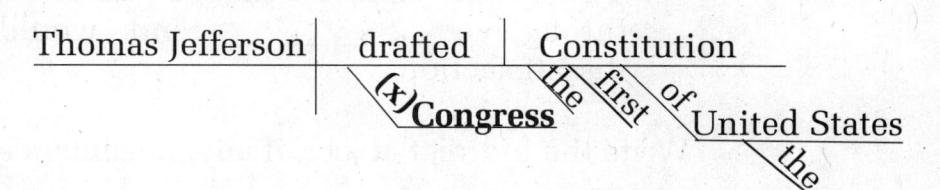

Notice that the indirect object (Congress) is attached beneath the verb by a slanted line as though it were a prepositional phrase with the preposition (x) understood and not stated.

Example 2 Diagram sentences a and b.

(a) Jefferson taught his peers the basic laws of government.

(b) This document gave the young nation guidelines.

Solution (a) We think, "Jefferson taught *to* his peers...." So, we diagram the sentence like this:

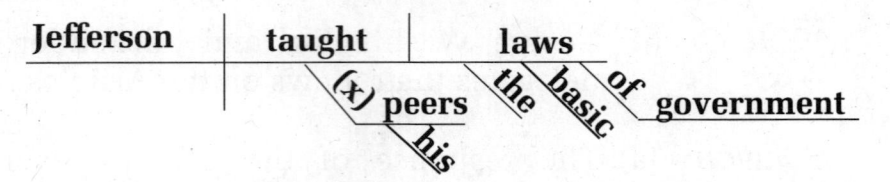

```
Jefferson | taught      | laws
              (x) peers    the  basic
                  his           of government
```

(b) We think, "This document gave *to* the young nation...." We diagram it like this:

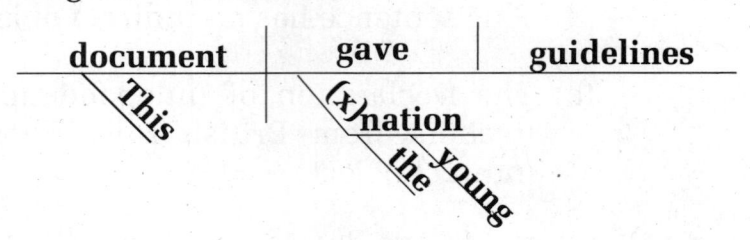

```
document | gave        | guidelines
  This     (x) nation
               the young
```

Practice For a–c, replace each blank with the correct vocabulary word.

a. At first, the colonists' rebellion didn't _____ the British.

b. Gradually, the new nation _____ out the old British ways.

c. The British believed that the colonists were just going through a _____ and would get over their dissatisfaction.

Write the indirect object, if any, in sentences d–g.

d. Thomas Jefferson presented John Hancock the Declaration of Independence to sign.

e. The Articles of Confederation replaced the Declaration of Independence.

f. The tour guide showed us the Liberty Bell.

g. The framers of the Constitution of the United States gave the new nation reasons for a stronger government.

For h and i, diagram each sentence.

i. Cal read Sal the history.

j. Judy delivered us pizza.

More Practice Write the indirect object, if any, in each sentence.

1. Please tell me the meaning of "separation of powers."

2. Have they given him the new document?

3. James Madison left us much correspondence and other writings.

4. Susan B. Anthony and Elizabeth Cady Stanton procured women's rights.

5. Monika and Hartwig gave Bryon a tour of Germany, their homeland.

6. I will write the Schaper Family a thank you note.

7. The police should issue that careless cyclist a warning.

Review Set 30 Choose the correct word to complete sentences 1–6.

1. A group of people unable to agree upon the verdict in a
(29) court case is called a (hung jury, filibuster, cicerone).

2. A (hector, consul, cicerone) guides sightseers through a
(17, 28) museum or other interesting landmark.

3. (Amiable, Gravid, Ambiguous) means "enlarged with
(12, 27) something, or pregnant."

4. Ms. Floobie suffers from the (delusion, illusion, allusion)
(26) that she is the Queen of Sheba.

5. The three philatelists have a (*pro tempore*, bicameral,
(8) common) interest in Scandinavian stamps.

6. A(n) (direct, indirect) object tells *to whom* or *for whom*
(30) the action is done.

7. Write whether the following sentence is declarative,
(1) interrogative, imperative, or exclamatory: Have you read *A Tale of Two Cities* by Charles Dickens?

8. Write whether this word group is a sentence fragment,
(2) run-on sentence, or complete sentence: *A Tale of Two Cities* is a sad account of man's inhumanity to man.

9. Write the proper, collective noun from this sentence: Many colorful birds live in Central America.

10. Write the compound, common noun from this sentence: Charles Dickens set his novel against the backdrop of the French Revolution.

11. For a–c, write the plural of each noun.
(a) ranch (b) maid of honor (c) Cathy

Write each word that should be capitalized in sentences 12 and 13.

12. did you study the french revolution in history, dad?

13. aunt emily wrote a song titled "my dog has black lips."

14. Write whether the following is a phrase or a clause: while Dr. Manette reverts to insanity

15. Write the indirect object in this sentence: Sydney Carton gives Lucie and Charles Darnay his greatest gift—his life.

16. Write each prepositional phrase and star each object of the preposition in this sentence: Besides the explorers, pirates were searching round about the island for the treasure.

17. Write three helping verbs that begin with the letter *h*.

18. For a–c, choose the correct past tense form of the irregular verb *be*.
(a) we (was, were) (b) they (was, were) (c) you (was, were)

For sentences 19 and 20, write the verb phrase and name its tense.

19. In May, the tall ship will have been sailing for fifteen months.

20. Since October, the ship has sailed all the way around the world twice.

For sentences 21 and 22, write the verb phrase and label it action or linking.

21. Sydney Carton appears calm and purposeful.

22. Carton exchanges places in prison with Charles Darnay.
(18)

For sentences 23 and 24, write the verb phrase and label it transitive or intransitive.

23. Does Cleo know the difference between suffrage and
(26) suffering?

24. Esau had traveled by camel through the desert for two
(26) hundred miles.

25. Write each adjective from this sentence: Charles Dickens
(23, 24) develops the character of Jarvis Lorry from a strict and proper businessman to a warm and sensitive one.

For sentences 26 and 27, write the verb phrase and label it active or passive voice.

26. Several trees had been uprooted by the fierce tornado.
(27)

27. Did that tornado uproot all those trees?
(27)

Diagram sentences 28–30.

28. Fred passed the queen a silver plate of spaghetti with
(29, 30) meatballs.

29. Stop laughing.
(16, 21)

30. Would you like to eat?
(19, 21)

LESSON 31 — The Period • Abbreviations

> **Dictation or Journal Entry**
>
> **Vocabulary:**
> *Hedonism* derives its meaning from a Greek word meaning "pleasure." *Hedonism* is the theory that pleasure is the highest good. Driven by *hedonism*, Ms. Fling spent each day at amusement parks, gourmet restaurants, and movie theaters.
>
> *Nestor,* an important character in the *Iliad*, was the oldest and wisest of the Greek warriors at Troy. Thus, a *nestor* is a leader in his or her field. The *nestor* of the U. S. Supreme Court happened to be the Chief Justice.

The Period Punctuation marks help the reader to understand the meaning of what is written. A **period** helps the reader to know where a sentence begins and ends, but there are other uses for the period as well.

Declarative Sentence A **declarative sentence** (statement) needs a period at the end.

> The people of New Hampshire greatly loved John Langdon.

Imperative Sentence An **imperative sentence** (command) needs a period at the end.

> Act now against British authority.

Initials We place periods after the **initials** in a person's name.

> M. E. Bradford
>
> B. D. Pistole

Outline In an **outline,** letters and numbers require a period after them.

> I. John Langdon
>   A. Merchant
>   B. Soldier
>   C. Political leader

Example 1 Add periods where they are needed in each expression.

(a) I The moderate Federalist position
   A Regulation of commerce
   B Establishment of military
   C Regulation of commerce

(b) Capture the infidels

(c) John Langdon was a member of the committee that made compromise possible and the Constitution acceptable

(d) According to L A Mayo, J Langdon spoke vehemently about restricting interstate tariffs

Solution (a) We place periods after the numbers and letters in an **outline.**

    I. The moderate Federalist position
       A. Regulation of commerce
       B. Establishment of military
       C. Regulation of commerce

(b) We place a period at the end of an **imperative sentence.** Capture the infidels.

(c) We place a period at the end of a **declarative sentence.**

John Langdon was a member of the committee that made compromise possible and the Constitution acceptable.

(d) We place periods after **initials** in a person's name. This is also a **declarative sentence.**

According to L. A. Mayo, J. Langdon spoke vehemently about restricting interstate tariffs.

Abbreviations Sometimes we shorten words by abbreviating them. **Abbreviations** often require periods, but not always. Because there are so many abbreviations, and because some abbreviations are used for more than one word, we check our dictionaries. Below are some common abbreviations that require periods. While it is important to become familiar with these, we do not generally use abbreviations in formal writing. **When in doubt, spell it out.**

Time of Day a.m. (Latin *ante meridiem*, "before noon")

p.m. (Latin *post meridiem*, "after noon")

Days of the Week
Sun. (Sunday)	Thurs. (Thursday)
Mon. (Monday)	Fri. (Friday)
Tues. (Tuesday)	Sat. (Saturday)
Wed. (Wednesday)	

Months of the Year
Jan. (January)	Apr. (April
Feb. (February)	May (no abbreviation)
Mar. (March)	June (no abbreviation)

	July (no abbreviation)	Oct. (October)
	Aug. (August)	Nov. (November)
	Sept. (September)	Dec. (December)
Proper Place Names	Dr. (Drive)	Rd. (Road)
	St. (Street)	Ave. (Avenue)
	Pl. (Place)	Blvd. (Boulevard)
	Mt. (Mount, Mountain)	Bldg. (Building)
Personal Titles	Mr. (Mister)	Miss (no abbreviation)
	Mrs. (Mistress; a married woman)	
	Ms. (any woman, especially one whose marital status is unknown)	
	Jr. (Junior)	Sr. (Senior)
	Dr. (Doctor)	Rev. (Reverend)
	Prof. (Professor)	Pres. (President)
	Gen. (General)	Capt. (Captain)
	Sen. (Senator)	Rep. (Representative)
Compass Directions	N. (north)	N.E. (northeast)
	S. (south)	N.W. (northwest)
	E. (east)	S.E. (southeast)
	W. (west)	S.W. (southwest)
Others	Co. (company)	etc. (Latin *et cetera*)
	Ltd. (Limited)	est. (estimated)
	Inc. (Incorporated)	cont. (continued)
	govt. (government)	anon. (anonymous)
	dept. (department)	misc. (miscellaneous)

Example 2   Write the abbreviation for each expression.

(a) Mistress   (b) November

(c) Saturday   (d) Drive

Solution   (a) **Mrs.**   (b) **Nov.**

(c) **Sat.**   (d) **Dr.**

In most of our writing, we spell out entire words and do not abbreviate. However, we use the following abbreviations even in formal writing:

> Personal titles such as Mr., Mrs., Jr., Ph.D., etc.
>
> Abbreviations that are part of a organization's legal name such as Inc., Co., Ltd., etc.
>
> Abbreviations used in expressions of time such as a.m., p.m., EST (eastern standard time), etc.
>
> A few others such as B.C. and A.D.

Example 3 Rewrite the following sentences using whole words instead of abbreviations that are not appropriate in formal writing.

(a) Mrs. Bartolo weighed one hundred twenty lbs. at the doctor's office.

(b) Michael Newkirk, D.D.S., extracted four wisdom teeth from the pres. of Spare Parts, Ltd., in Dec.

(c) In 49 B.C., Cleopatra was twenty yrs. old.

Solution (a) Mrs. Bartolo weighed one hundred twenty **pounds** at the doctor's office. (We keep the abbreviation **Mrs.** because it precedes a personal name and is used in formal writing, but we write out the entire word **pounds.**)

(b) Michael Newkirk, D.D.S., extracted four wisdom teeth from the **president** of Spare Parts, Ltd., in **December.** (We keep the abbreviation **D.D.S.** because it is acceptable in formal writing, but we write out the words **president** and **December.**)

(c) In 49 B.C., Cleopatra was twenty **years** old. (We keep the abbreviation **B.C.** because it is acceptable in formal writing, but we write out the word **years.**)

Practice Rewrite and add periods as needed in a–f.

    a. I New Hampshire's ratifying conventions
        A February, 1788
        B June, 1788

    b. John Langdon adjourned the convention in February to prevent a victory for Antifederalists

    c. Remember these dates

d. William H Harrison was born in Virginia

e. M A D D stands for "Mothers Against Drunk Driving"

f. The time changes from 11:59 pm to 12:00 am at midnight

For g–k, rewrite each sentence adding periods and making the necessary changes to abbreviations for formal writing.

g. Dr Yen received a degree from Harvard Univ last Feb

h. Mr Baker's dip recipe calls for two tsp of chili pepper.

i. In the mo of Feb, it appeared that the Constitution would not be ratified by NH.

j. New Hampshire lies on the SE side of Mass and on the E side of NY.

k. M E Bradford, Ph D, wrote the book called *Founding Fathers.*

l. Write the abbreviation for each expression.
   a. Wednesday b. August   c. Mister   d. Boulevard

For m and n, replace each blank with the correct vocabulary word.

m. Benjamin Franklin was labeled a _____ at the Constitutional Convention.

n. Pleasure-seeking Epicurians taught and pursued the principles of _____.

Review Set 31

Choose the correct word to complete sentences 1–5.

1. To (faze, phase, censor) is to perturb, disturb, or fluster.
(30)

2. A (hung jury, filibuster, cicerone) is a method of delaying legislative action by means of long speeches or prolonged debate.
(28, 29)

3. (Cicero, Filibuster, Hector) led the Trojan forces in the *Iliad* and killed several great Greek warriors.
(28, 29)

4. Gravid means (peaceful, belligerent, pregnant).
(27)

5. The grouchy lady refused to entertain guests. She was
(8, 9) (mutual, inhospitable, common).

Rewrite 6 and 7 placing periods where they are needed.

6.   I Punctuation marks
(31)   A Periods
                B Commas
                C Quotation marks

7. Mr Wang arrived at six pm for the dinner His wife came
(31) later

8. Rewrite this sentence adding periods and making
(31) necessary changes to abbreviations for formal writing:
Dr Payne's office bldg is on the corner of Green St and Sixth Ave

9. List the four types of sentences.
(1)

10. Write whether the following is a complete sentence, a
(2) sentence fragment, or a run-on sentence: Charlotte Bronte wrote *Jane Eyre* it is a psychological romance.

11. Replace the action verb in this sentence with one that
(3) might be more accurate or descriptive: Mrs. Curtis <u>went</u> around the track twice. (There is more than one answer.)

Write each word that should be capitalized in sentences 12 and 13.

12. jane eyre, i believe, is my favorite novel.
(9)

13. charlotte bronte sets the novel in northern england in the
(9, 25) 1800s.

14. In this sentence, write the verb phrase and name its tense:
(17) Jane Eyre is living at Gateshead Hall Manor with her aunt-in-law, Mrs. Reed.

15. In this sentence, write each noun labeling it concrete or
(4) abstract: Jane Eyre is subjected to mistreatment and hatred.

16. Write the plural of each noun.
(10, 11) (a) soprano   (b) grandchild   (c) potato

17. Write the four principal parts of the verb *clap*.
(13)

18. In this sentence, write the gerund and label its tense
(16) present or perfect: Having left Gateshead Hall Manor enabled Jane to start over at a different school.

19. Write whether the following is a phrase or a clause:
(20) advancing from pupil to teacher

20. Write each adjective from this sentence: Jane Eyre
(23, 24) supervises Adele, the little ward of Mr. Rochester, a princely and heroic master.

21. Write the indirect object in this sentence: Did Clark loan
(30) Peter his cape?

22. In this sentence, write each prepositional phrase, starring
(28) the object of each preposition: The hurricane had damaged all the buildings alongside of the boardwalk, except for the bank across from the post office.

23. In this sentence, write the verb phrase and label it action
(18) or linking: That story about the lady with twelve Siamese cats in her kitchen sounds interesting.

For sentences 24 and 25, write the verb phrase and label it active or passive voice.

24. Sometimes candidates are elected by a narrow margin of
(27) votes.

25. In November the community will elect a new school
(27) board member.

For sentences 26 and 27, write the verb phrase and label it transitive or intransitive.

26. Does your new yellow jacket glow in the dark?
(26)

27. Will you be wearing that snazzy yellow jacket at night?
(26)

Diagram sentences 28–30.

28. Robert bought his mother a bouquet of red carnations.
(29, 30)

29. Singing gives me much pleasure.
(16, 30)

30. Do we need to study?
(19, 21)

LESSON 32

Proofreading Symbols, Part 1

Dictation or Journal Entry

Vocabulary: The words *conscience* and *consciousness* are sometimes confused.

Our *conscience* is our sense of right and wrong. In order to maintain a clear *conscience*, the customer returned the excess change to the salesclerk.

Consciousness is awareness of one's surroundings, thoughts, and existence. Public *consciousness* of the politician's dishonesty changed the overall outlook of the election.

Conscientious and *conscious* are the adjective forms of these words.

Conscientious means "guided by one's conscience; scrupulous." The *conscientious* nurse attended to her patients carefully and tenderly.

Conscious means aware or cognizant. The nurse was *conscious* of the patient's need for attention.

Our goal is to apply the standards of written English to our writing. After writing and revising a first draft, we proofread to find and correct errors in grammar, usage, spelling, and punctuation. We use a set of standard **proofreading symbols** that all writers understand. The chart below shows some common proofreading symbols.

SYMBOL	EXAMPLE	MEANING
≡	paul Revere	Capitalize a lowercase letter.
/	the Next time	Make a capital letter lowercase.
∧	king of England	Insert a missing word, letter, or punctuation mark.
/	con︵scious (n)	Change a letter.
— or ℐ	the ~~the~~ reason	Leave out a word, letter, or punctuation mark.
⌒	news‿paper	Close up a space.
∾	consc︵ius	Change the order of the letters.
⊙	Mrs⊙Poof	Add a period.
#	dog#food	Add a space.

Example 1 Proofread this paragraph about Nicholas Gilman for mistakes in spelling and capitalization. Use the correct symbols for the needed changes.

nicholas gilman, the stereo type of a new englander, said few words but followed more dicisive Men. Gilman served as Governor of new Hampshire severel Times. John Langdon and Nicholas Gilman Traveled Togeather tothe Constitutional Convention. At the out break of the Revolution, Nicholas Gilman enlitsed in the continental arrmy.

Solution We proofread the paragraph in this way:

nicholas gilman, the stereo type of a new englander, said few words but followed more dicisive Men. Gilman served as Governor of new Hampshire severel Times. John Langdon and Nicholas Gilman Traveled Togeather tothe Constitutional Convention. At the out break of the Revolution, Nicholas Gilman enlitsed in the continental arrmy.

Example 2 Proofread this paragraph for mistakes in punctuation. Add the correct symbols for the needed changes.

Mr Gilman voted the moderate Federalist position at the Great Convention He supported the Constitution, vigorously, in New Hampshire and served, as one of New Hampshire's first, members to the House of Representatives

Solution We proofread the paragraph as follows:

Mr Gilman voted the moderate Federalist position at the Great Convention He supported the Constitution, vigorously, in New Hampshire and served, as one of New Hampshire's first, members to the House of Representatives

Example 3 Proofread these sentences for all mistakes.

One frenchdiplomat described nicholas Gilman as one of the Proudest men in in america.

Manny of his suppotrers consedered Nicholas Gilman very hand some man

Solution We proofread the sentences using the standard proofreading symbols.

One french/diplomat described nicholas Gilman as one of the Proudest men in in america.

Manny of his supporters consedered Nicholas Gilman^a very handsome man.

Practice For a–i, replace each blank with the correct symbol.

a. _____ Add a period.

b. _____ Make a capital letter lowercase.

c. _____ Add a space.

d. _____ Insert a missing word, letter, or punctuation mark.

e. _____ Capitalize a lowercase letter.

f. _____ Change a letter.

g. _____ Change the order of the letters.

h. _____ Close up a space.

i. _____ Leave out a word, letter, or punctuation mark.

j. Rewrite the following sentences as they are written. Then proofread them using the standard symbols.

Nicholas gilman retained, the confidince ofthe smal farmers and people people in New Hampshire

Poeple in Mr. Gilman's corner of america Found him trust worthy and pleasant.

For k–n, replace each blank with the correct vocabulary word.

k. Nicholas Gilman was _____ of the needs of the small farmer.

l. People admired him because he was _____ and hard-working.

m. Nicholas Gilman's _____ would not allow him to remain a member of the Federalist Party.

n. His _____ of the need for a stronger central government influenced his vote on political issues.

More Practice   See Master Worksheets.

Review Set 32   Choose the correct word to complete sentences 1–6.

1. The word (filibuster, cicerone, hedonism) comes from a Greek word meaning "pleasure."
   (31)

2. To faze is to (appease, lobby, disturb).
   (30)

3. To (alleviate, apportion, filibuster) is to obstruct legislative action by long speeches or debate.
   (24, 29)

4. A quorum is a (number, caucus, meeting) of people.
   (10)

5. Ambiguous statements are (clear, unclear, precise).
   (11)

6. (Do, Does) grammar appeal to you?
   (12)

7. Rewrite the following as it is, adding proofreading symbols to correct errors:
   (32)

   Joe adn i have been planting Corn since mon day We're tierd.

8. Write whether this sentence is declarative, interrogative, imperative, or exclamatory: Jane Austen wrote novels depicting early nineteenth-century manners.
   (1)

9. Write whether the following is a sentence fragment, run-on sentence, or complete sentence: Gleaming in the rosy light of a spectacular sunset over the ocean.
   (2)

10. Write the collective noun from this sentence: The Bennet Family consists of five beautiful daughters.
    (4)

11. Write the plural of each noun.
    (10, 11)
    (a) scenario   (b) photocopy   (c) birthday

Write each word that should be capitalized in sentences 12 and 13.

12. i have read jane austen's *pride and prejudice* and *sense and sensibility*, but i have not read her *mansfield park* and *persuasion*.
(9, 25)

13. hey, grandma, do you prefer british or american authors?
(9, 22)

14. Write the word from this list that is *not* a linking verb: is, am, are, was, were, be, being, been, look, feel, taste, that, smell, sound, seem, appear, grow, become, remain, stay
(18)

For sentences 15 and 16, write the verb phrase and name its tense.

15. This literature class will be studying the manners of the Victorian Age.
(17)

16. Hearing about new neighbors had delighted Mrs. Bennet.
(15)

For sentences 17 and 18, write the verb phrase and label it action or linking.

17. Mrs. Bennet is happy about the new, eligible bachelor.
(18)

18. Is Mr. Bingley, the eligible bachelor, courting Jane Bennet, the eldest girl?
(18)

19. Write whether the following is a phrase or a clause: with steadfast courage and determination
(20)

20. Write the infinitive in this sentence and label its tense present or perfect: Mrs. Bennet wants to capture a rich husband for each girl.
(19)

21. Write the present participle, past tense, and past participle of the verb *decline*.
(13)

22. Write the indefinite adjective in this sentence: Most students appreciate their teachers.
(24)

23. In this sentence, write the verb phrase and label it transitive or intransitive: Does Elizabeth Bennet see the hypocrisy of the Bingley sisters?
(26)

24. In this sentence, write the verb phrase and label it active
(27) or passive voice: Elizabeth Bennet is disliked by
Bingley's sisters.

25. Write the indirect object in this sentence: Will the
(30) Reverend Collins give Elizabeth a wedding ring?

26. Rewrite the following adding periods and making
(31) necessary changes to abbreviations for formal writing: On
Thurs, Feb 3, Mrs Lopez left for N Africa

27. Replace the blank with the singular present tense form of
(5) the verb.

Cars pass us.   A car _____ us.

Diagram sentences 28–30.

28. May I borrow your collection of humorous anecdotes?
(21, 29)

29. Did giggling give her the hiccups?
(21, 30)

30. Does your uncle like to read?
(21, 24)

LESSON 33

Coordinating Conjunctions

> **Dictation or Journal Entry**
>
> **Vocabulary:**
> Stentor, a Greek warrior in the *Iliad*, used his loud, powerful voice to deliver announcements and proclamations to the assembled Greek armies. Today, *stentorian* means a loud, powerful sound. The fitness instructor's *stentorian* voice permeated the entire building.
>
> The ancient Spartans had a reputation for being frugal, austere, and sternly disciplined. Today, the word *Spartan* means simple, frugal, and disciplined. A *Spartan* lifestyle allows for few luxuries.

Conjunctions are connecting words. They connect words, phrases, and clauses. There are three kinds of conjunctions: coordinating, correlative, and subordinating. In this lesson, we will learn to recognize coordinating conjunctions.

Coordinating Conjunctions We use a **coordinating conjunction** to join parts of a sentence that are equal, or similar in form. A coordinating conjunction connects a word to a word, a phrase to a phrase, or a clause to a clause. We call these sentence parts "elements." When joined by a conjunction, they are called "compound" parts.

Here are the common coordinating conjunctions:

and   but   or   nor   for   yet   so

They may join a word to another word.

peanut butter *and* jelly   cash *or* check
bread *and* butter   slowly *but* steadily
aggressive *yet* sensitive   conscious *or* conscience

They may join a phrase to another phrase.

to practice the skill *and* to take the test
on the airplane *or* aboard the ship
angering some people *but* appeasing others

They may connect a clause to another clause.

John Langdon served on the Continental Congress, *and* he financed a brigade against the British.

He was considered a patriot, *for* he sacrificed much for his country.

Example Underline each coordinating conjunction that you find in these sentences.

(a) We remember Elbridge Gerry from Massachusetts, for he signed the Declaration of Independence and the Articles of Confederation.

(b) Elbridge Gerry was an Antifederalist and an opponent to the Constitution, but economic insecurity under the Articles of Confederation drew him to the Great Convention.

(c) Most colonists despised war, yet they would not tolerate British interference or injustice.

(d) Mutual respect developed between Samuel Adams, John Hancock, and Elbridge Gerry, so they prepared the state of Massachusetts for war.

Solution (a) We remember Elbridge Gerry from Massachusetts, **for** he signed the Declaration of Independence **and** the Articles of Confederation.

(b) Elbridge Gerry was an Antifederalist **and** an opponent to the Constitution, **but** economic insecurity under the Articles of Confederation drew him to the Great Convention.

(c) Most colonists despised war, **yet** they would not tolerate British interference **or** injustice.

(d) Mutual respect developed between Samuel Adams, John Hancock, **and** Elbridge Gerry, **so** they prepared the state of Massachusetts for war.

Practice **a.** Memorize and write the seven coordinating conjunctions.

Write each coordinating conjunction, if any, that you find in sentences b–g.

b. As a Democratic-Republican, Elbridge Gerry gained favor and popularity.

c. He ran for governor of Massachusetts several times, but he was not successful until the age of sixty-five.

d. Some people think of Elbridge Gerry as a failure, yet he served in many political offices.

e. Elbridge Gerry served two terms as governor of Massachusetts, but he lost his bid for three terms, for the Federalists were angry about his attacks on their clergy and his redistricting of the state.

f. Have you heard of "gerrymandering," or the redistricting of an area to gain political control?

g. Elbridge Gerry participated significantly in our nation's history, so we read about his political views and actions in *Founding Fathers*.

For h and i, replace each blank with the correct vocabulary word.

h. Her _____ view of life explains her refusal to purchase a new television set with surround sound.

i. The _____ voice of the baseball announcer draws listeners from all over the country.

Review Set 33

Choose the correct word to complete sentences 1–5.

1. Our (conscience, consciousness, Nestor) is our sense of right and wrong.
(32)

2. The word *hedonism* comes from a Greek word meaning (pleasure, hospitality, generosity).
(31)

3. To (faze, phase, filibuster) is to introduce in stages.
(29, 30)

4. The (amiable, ambiguous, bellicose) flight attendant smiled and offered to help us.
(11, 12)

5. According to the last (caucus, lobby, census) there were only twenty-three people in Tinyville.
(10, 13)

Rewrite sentences 6 and 7, adding periods and making necessary changes to abbreviations for formal writing:

6. Mr Lu will meet us here on Thurs at nine am
(31)

7. At birth, Jasper W Zoot weighed ten lbs, two oz
(31)

8. Write the seven common coordinating conjunctions.
(33)

9. Write each coordinating conjunction from this sentence: Quan and Tom play tennis, but they do not play together, for Quan is a professional, yet Tom is only a beginner.
(33)

10. Write whether the following is a sentence fragment, run-on sentence, or complete sentence: Mr. Darcy is Mr. Bingley's wealthy and arrogant friend he falls in love with Elizabeth.
(2)

11. In this sentence, write the verb phrase and label it transitive or intransitive: Will Mr. Darcy ask Elizabeth to marry him?
(26)

12. For a–c, write the plural of each noun.
(10, 11) (a) leaf (b) louse (c) tax

Write each word that should be capitalized in sentences 13 and 14.

13. mr. darcy declares, "you must allow me to tell you how ardently i admire and love you."
(9)

14. eight-year-old adèle speaks a hodgepodge of french and english that mrs. fairfax cannot understand.
(22, 25)

15. Write the prepositional phrase and star the object of the preposition in this sentence: In a letter to Elizabeth, Mr. Darcy explains the reasons for his actions.
(28)

16. Write the four principal parts (present tense, present participle, past tense, and past participle) of the verb *lobby*.
(13)

For sentences 17 and 18, write the entire verb phrase and name its tense.

17. Elizabeth had been harboring her own pride and prejudice.
(17)

18. Lydia elopes with Mr. Wickham.
(5)

19. Write each adjective from this sentence: Young, impetuous Lydia Bennet marries Mr. Wickham.
(23, 24)

20. Rewrite the following as it is. Then add proofreading symbols to indicate corrections.
(32)
Jane an mR biingley becomed engaged.

21. In this sentence, write the verb phrase and label it active or passive voice: Mr. Darcy is proposing to Elizabeth again!
(27)

22. Rewrite this sentence using active voice: The snowman was built by Javier.
(27)

23. In this sentence, write the verb phrase and label it action or linking: Does Elizabeth seem happy about Mr. Darcy's wedding proposal?
(18)

24. Write whether this sentence is declarative, imperative, interrogative, or exclamatory: Do not insult my family!
(2)

25. Write the gerund in this sentence and label its tense present or perfect: We agreed that arguing would accomplish nothing.
(16)

26. Write whether the following is a phrase or a clause: when Elizabeth tells Mr. Bennet about her decision
(20)

27. Write the indirect object in this sentence: Elizabeth gives Mr. Bennet a plausible explanation.
(30)

Diagram sentences 28–30.

28. The stentorian voice of the preacher in the pulpit grabbed my attention.
(24, 29)

29. This good news gives me hope.
(21, 30)

30. Does your team hope to win?
(21, 24)

LESSON 34

Compound Subjects and Predicates • Diagramming Compounds

> **Dictation or Journal Entry**
> **Vocabulary:** The abbreviations *et al.* and *etc.* have Latin roots.
>
> *Et al.* comes from *et alii* meaning "and others." We use it in reference to additional people. Those attending the Constitutional Convention included John Langdon, Nicholas Gilman, *et al.*
>
> *Etc.*, from *et cetera*, also means "and others." We use it in reference to things and not people. For the upcoming exam, remember to study the Preamble, the Articles, the Bill of Rights, *etc.*

Compound Subjects

The predicate or verb of a sentence may have more than one subject, as in the sentence below.

John Langdon and *Nicholas Gilman* represented New Hampshire.

In the sentence above, the verb "represented" has two subjects: "John Langdon," "Nicholas Gilman." We call this a **compound subject.**

Compound Predicates

Likewise, a subject may have more than one predicate, as in the sentence below.

The *Bill of Rights* defines and safeguards fundamental individual rights.

In this sentence, the subject, "the Bill of Rights," has two predicates, "defines" and "safeguards." We call this a **compound predicate.**

Diagramming Compounds

To diagram a compound subject, predicate, direct object, or indirect object, we place each part of the compound on a separate, horizontal line. We write the conjunction on a vertical dotted line that joins the horizontal lines.

COMPOUND SUBJECT DIAGRAM:

Gerry and *Strong* submitted their votes.

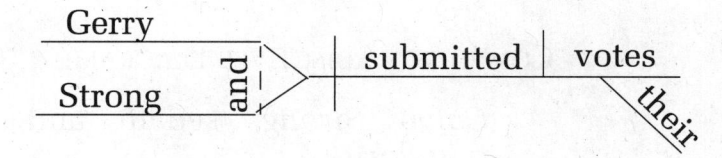

```
   Gerry
          \
           \  and  >—— submitted | votes
          /                         \their
   Strong
```

COMPOUND PREDICATE DIAGRAM:

The delegates discussed and debated the issues.

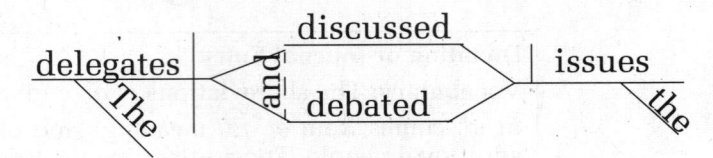

COMPOUND SUBJECT AND COMPOUND PREDICATE DIAGRAM:

Gerry and *Strong* supported and defended the Constitution.

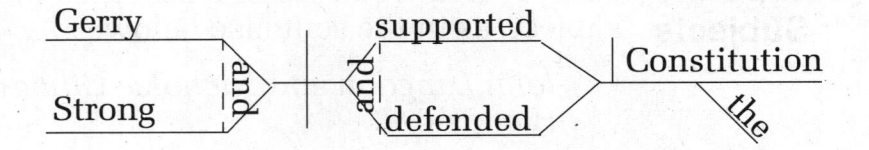

COMPOUND DIRECT OBJECT DIAGRAM:

Caleb Strong supported the *Great Compromise and annual *elections for representatives.

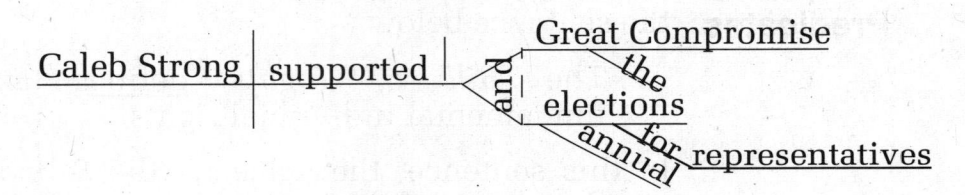

COMPOUND INDIRECT OBJECT DIAGRAM:

Strong gave (John Adams) and (the Federalists) his support.

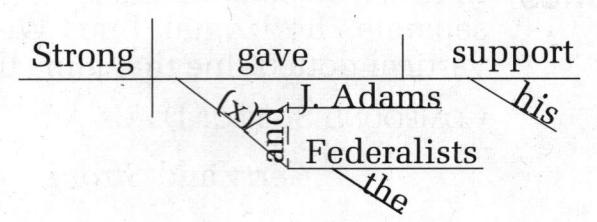

COMPOUND ADJECTIVES DIAGRAM:

Caleb Strong, sedate and stable, retained his popularity.

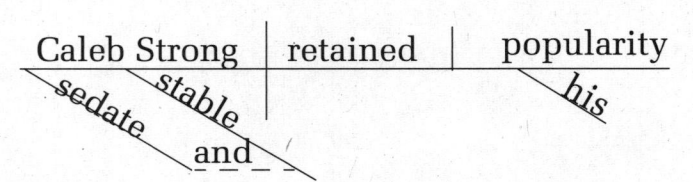

Example Diagram each sentence.

(a) John Adams and Caleb Strong opposed Thomas Jefferson.

(b) Strong favored and implemented the Federalist doctrine of national sovereignty.

(c) Nathaniel Gorham, Rufus King, and others experienced and survived financial failure.

Solution (a) This sentence contains a compound subject.

John Adams and *Caleb Strong* opposed Thomas Jefferson.

```
  John Adams  \
               >---+--- opposed | Thomas Jefferson
  Caleb Strong /  and
```

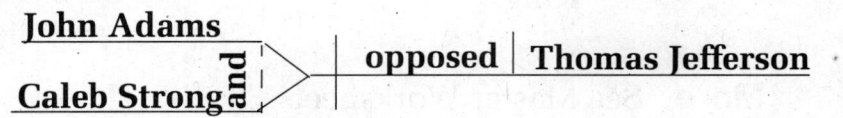

(b) This sentence has a compound predicate. The subject, *Strong*, did two things. He favored, and he implemented.

Strong favored and implemented the Federalist doctrine of state sovereignty.

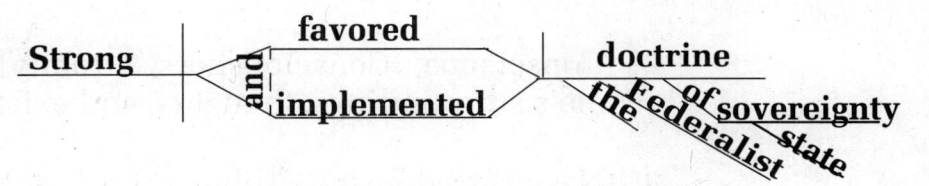

```
              favored
Strong |---+          +--- doctrine
           and              \of sovereignty
           implemented     the\Federalist\state
```

(c) This sentence has a compound subject (*N. Gorham, R. King, others*) and a compound predicate (experienced, survived).

Nathaniel Gorham, Rufus King, and *others* experienced and survived financial failure.

```
  N. Gorham                experienced
                \                       \
  R. King        >---+---<               +--- failure
                /and    and\             \financial
  others                    survived
```

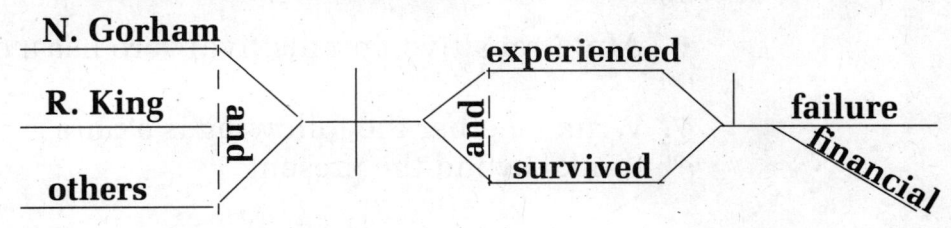

Practice For a and b, replace each blank with the correct vocabulary word(s).

a. Elbridge Gerry, Caleb Strong, Nathaniel Gorham, _____ served the state of Massachusetts in a variety of ways.

b. Representation, tax revenue, slave trade, _____ are some of the issues that complicated the passage of the U.S. Constitution.

Diagram sentences c–f.

c. Did Gorham lose money and property?

d. Alba read the boys and girls her report.

e. Faith, perseverance, and hard work saved the day.

f. The vocal and adamant Gorham recommended Rufus King.

More Practice See Master Worksheets.

Review Set 34 Choose the best word to complete sentences 1–6.

1. (Cicero, Hector, Stentor), a Greek warrior in the Iliad, used his loud, powerful voice to make announcements to the armies.
(28, 33)

2. (Conscience, Consciousness, Probity) is awareness of one's surroundings, thoughts, and existence.
(19, 32)

3. (Nestor, Hedonism, Filibuster) is the theory that pleasure is the highest good.
(29, 31)

4. A (filibuster, phase, cicerone) is a period or stage.
(29, 30)

5. (Can, May) you lift this heavy box for me?
(14)

6. A(n) (transitive, intransitive) verb has a direct object.
(26)

7. Write whether the following is a phrase or a clause: if you think beyond the present
(20)

8. In this sentence, write the verb phrase and label it action or linking: *To Kill a Mockingbird* remains a popular novel for all ages.
(18)

9. Write whether this word group is a complete sentence, sentence fragment, or run-on sentence: *To Kill a*
(2)

Mockingbird is a symbolic drama set in Southern Alabama in the early 1930s.

10. Write each compound noun from this sentence: Four disheveled sleepyheads shuffled into the classroom at daybreak.
(7)

11. From this sentence, write each noun and label its gender masculine, feminine, neuter, or indefinite: Percival, a rooster, creates mayhem amongst the hens every morning.
(7)

12. For a–c, write the plural of each noun.
(10, 11)
(a) elk   (b) sister-in-law   (c) busybody

Write each word that should be capitalized in sentences 13 and 14.

13. the house of representatives and the senate balance the power of the president of the united states.
(22, 25)

14. molly said, "hey, dad, tell me about boo radley."
(9, 22)

15. From this sentence, write the verb phrase and label it active or passive voice: Was that bridge designed by a famous engineer?
(27)

16. Write the prepositional phrase and star the object of the preposition in this sentence: Because of its length, this article continues at the back of the magazine.
(28)

17. From this sentence, write the adjective phrase and the noun it modifies: First Juan read the back of the book.
(29)

For sentences 18 and 19, write the verb phrase and name its tense.

18. For years, Boo's behavior has aroused the curiosity of Maycomb citizens.
(15)

19. Scout and Jem are trying to get Boo out of his house.
(17)

Write the correct verb form to complete sentences 20 and 21.

20. This month, Calpurnia (future perfect tense of *live*) with the Finches for five years.
(15)

21. Scout and Jem (present perfect tense of *experience*) Boo's kindness.
(15)

22. Rewrite the following, adding periods and making necessary corrections to abbreviations for formal writing: Dr Zoot asked if Sun is a day of rest in the state of Calif
(31)

23. Rewrite the following as it is. Then add proofreading symbols to indicate corrections.
(32)
Rhode IsLand isn't realy an island it's astate bordering massa chusetts.

24. Write the past participle of the verb *hurry*.
(13)

25. Write the seven common coordinating conjunctions.
(33)

26. Write the coordinating conjunction from this sentence: The townspeople are angry with Atticus, for he truly attempts to defend Tom.
(33)

Diagram each word of sentences 27–30.

27. To clean will require patience and endurance.
(19, 34)

28. Ms. Messy should scrub the floor beneath her kitchen table.
(21, 29)

29. Does Ms. Messy dread housecleaning?
(3, 21)

30. I loaned her my best bucket and a mop.
(30, 34)

LESSON 35 — Correlative Conjunctions

> **Dictation or Journal Entry**
>
> **Vocabulary:** The root *krat-* comes from the Greek word meaning "power."
>
> We combine the root with *demos*, the Greek word for "people," to form the word *democracy*, meaning rule by the people. People of other nations often envy our <u>democracy</u>.
>
> An *aristocracy* is a powerful nobility. Sometimes the *aristocracy* took advantage of the common people.
>
> A *bureaucrat* is an appointed government official. *Bureaucrats* do the day-to-day work that keeps our government working.
>
> A *plutocrat* is one who has power because of his or her wealth. In the late nineteenth century, wealthy industrialists became *plutocrats*.

Correlative Conjunctions Correlative conjunctions are similar to coordinating conjunctions in that they connect parts of a sentence that are equal, or parallel. Correlative conjunctions are always used in pairs. Here we list the most common ones:

both—and   either—or

neither—nor   not only—but also

The parts they join must be similar in form, or parallel.

> The writings of Elbridge Gerry created *both* American recruitment *and* patriotic fervor.
>
> Did *either* Samuel Adams *or* John Hancock serve with Gerry in the Second Continental Congress?
>
> *Neither* John Langdon *nor* Nicholas Gilman had faith in the Articles of Confederation.
>
> *Not only* the development of the Northwest Territory *but also* the retirement of the national debt concerned Elbridge Gerry.

Example 1 Underline the correlative conjunctions in each sentence.

(a) The new country needed both revenue and unity.

(b) Not only the war but also the economy moved Gerry to sound like a Federalist at times.

(c) Elbridge Gerry wanted neither a strong executive power nor an extensive court system.

Solution (a) The new country needed **both** revenue **and** unity.

(b) **Not only** the war **but also** the economy moved Gerry to sound like a Federalist at times.

(c) Elbridge Gerry wanted **neither** a strong executive power **nor** an extensive court system.

Diagramming We diagram correlative conjunctions this way:

Gorham wanted not only a sound currency but also regular tax revenue.

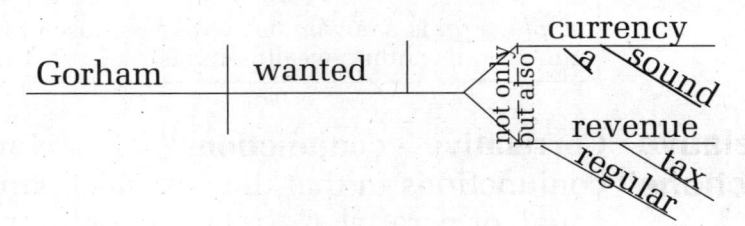

Example 2 Diagram this sentence:

Either the British or the colonists will rule the land.

Solution We diagram the correlative conjunctions as in the example above.

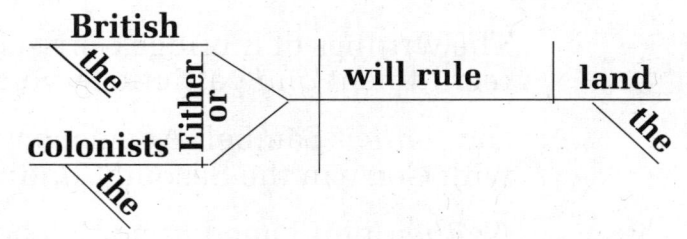

Practice a. Write the four common pairs of correlative conjunctions.

Write the correlative conjunctions from sentences b–e.

b. You may report on either the Revolutionary War or the Civil War.

c. Neither Cotesworth Pinckney nor John Marshall agreed on Elbridge Gerry's role in France.

d. Both Pinckney and Marshall returned to America before Gerry did.

e. Not only John Adams but also his friends ostracized Elbridge Gerry after the France fiasco.

f. Diagram this sentence:

He deserves neither disgrace nor ruin.

For g–j, replace each blank with the correct vocabulary word.

g. In the early twentieth century, reformers tried to limit the power of the wealthy _____.

h. Members of a(n) _____ often have noble titles or hereditary right to rule.

i. The U. S. Constitution is based on a firm belief in _____.

j. In order to receive a visa, the tourist had to speak to several _____.

Review set 35 Choose the correct word to complete sentences 1–5.

1. The abbreviation (*et al., e.g., i.e.*) means "and others" and
(34) refers to additional people.

2. (Stentorian, Spartan, Contemptible) means a loud,
(15, 33) powerful sound.

3. (Conscientious, Conscious, Gravid) means "guided by
(27, 32) one's conscience; scrupulous."

4. Hedonism is the theory that (charity, probity, pleasure) is
(31) the highest good.

5. Lying and cheating are (affectionate, amicable,
(12, 15) contemptible) behaviors.

6. Write whether the following sentence is declarative,
(1) exclamatory, imperative, or interrogative:

How do the townspeople feel about Mayella Ewell?

7. Write each word that should be capitalized in this
(9, 22) sentence: in *to kill a mockingbird,* harper lee depicts racism in the south.

8. Write the two abstract, common nouns from this
(4) sentence: Atticus Finch calls Maycomb's disease prejudice.

9. For a–c, write the plural of each noun.
(10, 11) (a) lady (b) delay (c) editor in chief

10. Write the prepositional phrases and star the objects of
(28) each preposition in this sentence: Because of a widespread drought, there was a catastrophic food shortage in Kenya during the summer of 2004.

11. For a–c, choose the correct form of the irregular verb *be*.
(12) (a) he (was, were) (b) you (was, were) (c) we (was, were)

12. In this sentence, write the verb phrase and label it action
(3, 18) or linking: Townspeople are threatening Atticus and his children.

13. In this sentence, write the verb phrase and label it
(26) transitive or intransitive: Leona's health has been improving since her vacation.

14. Write each adjective in this sentence: The unkempt and
(23, 24) ignorant Mayella still succeeds in swaying the prejudiced jury against gentle Tom Robinson.

15. Rewrite the following sentence, adding periods and
(31) making necessary changes to abbreviations for formal writing.
On Dec 1, at 8 a m, Gen Josh Lim led his soldiers to their remodeled barracks

16. Write the seven common coordinating conjunctions.
(33)

17. Write the correlative conjunction pair in this sentence:
(33) Not only Jem but also Scout receives an ethical awakening.

18. In this sentence, write the verb phrase and name its tense:
(15) Scout had dressed as a ham for the pageant.

19. In this sentence, write the gerund and label its tense
(16) present or perfect: Allison considered fishing but decided to swim instead.

20. In this sentence, write the infinitive and label its tense
(19) present or perfect: Elle likes swimming, but she chose to surf instead.

21. Write whether the following is a phrase or a clause: to get revenge on Atticus Finch
(20)

22. Write the present participle of the verb *hurry*.
(13)

23. In the following sentence, write the verb and label it active or passive voice: In a court of law, Atticus declares the equality of all people.
(27)

24. Write each abstract noun in this sentence: Equality must replace prejudice in our country.
(4)

25. Rewrite the following as it is and add proofreading symbols to indicate corrections:
(32)
Mrs Yu sees steam rising out of th manhole covers in Man hattan, Newyork.

26. Write four common pairs of correlative conjunctions.
(35)

27. Write the indirect object in this sentence: Dinah loaned Ann a three-pronged apple picker during harvest season.
(30)

Diagram sentences 28–30.

28. Both Chase and Lace expect to race.
(21, 35)

29. Cheating will give others a bad impression of you.
(16, 30)

30. Should Mr. Lu judge the pie-eating contest between the students and the teachers?
(29, 34)

LESSON 36

Diagramming Predicate Nominatives

> **Dictation or Journal Entry**
>
> **Vocabulary:** The words *stoic* and *sybaritic* trace their meanings back to ancient Greece.
>
> The Stoics belonged to a philosophical movement begun by a man named Zeno, who taught that people should be free from joy, grief, and any kind of passions in order to attain ultimate wisdom. Used as an adjective, *stoic* means indifferent to pleasure and pain. The *stoic* cook remained calm and dignified even when her kitchen was invaded by mice. Used as a noun, a *stoic* is one who is indifferent to pleasure and pain. I thought he was a *stoic*, for he never laughed at my jokes.
>
> In Italy, the Greeks founded the ancient city of Sybaris, which was known for its great wealth and hedonism. Therefore, the term *sybaritic* grew to mean extravagant and sensual. People wallowed in *sybaritic* pleasure at the hedonistic resort.

More than one name can identify people, animals, or things.

Lewis Carroll <u>is</u> a famous British *author*.

"Author" is another name for "Lewis Carroll."

Renames the Subject A **predicate nominative** is a noun that follows the verb and renames the subject person, animal, or thing. It explains or defines the subject and is identical with it. The subject and the predicate nominative are joined by a linking verb such as *am, is, are, was, were, be, being, been, become,* or *seem*. We remember that a linking verb does not show action, nor does it "help" the action verb. Its purpose is to connect the person, animal, or thing (the subject) to its new name (the predicate nominative).

Predicate nominatives are circled in the sentences below.

That *judge* is (Rufus King).

"Rufus King" renames "judge"

Rufus King <u>was</u> a conservative (statesman).

"statesman" renames "Rufus King"

If we reverse the subject and the predicate nominative as in the sentences below, the meaning of the sentence is not affected.

Rufus King <u>is</u> (that judge).

A conservative *statesman* <u>was</u> (Rufus King).

Identifying the Predicate Nominative

Reversing the subject and predicate in this manner helps us to identify the predicate nominative. If the linking verb is not a "to be" verb, we can replace it with a "to be" verb to determine whether there is a predicate nominative that renames the subject:

Rufus King remained a U.S. senator for twelve years.

Rufus King was a U.S. senator for twelve years.

↑
"to be" linking verb

Now we can reverse the subject and predicate, and we see that the predicate does indeed rename the subject. The meaning is the same, so we have identified a predicate nominative.

A U.S. senator for twelve years was Rufus King.

Predicate nominatives are more difficult to identify in interrogative sentences. Turning the question into a statement will help us.

Was Rufus King a high Federalist? (question)

Rufus King was a high Federalist. (statement)

In the statement above, we see that "Federalist" renames "Rufus King." Therefore, "Federalist" is a predicate nominative.

Compound Predicate Nominatives

Predicate nominatives may be compound, as in the sentence below.

Some of the representatives for Massachusetts were Caleb Strong, Nathaniel Gorham, and Rufus King.

Diagramming

In a diagram, the predicate nominative is indicated by a line that slants toward the right. Here we diagram the sentence above:

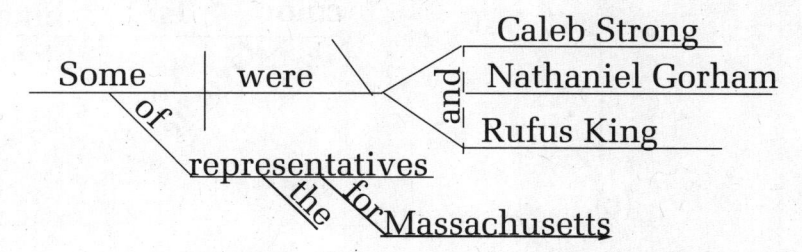

Below are more diagrams showing predicate nominatives.

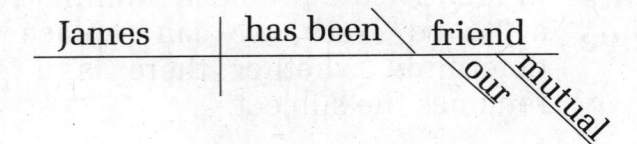

James has been our mutual friend.

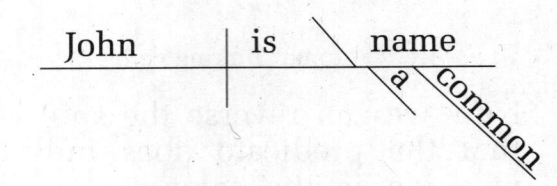

John is a common name.

Example Diagram the following sentences.
(a) Rufus King was a great orator, able diplomat, successful politician, and wise businessman.

(b) Is your favorite color blue?

(c) Lilibet and Jake were good friends.

Solution (a)

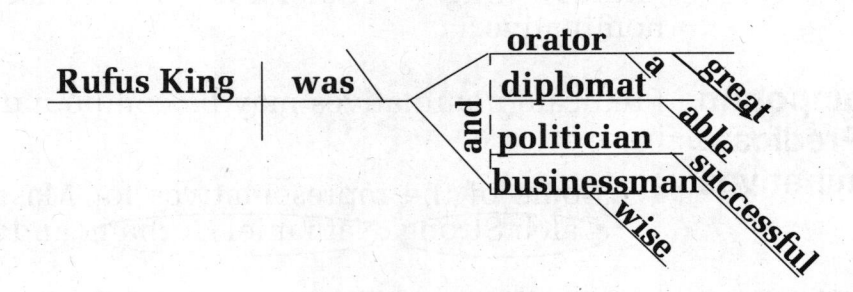

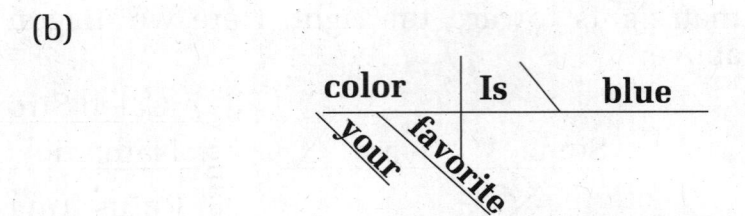

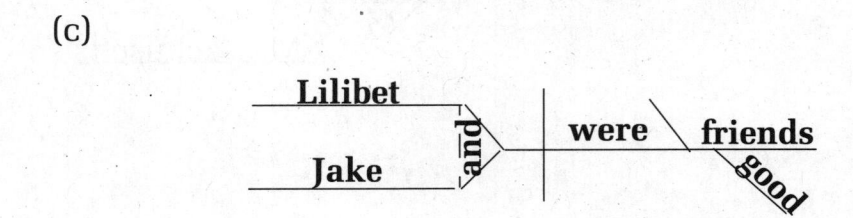

(b)

(c)

We remember that gerunds and infinitives can function as nouns. Therefore, a predicate nominative may be a gerund or an infinitive as in these sentences:

GERUND

Roger Sherman's occupation was *shoemaking*.

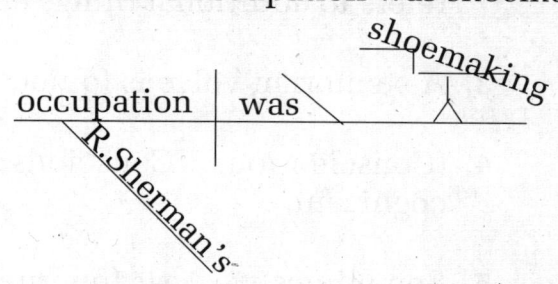

INFINITIVE

His goal was *to finish*.

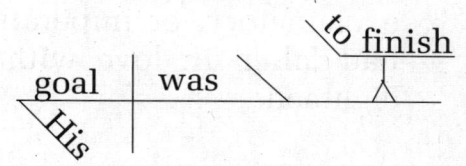

Practice For a–c, replace each blank with the correct vocabulary word.

a. The _____ rarely laughed or cried.

b. My _____ uncle showed no emotion during the funeral.

c. The _____ couple took one expensive cruise after another.

For d–g, diagram each sentence.

d. His hope for Connecticut was to compromise.

e. Sherman was the second-oldest man in the Great Convention.

f. Her joy has been her skating.

g. She became a trustworthy representative.

Review Set 36 Choose the correct word to complete sentences 1–5.

1. The root *krat-* comes from the Greek word meaning
(35) (guest, proof, power).

2. The abbreviation (*etc., eg., i.e.*) means "and others" and
(21, 34) refers to additional things and not people.

3. A stentorian voice is (quiet, loud, gentle).
(33)

4. (Conscientious, Conscious, Gravid) means aware, or
(27, 32) cognizant.

5. Sometimes we hear (quorums, recriminations, hospices),
(10, 16) or counter accusations, during a trial.

6. Write whether this sentence is declarative, interrogative,
(1) exclamatory, or imperative: Nick learns that Jay Gatsby had fallen in love with Daisy Buchanan at the age of eighteen.

7. Write the collective noun from this sentence: The party
(4) loaded into two cars and sped towards New York.

8. For a–c, write the plural of each noun.
(10, 11) (a) Wendy   (b) key   (c) ditch

9. Write each word that should be capitalized in this
(9) sentence: ernest hemingway wrote *the old man and the sea*, the story of a lonely, wise old fisherman.

10. Rewrite the following as it is. Then add proofreading
(32) symbols to indicate corrections.
Myrtle wilson wsa hit bya yellow care an killed

11. Write the four principal parts (present tense, present
(13) participle, past tense, past participle) of the verb *trap*.

12. Write whether the following is a phrase or a clause:
(20) riding in Gatsby's new yellow roadster

13. Write each prepositional phrase, starring the object of
(14, 29) each preposition from this sentence: Because of the car's description, Tom Buchanan believes Gatsby is Myrtle's killer.

14. From this sentence, write the verb phrase and label it transitive or intransitive: Daisy Buchanan had struck Myrtle Wilson while driving Gatsby's roadster.
⁽²⁶⁾

15. For a and b, choose the correct form of the verb.
⁽¹²⁾
(a) (Has, Have) you heard of an ouphe?
(b) (Do, Does) it seem like a true story?

16. From this sentence, write the verb phrase and name its
^(13, 15) tense: George Wilson sought revenge for Myrtle's death.

17. Write each adjective in this sentence: George, distraught,
^(23, 24) mistakenly shoots the unaware Gatsby.

Rewrite 18 and 19, adding periods and making necessary changes to abbreviations for formal writing.

18. I *The Great Gatsby*
⁽³¹⁾   A Genre
   B Setting
   C Principal characters

19. On Fri, Dr and Mrs Paziouros will move to 259 W Atara
⁽³¹⁾ St, Monrovia, CA, 91010

20. In this sentence, write the verb phrase and label it active
⁽²⁷⁾ or passive voice: Jay Gatsby was mourned only by Nick Carraway, the minister, Jay's dad, and an unknown man with owl-eyed glasses.

21. Write the seven common coordinating conjunctions.
⁽³³⁾

22. Write each coordinating conjunction from this sentence:
⁽³³⁾ Have you read *Macbeth* or *Romeo and Juliet*?

23. List the four most common pairs of correlative
⁽³⁵⁾ conjunctions.

Write each pair of correlative conjunctions from sentences 24 and 25.

24. Neither Daisy nor Myrtle dislikes Tom.
⁽³⁵⁾

25. Daisy will choose either Tom or Jay.
⁽³⁵⁾

26. From this sentence, write the verb phrase and label it
(3, 18) action or linking: Does that thin-sliced lunch meat smell rancid?

27. Write the predicate nominative from this sentence:
(36) Macbeth was a noble Scottish chieftain.

28. Write the infinitive from this sentence and label its tense
(19) present or perfect: To have secured the throne gave Lady Macbeth tremendous guilt.

Diagram sentences 29 and 30.

29. Both Prudence and Clotilda loaned the drama team
(30, 34) costumes for tonight's performance.

30. Boasting can be one's downfall.
(16, 36)

LESSON 37 — Noun Case

> **Dictation or Journal Entry**
>
> **Vocabulary:** Notice the difference between the adjectives *felicitous* and *fortuitous*.
>
> *Felicitous* means appropriate or fitting. Pledging allegiance to the flag is a *felicitous* way to begin the ceremony.
>
> *Fortuitous* means happening or produced by chance; accidental; lucky. Receiving fresh snow on the weekend designated for skiing is *fortuitous*.

We can group nouns into three **cases**: *nominative, possessive, and objective.* The case of the noun explains how the noun is used in the sentence.

Nominative Case

SUBJECT OF A SENTENCE

A noun is in the **nominative case** when it is the subject of a sentence. In the sentence below, the noun *man* is in the nominative case because it is the subject of the sentence.

> Next to Benjamin Franklin, the oldest *man* in the Great Convention was Roger Sherman.

PREDICATE NOMINATIVE

A noun is also in the **nominative case** when it is used as a predicate nominative. A predicate nominative follows a linking verb (to be verbs—is, am, are, was, were, etc.) and renames the subject. In the sentence below, *representative* renames the subject, Sherman. *Representative* is in the nominative case because it is a predicate nominative.

> Sherman was Connecticut's *representative*.

Below, we see verbals used as predicate nominatives:

> His passion is *to preach*. (infinitive)
>
> Your ideal job might be *proofreading*. (gerund)

Possessive Case

We are familiar with nouns that show possession or ownership. These nouns are in the **possessive case.** In the sentence below, the possessive noun *preacher's* is in the possessive case.

> The *preacher's* sermon gave me hope.

Example 1 Tell whether the italicized noun in each sentence is in the nominative case or the possessive case. If it is in the nominative case, tell whether it is the subject of the sentence or a predicate nominative.

(a) *Sherman* came from Connecticut.

(b) He was a skilled *politician.*

(c) Did *Connecticut's* citizens appreciate him?

(d) Her desire was *to stay.*

Solution (a) The word *Sherman* is in the **nominative case.** It is the **subject of the sentence.**

(b) The word *politician* is in the **nominative case.** It is a **predicate nominative**; it follows the linking verb *was,* and it renames the subject.

(c) *Connecticut's* is in the **possessive case.** It shows possession; it tells whose citizens.

(d) The infinitive *to stay* is in the **nominative case.** It functions as a predicate nominative.

Objective Case A noun is in the **objective case** when it is used as a *direct object*, an *indirect object*, or an *object of a preposition.*

Direct Object A noun or pronoun is called a **direct object** when it is the direct receiver of the action of the verb. Direct objects are starred in the sentences below.

Roger Sherman despised mob *rule.* (Roger Sherman despised who or what?)

Therefore, he issued a *warrant against Benedict Arnold.

In addition, he outlawed *scapegoating. (Gerund as a direct object)

Did he like *to hunt? (Infinitive as a direct object)

Indirect Object An **indirect object** is the noun or pronoun that tells "to whom" or "for whom" the action was done. In the following examples, the indirect objects are starred.

>Have you told *us everything?
>(Have you told everything to *us*?)
>
>Yale awarded *Sherman an honorary degree.
>(Yale awarded an honorary degree to *Sherman*.)
>
>Please hand *Mildred her diploma.
>(Please hand the diploma to *Mildred*.)

Object of a Preposition A noun or pronoun that follows a preposition is called the **object of a preposition**. Objects of the prepositions are starred in the examples below.

>on account of *impeachment   on top of the *desk
>
>outside of *New Haven   under the *influence
>
>except for the *Sons of Liberty   within a few *months

Example 2 For sentences, a–c, tell whether each italicized noun is a direct object, an indirect object, or the object of a preposition.

(a) After 1773, Sherman offered the *British* strong resistance.

(b) In the late 1760s, almanacs had recorded his *Loyalism*.

(c) The Parliament of *Great Britain* should not make America's laws.

Solution (a) *British* is an **indirect object**. It tells "to whom" the resistance was offered.)

(b) *Loyalism* is a **direct object**. It is the receiver of the action verb "had recorded."

(c) *Great Britain* is the **object of the preposition** "of."

Example 3 Tell whether the italicized noun is in the nominative, possessive, or objective case.

(a) Please describe a bicameral *government*.

(b) Sherman was *New Haven's* first mayor.

(c) "Father Sherman" became his *nickname*.

(d) He promised his *state* good leadership.

Solution (a) *Government* is a direct object. Therefore, it is in the **objective case.**

(b) *New Haven's* is a possessive noun. Therefore, it is in the **possessive case.**

(c) *Nickname* is a predicate nominative. It renames the subject. Therefore it is in the **nominative case.**

(d) *State* is an indirect object telling "to whom" he promised good leadership. Therefore, it is in the **objective case.**

Practice For sentences a–d, tell whether the italicized noun is in the nominative case or the possessive case. If it is in the nominative case, tell whether it is the subject of the sentence or a predicate nominative.

a. *To argue* would be contentious.

b. Tom's hobby is *woodcarving.*

c. Do you agree with the *politician's* opinion?

d. The *government* would have three branches.

For sentences e–g, tell whether the italicized noun is a direct object, an indirect object, or the object of a preposition.

e. Does the President serve at the *pleasure* of Congress?

f. Woodrow Wilson told the *people* the state of their union.

g. Did Andrew Jackson intimidate the *Supreme Court?*

For h–j, tell whether the italicized noun is in the nominative, possessive, or objective case.

h. *Campaigning* requires perseverance.

i. Above all, the candidate wanted *to win.*

j. People care about their *president's* morality.

For k and l, replace each blank with the correct vocabulary word.

k. The senator's _____ comments showed people his wisdom and sensitivity.

l. My encounter in the parking lot with the mechanic was _____, for I certainly needed help fixing my car at that moment.

Review Set 37 Choose the correct word or root to complete sentences 1–5.

1. The (bureaucrats, Stoics, plutocrats) believed that people should be free of any kind of passions.
   (35, 36)

2. The root (*crim-*, *bell-*, *krat-*) comes from a Greek word meaning "power."
   (35)

3. The abbreviation *et al.* means "and others" and refers to additional (people, things).
   (34)

4. The ancient (hedonists, Spartans, Romans) were frugal, austere, and sternly disciplined.
   (31, 33)

5. A consul is a government (law, official, count) working in a foreign country.
   (17)

6. In this sentence, write each noun and label its case nominative, objective, or possessive: Christie's stack of classical novels hit the floor with a thud.
   (37)

7. Write whether the following is a phrase or a clause: after Macbeth and Banquo heard the witch's prophecy
   (20)

8. In this sentence, write the verb phrase and label it action or linking: Macbeth believes these witches and their prophecies.
   (3, 18)

9. In this sentence, write the verb phrase and label it active or passive voice: Macbeth is tempted by power and fame.
   (27)

10. In this sentence, write the verb phrase and label it transitive or intransitive: Do the dark hags vanish?
    (21, 26)

11. In this sentence, write the infinitive and label its tense present or perfect: To usurp the throne would give Macbeth great pleasure.
    (19)

12. In this sentence, write the verb phrase and name its tense: Lady Macbeth has been plotting to murder King Duncan.
    (17)

13. Write the four principal parts of the verb *pop*.
(13)

14. Write each prepositional phrase, starring the object of each preposition in this sentence: According to plan, Lady Macbeth intoxicates the guards with drink, and Macbeth slays the King, planting the murder weapons on the guards.
(14, 28)

15. Rewrite this book title using correct capitalization: *the taming of the shrew*
(9)

16. Rewrite this outline using correct capitalization:
(9)
    i. *macbeth*
       a. type of work
       b. setting
       c. principal characters
       d. story overview

17. Rewrite the following as it is. Then add proofreading symbols to indicate corrections.
(32)
Every body but Banquo beleives that King duncan's sons mudered there father.

18. Rewrite the following adding periods and making necessary changes to abbreviations for formal writing.
(31)
Col Robert Andrews resides at 456 Doolittle St, Arcadia, TX

19. Write the predicate nominative(s) in this sentence:
(36)
William Shakespeare has become a famous English poet and dramatist.

20. Write the plural of each noun.
(10, 11)
  (a) attorney   (b) glassful   (c) fly

21. Write the seven common coordinating conjunctions.
(33)

22. Write the four common pairs of correlative conjunctions.
(35)

23. Write the indirect object(s) in this sentence: Granny gave Elle and Belle giant scoops of buttered broccoli with their yam and spinach casserole.
(30)

24. Write whether the following sentence is declarative, imperative, interrogative, or exclamatory: Lady Macbeth cannot clean her hands!

25. Write whether the following is a complete sentence, a sentence fragment, or a run-on sentence: Lacy Macbeth dies of guilt Macduff stabs Macbeth.

26. Write the present participle of the verb *spin*.

Diagram sentences 27–30.

27. Cheering will encourage the team.

28. To have booed would have demonstrated poor sportsmanship.

29. Are Jan and Jen sisters?

30. James painted me a picture of a sunset over the ocean.

LESSON 38 Diagramming Predicate Adjectives

> **Dictation or Journal Entry**
> **Vocabulary:** The roots *ven-* and *vent-* come from the Latin word *venire* meaning "come."
>
> An *advent* is a coming or arrival. *The advent of the computer* drastically changed the twentieth century.
>
> To *intervene* means to come between or to mediate between two opposing groups. A bystander *intervened* in the two boys' fight.

Describes the Subject We have learned that the predicate nominative *renames* the subject. The **predicate adjective** *describes* the subject. The predicate adjective follows a linking verb and gives more detail about the subject. See the example below.

A chili pepper is hot.

In the sentence above, the word "hot" is a predicate adjective. It describes "chili pepper"—hot "chili pepper."

We remember the common linking verbs such as *is, am, are, was, were, be, been, is being, will be,* and *have been*. Verbs like *become, seem, feel, appear, look, taste,* and *smell* also link the predicate adjective to the subject.

A chili pepper tastes hot.

Identifying Predicate Adjectives To help us identify the predicate adjective, we can replace a possible linking verb with a "to be" verb.

A chili pepper is spicy.
↑
"to be" verb

In the sentence above, we see that "spicy" describes the subject "chili pepper"—spicy "chili pepper." Therefore, "spicy" is a predicate adjective.

Compound Predicate Adjectives A predicate adjective may be compound as in the sentence below. Predicate adjectives are circled.

William Samuel Johnson was (reasonable) and (sedate).

Diagramming We diagram a predicate adjective in the same way we diagram a predicate nominative. Here is a diagram of the simple subject, linking verb, and predicate adjectives of the sentence above:

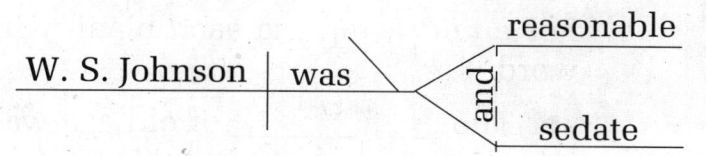

```
W. S. Johnson | was \ reasonable
                      and
                      sedate
```

reasonable and sedate William Samuel Johnson

Example Diagram the simple subject, linking verb, and predicate adjectives in sentences a–c.

(a) Does he appear successful?

(b) The attorney seemed cautious and conservative.

(c) His arguments were sensible and believable.

Solution (a)

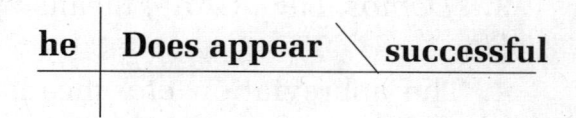

```
he | Does appear \ successful
```

(b)

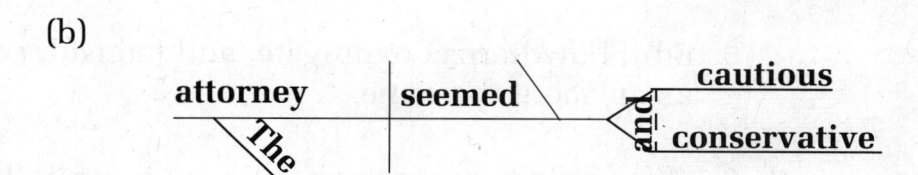

```
attorney | seemed \ cautious
  The              and
                   conservative
```

(c)

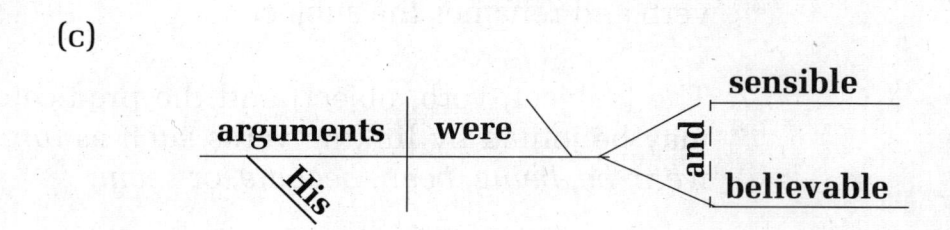

```
arguments | were \ sensible
  His             and
                  believable
```

Practice For sentences a–d, diagram the simple subjects, linking verbs, and predicate adjectives.

a. William Samuel Johnson's position on the Revolution was difficult.

b. Some states remained timid and obstinate.

c. His speech for equal representation in one house proved effective.

d. Did his voice sound confident?

For e and f, replace each blank with the correct vocabulary word.

e. The _____ of old age was apparent by her loss of memory and sagging skin.

f. The people of Connecticut asked William Samuel Johnson to _____ in their behalf.

Review Set 38 Choose the correct word or root to complete sentences 1–7.

1. After losing my beloved pet guinea pig, I appreciated your (felicitous, fortuitous, ambiguous) condolences.
(11, 37)

2. (Stoic, Sybaritic, Democratic) means indifferent to pleasure and pain.
(36)

3. (*Demos, Lev-, Grav-*) means "people."
(35)

4. The abbreviation *etc.* means "and others" and refers to additional (people, things).
(34)

5. Edit, bowdlerize, expurgate, and (consul, censor, census) mean about the same.
(17, 18)

6. A (common, concrete, predicate) noun follows a linking verb and renames the subject.
(36)

7. The (subject, verb, object) and the predicate nominative may be joined by linking verbs such as *am, is, are, was, were, be, being, been, become,* or *seem*.
(36)

8. Write the four principal parts (present tense, present participle, past tense, and past participle) of the verb *fry*.
(13)

9. In this sentence, write the verb phrase and label it action or linking: Does *Little Women* seem too sentimental for some readers?
(3, 18)

10. Write whether the following is a phrase or a clause: under the long green-paved avenues of gnarled oaks and of lichened beeches
(20)

11. Write whether the following sentence is declarative, interrogative, exclamatory, or imperative: Spend both your time and your money wisely.
(1)

12. Write whether this word group is a sentence fragment, run-on sentence, or complete sentence: Christmas looks bleak due to the Civil War Father is at the battlefront.
(2)

13. For a–c, write the plural form of each noun.
(11, 12) (a) justice of the peace   (b) bibliography   (c) life

14. Write each word that should be capitalized in this sentence: meg, jo, beth, and amy hope their father will return from the civil war before christmas.
(9)

15. Write the adjective phrase from this sentence followed by the noun it modifies: The oldest of the March girls is Meg.
(29)

Write the correct verb form to complete sentences 16 and 17.

16. Laurie, the grandson of the Marches' next-door neighbor, and Jo March (future of *become*) life-long friends.
(8)

17. In the past, the girls (past perfect of *demonstrate*) their talent, kindness, and grace.
(15)

18. In this sentence, write the verb phrase and name its tense: Meg will be marrying John Brooke soon.
(17)

19. Rewrite the following as it is. Then add proofreading symbols to indicate corrections.
(32)

One of of the grils becomes ill is it beth?

20. In this sentence, write the verb phrase and label it transitive or intransitive: Scarlet fever finally takes Beth March's life.
(26)

21. Write the indirect object in this sentence: Even during her illness, Beth gives everyone comfort.
(30)

22. Write each adjective in this sentence: The lonely Jo meets an older, German gentleman filled with a genteel love.
(23, 24)

23. Rewrite this outline adding periods as needed:
₍₉₎
    I Themes of *Little Women*
      A Joys of youth
      B Deep love of family

24. Write seven common coordinating conjunctions.
₍₃₃₎

25. Write the predicate nominative in this sentence: *Little Women* has remained a popular novel throughout the years.
₍₃₆₎

26. In this sentence, write the verb phrase and label it active or passive voice: It was written by Louisa May Alcott in 1869.
₍₂₇₎

Diagram sentences 27–30.

27. Does Bea like worrying and complaining?
_(16, 34)

28. My friend is becoming anxious.
₍₃₆₎

29. Is this a cause for worry?
_(29, 36)

30. To worry would be foolish.
_(19, 36)

LESSON 39 — Comparison Adjectives

> **Dictation or Journal Entry**
>
> **Vocabulary:** *Implicit* and *explicit* look similar but have different meanings.
>
> *Implicit* means "implied or hinted at; suggested, though not directly expressed." The lawyer made *implicit* accusations when questioning the witness.
>
> *Explicit*, an antonym of implicit, means clear and definite, leaving nothing unexplained. Mom gave *explicit* instructions not to wake the baby.

Adjectives are often used to compare nouns or pronouns. These **comparison adjectives** have three forms that show greater or lesser degrees of quality, quantity, or manner: positive, comparative, and superlative. Below are examples of the positive, comparative, and superlative forms of some adjectives.

POSITIVE	COMPARATIVE	SUPERLATIVE
clean	cleaner	cleanest
sharp	sharper	sharpest
high	higher	highest
light	lighter	lightest
pure	purer	purest

Positive   The positive degree, or basic form, describes a noun or pronoun without comparing it to any other. (Do not confuse *positive* with *good*. In this context, positive simply means "possessing the quality." The quality itself may be good, bad, or neutral.)

      Oliver Ellsworth is *eloquent*.

      That firefighter is *brave*.

      Hector looks *pale* today.

Comparative   The comparative form compares **two** persons, places, or things.

      Is Oliver Ellsworth *more eloquent* than Mr. Johnson?

      That firefighter is *braver* than I am.

      Hector looks *paler* than his brother.

Superlative The superlative form compares **three or more** persons, places, or things.

> Is Oliver Ellsworth the *most eloquent* of all?
>
> That firefighter is the *bravest* in the department.
>
> Of the three brothers, Hector looks the *palest*.

Example 1 Choose the correct adjective for each sentence.

(a) Connecticut is (small, smaller, smallest) than New York.

(b) Of the three flag poles, which is (tall, taller, tallest)?

(c) Jaime seems (perky, perkier, perkiest) than Hector.

Solution (a) Connecticut is **smaller** than New York. We use the comparative form because we are comparing two states.

(b) Of the three flag poles, which is **tallest?** We use the superlative form because we are comparing more than two.

(c) Jaime seems **perkier** than Hector. We use the comparative form because we are comparing only two people.

Forming Comparison Adjectives How we create the comparative and superlative forms of an adjective depends on how the adjective appears in its positive form. There are three main categories to remember.

One-Syllable Adjectives Most one-syllable adjectives become comparative by adding *er* to the ending; they become superlative by adding *est* to the ending.

> slight   slighter   slightest

Two-Syllable Adjectives that end in *y* When a two-syllable adjective ends in *y*, we create the comparative and superlative forms by adding *er* or *est*.

Positive	Comparative	Superlative
sleepy	sleepier	sleepiest
cozy	cozier	coziest
foggy	foggier	foggiest

Two or More Syllables Adjectives of two or more syllables usually form their comparative degree by adding "more" (or "less"); they form their superlative degree by adding "most" (or "least").

POSITIVE	COMPARATIVE	SUPERLATIVE
bellicose	more bellicose less bellicose	most bellicose least bellicose
explicit	more explicit less explicit	most explicit least explicit
stoic	more stoic less stoic	most stoic least stoic

There are exceptions to these guidelines. Below are a few examples of two-syllable adjectives whose comparative and superlative forms are created by adding *er* or *est*.

POSITIVE	COMPARATIVE	SUPERLATIVE
little (size, not amount)	littler	littlest
clever	cleverer	cleverest
quiet	quieter	quietest
simple	simpler	simplest
narrow	narrower	narrowest

* We check the dictionary if we are unsure how to form the comparative or superlative of a two-syllable adjective.

Spelling Reminders Remember that when adding *er* or *est* to the positive form of an adjective, we often must alter the word's original spelling. We apply the same rules we use when adding *ed* to form a past tense verb.

When an adjective ends with **two or more consonants,** *er* or *est* is simply added to the positive form of the adjective.

calm	calmer	calmest
strong	stronger	strongest

When an adjective ends with **a single consonant following one vowel,** we double the final consonant before adding *er* or *est*.

glad	gladder	gladdest
big	bigger	biggest

When an adjective ends with **a single consonant following two vowels,** we do not double the final consonant.

loud	louder	loudest
cruel	crueler	cruelest

When a one-syllable adjective ends in *w, x,* or *y* preceded by a vowel, we do not double the final consonant.

new	newer	newest
gray	grayer	grayest

When a two-syllable adjective ends with **y,** we change the *y* to *i* before adding the *er* or *est*.

dainty	daintier	daintiest
curly	curlier	curliest

When an adjective ends with a **silent e,** we drop the *e* and add *er* or *est*.

blonde	blonder	blondest
fine	finer	finest

Example 2 Complete the comparison chart by adding the comparative and superlative forms of each adjective.

POSITIVE	COMPARATIVE	SUPERLATIVE
(a) flat	_____	_____
(b) smart	_____	_____
(c) whiny	_____	_____
(d) nostalgic	_____	_____
(e) sure	_____	_____

Solution

POSITIVE	COMPARATIVE	SUPERLATIVE
(a) flat	**flatter**	**flattest**
(b) smart	**smarter**	**smartest**
(c) whiny	**whinier**	**whiniest**
(d) nostalgic	**more nostalgic**	**most nostalgic**
(e) sure	**surer**	**surest**

Practice For a–f, choose the correct adjective for each sentence, and tell whether it is positive, comparative, or superlative.

a. Oliver Ellsworth was (wise, wiser, wisest) than Benedict Arnold.

b. Mild Federalists wanted the (trim, trimmer, trimmest) government budget possible.

c. Oliver Ellsworth was a (vigorous, more vigorous, most vigorous) defender of states' rights.

d. Isn't this the (valuable, more valuable, most valuable) document of all?

e. This plant is (healthy, healthier, healthiest) than that one.

f. It is (snowy, snowier, snowiest) outside today.

For g and h, write the comparative and superlative form of each positive adjective.

g. rude   **h.** ambiguous

For i and j, replace each blank with the correct vocabulary word.

i. The doctor gave me _____, unquestionable orders to rest for five days.

j. We must read between the lines to find the author's _____, unstated conclusions.

Review Set 39

Choose the correct word to complete sentences 1–5.

1. The Latin word (*hospes, amare, venire*) means "come."
(38)

2. (Stoic, Sybaritic, Felicitous) means appropriate or fitting.
(36, 37)

3. A (bureaucrat, stoic, plutocrat) is indifferent to pleasure and pain.
(35, 36)

4. The Greek word *demos* means (simple, fault, people).
(35)

5. Probity is (incrimination, integrity, impeachment).
(19)

6. In this sentence, write whether the italicized noun is in the nominative, possessive, or objective case: William Golding's novel takes place on a tropical *island* after a nuclear war.
(37)

7. Write the four principal parts (present tense, present participle, past tense, and past participle) of the verb *trim*.
(13)

8. Write whether this sentence is declarative, interrogative, exclamatory, or imperative: In 1954, William Golding wrote *Lord of the Flies*, an ideological adventure novel.
(1)

9. Write whether the following is a phrase or a clause: after their plane crashed
(20)

10. In this sentence, write the verb phrase and label it action or linking: Jack proves cruel and power hungry.
(3, 18)

11. In this sentence, write the verb and label it transitive or intransitive: Ralph wanders out of the tropical jungle.
(26)

12. For a–c, write the plural of each noun.
(10, 11) (a) alto   (b) tablespoonful   (c) Henry

13. Rewrite the following as it is. Then add proofreading symbols to indicate corrections.
(32)
piggy want law and Order, butRalph prefers free dom

14. In this sentence, write the verb and label it passive or active voice: The conch shell symbolizes order in the boys' meetings.
(27)

15. Write the comparative form of the adjective *strong*.
(39)

16. Write the superlative form of the adjective *intelligent*.
(39)

17. Write the four common pairs of correlative conjunctions.
(35)

18. In this sentence, write the verb phrase and name its tense: By the end of the week, Jeffrey Robbins will have sketched all the main characters.
(15)

19. In this sentence, write the adjective phrase and the noun it modifies: A boy with thick glasses opposes the cruel boy, Jack.
(29)

20. Rewrite this sentence, adding periods and making necessary changes to abbreviations for formal writing: Dr Cough will give a special lecture in the library on S First St, on Vet Day, Nov 11
(31)

21. Write each predicate adjective from this sentence: Jack's words and actions became primitive and savage.
(36)

22. Write the predicate nominative from this sentence: Is Ralph a sensible leader?
(23, 36)

For sentences 23–25, replace each blank with the correct word.

23. We group nouns into three cases: _____, possessive, and objective.
(37)

24. The _____ of a noun explains how the noun is used in the sentence.
(37)

25. When a noun is a sentence subject or predicate nominative, it is in the _____ case.
(37)

26. From this sentence, write each gerund and label its tense present or perfect: In the distance, we could hear barking and howling.
(16)

27. From this sentence, write the infinitive and label its tense present or perfect: While I was setting the table, my yam and spinach casserole began to burn!
(19)

Diagram sentences 28–30.

28. Wally's little cousin might become an electrician.
(24, 36)

29. Alex loaned Pac and me his notes about ancient Greece.
(21, 30)

30. Has Mildred practiced reading and writing?
(16, 34)

LESSON 40 — Irregular Comparison Adjectives

> **Dictation or Journal Entry**
> **Vocabulary:** The roots *cep-*, *cap-*, and *cip-* come from the Latin verb *capere* meaning "to take or seize.".
> *Perceptible* means "noticeable; able to be taken in through the senses." The difference in the sounds of their voices was barely *perceptible*.
> *Susceptible* means "vulnerable, liable, and open to influence." Her weak arguments were *susceptible* to criticism.

Some adjectives have irregular comparative and superlative forms. We must learn these if we haven't already.

POSITIVE	COMPARATIVE	SUPERLATIVE
little (amount, not size)	less	least
good, well	better	best
bad, ill	worse	worst
far	farther	farthest
many, much, some	more	most

Little or Few? We use *little*, *less*, and *least* with things that cannot be counted. We use *few*, *fewer*, and *fewest* for things that can be counted.

> CANNOT BE COUNTED:
> He has *less* patience today than he had yesterday.

> CAN BE COUNTED:
> We will have *fewer* tests this semester.

Much or Many? We use *much* with things that cannot be counted, and we use *many* for things that can be counted.

> CANNOT BE COUNTED:
> There wasn't *much* debate.

> CAN BE COUNTED:
> *Many* delegates offered opinions.

Example 1 Choose the correct adjective for each sentence.

(a) Oliver Ellsworth had (little, less, least) interest in the ministry than in law.

(b) That was the (baddest, worst) tornado we had ever experienced.

(c) Dad has (less, fewer) vacation days this year than last year.

(d) (Many, Much) of the moderate or "cotton" Whigs trace their roots to Oliver Ellsworth.

Solution (a) Oliver Ellsworth had **less** interest in the ministry than in law. (The sentence is comparing two occupations, so we use the comparative form of "little.")

(b) That was the **worst** tornado we had ever experienced. ("Baddest" is not a word.)

(c) Dad has **fewer** vacation days this year than last year. ("Days" can be counted.)

(d) **Many** of the moderate or "cotton" Whigs trace their roots to Oliver Ellsworth. ("Whigs" can be counted.)

Avoid Double Comparisons We do not combine two comparatives or superlatives. In other words, we do not use *more* with *er,* or *most* with *est.*

NO: Julita was *more better* than Juanita at soccer.
YES: Julita was *better* than Juanita at soccer.

NO: Was Oliver the *most cleverest* essayist of all?
YES: Was Oliver the *cleverest* essayist of all?

Absolute Adjectives Some adjectives do not normally permit comparison. Adjectives that represent an ultimate condition (*square, round, maximum, equal, fatal, unique, dead*, etc.) cannot be increased by degree. For example, a square cannot be "squarer" than another square; it's either square or it's not! Therefore, we do not make comparisons with absolute adjectives. However, careful writers can modify them by using words like *almost, near,* and *nearly* instead of more/less and most/least.

NO: My house plant looks *deader* than yours.
YES: The withered plant is *nearly dead.*

Example 2 Choose the correct adjective for each sentence.
(a) The King was (nosier, more nosier) than the Queen.

(b) Yesterday was the (worst, most worst) day of my life.

(c) Crissy had the (most unique, unique) hairdo.

Solution (a) The King was **nosier** than the Queen. We do not combine two comparatives.

(b) Yesterday was the **worst** day of my life. We do not combine two superlatives.

(c) Crissy had the **unique** hairdo. *Unique* is an absolute adjective meaning "one of a kind." Something is either one of a kind or it's not, so we do not make comparisons with *unique*.

Practice For a–f, choose the correct adjective for each sentence.

a. Thomas Jefferson received (many, much) criticism from the Federalists.

b. Oliver Ellsworth created (many, much) new government agencies.

c. One of his (better, best) suggestions was the Judiciary Act.

d. Was he (more, most) effective at writing legislation than at preaching?

e. Penelope made (few, little) effort to quiet her yapping chihuahua.

f. I felt (better, more better) after the dictation test.

For g–i, replace each blank with the correct vocabulary word.

g. Small children are often _____ to colds, especially during the winter.

h. His fever was so slight that it was barely _____.

i. The Latin verb _____ means to "take or seize."

More Practice Choose the correct adjective for each sentence.

1. Connecticut has (little, less) land than Virginia.

2. Ellsworth negotiated (gooder, better) than Pinckney with the French Republic.

3. That brush fire was the (worse, worst) we've ever had.

4. Poppy feels (better, weller) today than she felt yesterday.

5. Her new computer is (reliabler, more reliable) than her old one.

6. She ate (more, most) salad than I did.

7. Which impostor is the (more conniving, most conniving) of the three?

8. Are you the (smarter, smartest) of the two?

9. Of the two delegates, Roger Sherman lived (farther, farthest) from the Connecticut River Valley.

10. Ellsworth missed (fewer, less) sessions than other delegates did.

11. Sherman had (fewer, less) absences than Elbridge Gerry.

12. Will we have (fewer, less) homework tonight?

Review Set 40 Choose the correct word to complete sentences 1–6.

1. (Implicit, Felicitous, Explicit) means implied, or hinted at.
  (39)

2. To intervene means to (live, sit, come) between, or to mediate.
  (38)

3. (Spartan, Stentorian, Fortuitous) means happening or produced by chance.
  (33, 37)

4. The ancient city of (Sparta, Troy, Sybaris) was known for its great wealth and hedonism.
  (36)

5. Democracy is rule by (animals, aristocrats, people).
  (35)

6. Of the two dogs, the Irish wolfhound is the (taller, tallest).
  (18, 39)

7. Write whether the following is a run-on sentence, complete sentence, or sentence fragment: Ralph soon regains his senses he becomes a leader again.
  (2)

8. Write whether this word group is a phrase or a clause: Simon, the loner who never believed in the beast
  (20)

9. Write the plural of each noun.
  (10, 11) (a) banjo   (b) tariff   (c) pony

10. Write each word that should be capitalized in this sentence: natalie is studying art history in florence, italy.
(9, 22)

11. From this sentence, write each prepositional phrase and star the object of each preposition: In addition to Simon, Piggy loses his life at the hands of Jack's mob.
(14, 28)

12. From this sentence, write the verb phrase and label it transitive or intransitive: One of Jack's boys steals Piggy's glasses.
(26)

13. Write the verb phrase from this sentence and label it action or linking: Does Piggy feel violated by the theft?
(3, 18)

14. In this sentence, write the verb phrase and name its tense: Roger has murdered Piggy.
(15)

15. Write the indirect object from this sentence: Piggy takes Ralph the conch shell.
(30)

16. Write each adjective from this sentence, and circle those that are articles: A white-uniformed naval officer rescues the filthy, stick-wielding boys.
(23, 24)

17. Write the four principal parts (present tense, present participle, past tense, and past participle) of the verb *plot*.
(13)

18. Write whether the italicized noun in this sentence is nominative, objective, or possessive case: Please hand *Woolie* today's vocabulary list.
(37)

19. Rewrite the following sentence, adding periods and making necessary changes to abbreviations for formal writing: On Fri morning, Dr Corndog parked too close to a fire hydrant on E Bay Ave
(31)

20. Write the predicate nominative in this sentence: The girl with the long brown braid is Brittney.
(36)

21. Write whether the italicized noun in the following sentence is a direct object, an indirect object, or the object of a preposition.
(37)
Jacob travels to the *desert* for dirt biking.

22. Write the gerund in this sentence and label its tense present or perfect: Having studied gave Jeb confidence for the difficult exam.
(16)

23. Write the infinitive in this sentence and label its tense present or perfect: After all that studying, Jeb hopes to pass.
(19)

24. Write the comparative and superlative forms of the adjective *silly*.
(39)

25. In this sentence, write the verb phrase and label it active or passive voice: Ms. Yee applies the grammar rules with accuracy and precision.
(27)

26. Rewrite the following as it is. Then add proofreading symbols to indicate corrections.
(32)
Emiko smile at at everyones she meets

27. Write whether the following sentence is declarative, imperative, exclamatory, or interrogative: For his summer project, Eagle Scout Andrew Yen led blind children on hikes.
(1)

Diagram sentences 28–30.

28. Pam enjoys both planting and harvesting.
(16, 34)

29. Have the seeds begun to sprout?
(19, 21)

30. Do these fruits and vegetables look fresh?
(34, 38)

LESSON 41 The Comma, Part 1: Dates, Addresses, Series

> **Dictation or Journal Entry**
>
> **Vocabulary:** Let us review the meanings of some expressions beginning with "all."
>
> *All ready* and *already* have different meanings. *All ready* means "completely prepared." I am *all ready* to take the Constitution test. *Already* means "before, or by this or that time; previously." The teacher has *already* instructed us on the meaning of the Preamble.
>
> *All right* means "satisfactory." Were your accommodations *all right*? Remember that "alright" is not a word; it is an incorrect spelling.
>
> *Altogether* and *all together* have distinct meanings. *Altogether* means "entirely, wholly, and completely." *Altogether* I memorized twenty-seven amendments to the Constitution. *All together* means "in a group." The students traveled to Washington D.C. *all together*.

Commas are another form of punctuation that we use to clarify the meaning of a phrase or a sentence. We use commas to group words that belong together and to separate those that do not.

Parts of a date We use commas to separate the **parts of a date.** When we write a complete date, we always place a comma between the day and the year.

> September 17, 1787

If a complete date appears in the middle of a sentence, we place a comma after the year.

> On September 17, 1787, thirty-nine men from twelve states came to sign the Constitution.

If the day of the week appears as part of the date, we place a comma after the day.

> We remember Monday, September 17, 1787.

Note: When just the month and the year appear in a sentence, no comma is required.

> People remember September 1787 as an important time in United States history.

Example 1 Place commas wherever they are needed in the parts of the date in this sentence:

> The Rivas Family visited Philadelphia on Thursday July 4 2002 and saw a parade near Independence Hall.

Solution We place a comma after the day of the week (Thursday). We also place a comma after the day (July 4). Lastly, we place a comma after the year, because the date appears in the middle of a sentence.

The Rivas Family visited Philadelphia on Thursday, July 4, 2002, and saw a parade near Independence Hall.

Parts of an Address We use commas to separate the **parts of an address** and the names of geographical places or political divisions.

The parts of a street address are separated by commas according to the following pattern:

house number and street, city, state and zip code

8317 Gilman Road, Elbridge, New Hampshire 55814

1744 Gerry Street, Wanamassa, NJ 07712

Note: We use the state abbreviation when addressing a letter or package.

We also use commas to separate the names of geographical places or political divisions.

Atlanta, Georgia, U.S.A.   Quito, Ecuador
Oxford, England, UK   Bejing, Zhangjiakou, China

If the city and state or country appear in the middle of the sentence, we place a comma after the state or country.

Alexander Hamilton was born in Nevis, West Indies, where his father was a trader.

Example 2 Place commas wherever they are needed in the parts of the address in these sentences.

(a) The document listed 27173 Sherman Road Marysville New York 11757 U.S.A.

(b) Alexander Hamilton served as captain of artillery when Trenton New Jersey was raided by George Washington.

Solution (a) We separate the parts of the address with commas. One comma goes after the house number and street, another goes between the city and the state, and another goes between the zip code and the country.

The document listed 27173 Sherman Road, Marysville, New York 11757, U.S.A.

(b) We place a comma between the city and the state, and another comma after the state because it is in the middle of a sentence.

Alexander Hamilton served as captain of artillery when Trenton, New Jersey, was raided by George Washington.

Words in a Series We use a comma to separate **three or more words or phrases in a series** as in the sentence below.

The "cotton" Whigs included Daniel Webster, Rufus Choate, and Robert Winthrop.

Supreme self-confidence, mild haughtiness, and slight hyperbole describe the character of Alexander Hamilton.

Example 3 Place commas as needed in this sentence:

Hamilton became a leader of the Federalist party a father of the republic a foil to milder nationalists and the most extreme nationalist.

Solution We separate the items in the series with commas.

Hamilton became a leader of the Federalist party, a father of the republic, a foil to milder nationalists, and the most extreme nationalist.

Practice For a–e, replace each blank with the correct vocabulary word(s).

a. _____, there were five delegates to the Constitutional Convention who wanted to abolish the existing states.

b. Alexander Hamilton had _____ been stigmatized for his origins.

c. As leader of the Federalist party, Alexander Hamilton was _____ to attack the Jeffersonians.

d. Standing _____, James Madison, John Dickinson, and Alexander Hamilton presented the arguments.

e. Hamilton believed it was _____ to establish a monarchy similar to that in Great Britain.

Rewrite sentences f–h, and place commas to separate parts of a date.

f. Hamilton's speech on June 18 1787 lasted for five hours!

g. On July 10 1787 the other delegates from New York left the Constitutional Convention in disgust.

h. Thanksgiving fell on Thursday November 28 in the year 2002.

Rewrite sentences i–k, and place commas to separate parts of an address.

i. The Constitutional Convention took place in Philadelphia Pennsylvania in 1787.

j. Anchorage Alaska has beautiful scenery.

k. Will you visit Dublin Ireland UK next summer?

Rewrite sentences l–n, and place commas to separate words in a series.

l. Hamilton dreamed of an American empire that would provide national happiness financial security and worldwide power.

m. Will strong central government create stability respect and ambition among its citizens?

n. January March May July August October and December have thirty-one days.

More Practice See Master Worksheets.

Review Set 41 Choose the correct word to complete sentences 1–11.

1. The Latin word (*venire, amare, capere*) means "to take or seize."

2. (Implicit, Fortuitous, Explicit) means implied, or hinted at.

3. Felicitous means (lucky, appropriate, extravagant).

4. The ancient city of Sybaris was known for its great wealth and (architecture, hedonism, literature).

5. (Democracy, Aristocracy, Bureaucracy) is a powerful nobility.

6. Bob has (less, fewer) tomato plants than I.

7. A(n) (concrete, abstract) noun names something that cannot be seen or touched.

8. Sue is the (younger, youngest) of the two sisters.

9. Jeb doesn't eat (much, many) mangoes.

10. A predicate adjective describes the sentence (subject, verb, object).

11. The predicate adjective follows a (linking, action) verb and gives more detail about the subject.

12. Rewrite this sentence adding periods and making necessary changes to abbreviations for formal writing: Miss Eltoe called from Mt Baldy to apologize for being late to her nine a m interview at the Holiday Craft Co

13. Write the plural of each noun.
    (a) deer   (b) stereo   (c) watch

14. Write each word that should be capitalized in this book title: *a connecticut yankee in king arthur's court*

15. Rewrite the following, adding commas as needed: George Washington was actually born on February 11 1732.

16. Write each prepositional phrase in this sentence, starring the object of each preposition: On his quest, Hank Morgan travels round about the countryside.
(14)

17. Write the verb phrase and name its tense: Hank Morgan is trying to restore justice in the land.
(17)

18. In this sentence, write the verb phrase and label it active or passive voice: Without any rights, Camelot's citizens have been oppressed.
(27)

19. Write each adjective in this sentence: The virtuous King Arthur always maintains a kingly demeanor and a righteous approach to life.
(23, 24)

20. Write the predicate adjective(s) in this sentence: In his rescue of King Arthur, Hank is clever and inventive.
(23, 38)

21. Write the verb phrase in this sentence and label it transitive or intransitive: Hank creates a modern American town in the midst of ancient Great Britain.
(21, 26)

22. Write the four principal parts (present tense, present participle, past tense, and past participle) of the verb *wheeze*.
(13)

23. In this sentence, write whether the italicized noun is nominative, objective, or possessive case: In his story about King Arthur's court, Mark Twain shifts between social *humor* and social disgust.
(37)

24. Write whether this word group is a phrase or a clause: before Merlin succumbs to the poisonous gas
(20)

25. Rewrite the following declarative sentence and make it interrogative: Margaret will proofread and edit this manuscript.
(1)

26. Write whether the following is a complete sentence, run-on sentence, or sentence fragment: Merlin casts one last spell on Hank he is to sleep for thirteen hundred years.
(2)

Diagram sentences 27–30.

27. The roses in the neighbor's garden smell fragrant.
(29, 36)

28. Mom's hydrangeas grew limp and colorless.
(18, 38)

29. Neither watering nor fertilizing revived the droopy hydrangeas.
(16, 35)

30. Does the weary gardener need to rest?
(19, 21)

LESSON 42 — Appositives

> **Dictation or Journal Entry**
>
> **Vocabulary:** The root *ag-* comes from a Latin word meaning "go, drive, lead, or do."
>
> An *agenda* is a list of things that need to be done. The *agenda* for this month's meeting includes old business, new business, and correspondence.
>
> *Agitate* is a verb meaning "to stir or excite." The impassioned speeches against British tyranny given by the Sons of Liberty *agitated* the crowds.

Appositives A group of words that immediately follows a noun to "rename" the noun or give more information about the noun is called an **appositive.** In the sentences below, we have underlined appositives.

Alexander Hamilton, <u>one of the authors of *The Federalist*</u>, represented New York at the Constitutional Convention.

The first Secretary of Treasury, <u>Alexander Hamilton</u>, established a financial system for funding the national and state debts.

The opportunist <u>Aaron Burr</u> shot and killed his arch enemy <u>Alexander Hamilton</u> in a duel.

Example 1 Identify the appositives from each sentence.

(a) Robert Yates, a decided Antifederalist, also represented New York at the Constitutional Convention.

(b) The leading Antifederalist propagandist, Abraham Yates, was the brother of Robert Yates.

Solution (a) The appositive, **"a decided Antifederalist,"** gives more information about the subject, "Robert Yates."

(b) The appositive, **"Abraham Yates,"** renames "the leading Antifederalist propagandist."

Improving Our Writing Using appositives skillfully can improve our writing. With an appositive, we can combine two choppy sentences to make one good one.

TWO CHOPPY SENTENCES:

Robert Yates was a slaveholder. Robert Yates opposed popular government.

ONE GOOD SENTENCE:
Robert Yates, a slaveholder, opposed popular government.

Example 2 Combine this pair of choppy sentences to make one good sentence by using an appositive.

John Lansing was an Antifederalist by principle and by connection. He was the wealthiest member of his party.

Solution We can make an appositive from the first sentence and combine it with the second sentence:

John Lansing, an Antifederalist by principle and by connection, was the wealthiest member of his party.

Or, we can make an appositive from the second sentence and combine it with the first sentence:

John Lansing, the wealthiest member of his party, was an Antifederalist by principle and by connection.

Diagramming the Appositive We diagram an appositive by placing it in parentheses beside the noun it describes or "renames." We place modifiers of the appositive directly underneath.

William Patterson of New Jersey, the spokesman for the small states, received support from Yates.

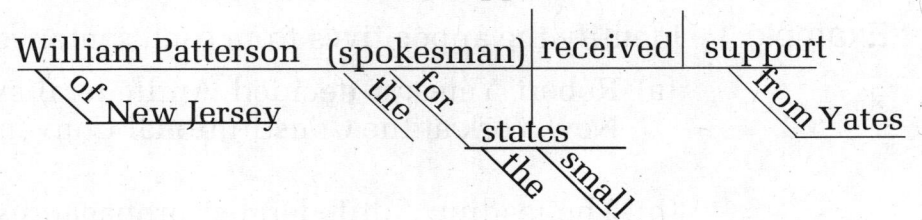

Example 3 Diagram this sentence:

The Federalist, a collection of eighty-five essays, supported ratification of the Constitution of 1787.

Solution We place the appositive, "collection," in parentheses beside the subject, "*The Federalist.*" We place the modifiers of "collection" underneath.

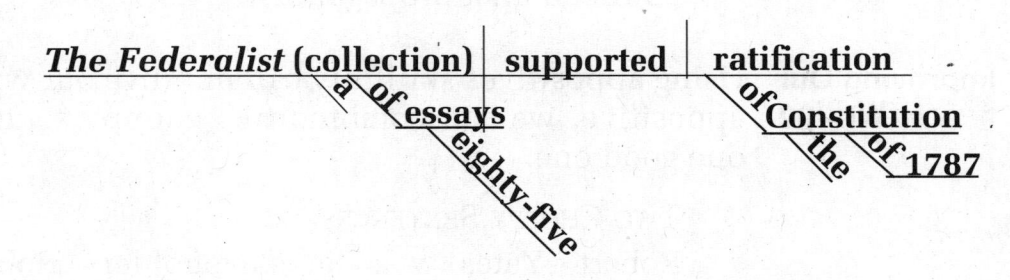

Practice For a–c, replace each blank with the correct vocabulary word.

a. William Paterson's _____ included equal representation of the small states in a unicameral legislature.

b. He proposed the Paterson Plan, which _____ those in favor of the Virginia Plan.

c. The root _____ comes from a Latin word meaning "go, drive, lead, or do."

For d and e, write the appositive from each sentence.

d. New Jersey's elder statesman, William Livingston, was one of the oldest, most prestigious, and respected members of the Constitutional Convention.

e. Livingston, a vigorous Whig, had lived with missionaries among the Mohawks on the frontier as a youth.

f. Diagram this sentence: Livingston, a talented writer, represented New Jersey.

For g and h, use an appositive to combine each pair of sentences to make one sentence.

g. Antifederalists were opponents of Federalists. Antifederalists believed that the Constitution gave too much power to the central government and too little to states.

h. James Madison wrote some of the Federalist Papers. The Federalist Papers were essays explaining that the new government would respect the rights of states and individuals.

Review Set 42 Choose the correct word to complete sentences 1–7.

1. I'm not hungry; I (all ready, already) ate dinner.
   (41)

2. The Latin verb *capere* means to (love, come, seize).
   (40)

3. Implicit means (lucky, implied, accidental).
   (39)

4. An (appropriation, advent, amendment) is a coming; an arrival.
   (23, 38)

5. Probity is (incrimination, integrity, impeachment).
(19)

6. Of the seven Siamese kittens, Leona was the (hungry, hungrier, hungriest).
(39)

7. I have (less, fewer) keys on my key ring than I had yesterday.
(40)

8. Write the verb phrase from this sentence and label it transitive or intransitive: Have you been waiting for me?
(26)

9. Write each noun from this sentence and circle the one that is collective: A pack of huskies violently attacks Curly, a dog from the ship.
(4)

10. Write each possessive noun from this list: shipmates, shipmate's, shipmates', husky's, huskies, huskies'
(7)

11. Write whether the following is a complete sentence, run-on sentence, or sentence fragment: Buck, a huge four-year-old Scottish-Saint Bernard cross-breed.
(2)

12. Write the plural of each noun.
(10, 11)   (a) radius   (b) portfolio   (c) wish

13. Write each word that should be capitalized in this sentence: aunt bea and uncle jake want to know who wrote "the emperor's new clothes."
(9, 22)

14. Rewrite the following adding commas as needed: Deb bathed the dog brushed the llama and fed the cats.
(41)

15. Write the verb phrase from this sentence and label it action or linking: Was *The Call of the Wild* written by Jack London?
(3, 18)

Write the correct verb form to complete sentences 16 and 17.

16. Manuel (present of *sell*) Buck to gold rushers.
(5)

17. Buck (future of *learn*) to survive in the wild.
(8)

18. Write each prepositional phrase from this sentence, starring the object of each preposition: In addition to many other lessons, Buck learns that he stands no chance against a man with a club.
(14)

19. Write each adjective from this sentence: Spitz, a sly-eyed and powerful lead dog, rivals Buck.
(23, 24)

20. Write the appositive from this sentence: Shah, my cousin's Russian Wolfhound, leapt into my lap.
(42)

21. Rewrite the following as it is. Then add proofreading symbols to indicate corrections.
(32)
Overtime, the domesticated Buck becaem a a wilder ness wolf

22. Rewrite this sentence adding periods and making necessary changes to abbreviations for formal writing: On the first Tues in Sept, Mr Levi B Green will be here at two p m to discuss the advantages of Richfoods, Inc
(31)

23. List the four most common pairs of correlative conjunctions.
(35)

24. Write the predicate nominative in this sentence: Over time, the domesticated Buck became a wilderness wolf.
(36)

For 25 and 26, write whether the italicized noun is nominative, objective, or possessive case.

25. *Buck's* name as lead pack dog became legendary.
(37)

26. Some dogs died of *starvation*.
(37)

27. Write whether the following is a phrase or a clause: to have survived the frigid water
(20)

28. Write the infinitive from this sentence and label its tense present or perfect: The pack is struggling to survive.
(19)

Diagram sentences 29 and 30.

29. Miss Informed, our new secretary, will give you important documents concerning our future plans.
(21, 42)

30. Is Miss Informed a reliable source of information?
(29, 36)

LESSON 43 The Comma, Part 2: Direct Address, Appositives, Academic Degrees

> **Dictation or Journal Entry**
>
> **Vocabulary:** The root *fin-* comes from a Latin word meaning "end" or "boundary."
>
> A *finale* is the last part or conclusion of any performance or course of action. The protagonist's soliloquy provided a satisfactory *finale* to the play.
>
> *Finite* means having definite limits or boundaries. The lawyer's arguments were infinite, but the time allowed to present them was *finite*.

In this lesson, we will discuss more uses for commas.

Nouns of Direct Address

A **noun of direct address** names the person who is being spoken to (the person who is receiving the information in the sentence). The noun can be the person's name or a "name" you are using for him or her. Nouns of direct address can appear anywhere in a sentence. We offset them with commas.

> Mr. Henneforth, do you remember which representative attending the Continental Congress had tuberculosis?
>
> Please, Maggie, name the British acts that offended the colonists in 1764–1765.
>
> How many representatives did New Jersey send to the Great Convention, Floyd?

There may be more than one noun of direct address in a sentence. Also, like any noun, a noun of direct address can be modified by adjectives. We offset the entire noun phrase with commas, as in the sentences below.

> Control your anger, Alexander and Aaron!
>
> Please, my reasonable colleagues, think about the example you are setting for future generations.

Example 1 Insert commas to separate the noun of direct address in the sentence below.

> I have heard Grandma and Grandpa that your great-grandparents fought in the Revolutionary War.

Solution We insert commas before and after "Grandma and Grandpa" because Grandma and Grandpa are being spoken to. They are nouns of direct address.

> **I have heard, Grandma and Grandpa, that your great-grandparents fought in the Revolutionary War.**

Appositives We have learned that an **appositive** is a word or group of words that immediately follows a noun to identify or give more information about the noun. In the sentence below, "a representative from New Jersey" is an appositive. Notice how commas offset it from the rest of the sentence.

> William Churchill Houston, <u>a representative from New Jersey</u>, attended the convention for less that two weeks because of illness.

In the sentence below, "John Fitch" is also an appositive. But it is not offset by a comma. Why?

> William Churchill Houston vigorously supported the steamboat built by the famous inventor <u>John Fitch</u>.

Essential and Nonessential Appositives Whether or not an appositive is offset with commas depends on how essential it is to the meaning of the sentence.

Let's look at the first sentence, above. If we remove the appositive, the sentence still makes sense:

> William Churchill Houston attended the convention for less than two weeks because of illness.

The phrase "William Churchill Houston" has already identified the person the sentence is about. The appositive "a representative from New Jersey" is informative but **nonessential** to the meaning of the sentence. **Nonessential appositives are offset with commas.**

Now let's remove the appositive from the second sentence:

> William Churchill Houston vigorously supported the steamboat built by the famous inventor.

The famous inventor? Which famous inventor? This sentence no longer makes sense. The appositive "John Fitch" is **essential** to the meaning of the sentence. **Essential appositives are not offset by commas.**

Example 2 Insert commas where necessary in the sentence below.

> David Brearly the able assistant of William Paterson helped prepare the New Jersey Plan.

Solution If we remove the appositive, "the able assistant of William Paterson," the meaning of the sentence is still clear. (David Brearly helped prepare the New Jersey Plan.) Therefore, it is a nonessential appositive and we offset it with commas.

David Brearly, the able assistant of William Paterson, helped prepare the New Jersey Plan.

Example 3 Insert commas where necessary in the sentence below.

Was New Jersey judge David Brearly appointed by President Washington?

Solution If we remove the appositive, "David Brearly," the reader is left to wonder *which* New Jersey judge and the meaning of the sentence is lost. Therefore, it is an essential appositive so we do not offset it with commas.

Was New Jersey judge David Brearly appointed by President Washington?

Academic Degrees When an **academic degree** or similar title follows a person's name, it is usually abbreviated. Here are some abbreviations you're likely to see:

M.D. (Doctor of Medicine)

D.D.S. (Doctor of Dental Surgery)

D.V.M. (Doctor of Veterinary Medicine)

Ph.D. (Doctor of Philosophy)

Ed.D. (Doctor of Education)

LL.D (Doctor of Laws)

D.D. (Doctor of Divinity)

R.N. (Registered Nurse)

L.P.N. (Licensed Practical Nurse)

M.B.A. (Master of Business Administration)

We use commas to offset academic degrees or other titles that follow a person's name.

Jonathan Dayton, LL.D., led the Federalist party in New Jersey for a quarter of a century.

Example 4 Insert commas to offset the academic degree in this sentence.

Dr. David Wheat D.V.M. might have treated the delegates' horses.

Solution Since "D.V.M." is an academic degree, it is offset with commas.

Dr. David Wheat, D.V.M., might have treated the delegates' horses.

Practice Rewrite sentences a–f, and place commas to offset nouns of direct address, appositives, and academic degrees.

a. Delegates please find your seats so that we can begin business promptly.

b. Did you realize Professor Cameron that Jonathan Dayton was the youngest delegate at the Constitutional Convention?

c. Jonathan Dayton a faithful follower of William Paterson was concerned with the rights of the small states.

d. Elias Boudinot an associate of Jonathan Dayton speculated in western lands.

e. Benjamin Franklin Ph.D. received his honorary degree from St. Andrews University.

f. Did James McHenry Ph.D. remain in his profession after independence was achieved?

For g–i, replace each blank with the correct vocabulary word.

g. The grand _____ of the fireworks display featured red, white, and blue explosions in the shape of a flag.

h. My strength is not infinite. My collapse near the end of the marathon proved that my endurance is _____.

i. The Latin root _____ means "end" or "boundary."

More Practice See Master Worksheets.

Review Set 43 Choose the correct word or root to complete sentences 1–10.

1. The root (*ven-, ag-, cep-*) means "go, drive, lead, or do."
(42)

2. Is Sid (already, all ready) for his sea voyage?
(41)

3. (Amiable, Implicit, Perceptible) means "noticeable; able to be taken in through the senses."
(39, 40)

4. Explicit means (implied, lucky, clear).
(39)

5. To (apportion, alleviate, intervene) is to come between, or to mediate.
(38)

6. The past tense of the verb *plan* is (planed, planned).
(5)

7. Paul and Jesse (is, am are) brothers.
(12)

8. A (positive, comparative, superlative) adjective compares three or more persons, places, or things.
(39)

9. A (positive, comparative, superlative) adjective compares two or more persons, places, or things.
(39)

10. A (positive, comparative, superlative) adjective describes a noun or pronoun without comparing it to any other.
(39)

11. Write whether the following is a sentence fragment, run-on sentence, or complete sentence: A loving relationship develops between Buck and his new master, John Thornton.
(2)

12. Write whether this word group is a phrase or a clause: since he was as faithful as the sunrise
(20)

13. Write each noun from this sentence and circle those that are feminine: Amanda writes poetry about a filly named Mercedes.
(7)

14. Write the plural of each noun.
(10, 11)   (a) stitch   (b) bay   (c) liability

15. Rewrite this sentence as it is. Then add proofreading symbols to indicate corrections.
(32)
One Time, Buck save John thornton's live.

16. In this sentence, write each prepositional phrase starring the object of each preposition: Elle lives across from Trung and down the street from the vegetable stand alongside the river.
(14)

17. Write the verb phrase from this sentence and name its tense: Had John Thornton been refusing to sell Buck?

18. Write the verb phrase from this sentence and label it active or passive voice: John and his friends were piling up bags of gold.

19. Write the verb phrase from this sentence and label it action or linking: Buck grows restless in captivity.

20. For a–c, write the comparative and superlative forms of each positive adjective.
   (a) low   (b) ambivalent   (c) subtle

21. Write the four principal parts (present tense, present participle, past tense, and past participle) of the verb *intervene.*

22. Use an appositive to combine this pair of sentences to make one sentence: Buck's prey was a bull moose. The bull moose was six feet tall and a formidable quarry.

23. Write the seven common coordinating conjunctions.

24. Rewrite this sentence adding periods and commas and making necessary changes to abbreviations for formal writing: Mr Yio arrived on Tues Oct 25 2004

25. Write whether the italicized noun in this sentence is nominative, objective, or possessive case: *Buck* attacks the Yeehat Indians for killing animals and men at the camp.

26. Write the gerund from this sentence and label its tense present or perfect: Fighting fails to fill a void in Buck's heart.

27. Rewrite this sentence adding commas as needed: My father Ivan Kutz volunteers at a hospital in Denver Colorado.

Diagram sentences 28–30.

28. Have Dan and Ann decided to stay?
(19, 34)

29. Did that political cartoonist give our President the benefit of the doubt?
(21, 29)

30. A magnanimous player avoids both gloating and complaining.
(16, 35)

LESSON 44

Overused Adjectives • Unnecessary Articles

> **Dictation or Journal Entry**
>
> **Vocabulary:** In our writing and speaking, we must use *any way* and *anyway* correctly.
>
> *Any way* means "in any manner." You may decorate the room *any way* you wish.
>
> *Anyway* means "in any case; nevertheless." The class period was almost over, but the professor introduced the new topic *anyway*.
>
> *Anyways* is not a word.

Overused Adjectives Sometimes we find ourselves using the same adjective over and over again. In this lesson we will learn to choose more vivid adjectives. Some of the adjectives that people use too often are as follows:

great	bad	rotten
nice	terrible	wonderful
good	awful	neat

While there is nothing wrong with the adjectives above, we should try to use more specific or interesting ones if we can. We can consult the dictionary or thesaurus for more choices.

WEAK: The U. S. Constitution is *good*!
BETTER: The U. S. Constitution is *innovative* (or *effective, brilliant, practical, impressive*).

WEAK: Benjamin Franklin was *great*.
BETTER: Benjamin Franklin was *clever* (or *accomplished, wise, intelligent, knowledgeable, witty, humorous, amusing*).

WEAK: The Articles of Confederation were *bad*.
BETTER: The Articles of Confederation were *deficient* (or *flawed, faulty, ineffective, inadequate, insufficient*).

Example 1 Rewrite each sentence replacing each over-used adjective with a more vivid one.

(a) Don't waste your time watching that *terrible* movie.

(b) George Whitefield was a *good* preacher.

(c) This apple tastes *bad*.

(d) Springer spaniels can be *nice* pets.

Solution   Our answers will vary. Here are some possibilities:

(a) Don't waste your time watching that **boring, crude, shoddy, substandard, frightening, horrid** movie.

(b) George Whitefield was a **dynamic, magnetic, brilliant, popular, powerful** preacher.

(c) This apple tastes **sour, fermented, rotten, mushy, bitter, bruised, old, unripe.**

(d) Springer spaniels can be **pleasant, agreeable, enjoyable, friendly, well-behaved, lively, adorable, entertaining** pets.

Unnecessary Articles   We have learned that the articles *a, an*, and *the* are adjectives. Sometimes they are used unnecessarily. Avoid these errors:

- We do not use *the* before "both."

   NO: *The both* of them represented Pennsylvania.
   YES: *Both* of them represented Pennsylvania.

   NO: Give *the both* of them your opinion.
   YES: Give *both* of them your opinion.

- We do not use *a* or *an* after phrases ending with "kind of," "sort of," or "type of."

   NO: James Madison was that *kind of a* politician.
   YES: James Madison was that *kind of* politician.

   NO: Do you like that *type of a* movie?
   YES: Do you like that *type of* movie?

Example 2   Rewrite each sentence correctly.

(a) I already showed the both of them our agenda.

(b) From what kind of a delusion does he suffer?

Solution   (a) **I already showed both of them our agenda.** (We remove the word *the*. It is not used before "both.")

(b) **From what kind of delusion does he suffer?** (We remove the word *a*. We do not use it after "kind of.")

Practice Rewrite sentences a–d replacing each over-used adjective with a more interesting one. Answers will vary.

    a. We sat through an *awful* filibuster.

    b. The cicerone was *good*.

    c. We had a *nice* picnic.

    d. This soap smells *bad*.

Rewrite sentences e and f correctly.

    e. That sort of a job does not appeal to me.

    f. Lucita brought the both of them to the meeting.

For g–j, replace each blank with *any way* or *anyway*.

    g. People warned Benjamin Franklin not to experiment with lightning, but he did _____.

    h. Was there _____ to channel the energy of lightning?

    i. You may dress _____ you like for the party.

    j. It is raining, but we'll mow the lawn _____.

More Practice See "Hysterical Fiction #3" in Master Worksheets.

Review Set 44 Choose the correct word to complete sentences 1–6.

    1. The root *fin-* means (take, end, come).
    (43)

    2. The root *ag-* means "go, drive, lead, or (do, seize, peace)."
    (42)

    3. Do you feel (alright, all right)?
    (41)

    4. (Perceptible, Explicit, Susceptible) means "vulnerable; open to influence."
    (40)

    5. The teacher might (intervene, apportion, alleviate) if the first graders begin to fight on the playground.
    (38)

    6. In the presidential election, Mrs. Prune received (less, fewer) votes than Mrs. Plump.
    (40)

7. Write whether this word group is a phrase or a clause: with his wild brothers in the wolf pack

8. A transitive verb has a direct object. Write the verb phrase in the following sentence and label it transitive or intransitive:

The Yeehats, an Indian tribe, are talking about an evil ghost dog.

9. Write each noun in this sentence and circle those that are abstract: Loneliness overcomes Buck at times.

10. Write the plural of each noun.
(a) tomato   (b) hobby   (c) runner-up

11. Rewrite this outline adding capital letters as needed:
   i. themes of the story
     a. survival of the fittest
     b. love for animals

12. Write each prepositional phrase from the following sentence starring the object of each preposition:

Except for his occasional return to John Mornton's camp, Buck lives like a wild animal in the forest.

13. Write whether the following is a complete sentence, run-on sentence, or sentence fragment:

Buck reflects on the past he howls long and mournfully.

14. For a–c, choose the correct form of the irregular verb *have*.

(a) Yesterday Derek (has, have, had) a cold.

(b) Now Stacey (has, have, had) a cold.

(c) Yeewa and Marus (has, have) matching hats.

15. In the following sentence, write the verb phrase and name its tense:

Jack London led a violent and adventurous life.

16. Write the verb phrase in the following sentence and label it action or linking: At fifteen, Jack London became a hobo.

17. Write each adjective in this sentence: The sinister Mephisto scolded God for creating a brutish man.

18. Write the four common pairs of correlative conjunctions.

19. Write the over-used article in this sentence: Shall we seize the both of those runaway geese?

20. Rewrite the following adding periods and making necessary changes to abbreviations for formal writing:

At two pm, Mr J B Cruz, Jr will be here to discuss career opportunities at Minnie's Catering Co in NYC

21. Rewrite the following adding commas as needed: Aunt Ella please send my mail to 1200 Dermit Drive Iowa City Iowa.

22. Write whether the italicized noun in the following sentence is in the nominative, objective, or possessive case:

Mephisto's bet with God is that Faust will sell his soul.

23. Use an appositive to combine this pair of sentences to make one sentence:

Faust expresses his indescribable discontent. Faust is a scholar-alchemist.

24. In the following sentence, write the verb phrase and label it active or passive voice:

Was Faust attempting to study his Bible?

25. Rewrite the following as it is. Then add proofreading symbols to indicate corrections.

The pooodle bark, growled, and ran a bout the house

Diagram sentences 26–30.

26. Congenial Irma is wise and resourceful.
(34, 36)

27. Jim's perspicacity saves him time and money.
(21, 30)

28. To work with cooperative people can be enjoyable.
(19, 38)

29. The two experts gave me a simple solution to my problem.
(21, 30)

30. Did you hear singing?
(16, 21)

LESSON 45

Verbals as Adjectives: Infinitives and Participles

> **Dictation or Journal Entry**
>
> **Vocabulary:** The root *ject-* comes from the Latin word *jacere* meaning "throw" or "hurl." We see it in familiar words like re*ject*, ob*ject*, and *eject*.
>
> *Conjecture,* which contains the root *ject-* (throw) and the prefix *con-* (together), means to "throw together" a theory based on few facts; to guess. Scientists *conjecture* that a large meteorite might someday impact the earth.
>
> *Trajectory* draws its meaning from *ject-* (hurl) and *trans-* (across). It literally means "hurling across." A *trajectory* is the curved path taken by a projectile such as a missile, meteor, or bullet. In order to hit her target, the archer carefully considered the *trajectory* of her arrow.

Infinitives We have learned that an infinitive can function as a noun—as the subject or as an object in a sentence. The infinitive can function as an adjective as well.

INFINITIVE AS A NOUN (SUBJECT):

To shout might wake the fugitives.

INFINITIVE AS AN ADJECTIVE:

This is no time *to shout*.

In the sentence above, "shout" modifies the noun, "time." Below, we italicize other infinitives that function as adjectives. Arrows point to the nouns that these adjectives modify.

She is the cicerone *to ask*.

His desire *to please* won him favor.

I saw her determination *to win*.

Diagramming Notice how we diagram an infinitive that is used as an adjective. We place the infinitive on stilts upon a slanted line underneath the word that the infinitive modifies.

Ben Franklin is the diplomat *to study*.

Ben Franklin | is \ diplomat
                    the to study

Example 1 Write the infinitive in each sentence and tell whether it is a noun or an adjective. If it is an adjective, tell which word it modifies.

(a) Would you like to rest?

(b) This is the place to rest.

Solution (a) **To rest** is the infinitive. It is the direct object and therefore a **noun.**

(b) **To rest** is the infinitive used as an **adjective modifying the word "place."**

Participles The **participle** is a verb form that usually ends in "ing" or "ed" but sometimes ends in "en," "d," or "t." The participle usually functions as an adjective.

That *crowing* rooster annoys me.

We cannot retrieve our *spoken* words.

The *bent* lightning rod still conducted electricity.

Example 2 Write the participle in each sentence and tell which noun it modifies.

(a) The stricken Benjamin Franklin recovered his health in time for the Great Convention.

(b) Had the aging grandfather of the republic earned universal respect?

(c) Did Madame Bluebell mourn her spent money?

Solution (a) The participle **stricken** modifies the noun **Benjamin Franklin.**

(b) The participle **aging** modifies the noun **grandfather.**

(c) The participle **spent** modifies the noun **money.**

The participle has three tense forms: present, past, and perfect.

PRESENT PARTICIPLE: *gravitating, lobbying*

PAST PARTICIPLE: *gravitated, lobbied*

PERFECT PARTICIPLE: *having gravitated, having lobbied*

Present participles are italicized in the sentences below:

That woman *voting* is Ms. Anthony.

The *adjourning* Congress had accomplished much.

Past participles are italicized in these sentences:

Spoilt people are never satisfied.

The *frightened* opossum bared its teeth.

Perfect participles are italicized in these sentences:

Having lobbied for better health care, the representative had pleased her constituents.

Having lost two elections, the candidate tried again.

Example 3 Write the participle in each sentence. Tell whether it is present, past, or perfect tense.

(a) Fried potatoes go well with eggs.

(b) Having known adversity, Blanca faced her future with determination and strength.

(c) I photographed the grazing heifer.

Solution (a) The participle, **fried,** is **past tense.**

(b) The participle, **having known,** is **perfect tense.**

(c) The participle, **grazing,** is **present tense.**

Diagramming The diagrams below show participles that function as adjectives. We place the participle on a slanted line below the noun it modifies.

That lady *singing* is my cousin.

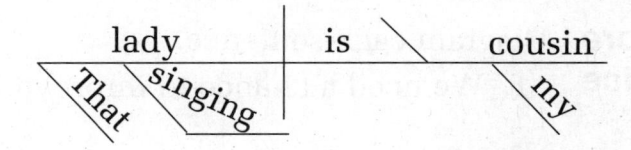

Have the police found the *stolen* vehicle?

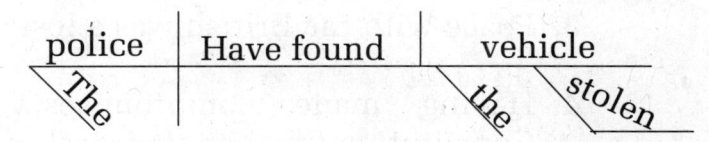

Having complained, I felt foolish.

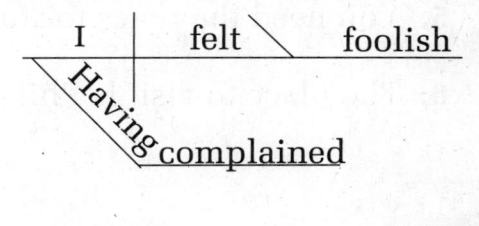

Practice For a–c, replace each blank with the correct vocabulary word.

    a. The _____ of a cannonball was difficult to predict during colonial times.

    b. One can only _____ what our nation would be like without the Constitution.

    c. The Latin root _____ means "throw" or "hurl."

For d and e, write the infinitive and tell whether it is a noun or an adjective. If it is an adjective, write the noun it modifies.

    d. The embarrassed delegate proceeded to blush.

    e. An agenda lists important issues to discuss.

For f–h, write the participle and the noun it modifies. Also, write whether it is present, past, or perfect tense.

    f. Having belonged to the landed magnates of New York, Gouverneur Morris represented Pennsylvania.

    g. Who appointed this practicing lawyer?

    h. The educated woman writes brilliantly.

Diagram sentences i and j.

    i. Important years to remember are 1776 and 1787.

    j. The frolicking ewe kicked the fence.

More Practice Diagram each sentence.

    1. We need a chance to improve.

    2. The man fighting was a Son of Liberty.

    3. Peace with the British was a lost cause.

    4. Having made compromises, the authors of the Constitution finished their task.

    5. You need the notes to study.

    6. The place to visit is Philadelphia.

Review Set 45 Choose the correct word to complete sentences 1–9.

1. (Anyways, Any way, Anyway) means "nevertheless."

2. The finale is the (first, middle, last) part.

3. A(n) (advent, agenda, aristocracy) is a list of things to do.

4. Yesterday I read two chapters, and today I read three, so (all together, altogether) I've read five chapters.

5. A pocket veto results when the (President, Republican, Democrat) holds a bill for more than ten days without signing it.

6. An (interrogative, exclamatory) sentence shows excitement or strong feeling and ends with an exclamation point.

7. A(n) (transitive, intransitive) verb has no direct object.

8. A(n) (appositive, preposition, conjunction) is a word or group of words that immediately follows a noun to rename the noun or give more information about it.

9. Violet is the (taller, tallest) of the twin sisters.

10. Rewrite this run-on sentence making two complete sentences: Faust finally divines that Mephisto is the Devil the two of them banter back and forth.

11. Write the plural of each noun.
 (a) Sunday (b) biography (c) half

12. Write each word that should be capitalized in this sentence: the allegorical, poetic drama titled *faust* takes place in a german city.

13. Write whether the following is a phrase or a clause: if they persist in concealing the truth

14. In this sentence, write the verb phrase and label it passive or active voice: Gretchen, Faust's lover and mother of his child, was saved by her faith.

15. For a–c, choose the correct form of the irregular verb *be*.

(a) We (was, were) phasing in a new language program.
(b) She (was, were) determined to learn Greek.
(c) The others (was, were) studying Latin.

16. Write the verb phrase from this sentence and label it action or linking: Despite fabulous wealth, Faust remains discontent.

17. Write the verb phrase in this sentence and name its tense: In the end, Faust will have received forgiveness from God.

18. Write the four principal parts (present tense, present participle, past tense, and past participle) of the verb *agitate*.

19. Write the proper adjective from this sentence: The English poet Christopher Marlowe wrote his own version of "Faust."

20. Write each predicate adjective from this sentence: Faust becomes compassionate and knowledgeable.

21. Write the pair of correlative conjunctions in this sentence: Both Christopher and Wagner borrow from Goethe's "Faust."

22. Rewrite this sentence adding periods and commas as needed: On Saturday June 2 Mrs Sanchez will hire plumbers roofers and electricians to fix up her house at 207 Brick Road Edmond Oklahoma

23. Write each predicate nominative from this sentence: Mephisto becomes a poodle, a nobleman, and a slave.

24. Write whether the italicized noun in this sentence is nominative, objective, or possessive case: The purpose of *man* is to overcome himself and achieve his true destiny.

25. Write the appositive in this sentence: Mephisto, the Devil, loses the battle for Faust's soul.

26. Rewrite the following as it is. Then add proofreading symbols to indicate corrections.

Though faust had sinned, he Still struggled towrads growth and know ledge.

Diagram sentences 27–30.

27. Can intervening friends help the lost soul?
(21, 45)

28. Was Silas, a prisoner of the Romans, singing?
(28, 42)

29. Singing gave him courage.
(16, 30)

30. Ms. Wire is the electrician to hire.
(36, 45)

LESSON 46 Pronouns and Antecedents

> **Dictation or Journal Entry**
>
> **Vocabulary:** Let us clarify the difference between the words *compose* and *comprise*.
>
> *Compose* means "to make up; to constitute." Eight associate justices plus one chief justice *compose* the U.S. Supreme Court.
>
> *Comprise* means "to include; to consist of." The U.S. Supreme Court *comprises* eight associate justices plus one chief justice.
>
> A common mistake is to use *comprise* for *compose*. Also, we do not use the phrase "is comprised of."

Pronouns A **pronoun** is a word that takes the place of a noun or a noun phrase. Rather than using the same noun over and over again, we use pronouns.

Without pronouns, our language would be tiresome:

> Mrs. Crankabit complains that other students sit on Mrs. Crankabit's bicycle at the gym. Mrs. Crankabit whines that some people in Mrs. Crankabit's class wear too much perfume, and Mrs. Crankabit gripes that Mrs. Crankabit's teacher makes the class too long. Mrs. Crankabit and Mrs. Crankabit's friend bellyache that the fan blows too much on Mrs. Crankabit and Mrs. Crankabit's friend. Mrs. Crankabit and Mrs. Crankabit's friend think that the music is too loud. Perhaps Mrs. Crankabit and Mrs. Crankabit's friend should cancel Mrs. Crankabit and Mrs. Crankabit's friend's memberships at the gym.

Pronouns (italicized) simplify the passage:

> Mrs. Crankabit complains that other students sit on *her* bicycle at the gym. *She* whines that some people in *her* class wear too much perfume, and *she* gripes that *her* teacher makes the class too long. Mrs. Crankabit and *her* friend bellyache that the fan blows too much on *them*. *They* think that the music is too loud. Perhaps *they* should cancel *their* memberships at the gym.

Pronouns are the words (such as *he, she, it, we, they*) we use to refer to people, places, and things that have already been mentioned. Pronouns are italicized in the examples below.

> James Madison proposed the Virginia Plan, and *he* continued to defend *it*.

In the sentence above, the pronoun *he* replaces "James Madison," and the pronoun *it* replaces "Virginia Plan."

Antecedents The noun or noun phrase to which the pronoun refers is called the **antecedent**. The prefix *ante* means "before", and the root *ced-* means "go." The antecedent usually "goes before" the pronoun. In the example above, "James Madison" and "Virginia Plan" are antecedents for the pronouns *he* and *it*.

Notice the antecedents for the pronouns *them* and *him* in this sentence:

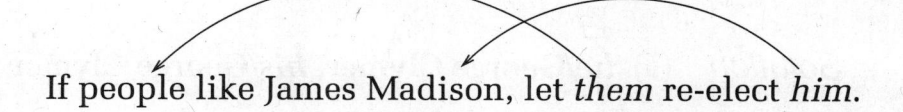

If people like James Madison, let *them* re-elect *him*.

The antecedent of the pronoun *them* is "people," and the antecedent of the pronouns *him* is "James Madison."

Often we find an antecedent in an earlier sentence:

Gouverneur Morris (antecedent) opposed slaveholders (antecedent). *He* attacked *them* vehemently.

Sometimes the antecedent comes after the pronoun:

Although *he* had inherited slaves, Gouverneur Morris (antecedent) called for the end of slavery.

An antecedent might be another pronoun:

Did *he* (antecedent) free all *his* slaves?

You (antecedent) might consult *your* history book.

A pronoun can also have more than one antecedent:

Alexander Hamilton (antecedent), John Jay (antecedent), and James Madison (antecedent) wrote the Federalist Papers; *they* argued the case for the Constitution.

Likewise, a noun can serve as the antecedent for more than one pronoun.

Gouverneur Morris (antecedent) demonstrated *his* patriotism as *he* performed *his* duties at the Constitutional Convention.

Example 1 List the pronouns in a–c. Beside each pronoun write its antecedent if there is one. (example: her/Annette)

(a) Although he had little influence on the other delegates, George Clymer still retained the respect of his colleagues.

(b) People admired Clymer. They appreciated his quietness, thoughtfulness, and modesty.

(c) Clymer was a man of wealth, but he shared it.

Solution (a) *he*/George Clymer, *his*/George Clymer

(b) *They*/People, *his*/ Clymer

(c) *He*/Clymer, *it*/wealth

Each pronoun needs a clear antecedent. The meaning of the sentence below is unclear because the antecedent is unclear:

Some say that *she* is a courageous peacemaker.
Who is a courageous peacemaker?
What is the antecedent of *she*?

The following sentences are unclear because they have more than one possible antecedent.

Lilly told Nadia about *her* parents.
Whose parents? Which is the antecedent of *her*?
Is it Lilly, or is it Nadia?

Bea asked Molly if *she* could play the piano.
Which is the antecedent of *she*?
Bea? Molly?

Clymer joined Meredith after *he* left.
Does *he* refer to Clymer or to Meredith?

To make our meaning clear, we can use nouns instead of pronouns, we can rearrange a few words, or we can rewrite the whole sentence:

Lilly told about Nadia's parents.

Bea asked if Molly could play the piano.

After Clymer left, he joined Meredith.

Example 2 Write the clearer sentence of each pair.

(a) While in Philadelphia, he called for complete independence.

While in Philadelphia, Clymer called for complete independence.

(b) Wilson and Clymer defended his home against an armed mob.

Wilson and Clymer defended Wilson's home against an armed mob.

Solution (a) We choose the second sentence because it clearly tells *who* called for independence.

While in Philadelphia, Clymer called for complete independence.

(b) We choose the second sentence because it clearly tells *whose* home they defended.

Wilson and Clymer defended Wilson's home against an armed mob.

Practice List the pronouns in a–c. Beside each pronoun write its antecedent if there is one.

a. Although Americans acted like radicals during the Revolution, they did not want to destroy the internal order of their society.

b. As he grew older, George Clymer fell away from the Federalist party.

c. Charles Townshend became prime minister of Great Britain in 1767. He taxed the colonies harshly.

For d and e, write the clearer sentence of each pair.

d. While Addy and Gaby were singing, she hit a wrong note.

While Addy and Gaby were singing, Addy hit a wrong note.

e. Gaby thought she had misread the music.

Gaby thought Abby had misread the music.

For f and g, replace each blank with the correct vocabulary word.

f. The delegation from Pennsylvania _____ Benjamin Franklin, Gouverneur Morris, George Clymer, and Thomas Mifflin.

g. Benjamin Franklin, Gouverneur Morris, George Clymer, and Thomas Mifflin _____ the Pennsylvania delegation.

Review Set 46

Choose the correct word or root to complete sentences 1–8.

1. The root (*bell-, plac-, ject-*) means "throw" or "hurl."
   (45)

2. I am tired, but I will exercise (anyways, any way, anyway).
   (44)

3. The (finale, agenda, plutocrat) is the last part, the end.
   (42, 43)

4. To (intervene, agitate, censor) is "to stir or excite."
   (38, 42)

5. We will march (altogether, all together) in a large group down Main Street.
   (41)

6. An action verb that has a direct object is called a (transitive, intransitive) verb.
   (26)

7. *This, that, those,* and *these* are called (descriptive, demonstrative, possessive) adjectives.
   (23)

8. *His, our, my, her, its, their,* and *your* are called (descriptive, demonstrative, possessive) adjectives.
   (24)

9. Write the correct verb form to complete this sentence: Charles Dickens (present of *focus*) on the plight of the poor.
   (5)

10. Write the four principal parts (present tense, present participle, past tense, and past participle) of the verb *flap*.
    (13)

11. Write each noun in this sentence and circle the one that is compound: The Ghost of Christmas Past provides flashbacks of Scrooge's childhood.
    (7)

12. Write each word that should be capitalized in this sentence: tonight uncle joe will read aloud from *a christmas carol* the second chapter, titled "the first of the three spirits."
    (9, 25)

13. Rewrite the following as it is. Then add proofreading symbols to indicate corrections.
(32)

Scrooge's nephew in vites Mr scroooge too him house for diner.

14. Write the plural of each noun.
(10, 11)
(a) person   (b) knife   (c) fox

15. Write whether the following is a phrase or a clause: when Jacob Marley appears to Scrooge
(20)

16. Write each prepositional phrase in this sentence starring the object of each preposition: On account of an *F*, Scrooge was sent home from the boarding school.
(14)

17. Write the verb phrase from this sentence and name its tense: Tomorrow we shall be examining Scrooge's relationship with Belle.
(17)

18. Write the comparative form of the adjective *hot*.
(39)

19. Write the superlative form of the adjective *hospitable*.
(39)

20. For this sentence, write the verb phrase and label it active or passive voice: Was Scrooge blaming the Ghost of Christmas Past for his pain?
(27)

21. Rewrite the following, adding commas and periods and making necessary changes to abbreviations for formal writing.
(31, 41)

On Wed Sept 5 2003 Sean-Carlos informed Dr Van Spronsen of his intention to attend the univ

22. Write whether the following is a complete sentence, sentence fragment, or run-on sentence: By the arrival of the Ghost of Christmas Present.
(2)

23. Write whether the italicized noun in this sentence is nominative, objective, or possessive case: The Ghost repeats Scrooge's own *words* about letting the poor die in order to "decrease the surplus population."
(37)

24. Write the verb phrase from this sentence and label it action or linking: Regarding his own words, Scrooge feels penitent.
(18)

25. Use an appositive to combine these sentences into one sentence: The Spirit's torch represents the "Christmas Spirit." The "Christmas Spirit" is the joy found in celebrating the Christmas season.
(42)

26. Write the over-used adjective from this sentence: What kind of a car does the Senator drive?
(44)

27. Write the antecedent for the italicized pronoun in this sentence: Unfortunately, Miss Informed cast *her* ballot for the wrong candidate.
(46)

28. Write seven common coordinating conjunctions.
(33)

Diagram sentences 29 and 30.

29. Having broken, the pipe began to leak.
(21, 45)

30. Can Lee and Ruth repair their broken water pipe?
(34, 45)

LESSON 47

The Comma, Part 3: Greetings and Closings, Last Name First, Introductory and Interrupting Elements, Afterthoughts, Clarity

> **Dictation or Journal Entry**
>
> **Vocabulary:** The root *tract-* comes from the Latin word *trahere* meaning "to drag or draw."
>
> A *retraction* is a withdrawal or taking back of something previously said. George Washington issued a *retraction* of his earlier praise of Thomas Mifflin's military prowess.
>
> *Intractable* means "not easily drawn back or controlled; stubborn." Washington's army suffered the *intractable* problems of hunger and fatigue.

Greeting We use a comma after the opening or **greeting** of a friendly letter.

Dear Dr. Lacy,

My dear grandfather,

Closing We use a comma after the **closing** of a letter.

Gratefully,

With love,

Example 1 Place commas where they are needed in the letter below.

Dear Dr. Imbus

Thank you for your quick diagnosis of my mother's condition.

Your appreciative patron
Kaylee

Solution We place commas after the greeting and closing of the letter.

Dear Dr. Imbus,

Thank you for your quick diagnosis of my mother's condition.

Your appreciative patron,
Kaylee

Last Name First When we alphabetize a list of names, we usually alphabetize by the person's last name. We place the last name first and the first name (followed by middle names, if any) last. They are separated by a comma, as shown:

> Anthony, Susan B.
> Carver, George Washington
> Poe, Edgar Allen
> Smith, Kate
> Zenger, John Peter

Other than in lists, we don't often write names this way. When we do, we are usually referring to a list. Quotations marks may indicate this:

> "Mifflin, Thomas" is listed as a delegate to the Constitutional Convention.
>
> Can you find "Thompson, Charles" in the index?

Example 2 Insert a comma where it is needed in the sentence below.

> To find out more about the first President of the United States, you might look in the encyclopedia under "Washington George."

Solution We use a comma when we place a last name first.

> To find out more about the first President of the United States, you might look in the encyclopedia under **"Washington, George."**

Comma = Pause When we speak, we often pause between words. If we wrote down exactly what we were saying, most of those pauses would be indicated by commas. Pauses usually occur when we insert words or phrases that interrupt the natural flow of the sentence. Notice how commas are used to offset the italicized words, phrases, and clauses in the sentences below.

> Thomas Mifflin is most noteworthy, *I think*, for his conspicuous role in bringing Pennsylvania to a full commitment of American independence.
>
> Thomas Mifflin was of distinguished Quaker origin, *for your information*.
>
> *No*, he was not my great-grandfather.

Introductory Elements An **introductory element** begins a sentence. It may refer to a previous sentence or express the writer's attitude about what is being said. An introductory element can also be a request or command. We place a comma after an introductory element.

> *As I remember*, Mifflin was a mild commercial Federalist and a man of wealth.
>
> *Unfortunately,* his political philosophy was not consistent.
>
> *Yes*, his outspoken opposition to the Stamp Act drew much attention.
>
> *Therefore,* we can read about him in history books.

A comma is not needed after an introductory adverb or short phrase that answers the question when, where, or how often.

> *Now* let us discuss the first amendment.
>
> *In some countries* people lack freedom of speech.
>
> *Last August* we visited Philadelphia.
>
> *Occasionally* Mom writes letters to the editor.

Interrupting Elements An **interrupting element** appears in the middle of a sentence, interrupting the flow from subject to verb to object, and should be set off with commas. An interrupting element can be removed without changing the meaning of the sentence.

> British sympathizers, *on the other hand,* were called Loyalists or Tories.
>
> Twenty percent of the colonists, *it is estimated*, supported Great Britain.

Afterthoughts **Afterthoughts** are similar to introductory and interrupting elements except that they are added to the ends of sentences and should be set off with commas.

> Native Americans supported the British, *by the way.*
>
> Slaves also joined the British, *if I remember correctly.*

Some afterthoughts turn the sentence into a question:

> The Patriots faced powerful foes, *didn't they?*

Example 3 Rewrite these sentences and use commas to offset introductory or interrupting elements and afterthoughts.

(a) Mifflin moreover favored the adoption of nonimportation agreements.

(b) Consequently he became involved in politics.

(c) He had strong opinions of course.

Solution (a) The word, "moreover," is not essential to the meaning of the sentence. It interrupts the flow of the sentence, so we offset it with commas.

Mifflin, **moreover,** favored the adoption of nonimportation agreements.

(b) The word "consequently" is an introductory element, so we place a comma after it.

Consequently, he became involved in politics.

(c) The words "of course" are an afterthought, so we offset them with a comma.

He had strong opinions, **of course.**

Clarity We use commas to **clarify the meaning** of sentences.

UNCLEAR: Because of Doc Susan has recovered.
CLEAR: Because of Doc, Susan has recovered.

UNCLEAR: After we ate the brass band played.
CLEAR: After we ate, the brass band played.

Example 4 Rewrite each sentence using a comma to make the meaning clear.

(a) Without Jenny Quan felt lonely.

(b) As I was watering the man next door hollered.

Solution (a) If we are talking about one person named Jenny Quan, then the sentence is incomplete. However, if Jenny and Quan are two different people, the sentence is complete. We use a comma to clarify the meaning:

Without Jenny, Quan felt lonely.

(b) Was I watering the man next door? Did I soak him with the hose? To avoid confusion, we insert a comma to clarify the meaning:

As I was watering, the man next door hollered.

Practice Rewrite a and b and insert commas as needed.

    a. Dear Thomas
        Congratulations on your promotion to brigadier general.
           Love
           Adele

    b. Use the index of your history book to find the writings of "Hamilton Alexander."

Rewrite sentences c–f, and insert commas to offset introductory or interrupting elements and afterthoughts.

    c. John Locke's *Two Treatises of Government* I believe talks about people's natural rights.

    d. Governments said Thomas Jefferson get their power from the consent of the governed.

    e. No the Articles of Confederation did not provide for a bicameral legislature.

    f. They failed to create effective leadership I have heard.

Rewrite sentences g and h, and insert commas to clarify the meaning.

    g. Ever since he has studied harder.

    h. Thanks to Kevin Jordan has transportation to school.

For i–k, replace each blank with the correct vocabulary word.

    i. Did the political candidate ever make a _____ of her derogatory statement concerning her opponent?

    j. The _____ criminal refused to cooperate with the police.

    k. The root _____ means "drag or draw."

More Practice See Master Worksheets.

Review Set 47 Choose the correct word to complete sentences 1–7.

1. (Conjecture, Comprise, Incriminate) means "to include, or consist of."

2. To (agitate, intervene, conjecture) is to "throw together" a theory based on few facts; to guess.

3. You may exercise (any way, anyways, anyway) you want.

4. (Implicit, Finite, Explicit) means having definite limits or boundaries.

5. In formal writing, we use "that is" instead of (*i.e.*, *e.g.*, *etc.*).

6. Vixen is the (louder, loudest) of the two barking dogs.

7. Dan (do, does) his chores before breakfast.

8. Write whether the following is a complete sentence, a run-on sentence, or a sentence fragment: Dickens foreshadows Tiny Tim's continued illness and seemingly certain death.

9. Write whether the following is a phrase or a clause: on behalf of every woebegone, hungry child in London

10. From this sentence, write the verb phrase and label it transitive or intransitive: Does Scrooge grieve over Tiny Tim's condition?

11. From this sentence, write the verb phrase and label it action or linking: Is the Ghost of Christmas Future a phantom?

12. From this sentence, write the verb phrase and label it active or passive voice: A group of businessmen are discussing Scrooge's death.

13. Write the plural of each noun.
    (a) Randy   (b) peach   (c) senator-elect

14. Write whether this sentence is declarative, interrogative, exclamatory, or imperative: Does anyone grieve for the dead Scrooge?

15. Rewrite the following as it is. Then add proofreading
(32) symbols to indicate corrections.

Scrooge refuse two reveel thee identity of the coprse

16. Rewrite the following, adding periods and commas as
(31, 41) needed: Grief compassion sympathy anger shock and disbelief normally accompany the death of a loved one

17. In this sentence, write each prepositional phrase, starring
(14) the object(s) of each preposition: Without exception, the people of London act happy about Scrooge's death.

18. Write the four principal parts of the verb *lobby*.
(13)

19. Write each adjective in this sentence: Scrooge's death
(23, 24) will allow a poor couple more time to repay their debt.

20. In this sentence, replace the italicized, over-used
(44) adjective with one that might be more descriptive: In the beginning of the story, Scrooge is a *bad* man.

21. Write four common pairs of correlative conjunctions.
(35)

22. Use an appositive to combine these two sentences to
(42) make one sentence: Now Scrooge is a new man. He promises to honor Christmas in his heart.

23. In this sentence, write each pronoun and its antecedent:
(46) The visits from the Christmas Spirits greatly alter Scrooge's attitudes, and he promises to keep their lessons in his heart.

24. Write the predicate nominative in this sentence: Scrooge
(36) is a changed man.

25. Write whether the italicized noun in this sentence is in
(37) the nominative, objective, or possessive case: Scrooge sends a huge *turkey* to the Cratchit home.

26. Write the indirect object in this sentence: Scrooge awards
(30) Bob Cratchit a raise in salary.

27. In this sentence, write the participle and the noun it
(45) modifies: Fred, shocked, welcomes Scrooge warmly into
his home.

28. In this sentence, write the infinitive and the noun it
(19) modifies: Scrooge appreciates the opportunity to
celebrate Christmas with those around him.

Diagram sentences 29 and 30.

29. Does that crowing rooster annoy you?
(21, 45)

30. Give me a chance to sleep.
(30, 45)

LESSON 48

Personal Pronouns

> **Dictation or Journal Entry**
>
> **Vocabulary:** How do we know when to use *any one* or *anyone*? *Every one* or *everyone*?
>
> When referring to a particular person or thing, we use *any one*. The teacher commented that *any one* of the delegates might be the topic of an oral report. *Anyone* means "anybody." I can't find *anyone* to help me.
>
> *Every one* refers to each one of a group of particular things or people. *Every one* of the students presented an oral report. *Everyone* means "all." *Everyone* snoozed during my presentation.

There are five categories of pronouns: personal, relative, indefinite, interrogative, and demonstrative. This lesson reviews personal pronouns.

Like nouns, **personal pronouns** refer to people and things (and also places, if you think of a place as an "it"). Personal pronouns are italicized in the following sentences.

I have researched *them*.

Have *you* read *my* report about *it* yet?

They suggest *we* use several different sources.

There are three forms of personal pronouns: person, number and case.

Person *First person* is the speaker: *I, me, mine, we, us, ours*

I shall appear in costume.

We shall laugh together.

That blunder was *mine*.

Second person is the person being spoken to: *you, yours*

Will *you* speak next?

All of *you* are welcome.

That portfolio is *yours*.

Third person is the person being spoken about: *he, she, it, him, her, his, hers, they, them, theirs*

He and *she* will dress like colonists.

Will *they* arrive on time?

The red cloak is *hers*.

Please present *it* to *them*.

Example 1 For each sentence below, write the pronoun and tell whether it is first person, second person, or third person.

(a) In that costume, you definitely resemble Alexander Hamilton.

(b) They described Thomas Fitzsimons as an "aristocrat."

(c) Let me wear the Martha Washington outfit.

Solution (a) ***You*** is **second person,** the person being spoken to.

(b) ***They*** is **third person,** the person being spoken about.

(c) ***Me*** is **first person,** the speaker.

Number Some personal pronouns are singular:

I, me, mine, you, yours, he, him, his, she, her, hers, it

Others are plural:

we, us, ours, you, yours, they, them, theirs

Example 2 For a–d, write each personal pronoun and tell whether it is singular or plural.

(a) They wore their costumes. (b) Mine was wrinkled.

(c) Tom ironed his. (d) Take a picture of them.

Solution (a) ***They*** is **plural.** (b) ***Mine*** is **singular.**

(c) ***His*** is **singular.** (d) ***Them*** is **plural.**

Case Case shows the job the pronoun is performing in the sentence.

Some pronouns are used as *subjects*:

> *He* joined the Federalists. *They* advocated a strong national government. *I* have not voted yet. Would *you* have supported the Federalists?

Others are used as *objects*:

> George Clymer joined *them* too. (direct object)
>
> Olga loaned *her* a wig. (indirect object)
>
> Government affects all of *us*. (object of a preposition)

Some pronouns show *possession*:

> *Yours* is on the counter.
>
> Did Olivia lose *hers*?
>
> Oliver borrowed *mine*.
>
> *Theirs* has disappeared.

Example 3 Write the pronoun and tell whether it shows possession or whether it is used as a subject or an object. If it is an object, tell what kind (direct object, indirect object, object of a preposition).

(a) Ernesto read her the story of the Boston Tea Party.

(b) Next summer, they might visit New England.

(c) Mr. Twaddell invited them to Philadelphia.

(d) Is yours in Boston also?

Solution (a) The pronoun **her** is an **indirect object.**

(b) The pronoun **they** is the **subject** of the sentence.

(c) The pronoun **them** is a **direct object.**

(d) The pronoun **yours** shows **possession.**

Practice For a and b, replace each blank with *everyone* or *every one*.

a. _____ of the delegates understood the importance of strengthening the government.

b. Is _____ ready to go?

For c and d, replace each blank with *anyone* or *any one*.

c. _____ of the delegates could have endorsed the patriot cause.

d. Did _____ leave early?

For sentences e–g, write the personal pronoun and tell whether it is first, second, or third person.

e. Reyna lobbied with me.

f. She appeased the loyalists.

g. Do you agree with James Madison?

For h and i, write the personal pronoun and tell whether it is singular or plural.

h. A historian might give us more information.

i. Please send me a postcard.

For j–m, write the personal pronoun and write whether it is used as a subject, direct object, indirect object, object of a preposition, or whether it shows possession.

j. Onping brought *him* a pair of boots.

k. Gia surprised *me* with a gift.

l. That powdered wig is *mine*.

m. *They* suffered great losses.

More Practice Write each personal pronoun from sentences 1–10, and tell whether it is first, second, or third person. Also tell whether it is singular or plural. (Example: 1. we, first person plural; you, second person singular)

1. May we serve you dinner tonight?

2. Weren't they bellicose?

3. Please loan him a jacket.

4. They're up there on stage performing their drama.

5. Are you acquainted with Robert Morris?

6. Everyone has voted except her.

7. Please vote according to your conscience.

8. I begged them to intervene.

9. They intervened on my behalf.

10. She toils conscientiously for us.

11.-20. Tell how each pronoun is used in sentences 1–10 above. Write "subject," "object," or "possession." (Example: 11. we—subject, you—object)

Review Set 48

Choose the correct word or root to complete sentences 1–11.

1. The root (*prob-, crim-, tract-*) means "to drag or draw."
   (47)

2. To comprise is to (guess, include, excite).
   (46)

3. To conjecture is to (excite, delay, guess).
   (45)

4. (Anyways, Any way, Anyway) means "in any manner."
   (44)

5. Gravity, which holds us to the earth, can also mean (crime, seriousness, lobby).
   (27)

6. Sarah (have, has) an energetic springer spaniel.
   (12)

7. The word to which a pronoun refers is called the (adjective, antecedent) of the pronoun.
   (46)

8. The prefix *ante* means (before, after).
   (46)

9. The root *ced-* means (stop, go).
   (46)

10. The antecedent usually goes (before, after) the pronoun.
    (46)

11. A (pronoun, adjective) is a word that takes the place of a noun.
    (46)

12. Write whether the following is a complete sentence, run-on sentence, or sentence fragment: Dashiell Hammett exposes the corruption and violence permeating American life in *The Maltese Falcon,* he gives us a glimpse into the lonelier side of life.
    (2)

13. Write whether the following is a phrase or a clause: since every character is trying to deceive all the others
(20)

14. Write each possessive noun from this list: nestors, nestor's, nestors', James's, Jameses, bureaucrats
(7)

15. From this sentence, write the verb phrase and label it action or linking: The author actually spent several years as a Pinkerton detective.
(3, 18)

16. Write the plural of each noun.
(10, 11)
(a) dairy   (b) waltz   (c) day

17. Write whether this sentence is declarative, interrogative, exclamatory, or imperative: Consider *The Maltese Falcon* a new genre of classical crime fiction.
(1)

18. Write each word that should be capitalized in this sentence: *the maltese falcon* takes place in san francisco, california, in the 1920s.
(9, 25)

19. Rewrite the following as it is. Then add proofreading symbols to indicate corrections.
(32)

The Main charcater is is sam Spade, a young ditective

20. In this sentence, write each prepositional phrase starring the object(s) of each preposition: Near the enemy encampment, the archers set guards, with arrow on string, at either end of the pass.
(14, 28)

21. Write the four principal parts of the verb *hurry*.
(13)

22. Write each adjective in this sentence: The beautiful and intelligent Brigid O'Shaughnessy hires some clever detectives to protect her.
(23, 24)

23. Rewrite this sentence adding periods and commas as needed: On Monday October 10 2005 Jacqueline auditioned for the part of Miss Wonderly
(31, 41)

24. Write the pair of correlative conjunctions from this sentence: The police believe that Spade killed not only Miles Archer but also Thursby.
(35)

25. Use an appositive to combine these two sentences to make one sentence: Miles Archer is Spade's older partner. Miles Archer is to tail Thursby.
(42)

26. From this sentence, write the verb phrase and label it active or passive voice: Lieutenants Dundy and Polhaus were questioning Sam Spade about the deaths.
(27)

Diagram sentences 27–30.

27. Sherry and her sister water and fertilize their African violets.
(21, 34)

28. They love gardening.
(16, 21)

29. The gardeners, exhausted, want a place to relax.
(21, 45)

30. That hammock between those two trees looks perfect.
(29, 38)

LESSON 49

Irregular Verbs, Part 2

> **Dictation or Journal Entry**
>
> **Vocabulary:** Familiar words like <u>duct</u>, pro<u>duce</u>, and re<u>duce</u> stem from the Latin verb *ducere* meaning "to lead." This root shows up in other words as well.
>
> *Conducive* means "tending to promote or encourage." It is almost always followed by the preposition *to*. A relaxed atmosphere is *conducive* to easy conversation and new friendships.
>
> A *deduction* is "a conclusion made by reasoning." Compiling the results of research, we can make certain *deductions*. *Deduction* also means "subtraction." The Internal Revenue Service allows taxpayers to take *deductions* for medical and dental expenses.

Regular verbs form the past tense by adding *d* or *ed* to the present tense of the verb. Irregular verbs form the past tense in different ways. There are no rules for forming their past tense and past participles. Fortunately, we recognize the principal parts of most irregular verbs just by hearing them. We must memorize the irregular verb parts that we do not know already.

Irregular verbs cause people the most trouble because it is easy to confuse the past tense and past participle.

   The commercial Federalists had chosen (NOT chose) Jared Ingersoll as their token Antifederalist.

   Jared Ingersoll began (NOT begun) to see the necessity of a stronger central government.

We can group some irregular verbs because they follow similar patterns. Here we list four groups of irregular verbs:

	Verb	Past Tense	Past Participle
1.	blow	blew	(has) blown
	know	knew	(has) known
	throw	threw	(has) thrown
	grow	grew	(has) grown
2.	bear	bore	(has) borne
	tear	tore	(has) torn
	wear	wore	(has) worn
	swear	swore	(has) sworn
3.	begin	began	(has) begun
	ring	rang	(has) rung
	shrink	shrank	(has) shrunk

	sing	sang	(has) sung
	drink	drank	(has) drunk
4.	choose	chose	(has) chosen
	freeze	froze	(has) frozen
	speak	spoke	(has) spoken
	break	broke	(has) broken
	steal	stole	(has) stolen

Example Write the correct verb form for sentences a–d.

(a) No one (knowed, knew, known) what Jared Ingersoll, Jr., really thought.

(b) He had (growed, grew, grown) displeased during Jefferson's first administration.

(c) After his association with Ben Franklin, Jared Ingersoll, Jr., had (shrink, shrank, shrunk) from the Loyalists.

(d) Finally, he (speaked, spoke, spoken) out against the Tories and his father.

Solution (a) No one **knew** what Jared Ingersoll, Jr., really thought.

(b) He had **grown** displeased during Jefferson's first administration.

(c) After his association with Ben Franklin, Jared Ingersoll, Jr., had **shrunk** from the Loyalists.

(d) Finally, he **spoke** out against the Tories and his father.

Practice For a–d, replace each blank with the correct vocabulary word.

a. The Latin word meaning "to lead" is _____.

b. Knowing that Jared Ingersoll, Sr. was a Tory, and that Jared Ingersoll, Jr., was a patriot allows us to make the _____ that Ingersoll family relationships were strained.

c. Mob rule and worthless currency proved _____ to an overhaul of the existing government.

d. Please take a ten percent _____ from the price of all old merchandise.

For e–o, write the correct verb form for each sentence.

e. Thomas Mifflin had (drinked, drank, drunk) too much liquor in his lifetime.

f. Yesterday we (sing, sang, sung) "Happy Birthday" to President Lincoln.

g. Alexander Hamilton's voice might have (ringed, rang, rung) out loudly during the Great Convention.

h. Jared Ingersoll, Jr., (sweared, swore, sworn) allegiance to the United States of America.

i. The colonists (wore, weared, worn) hats over their powdered wigs.

j. Jared Ingersoll, Jr., had (throwed, thrown, threw) his support behind a strict construction of the Constitution.

k. Late in 1778, he (break, broke, broken) with the Loyalists.

l. Later, Charles Jared Ingersoll (teared, tore, torn) himself away from the legal philosophies of his father and grandfather.

m. Since James Wilson refused to pay his debts, some believed that he had (stealed, stole, stolen) their money.

n. He had (blow, blew, blown) his chances for support from the people.

o. The water had (froze, frozen, frozed) overnight in the watering troughs.

More Practice Write the past tense and past participle of each verb.

1. bear   2. begin   3. blow   4. choose

5. drink   6. freeze   7. grow   8. know

9. ring   10. sing   11. speak   12. steal

13. swear **14.** tear **15.** throw **16.** wear

Review Set 49 Choose the correct word to complete sentences 1–12.

1. (Any one, Anyone) of the candidates might campaign in favor of this issue.
(48)

2. A(n) (conjecture, retraction, impeachment) is a withdrawal of something previously said.
(47)

3. (Compose, Incriminate, Conjecture) means "to make up, or constitute."
(46)

4. (Anyway, Anyways) is not a word.
(44)

5. (Judicious, Amicable, Gravid) means "wise, or sensible."
(12, 22)

6. We form the perfect verb tense by adding a form of the helping verb (be, have, do) to the past participle.
(15)

7. The (positive, comparative, superlative) form compares three or more persons, places, or things.
(39)

8. A (verb, conjunction, predicate nominative) follows a linking verb and re-names the subject.
(36)

9. A(n) (direct, indirect) object is the noun or pronoun that tells "to whom" or "for whom" the action was done.
(21, 30)

10. The pronoun *you* is (first, second, third) person.
(48)

11. The pronoun *they* is (singular, plural).
(48)

12. The pronoun *he* is (first, second, third) person, (singular, plural).
(48)

13. Write the verb phrase in this sentence and label it transitive or intransitive: Does Sam Spade give the police any information?
(21, 26)

14. Write each noun in this sentence and circle the one that is collective: The detective agency hopes to discover the truth.
(4, 7)

15. Write each word that should be capitalized in this sentence: on wednesday, aunt jenny asked, "have you ever read the book *a tale of two cities*?"

16. In this sentence, write the adjective phrase and then write the noun it modifies: Sam Spade is the main character in *The Maltese Falcon*.

17. Write the predicate adjective from this sentence: As Spade's secretary, Effie Perine proves efficient.

18. Write whether the following is a complete sentence, run-on sentence, or sentence fragment: Iva Archer accuses Sam Spade of murdering her husband.

19. Write whether the following is a phrase or a clause: laughing and shaking his head

20. Write the plural of each noun.
(a) turkey   (b) story   (c) dish

21. Write the four principal parts of the irregular verb *know*.

22. Write the past tense and past participle of the irregular verb *bear*.

23. Rewrite the letter below as it is. Then add proofreading symbols to indicate corrections.

> Dear miss Informed,
>   you said you would meetme at one pm what happened?
>   yours turly,
>   aunt Lilly

24. Use an appositive to combine these two sentences into one sentence: Miss Wonderly hires Sam Spade to find a missing person. The missing person is her seventeen-year-old sister.

25. Write the gerund in this sentence: Was killing a part of Miss Wonderly's plan?

26. Rewrite this sentence adding commas and periods and making necessary changes to abbreviations for formal writing: On Apr 3 2002 Mr and Mrs Steu gave birth to a six lb daughter and named her Calla Mary

27. Write each personal pronoun and its antecedent in this sentence: Tom asked Christina if she had his cell phone in her backpack.
(46)

28. From this sentence, write the participle and the noun it modifies: Wally pounded on the closed door.
(45)

Diagram sentences 29 and 30.

29. Will maracas, drums, and xylophones be the percussion instruments of our marching band?
(34, 45)

30. Percussion instruments can give our music decorative rhythms.
(21, 30)

LESSON 50 — Nominative Pronoun Case

> **Dictation or Journal Entry**
>
> **Vocabulary:** A final *e* makes the word *envelope* different from the word *envelop*.
>
> An *envelope* is a wrapper or container, used especially for mailing letters. I slid the birthday card into the *envelope*.
>
> To *envelop* means to wrap up, surround, or cover completely. Fog *enveloped* the highway, making visibility impossible.

Nominative Case We remember that nouns can be grouped into three cases: nominative, objective, and possessive. We also remember that the same is true of pronouns. In this lesson we will concentrate on the **nominative case.** A pronoun used as a subject or predicate nominative is in the nominative case.

He was apparently a humbug. (subject)

Our grouchiest relative was *he*. (predicate nominative)

Does *she* cast her pearls before swine? (subject)

The woman serving tea is *she*. (predicate nominative)

Example 1 Complete this chart by replacing each blank with the correct nominative case pronoun.

Number	Person	Case NOMINATIVE (subject)
Singular	First	____
	Second	____
	Third (masc.)	____
	(fem.)	____
	(neuter)	____
Plural	First	____
	Second	____
	Third	____

Solution We complete the chart as follows:

Number	Person		Case NOMINATIVE (subject)
Singular	First		*I*
	Second		*you*
	Third	(masc.)	*he*
		(fem.)	*she*
		(neuter)	*it*
Plural	First		*we*
	Second		*you*
	Third		*they*

Subjects These sentences use nominative case personal pronouns as subjects:

I remember Thomas Paine.

He published a pamphlet about liberty.

When we use the pronouns *I* or *we* as part of a compound subject, we politely refer to ourselves last:

Mom and *I* flew to Great Britain.

Mr. Twaddell and *we* might rock the boat.

Example 2 Write the sentence that is more polite.

We and Adele will address the envelopes.

Adele and we will address the envelopes.

Solution It is more polite to refer to ourselves (we) last.

Adele and we will address the envelopes.

Example 3 Write a sentence using a nominative case personal pronoun as a subject.

Solution Your answer will be unique. Here are some examples of pronouns used as subjects:

***It* startled the deer.**

***They* vanished into the woods.**

***You* and *she* have agitated your listeners.**

Predicate Nominatives These sentences use nominative case personal pronouns as predicate nominatives:

> James Wilson is *he* in the photo.
>
> Alison is *she* alongside the gentleman.

Predicate nominatives can also be compound:

> The lawyers were John Dickinson and *he*.
>
> The parents of James Wilson were *she* and *he*.

Example 4 Write a sentence using a nominative case pronoun as a predicate nominative.

Solution Your answer will be unique. Here are some correct examples:

> **The last presenter was *I*.**
>
> **The most amiable negotiators were *they*.**
>
> **That stoic, expressionless sales clerk is *he*.**

Practice

a. Study the nominative case pronoun chart from Example 1. Then try to reproduce it from memory. You may abbreviate. (Example: 1st, 2nd, 3rd, sing. pl.)

b. Unscramble these words to make a sentence with a personal pronoun as a subject:

called the of America for they independence

c. Unscramble these words to make a sentence with a personal pronoun as a predicate nominative:

red vest the he was Loyalist the in

d. Write the sentence that is more polite:

I and she will march in the parade.

She and I will march in the parade.

e. Write each nominative case pronoun from this list:

me	him	I	she	them
they	he	her	we	us

Choose the nominative case pronoun for sentences f–i.

f. The lady beside James Wilson is (she, her).

g. The bureaucrats were (them, they) in the elevator.

h. The man in the lab coat was (him, he).

i. It is (I, me) who must scour the pans.

For j–m, replace each blank with *envelope* or *envelop*.

j. Sometimes clouds _____ the mountain peak.

k. My friend's letter arrived in a green _____.

l. Lucy placed a postage stamp on her _____.

m. Families _____ new puppies with love and attention.

Review Set 50 Choose the correct word(s) to complete sentences 1–10.

1. The Latin word (*amare, hospes, ducere*) means "to lead."
(49)

2. Is (any one, anyone) home?
(48)

3. A retraction is a (guess, law, withdrawal).
(47)

4. To compose is to (agree, make up, influence).
(46)

5. To apportion is to give out (pizza, parts, advice).
(23)

6. Of my six cousins, Dora is the (more, most) amiable.
(40)

7. We call the personal pronouns *I, me, mine, we, us,* and *ours* the "speaker," or (first, second, third) person.
(48)

8. We call the personal pronouns *you* and *yours* the "person spoken to," or (first, second, third) person.
(48)

9. During yesterday's trial, the defendant (wear, wore, worn) a contemptuous frown.
(49)

10. Had this grumpy defendant actually (steal, store, stolen) the jewels?
(49)

11. Write the plural of each noun.
(10, 11) (a) jury   (b) sheep   (c) wolf

12. In this sentence, write the verb phrase and name its tense:
(15) Had Sam Spade searched Miss Wonderly's apartment for clues of the falcon's whereabouts?

13. Write whether the following is a phrase or a clause: that *La Paloma* was the only vessel sailing in from Hong Kong

14. Write whether the following is a complete sentence, run-on sentence, or sentence fragment: Keeled over, dead, with the falcon in his hand.

15. In this sentence, write the verb phrase and label it action or linking: Sam Spade correctly identifies Miss Wonderly as the murderer.

16. Rewrite this story title using correct capitalization: "uncle wiggily and the crawly snake"

17. Write the correct verb form to complete this sentence: Suddenly it (past tense of *begin*) to rain.

18. Write the comparative and superlative forms of the adjective *conscientious*.

19. Rewrite the letter below, adding capital letters and correct punctuation marks.

dear aunt Lilly
    i lost my watch please forgive me
        regretfully
        miss informed

20. Write the participle used as an adjective in this sentence: With pleading eyes, Miss Wonderly begs Spade to let her go.

21. In this sentence, write the verb phrase and label it transitive or intransitive: Lightning flashed in the night sky.

22. Write whether the italicized noun is nominative, objective, or possessive case: To keep cool, Babe Ruth wore a cabbage *leaf* under his baseball cap.

23. Write each pronoun and its antecedent from this sentence: Douglas MacArthur's mother accompanied him to West Point to make sure he studied.

24. Write the four principal parts of the irregular verb *sing*.

25. For a and b, write the past tense and past participle of each verb.
(49)
 (a) throw (b) tear

26. Write the gerund from this sentence and label its tense
(16) present or perfect: Marie Taglioni, the first prima donna ballerina, initiated dancing on the toes.

27. In this sentence, write the verb phrase and label it active
(27) or passive voice: Was that tutu worn by Marie Taglioni?

28. Write seven common coordinating conjunctions.
(33)

Diagram sentences 29 and 30.

29. We hope to have reconciled.
(21, 45)

30. My dog Boomer offered me his wounded right paw to
(42, 45) shake.

LESSON 51 — Objective Pronoun Case

> **Dictation or Journal Entry**
>
> **Vocabulary:** The Latin verb *sequi* gives us the root *sec-* or *sequ-*, meaning "to follow," as in the familiar words *sequel* and *second*.
>
> *Consequential* means "following as an effect or conclusion; resultant." Business losses continued, so the *consequential* bankruptcy was no surprise.
>
> A *sequence* is a fixed condition or order of one thing following directly after another. Are you familiar with the *sequence* of events leading up to the Revolutionary War?

Pronouns are **objective case** when they are used as direct objects, indirect objects, or objects of a preposition.

>   Robert Morris joined *them. (direct object)
>
>   Lee offered *me two orphaned mice. (indirect object)
>
>   Zena rode with *us. (object of a preposition)

Objective case pronouns can be compound. We politely mention ourselves last.

>   The camera flash temporarily blinded *her* and *us*.
>
>   Binh loaned *him* and *me* some golf clubs.
>
>   Ernesto sang with *them* and *me*.

Example 1 Choose the sentence that is more polite.

>   Grandma baked squash for me and her.
>
>   Grandma baked squash for her and me.

Solution It is more polite to mention ourselves last.

Grandma baked squash for her and me.

Example 2 Complete this chart by replacing each blank with the correct objective case pronoun.

Number	Person		Case OBJECTIVE
Singular	First		___
	Second		___
	Third	(masc.)	___
		(fem.)	___
		(neuter)	___
Plural	First		___
	Second		___
	Third		___

Solution We complete the chart as follows:

Number	Person		Case OBJECTIVE
Singular	First		*me*
	Second		*you*
	Third	(masc.)	*him*
		(fem.)	*her*
		(neuter)	*it*
Plural	First		*us*
	Second		*you*
	Third		*them*

Direct Objects The following sentences have personal pronouns as direct objects. Notice that they are objective case pronouns.

The king banished *them.

Manuel surprised *me.

I thanked *him.

Example 3 Write a sentence using a pronoun as a direct object.

Solution Answers will vary. Here are some examples:

Robert Morris intrigues *her*.

Mr. Morris does not interest Bert or *me*.

That senator opposes *it*.

Indirect Objects These sentences have personal pronouns as indirect objects. They are objective case.

Scot ordered *her some new software.

The company denies *him and *me our refund.

Debby scrambled *us some eggs.

Example 4 Write a sentence using an objective case personal pronoun as an indirect object.

Solution Our answers will vary. Here are some possibilities:

The docent offered *us* a map.

Some children sold *them* bottled water.

Mr. Monotone read *her* and *me* his entire thesis.

Objects of a Preposition The sentences below have personal pronouns used as objects of a preposition. Of course they are objective case.

A helicopter hovered near *her.

Dr. Kutz spoke on behalf of *them and *me.

Patriots shouted around *us.

Example 5 Write a sentence using a personal pronoun as an object of a preposition.

Solution Here are some possible answers:

Robert Morris's firm ruled over *them*.

The firm earns money from *you* and *us*.

My team won in spite of *me*.

Practice a. Study the objective case pronoun chart from Example 1. Then try to reproduce it from memory.

b. Unscramble these words to make a sentence with a personal pronoun as a direct object:

aggravated   King George   us   and   Patriots   the

c. Unscramble these words to make a sentence with a personal pronoun as an indirect object:

told   docent   them   a   the   history

d. Unscramble these words to make a sentence with a personal pronoun as an object of a preposition:

apricots   Liza   with   canned   me   and   him

e. Write the sentence that is more polite.
Aunt Sukey winked at my cousin and me.
Aunt Sukey winked at me and my cousin.

f. Write each objective case pronoun from this list:

| me | him | I | she | them |
| they | he | her | we | us |

Choose an objective case pronoun for sentences g–i.

g. Will the tour leave without my friend and (I, me)?

h. The cicerone gave Jasper and (she, her) a map.

i. Wealthy Robert Morris led Charles Willing and (they, them) to prosperity.

For j–l, replace each blank with the correct vocabulary word.

j. In a dictionary, we find words in an alphabetical _____.

k. After repeated tardiness, the loss of one's job may be _____.

l. The roots *sec-* and *sequ-* mean "to _____."

Review Set 51

Choose the correct word(s) to complete sentences 1–12.

1. (Envelope, Envelop) is a verb.
(50)

2. The Latin word *ducere* means to (throw, love, lead).
(49)

3. (Every one, Everyone) of the peaches has fallen from the tree.
(48)

4. (Intractable, Judicious, Gravid) means "not easily drawn back or controlled; stubborn."
(47)

5. An (indirect democracy, affection, appropriation) is something set aside for someone, especially money.
(23)

6. *He, him, his, she, her, hers,* and *it* are (first, second, third) person pronouns.
(48)

7. Pronoun (gender, case) shows the job the pronoun performs in the sentence.
(50)

8. Judy thought she (know, knew, known) all the planets of the solar system.
(49)

9. She has (grow, grew, grown) wiser with age.
(49)

10. Have you (tear, tore, torn) up all the expired coupons?
(49)

11. Has the phone (ring, rang, rung) in the last half hour?
(49)

12. Of the two architects, Lee has drawn the (good, better, best) design.
(40)

13. Write whether the following is a phrase or a clause: at Henry VIII's deathbed
(20)

14. Write the plural of each noun.
(10, 11)
    (a) factory   (b) chimney   (c) loaf

15. In this sentence, write the verb phrase and label it action or linking: Anita Bryant sang "The Battle Hymn of the Republic" at Lyndon B. Johnson's funeral in 1973.
(3, 18)

16. Rewrite the letter below as it is. Then add proofreading symbols to indicate corrections.
(25, 32)

    deerKatrina,
        please thank grandma for Making those squash pies they was delicoius

                grate fully,
                Leling

17. For a and b, write the past tense and past participle of each irregular verb.
(49)
    (a) choose   (b) break

18. Write the comparative and superlative form of the adjective *susceptible*.
(39)

Replace each blank with the correct word to complete sentences 19 and 20.

19. We can group nouns into three cases: nominative case, _____ case, and possessive case
(50)

20. A noun is in the _____ case when it is the subject of a sentence or when it is used as a predicate nominative.
(50)

21. Rewrite this sentence in the active voice: That fir tree was planted by my neighbor.
(27)

22. Use an appositive to combine these two choppy sentences to make one longer sentence:
(42)

Georges Bizet wrote the opera *Carmen*.
Georges Bizet was a French composer.

23. Write whether the italicized pronoun in the following sentence is nominative, objective, or possessive case:
(37)

The physicians did *their* duty in hiding King Henry VIII's dying condition.

24. From the following sentence, write each pronoun and its antecedent:
(46)

Napoleon adopted the bumblebee as his official emblem.

25. Write the participle used as an adjective in this sentence: Crackling fireworks awoke Jason and Nathan in the middle of the night.
(45)

26. Write each adjective from the following sentence and circle the one that is sometimes over-used:
(44)

The good artist Leonardo Da Vinci wrote on many diverse subjects.

27. Write the correlative conjunction pair from the following sentence:
(35)

Both Mother Teresa (Calcutta, India) and Lech Walesa (Poland) received the Nobel Peace Prize in 1979.

Diagram sentences 28–30.

28. Having hesitated, she had no desire to continue.
(21, 45)

29. Do both Annie and she enjoy cooking?
(19, 34)

30. The gentleman with the microphone is he.
(29, 36)

LESSON 52 — Personal Pronoun Case Forms

Dictation or Journal Entry

Vocabulary: The words *disinterested* and *uninterested* seem similar but have different meanings.

Disinterested means impartial, neutral, or dispassionate. Molly was interested in the debate, but she took a *disinterested* position; she did not choose sides. A *disinterested* jury returns the fairest judgment.

Uninterested means indifferent and unconcerned. An *uninterested* jury might miss important facts concerning a case because of boredom or distraction. The yawning audience seemed *uninterested* in my lecture on Scandinavian postage stamps.

Case Forms   The following chart helps us to sort out the three personal pronoun **case forms:** (1) If a pronoun is a subject or predicate nominative, it is *nominative case*. (2) A pronoun used as a direct object, indirect object, or object of a preposition is *objective case*. (3) If a pronoun shows possession, it is *possessive case*.

		CASE		
NUMBER	PERSON	NOMINATIVE (subject)	OBJECTIVE	POSSESSIVE
Singular	First	*I*	*me*	*mine*
	Second	*you*	*you*	*yours*
	Third (masc.)	*he*	*him*	*his*
	(fem.)	*she*	*her*	*hers*
	(neuter)	*it*	*it*	
Plural	First	*we*	*us*	*ours*
	Second	*you*	*you*	*yours*
	Third	*they*	*them*	*theirs*

Example 1   Tell whether each italicized pronoun is nominative, objective, or possessive case.

(a) Gouverneur Morris and *he* represented the commercial Federalists.

(b) Congress gave *him* authority over the disordered finances of the new nation.

(c) *His* was the largest contribution.

Solution   (a) **nominative case**

(b) **objective case**

(c) **possessive case**

The pronoun case form depends on how the pronoun is used in the sentence. We refer to the chart above to decide which pronoun is correct for this sentence:

(We, Us) delegates are considering alternatives.

The pronoun identifies "delegates" which is the subject of the sentence. We use the nominative case pronoun *we* (NOT *us*) as a subject. Therefore, we write

We delegates are considering alternatives.

Example 2 Tell how the pronoun is used in each sentence (subject, direct object, indirect object, object of a preposition, or possession).

(a) Congress liked *him* for his extraordinary skills.

(b) That financial plan was *his*.

(c) *They* agreed with Robert Morris's suggestion for paying war debts.

(d) Morris had argued with *them* over debt payment.

(e) Robert Morris gave *her* his opinion.

Solution (a) *Him* is a **direct object.**

(b) *His* shows **possession.**

(c) *They* is the **subject.**

(d) *Them* is the **object of the preposition "with."**

(e) *Her* is an **indirect object.**

Example 3 Determine how the pronoun is used in each sentence. Then refer to the chart above to help you choose the correct pronoun. Rewrite each sentence correctly.

(a) Both John Dickinson and (he, him) opposed the Declaration of Independence, yet Robert Morris signed it.

(b) Robert Morris provided funds for Washington's army and (they, them).

(c) The war profited Charles Willing and (he, him).

Solution (a) The pronoun is a **sentence subject,** so we choose the nominative case pronoun **he.**

Both John Dickinson and **he** opposed the Declaration of Independence, yet Robert Morris signed it.

(b) The pronoun is the **object of the preposition "for,"** so we choose the objective case pronoun **them.**

Robert Morris provided funds for Washington's army and **them.**

(c) The pronoun is a **direct object,** so we choose the objective case pronoun **him.**

The war profited Charles Willing and **him.**

Practice For a–c, tell whether the pronoun is nominative, objective, or possessive case.

a. Robert Morris shared with *them* his money and ingenuity.

b. Roger Sherman and Robert Morris were *they* who signed all three of the nation's documents.

c. *His* was a generous gift.

For d–i, tell how the pronoun is used in each sentence (subject, predicate nominative, direct object, indirect object, object of a preposition, possession).

d. That cloudburst drenched *me.*

e. Is this signature *yours*?

f. *We* researched John Dickinson.

g. Patriots gave *him* the nickname "Penman of the Revolution."

h. Dickinson argued against *them* on some issues.

i. It was *he* who wrote "Letters from a Farmer in Pennsylvania."

For j and k, choose the correct pronoun.

j. (We, Us) students will re-enact the Great Convention.

k. Ben Franklin will stand beside Robert Morris and (*I, me*).

For l and m, replace each blank with the *disinterested* or *uninterested*.

l. Some _____ mediators are struggling to satisfy the demands of both of the warring parties.

m. The _____ bystander paid no attention to the arguing bureaucrats.

Review Set 52 Choose the correct word to complete sentences 1–6.

1. The Latin word (*ducere, venire, sequi*) means "to follow."
(51)

2. (Envelope, Envelop) is a noun.
(50)

3. (Conducive, Bicameral, Ambiguous) means "tending to promote or encourage."
(49)

4. Is (Every one, Everyone) here?
(48)

5. Alleviate means to (lighten, edit, condemn).
(24)

6. A (clause, phrase) is a group of words with a subject and a predicate.
(20)

7. Write the plural of each noun.
(10, 11) (a) inch   (b) foot   (c) yardstick

8. Write the verb phrase in this sentence and label it transitive or intransitive: Edgar Allen Poe wrote poetry filled with gothic imagery.
(21, 26)

9. Rewrite the following sentence so that it is in active voice: Dark surroundings and ghostly symbols were used by Poe to create a sense of fear.
(27)

10. Write the four principal parts of the irregular verb *swear*.
(49)

11. Write the comparative and superlative forms of the adjective *little*, meaning "amount."
(40)

12. Rewrite the following as it is. Then add proofreading symbols to indicate corrections.
Voltaire, a french Writer and philsopher, was was bornin paris on november 21, 1694.

13. Rewrite this sentence adding capital letters, periods, and commas as needed: of course mom i shall help you weed the garden dump the trash and feed the dog

14. Write the seven common coordinating conjunctions.

15. Write the verb phrase from this sentence and label it action or linking: Did *The Fall of the House of Usher* seem gothic and scary?

16. In this sentence, write the verb phrase and name its tense: An unidentified narrator will be introducing all the story's characters.

17. Use an appositive to make one sentence from the following two sentences: Roderick Usher wrote the Narrator and requested his presence at the ancestral Usher home. The Narrator was Roderick's one personal friend.

18. Write each pronoun and its antecedent in this sentence: The Narrator swallowed his fear as he approached Roderick Usher's inner chamber.

19. Write whether the following is a phrase or a clause: pallid skin like that of a corpse

20. Reproduce the nominative case pronoun chart. You may abbreviate "1st, 2nd, 3rd, sing. pl., etc."

21. Write each possessive noun from this list: aristocracies, aristocracy's, nestors, nestor's, nestors'

22. Unscramble these words to make a sentence with a personal pronoun as a predicate nominative:
    is   emcee   the   she

23. For a and b, write the past tense and past participle of
(49) each irregular verb.
(a) blow   (b) shrink

24. Which sentence below is more polite? Write A or B.
(50, 52) A. He and I will apportion the money fairly.
B. I and he will apportion the money fairly.

25. Write the participle used as an adjective in this sentence:
(45) Usher's terrifying appearance unnerves the Narrator.

26. Write each gerund in this sentence: Two of my hobbies
(16, 36) are fishing and reading.

Diagram sentences 27–30.
27. Would you like a judicious person to intervene?
(21, 45)
28. Bake us some of your English muffins with raisins and
(29, 30) nuts.

29. Hiking, Vinita began whistling.
(16, 21)

30. The winners of the whistling competition might have
(34, 36) been she and I.

LESSON 53

Possessive Pronouns and Possessive Adjectives • Diagramming Pronouns

> **Dictation or Journal Entry**
>
> **Vocabulary:** The two adjectives *apollonian* and *bacchanalian* derive their meanings from Greek and Roman gods.
>
> The Greek god Apollo is associated with calm rationality. Therefore, *apollonian* means "harmonious, serene, well-balanced, ordered, rational, and calm." Robert Morris's *apollonian* personality won him admiration and trust in Pennsylvania.
>
> Bacchus was the Roman god of wine and frenzy. Consequently, the word *bacchanalian* means "frenzied, riotous, wanton, and debauched." Those who care about their reputations avoid *bacchanalian* events.

Possessive Pronouns We have learned that a pronoun takes the place of a noun. The possessive pronouns *mine*, *yours*, *his*, *hers*, *ours*, and *theirs* replace nouns to tell "whose."

That's *yours,* not *mine.*

His has stripes, but *hers* has polka dots.

Theirs look delicious, so why don't *ours?*

Notice that in each of the sentences above, the possessive pronoun **replaces a noun** and stands alone.

Possessive Adjectives There is another group of words that is very similar to possessive pronouns except that they **come before a noun** rather than replace it. These words are the possessive adjectives *my, your, his, her, its, our*, and *their*.

Your cow ate *my* corn.

Her sister likes *his* brother.

Their sheep are grazing in *our* pasture.

In each of the sentences above, the possessive adjective comes before a noun to tell "whose."

Many people consider these words pronouns. Others see them as adjectives because they always come before nouns to modify them. What is important is using them correctly.

POSSESSIVE ADJECTIVE (IN FRONT OF A NOUN)	POSSESSIVE PRONOUN (STANDING ALONE)
my	mine
your	yours
his	his

her	hers
its	its *(very seldom used)*
our	ours

Errors to Avoid Possessive pronouns do not have apostrophes. The words *yours, hers, its,* and *ours* are already possessive.

> INCORRECT: I borrowed Dad's keys but not **your's**.
> CORRECT: I borrowed Dad's keys but not **yours**.

> INCORRECT: That scruffy kitten is **her's** to love.
> CORRECT: That scruffy kitten is **hers** to love.

Also, we must not confuse contractions and possessive adjectives.

POSSESSIVE ADJECTIVE	CONTRACTION	
your	you're	(you are)
their	they're	(they are)
its	it's	(it is)

Example 1 Choose the correct word to complete each sentence.

(a) Is that pen (yours, your's)?

(b) (It's, Its) ink has dried up.

(c) Do you believe (it's, its) useless?

(d) The responsibility is (theirs, their's).

Solution (a) Is that pen **yours**?

(b) **Its** ink has dried up.

(c) Do you believe **it's** useless?

(d) The responsibility is **theirs.**

Diagramming Pronouns We diagram pronouns in the same way we diagram nouns.

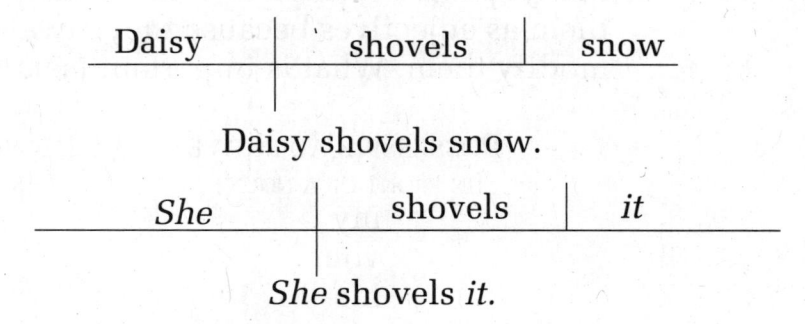

```
  Daisy   |  shovels  |  snow
          |
```

Daisy shovels snow.

```
   She    |  shovels  |  it
          |
```

She shovels *it.*

Diagramming a sentence helps us determine which pronoun to use, because it clearly shows *how* the pronoun is used in the sentence. We diagram the main parts of the sentence below to help us choose the correct pronoun:

Squirrels frolicked beside Kim and (*I, me*).

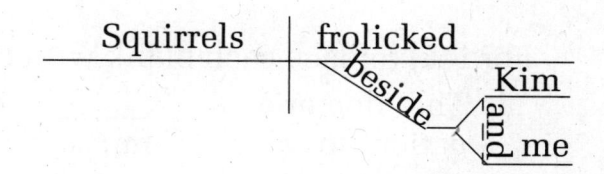

We see from the diagram that the pronoun is an object of the preposition *beside*, so we choose the objective case pronoun *me*.

Squirrels frolicked beside Kim and *me*.

Example 2 Diagram the following sentence in order to choose the correct pronoun. Then rewrite the sentence correctly.

Dickinson and (he, him) signed the document.

Solution We diagram the sentence this way:

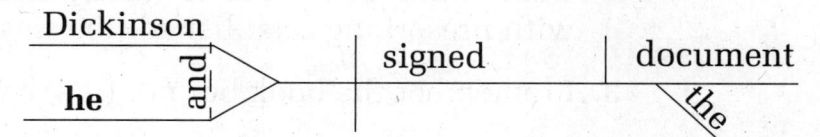

We see from our diagram that the pronoun is part of the subject of the sentence, so we choose the nominative case pronoun **he**.

Dickinson and **he** signed the document.

Practice Diagram sentences a–c choosing the correct pronoun. Then choose the correct word to complete the sentence.

a. The teacher and (we, us) thanked the docent.

b. Mail Fiona and (me, I) a copy.

c. Ivan sent Anton and (she, her).

Choose the correct word to complete sentences d–h.

d. The old plan was ineffective; (it's, its) weaknesses outweighed (it's, its) strengths.

e. Those suggestions were (theirs, their's).

f. Please give us (your, you're) ideas.

g. (They're, Their) in agreement with the Old Whig tradition.

h. (Its, It's) fortuitous that we met at the library.

For i–k, replace each blank with the correct vocabulary word.

i. The doctor's _____ demeanor helped his sick patient to remain calm.

j. Respectable citizens stayed away from the _____ party on the beach.

k. The adjectives *apollonian* and *bacchanalian* come from the names of Greek and Roman _____.

More Practice Choose the correct word(s) to complete each sentence.

1. Many Quakers made (their, there) homes in Delaware.

2. Some people are determined to put (their, there, they're) trust in the law, not men; (their, there, they're) concerned with preserving established liberties.

3. I remember the book but not (it's, its) author.

4. England's history is longer and more varied than (ours, our's).

5. My country has divided powers, but (hers, her's) has a dictator.

6. Is this postcard (yours, your's)?

7. Did you bring (you're, your) brothers with you?

8. Yes, (they're, their) waiting for me over (there, they're, their) beside the monument.

9. A goldfinch made (it's, its) nest in my pecan tree, and now (it's, its) laying eggs.

10. (You're, Your) not allowed to ride (you're, your) bike in the park.

Review Set 53 Choose the correct word to complete sentences 1–8.

1. Disinterested means (uninterested, impartial, angry).
(52)

2. The Latin word *sequi* means "to (love, lead, follow)."
(51)

3. Snow may (envelope, envelop) a vehicle.
(50)

4. Conducive means "tending to (encourage, discourage, disrupt)."
(49)

5. (Levity, Probity, Gravity) is frivolity; lack of appropriate seriousness.
(24)

6. Please loan Lisa and (her, she) a basketball.
(51)

7. Is this basketball (yours, your's)?
(53)

8. A possessive (noun, pronoun) has no apostrophe.
(53)

9. Write the plural of each noun.
(10, 11)
(a) city   (b) man   (c) rule of thumb

10. Rewrite this sentence so that it is in active voice: Everyone in the crowd was annoyed by the hoodlum's intractable behavior.
(27)

11. Write the four principal parts of the irregular verb *grow*.
(13)

12. Write the comparative and superlative forms of the adjective *crazy*.
(39)

13. Rewrite the following as it is. Then add proofreading symbols to indicate corrections.
(32)

Mr usher had a a sistre her name was Alfie

14. Rewrite this story title using correct capitalization: "the making of an explorer."
(9)

15. From this sentence, write the verb phrase and label it action or linking: Madeline Usher attacked her brother for his cruelty.
(3, 18)

16. Write four common pairs of correlative conjunctions.
(35)

17. From this sentence, write the verb phrase and name its tense: The Narrator will flee the Usher mansion in terror.
(8)

18. Use an appositive to make one sentence from the following two sentences:

The Russian artist Marc Chagall painted *I and the Village*.

I and the Village is an abstract painting that looks like something from a dream.

19. Write the pronoun and its antecedent in this sentence: The Narrator watched the Usher mansion as it crumbled and fell into the dark lake.

20. Write whether the following is a phrase or a clause: valued for its imaginative details

21. Reproduce the objective case pronoun chart from Lesson 52. You may abbreviate "1st, 2nd, 3rd, sing. pl., etc."

22. Which sentence below is more polite? Write A or B.
   A. Please wait for me and him.
   B. Please wait for him and me.

23. In the following sentence, write the infinitive and label it an adjective or a noun:

I have an intriguing mystery to read.

24. For a and b, write the past tense and past participle of each irregular verb.
   (a) speak   (b) steal

25. Write the participle used as an adjective in this sentence: The lying witness did not convince me.

26. In the following sentence, write the gerund and label its tense present or perfect:

Having won the Tour de France once made the competitor want to race again.

27. Write the collective noun in this sentence: Tomorrow we shall hear what the jury has decided.

Diagram sentences 28–30.

28. We, the jurors, might need several hours to decide.
(42, 45)

29. Has the jury finished deliberating?
(16, 21)

30. Dan and I were members of a hung jury.
(34, 36)

LESSON 54

Dependent and Independent Clauses • Subordinating Conjunctions

> **Dictation or Journal Entry**
> **Vocabulary:** Let us clarify the meaning of the words *biannual*, *biennial*, *bimonthly* and *biweekly*.
> *Biannual* means twice a year, or "semiannual." The company's *biannual* meetings occur in June and December.
> *Biennial* means every two years. Cleaning my garage has become a *biennial* event although it should be an annual event.
> *Bimonthly* and *biweekly* are ambiguous. *Bimonthly* can mean twice a month or every two months. *Biweekly* can mean twice a week or every two weeks. For that reason, it is clearer to use more specific terms such as "twice a week" or "every two months" instead.

Independent Clauses There are two types of clauses. One type is the **independent clause,** also called the main clause. An independent clause expresses a complete thought. It makes sense all by itself.

Ambiguous terms confuse us.

Dickinson drafted the Articles of Confederation.

Dependent Clauses A **dependent clause** is the other type of clause. It cannot stand by itself and is sometimes called the subordinate clause. Alone, it does not make sense.

If the word seems ambiguous

Since John Dickinson spoke for the colonies

Although the clauses above each contain a subject and a predicate, but they do not make sense; they sound incomplete. However, if we remove the introductory words, "if" and "since," they become independent clauses. Standing alone, they make sense:

The word seems ambiguous.

John Dickinson spoke for the colonies.

Example 1 For a–d, tell whether the clauses are dependent or independent.

(a) when John Dickinson published *Letters from a Farmer in Pennsylvania*

(b) he explained the colonists' feelings toward policies of the British

(c) until he had petitioned the king

(d) he also wrote "Song of the Farmer," the anthem of the Revolution

Solution (a) This is a **dependent** clause. It depends on another clause in order to make sense.

(b) This is an **independent** clause. It can stand by itself and does not require another clause in order to make sense.

(c) This is a **dependent** clause. Alone, it makes no sense.

(d) This is an **independent** clause. Standing alone, it makes sense.

Subordinating Conjunctions

A **subordinating conjunction** introduces a dependent clause. We can turn an independent clause into a dependent clause by adding a subordinating conjunction. In the dependent clauses below, *while* and *unless* are subordinating conjunctions.

INDEPENDENT CLAUSE	DEPENDENT CLAUSE
He spoke eloquently.	*While* he spoke eloquently,...
He lost the argument.	*Unless* he lost the argument,...

Here we list some common subordinating conjunctions:

after	*because*	*so that*	*when*
although	*before*	*than*	*whenever*
as	*even though*	*that*	*where*
as if	*if*	*though*	*wherever*
as soon as	*in order that*	*unless*	*while*
as though	*since*	*until*	

Many of these words also function as prepositions. Sometimes phrases begin with prepositions such as *after*, *before*, *since* or *until*. In this case, these words are not subordinating conjunctions but prepositions. Remember that a clause has both a subject and a verb. Notice how the word *after* is used in the two sentences below.

SUBORDINATING CONJUNCTION:
John Dickinson joined the Continental Congress *after* he wrote a "Petition to the King." (*after he wrote a "Petition to the King"* is a **clause**)

PREPOSITION:
John Dickinson joined the Continental Congress *after* this petition. (*after this petition* is a prepositional **phrase**. It lacks a subject and predicate.)

Example 2 Identify the subordinating conjunctions in the following sentences.

(a) If a revolution were necessary, John Dickinson desired one on proper grounds.

(b) He finally accepted the Declaration of Independence even though he had spoken against it.

Solution (a) ***If*** is the subordinating conjunction which introduces the dependent clause, "If a revolution were necessary."

(b) ***Even though*** is the subordinating conjunction which introduces the dependent clause, "even though he had spoken against it."

Practice For a–d, tell whether the clauses are dependent or independent.

a. as soon as they had voted

b. the brigadier general of the Pennsylvania militia assumed his duties

c. he primarily objected to the timing

d. that we should avert disaster

Write each subordinating conjunction in sentences e–g.

e. Because he disapproved of Jefferson's vehement language, Dickinson disliked the Declaration of Independence.

f. The Declaration of Independence was adopted even though the states were not united.

g. Until Dickinson accepted a definition of America outside the stream of British history, he disapproved of the fashionable ideas.

For h–k, replace each blank with the correct vocabulary word(s).

h. On even-numbered years, we make our _____ visit to Washington, D.C.

i. The school provides for _____ field trips in October and April to motivate the students.

j. The ambiguous term *bimonthly* can mean "_____ a month" or "every other month."

k. The ambiguous term *biweekly* can mean "twice a week" or "every _____ week."

More Practice See Master Worksheets.

Review Set 54 Choose the correct word(s) to complete sentences 1–11.

1. (Apollonian, Bacchanalian, Stentorian) means "harmonious, serene, calm, and rational."
(53)

2. Uninterested means (disinterested, indifferent, passionate).
(52)

3. (Bellicose, Amiable, Consequential) means "following as an effect or conclusion; resultant."
(51)

4. Suffrage is the right to (life, bear arms, vote).
(25)

5. Guy's pencil drawing created the (delusion, illusion, allusion) of three dimensions.
(26)

6. Is this hockey stick (your's, yours) or Matt's?
(53)

7. I am searching for (its, it's) owner.
(53)

8. (Him, he) and Oscar are polishing the fire truck.
(50)

9. (Your, You're) encouraging words have cheered me.
(53)

10. In the race between José and Juan, José was (faster, fastest).
(39)

11. Lana had never (sang, sung) "God Bless America" before.
(49)

12. From this sentence, write the verb phrase and name its tense: Tom Canty, a pauper boy, was listening to Father Andrew.
(17)

13. From memory, reproduce the nominative case pronoun chart. You may abbreviate.
(50)

14 From this sentence, write each noun and circle the two
(4) that are abstract: Poverty makes life difficult for the Canty Family.

15. Rewrite the following as it is. Then add proofreading
(32) symbols to indicate corrections.

Mom warned, "oh, what a tangled web we weave when first we practice too deceive" this was a quote form sir Walter Scott's poem "marmion."

16. Write whether the following is a phrase or a clause: while
(20) another English lad is born into the rich and royal Tudor Family

17. Write the over-used adjective from the sentence below.
(23, 44) Then write one that is more descriptive.

Miss Yu gave a good farewell speech.

18. Write the four principal parts of the irregular verb *know*.
(13)

19. From this sentence, write each adjective or word used as
(24) an adjective and circle the one that is demonstrative: These joyous parents celebrate the arrival of Britain's heir.

20. Write the infinitive from the sentence below. Then write
(19, 21) how it functions in the sentence.

In *The Prince and the Pauper*, Mark Twain has a contrast to develop.

21. From this sentence, write the verb phrase and label it
(21, 26) transitive or intransitive: The new-fallen snow must have glistened in the moonlight.

Replace each blank with the correct word to complete sentences 22 through 24.

22. A noun or pronoun used as a direct object, an indirect
(51) object, or an object of a preposition is in the _____ case.

23. The word to which a pronoun refers is called the
(46) _____.

24. A noun or pronoun used as a subject or predicate nominative is in the _____ case.

25. From this sentence, write the verb phrase and label it linking or action: Because of his education, intelligence, and grace, Tom Canty seems wiser than others his age.

26. For a and b, write the plural of each noun.
(a) son-in-law   (b) mouthful

27. Rewrite this sentence so that it is in active voice: Tom Canty is invited into the palace by Edward Tudor.

28. Use an appositive to make one sentence from these two sentences: Mark Twain was a social and political satirist. Mark Twain wrote *The Prince and the Pauper*.

Diagram sentences 29 and 30.

29. Did reading spark Dell's ambition to investigate?

30. Having read, Dell felt curious.

LESSON 55

Gerunds Versus Participles and Verbs • Gerund Phrases

> **Dictation or Journal Entry**
> **Vocabulary:** The adjectives *Delphic* and *Dionysian* come from ancient Greece.
> *Delphic* comes from the Greek city of Delphi, the location of a temple to Apollo. In Delphi, there was a woman who supposedly foretold the future for Apollo. Priests frequently misinterpreted her prophecies. Therefore, the word *Delphic* means "unclear, ambiguous, or obscure." A few *Delphic* statements convinced the judge that the witness was not reliable.
> *Dionysian* comes from Dionysus, the Greek forerunner of Bacchus. Dionysus gave the human race its first wine. Worship of Dionysus involved frenzied celebrations with much drunkenness. Therefore, the word *Dionysian* means "wildly uninhibited, frenzied, unrestrained, undisciplined; bacchanalian." We sensed the *Dionysian* spirit in New Orleans during Mardi Gras.

Gerunds Vs. Participles and Verbs

We remember that a gerund may be the present participle of a verb (the *-ing* form) functioning as a noun. The gerund can be a sentence subject, a direct object, an object of a preposition, or a predicate noun. We also recall that not every word ending in *-ing* is a gerund. Some are verbs or participles. To determine if the *-ing* word is a gerund, we must examine how it is used in the sentence.

Gerunds:

 Sweeping is my job. (sentence subject)

 The politician enjoyed *speaking*. (direct object)

 Rosa's favorite pastime is *singing*. (predicate noun)

 Erin has a flair for *yodeling*. (object of preposition)

Participles:

 The twins wore *matching* outfits. (adjective)

 That woman *standing* is a new employee. (adjective)

Verbs:

 She *has been standing* for hours.

 Erin *is yodeling* again.

Example 1 Write whether the *-ing* word in each sentence is a verb, participle, or gerund.

(a) Raymond has been complaining all day.

(b) The complaining customer raised her voice at me.

(c) Complaining will not solve your problem.

Solution (a) **Has been complaining** is a present perfect progressive tense **verb.**

(b) **Complaining** is a **participle.** It is used as an adjective modifying "customer."

(c) **Complaining** is a **gerund.** It is the subject of the sentence.

Gerund Phrases A **gerund phrase** contains a gerund and its objects and modifiers. It is always used as a noun. The gerund phrase may have adjectives, adverbs, direct objects, or prepositional phrases within it. We will learn about adverbs in a later lesson. Gerund phrases are italicized below.

Matching the colors proved impossible.
(gerund + direct object)

Effective governing will increase your popularity.
(adjective + gerund)

Luis likes *dancing with Liza.*
(gerund + prepositional phrase)

Below, we show how gerund phrases function in sentences:

SENTENCE SUBJECT:
Having spent his life in public service earned Gunning Bedford respect.

DIRECT OBJECT:
He favored *compromising on equal representation.*

OBJECT OF A PREPOSITION:
He devised a plan for *protecting his neighbors.*

PREDICATE NOUN:
His goal was *helping the cause of education.*

Example 2 Write the gerund phrase in each sentence. Then write whether the phrase functions as a sentence subject, direct object, object of a preposition, or a predicate noun.

(a) The politician's job is promoting fair legislation.

(b) Relieving poverty is a challenge.

(c) Do you have an idea for aiding the poor?

(d) Perhaps some regret having voted for me.

Solution (a) **Promoting fair legislation** functions as a predicate noun.

(b) **Relieving poverty** is the subject of the sentence.

(c) **Aiding the poor** is the object of the preposition "for."

(d) **Having voted for me** is the direct object of the sentence.

A noun or pronoun that precedes a gerund or gerund phrase, is possessive, for a gerund is a noun.

Her introducing the guests was punctilious.
(*Her introductions*)

Because of *Mimi's criticizing the cook,* no one ate.
(*Mimi's criticism*)

No one appreciates *our complaining.*
(*our complaints*)

Example 3 Choose the possessive noun or pronoun to precede each gerund phrase.

(a) They disapproved of (me, my) questioning their integrity.

(b) (Kerry, Kerry's) playing drums adds volume to the music.

(c) Jenny likes (us, our) decorating her room with flowers.

Solution (a) They disapproved of **my** questioning their integrity.

(b) **Kerry's** playing drums adds volume to the music.

(c) Jenny likes **our** decorating her room with flowers.

Practice For a–c, replace each blank with the correct vocabulary word.

a. The _____ atmosphere of the beach party alerted neighbors to potential danger.

b. His _____ statement left me wondering.

c. _____ means the same as bacchanalian.

For d–g, write the gerund phrase and tell how it functions in the sentence (subject, predicate nominative, direct object, or object of a preposition).

d. George Read favored protecting the interests of the smaller states.

e. Our wearing red, white, and blue on Wednesdays originated with Mrs. Welch.

f. Before holding any political positions, George Read practiced law in Philadelphia.

g. Kurt's favorite night time activity is reading mystery stories.

Choose the correct word to precede the gerund phrase in h–j.

h. Did they appreciate (him, his) speaking against the Stamp Act?

i. (You, Your) presenting a thorough biography of George Read gave me a picture of his political stance.

j. Annabel gets excited about (me, my) sharing the fascinating facts about the delegates.

For k–m, write whether the *-ing* word is a gerund (noun), participle (adjective), or verb.

k. Is presiding with humility possible?

l. He had been presiding for four years.

m. The presiding board member called the session to order.

More Practice Write each gerund phrase and tell whether it functions as a sentence subject, direct object, object of a preposition, or predicate noun.

1. Dale tried the old fashioned method of building furniture without nails.

2. Her snoring woke me.

3. They applauded her for telling the truth.

4. She denied spying on the British.

5. Spying on them would be foolish.

6. Thoreau placed great value on living simply.

7. Her passion was collecting antique spoons.

8. She resents his pestering her.

Review Set 55

Choose the correct word to complete sentences 1–10.

1. (Biannual, Biennial) means twice a year, or semiannual.
(54)

2. (Apollonian, Bacchanalian, Stentorian) means "frenzied, riotous, wanton, and debauched."
(33, 53)

3. A(n) (uninterested, disinterested) person is impartial, neutral, or dispassionate.
(52)

4. Consequential means (warlike, friendly, resultant).
(51)

5. To hector means to (guide, bully, agree).
(28)

6. I appreciate (you, your) sweeping the porch.
(53)

7. Our lawn is greener than (theirs, their's).
(53)

8. My tree has as (much, many) avocados as yours does.
(40)

9. Yesterday, their border collie (steal, steals, stole) our newspaper.
(49)

10. The border collie chasing butterflies is (her, she).
(36, 50)

11. Write whether the following is a complete sentence, sentence fragment, or run-on sentence: Edward Tudor and Tom Canty switch identities, Edward is not accustomed to a beggar's life.
(2)

12. Write whether the following is a phrase or a clause: singing a long song about working on a railroad
(20)

13. Rewrite this sentence, adding periods, commas, and capital letters and making necessary changes to abbreviations for formal writing: miss ogaz said "on sat nov 16 2003 i practiced my spanish dance steps watched a british movie and mopped the kitchen floor"
(25, 41)

Replace each blank with the correct word to complete sentences 14–16.

14. Clauses may be either independent or _____.
(54)

15. The _____ of a noun explains how the noun is used in a sentence.

16. Nouns and pronouns are in the _____ case when they are used as direct objects, indirect objects, or objects of a preposition.

17. For a–c, write whether the *-ing* word in each sentence is a verb, participle, or gerund.

   (a) Did the howling coyotes keep you awake last night?

   (b) The coyotes' howling kept me awake.

   (c) The coyotes have been howling every night this week.

18. From this sentence, write the verb phrase and label it transitive or intransitive: Miles Hendon, a kind-hearted nobleman, rescues Edward Tudor from the ridicule of the crowds.

19. From this sentence, write the verb phrase and name its tense: Next month, Phil will have been singing in the choir for six years.

20. Write the seven common coordinating conjunctions.

21. From this sentence, write the verb phrase and label it linking or action: Did the nobleman's brother assume control of the family business?

22. Write the plural of each noun.
   (a) eyelash   (b) box   (c) lily

23. Write the four principal parts of the irregular verb *wear*.

24. From this sentence, write the dependent clause, circling the subordinating conjunction: While Edward Tudor lives as a beggar, he witnesses the inhumanity of British justice.

25. Which sentence is more polite? Write A or B.
   A. Please call me and Jan.   B. Please call Jan and me.

26. Unscramble these words to make an interrogative sentence with a personal pronoun as a direct object:
   her   shall   we   recommend   Dudley   and

27. Rewrite the following as it is. Then add proofreading symbols to indicate corrections.

tom enjoy being prinse but is glad to give up up the throne after awhile

28. Rewrite this sentence so that it is in active voice: The living room was vacuumed by Robert.

Diagram sentences 29 and 30.

29. My neighbor Diana loaned me two cups of flour for the pie crust.

30. Having burned, the pie tasted dry and bitter.

LESSON 56   Participle Phrases • Diagramming Participle and Gerund Phrases

> **Dictation or Journal Entry**
>
> **Vocabulary:** *Flair* and *flare* are homophones, words with the same sound but with different spellings and meanings. *Flair* is a noun; *flare* is either a noun or a verb.
>
> *Flair* is perceptiveness, discernment, or a natural talent or aptitude. She has a *flair* for arranging her garden flowers into beautiful bouquets.
>
> A *flare* (noun) is a flame or bright blaze of light. *Flares* lined the highway to warn motorists of the road block.
>
> *Flare* (verb) means "to blaze with a sudden burst of flame" or "to burn brightly." The small flame *flared* when I blew on it.

We remember that participles are verbals that function as adjectives. Most participles end in "ing" or "ed," but some end in "en," "d," or "t." They have three tenses:

PRESENT:	flaring, enveloping
PAST:	flared, enveloped
PERFECT:	having flared, having enveloped

Participle Phrases   A **participle phrase** contains a participle and its objects and modifiers. It is used as an adjective to modify a noun or pronoun. Participle phrases are italicized in the sentences below.

Protected by wealth and influence, Richard Bassett enjoyed local political popularity.
   (modifies "Richard Bassett")

Having been abandoned by his parents, he was raised by a wealthy kinsman.
   (modifies "he")

Flaring with each gust of wind, the fire raged out of control.
   (modifies "fire")

A newscaster in a helicopter photographed flames *enveloping the canyon*.
   (modifies "flames")

Before trying to identify a participle phrase, we first find the simple subject and simple predicate of the sentence. Then we look for the participle phrase.

simple subject ↓   ↓ simple predicate
   Richard Bassett <u>favored</u> laws protecting the local citizens.

In the sentence above, "protecting the local citizens" is a participle phrase modifying "laws."

We may find a participle phrase either before or after the word it modifies. A sentence becomes confusing if there are too many words between the participle phrase and the word it modifies.

Richard missed his family *sitting on the bench.* (Who is sitting on the bench, Richard or his family?)

This is easier to understand:

Sitting on the bench, Richard missed his family.

Example 1 For each sentence, write the participle phrase and the noun or pronoun that it modifies.

(a) Following the leadership of John Dickinson, Richard Bassett was one of the most loyal Federalists.

(b) Using his presidential authority, John Adams named Richard Bassett as one of the notorious "midnight judges."

(c) Democratic-Republicans, elected to office, abolished Richard Bassett's seat on the U. S. Circuit Court.

Solution (a) **Following the leadership of John Dickinson** modifies **Richard Bassett.**

(b) **Using his presidential authority** modifies **John Adams.**

(c) **Elected to office** modifies **Democratic-Republicans.**

Diagramming Participle and Gerund Phrases

THE PARTICIPLE PHRASE

We diagram the participle phrase under the word it modifies.

Leading an abolition movement, Richard Bassett freed his slaves.

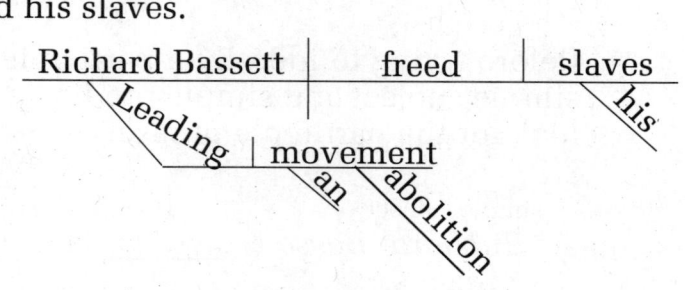

THE GERUND PHRASE

We diagram the gerund phrase to show how the gerund functions in the sentence.

Rehearsing for a speech gives the speaker more confidence.

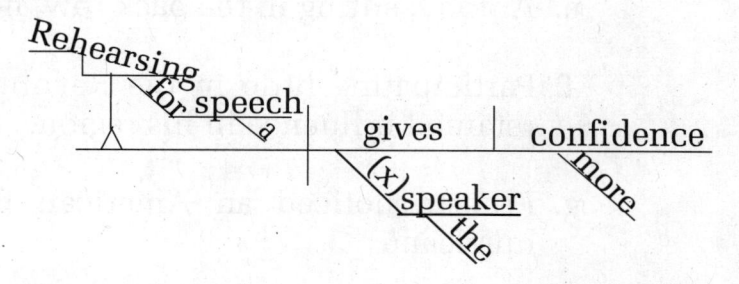

Example 2 Diagram each sentence.

(a) Her flair was decorating a home.

(b) Complementing the red carpet, the curtains were blue and yellow.

Solution (a)

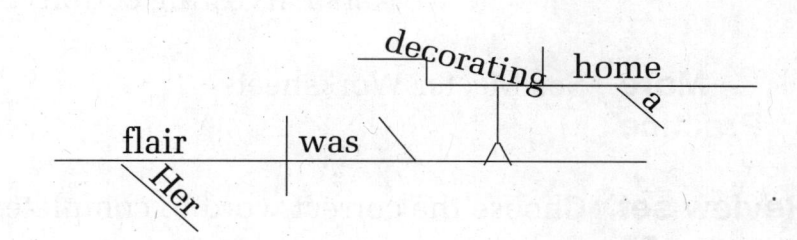

(b)

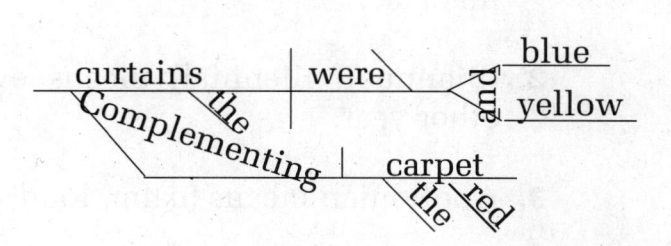

Practice For a–d, replace each blank with the correct vocabulary word.

a. When wind fans campfires, they often _____ brightly.

b. Richard Bassett's _____ for politics resulted in his term as a U.S. Senator.

c. A _____ shot into the sky signaled the beginning of the firework display.

d. _____ are words with the same sound but with different spellings and meanings.

For e–h, write the participle phrase and the noun or pronoun it modifies.

e. Antony, sitting in the back row, never said a word.

f. Participating little in the Revolution, Jacob Broom still retained influence in his region.

g. Ernesto noticed an American flag torn by the fierce hurricane.

h. The tourist admired Delaware's first cotton mill, built by Jacob Bloom.

Diagram sentences i and j.

i. Building a cotton mill required ingenuity.

j. The workers harvesting cotton look weary.

More Practice See Master Worksheets.

Review set 56 Choose the correct word to complete sentences 1–11.

1. (Delphic, Dionysian, Bacchanalian) means ambiguous, or unclear.
   (53, 55)

2. (Biannual, Biennial) means every two years, or every other year.
   (54)

3. Apollonian means (calm, loud, frenzied).
   (53)

4. A(n) (uninterested, disinterested) person is indifferent and unconcerned.
   (52)

5. A filibuster is a method of (speeding, helping, delaying) legislative action.
   (29)

6. When used as the subject of a sentence, a noun or pronoun is in the (nominative, objective) case.
   (50)

7. Has Elmer (wore, worn) those same socks every day this week?
   (49)

8. This briefcase is mine; (your's, yours) is under that chair.

9. The present participle of a verb functioning as a noun is a(n) (infinitive, gerund, preposition).

10. The executor of the estate will apportion the funds among the siblings and (he, him).

11. Which is the (more, most) complete of the two agendas?

12. Write the plural of each noun.
(a) Abby (b) caddy (c) grant-in-aid

13. Write each predicate adjective in this sentence: Frederic Henry, an American soldier, was young and handsome.

14. In this sentence, write the verb phrase and name its tense: Frederic Henry was returning to the Italian front.

15. Write four pairs of correlative conjunctions.

16. Rewrite this sentence so that it is in active voice: A British nurse was met by Lieutenant Rinaldi.

17. Write whether the following is a phrase or a clause: to hide their mutual attraction

18. In this sentence, write the verb and label it transitive or intransitive: World War I affected the soldiers in different ways.

19. In this sentence, write the verb and label it action or linking: Rinaldi became discouraged and ill.

20. Write the four principal parts of the irregular verb *drink*.

21. Rewrite the following, adding periods, commas, and capital letters and making necessary changes to abbreviations for formal writing:

dear professor droner

on thurs nov 13 2003 you gave a lecture titled "the social and cultural history of the ancient world" I do not remember the last half of it

regretfully

ms snoozer

22. Use an appositive to make one sentence from these two
(42) sentences: The Nile is the longest river in the world. The
Nile flows north through Egypt and empties into the
Mediterranean Sea.

23. Write the objective case, third person plural pronoun.
(51)

24. In this sentence, write each pronoun and its antecedent:
(46) Malia said she would leave her gila monster at home.

25. Rewrite the following as it is. Then add proofreading
(32) symbols to indicate corrections.
Frederic desserts the italian army and trys two find
Catherine

26. Write whether this sentence is true or false: Possessive
(53) pronouns have apostrophes.

27. In this sentence, write the dependent clause, circling the
(54) subordinating conjunction: As the police chased
Frederic, he and Catherine fled to Switzerland.

Diagram sentences 28–30.

28. I saw Benito sneaking some food for a snack.
(21, 55)

29. Snatching a bag of carrots, he left me the cookies, chips,
(30, 55) and soda.

30. Nourishing his body was Benito's goal.
(36, 55)

LESSON 57

Reflexive and Intensive Personal Pronouns

> **Dictation or Journal Entry**
>
> **Vocabulary:** The adjectives *jovial* and *mercurial* come from the names of Roman gods.
>
> The Romans' chief god was Jove, or Jupiter. Although his anger could destroy someone instantly, Jove was generally a fatherly, sociable, and cheerful figure. Therefore, the word *jovial* means merry, jolly, and mirthful. The card pictured Santa Claus with his *jovial* countenance.
>
> The ancient Roman god Mercury was a speedy messenger with winged cap and sandals, who was thought to be eloquent and clever. The planet Mercury was so named because it is the fastest, and the liquid metal was named mercury because it is nearly impossible to hold. The word *mercurial* came to mean unpredictable, changeable, volatile, and fickle. The saleswoman's *mercurial* temperament made friendships with other employees difficult.

Reflexive Personal Pronouns

Reflexive pronouns end in "-self" or "-selves." A reflexive pronoun throws the action back upon the subject of the sentence. It is a necessary part of the sentence and cannot be omitted. **The antecedent of a reflexive pronoun is always the subject of the sentence.** The singular reflexive pronouns are *myself, yourself, himself, herself,* and *itself.*

A delegate may not appoint *himself*.

You will reward *yourself* if you work hard.

The plural reflexive pronouns are *ourselves, yourselves,* and *themselves.*

Can babies protect *themselves*?

We have acquainted *ourselves* with each candidate.

Like all pronouns, reflexive pronouns match their antecedents in person, number, and gender; are used as direct objects, indirect objects, and objects of a preposition; and are diagrammed like this:

INDIRECT OBJECT:

Gia built *herself* a log cabin.

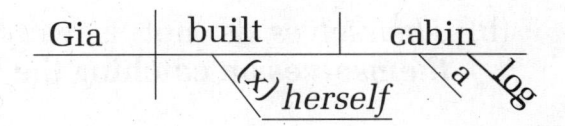

```
Gia  |  built  |  cabin
           \(×) herself    \a \log
```

www.saxonhomeschool.com
©Houghton Mifflin Harcourt Publishers, Inc.

349

Grammar and Writing 8
Student Edition, 9781419098581

DIRECT OBJECT:
Lorenzo injured *himself*.

Lorenzo | injured | *himself*

OBJECT OF A PREPOSITION:
Delegates were bickering among *themselves*.

Delegates | were bickering
　　　　　　among *themselves*

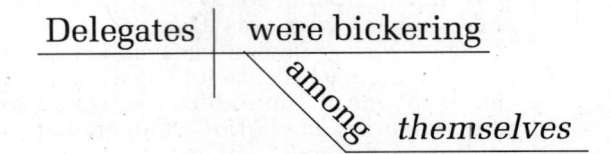

Errors to Avoid We do not use *hisself* and *theirselves*. They are not words.

NO: Jacob Broom chastised *hisself*.
YES: Jacob Broom chastised *himself*.

NO: They presented *theirselves* as reasonable men.
YES: They presented *themselves* as reasonable men.

We do not use reflexive pronouns in place of the simple personal pronoun.

NO: Maricruz and *myself* will feed the sheep.
YES: Maricruz and *I* will feed the sheep.

Example 1 Choose the correct personal pronoun for each sentence.

(a) Sarah and (myself, I) researched Jacob Broom.

(b) Naomi and Rita prided (theirselves, themselves) on catching the largest bass in the lake.

Solution (a) We do not use a reflexive pronoun in place of a personal pronoun. **Sarah and *I* researched Jacob Broom.**

(b) *Theirselves* is not a word. **Naomi and Rita prided *themselves* on catching the largest bass in the lake.**

Intensive Personal Pronouns **Intensive personal pronouns** have the same form as reflexive personal pronouns. However, they are used to emphasize or intensify another noun or pronoun. We can leave the intensive pronoun out of a sentence without changing the meaning of the sentence. The antecedent is whatever word the intensive pronoun emphasizes; it need not be the subject of the sentence. Notice that the sentences below make sense without the intensive pronoun.

The librarian *herself* designed the shelves.

Kim and Kay *themselves* carried the luggage.

I'll slice the pie *myself.*

Can you find the information *yourself*?

Again, we do not use *hisself* and *theirselves.* They are not words. Also, we do not replace simple personal pronouns with intensive pronouns.

We diagram intensive personal pronouns like this:

You must shear the sheep *yourselves.*

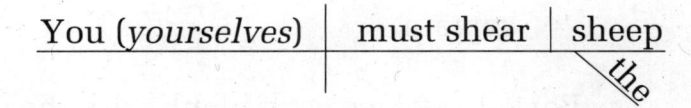

| You (*yourselves*) | must shear | sheep |

They harvested the corn *themselves.*

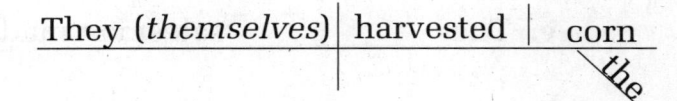

| They (*themselves*) | harvested | corn |

Example 2 Choose the correct personal pronoun for each sentence.

(a) Mabel and I will scrutinize the records (ourself, ourselves).

(b) Washington (hisself, himself) led the troops to victory.

(c) Perhaps the hikers will blaze a new trail (*theirselves, themselves*).

Solution (a) The intensive pronoun must be plural because its antecedent is plural. **Mabel and I will scrutinize the records *ourselves.***

(b) *Hisself* is not a word. **Washington *himself* led the troops to victory.**

(c) *Theirselves* is not a word. **Perhaps the hikers will blaze a new trail *themselves.***

Practice Choose the correct personal pronoun for sentences a–d.

    a. Neither Fritz nor (myself, I) realized that Luther Martin was an old Whig and legalist.

    b. Luther Martin wrote *The Genuine Information* (hisself, himself).

    c. (You, Yourself) may visit Mount Vernon, the home and tomb of George Washington.

    d. While in Philadelphia, they aligned (theirselves, themselves) with the Antifederalists.

    e. Diagram this sentence: Martin himself defended the captain.

For f–i, replace each blank with the correct vocabulary word.

    f. Did a _____ temperament cause Alexander Hamilton to enter a duel with Aaron Burr?

    g. The _____ salesman made people laugh.

    h. A _____ person is happy.

    i. A _____ personality is changeable and unpredictable.

More Practice Choose the correct personal pronoun for each sentence.

    1. Luther Martin (himself, hisself) said that only "total ignorance of human nature" could justify a strong central government.

    2. Antifederalists agreed among (theirselves, themselves).

    3. They attempted to settle the dilemma (theirself, themselves).

    4. Hansel and (I, myself) outlined the major points of the New Jersey Plan.

    5. Horatio showed Elisa and (me, myself) a book about the British monarchy.

    6. I think Sylvia and Frank ate the whole pie (theirselves, themselves).

7. Samuel Chase and (he, himself) grew interested in the politics of transition.

8. Luther Martin delivered fifty-three speeches (hisself, himself) at the Constitutional Convention.

9. He and John Mercer refused to sign the Constitution (theirselves, themselves), but other Antifederalists did.

10. I believe Mr. Martin and (she, herself) tried to restrain the Tories in Maryland.

Review Set 57

Choose the correct word to complete sentences 1–9.

1. *Flair* and *flare* are (synonyms, antonyms, homophones).
(56)

2. (Delphic, Apollonian, Dionysian) means Bacchanalian, or frenzied.
(53, 55)

3. To phase is to (lobby, introduce, filibuster) in stages.
(30)

4. A (nestor, hector, cicerone) is a leader in his or her field.
(28, 31)

5. Conscientious means "guided by (conscience, hedonism, Cicero).
(32)

6. A (first, second, third) person pronoun indicates the speaker.
(48)

7. *You* and *yours* are (first, second, third) person pronouns.
(48)

8. Both Pam and (him, he) were eager to board the train.
(48, 50)

9. That judicious comment was (her's, hers).
(48, 53)

10. Write the plural of each noun.
(10, 11) (a) louse   (b) Nancy   (c) trench

11. Rewrite the following sentence, adding periods, commas, and capital letters and making necessary changes to abbreviations for formal writing.
(9, 31)

my aunt and i sailed on a junk down the yangtze r in china last fri the seventh of oct

12. Rewrite this sentence so that it is in active voice: Those reservoirs were built by the ancient Egyptians.
(27)

13. Write the seven common coordinating conjunctions.
(33)

14. In this sentence, write the verb phrase and label it action
(3, 18) or linking: At the end of *A Farewell to Arms*, Frederic is wandering the streets in despair.

15. From this list, write the two sentence types that may end
(1) with a period: interrogative, exclamatory, imperative, declarative

16. Rewrite the following as it is. Then add proofreading
(32) symbols to indicate corrections.

Dr Payne did my foot sergury did he do your's also?

17. From this sentence, write the personal pronoun and
(52) name its case: The pet owl traveling with Florence Nightingale was hers.

18. In this sentence, write the verb phrase and label it
(21, 26) transitive or intransitive: Widening into a broad delta, the Ganges River flows into the Indian Ocean.

19. Write whether the following is a phrase or a clause:
(20) breaking into the dean's office to check on grades

20. In this sentence, write the dependent clause, circling the
(54) subordinating conjunction: Even though Fidel Castro is the communist national leader of Cuba, Juanita, his sister, is an ardent anti-communist.

21. Which sentence is more polite? Write A or B.
(28, 51)
   A. The envelope was addressed to me and him.
   B. The envelope was addressed to him and me.

22. Write whether the following is a complete sentence,
(2) sentence fragment, or run-on sentence: Archbishop of Krakow, Pope John Paul II.

23. Write each possessive pronoun from this list: your,
(53) they're, his, her's, it's, its, their, you're

24. Choose the possessive noun or pronoun to precede the
(16, 53) gerund phrase in this sentence: (Grandpa, Grandpa's) whistling drove Hamoon crazy.

25. Write the superlative form of the adjective *jovial*.
(39)

26. Write the four principal parts of the irregular verb *ring*.
(13, 49)

27. Use an appositive to make one sentence from these two sentences: The Volga River begins north of Moscow, Russia, and flows into the Caspian Sea. The Volga River is the longest in Europe.
(42)

Diagram sentences 28–30.

28. My cousin Dale bought himself a run-down house to repair.
(42, 56)

29. Having sanded the front door, Dale prepared to paint.
(21, 56)

30. Will restoring old homes become his livelihood?
(36, 55)

LESSON 58

The Comma, Part 4: Descriptive Adjectives, Dependent Clauses

> **Dictation or Journal Entry**
> **Vocabulary:** We often see the words *libel* and *slander* together. Let us clarify their meanings.
>
> *Slander* is the act or crime of uttering a false and malicious statement about another person that is damaging to that person's reputation or well-being. Rumors full of *slander* hurt the politician's chances for re-election.
>
> *Libel* is the act or crime of damaging a person's reputation by way of pictures, signs, or written or printed words. The politician sued the local newspaper for *libel*.

We remember that commas indicate the natural pauses in our speech. Let us review other uses for commas.

Descriptive Adjectives We use a comma to separate two or more **descriptive adjectives.** In the sentence below, we use a comma to separate the two descriptive adjectives, "tireless" and "energetic."

> The *tireless, energetic* Luther Martin became an eminent lawyer in America.

However, if one adjective is a color, we do not use a comma to separate it from another adjective.

> The *old-fashioned black* dress of Luther Martin was a familiar sight on the streets of Baltimore.

One way to decide whether a comma is needed is to insert the word "and" between the adjectives.

> IF YOU COULD SAY: It was a *chilly and blustery* day.
> YOU DO NEED A COMMA: It was a *chilly, blustery* day.
>
> YOU WOULDN'T SAY: She had *short and brown* hair.
> SO YOU DON'T NEED A COMMA: She had *short brown* hair.

Example 1 Insert commas where they are needed in the sentences below.

(a) The coarse braided white wigs worn by the colonists lost popularity in time.

(b) Luther Martin gave Sir William Howe a fervent thoughtful response.

Solution (a) We place a comma between the two adjectives "coarse" and "braided," but we do not place a comma before the color adjective "white."

The *coarse, braided white* wigs worn by the colonists lost popularity in time.

(b) We separate the adjectives "fervent" and "thoughtful" with a comma.

Martin gave Sir William Howe a *fervent, thoughtful* response.

Dependent Clauses We remember that a **dependent clause** cannot stand alone, while an independent clause, or main clause, makes sense without the dependent clause. We use a comma after a **dependent clause** when it comes before the main clause.

Because he served so long, Luther Martin is a legend.
    (DEPENDENT CLAUSE)   (INDEPENDENT/MAIN CLAUSE)

However, we do not use a comma when the dependent clause follows the main clause.

Luther Martin is a legend because he served so long.
(INDEPENDENT/MAIN CLAUSE)   (DEPENDENT CLAUSE)

Example 2 Insert commas if needed in the sentences below.

(a) Since he had access to scholarly resources as attorney general he undertook a careful and profound study of law.

(b) He became a leading attorney in Maryland because he had gained so much knowledge.

Solution (a) We place a comma after the dependent clause, "Since he had access to scholarly resources as attorney general," because it comes before the main clause.

Since he had access to scholarly resources as attorney general, he undertook a careful and profound study of law.

(b) No comma is needed in this sentence, because the dependent clause follows the main clause.

Practice Rewrite sentences a–c, and insert commas to separate descriptive adjectives.

a. The preoccupied near-sighted Luther Martin bumped into a cow, tipped his hat, and apologized.

b. A disgusted disillusioned delegate left the convention early.

c. Frequent red flags warned the Antifederalists of the futility in opposing the Constitution.

Rewrite sentences d–f, and insert a comma after each dependent clause.

d. Because Luther Martin supported Samuel Chase some scholars believe he opposed the Constitution for financial reasons.

e. Even though this seems reasonable other scholars believe otherwise.

f. While some people doubted his motives he actually had good intentions.

For g and h, replace each blank with the correct vocabulary word.

g. Some Tories used _____ in pamphlets to create disgust toward the Patriots.

h. When running for political office, it is tempting for politicians to give speeches full of _____ to discredit their opponents.

More Practice

See Master Worksheets.

Review Set 58

Choose the correct word to complete sentences 1–10.

1. (Jovial, Mercurial, Dionysian) means merry, jolly, and mirthful.
(55, 57)

2. (Flair, Flare) is perceptiveness, discernment, or natural talent.
(56)

3. Delphic means (unclear, loud, frenzied).
(55)

4. Bacchanalian means (calm, serene, frenzied).
(53)

5. Greta is uninterested; she is (unconcerned, impartial, neutral).
(52)

6. Please accompany Simon and (myself, me) to the county fair.
(21, 51)

7. Could a pirate have moved that heavy treasure chest (hisself, himself)?
(57)

8. *She, her,* and *hers* are (first, second, third) person
(52) pronouns.

9. I sent an email to Luis and (he, him).
(28, 51)

10. This travel itinerary is (their's, theirs), not (our's, ours).
(53)

11. Write the plural of each noun.
(10, 11)
(a) itinerary   (b) letter of credit   (c) placebo

12. Rewrite the following letter, adding periods, commas,
(9, 47) and capital letters and making necessary changes to
abbreviations for formal writing.

dear uncle william

officer green's salad i believe calls for one lb of chopped spinach one tsp of crushed garlic and three california peppers i hope you enjoy it

love

sal

13. In the following sentence, write each prepositional
(14, 28) phrase, starring the object of each preposition:

According to the encyclopedia, the duck-billed platypus lives along the bank of a river in Australia.

14. Write the reflexive pronoun in this sentence:
(57)

In *The Old Man and the Sea*, Santiago prides himself in his skill and discipline.

15. Write whether the following sentence is declarative,
(1) imperative, interrogative, or exclamatory:

Work quickly but carefully.

16. Write the adjective that should be omitted from the
(44) following sentence:

Professor Droner is the kind of a teacher whom most people avoid.

17. From this sentence, write each personal pronoun and
(48, 50) name its case:

He admires Joe DiMaggio for his athletic skill and discipline.

18. In the following sentence, write the verb phrase and label it transitive or intransitive:

Does Professor Droner speak in a monotone?

19. Rewrite the following as it is. Then add proofreading symbols to indicate corrections.

Young Manolin brang food an bait to to Santiago's shack

20. In the following sentence, write the dependent clause, circling the subordinating conjunction:

Santiago dreams of lions whenever he falls asleep.

21. Rewrite the following sentence so that it is in active voice:

The closing hymn was sung by a baritone.

22. Write whether the following is a complete sentence, sentence fragment, or run-on sentence:

Santiago hooks a lavender marlin it is the biggest fish he has ever seen!

23. Write the gerund phrase in this sentence:

The huge marlin continues towing the boat.

24. Choose the possessive noun or pronoun to precede the gerund phrase in the following sentence:

I appreciate (Tom, Tom's) cleaning the chicken coop every day.

25. Write the comparative form of the adjective *silly*.

26. Write the four principal parts of the verb *wrap*.

27. Use an appositive to make one sentence from these two sentences:

A delta is a broad, fan-shaped deposit of mud and sand.

Flowing into the Indian Ocean, the Ganges River widens into a delta.

Diagram sentences 28–30.

28. Did your dog Penny eat the entire cheesecake herself?
(21, 42)

29. Having consumed the whole cheesecake, Penny burped.
(24, 56)

30. Training a frisky beagle with a mind of its own proved difficult.
(36, 56)

LESSON 59

Compound Sentences • Coordinating Conjunctions

> **Dictation or Journal Entry**
> **Vocabulary:** The Greek root *amphi-* and the Latin root *ambi-* mean "on both sides" or "around." We see these roots in familiar words such as <u>amphi</u>bian, <u>amphi</u>theater, and <u>ambi</u>guous.
> *Ambivalent* means "having conflicting feelings or attitudes about an object, person, or idea." *Ambivalent* about the measure, Harry could not decide how to vote.
> *Ambidextrous* means "able to use both the right and left hands with equal ease." An *ambidextrous* pitcher gives a baseball team more options when facing a good hitter.
> *Ambient* means "completely surrounding; encompassing." The *ambient* noises might interfere with a student's ability to concentrate.

Compound Sentences Two or more simple sentences (independent clauses) joined by a connecting word like *and*, *or*, or *but* form a compound sentence. Only sentences closely related in thought can be joined to form a compound sentence. Below, we connect two simple sentences to form a compound sentence.

TWO SIMPLE SENTENCES:

Luther Martin proposed the electoral college.

He opposed the reelection of presidents.

ONE COMPOUND SENTENCE:

Luther Martin proposed the electoral college, but he opposed the reelection of presidents.

Here we diagram the simple subjects and simple predicates of the compound sentence above:

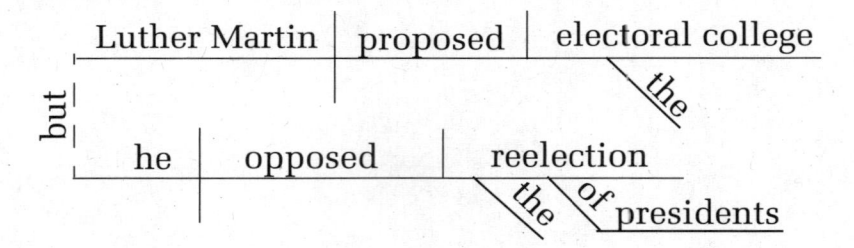

```
        Luther Martin | proposed | electoral college
                                          \the
     but
        he | opposed | reelection
                          \the \of presidents
```

Notice that the compound sentence is made up of two independent clauses which can each stand alone and make sense. Remember that any number of independent clauses can be joined to form a compound sentence. For example, here we join four independent clauses (simple sentences) to form one compound sentence:

Sergio arrived early, and Ilbea came on time, but Liz was a little late, and Bill never showed up at all.

Coordinating Conjunctions

A **coordinating conjunction** may join two simple sentences to form a compound sentence. We have learned that the following are coordinating conjunctions:

    and but or nor for yet so

Notice how coordinating conjunctions are used in the compound sentences below.

AND INDICATES ADDITIONAL INFORMATION:
The ambidextrous painter used two brushes, **and** her colors ran together.

BUT SHOWS CONTRAST:
The critters created ambient commotion, **but** Debby slept through it.

OR SHOWS A CHOICE:
Ambivalent representatives must make up their minds, **or** they will lose votes in the next election.

Conjunctions may also connect the parts of a compound subject or predicate. Do not confuse a compound subject or a compound predicate with a compound sentence. Remember that a compound sentence has both a subject and a predicate on each side of the conjunction. A compound sentence follows this pattern:

subject predicate, (conjunction) *subject* predicate
Ann should study, (or) *she* might fail.
Martha is working, (but) *Mary* is sitting.
Tom washed windows, (and) *Jacob* dusted tables.

Example 1 Tell whether each sentence is simple or compound. If it is compound, write the coordinating conjunction which joins the two independent clauses.

(a) James McHenry had many possessions, but his wealth was inherited.

(b) He came from a prosperous family, and he looked like a gentleman.

(c) James McHenry practiced medicine for a short while and served under the redoubtable Dr. Benjamin Rush.

(d) Most Ulster Presbyterians resented British authority, so the Stamp Act gave them a real excuse to rebel.

Solution   (a) We find a subject and a predicate on each side of the conjunction: *James McHenry* <u>had</u> (conjunction), *wealth* <u>was</u>. Therefore, the sentence is **compound**. The coordinating conjunction **but** joins the two independent clauses.

(b) This sentence is **compound**. It consists of two independent clauses joined by the coordinating conjunction **and**.

(c) This is a **simple** sentence. It is a single, independent clause with one subject (James McHenry) and a compound predicate (practiced/served).

(d) This is a **compound** sentence. Two independent clauses are joined by the coordinating conjunction **so**.

Diagramming   To diagram the simple subjects and simple predicates of a compound sentence, we follow these steps:

1. Diagram each simple sentence, one below the other.
2. Join the two sentences with a dotted line on the left side.
3. Write the conjunction on the dotted line.

Below, we diagram the simple subjects and simple predicates of this compound sentence:

Allison enjoys surfing, for she is athletic.

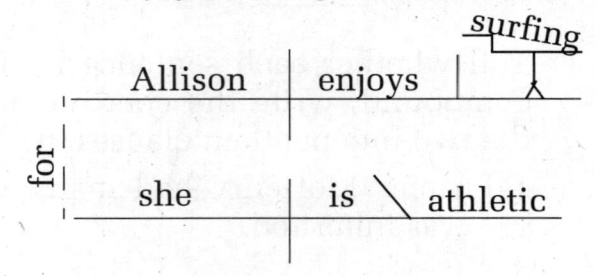

```
                           surfing
        Allison  |  enjoys  | /\
     _|_____
    |
 for|
    |_____
        she      |  is  \  athletic
```

Example 2   Diagram this compound sentence:

James McHenry remained a Federalist, but many of his associates became Democratic-Republicans.

Solution   We diagram the simple subject and simple predicate of each simple sentence and place them one below the other. Then we join them with a dotted line on which we write the coordinating conjunction, "but."

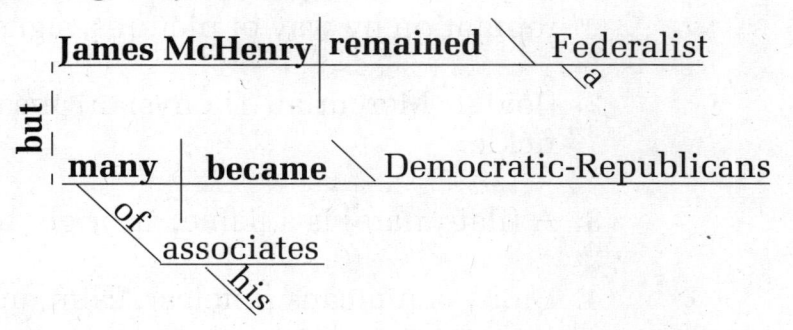

```
    James McHenry | remained \ Federalist
                              \a
but
    many | became \ Democratic-Republicans
         \of
          \associates
           \his
```

Practice For a–e, tell whether each sentence is simple or compound. If it is compound, write the coordinating conjunction which joins the two or more independent clauses.

a. Daniel of St. Thomas Jenifer befriended those in authority and represented Maryland's aristocracy.

b. He served the public, yet he sought chances for promotion.

c. Daniel of St. Thomas Jenifer had a flair for hospitality, so he threw wonderful parties.

d. Missy visited the old plantation, but she didn't see any tobacco fields.

e. Frivolous yet dignified aristocrats waltzed to the minuet and chatted amongst themselves.

f. Following Example 2, diagram this compound sentence:

The train has arrived, so we must depart.

For g–j, replace each blank with the correct vocabulary word.

g The roots *amphi-* and _____ mean "on both sides" or "around."

h. The troops knew they were in grave danger because of the _____ enemy strongholds.

i. The _____ author held a pen in each hand.

j. Max did not know whether to trust me or not; he was _____.

Review Set 59 Choose the correct word to complete sentences 1–10.

1. (Slander, Libel) is the crime of damaging a person's reputation by way of pictures, signs, or written words.
  ⁽⁵⁸⁾

2. (Jovial, Mercurial, Dionysian) means unpredictable and fickle.
  ⁽⁵⁵, ⁵⁷⁾

3. A (flair, flare) is a flame, or bright blaze of light.
  ⁽⁵⁶⁾

4. Dionysian means (unclear, calm, unrestrained).
  ⁽⁵⁵⁾

5. The word (stentorian, Spartan, contemptuous) means simple, frugal, and disciplined.
  ⁽¹³, ³³⁾

6. Alex and (me, myself, I) counted seven foreign ambassadors at the World's Fair.
  ⁽⁴⁸, ⁵⁰⁾

7. Did Amanda and Alfred build that tool shed (theirselves, themselves)?
  ⁽⁵⁷⁾

8. *I, me, we, us, mine,* and *ours* are (first, second, third) person pronouns.
  ⁽⁵²⁾

9. Bryon sent flowers to Kay and (she, her) on Mother's Day.
  ⁽²⁸, ⁵¹⁾

10. That noisy rooster was (yours, your's), not (ours, our's).
  ⁽⁵³⁾

11. Write whether this sentence is simple or compound: Grumbling about the high prices and the drab colors, Meg stomped out of the clothing store.
  ⁽⁵⁹⁾

12. Write the plural of each noun.
  ⁽¹⁰, ¹¹⁾ (a) platypus   (b) zero   (c) mousetrap

13. Rewrite the following, adding periods, commas, and capital letters as needed:
  ⁽⁹, ⁴⁷⁾
    after she had shaken hands with a hundred people at the reception ms li wanted to get out of her sunday suit toe-pinching high heels and heavy clip-on earrings

14. Write the intensive personal pronoun in this sentence: Does Santiago see the sharks himself?
  ⁽⁵⁷⁾

15. Write the adjective that should be omitted from this sentence: I thought the both of them had lost their minds!
  ⁽⁴⁴⁾

16. From this sentence, write the personal pronoun and name its case: Santiago uses his spear on the marlin, which has fought for three days.
₍₅₂₎

17. In this sentence, write the verb phrase and label it transitive or intransitive: Are hammerheads and other sharks devouring the marlin?
_(21, 26)

18. Rewrite the following as it is. Then add proofreading symbols to indicate corrections.
₍₃₂₎

the next morning, the othre fisher men finded the skeleton off the marlin

19. In this sentence, write the dependent clause, circling the subordinating conjunction: When the smoke alarm went off, Dudley knew his frozen pizza was ready.
₍₅₄₎

20. Rewrite this sentence so that it is in active voice: That pizza with the crispy crust was baked by Dudley.
₍₂₇₎

21. Write whether the following is a complete sentence, sentence fragment, or run-on sentence: Scoundrels gloating over other people's calamity.
₍₂₎

22. Write the infinitive phrase in this sentence: More than anything else, Santiago wanted to catch the big marlin.
_(45, 56)

23. Write the participial phrase in this sentence: Noah and his three sons built an ark of cypress wood coated with pitch.
₍₅₆₎

24. Write the gerund phrase in this sentence: Again, Santiago begins dreaming about lions.
_(28, 56)

25. Write the superlative form of the adjective *peaceful*.
₍₃₉₎

26. Write the four principal parts of the verb *envelop*.
_(13, 49)

27. Use an appositive to make one sentence from these two sentences: Tchaikovsky was a Russian composer. Tchaikovsky wrote a famous ballet called *The Nutcracker*.
₍₄₂₎

28. Write each noun from this sentence and circle those that are abstract: This book contains themes of courage, endurance, and noble suffering.
(4)

Diagram sentences 29–30.

29. Noah had work to do.
(21, 56)

30. He and his three sons built an ark of cypress wood coated with pitch.
(21, 56)

LESSON 60

The Comma, Part 5: Compound Sentences, Direct Quotations

> **Dictation or Journal Entry**
> **Vocabulary:** The words *tortuous* and *torturous* look similar but have different meanings.
> *Tortuous* means full of bends, twists, and turns. The hikers found the *tortuous* trail difficult to follow.
> *Torturous* means painful and agonizing. The prisoners endured *torturous* treatment at the hands of the enemy.

Compound Sentences We remember that two sentences or independent clauses joined by a coordinating conjunction (*and, but, or, for, nor, yet, so*) is called a compound sentence. We place a comma after the first independent clause and before the coordinating conjunction in a compound sentence.

> The tortuous path climbed upward, *and* Lilly was out of breath.

> Lilly finished the marathon, *but* the last few miles were torturous.

We have memorized these *coordinating conjunctions*, which signal the need for a comma in a compound sentence.

> and   but   or   nor   for   yet   so

Example 1 Identify the coordinating conjunction in each compound sentence.

(a) A stronger central government could end the chaos, but it might oppress the people.

(b) Daniel Carroll favored property protection, for he owned a lucrative tobacco plantation.

(c) The aristocrat had a voice of authority in Maryland, so people listened to him.

Solution (a) **but**   (b) **for**   (c) **so**

Example 2 Insert a comma before the coordinating conjunction to separate the two independent clauses in the sentences below.

(a) Daniel Carroll disliked the idea of revolution yet he helped to gather supplies for the American troops.

(b) The Patriots must discipline themselves or the British will defeat them.

We place a comma after the first independent clause and before the coordinating conjunction.

(a) Daniel Carroll disliked the idea of revolution, *yet* he helped to gather supplies for the American troops.

(b) The Patriots must discipline themselves, *or* the British will defeat them.

Direct Quotations We use a comma or commas to offset the exact words of a writer or speaker, a **direct quotation**, from the rest of the sentence.

Great Grandma Parrot explained, "My father was a Loyalist, so he fought on the side of the British."

"However," she continued, "my husband joined the Patriots."

"I felt rather ambivalent during the war," she said.

Notice that the comma stays next to the word it follows. If a comma follows a direct quote, the comma goes inside the quotation marks.

YES: "This is boring," said Stephen.
NO: "This is boring", said Stephen.

Example 3 Rewrite sentences a and b, and insert commas as needed to separate direct quotations.

(a) "After his European travels" shared Professor Erudite "Daniel Carroll married and settled down on the plantation."

(b) "He wanted a new constitution rather than a revision of the Articles of Confederation" said the professor.

Solution (a) We use commas to set apart the professor's words.

"After his European travels," shared Professor Erudite, "Daniel Carroll married and settled down on the plantation."

(b) We place a comma after the professor's words.

"He wanted a new constitution rather than a revision of the Articles of Confederation," said the professor.

Practice   a. List the seven coordinating conjunctions.

For b–d, write the coordinating conjunction in each sentence.
  b. The Articles of Confederation failed, for the government had too little power.

  c. Daniel Carroll did not seek fame, yet he spoke on twenty occasions at the Constitutional Convention.

  d. He never desired a political office, and he shunned serious politics.

Rewrite sentences e and f, and insert a comma before a coordinating conjunction in a compound sentence.
  e. Passionate Federalists lived in Maryland but there were ardent Antifederalists as well.

  f. Samuel Chase spoke against the Constitution so Daniel Carroll replied to him in the article, "A Friend to the Constitution."

Rewrite sentences g and h, and insert commas to separate direct quotations.
  g. "John Francis Mercer" writes M. E. Bradford "was an ardent Antifederalist connected with the Samuel Chase faction in Maryland."

  h. Mr. VanLeeuwen said "John Francis Mercer even viewed the Articles of Confederation as a threat to state sovereignty."

For i–l, replace each blank with the correct vocabulary word.
  i. The course of the river was not straight; it was _____, curving around hills and meandering through meadows.

  j. Climbing a rocky cliff barefoot would be _____.

  k. _____ means twisted.

  l. _____ means painful.

More Practice   See Master Worksheets. Insert commas where they are needed in these sentences.

Review set 60 Choose the correct word or root to complete sentences 1–11.

1. The Latin root (*sequi-, ambi-, tract-*) means "on both sides" or "around."

2. (Slander, Libel) is the crime of saying something that damages a person's reputation.

3. Jovial means (unpredictable, sad, merry).

4. To (flair, flare) is to burn brightly.

5. The drama group included Nien, Liezl, Naomi, (*etc., et al.*).

6. The students designed the science laboratory (theirselves, themselves).

7. The plan appeared ludicrous to my friends and (me, myself, I), so we laughed.

8. Liezl and (she, her) seem judicious; they exercise good judgment.

9. The statement, "Possessive pronouns have apostrophes," is (true, false).

10. Yesterday, some hoodlums (stealed, stole, stolen) my mother's potted geranium.

11. I appreciate (them, there, their) intervening to save my reputation.

12. Write the plural of each noun.

    (a) piano   (b) bookshelf   (c) shoebox

13. Rewrite the following, adding periods, commas, and capital letters as needed: aunt emma and uncle fred took an alaskan vacation they paddled in a kayak around a lake viewed glaciers from a helicopter and fished for salmon in a stream

14. Write whether the following is a phrase or a clause: Anne Morrow Lindberg, the wife of Charles

15. In this sentence, write the verb phrase and label it action
(3, 18) or linking: Ralph Bunche and Martin Luther King, Jr., were winners of the Nobel Peace Prize.

16. In this sentence, write each prepositional phrase, starring
(14, 28) the object of each preposition: According to election law, candidates for public office are prohibited from campaigning within one hundred feet of a polling place.

17. Write whether the following is a complete sentence,
(2) sentence fragment, or run-on sentence: In 1962, two famous spies were exchanged, the U.S. traded Rudolph Abel for Francis Gary Powers.

18. From this sentence, write the personal pronoun and
(46, 50) name its case and its antecedent: Hank Aaron was he who broke Babe Ruth's home run record.

19. Rewrite the following as it is. Then add proofreading
(32) symbols to indicate corrections.

Please remind ms Flake that posessive pronouns donot have apos trophie's.

20. From this sentence, write the dependent clause, circling
(54) the subordinating conjunction: Although many actors have portrayed Tarzan, Johnny Weissmuller was the first.

21. Use an appositive to make one sentence from these two
(42) sentences: The Amazon is the world's second longest river. The Amazon starts in the Andes Mountains in Peru and flows through the rain forest in Brazil.

22. Write the gerund phrase in this sentence and label its
(55, 56) tense present or perfect: Having lost his car keys gave Jeb a large dose of anxiety when it was time to leave for work.

23. Write the participial phrase in this sentence: In the
(55, 56) distance, I could hear someone singing the railroad song.

24. Write whether this sentence is simple or compound: Our
(59) words have the power to create, not only on paper, but also in the life of another person.

25. Write the comparative form of the adjective *tortuous*.
(39)

26. Write the four principal parts of the irregular verb *choose*.
(13, 49)

27. Write each coordinating conjunction in this sentence: Would you like ham and cheese, or do you prefer peanut butter and jelly?
(33)

28. Rewrite this sentence so that it is in active voice: The floor was swept and the windows were washed by Roger.
(27)

Diagram sentences 29 and 30.

29. Eva has admired Sam's repairing automobile engines.
(21, 56)

30. Sam, an excellent mechanic, likes Eva, yet he remains a single man.
(42, 59)

LESSON 61   Relative Pronouns • Diagramming the Dependent Clause

> **Dictation or Journal Entry**
> **Vocabulary:** The Greek preposition *epi-*, which is commonly used as a prefix in the forms *epi-, ep-,* and *eph-,* means "on, upon," "in addition to," and "for, against."
>
> <u>Ephemeral</u> means "lasting *for* a day;" "fleeting; momentary." An actor's popularity is generally *ephemeral.*
>
> <u>Epidermis</u> is the outer, nonsensitive, nonvascular layer of skin overlying the inner, sensitive layer or "dermis." The *epidermis* of some people reacts to soap and wool by breaking out in a rash.

Relative Pronouns

Relative pronouns play the part of the subject or object in clauses (sentences within sentences).

John Francis Mercer, *who* represented Maryland at the Constitutional Convention, returned home disgruntled.

The citizens, with *whom* we may identify, were not regarded as capable of voting intelligently.

Relative pronouns often refer to nouns that have preceded them, making the sentence more compact.

WORDY:

Beside his driveway, Bob planted day lilies full of colossal blooms; these colossal blooms were vivid but ephemeral.

COMPACT:

Beside his driveway, Bob planted day lilies full of colossal blooms *that* were vivid but ephemeral.

Simple The following are simple relative pronouns:

who, whom, whose, what, which, that

WHO REFERS TO PEOPLE (OR PERSONIFIED ANIMALS—ANIMALS GIVEN NAMES):

John Mercer, *who* was reluctant to allow direct voting by all people, wanted to restrict suffrage.

My cat Bingo Bailey, *who* sleeps at the foot of my bed, chases mice during the night.

WHICH REFERS TO ANIMALS OR THINGS, BUT **NOT** PEOPLE:

Voting, *which* was a point of contention at the Constitutional Convention, was settled by the Electoral College.

The elephant, *which* symbolizes the Republican Party, often appears in the editorial section of the newspaper.

THAT REFERS TO PEOPLE, ANIMALS, OR THINGS:

The ladies *that* manage this department have gone home sick.

The animal *that* represents the Democratic Party is the donkey.

The twenty speeches *that* John Francis Mercer delivered seemed contentious and negative.

Remember that **we do not use *which* for people.**

Example 1 Choose the correct relative pronoun for each sentence.

(a) John Mercer, (who, which) spoke with passion during the convention, left outraged after eleven days.

(b) Thomas Jefferson's thoughts, (who, which) reflected the opinions of many, labeled John Mercer as vain and ambitious.

(c) The man (which, that) John Mercer vehemently opposed was Alexander Hamilton.

Solution (a) We choose **who** because it refers to "John Mercer," a person. We do not use *which* for people.

(b) We choose **which** because it refers to "thoughts," a thing. We do not use *who* for things.

(c) We choose **that** because it refers to "man," a person. We do not use *which* for people.

Errors to Avoid The relative pronoun *who* can cause problems, because it changes form depending on the part it plays in the clause:

SUBJECT	OBJECT	POSSESSIVE
NOMINATIVE CASE	OBJECTIVE CASE	POSSESSIVE CASE
who	*whom*	*whose*

In the sentences below, we diagram the sentence within the sentence (dependent clause) to show how the pronoun is used.

SUBJECT:

John Mercer, who opposed Hamilton, argued for days at the convention.

```
  who   |  opposed  |  Hamilton
```

OBJECT:

George Washington, whom we know, chaired the Constitutional Convention.

```
  we  |  know  |  whom
```

POSSESSIVE:

George Washington, whose leadership was indispensable, embodied the colonists' sense of nationality.

```
  leadership  |  was \ indispensable
       \whose
```

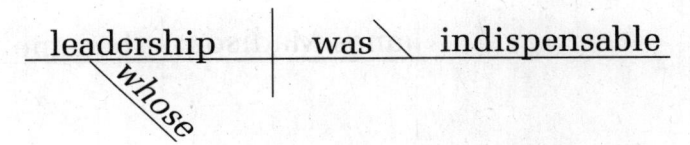

Diagramming the Dependent Clause

Now let us diagram an entire complex sentence, showing both the dependent and independent clauses. Notice how we attach this kind of a dependent clause to the independent clause using a dotted line between the relative pronoun and its antecedent. We place the dependent clause below the independent clause.

George Washington, whom I admire, commanded the Patriot troops.

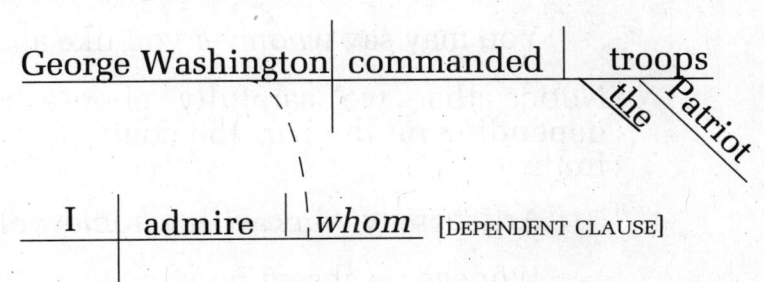

```
  George Washington | commanded | troops
                                   \the \Patriot

          I  |  admire  |  whom   [DEPENDENT CLAUSE]
```

377

Example 2 Diagram the sentence to help you determine whether the relative pronoun is a subject or an object. Then choose the correct pronoun form.

(a) George Washington, (who, whom) many idolized, opposed anarchy.

(b) James Madison, (who, whom) drafted the Constitution, became our fourth president

Solution (a) George Washington, **whom** many idolized, feared anarchy in democracy. (object)

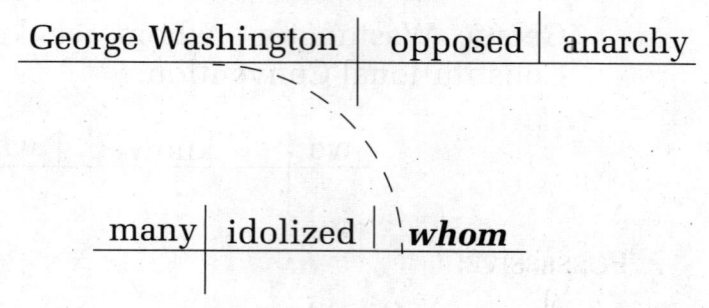

```
George Washington | opposed | anarchy


       many | idolized | whom
```

(b) James Madison, **who** drafted the Constitution, became our fourth president. (subject)

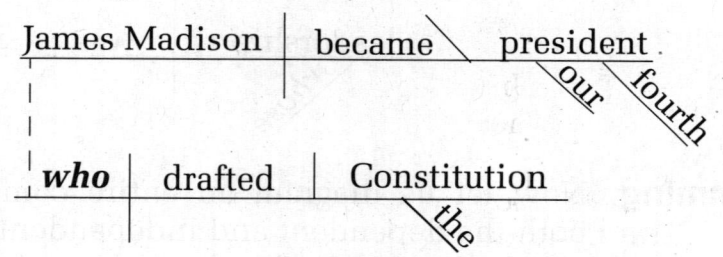

```
James Madison | became \ president
                              \our \fourth
    who | drafted | Constitution
                        \the
```

Compound The following are compound relative pronouns:

whoever   whomever   whosoever
whatever   whatsoever   whichever

Suzi may ride *whichever* bike she wants.

You may say *whatever* you like about my new haircut.

Notice that we carefully choose *whoever* or *whomever* depending on the part the compound relative pronoun plays in the clause.

Artists may work with *whomever* they want. (object)

Whoever is absent must make up the work. (subject)

Example 3 Choose the correct compound relative pronoun for this sentence:

(*Whoever, Whomever*) wants to serve lunch should arrive by noon.

Solution **Whoever** wants to serve lunch should arrive by noon. The pronoun is the subject, so we choose the *who* form.

Practice Choose the correct relative or appositive pronoun for sentences a–e.

  a. George Washington, (who, which) rode a white horse, battled hunger and cold at Valley Forge.

  b. George William Fairfax, (whom, who) George Washington befriended, surveyed the Shenandoah Valley.
  Think G. Washington | befriended | ?

  c. I will accept (whoever, whomever) you choose for the job.

  Think   I | will accept | ?

  d. Unfortunately, the brother (that, which) Dora admired most fell ill.

  e. Governor Robert Dinwiddie, (who, whom) Washington served, ordered the French to leave the region.

  Think   Washington | served | ?

  f. Diagram this sentence:

  Bo wants a dog that will guard his home.

For g–i, replace each blank with the correct vocabulary word.

  g. The _____ of an elephant is wrinkled, rough, and hairy.

  h. The prefix _____ means "above," "over," or "upon."

  i. George Washington's fame was not _____.

More Practice Choose the correct relative pronoun for each sentence.

1. George Washington was given command over all (whom, who) defended the borders of Virginia.

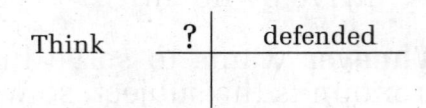

   Think | ? | defended |

2. George Washington, (whom, who) displayed exemplary conduct, won international fame after the Battle of Monongahela.

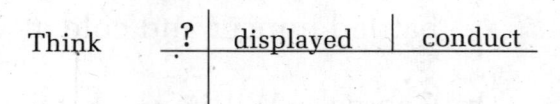

   Think | ? | displayed | conduct |

3. The French, (who, whom) the colonists sought, evaded George Washington's troops.

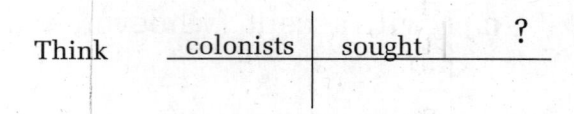

   Think | colonists | sought | ? |

4. The officials with (who, whom) he pleaded refused to cooperate.

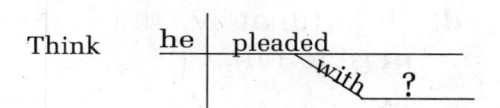

   Think | he | pleaded | with ? |

5. The young officers (who, whom) Washington commanded considered him a mentor.

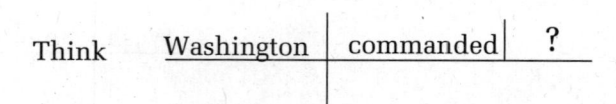

   Think | Washington | commanded | ? |

6. Those (who, whom) saw him in action appreciated his bravery.

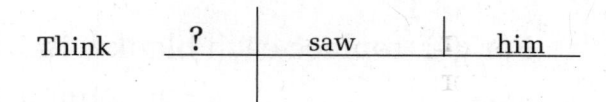

   Think | ? | saw | him |

7. We will always remember those (who, which) fought in the Revolutionary War.

Review Set 61

Choose the correct word(s) to complete sentences 1–13.

1. (Tortuous, Torturous) means full of bends, twists, and turns.

2. (Jovial, Dionysian, Ambivalent) means "having conflicting feelings or attitudes about an object, person, or idea."

3. (Slander, Libel) involves spoken words.

4. Mercurial means (unpredictable, merry, mirthful).

5. A (bureaucrat, Spartan, plutocrat) is an appointed government official.

6. My grandpa seized the intruder (hisself, himself).

7. He and Grandma (was, were) both prepared to defend (theirselves, themselves).

8. The intruder and (them, they, themselves) scuffled vigorously over a valuable painting.

9. "It's not (your's, yours)!" shouted Grandpa.

10. Before the police arrived, the intruder had (grew, grown) weary.

11. He had (begin, began, begun) searching for a way of escape.

12. He could no longer tolerate (them, their) pounding him with pillows.

13. A (subordinating, coordinating) conjunction may join two simple sentences to form a compound sentence.

Rewrite 14 and 15, adding periods, commas, and capital letters as needed.

14. grandpa said, "if you help me we can tie up this intruder so that he doesn't escape"

15. dear grandma and grandpa
(25, 47)

    since you captured the intruder he cannot bother anyone else i am proud of you for you are courageous

with admiration

jaime

16. Write whether this sentence is in active or passive voice:
(27) Lew Wallace wrote *Ben-Hur: A Tale of the Christ.*

17. Write the possessive case, second person, singular or
(48, 52) plural personal pronoun.

18. In this sentence, write the verb phrase and label it
(21, 26) transitive or intransitive: The tale begins with an account of Jesus' humble birth.

19. Rewrite the following as it is. Then add proofreading
(32) symbols to indicate corrections.

The architect from pasadena showed me me the building plan i like it.

20. Write the plural of each noun.
(10, 11)
  (a) oasis   (b) calf   (c) theory

21. From this sentence, write the dependent clause, circling
(54) the subordinating conjunction: *Ben-Hur* takes place when Jesus lived in Judea.

22. Use an appositive to make one sentence from these two
(42) sentences: William Shakespeare used interesting metaphors in his writing. Metaphors are figures of speech.

23. In this sentence, write the participial phrase followed by
(56) the word it modifies: Infuriated by Messala's prideful attitude, Judah Ben-Hur goes to Rome to become a soldier.

24. Write the intensive personal pronoun in this sentence:
(57) Jenny mopped the floor and cleaned the refrigerator herself.

25. Write the superlative form of the adjective *jovial*.
(39)

26. Write the four principal parts of the irregular verb *tear*.
(13, 49)

For 27 and 28, write whether the sentence is simple or compound. If it is compound, write the coordinating conjunction that joins the two independent clauses.

27. Miss Huynh can translate this message, for she speaks
(33, 59) many different languages.

28. On Tuesday, Miss Huynh attended the committee
(59) meeting and gave a long, detailed report concerning the state budget.

Diagram sentences 29 and 30.

29. Amy was timid, so she disliked confronting people.
(56, 59)

30. Twisting my ankle hindered my progress, but I
(56, 59) completed the rest of the hike.

LESSON 62

The Comma, Part 6: Nonessential Parts • *That* or *Which*

> **Dictation or Journal Entry**
>
> **Vocabulary:** The Latin word *primus* gives the English language its prefix *prim-*, meaning "first," as in the familiar words <u>prim</u>ary, <u>prim</u>er, <u>prim</u>ate, and *primitive*.
>
> *Primogeniture* is the state of being the firstborn of children of the same parents. *Primogeniture* is also the right of the eldest son to inherit his father's entire estate. *Primogeniture* arose in England to prevent the division of estates among many sons. Americans, under a campaign led by Thomas Jefferson, were most eager to abolish the practice of *primogeniture*. Most of the existing monarchies still descend by the law of *primogeniture*.
>
> *Primal* is an adjective meaning "original" or "first in importance." The *primal* Constitution contained no Bill of Rights. The *primal* concern of George Washington was to protect the people from chaos.

Nonessential Parts Parts of a sentence that modify other parts are sometimes essential to the meaning of the sentence and sometimes not. When a modifying word, phrase, or clause is not necessary for the meaning of a sentence, we call it **nonessential,** and we set it off by commas. **Nonessential parts** are underlined in the sentences below.

NONESSENTIAL WORD

George Washington's wife, <u>Martha</u>, was the wealthy widow of Daniel Parke Custis.

NONESSENTIAL PHRASE

George Washington, <u>in his blue-and-buff uniform of the Virginia militia</u>, attended the Second Continental Congress.

NONESSENTIAL CLAUSE

Samuel and John Adams, <u>who had organized the New England Militia</u>, decided to turn the army over to the Continental Congress.

Essential and nonessential parts are underlined in the sentence pairs below. Notice that nonessential parts are set off by commas while essential parts are not. Compare each pair of sentences.

> no commas = *essential*
> commas = *nonessential*

The woman <u>who called you</u> is my mother.
(essential—tells *which* woman. There may have been many women.)

My mother, <u>who called you</u>, sells cosmetics.
(nonessential—the writer only had one mother. The clause only adds information.)

Our rabbit <u>Peter</u> doesn't like carrots. (essential—The lack of commas indicates that the writer must have more than one rabbit.)

Our rabbit, <u>Peter</u>, doesn't like carrots. (nonessential—The commas indicate that the writer must have only one rabbit, whose name is Peter.)

Mike wrote to his sister <u>Elyse</u>. (essential—The lack of a comma indicates that the writer must have more than one sister.)

Mike wrote to his sister, <u>Elyse</u>. (nonessential—The comma indicates that the writer has only one sister.)

Example 1 Write whether each underlined expression is essential or nonessential.

(a) The turning point <u>that scholars acknowledge</u> was Valley Forge.

(b) The turning point, <u>which was Valley Forge</u>, demonstrated the Patriots' perseverance.

Solution (a) The lack of commas indicates that this clause is **essential.** It tells *which* turning point. Perhaps people other than scholars see a different turning point in the war.

(b) The commas indicate that this clause is **nonessential.** It adds information, but it is not necessary for the meaning of the sentence.

That or Which In adjective clauses, the use of **that** or **which** depends on whether the clause is essential or nonessential. We use **that** for essential clauses. We use **which** for nonessential clauses, and we set them off with commas.

ESSENTIAL CLAUSE

    The battle **that ended the Revolutionary War** was at Yorktown.

NONESSENTIAL CLAUSE

    Yorktown, **which supposedly provided protection for the British troops**, failed to do so.

ESSENTIAL CLAUSE

    A treaty **that was signed in Paris** officially ended the war.

NONESSENTIAL CLAUSE

    The Treaty of Paris, **which was signed in 1783,** allowed George Washington to return to private life.

Example 2 Choose *that* or *which* for each sentence.

(a) Nate wrote an editorial (that, which) slandered a politician.

(b) His article, (that, which) was published last Tuesday, accuses the politician of perjury and treason.

Solution (a) Nate wrote an editorial **that** slandered a politician. (The clause is not set off by commas. Therefore, we know that it is an essential clause, so we choose *that*.)

(b) His article, **which** was published last Tuesday, accuses the politician of perjury and treason. (The clause is set off by commas, which indicate a nonessential clause. Therefore, we choose *which*.)

Practice For a–c, replace each blank with the correct vocabulary word.

a. The _____ purpose of the Mount Vernon Conference was to settle disputes between Maryland and Virginia.

b. Believing that _____ was unfair, Americans chose to evenly distribute inheritances among siblings.

c. The _____ document of the young nation was the Declaration of Independence.

For d–f, write whether the underlined expression is essential or nonessential.

d. The Annapolis Convention, <u>which in turn called for the Constitutional Convention</u>, pleased George Washington.

e. The man <u>who convened the Constitutional Convention</u> was Robert Morris.

f. George Washington, <u>who spoke only once in the Convention</u>, wielded his power thoughtfully and responsibly.

For g–j, choose *that* or *which*.

g. George Washington's responses, (that, which) were sage and temperate, matched those of Ben Franklin.

h. Partisan politics, (which, that) George Washington deplored, emerged during his second term as president.

i. The job (that, which) George had accepted proved exceedingly difficult.

j. The museum displays a wig (that, which) might have belonged to George Washington.

Review Set 62

Choose the correct word to complete sentences 1–10.

1. The Greek prefix *epi-* means (inner, not, upon).
(61)

2. (Tortuous, Torturous) means painful and agonizing.
(60)

3. (Mercurial, Apollonian, Ambidextrous) means "able to use both the right and left hands with equal ease."
(59)

4. (Slander, Libel) involves written words or pictures.
(58)

5. Drivers can (avert, alert, advert) accidents by driving more slowly in bad weather.
(2)

6. During the nutrition lecture, Kim and (me, myself, I) gravitated toward the doughnut shop.
(50)

7. Mr. Eupepsia and (them, they) tried to prick my conscience.
(50)

8. Mr. Eupepsia, (who, whom, which) lectures on nutrition, suggested that poor eating habits can make people susceptible to disease.
(61)

9. Had he (know, knew, known) about my visits to the doughnut shop?
(49)

10. I resent (him, his) pointing out my weaknesses.
(53)

11. Rewrite this sentence so that it is in active voice: Were the Romans driven out of Judah by Ben-Hur?
(27)

12. Write whether this clause is dependent or independent: As he watched a detested Roman leader arrive
(54)

Rewrite 13 and 14, adding periods, commas, and capital letters as needed.

13. latin which was the language spoken in ancient rome influenced the development of other languages
(61, 62)

14. french spanish italian and portuguese are called romance languages for they developed out of latin
(22, 41)

15. Write whether the following is a complete sentence, sentence fragment, or run-on sentence: I understand that Ben-Hur accidently killed Valerius Gratus.
(2)

16. Write the nominative case, first person, plural personal pronoun.
(50)

17. For sentences a and b, write the verb phrase and label it action or linking.
(3, 18)

(a) Senator Green has been feeling ambivalent about the environmental bill before the legislature.

(b) She has been feeling pressure from her constituents.

18. From the following sentence, write each pronoun and name its case and its antecedent:
(46)

Ben-Hur feels betrayed when he recognizes his friend Messala as one of the arresting soldiers.

19. Write the plural of each noun.
(10, 11)

(a) James (b) Lopez (c) Jerry

20. From the following sentence, write the dependent clause, circling the subordinating conjunction:
(54)

While Ben-Hur is on the way to Nazareth, he meets Jesus for the first time.

21. In the following sentence, write the verb phrase and name its tense:
(15)

Ben-Hur had saved the Roman ship's captain, Arrius.

22. Use an appositive to make one sentence from the following two sentences:
(42)

In the year 44 B.C., Julius Caesar was assassinated on the Ides of March. Julius Caesar was a Roman dictator.

23. Write the gerund phrase in the following sentence and label its tense present or perfect:
(17, 55)

Arrius reciprocates Ben-Hur's kindness by adopting him as his own son.

24. In the following sentence, write the participial phrase followed by the word it modifies:
(45, 46)

Having trained as a Roman soldier, the elderly servant doesn't trust Ben-Hur.

25. Write the comparative form of the adjective *bellicose*.
(39)

26. Write the four principal parts of the irregular verb *freeze*.
(13, 49)

For 27 and 28, write whether the sentence is simple or compound. If it is compound, write the coordinating conjunction that joins the two independent clauses.

27. Ben-Hur watches the chariot race, and he spies Messala as one of the drivers.
(59)

28. In the great coliseum, Ben-Hur challenges Messala to a chariot race and wins.
(59)

Diagram sentences 29 and 30.

29. Every architect who submits a building plan will receive
(21, 61) a personal letter in response.

30. Having drunk several cups of coffee, Henry tried to draw,
(56, 59) but his hand was unsteady.

LESSON 63 Pronoun Usage: Appositions and Comparisons

> **Dictation or Journal Entry**
>
> **Vocabulary:** Let us clarify the meaning of the body positions *prone* and *supine*.
>
> *Prone* means "lying with the face or front downward; prostrate." While lying *prone* of the beach, the shipwrecked sailor rested his forehead on his arms to keep the sand out of his mouth. The word *prone* can also mean "naturally inclined; disposed." Some people are *prone* to talk too much.
>
> *Supine* means "lying on the back with the face turned upward." While lying *supine* on the beach, the shipwrecked sailor covered his face with his hat to keep the sun out of his eyes. The word *supine* also means "having moral or mental indifference; apathetic." The Patriots resented those who were *supine* slaves to British authority.

Written vs. Spoken Language

The traditional rule for pronouns is that a pronoun following a form of "be" must be in the nominative case, as in the examples below:

It is *I*.

Was it *they* who called?

We knew it was *she*.

When we write, we should follow this rule. When we are speaking, however, we tend to be less formal. Our ear tells us that in casual conversation, "It is I" sound stiff. Instead, we are more likely to say:

It is *me*. (conversation)

Was it *them* who called? (conversation)

We knew it was *her*. (conversation)

Remember that this relaxed pronoun usage is acceptable in casual conversation, but would be unacceptable in formal speech or any form of writing.

Now we will discuss two more areas that often cause trouble in pronoun usage.

Appositions

We remember than an appositive renames a person or thing. An **apposition** is a pronoun used to rename a noun for emphasis.

Only one person, *he*, will preside over the meeting.

The two political parties, *they* and *we*, will run candidates against each other.

The apposition must be in the same case form as the noun it renames. Consider the examples below.

> SUBJECT:
> *We* (NOT *us*) Federalists favor a strong central government.
>
> OBJECT:
> George Washington gave *us* (NOT *we*) Americans a role model to emulate.
>
> SUBJECT:
> Both candidates, John Adams and *he* (NOT *him*) wanted to speak at the assembly.

Example 1 Choose the correct apposition for this sentence:

> The two friends, Gouverneur Morris and (he, him), learned to respect one another.

Solution The apposition, "Gouverneur Morris and he," renames "friends," which is the sentence subject, so we use the nominative case pronoun:

> The two friends, Gouverneur Morris and **he,** learned to respect one another.

Comparisons In comparison sentences, a verb is sometimes omitted (often after *than* or *as*).

> No one tried harder than *he*. ("did" is omitted)
>
> We play the violin as well as *they*. ("do" is omitted)

Notice that the pronouns in the sentences above are in the nominative case because they are used as subjects of clauses whose verbs are understood (not stated).

The pronoun used in a comparison is important because it can change the meaning of the sentence:

> Rosa likes jazz as much as *he*. ("does" is omitted)
> [MEANING: Rosa likes jazz as much as he does.]
>
> Rosa likes jazz as much as *him*. ("she likes" is omitted)
> [MEANING: Rosa likes jazz as much as she likes him.]

Example 2 Choose the correct pronoun for the following sentences.

(a) Our team scored more points than (*they, them*).

(b) I speak French as well as (*he, him*).

Solution (a) Our team scored more points than **they**. ("did" is omitted)

(b) I speak French as well as **he**. ("does" is omitted)

Practice Choose the correct pronoun for sentences a–e.

a. (We, Us) students memorized George Washington's famous lines.

Think   ? | memorized

b. It is acceptable to (we, us) students to delay the exam.

Think   to ?

c. The docent gave (we, us) tourists the history of the state capitol building.

Think   docent | gave | ?

d. Binh is better at problem solving than (I, me). ["am" omitted]

e. They bicker over issues as often as (*we, us*). ["do" omitted]

For f–i, replace each blank with the correct vocabulary word.

f. We must take a firm stand; we must not act _____ about immorality.

g. Lying _____ outdoors, Leslie gazed into the blue sky.

h. After the race, Blythe lay _____ and breathed into the crabgrass.

i. Are you _____ to procrastinate?

More Practice Choose the correct pronoun for each sentence.

1. John Adams was much shorter than (he, him). ["was" omitted]

2. (We, Us) Americans appreciate our heritage.

Think   ? | appreciate

3. The guide showed (we, us) students the original document of the Constitution.

   Think | guide | showed | ? |

4. Lucinda and (her, she) will brush the horses.

   Think | ? | will brush |

5. George Washington nominated two friends, John Adams and (he, him).

   Think | G. Washington | nominated | ? |

6. George had more wooden teeth than (she, her). ["had" omitted]

7. James Madison spoke more frequently than (he, him). ["spoke" omitted]

8. We commute as far as (they, them). ["do" omitted]

9. (We, Us) girls toured Mount Vernon.

   Think | ? | toured |

10. The bus driver's detour made (we, us) tourists nervous.

    Think | detour | made | ? |

Review Set 63

Choose the correct word to complete sentences 1–14.

1. The Latin word (*amare, primus, sequi*) means "first."
(62)

2. The Greek prefix meaning "on" is (*penta-, epi-, endo-*).
(61)

3. Tortuous means full of (pain, turns, laughter).
(60)

4. (Bacchanalian, Biannual, Ambient) means "completely surrounding."
(59)

5. We describe things that happened before the American Civil War as (bellicose, antebellum, bicameral).
(3)

6. We use commas to set off (essential, nonessential) parts of a sentence.

7. Jesse and (him, himself, he) were scheming together.

8. This reply is from Rosita, (who, whom) they invited to dinner.

9. Is anyone busier than (her, she)?

10. (We, Us) firefighters risk our lives for others.

11. The bandit (who, which, whom) robbed the train lost his bandana as he fled.

12. (Who, Whom) is an objective case pronoun.

13. My parents encourage (me, my) studying Latin.

14. The pronoun *who* is in the (nominative, objective) case.

Rewrite 15 and 16, adding periods, commas, and capital letters and making necessary changes to abbreviations for formal writing.

15. redheaded eric a fierce viking sailed west past iceland and discovered greenland

16. on tues nov fourth in hampton virginia col. peterson will present a documentary on the adventurous explorer leif ericson

17. Write the possessive case, third person, plural personal pronoun.

18. In this sentence, write the verb phrase and label it transitive or intransitive: Messala hires two brutes to murder Ben-Hur.

19. In the following sentence, write each prepositional phrase and star the object of each preposition:

Because of the disarray in my garage, I could not find a wrench in spite of the large conglomeration of tools and gadgets scattered round about the work area.

20. Write the plural of each noun.
(a) firefly   (b) lunch   (c) dairy

21. From the following sentence, write the dependent clause, circling the subordinating conjunction:

As soon as he escapes, Ben-Hur begins looking for his mother and sister.

22. Rewrite the following as it is. Then add proofreading symbols to indicate corrections.

My bird book is vary old the brids may have evolved since itwas wrote.

23. Rewrite this sentence so that it is in active voice: The soldier abusing a Jewish man is slain by Ben-Hur.

24. In the following sentence, write the participial phrase followed by the word it modifies:

Ben-Hur slays the soldier abusing a Jewish man.

25. Write the superlative form of the adjective *good*.

26. Write the four principal parts of the verb *drop*.

27. Write whether the underlined expression in the following sentence is essential or nonessential:

My dog Dinah howls high, soprano notes.

Diagram sentences 28–30.

28. I like to swim, but Bob prefers to surf.

29. Collecting large, scary-looking insects is Mandy's secret hobby.

30. The student chasing giant cockroaches is she.

LESSON 64

Interrogative Pronouns

> **Dictation or Journal Entry**
>
> **Vocabulary:** English borrows the Latin phrases *modus operandi* and *modus vivendi*.
>
> A *modus operandi* is a manner of work; a method of operation; a usual way of doing something. Can you develop a more efficient *modus operandi* for completing your assignments?
>
> A *modus vivendi* is a manner of living; a practical arrangement that is acceptable to all concerned. The divorced parents put aside their differences to establish a *modus vivendi* concerning visitation with their children's best interests at heart.

When a relative pronoun introduces a question, it is called an **interrogative pronoun.** *Who, whom, whose, what, that, which, whoever, whichever,* and *whatever* are interrogative pronouns.

Who is James Madison?

What did he contribute?

Which was his state?

Whom did he defend?

Whoever would believe that?

A sentence doesn't have to end with a question mark in order to contain an interrogative pronoun. Sometimes an interrogative pronoun introduces a question that is contained inside a declarative sentence:

She asked *who* was on the ballot.

Yin wondered *what* they believed.

Kim didn't know *which* would work better.

Example 1 Write each interrogative pronoun that you find in each sentence.

(a) Winnie couldn't imagine what had happened to him.

(b) Who called James Madison "little and ordinary"?

(c) The historian had not concluded which was the more reliable account.

(d) Whose are these research papers?

Solution   (a) **what**   (b) **who**   (c) **which**   (d) **whose**

Who or Whom In order to decide whether we should use *who* or *whom*, we must determine what part the interrogative pronoun plays in the sentence. If it functions as a subject or predicate nominative, we use *who*.

Who submitted the Virginia plan? (subject)

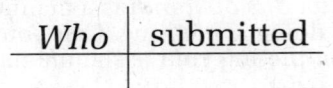

$$\text{Who} \mid \text{submitted}$$

Who offered the New Jersey plan? (subject)

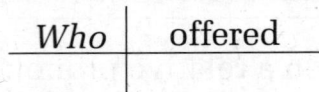

$$\text{Who} \mid \text{offered}$$

The new senator is *who*? (predicate nominative)

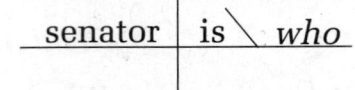

$$\text{senator} \mid \text{is} \setminus \text{who}$$

If the interrogative pronoun is an object (direct object, indirect object, object of a preposition), we use *whom*.

Whom did Madison oppose? (direct object)

$$\text{Madison} \mid \text{did oppose} \mid \text{Whom}$$

To *whom* did Paterson present his plan? (object of a preposition)

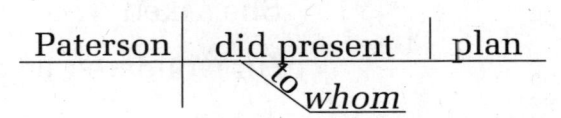

$$\text{Paterson} \mid \text{did present} \mid \text{plan}$$
$$\text{to whom}$$

To check to see that we have used *who* or *whom* correctly, we can turn the questions above into statements and substitute *he/she* for *who*, and *him/her* for *whom*:

> RIGHT: Madison <u>opposed</u> *him/her*.
> WRONG: Madison <u>opposed</u> *he/she*.

> RIGHT: Paterson <u>presented</u> his plan to *him/her*.
> Wrong: Paterson <u>presented</u> his plan to *he/she*.

Errors to Avoid Do not confuse *whose* and *who's*. *Whose* is a possessive or interrogative pronoun. *Who's* is a contraction for "who is." Remember, possessive pronouns do not have apostrophes.

Who's the author? (Who is the author?)

Whose signature is that?

Example 2 Choose the correct interrogative pronoun for each sentence.

(a) (Who, Whom) became the fourth President?

(b) (Who, Whom) did they elect?

(c) To (who, whom) were you speaking?

(d) This wig belongs to me, but (who's, whose) is that?

Solution (a) The pronoun is used as the subject, so we choose *who*.

Who became the fourth President?

(b) We change the question into a statement: They elected (who, whom). Then we substitute *he* or *she* for *who*, and *him* or *her* for *whom* to see which is correct.

"They elected *him* or *her*," is correct.
NOT "They elected *he* or *she*."

The pronoun is used as an object, so we choose *whom*.

Whom did they elect?

| they | did elect | *Whom* |

(c) The pronoun is used as an object of a preposition, so we choose *whom*.

To **whom** were you speaking?

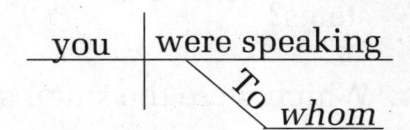

| you | were speaking |
         \ To
          \ whom

(d) *Who's* is a contraction for "who is." We choose *whose* because it is the interrogative pronoun.

This wig belongs to me, but **whose** is that?

Adjective or Pronoun? When *which, whose,* and *what* come before nouns, they are adjectives. When *which, whose,* and *what* stand alone, they are interrogative pronouns.

ADJECTIVE: *Which* pen has blue ink?
PRONOUN: *Which* has blue ink?

ADJECTIVE: *What* book fell off the shelf?
PRONOUN: *What* fell off the shelf?
ADJECTIVE: *Whose* glasses are these?
PRONOUN: *Whose* are these?

Example 3 Tell whether the italicized word in each sentence is an adjective or an interrogative pronoun.

(a) *Whose* influence restrained James Madison?

(b) I wonder *what* Patrick Henry meant.

(c) *What* kind of man was William Paterson?

(d) *Which* of the two had the better idea?

Solution (a) *Whose* comes before the noun *influence*, so it is an **adjective.**

(b) *What* stands alone as the direct object, so it is an **interrogative pronoun.**

(c) *What* precedes the abstract noun *kind*, so it is an **adjective.**

(d) *Which* stands alone as the subject; it does not come before a noun. Therefore it is an **interrogative pronoun.**

Practice For a–c, write the interrogative pronoun, from each sentence.

a. Do you know who defended the interests of the small states?

b. Which were the small states?

c. Whose is that notebook?

For d–f, choose the correct interrogative pronoun for each sentence.

d. With (who, whom) was James Madison linked in writing *The Federalist*?

e. (Who's, Whose) are those detailed records?

f. (Who, Whom) is called the "Father of the Constitution"?

For g and h, tell whether the italicized word is an adjective or an interrogative pronoun.

g. *What* do you know about James Madison?

h. *Which* delegates represented the small states?

For i and j, replace each blank with the correct vocabulary word.

i. The concerned father worked out a _____ for getting along with his rebellious son.

j. The foreman made it known that a more effective _____ was necessary in order to increase the company's production.

More Practice Choose the correct word to complete each sentence.

1. (Who's, Whose) running for President?

2. (Who's, Whose) plantation was named Montpelier?

3. (Who, Whom) plowed the field?   ? | plowed

4. To (who, whom) did that plantation belong?

5. (Who, Whom) are you criticizing?   you | are criticizing | ?

6. (Who's, Whose) the slave picking cotton?

7. (Who's, Whose) red bandana is that?

8. With (who, whom) would you like to discuss current politics?

9. (Who, Whom) will plant the next crop.   ? | will plant

10. (Who, Whom) might we nominate for our next President?
    we | might nominate | ?

Review Set 64 Choose the correct word to complete sentences 1–14.

1. Prone and (judicious, sybaritic, supine) are body positions.
(63)

2. The Latin word *primus* means (last, love, first).
(62)

3. (Torturous, Ephemeral, Ambivalent) means "lasting for a day."
(61)

4. Torturous means full of (turns, pain, laughter).
(60)

5. The (bellicose, bicameral, pacifist) protester shouted angrily and punched innocent bystanders.
(3)

6. Maria swam faster than (I, me).
(63)

7. Dad promised my brother and (me, myself, I) a camping trip in the Sierras.
(21, 51)

8. We were discussing Ben Franklin, (who, whom) we studied last semester.
(61)

9. (We, Us) basketball players are accustomed to rigorous training.
(63)

10. (Who's, Whose) tennis racquet is this?
(64)

11. Mr. Eupepsia and (her, herself, she) drank carrot juice with basil.
(50)

12. The youngest stallion, (which, that) had jumped the fence, trotted down the dusty trail.
(61)

13. His friends are tired of (him, his) boasting.
(53)

14. The pronoun *whom* is in the (nominative, objective) case.
(52)

Rewrite 15 and 16, adding periods, commas, and capital letters and making necessary changes to abbreviations for formal writing.

15. dear professor droner
(9, 47)
    unfortunately i slept through your lecture on world history so i failed the exam on fri
    if you will give me a second chance i will do better next time
                      your student
                      ima snoozer

16. dr droner my history teacher lectured for three hrs and twenty min last tues
(31, 43)

17. Write the objective case, first person, singular personal pronoun.
(52)

18. Write whether the underlined expression in the following sentence is essential or nonessential:
(62)

Our two border terriers, <u>Rocky and Spike</u>, received awards at the dog show.

19. In the following sentence, write the verb phrase and label it action or linking:
(3, 18)

Does Ben-Hur train three legions of Jewish soldiers?

20. Write the plural of each noun.
(10, 11)

(a) tragedy   (b) Commander in Chief   (c) Tony

21. From the following sentence, write the two dependent clauses, circling the subordinating conjunction for each clause:
(54)

When Ben-Hur hears that the King of the Jews has arrived in Jerusalem, he has to see for himself.

22. Rewrite the following as it is. Then add proofreading symbols to indicate corrections.
(32)

Jesus look calm and kind he looks li ke a king.

23. Write whether the following is a phrase or a clause: like the Son of the living God
(20)

24. Rewrite the following sentence so that it is in active voice:
(27)

Through the compliments of friends, Casper is encouraged.

25. Write the comparative form of the adjective *bad*.
(40)

26. In the following sentence, write the verb phrase and name its tense:
(17)

Ben-Hur's mother and sister were also looking for Jesus.

27. In the following sentence, write the participial phrase followed by the word it modifies:
(56)

Having healed Ben-Hur's mother and sister of leprosy, Jesus reunites the family.

Diagram sentences 28–30.

28. Using today's newspaper, Len folded me a rain hat.
(21, 56)

29. Folding paper rain hats is Len's specialty.
(36, 56)

30. The voice instructor who taught me to sing has become famous.
(21, 61)

LESSON 65 — Quotation Marks, Part 1

> **Dictation or Journal Entry**
> **Vocabulary:** Let us clarify the meanings of the similar words *loath* and *loathe*.
> *Loath* is an adjective meaning reluctant and unwilling. Initially, the smaller states were *loath* to accept state representation based on population.
> *Loathe* is a verb meaning to detest, hate, or abhor. Aaron Burr *loathed* Alexander Hamilton and killed him in a duel.

Direct Quotation

A **direct quotation** gives a speaker's exact words. To indicate a direct quotation, we enclose the speaker's words in quotation marks.

James Madison said, "In framing a government which is to be administered by men over men, the great difficulty lies in this: you must first enable the government to control the governed; and in the next place, oblige it to control itself."

"In framing a system which we wish to last for ages, we should not lose sight of the changes which ages will produce," he continued.

Notice that in each of the examples above, the punctuation mark following the direct quotation appears **inside** the quotation marks.

Example 1 Place quotation marks where they are needed in the sentence below.

Your President may easily become a King, thundered Patrick Henry.

Solution We place quotation marks before and after Patrick Henry's words.

"Your President may easily become a King," thundered Patrick Henry.

Direct Quotation with Explanatory Note

Sometimes a direct quotation is interrupted by an **explanatory note** such as *he said, she replied, the teacher explained*, etc. We enclose in quotation marks only the direct quotation parts, not the explanatory note. Notice that both parts of the direct quotation are enclosed in quotation marks.

"All men having power," observed James Madison, "ought to be distrusted."

"There will be no checks," warned Patrick Henry, "no real balances in this government."

Example 2 Place quotation marks where they are needed in the sentence below.

> Since the states never possessed the essential rights of sovereignty, insisted James Madison, the people would not be less free as members of one great Republic than as members of thirteen small ones.

Solution We place quotation marks around both parts of James Madison's direct quotation, but we do not enclose the explanatory note (insisted James Madison) in quotation marks.

> **"Since the states never possessed the essential rights of sovereignty," insisted James Madison, "the people would not be less free as members of one great Republic than as members of thirteen small ones."**

Indirect Quotations An **indirect quotation** tells about what someone said, but it does not give the speaker's exact words. We do not use quotation marks with indirect quotations.

> James Madison declared that the assumption of safety from despotism in small states was ridiculous.

> He insisted that the Constitution would provide a government neither wholly federal, nor wholly national.

Example 3 Add quotation marks if needed to the sentence below.

> James Madison emphasized that there were restraints built into the system.

Solution **No quotations marks** are necessary, because this is not a direct quotation. It is an **indirect quotation.**

Practice For a–e, rewrite correctly each sentence that needs quotation marks. If the sentence does not need quotation marks, write "none."

a. Madison told the Antifederalists that the Constitution was just what they had in mind.

b. He said that stronger national authority was necessary to collect a tax, pay the public debts, and defend the frontiers.

c. The powers of the government relate to external objects, said Madison, and are but few.

d. Of all the dispositions and habits which lead to political prosperity, said George Washington, Religion and Morality are indispensable supports.

For e and f, replace each blank with the correct vocabulary word.

e. Did Patrick Henry _____ the political beliefs of James Madison?

f. George Mason and Patrick Henry were _____ to accept the Constitution without further protection of the states' liberties.

More Practice See Master Worksheets.

Review Set 65 Choose the correct word to complete sentences 1–13.

1. A (deduction, retraction, modus operandi) is a method of operation, or a usual way of doing something.
   (64)

2. Prone means lying with the face or front (downward, upward).
   (63)

3. (Primogeniture, Ephemeral, Dionysian) is the state of being the firstborn of children of the same parents.
   (62)

4. (Epidermis, Trajectory, Suffrage) is the outer layer of skin.
   (61)

5. A legislature having two branches, chambers, or houses is (bellicose, bicameral, antebellum).
   (4)

6. They have fewer weeds in their yard than (we, us, ourselves).
   (63)

7. Ralph and (we, us, ourselves) plan to pull weeds tomorrow.
   (50)

8. Of all the waiters and waitresses, Mr. Able is the (clumsier, clumsiest).
   (39)

9. He apologized to (we, us) restaurant patrons.
   (51, 63)

10. Is that broken plate (yours, your's)?
(53)

11. Did you notice (him, his) spilling gravy on my sleeve?
(53)

12. The pronoun (*who, whom*) is in the objective case.
(51, 61)

13. The computer (that, which) I used for research has crashed.
(62)

14. Rewrite the following as it is. Then add proofreading symbols to indicate corrections.
(32)

Lew wallace's *Ben-Hur* are a mitxure off history an intrigue

15. Rewrite the following, adding capital letters and punctuation marks as needed:
(25, 41)

in his inaugural address, on january 20 1961 president john f kennedy proclaimed the rights of man come not from the generosity of the state but from the hand of god

16. Rewrite this sentence so that it is in active voice: Fewer details were expected by the reader.
(27)

17. Write the possessive case, second person, singular or plural personal pronoun.
(52)

18. In this sentence, write the verb phrase and name its tense: By the end of the novel, Ben-Hur will be celebrating love.
(17)

19. In this sentence, write the verb phrase and label it action or linking: Ben-Hur becomes peaceful and forgiving.
(3, 18)

20. From this sentence, write the dependent clause, circling the subordinating conjunction: While *Ben-Hur* chronicles a man's rise out of slavery, it also portrays a man's victory over anger.
(54)

21. Write the plural of each noun.
(10, 11)
  (a) yourself (b) pocketful (c) analysis

22. Write whether the underlined expression in this sentence is essential or nonessential: My father, <u>Richard Curtis</u>, deserves a round of applause.
(62)

23. Write whether the following is a phrase or a clause: because he forgave his enemies
(20)

24. Write the superlative form of the adjective *good*.
(40)

25. Write the four principal parts of the verb *shop*.
(13)

26. Write the gerund phrase in this sentence: Apologizing for our mistakes can heal some big wounds.
(16, 55)

27. In this sentence, write the participial phrase followed by the word it modifies: Leaping like a kangaroo, Ieling flew easily over the hurdles.
(55, 56)

Diagram sentences 28–30.

28. Mr. Able, whom we have hired, has dropped two entrées of spaghetti.
(21, 61)

29. Having noticed his clumsiness, we asked him to leave.
(30, 56)

30. Should we have given him another chance to improve?
(21, 45)

LESSON 66

Quotation Marks, Part 2

> **Dictation or Journal Entry**
>
> **Vocabulary:** *Ad hoc* and *ad hominem* are two more expressionss borrowed from Latin.
>
> *Ad hoc* means "for a specific and limited purpose." The school formed an *ad hoc* committee to examine dress code violations and recommend improvements to current policy.
>
> *Ad hominem* means "using prejudice and emotion rather than intellect or reason." In an *ad hominem* campaign, the candidates sought to belittle one another rather than to discuss the issues.

Speaker Changes A set of quotation marks can contain the words of only one speaker. When the speaker changes, we use a new set of quotation marks. Also, when writing dialogue (conversation), we start a new paragraph every time the speaker changes.

Notice how quotation marks are used with changing speakers in this excerpt from *The Long Valley*.

> "Won't you tell any more stories?" Jody asked.
>
> "Why, sure I'll tell them, but only when—I'm sure people want to hear them."

Example 1 Rewrite the following conversation from *The Long Valley*, inserting quotation marks as needed.

> I like to hear them, sir.
>
> Oh! Of course you do, but you're a little boy. It was a job for men, but only little boys like to hear about it.
>
> I'll wait outside for you, sir.

Solution We know that a new paragraph means that the speaker has changed. We place quotation marks around the actual words of each speaker.

> **"I like to hear them, sir."**
>
> **"Oh! Of course you do, but you're a little boy. It was a job for men, but only little boys like to hear about it."**
>
> **"I'll wait outside for you, sir."**

Titles Titles of short literary words are enclosed in quotation marks. This includes short stories, parts of books (chapters, lessons, sections, etc.), essays and sermons, one-act plays, newspaper and magazine articles, and short poems. We also enclose in quotation marks the titles of songs.

Geoffrey Chaucer's *Canterbury Tales* includes such short tales as "The Knight's Tale," "The Nun's Tale," "The Priest's Tale," and "The Miller's Tale."

Walt Whitman wrote "I Hear America Singing."

"The Leader of the People" is a short story in a collection entitled *The Long Valley*.

Note that we do not use quotation marks for larger literary works such as books, plays, movies, or operas. Instead, these are italicized or underlined (Les Miserables, *Canterbury Tales*).

Example 2 Rewrite the sentences below, inserting quotation marks where they are needed.

(a) During the Christmas season, we hear the popular song The Twelve Days of Christmas.

(b) Anh Tran recited the poem 'Twas the Night Before Christmas.

(c) Have you read the essay titled The Silver Wig?

Solution (a) We place quotation marks around "The Twelve Days of Christmas" because it is a song title. **During the Christmas season, we hear the popular song "The Twelve Days of Christmas."**

(b) We enclose "'Twas the Night Before Christmas" in quotation marks because it is a poem. **Anh Tran recited the poem "'Twas the Night Before Christmas."**

(c) We enclose the essay title, "The Silver Wig," in quotation marks. **Have you read the essay titled "The Silver Wig"?**

Practice For a–d, replace each blank with the correct vocabulary word.

a. _____ remarks seem out of place during a formal debate.

b. The city formed a committee _____ in order to purchase new recreational equipment for the park.

c. In an emotive, _____ retort, Ms. Hoot reminded the court of her opponent's large tattoo.

d. The purpose of this _____ group is to plan the next social event for the school.

e. Rewrite this dialog from "The Leader of the People," and insert quotation marks where they are needed.

> Jody ran into the kitchen. We got a letter! he cried.
> His mother looked up from a pan of beans. Who has?
> Father has. I saw it in his hand.
> Carl strode into the kitchen then, and Jody's mother asked, Who's the letter from, Carl?

Rewrite sentences f–h, inserting quotation marks as needed.

f. The Used Car Lot is a chapter from John Steinbeck's *The Grapes of Wrath*.

g. Have you heard the song Winter Wonderland?

h. James Thurber wrote an essay entitled The American Literary Scene.

More Practice See Master Worksheets.

Review Set 66 Choose the correct word(s) to complete sentences 1–15.

1. (Loath, Loathe) is an adjective meaning reluctant and unwilling.
(65)

2. A (*writ of habeas corpus, modus vivendi*) is a manner of living.
(64)

3. Supine means lying on the back with the face turned (downward, upward).
(63)

4. Primogeniture is the right of the (eldest, youngest) son to inherit his father's entire estate.
(62)

5. Phoniness and (affection, affectation, impeachment) mean almost the same.
(5)

6. Julius plays the trumpet louder than (I, me).
(63)

7. Alex and (me, myself, I) plan to run five miles today.
(50)

8. Of the two house finches, the male is the (more, most) colorful.
(40)

9. The coach handed medals to (we, us) distance runners.
(28, 63)

10. These medals are (ours, our's).
(53)

11. The relative pronoun (*who, which, that*) may refer to people, animals, or things.
(61)

12. The relative pronoun (*who, which*) may refer to animals or things.
(61)

13. My sister ignored (me, my) singing "The Bear Went Over the Mountain."
(53)

14. The drama, (which, that) involved a cruel curmudgeon, ended happily.
(62)

15. The pronoun (*who, whom*) is in the nominative case.
(61)

16. Rewrite the following, adding periods, commas, and capital letters as needed and making necessary changes to abbreviations for formal writing:
(9, 31)

dear ms snoozer

grades have closed so i cannot give you a second chance on the exam

fortunately you will have another opportunity to hear my lecture this thurs feb 2 at the public library on maple ave

sincerely

dr droner

17. Write the nominative case, first person, singular personal pronoun.
(52)

18. Use an appositive to make one sentence from these two sentences: Galileo was a modest and enthusiastic professor. Galileo performed the bulk of his scientific work at the University of Padua.
(42)

19. In the following sentence, write the verb phrase and label it transitive or intransitive:

Had the entire earth frozen?

20. From the following sentence, write the dependent clause, circling the subordinating conjunction:

Galileo continued to publish the results of his research even though the Pope condemned Galileo's findings.

21. For a and b, write the plural of each noun.

(a) donkey (b) lady (c) hypothesis

22. Write whether the underlined expression in the following sentence is essential or nonessential:

Macadamia trees, <u>which produce delicious nuts</u>, require temperate to tropical climates.

23. Write whether the following is a phrase or a clause:

pitted with craters and covered with mountainous ranges

24. Rewrite the following, adding capital letters and punctuation marks as needed:

lucy kept on humming the song take me out to the ball game

25. Write the superlative form of the adjective *bad*.

26. Rewrite the following letter as it is. Then add proofreading symbols to indicate corrections.

Dear mrs Chesterfield,

   My base ball broke your stained glass window i'm sorry how much do i oew you?

sincerely,
Frankie Howard

27. In the following sentence, write the participial phrase followed by the word it modifies:

Devastated by his wife's death and his own blindness, Galileo succumbed to death.

Diagram sentences 28–30.

28. Offering advice might be easy, but receiving it can be difficult.
(36, 56)

29. Will they appreciate my attempt to help?
(21, 45)

30. Could my giving advice destroy the friendship between them and me?
(29, 56)

LESSON 67

Demonstrative Pronouns

> **Dictation or Journal Entry**
>
> **Vocabulary:** Let us clarify the meanings of the similar words *grisly* and *grizzly*.
>
> *Grisly* is an adjective meaning "causing horror, revulsion, or fear; gruesome." *An account of a grisly accident appeared on the front page of the newspaper.*
>
> A *grizzly* is a North American brown bear that is endangered everywhere except in Alaska. *The early settlers in California greatly feared the grizzly bear.*
>
> *Grizzly* can also mean "grayish." *The actor's grizzly hair distinguished him from the younger men.*

Pointers   *This*, *that*, *these*, and *those* are **demonstrative pronouns**. Some people call them "pointing pronouns" because they seem to point out the person or thing being referred to, distinguishing it from others.

This is a portrait of James Madison.

That is his estate.

These were his resolutions.

Those make interesting exhibits.

A demonstrative pronoun must agree in number with its antecedent (the noun that it points out).

SINGULAR:	*This* is a grizzly bear.
PLURAL:	*These* are grizzly bears.
SINGULAR:	*That* is a grisly photograph.
PLURAL:	*Those* are grisly photographs.

This, These   We use *this* and *these* to point out persons or things that are nearby in space, time or awareness.

This is Montpelier.

These are antiques.

That, Those   We use *that* and *those* to point out persons or things that are farther away.

That is typical colonial dress.

Those are boots worn by colonial men.

Errors to Avoid   We never add "here" or "there" to a demonstrative pronoun.

NO: This *here* is Madison's handwriting.
YES: This is Madison's handwriting.

NO: That *there* looks like his pen.
YES: That looks like his pen.

We do not use "them" in place of "these" or "those."

NO: *Them* represent our heritage.
YES: *These* represent our heritage.

NO: *Them* wigs seem uncomfortable.
YES: *Those* wigs seem uncomfortable.

Adjective or Pronoun The demonstrative pronouns *this*, *that*, *these*, and *those* also function as demonstrative adjectives.

It is easy to tell the difference. If they stand alone, they are demonstrative pronouns. If they come before a noun, they are demonstrative adjectives.

These are primal. (pronoun)

These drafts are primal. (adjective)

James Madison penned *this*. (pronoun)

James Madison penned *this* draft. (adjective)

Example Choose the correct demonstrative pronoun for each sentence, and write the noun that it points to.

(a) (This here, This) is a man who despised abolitionists.

(b) Is (that, those) the reason he refused to free his slaves?

(c) (This, These) are my dreams for the future.

(d) (Them, Those) are her aspirations.

Solution (a) **This man.** We do not add "here" to demonstrative pronouns.

(b) **that reason.** A demonstrative pronoun must agree in number with its antecedent.

(c) **These dreams**

(d) **Those aspirations**

Practice For a–c, replace each blank with the correct vocabulary word.

a. Several California newspapers and restaurants are named after the _____ bear.

b. The lions attacking the zebra was a _____ sight.

c. Grandpa covered his _____ hair with his baseball cap.

For d–h, choose the correct demonstrative pronoun, and write the noun it points to.

d. (This, These) is an early American statesman.

e. (That, Those) are his opinions.

f. (This, These) is Orange County, Virginia.

g. (These, That) are James Madison's friends.

h. (This, This here) president helped Jefferson found the University of Virginia.

i. Replace the blank with the correct word. A demonstrative pronoun is sometimes called a _____ pronoun.

Review Set 67 Choose the correct word(s) to complete sentences 1–12.

1. (*Ad hoc, Ad hominem*) means "for a specific and limited purpose."
(66)

2. (Loath, Loathe) is a verb meaning to detest, hate, or abhor.
(65)

3. Supine and (primal, conducive, prone) are body positions.
(63)

4. Fondness and (affection, affectation, impeachment) have similar meanings.
(5)

5. If we calm or satisfy people, we (instruct, appease, bewilder) them.
(6)

6. Angela and (me, myself, I) pitched our tents and dug a well.
(50)

7. Angela worked harder than (me, I).
(63)

8. (That there, That) well is (their's, theirs, there's); this one is (our's, ours).
_(53, 67)_

9. Of the two wells, ours is the (deeper, deepest).
_(39)_

10. (This here, This) meadow belongs to (we, us) pioneers.
_(63, 67)_

11. John Paul Jones, (who, which) commanded the *Bonhomme Richard*, engaged in an intense naval combat with the British.
_(61)_

12. The large British convoy (which, that) fought against John Paul Jones finally surrendered after hours of fighting.
_(62)_

13. From this sentence, write the verb phrase and name its tense: Is Robert Walton trying to sail to the North Pole?
_(17)_

14. Rewrite the following as it is. Then add proofreading symbols to indicate corrections.
_(32)_
Victor Frankenstein became obsesssed with the idea off craeting life it self.

15. Which sentence is more polite? Write A or B.
_(51)_
A. Angela enjoyed digging with me and him.
B. Angela enjoyed digging with him and me.

16. Rewrite the following, adding periods, commas, and capital letters as needed and making necessary changes to abbreviations for formal writing:
_(31, 41)_
dear professor droner
   by fri dec 19 2003 i will no longer be enrolled at this university i plan to transfer to the univ of southern calif so i will not be able to attend your lecture
regretfully
ima snoozer

17. Write the nominative case, third person, plural personal pronoun.
_(52)_

18. Use an appositive to make one sentence from these two sentences: Frankenstein was Victor's creation. Now Frankenstein demands a mate.
_(42)_

19. In this sentence, write the verb phrase and label it action or linking: To Victor, this idea sounds disgusting.
_(3, 18)_

20. From this sentence, write the dependent clause, circling the subordinating conjunction: The monster flees after he kills Victor's bride.
(54)

21. Write the plural of each noun.
(10, 11) (a) brother-in-law (b) step-sister (c) crisis

22. Rewrite this sentence so that it is in active voice: The story was told to Robert Walton by Victor.
(27)

23. Write whether the following is a phrase or a clause: who dies at the end of the story
(20)

24. Rewrite the following, adding capital letters and punctuation marks as needed: i think said amanda that john paul jones named his ship in honor of benjamin franklin author of *poor richard's almanac*
(43, 65)

25. Write the superlative form of the adjective *courageous*.
(39)

26. Write the four principal parts of the verb *hurry*.
(13)

27. In this sentence, write the participial phrase followed by the word it modifies: The monster, standing over Victor's body, begs the dead scientist's forgiveness.
(56)

Diagram sentences 28–30.

28. That grouchy rancher might resent our agitating either his herd of cattle or his flock of sheep.
(21, 56)

29. Slander and libel are similar crimes.
(34, 36)

30. Will Nelly take the trolley, or will she ride that old bike with flat tires?
(21, 59)

LESSON 68 — Indefinite Pronouns

> **Dictation or Journal Entry**
>
> **Vocabulary:** The root *vor-* comes from the Latin verb *vorare*, meaning "to eat." The ending *ivorous* appears in words like *frug<u>ivorous</u>* (fruit-eating), *gran<u>ivorous</u>* (grain-eating), etc.
>
> *Carnivorous* means "meat-eating or flesh-eating." The zookeepers fed chunks of meat to the *carnivorous* animals.
>
> *Herbivorous* means "plant-eating." One dinosaur, the *herbivorous* Diplodocus, used its thick tail as a deadly weapon against carnivorous enemies.

A pronoun that does not have a known antecedent is called an **indefinite pronoun.** It refers to a person or thing only generally.

Singular Some indefinite pronouns refer to only one person or thing. They are singular and take singular verbs:

another	*anybody*	*anyone*
anything	*neither*	*either*
everybody	*everyone*	*everything*
each	*nobody*	*no one*
nothing	*other*	*one*
somebody	*someone*	*something*
much		

Everybody in her classes <u>appreciates</u> her humor.

Each of the students <u>laughs</u> at her jokes.

Neither of the teachers <u>remembers</u> my name.

Nothing <u>is</u> more frustrating.

Plural The following indefinite pronouns refer to more than one person or thing. They take plural verbs:

several	*both*	*few*
ones	*many*	*others*

Both of them <u>favor</u> herbivorous pets.

Few of their sheep <u>need</u> shearing.

Many in the flock <u>are</u> lost.

Others <u>seem</u> hungry.

Either Singular or Plural Some indefinite pronouns can be singular or plural depending on their use in the sentence:

all   any   most
none   some

They are plural when they refer to things that can be counted.

Most of the rooms <u>are</u> blue.

They are singular when they refer to things that cannot be counted.

Most of the house <u>is</u> blue.

Example 1 Write each indefinite pronoun and tell whether it is singular or plural in the sentence.

(a) I hope that all of the carnivores have been fed.

(b) I believe much of the opposition to the Constitution was led by George Mason.

(c) Today, many in Virginia remember George Mason.

(d) Has most of the food been prepared?

(e) Has all of the house been freshly painted?

(f) Of course, none of the delegates agree with the entire document.

Solution (a) ***all*, plural** (can be counted)   (b) ***much*, singular**

(c) ***many*, plural**   (d) ***most*, singular**

(e) ***all*, singular** (cannot be counted) (f) ***none*, plural** (can be counted)

Example 2 Choose the correct verb form (singular or plural) to match the indefinite pronouns in each sentence.

(a) (Is, Are) *all* of you familiar with George Mason?

(b) *Few* in Virginia (have, has) forgotten him.

(c) *Many* of us (realize, realizes) that he refused to sign the Constitution.

(d) (Is, Are) *anything* more important than our Bill of Rights?

Solution (a) **Are** *all* of you familiar with George Mason?

(b) *Few* in Virginia **have** forgotten him.

(c) *Many* of us **realize** that he refused to sign the Constitution.

(d) **Is** *anything* more important than our Bill of Rights?

Adjective or Pronoun? Just like demonstrative pronouns, when indefinite pronouns are placed before nouns, they function as indefinite adjectives.

Some recall the dates. (pronoun)

Some students recall the dates. (adjective)

Agreement with Antecedents If an indefinite pronoun is the antecedent for a personal pronoun, the personal pronoun must agree in number, person, and gender with its antecedent.

SINGULAR: *Everything* serves *its* purpose.
(antecedent)   (personal pronoun)

PLURAL: *Both* serve *their* purpose.
(antecedent) (personal pronoun)

There is an exception. When writing, we do not use the plural *their* with the singular *everyone, everybody*, etc. When speaking, however, it has become acceptable to use *their* when *him* or *her* would sound awkward.

SPOKEN: *Everybody* does *their* part.

WRITTEN: *Everybody* does *his* or *her* part.

Example 3 Choose the correct personal pronoun to match the antecedent.

(a) Most of the delegates represent (their, his/her) states faithfully.

(b) Everybody believes (their, his/her) opinion is correct.

(c) However, nobody ridicules (their, his/her) neighbor.

Solution (a) The antecedent *most* is plural; it refers to delegates, which can be counted. Therefore, we choose a plural personal pronoun—**their**.

Most of the delegates represent **their** states faithfully.

(b) The antecedent *everybody* is singular, so we choose a singular pronoun—**his/her**.

Everybody believes **his or her** opinion is correct.

(c) The antecedent *nobody* is singular, so we choose a singular personal pronoun—**his or her**.

However, nobody ridicules **his or her** neighbor.

Practice For sentences a and b, write the indefinite pronoun and tell whether it is singular or plural.

   a. All of them treasure their freedom.

   b. Nothing justifies imprisonment without just cause.

For sentences c–e, choose the correct verb form to match the indefinite pronoun.

   c. *None* of the leaders (agree, agrees) with every aspect of the issue.

   d. (Do, does) some of the members desire a stronger central government?

   e. *Each* of the candidates (speak, speaks) in turn.

For f–h, choose the correct personal pronoun and verb form to match the indefinite pronoun antecedent.

   f. *Several* of the leaders (share, shares) the opinion of (their, his/her) political party.

   g. *Everything* in the news (is, are) scrutinized for (its, their) accuracy.

   h. *One* of my friends (want, wants) to nominate (their, his/her) sister for President.

For i–k, replace each blank with the correct vocabulary word.

   i. The Latin verb _____ means "to eat."

j. Animals that eat buffalo, venison, and other types of meat are _____.

k. The _____ sheep grazed in the green pasture chewing their cud and consuming only grass and grains.

More Practice Tell whether each indefinite pronoun is "singular," "plural," or "either."

1. most   2. both   3. anybody   4. neither

5. either   6. some   7. everyone   8. few

9. everything   10. ones   11. each   12. many

13. something   14. nothing   15. others   16. some

17. another   18. several   19. none   20. all

Review Set 68 Choose the correct word(s) to complete sentences 1–14.

1. (Grisly, Grizzly) means gruesome.
(67)

2. (Ad hoc, Ad hominem) means "using emotion rather than reason."
(66)

3. Loath is a(n) (adjective, verb, noun).
(65)

4. The Latin root *plac-* means (fight, argue, appease).
(6)

5. The Latin root *pac-* means (war, peace, party).
(6)

6. The First Lady waved to my sister and (me, myself, I) as she passed.
(28, 51)

7. Senator Dill has more powerful constituents than (he, him).
(63)

8. (Who's, Whose) conjecture was that?
(64)

9. The flowers (which, that) Tim sent to Esther arrived on her birthday.
(62)

10. I was astounded, for (us, we) Knights effortlessly won the volleyball game against the Panthers.
(63)

11. My friends acted embarrassed by (me, my) singing "Polly Wolly Doodle" as we strolled through the mall.

12. Will the general manager appoint the committee chairperson (hisself, himself)?

13. (Them, Those) charlatans like to hear (theirselves, themselves) talk.

14. Nobody in these apartments (appreciates, appreciate) cockroaches indoors.

15. Rewrite the following, adding capital letters and punctuation marks as needed: mary shelly the author of *frankenstein* liked to exchange scary stories with friends

16. From this sentence, write the verb phrase and name its tense: Have you finished reading *Frankenstein* yet?

17. Write the objective case, third person, plural personal pronoun.

18. Use an appositive to make one sentence from these two sentences: *Frankenstein* spawned two new literary genres. These genres were science fiction and horror.

19. In this sentence, write whether the underlined expression is essential or nonessential: The goose <u>that stole my sandwich</u> had a red band around its leg.

20. From this sentence, write the dependent clause, circling the subordinating conjunction: Since Mary Shelly was vacationing with some of England's greatest writers, she was hesitant to share her masterpiece.

21. In this sentence, write the verb phrase and label it action or linking: Mary Shelly portrayed the ethical dangers of experimenting with life.

22. Rewrite this sentence so that it is in active voice: *The Time Machine* was written by H. G. Wells.

23. Rewrite the following as it is. Then add proofreading symbols to indicate corrections.

An inquistive scientist beleives in in travel threw time

24. Write whether the following is a phrase or a clause: as he frantically searches for his time machine
(20)

25. Write the comparative form of the adjective *noisy*.
(39)

26. Write the four principal parts of the irregular verb *steal*.
(13)

27. In this sentence, write the participial phrase followed by the word it modifies: Engulfed by the fear of losing contact with his own age, the Time Traveler flies into a desperate search for his time machine.
(56)

Diagram sentences 28–30.

28. Will gathering rocks or seashells entertain Emily and him?
(21, 56)

29. Are both Arizona and New Mexico Southwest states?
(35, 36)

30. Debby, whom you have met, will demonstrate glassblowing.
(21, 61)

LESSON 69

Italics or Underline

> **Dictation or Journal Entry**
>
> **Vocabulary:** Notice the difference between the similar words *lightning* and *lightening*.
>
> *Lightning* is a brilliant electrical discharge in the atmosphere. *Lightning* and thunder accompanied the violent hail storm.
>
> *Lightening* means making lighter or brighter. She is *lightening* the paint color by adding white.
>
> *Lightening* can also mean "making less heavy; reducing the weight or load." I am *lightening* my burden by leaving the heavy items behind.

The word **italics** refers to a slightly slanted style of type that is used to indicate titles of larger literary works or to bring special emphasis to a word of phrase in a sentence. The book title below is in italics.

London Public Ledger

When we handwrite material, or when the italic style of type is not available, we **underline** the word or words that require italics in print.

London Public Ledger

Here are some of the main categories of words and phrases that should be italicized or underlined.

Longer Literary Works, Movies, CD's, etc. We italicize or underline titles of books, magazines, newspapers, pamphlets, plays, book-length poems, television shows, movies, films, record albums, tapes, and CD's.

Grandpa enjoyed reading *Life Magazine*.

Tonight, Dad and I will watch Gone with the Wind.

Ships, Planes, and Trains We italicize or underline the names of ships, planes, and trains. (Words such as "The" and "U.S.S." are not treated as part of the vehicle's name.)

Howard Hughes named his plane the *Spruce Goose*.

Most colonists appreciated the hardships suffered by their predecessors on the Mayflower.

Paintings and Sculptures We italicize or underline the names of famous paintings, sculptures, and other works of art.

> The French sculptor Rodin fashioned *The Thinker* out of bronze.

> Vincent van Gogh painted the famous <u>Starry Night</u>.

Example 1 For sentences a–e, underline all words that should be italicized in print.

(a) Charles Lindbergh completed the first solo, non-stop, transatlantic flight in the Spirit of St. Louis.

(b) Leaves of Grass is a book-length poem written in neither rhyme nor blank verse, but in a sort of excited prose.

(c) Rembrandt van Rijn painted Return of the Prodigal Son.

Solution (a) We underline **<u>Spirit of St. Louis</u>** because it is the name of an airplane.

(b) **<u>Leaves of Grass</u>** is a book-length poem.

(c) **<u>Return of the Prodigal Son</u>** is a famous painting.

Words as Words We italicize or underline a word when the sentence calls attention to the word **as a word.**

> To use *gonna* for *going to* is improper.

> The word *lobby* can be either a verb or a noun.

> Dinah wrote *there* when she meant *their*.

This is also true for numerals and lowercase letters.

> Unfortunately, my handwritten *o* looked like an *a*, so the word *cot* looked like *cat*. In addition, my *5*'s looked like *s*'s.

Foreign Words and Phrases We italicize or underline foreign words not commonly used in everyday English language. We also italicize or underline scientific terms.

> At a market in France, we bought some *fromage*, or cheese.

> Dad often uses *adios* to bid people farewell.

Genus and Species Names We italicize or underline the scientific names for a genus, species, or subspecies.

> To learn about the gum tree, you must look under its scientific name, *Eucalyptus*.
>
> Mollies are a tropical fish of the genus *Mollienesia*.

Example 2 For sentences a and b, underline all parts that should be italicized in print.

(a) The numbers 8 and 0 looked similar in the digital display.

(b) The Spanish teacher explained that tarea means "homework."

Solution (a) We underline **8** and **0** because these numbers are used out of context.

(b) **Tarea** is a foreign word.

Practice For a–d, replace each blank with the correct vocabulary word.

a. A flash of _____ sent the frightened children scurrying under their beds as the winter storm unleashed its fury.

b. We are _____ the color of the fabric by soaking it in chlorine bleach.

c. A _____ rod protects a building during a thunder storm by conducting the electricity to the ground.

d. I am _____ tomorrow's homework load by doing extra work today.

Write and underline the words that should be italicized in sentences e–i.

e. Mimi found a new squash recipe in her local newspaper, The Purple Mountain Muse.

f. Please do not use huh when you want me to repeat something.

g. The mockingbird, or mimus polyglottos, sings an exuberant song both day and night.

h. The French use bonjour to greet each other in the morning.

i. The Nina was one of the three ships under the command of Columbus when he made his first voyage to America in 1492.

More Practice See Master Worksheets.

Review set 69 Choose the correct word(s) to complete sentences 1–13.

1. The Latin verb (*amare, venire, vorare*) means "to eat."
(68)

2. (Grisly, Grizzly) is a North American brown bear.
(67)

3. Loathe is a(n) (adjective, verb, noun).
(65)

4. The Latin term *pro tempore* means (forever, for a little while, in the past).
(7)

5. Glenda and Wassim are in love. Their affectionate feelings are (impeachable, mutual, democratic).
(8)

6. Kyle and (him, himself, he) created the website (themselves, theirselves).
(57)

7. Miss Tran drives farther than (me, myself, I) every day.
(63)

8. Not everybody (wash, washes) (their, his/her) car weekly.
(68)

9. The music, (which, that) sounded like Mozart, made me nostalgic.
(62)

10. Will you meet with (us, we) clarinet players after the parade?
(63)

11. (Him, His) playing Haydn's sonatas on the piano creates a soothing atmosphere.
(53)

12. Did you see (them, those) lightning flashes?
(67)

13. Neither of us (remember, remembers) which indefinite nouns take singular verbs.
(68)

14. Rewrite this sentence adding capital letters and punctuation marks as needed: unfortunately said ernie i missed the bus on elm street so i took a taxi instead

15. Write the plural of each noun.
(a) parenthesis   (b) armload   (c) virtuoso

16. Rewrite the following as it is. Then add proofreading symbols to indicate corrections.

Henry James writed The turn Of the Screw, a early pyschological thriller I read it last year.

17. Write the nominative case, first person, plural pronoun.

18. Use an appositive to make one sentence from these two sentences: Manatees are nonaggressive herbivores. Herbivores are plant-eating animals.

19. In this sentence, write whether the underlined expression is essential or nonessential: The trail, <u>which is narrow and rocky</u>, ascends to eleven thousand feet above sea level.

20. From this sentence, write the dependent clause, circling the subordinating conjunction: While the mystery surrounding the death of the previous governess causes some alarm, the new woman takes the job.

21. In this sentence, write the verb phrase and label it transitive or intransitive: After the volleyball game, we were jumping for joy!

22. In this sentence, write the indefinite pronoun and label it singular, plural, or either: I don't know if either of the mathematicians has the correct answer.

23. Write the reflexive pronoun in this sentence: The new governess judges the children herself.

24. Write whether the following is a complete sentence, sentence fragment, or run-on sentence: Peter Quint, a former valet, appears to the princess.

25. Write the comparative form of the adjective *good*.

26. Rewrite this sentence so that it is in active voice: The governess is puzzled by the children's secrecy.
(27)

27. In this sentence, write the participial phrase followed by the word it modifies: Having learned about Mr. Quint and Miss Jessel, the governess ponders the children's secrecy.
(56)

28. Write and underline each word that should be italicized in this sentence: Nihao is a Chinese greeting.
(69)

Diagram sentences 29 and 30.

29. Chris likes building small houses for the cardinals.
(16, 21)

30. Those quarreling cousins sound immature.
(38, 56)

LESSON 70 — Irregular Verbs, Part 3

> **Dictation or Journal Entry**
>
> **Vocabulary:** The Latin verb *credere* means "to believe" and forms the base of familiar words like *credible*, *incredible*, *credentials*, etc.
>
> *Credence* is belief, especially in the statements of others. Let's not give *credence* to rumors.
>
> *Credulity* is the willingness to believe, accept, or trust without sufficient evidence; gullibility. With *credulity*, Manny listened attentively as I told the tall tale.

We have already learned that there are no rules for forming the past tense and past participle of irregular verbs. In this lesson, we will look at some additional irregular verbs.

Remember that we must memorize the principal parts of irregular verbs. To test yourself, cover the past and past participle forms, then try to write or say the past and past participle for each verb. Make a new list of the ones you miss, and work to memorize them.

VERB	PAST	PAST PARTICIPLE
beat	beat	(has) beaten
bite	bit	(has) bitten
bring	brought	(has) brought
build	built	(has) built
burst	burst	(has) burst
buy	bought	(has) bought
catch	caught	(has) caught
come	came	(has) come
cost	cost	(has) cost
dive	dove	(has) dived
drag	dragged	(has) dragged
draw	drew	(has) drawn
drown	drowned	(has) drowned
drive	drove	(has) driven
eat	ate	(has) eaten
fall	fell	(has) fallen
feel	felt	(has) felt
fight	fought	(has) fought
flee	fled	(has) fled
flow	flowed	(has) flowed

fly   flew   (has) flown
forsake   forsook   (has) forsaken

Example 1   Write the past tense and past participle forms of each verb.
(a) fly   (b) bite   (c) flee   (d) dive

Solution   (a) fly, **flew, (has) flown**

(b) bite, **bit, (has) bitten**

(c) flee, **fled, (has) fled**

(d) dive, **dove, (has) dived**

Example 2   Write the correct verb form for each sentence.
(a) George Mason (brang, brought, brung) his thoughts together in the Fairfax Resolves.

(b) He had not (forsook, forsaken, forsake) his conscience.

(c) George Mason (draw, drew, drawn) up the Fairfax Resolves knowing that war was almost inevitable.

Solution   (a) George Mason **brought** his thoughts together in the Fairfax Resolves.

(b) He had not **forsaken** his conscience.

(c) George Mason **drew** up the Fairfax Resolves knowing that war was almost inevitable.

Errors to Avoid   People sometimes treat a regular verb as if it were irregular. For example, the past tense of *drag* is *dragged*, not "drug." The past tense of *drown* is simply *drowned*, not "drownded." Avoid these errors by memorizing the irregular verbs and consulting a dictionary when in doubt. If the dictionary does not list the verb's principle parts, the verb is regular.

Practice   For a–h, write the past and past participle form of each verb.
a. catch   b. fight   c. eat   d. feel

e. beat   f. drive   g. flow   h. fall

For i–n, write the correct verb form for each sentence.

i. George Mason (build, builded, built) his home, Gunston Hall, in Maryland.

j. He had (buy, buyed, bought) sixty thousand acres of land in western Virginia and Kentucky.

k. Sixty thousand acres (cost, costed, costs) very little then compared to today's prices.

l. He had (comed, came, come) to the conclusion that independence was necessary.

m. When change comes along, do you (drag, dragged, drug) your feet, or move reluctantly, like many of the colonists did?

n. Many colonists must have (eat, eaten, ate) with wooden dentures.

For o–q, replace each blank with the correct vocabulary word.

o. We gain the _____ of our friends when we speak the truth and keep our promises.

p. The Latin verb meaning "to believe" is _____.

q. I bought the product with _____, not knowing the salesperson was a fraud.

More Practice See Master Worksheets.

Review set 70 Choose the correct word to complete sentences 1–13.

1. (Lightning, Lightening) is a brilliant electrical discharge in the atmosphere.
(69)

2. The Latin verb *vorare* means to (love, eat, come).
(68)

3. (Grisly, Grizzly) means "grayish."
(67)

4. The hot, barren desert is (bellicose, bicameral, inhospitable) to tropical plants.
(9)

5. We might organize a (quorum, caucus, hospice) to
(9, 10) discuss the improvement of our town's recreation facilities.

6. Mervyn asked advice from two women, Candace and
(63) (she, her).

7. Dr. Chu (himself, hisself) arrived at the hospital before
(57) (we, us).

8. *Several, both, few, ones, many,* and *others* are always
(68) (singular, plural) indefinite pronouns.

9. The humming birds (which, that) come to my feeder get
(62) plenty to eat.

10. Did you see (we, us) trombone players as we marched
(63) with the band down Main Street?

11. The team was weary of (him, his) complaining.
(53)

12. This parking place is his, not (their's, theirs).
(53)

13. Neither of the colors (match, matches) the sofa.
(68)

Rewrite 14 and 15, adding capital letters and punctuation marks as needed.

14. my dad read me a chapter titled turning on the light but i
(9, 66) didn't understand it for it was too technical

15. yes said ms wong we shall review the history of france
(60, 66) next monday

16. Write the correct verb form in this sentence: The
(5) President (present tense of *rely*) on his cabinet for advice.

17. Write the objective case, first person, plural pronoun.
(51)

18. In the sentence that follows, write the verb phrase and
(8) name its tense: Shall we squeeze these lemons to make lemonade?

19. In this sentence, write whether the underlined
(62) expression is essential or nonessential: Ironically, the

global warming meeting, which was held in Oregon, was postponed because of ice, snow, and freezing rain.

20. From this sentence, write the dependent clause, circling the subordinating conjunction: I'll play tennis with you as soon as I finish this homework assignment.
(54)

21. Rewrite the following sentence so that it is in active voice: The governess was surprised by the ending.
(27)

22. In this sentence, write the indefinite pronoun and label it singular, plural, or either: Several of the nurses have gone to help the suffering in other countries.
(68)

23. Rewrite the following as it is. Then add proofreading symbols to indicate corrections.
(32)

Andrew listens too his conscience he is is not afriad to stand alone.

24. Write whether the following is a phrase or a clause: clicking her shiny, new, monogrammed ball-point pen with three colors of ink.
(20)

25. Write the superlative form of the adjective *conducive*.
(39)

26. Write the four principal parts of the verb *bring*.
(13)

27. In this sentence, write the infinitive used as an adjective: Since she was tired of standing, Isabel was looking for a place to sit.
(45)

28. Write and underline each word that should be italicized in this sentence: In a New York art center, we saw Alexander Liberman's exceptionally large sculpture called Iliad.
(69)

Diagram sentences 29 and 30.

29. One of my friends endured running the marathon.
(56, 68)

30. Were the geologists, whom we met, studying the soil on Mars?
(21, 61)

LESSON 71

Irregular Verbs, Part 4

> **Dictation or Journal Entry**
> **Vocabulary:** The meanings of *noisome* and *noisy* are unrelated.
> *Noisome* means offensive, especially to the smell. It also means harmful, or injurious. We could barely breathe because of the *noisome* fumes.
> *Noisy* means making noise or racket. A *noisy* mob thronged the ticket booth before the concert.

In this lesson, we will review more irregular verbs, whose principal parts we must memorize. To test yourself, cover the past and past participle forms, then try to write or say the past and past participle for each verb. Make a new list for yourself of the forms you miss, and work to memorize them.

VERB	PAST	PAST PARTICIPLE
give	gave	(has) given
go	went	(has) gone
hang (execute)	hanged	(has) hanged
hang (dangle)	hung	(has) hung
hide	hid	(has) hidden, hid
hold	held	(has) held
lay	laid	(has) laid
lead	led	(has) led
lend	lent	(has) lent
lie (recline)	lay	(has) lain
lie (deceive)	lied	(has) lied
lose	lost	(has) lost
make	made	(has) made
mistake	mistook	(has) mistaken
put	put	(has) put
raise	raised	(has) raised
ride	rode	(has) ridden
rise	rose	(has) risen
run	ran	(has) run
see	saw	(has) seen
sell	sold	(has) sold

Example 1 Write the past and past participle forms of each verb.

(a) lie (deceive) (b) lie (recline)

(c) hang (dangle) (d) hang (execute)

Solution (a) lie, **lied, (has) lied**

(b) lie, **lay, (has) lain**

(c) hang, **hung, (has) hung**

(d) hang, **hanged, (has) hanged**

Example 2 Write the correct verb form for each sentence.

(a) George Mason (give, gave, given) his reasons for opposing the Constitution.

(b) He (see, saw, seen) the flaws of human nature.

(c) George Washington had (mistake, mistook, mistaken) the honest intentions of George Mason.

Solution (a) George Mason **gave** his reasons for opposing the Constitution.

(b) He **saw** the flaws of human nature.

(c) George Washington had **mistaken** the honest intentions of George Mason.

Practice For a–h, write the past and past participle form of each verb.

a. make   **b.** raise   **c.** lose

d. hide   **e.** hold   **f.** lay

g. ride   **h.** rise   **i.** lend

For j–m, write the correct verb form for each sentence.

j. George Wythe (lead, led, leaded) a protest against the Stamp Act.

k. Later, he (go, went, gone) to Philadelphia to sign the Declaration of Independence.

l. The judge had (put, putted, putten) his gavel on the podium.

m. Had he ever (run, ran, runned) for a seat in the House of Burgesses?

For n and o, replace each blank with the correct vocabulary word.

n. The _____ engine shook the windows of my home.

o. Rotten eggs emit a _____ odor.

More Practice See Master Worksheets.

Review set 71 Choose the correct word to complete sentences 1–14.

1. The Latin verb (*vorare, amare, credere*) means "to believe."
(70)

2. (Lightning, Lightening) means making lighter or brighter.
(69)

3. Carnivorous means meat-(grinding, eating, ball).
(68)

4. Ambivalent attitudes are (decisive, conflicting, hospitable).
(59)

5. Although they did not know one another, the two students worked well together. They had an (ambivalent, amicable, ambiguous) relationship.
(12)

6. We use the relative pronoun (who, whom) for the subject of a sentence.
(61)

7. If the relative pronoun functions as an object, we use (who, whom).
(61)

8. Not everyone (appreciate, appreciates) a weasel on (their, his or her) property.
(68)

9. The creek, (that, which) freezes in winter, runs through my backyard.
(62)

10. (We, Us) algebra students try to help one another.
(63)

11. The captain encouraged (us, our) resting before the big race.
(53, 63)

12. I found (this, this here) treasure in the attic.
(67)

13. Puddleglum, (who, whom) the reader will remember, has a rather pessimistic disposition.
(61)

14. Alice has (brung, bringed, brought) that white rabbit to school every day this week.
(70)

15. Rewrite the following as it is. Then add proofreading symbols to indicate corrections.
(32)

This novel is about a youngman whom sells his sole for worldly vanity

16. Rewrite the following so that it is in active voice: Dorian Gray is tempted by Henry Wotton.
(27)

17. Write the possessive case, first person, plural pronoun.
(52)

18. Write the indefinite pronoun in this sentence and label it singular, plural, or either: Has everybody studied for the Constitution test?
(68)

19. In this sentence, write whether the underlined expression is essential or nonessential: My watch, which needs a new battery, is running behind today.
(62)

20. From this sentence, write the dependent clause, circling the subordinating conjunction: Miss Informed thought that today was a holiday.
(54)

21. In this sentence, write the verb phrase and label it transitive or intransitive: Bonnie might have been snoring loudly with her head under a pillow.
(26)

22. Write the five indefinite pronouns from this list that can be either singular or plural depending on their use in the sentence: nobody, all, both, none, someone, many, any, some, most
(68)

23. In the following sentence, write the gerund phrase and label its tense present or perfect: Having mastered the irregular verbs allowed Zack to score high on the test.
(15, 55)

24. Write whether the following is a complete sentence, sentence fragment, or run-on sentence: Imagining the punctual arrival of a horse and carriage.
(2)

25. For a–c, write the plural of each noun.
(10, 11) (a) trunkful   (b) Justice of the Peace   (c) calamity

26. Write the four principal parts of the irregular verb *build*.
(13, 70)

27. Use an appositive to make one sentence from the
(42) following two sentences: Albrecht Dürer was a German artist who lived over five hundred years ago. Albrecht Dürer painted a realistic, lifelike picture called *Young Hare*.

28. Write and underline each word that should be italicized
(69) in the following sentence: From cut-out pieces of colored paper stuck on a white background, Matisse created his abstract picture called The Snail.

Diagram sentences 29 and 30.

29. Waxing his car is the deputy's favorite pastime.
(36, 56)

30. Who is that deputy waxing his car?
(36, 56)

LESSON 72

Irregular Verbs, Part 5

> **Dictation or Journal Entry**
>
> **Vocabulary:** Let us examine the words *literally* and *figuratively*.
>
> *Literally* means word for word; in the literal or strict sense rather than in the figurative sense. Don't take his fish story *literally*.
>
> *Figuratively* means involving a figure of speech; metaphorically; not literally. *To beat around the bush* is a figurative expression. William Shakespeare uses the garden literally as his subject, but he uses it *figuratively* to represent the world.

In this lesson, we will review the last group of irregular verbs, whose principal parts we must memorize. To test yourself, cover the past and past participle forms, then try to write or say the past and past participle for each verb. Make a new list for yourself of the forms you miss, and work to memorize them.

Verb	Past	Past Participle
set	set	(has) set
shake	shook	(has) shaken
shine (light)	shone	(has) shone
shine (polish)	shined	(has) shined
shut	shut	(has) shut
sit	sat	(has) sat
slay	slew	(has) slain
sleep	slept	(has) slept
spring	sprang, sprung	(has) sprung
stand	stood	(has) stood
strive	strove	(has) striven
swim	swam	(has) swum
swing	swung	(has) swung
take	took	(has) taken
teach	taught	(has) taught
tell	told	(has) told
think	thought	(has) thought
wake	woke, waked	(has) waked
weave	wove	(has) woven
wring	wrung	(has) wrung
write	wrote	(has) written

Example 1 Write the past and past participle forms of each verb.

(a) swim (b) wring (c) spring (d) sleep (e) weave

Solution (a) swim, **swam, (has) swum**

(b) wring, **wrung, (has) wrung**

(c) spring, **sprang or sprung, (has) sprung**

(d) sleep, **slept, (has) slept**

(e) weave, **wove, (has) woven**

Example 2 Write the correct verb form for each sentence.

(a) John Blair, Jr. (stand, stood, standed) behind Britain for as long as he could.

(b) Sadly, many soldiers had been (slayed, slaid, slain) by the end of the war.

(c) Leaders of the Revolution (thinked, thought) highly of John Blair, Jr.

Solution (a) John Blair, Jr. **stood** behind Britain for as long as he could.

(b) Sadly, many soldiers had been **slain** by the end of the war.

(c) Leaders of the Revolution **thought** highly of John Blair, Jr.

Practice For a–f, write the past and past participle form of each verb.

a. shut **b.** shine (light) **c.** shine (polish)

d. shake **e.** strive **f.** wake

For g–l, write the correct verb form for each sentence.

g. John Blair, Jr.'s parents had (teached, taught) him conservative values.

h. Frederick Horner (write, wrote, written) *History of the Blair, Banister, and Braxton Families.*

i. A helpful cicerone (telled, told) the guests what each of the signers of the Constitution had contributed.

j. John Blair, Jr. (strive, strove, striven) to peacefully protest the policies of the British government.

k. The lifeguard has (swim, swam, swum) her laps.

l. Edmund Randolph (swing, swang, swung) back and forth from Federalist to Antifederalist.

For m–p, replace each blank with *figuratively* or *literally*.

m. Through the use of similes, metaphors, and other literary devices, poets express their thoughts _____.

n. The driver _____ ran out of gas and his car came to a halt.

o. I was speaking _____ when I said that I would "give you a hand."

p. I did not take it _____ when he encouraged me to "hit the books."

More Practice See Master Worksheets.

Review set 72 Choose the correct word to complete sentences 1–14.

1. (Noisome, Noisy) means making noise or racket.
(71)

2. The Latin verb *credere* means to (eat, love, believe).
(70)

3. (Lightning, Lightening) means making less heavy.
(69)

4. Herbivorous means plant-(fertilizing, eating, growing).
(68)

5. The government takes a (quorum, census, hospice) to determine how many people live in certain areas.
(13)

6. To (who, whom) are you referring?
(61)

7. That drummer, (who, whom) we heard at the concert, might be famous someday.
(61)

8. Each of the artists (need, needs) (their, his/her) own gallery to display paintings.

9. The bus (that, which) just arrived will leave in fifteen minutes.

10. (We, Us) apple pickers worked ten hours yesterday.

11. Ima Snoozer appreciates (me, my) nudging her during Professor Droner's lectures.

12. (Those, Them) badminton players have wrecked three shuttlecocks this afternoon.

13. Is this racquet (her's, hers)?

14. Yesterday, Mario gathered his courage and (dived, dove) into the chilly lake.

Rewrite 15 and 16, adding capital letters and punctuation marks as needed.

15. banishing the procrastinators the sluggards and the hoodlums the queen keeps only the punctual the diligent and the conscientious in her palace

16. next tuesday said tina i shall fly from denver colorado to dallas texas

17. Write the possessive case, third person, singular (masculine) pronoun.

18. Write the indefinite pronoun in this sentence and label it singular, plural, or either: Much is required of Professor Angles's geometry students.

19. In this sentence, write whether the underlined expression is essential or nonessential: Miss Beagle's leather leash, <u>which hung near the back door</u>, looked old and worn.

20. Write the intensive personal pronoun in this sentence: The queen herself must discern who is a trustworthy citizen and who is a swindler, or a fake.

21. From this sentence, write the infinitive and tell whether it functions as a noun or an adjective: I think Lord Chestnut is the phony to expose.
(19, 45)

22. In this sentence, write the participial phrase followed by the word it modifies: Pontificating loudly from the balcony, Lord Chestnut has everyone's rapt attention.
(56)

23. Rewrite the following as it is. Then add proofreading symbols to indicate corrections.
(32)

Dorian gray will give his soul too stay yung

24. From this sentence, write the personal pronoun and its antecedent: Does Lord Chestnut really believe he can fool the queen?
(46)

25. Write the comparative form of the adjective *little* (amount).
(40)

26. Write the four principal parts of the irregular verb *eat*.
(13, 70)

27. Rewrite the following so that it is in active voice: Is the portrait of Dorian Gray destroyed by the artist Basil Hallward?
(27)

28. Write and underline each word that should be italicized in this sentence: The scientific name for lobster, a decapod crustacean found in North Atlantic waters, is Homarus americanus.
(69)

Diagram sentences 29 and 30.

29. The silliest jesters were my sister and he.
(24, 36)

30. My friend Ann enjoys photographing desert sunsets and sketching horned toads.
(21, 56)

LESSON 73

The Exclamation Mark • The Question Mark • The Dash

> **Dictation or Journal Entry**
>
> **Vocabulary:** The Latin word for "faith" is *fides,* which gives us the English root *fid-,* as in the familiar words *confid*ence, in*fid*el, and *fid*elity.
>
> An *affidavit* is a written declaration certified before a judge or other authority. A police officer must file an *affidavit* in order to receive a search warrant.
>
> As a noun, a *fiduciary* is a person chosen to manage the property or affairs of another. A *fiduciary* will dispense the assets of the deceased as directed by the trust.
>
> As an adjective, *fiduciary* means relating to a thing held in trust. Bob will oversee his brother's *fiduciary* estate.

Almost every sentence ends with one of three punctuation marks. The period, the exclamation mark, and the question mark are called final, or terminal, punctuation marks.

Exclamation Mark   We use an **exclamation mark** after an exclamatory sentence (a sentence showing strong emotion).

>   Come and look! The sunset is beautiful!

We can also use an exclamation mark after a word or phrase showing strong emotion. We call this an **interjection.**

>   Wow! What a sight!
>
>   Whoa! Slow down, Tiger!

We limit our use of exclamation marks, for they are like shouting. One who shouts all the time is soon ignored, so we use exclamation marks sparingly.

Question Mark   We place a **question mark** at the end of an interrogative sentence (one that asks a question).

>   Are you familiar with George Wythe?
>
>   Did he draft a petition to the British Crown against the Stamp Act?

With Quotation Marks   When using exclamation marks and question marks with quotation marks, we must decide whether to place the final punctuation mark *inside* or *outside* the quotation marks. We do this by determining if the final punctuation mark punctuates the whole sentence or just the part in quotation marks.

In the sentence below, only the words in quotation marks ask a question. The question mark punctuates only the direct quotation, so it goes *inside* the quotation marks.

"Will you be here tomorrow?" asked the teacher.

In the next sentence, the question mark punctuates the whole sentence, so it goes *outside* the quotation marks:

Did you know that the Virginia state seal, *Sic Semper Tyrannis*, means "thus ever to tyrants"?

Example 1 Rewrite sentences a–d and insert exclamation and question marks as needed.

(a) Who first called for the political independence of the colonies

(b) You're so brilliant

(c) Did Wythe convince his fellow legislators with his argument

(d) Incredible He trained such famous lawyers as John Marshall, James Monroe, and Henry Clay

Solution (a) This interrogative sentence requires a question mark.

Who first called for the political independence of the colonies?

(b) **You're so brilliant!** (exclamatory sentence)

(c) This interrogative sentence requires a question mark.

Did Wythe convince his fellow legislators with his argument?

(d) **Incredible! He trained such famous lawyers as John Marshall, James Monroe, and Henry Clay!** Interjections and exclamatory sentences require exclamation marks.

Dash Another punctuation mark that we must use sparingly is the **dash.** The dash can indicate a sudden change in thoughts, an interruption in the flow of the sentence, faltering speech, or an abrupt halt to speech.

George Wythe submitted a list of corrective alterations—yes, it upset some people—to the Virginian ratification convention.

This scholar—um, if I remember right—was seventy when he mastered the Hebrew language.

James McClurg—please pay close attention—was one of the most ill-suited delegates.

A dash can also be used to offset certain words or phrases for emphasis.

George Washington, James Madison, George Mason, and George Wythe—these and other Virginians served at the Constitutional Convention.

One of the most distinguished was George Wythe—lawyer, jurist, professor, and statesman.

He became a professor of law at William and Mary—the first American to hold such a position.

Errors to Avoid We do *not* use a dash in place of a period. The following is *incorrect*:

James McClurg was a respected member of the medical profession—He was a high Federalist interested in protecting large investments.

The two, separate sentences above must be separated by a period, not a dash:

James McClurg was a respected member of the medical profession. He was a high Federalist interested in protecting large investments.

Example 2 Rewrite sentences a–c, inserting dashes where they are needed.

(a) James McClurg let me think came from a family of physicians.

(b) He received his M.D. from the University of Edinburgh perhaps the finest medical school in the world.

(c) "Watch out for the" said Zena as James tripped on the hose.

Solution (a) We place a dash to indicate an interruption in the flow of the sentence. **James McClurg—let me think—came from a family of physicians.**

(b) We use a dash for emphasis. **He received his M.D. from the University of Edinburgh—perhaps the finest medical school in the world.**

(c) We use a dash to indicate an abrupt halt to speech. **"Watch out for the—" said Zena as James tripped on the hose.**

Practice Rewrite sentences a–d and place exclamation marks and question marks where they are needed.

   a. Impressive Look what you have accomplished

   b. Do you know who served as surgeon for the Virginia militia

   c. Was it James McClurg

   d. Good deduction You're right

Rewrite sentences e–g, inserting dashes where they are needed.

   e. Volume One of the journal was dedicated to let's see James McClurg.

   f. James McClurg deplored the leaders of his state George Mason, John Blair, and Edmund Randolph.

   g. Gus said, "Don't bump into the" as Oscar hit the wall.

For sentences h–k, replace each blank with the correct vocabulary word.

   h. One of the _____ duties of the accountant was to see that the trust funds were fairly distributed.

   i. The Latin word for "faith" is _____.

   j. Please file an _____ with the judge before examining the stolen property.

k. In order to demonstrate integrity and intelligence, the trustee hired a _____ to administer the will.

More Practice See "Hysterical Fiction #4" in Master Worksheets.

Review set 73 Choose the correct word(s) to complete sentences 1–14.

1. (Literally, Figuratively, Bienially) means "word for word."

2. (Noisome, Noisy) means offensive, especially to the smell.

3. Credence is (distrust, belief, doubt).

4. (Can, May) Herbert run a mile?

5. One who shows scorn is (admirable, amiable, contemptuous).

6. Meg (wave, waves) to people (that, who) wave to her whether she recognizes them or not.

7. She may wave to (whoever, whomever) she wishes.

8. Neither of the sisters (want, wants) that old gray raincoat in (their, her) closet.

9. A large red envelope, (that, which) contained four one-dollar bills, appeared on my desk last Tuesday.

10. The new band director had been waiting for (us, we) drummers.

11. The mail carrier dislikes (Rex, Rex's) barking, snarling, and jumping fences.

12. (Those, Them) seats are (our's, ours), but these are (your's, yours).

13. Last night I (see, saw, seen) two skunks under (that, that there) peach tree.

14. Oh dear, squirrels have (bite, bit, bitten) holes in our hammock!

15. Rewrite the following adding capital letters and punctuation marks as needed: if you will pay attention i shall read you a chapter titled forgiveness brings healing
(9, 66)

16. Rewrite the following as it is. Then add proofreading symbols to indicate corrections.
(32)

Lord Henry Leads Dorian Gray downthe path off evel.

17. Write the possessive case, third person, singular (feminine) personal pronoun.
(53)

18. For sentences a and b, write the verb phrase and label it action or linking.
(3, 18)

(a) Has Manny proved his point?

(b) Did Manny prove trustworthy?

19. In this sentence, write whether the underlined expression is essential or nonessential: An envelope that contained four one-dollar bills was lost in the shuffle.
(62)

20. Write whether the following is a phrase or a clause: when Dorian invites Lord Henry and Basil Hallward to meet his new love
(20)

21. From this sentence, write the gerund phrase: Your assignment, class, will be evaluating your essays.
(55, 56)

22. Write whether the following is a complete sentence, sentence fragment, or run-on sentence: Resolved to live a pure life and marry Sibyl Vane, Dorian learns that she is dead.
(2)

23. Write the correct verb form in this sentence: Jan hoped Van (past perfect tense of the verb *come*) to bring her a new puppy.
(15, 70)

24. In this sentence, write the dependent clause, circling the subordinating conjunction: My sister grimaces whenever I talk about baking rhubarb pies.
(54)

25. Write the plural of each noun.
(10, 11)

(a) thesis   (b) Curtis   (c) editor in chief

26. Write the four principal parts of the irregular verb *fall*.
_(13, 70)

27. Rewrite the following so that it is in active voice: A life of wild joys was pursued by Dorian Gray.
₍₂₇₎

28. In the following sentence, write and underline each word that should be italicized: The Merrimac and the Monitor were iron clad ships used during the American Civil War.
₍₆₉₎

Diagram sentences 29 and 30.

29. Neither of the brothers remembers the combination to the padlock.
_(21, 68)

30. Did you see the nice person who left me that red envelope?
_(21, 61)

LESSON 74

Subject-Verb Agreement, Part 1

> **Dictation or Journal Entry**
>
> **Vocabulary:** The root *curr-*, or *curs-*, comes from the Latin verb *currere* meaning "to run," as in the familiar words *current* and *excursion*.
>
> *Cursory* means hasty, rapid and superficial; not thorough. The customer relations employee gave a *cursory* report of the customer's complaint.
>
> *Concurrent* means happening simultaneously; existing or occuring at the same time. The Allies made *concurrent* attacks by land, sea, and air against the Axis in World War II.

Just as a pronoun must agree with its antecedent, a verb must agree with the subject of the sentence in **person** and **number**.

Person Verbs and personal pronouns are the only parts of speech that change their form to show person (point of view).

When we learned about the irregular verbs *be*, *have*, and *do* in Lesson 12, we used a chart similar to the one below. Here we show two regular verbs (*talk* and *discuss*) and one irregular verb (*be*) in the first, second, and third person. (Most regular verbs form the third person singular by adding *-s* or *-es*. The irregular verbs must be memorized.)

	SINGULAR	PLURAL
1ST PERSON	**I** talk, discuss, am	**we** talk, discuss, are
2ND PERSON	**you** talk, discuss, are	**you** talk, discuss, are
3RD PERSON	**he** talks, discusses, is	**they** talk, discuss, are

If the subject of a sentence is in the **first person** (I, we), the verb must also be in the first person:

I talk to them daily.   *We* discuss each issue.

I am hospitable.   *We* are amiable.

If the subject of a sentence is in the **second person** (you), the verb must also be in the second person:

You talk daily.

If the subject of a sentence is in the **third person** (he, she, it, or any noun), the verb must also be in the third person:

She talks every day.   *They* talk every day.

Jan discusses each detail.   *People* discuss each detail.

The teacher is jovial.   *The teachers* are jovial.

Number If the subject of a sentence is **singular,** the verb must also be singular:

I <u>advocate</u> a limited federal union.

He <u>supports</u> a stronger central government.

If the subject of a sentence is **plural,** the verb must also be plural:

We <u>advocate</u> a limited federal union.

They <u>support</u> a stronger central government.

Compound Subjects We must carefully determine whether the subject of a sentence is singular or plural.

Compound subjects joined by *and* are considered plural and require a plural verb.

Maisy and *Daisy* <u>agitate</u> the crowd.

Snow and *sleet* <u>envelop</u> the neighborhood.

Compound subjects joined by *or, nor, either-or,* or *neither-nor* can be singular or plural, depending on the subjects themselves:

- If both subjects are singular, we use a singular verb.

    Neither *Nien* nor *Liezl* <u>knows</u> the answer.

    Either *jam* or *honey* <u>tastes</u> sweeter than molasses.

- If both subjects are plural, we use a plural verb.

    Neither the *Federalists* nor the *Antifederalists* <u>have</u> all the answers.

    Either *debtors* or *mobs* <u>rule</u> in weak governments.

- If one subject is singular and the other is plural, the verb should agree with the subject nearest it.

    Neither *Randolph* nor the *"old lions"* <u>favor</u> strong central government.

    Either the *people* or their *representative* <u>argues</u> the case.

Example Choose the correct verb form for each sentence.

(a) Either butter or margarine (coat, coats) the popcorn.

(b) The maids-in-waiting (wear, wears) flowers in their hair.

(c) Politics and law (occupy, occupies) the delegates.

(d) Neither the powdered wigs nor the wooden teeth of colonial times (suit, suits) us today.

Solution (a) When compound singular subjects are joined by *either-or*, we use a singular verb form: Either butter or margarine **coats** the popcorn.

(b) The subject, "maids-in-waiting," is plural, so we use the plural verb form: The maids-in-waiting **wear** flowers in their hair.

(c) A compound subject joined by *and* uses a plural verb form: Politics and law **occupy** the delegates.

(d) Compound plural subjects joined by *neither-nor* require a plural verb form: Neither the powdered wigs nor the wooden teeth of colonial times **suit** us today.

Practice For a–f, choose the correct verb form for each sentence.

a. Edmund Randolph (suggest, suggests) a completely new government.

b. The delegates (listen, listens) intently to Edmund Randolph's proposal.

c. The representation in the Senate, the North's refusal to count only three-fifths of the slaves, and the single executive (displease, displeases) Randolph.

d. Neither Edmund Randolph nor George Mason (sign, signs) the Constitution in its finished form.

e. Either lies or a mistake (explain, explains) the end of Randolph's political career.

f. Historical writing and legal cases (absorb, absorbs) Randolph later in life.

For g–l, replace each blank with the correct vocabulary word.

g. The attacks on Edmund Randolph's motives and character came _____ with his appointment as secretary of state.

h. The Latin verb _____ means "to run."

i. The _____ judgment of Edmund Randolph's actions has been refuted and withdrawn.

More Practice Choose the correct verb form for each sentence.

1. Neither the watermelon nor the raspberries (taste, tastes) ripe.

2. Either the flutes or the piano (sound, sounds) out of tune.

3. The lory and the parrot (live, lives) in groups.

4. The sparrow and the finch (grow, grows) to about five inches long.

5. All doves (is, are) monogamous.

6. They (love, loves) their mates till death.

7. Either a crow or a raven (was, were) bathing in the puddle.

8. A pigeon and a dove (was, were) pecking for seeds.

9. Either the nightengales or the robin (was, were) laying eggs.

10. Mynas and starlings (has, have) soft bills.

Review set 74 Choose the correct word to complete sentences 1–14.

1. The Latin word for "faith" is (*vorare, primus, fides*).
(73)

2. (Literally, Figuratively, Bienially) means metaphorically.
(72)

3. The meanings of noisome and noisy are (similar, unrelated, unclear).
(71)

4. (Retraction, Deduction, Credence) is belief.
(70)

5. If we show that someone is guilty, we (avert, incriminate, appease) him or her.
(16)

6. Have you met the photographer (who, whom) took these pictures?
(61)

7. I asked Sam and (she, her) to photograph the kittens.
(51)

8. Neither of these socks (has, have) (their, its, it's) mate.
(53, 68)

9. The avocados (which, that) I picked yesterday will ripen in a week.
(62)

10. (We, Us) history students have been discussing the Great Depression.
(63)

11. Sid disliked (Rob, Rob's) leaving dirty socks on the floor.
(7)

12. (Those, Them) dirty socks (was, were) worn out.
(12, 67)

13. (Their, There, They're) elastic had (all ready, already) lost its elasticity.
(41, 53)

14. By ten o'clock, Sid had (took, taken) all Rob's socks to the laundromat.
(72)

15. Rewrite the following, adding capital letters and punctuation marks as needed: hey yelled rob where are my socks
(65, 73)

16. Rewrite the following as it is. Then add proofreading symbols to indicate corrections.
(32)

Basil Hallwood beged DorianGray two re pent of his sins.

17. Write the possessive case, second person (either singular or plural) pronoun.
(52)

18. In the following sentence, write the verb phrase and label it transitive or intransitive: Dorian's mask of youth saved his life but not his conscience.
(26)

19. In the sentence that follows, write whether the underlined clause is essential or nonessential: Rob's socks, <u>which have no elasticity</u>, are at the laundromat.
(62)

20. In the following sentence, write the pronoun and its antecedent: Dorian Gray valued his own youthful, innocent face.
(46)

21. From the following sentence, write the infinitive and label it a noun or an adjective: Rob has a problem to solve.
(19, 45)

22. Write the superlative form of the adjective *exuberant*.
(39)

23. From the sentence that follows, write the indefinite pronoun and label it singular or plural: Unfortunately, some of the elastic has rotted.
(68)

24. From the following sentence, write the dependent clause, circling the subordinating conjunction: Will Rob buy new socks before he throws away the old ones?
(54)

25. Write the four principal parts of the irregular verb *tell*.
(13, 72)

26. Use an appositive to make one sentence from these two sentences: Lord Henry was the devil's advocate. Lord Henry had poisoned Dorian's soul.
(42)

27. Write the plural of each noun.
(10, 11)   (a) elf   (b) latch   (c) secretary

28. Write and underline each word that should be italicized in the following sentence: In C.S. Lewis's novel called The Horse and His Boy, we learn how a talking horse and a young prince save Narnia from enemy invasion.
(69)

Diagram sentences 29 and 30.

29. A hoodlum plotted to steal my backpack, but Jenny exposed the scheme.
(19, 21)

30. Does either of the mechanics enjoy repairing antique cars?
(21, 56)

LESSON 75 — Subject-Verb Agreement, Part 2

> **Dictation or Journal Entry**
>
> **Vocabulary:** Two letters make a significant difference in meaning between *limp* and *limpid*.
>
> As a noun, a *limp* is a lame movement or gait. The girl's *limp* made it impossible for her to walk in high heels.
>
> As a verb, to *limp* is to walk lamely or with an uneven gait, favoring one leg. The injured soccer player *limped* off the field.
>
> As an adjective, *limp* means lacking firmness; wilted. After a few days, the *limp* rose slumped over the edge of the vase.
>
> *Limpid* is an adjective meaning clear, lucid, or transparent. We could easily see several trout swimming in the *limpid* lake.

For subject-verb agreement, we must first identify the subject of the sentence and then determine whether it is singular or plural.

Words Between the Subject and Verb

Words that come between the subject and the verb must not distract us. We must be aware of prepositional phrases, appositives, and other works that might be mistaken for the subject of the sentence. Diagramming, at least mentally, the simple subject and simple predicate helps us to determine which verb form to use.

A calendar listing all of the school holidays (was, were) sent to all students.

    calendar | was (not were)

That bouquet of limp flowers (need, needs) water.

    bouquet | needs (not need)

William Davie, among other delegates, (prefer, prefers) that the Senate be weighted to represent wealth and property.

    William Davie | prefers (not prefer)

Example 1 Diagram the simple subject and simple predicate in order to show the correct verb form for each sentence.

(a) A union allowing local prejudices and interests (appeal, appeals) to many colonists.

(b) William Davie, with the help of others, (fight, fights) for ratification in North Carolina.

(c) The bickering between politicians (is, are) sometimes vehement.

Solution (a) A union allowing local prejudices and interests **appeals** to many colonists.

<u>union</u> | <u>appeals</u>

(b) William Davie, with the help of others, **fights** for ratification in North Carolina.

<u>William Davie</u> | <u>fights</u>

(c) The bickering between politicians **is** sometimes vehement.

<u>bickering</u> | <u>is</u>

Reversed Subject-Verb Order   If the subject follows the verb, we carefully identify the subject and make the verb agree with it.

East of the Appalachian Mountains (lie, lies) North Carolina.

<u>North Carolina</u> | <u>lies</u>

There in the lower house of North Carolina (sit, sits) William Davie.

<u>William Davie</u> | <u>sits</u>

Here (comes, come) the peace commissioners from France.

<u>commissioners</u> | <u>come</u>

Now there (is, are) diplomats to negotiate the treaty.

<u>diplomats</u> | <u>are</u>

Example 2 Diagram the simple subject and simple predicate in order to show the correct verb form for each sentence.

(a) Here (is, are) a picture of William Davie's distinguished Scottish ancestors.

(b) There, at Tivoli, South Carolina, (live, lives) the memories of his grandfather.

(c) Into the meeting hall (come, comes) one of the most outspoken delegates.

Solution (a) Here **is** a picture of William Davie's distinguished Scottish ancestors.

| picture | is |

(b) There, at Tivoli, South Carolina, (live, lives) the memories of his grandfather.

| memories | live |

(c) Into the meeting hall **comes** one of the most outspoken delegates.

| one | comes |

Practice Diagram the simple subject and simple predicate in order to determine the correct verb form for sentences a–d.

a. There in the library (was, were) stories about people in North Carolina.

b. Listed as occupations of Hugh Williamson (was, were) preacher and physician.

c. The list of his many occupations (read, reads) as follows: preacher, physician, land speculator, scientist, and North Carolina politician.

d. Astronomy, eels, and electricity (is, are) his special interests.

For e–h, replace each blank with the correct vocabulary word(s).

e. In *A Christmas Carol*, the crippled Tiny Tim walked with a _____.

f. The vase was made of pure and _____ crystal.

g. A blister on my right heel caused me to _____.

h. In the rain, her fancy hairdo became _____.

More Practice Choose the correct verb form for each sentence.

1. A bird with long blue tail feathers (sit, sits) on my window sill.

2. That bag of potatoes (smell, smells) rotten.

3. What classes (is, are) John taking this semester?

4. Here (comes, come) the racing cyclists!

5. There (is, are) many different shades of green.

6. The sound of the gulls (remind, reminds) me of the ocean.

7. The music from distant bagpipes (make, makes) Mrs. Anderson nostalgic.

8. Every one of the cyclists (is, are) wearing a helmet.

9. On that street (lives, live) two of my cousins.

10. Over the Rocky Mountains (fly, flies) the jet.

Review set 75 Choose the correct word to complete sentences 1–14.

1. The Latin verb (*credere, vorare, currere*) means "to run."
(74)

2. The Latin word *fides* means (eat, first, faith).
(73)

3. To "lose your marbles" is a (literal, figurative) expression.
(72)

4. A (caucus, census, consul) looks after the interests of his or her country in a foreign country.
(17)

5. Blame, condemn, and (censor, censure, census) mean about the same.
(18)

6. You may study with (whoever, whomever) you want.
(61)

7. Sid and (her, she) washed Rob's socks.
(50)

8. Not everyone (wash, washes) (their, his or her) own clothes.
(53, 68)

9. This live oak tree, (which, that) was once a tiny seedling, now stands sixty feet tall.
(62)

10. The coach has been lecturing (we, us) tennis players about the importance of sufficient sleep.
(63)

11. Professor Tough does not indulge (us, our) wasting time in class.
(53, 63)

12. Neither the brussel sprouts nor the cabbage (taste, tastes) good without cheese sauce.
(68)

13. That mistake was mine, not (her's, hers).
(53)

14. Have you (mistook, mistaken) me for a movie star?
(71)

15. Rewrite the following as it is. Then add proofreading symbols to indicate corrections.
(32)

The theme off "Our Town," by Thornton wilder, isthe magic of the the mundane.

16. Rewrite the letter below, adding capital letters and punctuation marks as needed.
(25, 47)

dear mr wilder
    your play helps people to treasure everyday life
your fan
sophia

17. Write the seven common coordinating conjunctions.
(33)

18. In this sentence, write the verb phrase and label it action or linking: Did the protagonist appear desperate?
(3, 18)

19. In this sentence, write whether the underlined clause is essential or nonessential: Oh dear, the boxes <u>that contain our textbooks</u> are sitting out in the rain!
(62)

20. Write whether the following is a phrase or a clause: our common and fragile humanity
(20)

21. In the sentence that follows, write the infinitive and label it a noun or an adjective: Do we need to bring those boxes in out of the rain?
(19, 45)

22. Write the three personal pronoun case forms.
(52)

23. In the following sentence, write the indefinite pronoun and label it singular or plural: Does each of the boxes contain a dozen grammar books?
(68)

24. In the following sentence, write the dependent clause, circling the subordinating conjunction: The peacock may be a symbol if it represents vanity and ostentation.
(54)

25. Write the four principal parts of the irregular verb *go*.
(13, 71)

26. From the sentence that follows, write the participial phrase followed by the noun it modifies: Using the simplest scenery and props, the Stage Manager describes life as it unfolds.
(56)

27. Rewrite the following sentence so that it is in active voice: Were the stars obscured by a haze last night?
(27)

28. Write and underline each word that should be italicized in the following sentence: The weather forecast, according to the Mud Valley Herald, calls for thunderstorms and heavy rain.
(69)

Diagram sentences 29 and 30.

29. Do you have a promise to keep?
(21, 45)

30. That hawk, the one with a fish in its beak, might be an osprey.
(36, 42)

LESSON 76

Subject-Verb Agreement, Part 3

> **Dictation or Journal Entry**
>
> **Vocabulary:** The Latin verb *flectere* means "to bend" and gives us the root *flex/flect*, as in the familiar words *flexible* and *reflect*.
>
> A *flexor is* a muscle that bends or flexes the body. There are three *flexors* that move the big toe: *flexor digiti minimi brevis, flexor digitorum brevis, flexor digitorum longus.*
>
> To *genuflect* is to bend the knee, as in worship or respect. As they entered the sanctuary, the worshipers *genuflected* before sitting in the pews.

Indefinite Pronouns

We remember that some indefinite pronouns are singular, some are plural, and some can be either. If an indefinite pronoun is the subject of a sentence, the verb must agree with it in number. (See Lesson 68 for the complete list of indefinite pronouns.)

SINGULAR *Nobody* <u>is</u> here.

PLURAL *Few* <u>are</u> there.

SINGULAR *Some* <u>was</u> slanderous.

PLURAL *Some* <u>were</u> ambivalent.

Sometimes people are confused when a prepositional phrase comes between the subject and predicate. Diagramming the simple subject and simple predicate helps us to see which verb is correct.

Neither of the North Carolina delegates (was, were) decidedly Federalist.

Neither | was

One of them (was, were) a physician and preacher.

One | was

Each of the students (hope, hopes) to visit Washington, D.C.

Each | hopes

Somebody with little, round spectacles (is, are) addressing the Senate.

Somebody | is addressing

Example 1 Choose the correct verb form for each sentence.

(a) Everyone (were, was) listening carefully.

(b) Neither of the tours (include, includes) a trip to the Smithsonian Institute.

Solution (a) The indefinite pronoun *everyone* takes a singular verb: Everyone **was** listening carefully.

(b) The indefinite pronoun *neither* takes a singular verb: Neither of these tours **includes** a trip to the Smithsonian Institute.

Plural Nouns We remember that words like *slacks, shears, scissors, tweezers,* and *pants* use a plural verb, for they are plural.

Only sharp *scissors* cut fabric.

Wool *pants* attract moths.

Contractions We use contractions cautiously, expanding them, if necessary, to be sure the subjects and verbs agree.

Hugh Williamson wasn't (was not) unreasonable.
They weren't (were not) unreasonable.

The *Smithsonian Institute* isn't (is not) in Pennsylvania.
We aren't (are not) in Pennsylvania.

Professor Prune doesn't (does not) have wrinkles.
They don't (do not) have wrinkles.

Jasper hasn't (has not) found his escaped parakeet.
Jasper and *Theo* haven't (have not) found the bird.

Errors to Avoid We use the contraction *there's* ("there is" or "there has") only with singular subjects.

There's (there is) only one *hotspur* in the crowd.

There's (there has) been *debate* among the states.

We do NOT use the contraction *there's* with plural subjects.

NO: There's several *issues* to discuss.

YES: There are several *issues* to discuss.

Ain't is not a word. We do not use it for *isn't, hasn't, aren't,* or *haven't.*

Suffrage isn't (NOT ain't) the only cause for dispute.

He hasn't (NOT ain't) adjourned the meeting yet.

Example 2 Choose the correct verb form for each sentence.

(a) These pinking shears (keep, keeps) the fabric from fraying.

(b) Richard Dobbs Spaight (don't, doesn't) accept opposition well.

(c) The angry gentleman (hasn't, haven't) forgiven John Stanley.

(d) Richard Dobbs Spaight (ain't, isn't) willing to be called a liar and a scoundrel.

Solution (a) *Shears* is a plural subject, so we use a plural verb: These pinking shears **keep** the fabric from fraying.

(b) *Richard Dobbs Spaight* is a singular subject, so we use the singular verb: Richard Dobbs Spaight **doesn't** accept opposition well.

(c) *Gentleman* is a singular subject, so we use a singular verb: The angry gentleman **hasn't** forgiven John Stanley.

(d) *Ain't* is not a word, so we choose *isn't*: Richard Dobbs Spaight **isn't** willing to be called a liar and a scoundrel.

Practice For a–e, choose the correct verb form or contraction for each sentence.

a. Richard Dobbs Spaight (ain't, isn't) the only man who has died in a duel.

b. Tweezers (help, helps) the philatelist to handle stamps without damaging them.

c. Alexander Hamilton and Richard Dobbs Spaight (wasn't, weren't) peacemakers.

d. (There's, There are) politicians with integrity.

e. Each of the leaders (speak, speaks) from experience.

For f–h, replace each blank with the correct vocabulary word.

f. The Latin verb _____ means "to bend."

g. An ambassador expects to _____ before a foreign monarch.

h. The hip _____ assists in bending the knees.

More Practice Choose the correct verb form or each sentence.

1. Tongs (allow, allows) us to serve salad neatly.
2. Warm pajamas (was, were) needed in winter.
3. That class (ain't, isn't) what I expected.
4. Everyone in my classes (complain, complains) about the amount of homework.
5. Everybody at the computers (want, wants) help.
6. Nobody in the upper grades (expect, expects) an easy assignment.
7. Either of them (work, works) well independently.
8. Each of us (plan, plans) to finish college.
9. Neither of the cats (sleep, sleeps) on the couch.
10. Of course, anyone (hope, hopes) to live a long, happy life.
11. One of the delegates (leave, leaves) the convention in a fit of anger.
12. He (don't, doesn't) say much.
13. The others at the convention (wasn't, weren't) listening to him.
14. Federalists and Antifederalists (ain't, aren't) bickering as much as they were previously.

Review set 76 Choose the correct word(s) to complete sentences 1–14.

1. (Limp, Limpid, Cursory) means clear, lucid, or transparent.
   (75)

2. The Latin verb *currere* means to (believe, eat, run).
   (74)

3. A(n) (affidavit, fiduciary, primogeniture) is a written declaration affirmed before an authority.

4. I speak (literally, figuratively) when I tell you that I haven't finished my homework.

5. Approbation is (condemnation, commendation, blame).

6. (Who, Whom) left the ice cream out?

7. Don't blame Liz and (I, me).

8. Neither of the sisters (want, wants) (their, her) diary read aloud.

9. Miss Match, (who, which) takes pride in her fashion, wore reddish orange sandals with magenta nylons.

10. May (we, us) soccer players please practice on this field today?

11. We were grateful for (him, his) caring for our hamster while we were away.

12. Outside the corral (stand, stands) two stunning black stallions.

13. (There, Their, They're) stomping (there, their, they're) hooves in fury.

14. Neither of the jockeys (have, has) (rode, ridden) either of these stallions.

15. Rewrite the sentence below as it is. Then add proofreading symbols to indicate corrections.

   during the Great Depression which lasted From 1929 to 1939 millions of americans lost thier jobs their homes and their financial security

16. Rewrite the following, adding capital letters and punctuation marks as needed: Furthermore said uncle sid i lived in iowa during the 1930s food and other supplies were rationed so it was a difficult time for everyone

17. Write the gerund phrase in the following sentence: We passed the time by playing chess.
_(55, 56)

18. In the following sentence, write the verb phrase and name its tense: Riding in the hay-baling tractor out in the fields, my friend April has been sneezing uncontrollably throughout the morning.
_(15, 17)

19. In this sentence, write whether the underlined clause is essential or nonessential: Her nose, <u>which resembles a shiny light bulb</u>, is red and raw.
₍₆₂₎

20. Write whether the following is a complete sentence, sentence fragment, or run-on sentence: Anne Frank's diary covers a span of two years the family was hiding in Amsterdam.
₍₂₎

21. Write the comparative form of the adjective *bad*.
₍₄₀₎

22. Write the objective case, first person, plural personal pronoun.
₍₅₁₎

23. In the following sentence, write the indefinite pronoun and label it singular or plural: I think some of the hay bales have been loaded into a truck already.
_(46, 68)

24. In the following sentence, write the pronoun and its antecedent: April insists that she doesn't need any antihistamine.
_(46, 50)

25. Write the four principal parts of the irregular verb *give*.
_(49, 70)

26. Use an appositive to make one sentence from these two sentences:
₍₄₂₎

In Samuel Taylor Coleridge's poem, "Rime of the Ancient Mariner," the Mariner kills an albatross, which is later tied around his neck. An albatross is a web-footed sea bird.

27. Write the plural of each noun.
_(10, 11) (a) birch   (b) bay   (c) self

28. Rewrite the following sentence so that it is in active voice: In *Moby Dick*, a shipmate's coffin floating in the ocean is clung to by Ishmael.
₍₂₇₎

Diagram sentences 29 and 30.

29. Much of the grain in the field looks golden and ripe.
(36, 68)

30. The usher who seated us was wearing strong perfume.
(21, 61)

LESSON 77 Subject-Verb Agreement, Part 4

> **Dictation or Journal Entry**
>
> **Vocabulary:** Let us learn to distinguish between the verbs *denote* and *connote*.
>
> To *denote* is to be an indication or sign of; mean. A scowl often *denotes* anger.
>
> To *connote* is to imply or suggest a meaning in addition to the literal meaning. Green denotes a color; but it *connotes* life, newness, vitality, and hope.

In this lesson, we will review agreement between subjects and verbs when the subject is a collective noun or a singular noun that seems to be plural.

Collective Nouns   A collective noun refers to a group or unit. The following words are collective nouns:

committee	*staff*	*faculty*	*team*
species	*army*	*pair*	*couple*
series	*gallows*	*arms*	*accommodations*
contents	*clothes*	*archives*	*congratulations*

We use a singular verb if the collective noun refers to one unit.

The *headquarters* <u>employs</u> one thousand workers.

This *species* <u>exists</u> only in the Amazon Jungle.

We use a plural verb if the collective noun refers to individuals within a group. The helping verb must also be plural.

The *couple* <u>are</u> eating at different restaurants tonight.

The teaching *staff* <u>arrive</u> for class at various times.

Special Singular Nouns   Some singular nouns appear to be plural, but they are not. The following singular nouns require a singular verb:

mumps	*measles*	*news*	*lens*

News <u>is</u> labeled "yellow journalism" if it exaggerates the facts.

Mumps <u>causes</u> one's cheeks to swell.

Special Singular or Plural Nouns

Some nouns have the same form whether they are singular or plural. *Corps, series, means, species,* and *gross,* as well as many animal names (*deer, trout, bison, salmon,* etc.), are some examples. Use the meaning of the sentence to decide which verb form to use.

SINGULAR: This *corps* of engineers <u>is</u> the most reliable.

PLURAL: Several other *corps* <u>are</u> interested in the job.

SINGULAR: That *sheep* <u>was</u> in the pasture.

PLURAL: Two *sheep* <u>were</u> wandering.

Finally, nouns that end in *-ics*, such as *mathematics, economics, ethics, athletics, acoustics,* and *politics,* can also be either singular or plural, depending on their meaning in the sentence. If we are referring to a body of knowledge, the noun is singular. If we are referring to a series of actions, the noun is plural:

Politics <u>is</u> a divisive subject.

Her *politics* <u>are</u> manipulative.

Example Choose the correct verb form for each sentence.

(a) Mathematics (use, uses) numbers to express quantities symbolically.

(b) Congress (pass, passes) new bills during each session.

(c) The militia (tether, tethers) their horses to the trees near camp.

(d) Measles (cause, causes) an eruption of red spots.

Solution (a) Mathematics **uses** numbers to express quantities symbolically. ("Mathematics" is a singular noun in this sentence, for it refers to a body of knowledge.)

(b) Congress **passes** new bills during each session. ("Congress" is a collective noun referring to a unit.)

(c) The militia **tether** their horses to the trees near camp. ("Militia" is a collective noun referring to the individuals within the group in this case.)

(d) Measles **causes** an eruption of red spots. ("Measles" is a singular noun.)

Practice Choose the correct verb form for sentences a–g.

a. The headquarters of the United States of America (remain, remains) in Washington, D.C.

b. The evening news (keep, keeps) the public informed of current events.

c. Aerobics (provide, provides) stimulation for the heart and the lungs.

d. Economics (examine, examines) the distribution and consumption of goods.

e. The staff (park, parks) their cars in the distant lot.

f. The pride of lions (have, has) returned to the plain.

g. The contents of this book (is, are) located just after the title page.

For h–k, replace each blank with *denotes* or *connotes*.

h. A red rose _____ a beautiful flower.

i. A red rose _____ love.

j. White _____ a color.

k. White _____ purity.

Review Set 77 Choose the correct word(s) to complete sentences 1–14.

1. The Latin verb (*currere, sequi, flectere*) means "to bend."

2. (Concurrent, Limpid, Limp) means lacking firmness; wilted.

3. (Contemptible, Cursory, Conscientious) means hasty, rapid, and superficial; not thorough.

4. A(n) (affidavit, fiduciary, primogeniture) is a person chosen to manage the property of another.

5. We find the terms *pocket veto* and *ex post facto* in the (Bible, Constitution, Declaration of Independence).

6. (Have, Has) this series of novels captured your interest?
<small>(12, 77)</small>

7. Economics (was, were) a challenging subject for the business majors at the university.
<small>(12, 77)</small>

8. You may mail an application to (whoever, whomever) qualifies for the job.
<small>(61, 64)</small>

9. Ross and (he, him) will qualify once they receive (there, they're, their) high school diplomas.
<small>(50, 53)</small>

10. Not everyone (pass, passes) the test before (their, his or her) eighteenth birthday.
<small>(53, 68)</small>

11. Does Zelda appreciate (you, your) tutoring her in English?
<small>(21, 53)</small>

12. Neither the finches nor the macaw (sleeps, sleep) during our band practice.
<small>(5, 68)</small>

13. My parakeet is blue, but (hers, her's) is green.
<small>(53)</small>

14. If I had known you were (there, their), I would have (went, gone) to meet you.
<small>(53, 71)</small>

15. Rewrite the following sentence as it is. Then add proofreading symbols to indicate corrections.
<small>(32, 69)</small>

Dr Pain say that my ambiguous state ments confuze her.

16. Rewrite the letter below, adding capital letters and punctuation marks as needed.
<small>(25, 47)</small>

dear mr van winkle

why did you sleep twenty years were you tired

sincerely

mr longfellow

17. Write four common pairs of correlative conjunctions.
<small>(35)</small>

18. In the following sentence, write the verb phrase and label it transitive or intransitive:
<small>(26)</small>

Did Sancho Panza follow Don Quixote on his escapades?

19. In the following sentence, write whether the underlined clause is essential or nonessential:

President John F. Kennedy, <u>who wrote *Profiles in Courage*</u>, won a Pulitzer Prize.

20. Write whether the following is a phrase or a clause:

a play based on the life of Cyrano de Bergerac

21. In the following sentence, write the infinitive phrase and label it a noun or an adjective:

Does Casper have a mystery to unravel?

22. Write the three personal pronoun case forms.

23. In the following sentence, write the indefinite pronoun and label it singular or plural:

Was any of the pancake syrup tainted with sausage grease?

24. In the following sentence, write each dependent clause, circling each subordinating conjunction:

Since I know that wise people take advice, I shall consider what you say.

25. Write the four principal parts of the irregular verb *strive*.

26. In the sentence below, write the participial phrase followed by the noun it modifies.

Jo stomped out grumbling about high prices.

27. Write whether the following sentence is in active or passive voice:

William Wordsworth was followed by Lord Tennyson as Poet Laureate.

28. Write and underline each word that should be italicized in the following sentence:

The famous Dutch artist Rembrandt van Rijn painted Belshazzar's Feast, showing Belshazzar's surprise at the handwriting on the wall.

Diagram sentences 29 and 30.

29. Signing her name, my friend Zoe promised me her
(42, 56) support.

30. Zoe will either make phone calls or write letters.
(21, 35)

LESSON 78

Negatives • Double Negatives

> **Dictation or Journal Entry**
>
> **Vocabulary:** The Latin prefix *post-* means "after," as in the familiar words *post*script and *post*date.
>
> *Posterior* is an adjective meaning situated toward the back; rear. The *posterior* part of the body includes muscles such as *trapezius* and *gluteus maximus*. Posterior is also used as a noun meaning buttocks. After sliding down the riverbank, my *posterior* was covered with mud.
>
> *Posthumous* means "published after the death of the author" or "occurring after one's death." While the scientist received no special recognition during her lifetime, her country gave her a *posthumous* award for her scientific discovery.

Negatives Negatives are modifiers, usually adverbs, that mean "no" or "not." We will review adverbs later. In this lesson we will discuss the proper use of negatives. Negatives are italicized in the sentences below.

Jim *never* rides that wild stallion.

The wandering burro had *nowhere* to go.

We have *barely* enough hay for the mule.

We do *not* know what the future holds.

Here is a list of common negatives:

no	*not*	*never*
hardly	*scarcely*	*barely*
nowhere	*none*	*no one*
nothing	*nobody*	

We see from the list above that the word *not* is a negative. Therefore, the contraction *n't* is also a negative:

We do*n't* know what the future holds.

Sorry, I was*n't* thinking.

I had*n't* planned ahead.

Example 1 Write each negative that you find in these sentences.

(a) Richard Dobbs Spaight hardly paid any attention to his plantation.

(b) He scarcely had time for his family.

(c) I didn't call anybody, so nobody knew that I wasn't coming.

(d) The ferry was nowhere in sight.

Solution (a) **hardly** (b) **scarcely**

(c) **n't, nobody, n't** (d) **nowhere**

Double Negatives We use only one negative to express a negative idea. In the English language, two negatives in the same clause "cancel each other out" and the idea becomes positive again. Therefore, it is incorrect to use two negatives with one verb. We call this a **double negative,** and we avoid it.

NO: Milly *never* accepts *no* help. (double negative)
YES: Milly *never* accepts help.
YES: Milly accepts *no* help.

NO: That person has*n't no* conviction. (double negative)
YES: That person has*n't* conviction.
YES: That person has *no* conviction.

NO: Moe does*n't* want *no* advice. (double negative)
YES: Moe does*n't* want advice.
YES: Moe wants *no* advice.

Example 2 Choose the correct word to complete each sentence. Avoid double negatives.

(a) Alexander Martin (would, wouldn't) hardly acknowledge the value of the Constitution.

(b) He didn't have (nothing, anything) good to say about it.

(c) The orators weren't using (any, no) microphones.

Solution (a) Alexander Martin **would** hardly acknowledge the value of the Constitution. (The words "wouldn't" and "hardly" are both negatives. We may use only one negative to express an idea, so we choose "would.")

(b) He didn't have **anything** good to say about it. (The words "didn't" and "nothing" are both negatives. To avoid double negatives, we choose "anything.")

(c) The orators weren't using **any** microphones. (The words "weren't" and "no" are both negatives. To avoid double negatives, we choose "any."

Correcting Double Negatives

To correct a double negative, we can replace one of the negatives with a positive word. Study the positive forms of the negatives below:

NEGATIVE		POSITIVE
hardly	→	almost
no	→	any, a
nobody	→	anybody
nowhere	→	anywhere
never	→	ever
neither	→	either
none	→	any
no one	→	anyone
nothing	→	anything

Benito did*n't* hear *nothing*. (anything, *nothing* crossed out)

Annie Mae has*n't* *no* surf board. (a, *no* crossed out)

Ashley *never* wants *no* help. (any, *no* crossed out)

Example 3 Rewrite this sentence and correct the double negative:

There wasn't nobody home.

Solution We replace the second negative, *nobody*, with a positive form—*anybody*:

There wasn't *anybody* home.

Remember that a sentence can contain more than one negative, as long as they are not in the same clause. The sentence below is not an example of a double negative because each negative is in a different clause.

Josh *didn't* study, so he has *no* confidence.

Rare Exceptions On rare occasions, we might use a double negative for effect. Look at the following sentences:

The test was so important, I *couldn't not* study!

I *scarcely, scarcely* remember the incident.

The double negative is deliberate in these sentences. Most double negatives, however, are unintended and incorrect. They are often heard in speech, but that is no excuse for using them.

Practice Choose the correct word to complete sentences a–e.

a. The protesting colonists hardly (never, ever) agreed with British policies.

b. During the Battle of Germantown, Alexander Martin (could, couldn't) find no familiar faces.

c. George Washington had never seen (anything, nothing) like Alexander Martin's confusion.

d. The army didn't (never, ever) court-martial him for his cowardice.

e. The army didn't charge him with (no, any) wrongdoing.

For f–i, replace each blank with the correct vocabulary word.

f. Were there ever any _____ charges against Alexander Martin for his cowardice during the Battle of Germantown?

g. Unfortunately, I landed on a cactus on my _____.

h. The prefix meaning "back" or "after" is _____.

i. The _____ side of a photograph is generally white.

More Practice Choose the correct word to complete these sentences.

1. The defendant didn't have (no, an) alibi.

2. The judge didn't believe (nothing, anything) he said.

3. He hadn't gone (nowhere, anywhere) that day.

4. A potential witness screeched, "I didn't see (nothing, anything)!"

5. The prosecutor had hardly (no, any) evidence.

6. The jury had scarcely (no, any) time to deliberate.

7. I hadn't (ever, never) attended a trial before.

8. The lawyer didn't argue about (none, any) of my statements.

9. I didn't see (no one, anyone) leave the courtroom.

10. She doesn't want to hear (either, neither) testimony.

Review set 78

Choose the correct word to complete sentences 1–15.

1. To denote is to (connote, mean, limp).
(77)

2. The Latin verb *flectere* means to (follow, bend, eat).
(76)

3. To (loathe, slander, limp) is to walk lamely or with an uneven gait.
(75)

4. (Contemptible, Cursory, Concurrent) means happening simultaneously.
(74)

5. In formal writing, we use "that is" instead of (*i.e., e.g., etc.*).
(21, 34)

6. For (who, whom) are you buying this gift?
(51)

7. (Me and him, Him and me, He and I) are buying the fruitcake for (you and she, you and her).
(53, 68)

8. Only one of the politicians (is, are) using (their, his or her) common sense.
(53, 74)

9. A new virus, (that, which) my brother and I inadvertently sent, crashed our parents' computer.
(62)

10. (We, Us) brothers apologized to our parents.
(63)

11. Mom and Dad say they are tired of (us, our) sending them emails instead of talking face to face.
(53)

12. That league of voters (want, wants) to change public opinion.
(5, 77)

13. Melody has hers, but she (don't, doesn't) have (your's, yours).
(12, 53)

14. Has Patricia (swam, swum) sixty laps of the pool?
(71, 72)

15. The tuxedo pants (has, have) suspenders.
(12, 77)

16. Rewrite the following, adding capital letters and correct punctuation marks: all right replied rawlin i will feed the chickens collect the eggs and clean the coop while you caleb are surfing at newport beach
(9, 65)

17. In this sentence, write the gerund phrase: Could thinking about other people's needs make us less selfish?
(55, 56)

18. In this sentence, write the verb phrase and name its tense: Throughout the month of August, our garden had been producing a plethora of zucchini.
(15, 17)

19. In this sentence, write whether the underlined clause is essential or nonessential: The squirrel that chewed my hammock lives high in the old oak tree.
(62)

20. From this sentence, write the dependent clause, circling the subordinating conjunction: Did you try to repair the hammock after the squirrel chewed it?
(54)

21. Write the comparative form of the adjective *generous*.
(39)

22. Write the nominative case, third person, plural personal pronoun.
(52)

23. In this sentence, write the indefinite pronoun and label it singular or plural: Certainly, much of this music is too difficult for beginning piano students.
(68)

24. In this sentence, write the pronoun and its antecedent: Mrs. Curtis doesn't know if she will have time today to wash the pick-up truck.
(46)

25. Write the four principal parts of the irregular verb *sleep*.
(71, 72)

26. Rewrite the following as it is. Then add proofreading symbols to indicate corrections.
(9, 32)

In teh poem "Casey at Bat," fivethousand fan saw casey strike out.

27. Write the plural of each noun.
(10, 11) (a) Sherry (b) bagful (c) son-in-law

28. Write and underline each part that should be italicized in
(69) this sentence: In the phone book, we find many entries under C due to the many Coopers and Changs.

Diagram sentences 29 and 30.

29. Take him these two gallons of nonfat milk.
(21, 29)

30. Do you have time to wash my muddy, dented pick-up
(24, 56) truck?

LESSON 79 — The Hyphen: Compound Nouns, Numbers

> **Dictation or Journal Entry**
> **Vocabulary:** Let us make a clear distinction between the words *flaunt* and *flout*.
> To *flaunt* is to make a bold, conspicuous, gaudy display in public. The actress flaunted her six-carat diamond in front of the media.
> To *flout* is to treat with contempt or disdain; to mock; to scoff at; to defy. The rebellious student *flouted* school uniform policy by wearing an outlandish outfit to class.

The **hyphen** is a punctuation mark used in connecting elements of compound words and in expressing numbers.

Compound Nouns We have learned that some compound nouns are hyphenated. There are no absolute rules for spelling a compound noun as one word, as two words, or hyphenated. However, certain categories of compound nouns are usually (but not always) hyphenated.

- Compound nouns that end in prepositional phrases:

    right-of-way   father-in-law   stick-in-the-mud
    free-for-all   man-about-town   attorney-at-law

- Compound nouns containing the prefix *ex-* or *-self* or the suffix *-elect*:

    ex-President   self-discipline   President-elect

- Compound nouns that are units of measurement:

    board-foot   man-hour   light-year

- Compound nouns that end with the prepositions *in*, *on*, or *between*:

    check-in   stand-in   trade-in
    add-on   goings-on   go-between

Nouns without Nouns? The English language is so flexible that we can create nouns from almost any part of speech. Look at the last category (compound nouns that end with prepositions) and notice that some of them don't contain an actual noun. Following are more examples of compound nouns formed from other parts of speech. We join the elements (words) with hyphens.

    go-getter   know-it-all   has-been
    get-together   look-alike   hand-me-down
    sit-up   cure-all   lean-to

The dictionary lists many of these words. But no dictionary can show every single combination of words that might make up a compound noun. If you have the need for a unique combination, do what experienced writers do: use any similar words you can find in the dictionary to decide how to punctuate your compound noun.

Example 1 Write the words that should be hyphenated in sentences a–c.

(a) They memorized word for word an entire chapter from the *King James Bible*.

(b) Because of a mix up in signals, Joe fumbled the ball.

(c) The sun is more than eight light minutes away from Earth.

Solution (a) **Word-for-word** is a compound ending in a prepositional phrase.

(b) We check the dictionary and find that **mix-up** requires a hyphen to connect the preposition *up* to the first part of the compound word.

c) We use a hyphen in **light-minutes** because it is a unit of measurement.

Numbers Hyphens are often used to join elements in the expression of numbers, inclusive sets or sequences, and fractions.

Numbers as Words We use a hyphen in compound numbers from twenty-one to ninety-nine:

>forty-nine, seventy-six, thirty-three, etc.

A Range of Numbers We use a hyphen to indicate a range of numbers or an inclusive set or sequence.

>pages 14–29   the years 1985–1995
>40–50 percent   the week of April 12–19
>scores 98–107

Because the hyphen takes the place of pairs of words such as *from/through*, *from/to*, or *between/and*, we do not use one of the words and a hyphen.

>INCORRECT: between 1995–2003

>CORRECT: between 1995 and 2003

Example 2 Write the numbers and fractions that should be hyphenated in sentences a–d.

(a) In Charleston, South Carolina, a newspaper obituary honored the deceased John Rutledge, 1739 1800.

(b) John Rutledge became Associate Justice when he was fifty one years old.

(c) The game scores of the volleyball match were 15 12, 11 15, and 15 3.

Solution (a) **1739–1800** is hyphenated because it indicates the span of years of a person's life.

(b) **Fifty-one** is hyphenated because it is a number between 21 and 99.

(c) **15-12, 11-15, 15-3** are hyphenated because they are game scores from a volleyball match.

Practice For a–d, replace each blank with the correct vocabulary word.

a. Show-offs like to _____ their money in front of other people.

b. The disrespectful siblings _____ their parents' curfew rules by staying out past midnight.

c. To display conspicuously is to _____.

d. To defy is to _____.

For e–g, write each expression that should be hyphenated.

e. When Lisa moved to another town, her friends gave her a warm send off.

f. The standardized exam allowed twenty five minutes for the vocabulary section and forty eight minutes for the reading comprehension section.

g. My ninety year old friend still drives her car to the market.

More Practice

For 1–4, use words to write each number.

1. 31   **2.** 46   **3.** 72   **4.** 89

Write each expression that should be hyphenated in sentences 5–10.

5. The soccer team favored to win the tournament lost to the underdogs, 1 0.

6. A sign in sheet records the presence of each delegate.

7. Was the administration involved in a cover up?

8. During the long sea voyage, Lydia hardly noticed the up and down motion of the ship.

9. Your great grandfather is my father in law's father.

10. The event was completely disorganized; it was a free for all.

Review set 79

Choose the correct word to complete sentences 1–14.

1. The Latin prefix (*post-*, *ambi-*) means "after."
(78)

2. To connote is to (slander, suggest, envelop) a meaning in addition to the literal meaning.
(77)

3. A (fiduciary, flexor, quorum) is a muscle that bends the body.
(76)

4. Limpid means (cloudy, delphic, clear).
(75)

5. To (censor, gravitate, incriminate) is to be drawn toward something.
(27)

6. There are three kinds of verbals: the gerund, the infinitive, and the (preposition, participle).
(16, 45)

7. (Me and her, Her and me, She and I) will brainstorm with (you and he, you and him).
(50, 51)

8. Neither of the weary nurses (have, has) finished (their, his or her) twelve-hour shift yet.
(53, 76)

9. We couldn't see (no, any) stars in the sky last night.
(78)

10. Debby has adopted more dogs and cats than (me, I).
(63)

11. Bob said he likes (me, my) washing windows along with him.
(53, 55)

12. That team of workers (accomplish, accomplishes) more than the others.
(5, 77)

13. (Wasn't, Weren't) there scissors in the drawer?
(12, 77)

14. My aunt has (wove, woven) some intricate designs in her baskets.
(15, 72)

15. Rewrite the following sentence so that it is in active voice: Plato and other "pagan" philosophers were ridiculed by Dante in *The Divine Comedy.*
(27)

16. Rewrite the following, adding capital letters and correct punctuation marks: last tuesday march 3 i found several pizza coupons that had expired on december 31 1998
(9, 41)

17. In this sentence, write the infinitive and label it a noun or an adjective: Struggling with a difficult sentence diagram, the frustrated student began to scream.
(19, 45)

18. In this sentence, write the verb phrase and name its tense: Saint Thomas Aquinas had earned Dante's praise and respect as a godly philosopher.
(15, 17)

19. In this sentence, write whether the underlined clause is essential or nonessential: The gray squirrel, <u>which chewed my hammock</u>, lives high in the old oak tree.
(62)

20. From this sentence, write each dependent clause, circling each subordinating conjunction: Working on the difficult sentence diagram, I kept my composure even though I wanted to scream with frustration as other students were doing.
(54)

21. Write the four common pairs of correlative conjunctions.
(35)

22. Write the nominative case, third person, singular (neuter gender) personal pronoun.
(50)

23. In this sentence, write the indefinite pronoun and label it singular or plural: You will probably find that most of the fresh peach ice cream has been consumed.
(68)

24. In this sentence, write each prepositional phrase and star
(14, 28) the object of each preposition: Sherlock Holmes enjoyed beekeeping in addition to sleuthing.

25. Write the four principal parts of the irregular verb *run*.
(13, 71)

26. In this sentence, write the verb phrase and label it action
(3, 18) or linking: Does Hercules look courageous after slaying the Nemean Lion?

27. Write whether the following is a complete sentence,
(2) sentence fragment, or run-on sentence: Weary pilgrims staggering through the slough of despair.

28. Rewrite the following as it is. Then add proofreading
(9, 32) symbols to indicate corrections.

St Paul was in spired to write, "for now we see threw a glass darkly...."

Diagram sentences 29 and 30.

29. Does diagramming sentences increase your
(16, 21) understanding of sentence structure?

30. Darby likes playing ping-pong, but Meg prefers shooting
(21, 56) baskets.

LESSON 80

Adverbs that Tell "How"

> **Dictation or Journal Entry**
>
> **Vocabulary:** Homer's *Odyssey* gives the English language the words *odyssey* and *Penelope*.
>
> In Homer's *Odyssey,* Odysseus spends twenty years traveling home from the Trojan War. During these years, Odysseus experiences great adventures and learns much about himself. Therefore, an *odyssey* is a long journey of wanderings full of adventures and trials. The family's trip to British Columbia was an *odyssey* that none of them would ever forget.
>
> Odysseus's faithful wife, *Penelope*, waits patiently for her husband to return from Troy. She fends off potential suitors by saying that she cannot remarry until she finishes weaving her father-in-law's funeral shroud. A *Penelope* is a patient, perfect, and faithful wife. While Sergeant Lopez was separated from his family during his tour of duty abroad, he hoped his wife would be a *Penelope*.

Adverbs are descriptive words that "modify" or add information to verbs, adjectives, and other adverbs. They answer the questions "how," "when," "where," and "how much" (or "to what extent"). The italicized adverbs below modify the verb *served*:

> How: Mr. Pinckney served *conscientiously*.
>
> When: He served *yearly*.
>
> Where: He served *there*.
>
> How Much: He served *frequently*.

"How" An adverb that tells "how" usually modifies the verb or verb phrase and often ends in the suffix *-ly*. For example, let's think about how Charles C. Pinckney governed:

> Charles C. Pinckney governed *cautiously*.

Charles C. Pinckney might have governed *responsibly, expertly, recklessly, cleverly, irresponsibly,* or *inconsistently*. These adverbs answer the question "how" he governed.

Example 1 Write the adverbs that tell "how" from this sentence:

> Nadine spoke graciously, gently, and modestly to her younger sister.

Solution The adverbs **graciously, gently,** and **modestly** tell "how" Nadine spoke.

Suffix -ly We remember that descriptive adjectives often end with suffixes such as *-able, -ful, -ive,* or *-ous*. Adjective and adverb forms of some nouns are listed below. Notice that the adverb is formed by adding -ly to the adjective.

Noun	Adjective	Adverb
faith	faithful	faithfully
exuberance	exuberant	exuberantly
majesty	majestic	majestically
peace	peaceful	peacefully
joy	joyful	joyfully
patience	patient	patiently
sincerity	sincere	sincerely
play	playful	playfully

Of course, not every word that ends in -ly is an adverb. *Ghastly, hilly, lively, orderly,* and *friendly* are all adjectives.

Adjective or Adverb? Some words, such as *hard, fast, right, early,* and *long,* have the same form whether they are used as adjectives or adverbs. However, we can always tell how the word is being used because an adjective modifies a noun or pronoun, and an adverb modifies a verb, adjective, or other adverb.

ADJECTIVE: I sat on *hard* concrete. (modifies the noun "concrete")

ADVERB: She worked *hard.* (modifies the verb "worked")

ADJECTIVE: It was a *fast* speed. (modifies the noun "speed")

ADVERB: Lilly walks *fast.* (modifies the verb "walks")

ADJECTIVE: Make a *left* turn at the corner.

ADVERB: Please turn *left* at the corner.

ADJECTIVE: We attended a *late* meeting.

ADVERB: We met *late.*

We look carefully to distinguish between an adverb and a predicate adjective. Consider the following sentence:

The new student felt lonely.

It might seem that *lonely* tells "how" the student felt. But we remember that we can identify a predicate adjective by replacing a possible linking verb (felt) with a "to be" verb:

The new student *was* lonely. (lonely student)

The word *lonely* describes the student, not the act of feeling. It is an adjective. Compare this to a sentence containing an action verb:

> The new student works silently.

If we replace an action verb with a "to be" verb, the sentence no longer makes sense:

> The new student *is* silently? (silently student?)

Silently does not describe the student. It describes the act of working. It is an adverb.

Example 2 Tell whether the italicized word in each sentence is an adjective or adverb. Also, tell which word or phrase it modifies.

(a) Please stand *still* for the photo.

(b) The *still* water in the late was crystal clear.

(c) After the storm, the water grew *still*.

Solution (a) The word *still* is an **adverb that modifies the verb "stand."** *Still* tells "how" to stand.

(b) The word *still* is an **adjective. It modifies the noun "water."** *Still* tells "what kind" of water.

(c) The word *still* is a predicate **adjective modifying the noun "water."**

Practice For sentences a–c, write each adverb that tells "how" and tell what word or phrase it modifies.

a. Charles Cotesworth Pinckney, from South Carolina, fought publicly and wholeheartedly for the Constitution.

b. Viciously and methodically, Antifederalists criticized the Constitution.

c. Everyone sincerely believed that they were right.

For d–g, tell whether the italicized word is an adjective or an adverb, and give the word or phrase it modifies.

d. Charles Pinckney seemed *lively*.

e. He sought the center stage *habitually* and *heroically*.

f. On the whole, the Constitutional Convention appeared *orderly*.

g. Charles Pinckney's political affiliations *generally* opposed those of Charles Cotesworth Pinckney, his distinguished second cousin.

For h–k, replace each blank with the correct vocabulary word.

h. Homer's _____ provided the English language with descriptive words.

i. A woman like Mary Bailey in *It's a Wonderful Life* is an example of a _____.

j. Odysseus experienced perilous adventures and moral growth as a result of his _____.

k. The couple's unforgettable _____ in Germany imprinted itself on their minds and hearts.

Review set 80 Choose the correct word to complete sentences 1–15.

1. To (flaunt, flout, flex) is to made a bold, conspicuous, gaudy display in public.
(79)

2. The Latin prefix *post-* means (before, near, after).
(78)

3. To (alleviate, compose, denote) is to mean literally.
(77)

4. To (genuflect, alleviate, faze) is to bend the knee.
(76)

5. Jurisdiction is (seriousness, power, blame).
(22)

6. Words like *no, hardly, none, scarcely,* and *barely* are examples of (appositives, adjectives, negatives).
(78)

7. Danae and (they, them) have been grooming race horses.
(50)

8. Each of the race horses (have, has) (their, its) own groomer.
(53, 68)

9. Peter says he hasn't (ever, never) seen such tall stallions.
₍₇₈₎

10. (Me and him, He and I, Him and me) worked longer than you and (her, she).
_(50, 51)

11. Please send (us, we) preschool teachers your empty milk containers.
_(21, 51)

12. A pallet of new grammar books (is, are) sitting in the warehouse.
₍₇₇₎

13. (Is, Are) measles as contagious as chicken pox?
_(12, 77)

14. I (saw, seen) a glorious sunrise this morning!
₍₇₁₎

15. John, James, and (me, myself, I) mended the fences.
₍₅₀₎

16. Rewrite the following, adding capital letters and correct punctuation marks, including hyphens: one third of my class has already read the first fifty two chapters of the spanish novel said ms flores the department head
_(65, 79)

17. In this sentence, write the participial phrase followed by the word it modifies: Having completed her essay, Blanca slumped in the chair and sighed with relief.
₍₅₆₎

18. In this sentence, write the verb phrase and name its tense: Jacob is memorizing the five rolls, or scrolls, of the Jewish Torah.
₍₁₇₎

19. In this sentence, write whether the underlined clause is essential or nonessential: The squirrel <u>that lives in the oak tree</u> chattered incessantly until noon.
₍₆₂₎

20. From this sentence, write the dependent clause, circling the subordinating conjunction: Julita sang "God Bless America" a cappella even though she had a sore throat.
₍₅₄₎

21. Write the plural of each noun. Use the dictionary if you are not sure.
_(10, 11)

(a) basketful   (b) cliff   (c) axis

22. Write the objective case, third person, singular (masculine gender) personal pronoun.
₍₅₂₎

23. In this sentence, write the indefinite pronoun and label it
(68) singular or plural: Strangely, most of the pumpkin ice cream pie has disappeared from the freezer.

24. Write the superlative form of the adjective *hungry*.
(39)

25. Write the four principal parts of the irregular verb *lose*.
(13, 71)

26. In this sentence, write the verb phrase and label it
(26) transitive or intransitive: Are some of the high school students complaining about homework?

27. Write whether the following is a complete sentence,
(2) sentence fragment, or run-on sentence: Martin Luther King wrote *Why We Can't Wait*.

28. Write and underline each word that should be italicized
(69) in this sentence: This Friday, my friends and I are going to see the musical play Les Miserables.

Diagram sentences 29 and 30.

29. Having failed the test on diagramming sentences, Petunia
(38, 56) felt discouraged.

30. The engineer whom we hired dislikes designing large
(21, 61) bridges.

LESSON 81

Using the Adverb *Well*

> **Dictation or Journal Entry**
>
> **Vocabulary:** Let us discuss two political terms, *gerrymandering* and *constituent*.
>
> *Gerrymandering* is the practice of redrawing the boundary lines of congressional districts in order to favor a certain party's candidates. Elbridge Gerry was governor of Massachusetts in 1812, when district boundaries were redrawn for the first time. One district resembled the shape of a salamander. Thus, *Gerry* plus *salamander* created the word *gerrymander,* meaning any unfair and partisan reapportionment of election districts. The party's ploy of *gerrymandering* resulted in unfair representation.
>
> In politics, a *constituent* is one who elects another as a representative in public office. Voters are *constituents*, for they cast their votes for a candidate to represent them.

Good The words *good* and *well* are frequently misused. *Good* is a descriptive adjective or a predicate adjective. It describes a noun or pronoun, as in these sentences:

Was Pierce Butler a good speaker?
(descriptive adjective modifying "speaker")

He came from a good family.
(descriptive adjective modifying "family")

That historical novel sounds good.
(predicate adjective describing "novel")

Well The word *well* is usually an adverb. It modifies an action verb and explains "how" someone does something.

Most people spoke well of him.

They recovered well from financial losses.

How well do you know him?

We do not use the word *good* as an adverb. Instead, we use *well*. See these examples:

NO: Debby edits *good.*
YES: Debby edits *well.*

NO: This cotton gin works *good.*
YES: This cotton gin works *well.*

Example 1 Replace each blank with *well* or *good*.

(a) Did Pierce Butler advise his colleagues _____?

(b) Yes, he was a _____ advisor—cautious and prudent.

(c) His cosmopolitan experiences served him _____ in the Convention.

(d) He believed the Constitution was a _____ document.

Solution (a) Did Pierce Butler advise his colleagues **well**? *Well* is an adverb telling "how" Pierce Butler advised.

(b) Yes, he was a **good** advisor—cautious and prudent. *Good* is an adjective modifying the noun "advisor."

(c) His cosmopolitan experiences served him **well** in the Convention. *Well* is an adverb, which modifies the verb "served" and tells "how" his experiences served him.

(d) He believed the Constitution was a **good** document. *Good* is an adjective modifying the noun "document."

Feeling Well? The word *well* is used as an adjective when referring to the state of one's health. You feel *good* about passing a test, for example, but when you wish to state that you are in good health, it is preferable to say that you are *well*.

I feel *well* today.

Is Jill *well*, or is she still ill?

Example 2 Choose either *well* or *good* to complete each sentence.

(a) Pierce Butler had a (good, well) feeling about his fugitive-slave clause in the Constitution.

(b) Having been blessed with good health, Pierce Butler felt (good, well) until his death at seventy-seven.

Solution (a) Pierce Butler had a **good** feeling.... (We use *good* because it is an adjective modifying "feeling." Also, it does not refer to one's health.)

(b) Having been blessed with good health, Pierce Butler felt **well** until his death at seventy-seven. (It is preferable to use the word *well* to describe how one feels.)

Practice Choose the correct descriptive word for sentences a–e.

a. The delegates worked together (good, well) to create an acceptable document.

b. They did a (good, well) job by compromising to satisfy all the states.

c. They learned to debate (good, well).

d. James Monroe was a (good, well) friend to Pierce Butler.

e. John E. Calhoun did not feel (good, well) in his last year in the Senate.

For f–h, replace each blank with the correct vocabulary word.
f. Voting on bills, most of the Senators tried to please their _____.

g. _____ is an unfair redrawing of voter district boundaries.

h. _____, the voters that a legislator represents, exercise considerable influence.

More Practice Choose the correct descriptive word for each sentence.
1. Those glasses look (good, well) on you!
2. How (good, well) do you know the Presidents?
3. Do you sing (good, well)?
4. With practice, you might become a (good, well) singer.
5. Your soprano solo sounded (good, well).
6. Julita is feeling (good, well) today.
7. Christina skates (well, good) for her age.
8. Allison has a (good, well) disposition for nursing.
9. Onping recites Shakespeare very (good, well).
10. Ah, that vegetable soup smells (good, well)!

Review set 81 Choose the correct word to complete sentences 1–15.
1. (Odysseus, Penelope, Dionysus) spent twenty adventuresome years traveling home from the Trojan War.
   (80)

2. To (flaunt, flout, appease) is to treat with contempt; to mock; to defy.
   (79)

3. Posterior means situated toward the (front, back, middle).
(78)

4. To (denote, connote, envelop) is to imply, or suggest a
(77) meaning in addition to the literal meaning.

5. Judicious means (funny, sensible, heavy).
(22)

6. *Now, then, soon, often,* and *here* function in sentences as
(80) (nouns, adverbs, adjectives).

7. (Her and me, Me and her, She and I) swam farther than
(50, 63) you and (him, he).

8. Grandma appreciated (us, our) mowing and edging her
(50, 53) lawn.

9. "Cars can't wash (theirselves, themselves)," said Aunt
(57) Mabel.

10. (Isn't, Ain't, Aren't) there any hair clippers in that
(78) cupboard?

11. Liz has (her's, hers), but she (don't, doesn't) have (their's,
(53, 78) theirs).

12. The young artist (who, whom) you met in the gallery
(61) could become famous for his primitive-looking clay pots.

13. The clay pot (that, which) he fired yesterday cracked in
(62) several places.

14. The rabbits have (ate, eaten) all the cauliflower.
(70)

15. Of the two villains, Sher Khan seemed the (meaner,
(39) meanest).

16. Rewrite the following, adding capital letters and correct
(31, 66) punctuation marks, including hyphens: the monday
before last dr baker spent twenty five minutes reading us
a short story by hans christian andersen its title was the
princess and the pea

17. For a–c, write whether the *-ing* word in each sentence is a
(55) verb, participle, or gerund.
   (a) Sometimes the dog's digging infuriates me.

(b) Shall I chastise the dog digging holes in my yard?
(c) Spike is digging an escape route under the fence!

18. Rewrite the following sentence so that it is in active voice: Several captivating stories by Dr. Seuss were read by the librarian to all fifty children.

19. In this sentence, write whether the underlined clause is essential or nonessential: That ambiguous sentence, <u>which contained a pronoun lacking a clear antecedent</u>, confused me.

20. From this sentence, write the dependent clause, circling the subordinating conjunction: Drizella and Anastasia refuse to let Cinderella go to the ball so that the prince will never see Cinderella.

21. Write the seven common coordinating conjunctions.

22. Write the nominative case, third person, singular (masculine gender) personal pronoun.

23. For sentences a and b, write whether the italicized word functions as an adjective or an adverb.
(a) Monty is working *hard*.
(b) Removing a tree stump is *hard* work.

24. From this sentence, write the pronoun followed by its antecedent: As Kurt smacked the ball to left field, he heard the crowd cheer.

25. Write the four principal parts of the irregular verb *catch*.

26. Write whether the following is a phrase or a clause: in the eyes of most high school students living in America today

27. From this sentence, write each prepositional phrase and star the object of each preposition: In spite of the darkness, the animal rescue team searched throughout the night for the escaped cougar from the local zoo.

28. Write whether the following is a complete sentence, a sentence fragment, or a run-on sentence: The apocalyptic *Four Horsemen* represent war, famine, death, and one unknown they are on mounts of red, black, pale, and white.

Diagram sentences 29 and 30.

29. The senator's voice sounded stentorian but amiable.
(24, 38)

30. My bewildered teacher asked me to explain my poor test score.
(21, 56)

LESSON 82   The Hyphen: Compound Adjectives

Dictation or Journal Entry

Vocabulary: The words *later* and *latter* differ in spelling by only one letter but have very different meanings.

Later is the comparative form of the adjective or adverb *late*, meaning "coming or appearing after a certain time." Scot arrived *later* than Debby.

Latter refers to the second of the two mentioned. In the Constitutional Convention, Charles Pinckney and Pierce Butler both represented South Carolina; the *latter* was a true aristocrat.

We have seen how hyphens are used in compound nouns and with numbers. In this lesson we will learn more uses for hyphens.

Compound Adjectives Just as we combine words to form compound nouns, we can combine words to form **compound adjectives**. A compound adjective is a group of words that works *as a unit* to modify a noun with a single thought. It is not a list of adjectives, each modifying a noun in its own way.

> COMPOUND ADJECTIVE: *heart-shaped* sandwiches
>
> TWO ADJECTIVES: *fancy, little* sandwiches
>
> COMPOUND ADJECTIVE: *homemade* pie
>
> TWO ADJECTIVES: *rich, creamy* pie
>
> COMPOUND ADJECTIVE: *green* and *yellow* shirt
>
> THREE ADJECTIVES: *clean brown work* shirt

As shown above, compound adjectives can be spelled as one word, left as separate words, or hyphenated. How they appear is sometimes a matter of rule but is often a matter of custom or style. The following guidelines will help you form many compound adjectives confidently.

Clarity Our goal is to make our meaning as clear as possible to the reader. When we use hyphens to join two or more words, it helps the reader understand that the words are to be read as a single unit. This prevents confusion. Consider this sentence:

> The government owned land in the desert is not for sale.

The reader, seeing a subject (government), a verb (owned), and a direct object (land), is likely to misread the sentence. So we hyphenate the compound adjective for greater clarity:

The government-owned land in the desert is not for sale.

Borrowed phrases and clauses One of the ways we modify nouns is by borrowing descriptive phrases and clauses and using them as compound adjectives. Hyphens help join words that work as a unit to modify a noun.

Prepositional phrases When we use a prepositional phrase to modify a noun, it is functioning as a compound adjective. If it comes *before* the noun, it should be hyphenated.

I want an *up-to-date* weather report.

(Please bring the weather report *up to date*.)

We are *out-of-town* guests.

(We guests come from *out of town*.)

Words out of order When we borrow a descriptive phrase or clause and place it before a noun, we often eliminate or rearrange some of the words. To help them express a single thought, words that are out of their normal order can be held together by hyphens.

He likes *chocolate-covered* cherries.

(The cherries are *covered with chocolate*.)

The *grouchy-looking* clerk frowned at me.

(The clerk *looked grouchy*.)

An exception We *do not* use a hyphen in a compound adjective that begins with an adverb ending in *-ly*.

some *nicely kept* offices, a *securely fastened* padlock

the *freshly painted* fence, my *painfully swollen* elbow

Number + unit of measure We use a hyphen when joining a number to a unit of measure to form a compound adjective.

24-inch bike, *three-mile* race, *five-year* plan

We *do not* use a hyphen when the number alone modifies the noun:

24 inches, three miles, five years

Fractions We use a hyphen in a fraction that functions as an adjective.

The bill passed with a *two-thirds* majority.

Our gas tank is *three-fourths* full.

If the numerator or the denominator of a fraction is already hyphenated, *do not* use another hyphen:

A five twenty-fifths increase equals a *one-fifth* increase.

We *do not* use a hyphen if the fraction functions as a noun.

Two thirds of my friends like spinach.

Example 1 Write the words that should be hyphenated in sentences a–e.

(a) She buys jelly filled doughnuts.

(b) We've had below average precipitation.

(c) That was a sour tasting lemon drop.

(d) Jasmine had a three inch growth spurt last month.

(e) Three fourths of the students left early.

Solution (a) We hyphenate **jelly-filled** because the words work as unit to modify the noun *doughnuts* with a single thought: filled with jelly.

(b) We hyphenate **below-average** because it is a prepositional phrase that comes before and modifies the noun *precipitation*.

(c) We hyphenate **sour-tasting** to help it retain its meaning (something that tastes sour).

(d) We hyphenate **three-inch** because it is a compound adjective formed by a number and a unit of measure.

(e) **None.** We do not hyphenate the fraction three fourths because it is functioning as a noun.

Dictionary clues Remember, dictionaries cannot contain all the compound words we can create. If you are faced with an unfamiliar compound, you can search the dictionary for similar compounds and use them as clues.

Other uses for hyphens We use hyphens to avoid confusion or awkward spelling, and to join unusual elements.

With prefixes and suffixes If you add a prefix or suffix to a word, and the resulting word is misleading or awkward, use a hyphen for clarity.

I will *re-cover* (not *recover*) the chair with new fabric.

It had a hard, *shell-like* (not *shelllike*) surface.

The *fall-like* (not *falllike*) weather is refreshing

Also, use a hyphen to join a prefix to any proper noun.

pro-American, mid-August, post-World War II

Letter + word, number + number Hyphens are used to combine unusual elements into single expressions.

When a letter (or group of letters) modifies a word in a compound noun or adjective, a hyphen is often used.

A-frame, L-shaped, G-rated, U-turn, t-shirt

We can also use a hyphen to join numbers in expressions such as the following:

The final score was *68-87*.

We have a *fifty-fifty* chance of winning the coin toss.

Example 2 Write the words, if any, that should be hyphenated in sentences a–d. Be prepared to use the dictionary.

(a) I want to repress my wrinkled shirt.

(b) Were the protestors antiChristian?

(c) Jake needs a c clamp for his project.

(d) A hundred votes were split sixty forty.

Solution (a) We hyphenate **re-press** to avoid misleading the reader.

(b) We hyphenate **anti-Christian** because we are joining a prefix and a proper noun.

(c) We consult the dictionary and find that **c-clamp** is a hyphenated term.

(d) We use a hyphen to form the expression **sixty-forty**.

Practice Write the words, if any, that should be hyphenated in sentences a–e.

a. G rated movies provide all ages with appropriate entertainment.

b. I will research my desk for that lost document.

c. The self nominated candidate lacked the support of others.

d. The rapidly flowing current carried us downstream.

e. We'll need a ten foot extension ladder.

For f–i, replace each blank with *later* or *latter*.

f. If Christie had to choose between vanilla and chocolate, she would choose the _____.

g. The vacancy on the Supreme Court will be filled _____.

h. We looked up the words *felicitous* and *fortuitous* and found that the _____ means lucky.

i. Now we are working, but _____ we will play.

Review set 82

Choose the correct word to complete sentences 1–15.

1. (Flaunting, Censuring, Gerrymandering) is the practice of redrawing the boundary lines of congressional districts.
(81)

2. A(n) (odyssey, Penelope, modus operandi) is a long journey, full of adventures and trials.
(80)

3. To flout is to (sing, sleep, defy).
(79)

4. Posthumous means published (before, after, during) the death of the author.
(78)

5. Money set aside for something is a(n) (caucus, appropriation, jurisdiction).
(23)

6. Quickly proofreading the essay, I (could, couldn't) find no obvious errors.
(78)

7. Beth thinks that physics (is, are) easy.
(12, 77)

8. A flock of geese (has, have) landed near the pond.
(12, 77)

9. (Us, We) recording artists are building a sound room.
(50, 63)

10. (Her and me, Me and her, She and I) cannot lift as much weight as (he, him).
(50, 63)

11. The kitten (don't doesn't) have (no, any) catnip.

12. One of the kittens often (leave, leaves) (their, its) muddy footprints on the hood of my car.

13. Sometimes I see the mother cat and (they, them) sleeping underneath the picnic table.

14. Have you ever (drove, driven) across the country?

15. Alba, please tell Ilbea and (me, myself, I) your secret.

16. Rewrite the following, adding capital letters and correct punctuation marks, including hyphens: my recipe said gloria calls for four and three fourths cups of well sifted flour two cups of sugar and six bananas it makes twenty four muffins

17. For a–c, write whether the *-ing* word in each sentence is a verb, participle, or gerund.
  (a) The whistling of the wind kept me awake.
  (b) I yelled at the whistling wind.
  (c) The wind was whistling through the trees.

18. In this sentence, write the verb phrase and name its tense: Perry Mason, the lawyer, has lost only one case.

19. From this sentence, write the dependent clause, circling the subordinating conjunction: We shall give you the financial report as soon as the audit is complete.

20. In this sentence, write whether the underlined clause is essential or nonessential: The county audit, <u>which was completed last month</u>, found gross mismanagement of public funds.

21. Write the plural of each noun.
  (a) Kris   (b) sheaf   (c) editor-in-chief

22. Write the nominative case, third person, singular (feminine gender) personal pronoun.

23. For sentences a and b, write whether the italicized word functions as an adjective or an adverb.
  (a) The sprinters ran *fast*.

(b) It was a *fast* race.

24. Use an appositive to make one sentence from these two
(42) sentences: Aunt Helen often repeats her favorite old saying. Her favorite old saying is, "A stitch in time saves nine."

25. Write the four principal parts of the irregular verb *cost*.
(13, 70)

26. Write the comparative form of the adjective *tasty*.
(39)

27. Rewrite the following as it is. Then add proofreading
(32) symbols to indicate corrections.

Alice had a curious dreem you can read about it in *Alice in Wonder land.*

28. Write and underline each word that should be italicized
(69) in this sentence: Ms. Packrat has been searching the classified section of the Los Angeles Times for antique can openers, typewriters, and old shoes.

Diagram sentences 29 and 30.

29. Stomping her foot, the toddler gave the baby-sitter a
(30, 56) defiant look.

30. Does the baby-sitter regret having ignored the advice of
(21, 56) the child's psychologist?

LESSON 83

Adverbs that Tell "Where"

> **Dictation or Journal Entry**
>
> **Vocabulary:** The terms *eminent domain* and *enacting clause* are legal terms.
>
> *Eminent domain* is the government's right to take land for public use. The Federal government may exercise its right of *eminent domain* to purchase all property needed to build an interstate highway.
>
> "Be it enacted by the Senate and the House of Representatives" is the *enacting clause* found on each bill before Congress. The entire bill is scrapped if a majority votes to strike the *enacting clause*.

We have identified adverbs that tell "how." In this lesson, we will review adverbs that tell "where." Again, let's think about how Charles Pinckney served:

Charles Pinckney served *enthusiastically*.

"Where" Now, let's think about **where** Charles Pinckney served:

Charles Pinckney served *nearby*.

He might also have served *downtown, uptown, everywhere, somewhere, here, there,* or *anywhere*.

Here are some common adverbs that tell "where:"

nearby	anywhere	up	in
far	everywhere	here	out
down	nowhere	there	home
uptown	somewhere	upstream	inside
downtown	around	downstream	outside

We remember that words like *in, out,* and *down* can also be prepositions. But in order to function as a preposition, a word must have an object. When a word like *in, out, up,* or *down* does not have an object, it is an adverb.

PREPOSITION: She stomped *out* the door. (object "door")

ADVERB: She stomped *out*. (no object)

Example 1 For sentences a–d, write each adverb that tells "where," and give the verb or verb phrase that it modifies.

(a) Pinckney's enthusiastic support of a stronger government trickled home.

(b) Did he travel far to spread his views?

(c) Here and there, he found political allies.

(d) Pinckney rumored everywhere that Great Britain's constitution was the best in the world.

Solution (a) The adverb **home** tells "where" Pinckney's support **trickled**.

(b) The adverb **far** modifies the verb **did travel** and tells "where."

(c) The adverbs **here** and **there** modify the verb **found**, telling "where" he found political allies.

(d) The adverb **everywhere** modifies the verb **rumored**, telling "where" Pinckney rumored.

Diagramming We diagram adverbs just as we do adjectives. We write the adverb on a slanted line under the word it modifies. Here we diagram a sentence containing an adverb:

Charles Pinckney served *nearby*.

Charles Pinckney | served
                        \nearby

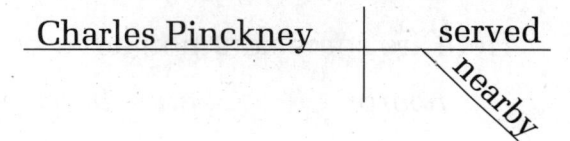

Example 2 Diagram this sentence: Is Luisa rowing upstream?

Solution We see that the adverb *upstream* tells "where" Luisa is rowing, so we diagram the sentence like this:

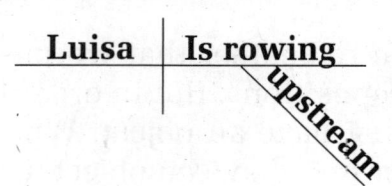

Luisa | Is rowing
              \upstream

Practice Write each adverb that tells "where" in sentences a–d, then write the verb or verb phrase it modifies.

a. Pinckney stands out among his peers.

b. He has come up in my opinion.

c. Were you following him around?

d. Luisa has traveled nowhere.

Diagram sentences e and f.

   e. Bob and Christie looked everywhere.

   f. They had lost their keys somewhere.

For g and h, replace each blank with the correct vocabulary word(s).

   g. The Congressional secretary included the mandatory _____ before submitting a copy of the bill to each politician.

   h. The right of _____ might permit the government to purchase your property for building a railroad.

Review set 83 Choose the correct word to complete sentences 1–15.

1. (Later, Latter) is the comparative form of the adjective or adverb *late*.
   (82)

2. Gerrymandering is the practice of (crossing, redrawing, ignoring) the boundary lines of congressional districts in order to favor a certain party's candidates.
   (81)

3. An odyssey is a long (ponytail, journey, meeting).
   (80)

4. Levity is (giddiness, seriousness, blame).
   (24)

5. Women in the United States now have (gravity, recrimination, suffrage); they can vote.
   (25)

6. Chicken noodle soup tastes (good, well).
   (81)

7. Can (me and her, her and me, she and I) meet you and (he, him) for breakfast?
   (50, 51)

8. Joe (doesn't, don't) approve of (me, my) wasting time.
   (12, 55)

9. Julita and (me, myself, I) play tennis on Tuesdays.
   (50)

10. Mathematics (isn't, ain't, aren't) too difficult if you do your homework.
    (77)

11. Jenny (doesn't, don't) have either (your's, yours) or (her's, hers).
    (12, 53)

12. The artist (who, whom) painted this portrait sells his work online.

13. The new gallery, (that, which) opens next Monday, will display several of his pieces.

14. Have you ever (rode, ridden) a horse in a parade?

15. Of all the comments, yours was the (more, most) helpful and complimentary.

16. Rewrite the following, adding capital letters and punctuation marks as needed: pardon me mrs curtis but isn't this a one way street asked fernando

17. For a–c, write whether the *-ing* word in each sentence is a verb, participle, or gerund.
  (a) Chirping finches gather around the thistle.
  (b) Are the finches chirping in unison?
  (c) That finch likes chirping to his friend.

18. In the following sentence, write the verb phrase and name its tense: Have you studied for Friday's dictation test?

19. In the following sentence, write whether the underlined clause is essential or nonessential: The lightning <u>that struck my neighbor's palm tree</u> also caused a power outage.

20. From the following sentence, write the dependent clause, circling the subordinating conjunction: Calamity seemed to follow Jane wherever she went.

21. From this sentence, write the indefinite pronoun and label it singular or plural: Unfortunately, most of the banana muffins have burned.

22. Write the nominative case, second person, personal pronoun.

23. For a–c, write whether the italicized word functions as an adjective or an adverb.
  (a) Jeb's latest novel was published *posthumously*.
  (b) Does the main character appear *homely*?

(c) A *lonely* outcast shuffled down Main Street.

24. Write whether the following is a phrase or a clause: outside the jurisdiction of the city government
(20)

25. Write the four principal parts of the irregular verb *feel*.
(13)

26. Rewrite the following sentence so that it is in active voice: I was admonished by my parents not to climb the tree during a thunderstorm again.
(27)

27. In this sentence, write the infinitive, labeling it an adjective or a noun: Maxwell has twenty-two thank-you notes to write.
(45)

28. Rewrite the following as it is. Then add proofreading symbols to indicate corrections.
(32)

Mr Abernathy says that his aunt might havebeen acquainted with the Queen Scotland.

Diagram sentences 29 and 30.

29. Collecting old shoes is Ms. Packrat's new hobby.
(16, 36)

30. Stacking up her shoeboxes, Ms. Packrat is neatly organizing her collection.
(56, 80)

LESSON 84

Word Division

> **Dictation or Journal Entry**
>
> **Vocabulary:** Let's learn the history of the adjectives *procrustean* and *protean*.
>
> According to Greek legend, Procrustes was a robber who mutilated or stretched his victims to make them fit the length of his bed. Therefore, *procrustean* came to mean "taking no account of individual differences; cruelly making everything the same; forcing conformity." The *procrustean* store manager insisted that all his employees dye their hair the same color.
>
> *Protean* traces back to a character named Proteus in *Odyssey*. Menelaus needed to capture Proteus to discover how to get home to Sparta. The problem was that Proteus had the ability to change into any shape that he chose. Thus, *protean* means "readily assuming different shapes; variable." The *protean* actress was able to play many different roles.

When writing, we use a hyphen to divide a word if we run out of room at the end of a line. It is important to know *where* (or *whether*) to divide a word. Using a computer does not free us from this responsibility. Many "automatic" word divisions are unacceptable in good writing.

We observe the following guidelines when dividing a word.

Between syllables Words can be divided only between syllables. We check the dictionary if we are in doubt about how a word is divided. The hyphen always appears with the first half of the word.

     par- tial   mo- tive   par- ent   mort- gage

One-letter syllables A one-letter syllable should not be divided from the rest of the word.

     uten- sil (not u- tensil)

     amia- ble (not a- miable)

     media (not medi- a)

Because of this, two-syllable words such as the following are never divided:

     amaze   lucky   ideal   icon

When a word contains a one-letter syllable, we divide the word *after* that syllable.

     presi- dent (not pres- ident)

     nega- tive (not neg- ative)

     incrimi- nate (not incrim- inate)

Compound words Divide a compound word between its elements. If the word is already hyphenated, divide it *after* the hyphen.

> silver- ware (not sil- verware)
>
> super- market (not supermar- ket)
>
> brother- in- law (not bro-ther-in-law)

Prefixes and suffixes Divide a word after a prefix or before a suffix.

> re- consider (not recon- sider)
>
> defense- less (not de-fenceless)

Longer words Some longer words contain more than one possible dividing place. We divide them as needed to fit the line.

> car- nivore *or* carni-vore
>
> fan- tanstic *or* fantas- tic

Do not divide Some words and expressions are never divided.

One-syllable words One-syllable words cannot be divided, no matter how many letters they contain. Remember that even when you add *-ed*, some words are still one syllable.

> breathe   feigned   mouthed   straight

Short words Words with four letters should not be divided even if they are more than one syllable.

> many   liar   pity   very

Also, we do not divide contractions or abbreviations.

> wouldn't   they'll   o'clock

Example Use hyphens to divide each of the words. Remember that not all words should be divided. Use the dictionary if necessary.

(a) whisper   (b) among   (c) genuflect

(d) ravenous   (e) sleepyhead   (f) marched

Solution (a) We divide between syllables: **whis- per**

(b) We do not divide a one-letter syllable from the rest of the word. **Among** cannot be divided.

(c) We divide a word *after* a single-letter syllable: **genu- flect**

(d) We divide a word *before* a suffix: **raven- ous**

(e) We divide a compound word between its elements: **sleepy- head**

(f) We do not divide one-syllable words. **Marched** cannot be divided.

Practice Use a hyphen to divide words a–f. Not all the words should be divided. Use a dictionary if you are not sure.

a. flaut
b. eminent
c. odorous

d. noisy
e. wouldn't
f. sixty-four

For g–j, replace each blank with the correct vocabulary word.

g. The figure from Greek mythology who could change shapes at will was _____.

h. The Grecian figure who showed no mercy toward his victims was _____.

i. Uriah Heep was a _____ character, for he could be syrupy sweet one second and ruthlessly vindictive the next.

j. The _____ dictator's policies were arbitrary and violent.

More Practice Hyphenate each word correctly. Use the dictionary if you are not sure.

1. planned
2. wasn't
3. connote
4. closed
5. Procrustes
6. posthumous
7. hadn't
8. constituent
9. affidavit
10. photocopy
11. credence
12. cursory
13. concurrent
14. heptagon
15. stepmother
16. oxygen
17. matron-of-honor
18. herbivorous

19. hemisphere 20. lightning

Review Set 84

Choose the correct word(s) to complete sentences 1–15.

1. (Eminent domain, Habeus corpus, Enacting clause) is the government's right to take land for public use.
 (83)

2. Our flight is (later, latter) than yours.
 (82)

3. A (constituent, Penelope, consul) is one who elects another as a representative in public office.
 (81)

4. A(n) (odyssey, Penelope, cicerone) is a patient and faithful wife.
 (80)

5. Gracie did not discuss her previous job, but she made a(n) (delusion, illusion, allusion) to it.
 (26)

6. At the beginning of *The Grapes of Wrath*, Tom Joad (don't, doesn't) have (no, a) job.
 (12, 18)

7. Mumps (is, are) an uncomfortable childhood disease.
 (77)

8. A pride of lions (was, were) moving across the plain.
 (76, 77)

9. Please give (us, we) travelers the train schedule.
 (51, 63)

10. The Joad Family is displaced. Is Jim Casy as displaced as (they, them)?
 (63)

11. Jenny likes singing. Phil and (she, her) (sing, sings) beautifully together.
 (50, 74)

12. Each of the characters (have, has) (their, his or her) own personality.
 (53, 76)

13. (Them, Those) displaced tenant farmers headed to California for sunshine and better wages.
 (67)

14. The Joads and (them, themselves, they) traveled together as far as the Colorado River.
 (50)

15. The wind (blew, blown) over the barren ground.
 (49)

16. Rewrite the following, adding capital letters and correct punctuation marks: yes tom admitted i served time in prison for a terrible crime

17. For a–c, write whether the *-ing* word functions as verb, participle, or gerund.
(a) Migrant camps were full of *suffering* laborers.
(b) The Joad children were *suffering* from hunger.
(c) Did the government camps end the *suffering*?

18. In the following sentence, write the verb phrase and name its tense: The Joads have been picking peaches and cotton to survive.

19. Write whether the following sentence is true or false: In an adjective clause, the use of *that* or *which* depends on whether the clause is essential or nonessential.

20. From the following sentence, write the dependent clause, circling the subordinating conjunction: When Rose of Sharon's baby arrived, it was stillborn.

21. Use an appositive to make one sentence from the two sentences below.
Steinbeck's *The Grapes of Wrath* is a masterpiece.
It portrays a family's optimism despite a harsh struggle against death and greed.

22. Write the possessive case, second person, personal pronoun.

23. For a and b below, write whether the italicized word functions as an adjective or an adverb.
(a) *Appallingly* harsh events fail to destroy the Joads' optimism.
(b) John Steinbeck had a *lively* imagination.

24. Write whether the following is a phase or a clause: after Rose of Sharon's husband sneaks off, abandoning her

25. Write the four principal parts of the irregular verb *set*.

26. Write the superlative form of the adjective *destructive*.

27. For a–c, write the plural of each noun.
(10, 11)
    (a) category   (b) genius   (c) testimony

28. Write and underline each word that should be italicized in the following sentence: Norman Rockwell painted three hundred eighteen covers for The Saturday Evening Post.
(69)

Diagram sentences 29 and 30.

29. The migrant workers asked Jim Casy to plead their cause.
(30, 56)

30. Jim Casy, a preacher, was a labor agitator.
(36, 42)

LESSON 85 — Adverbs that Tell "When"

> **Dictation or Journal Entry**
> **Vocabulary:** *Ascent* and *assent* are homophones, words that sound alike but differ in spelling and meaning.
>
> *Ascent* is upward movement. William Few made a rapid *ascent* to a position of leadership in Georgia.
>
> As a verb, *assent* means "to express agreement." The states must *assent* to the Constitution before it can be enacted. As a noun, an *assent* is an agreement, or concurrence. The states finally gave their *assent* to the plan.

We have reviewed adverbs that tell "how" and "where." In this lesson, we will review adverbs that modify a verb and tell "when." Again, let us think about how and where Charles Pinckney served:

How: Charles Pinckney served *responsibly*.

Where: Charles Pinckney served *here*.

"When" Now we will think about "when" Charles Pinckney served:

When: Charles Pinckney served *daily*.

He might also have served *later*, *today*, *then*, *nightly*, or *monthly*.

The following common adverbs tell "when":

before	when	late	soon
yearly	tonight	after	monthly
hourly	early	today	tomorrow
now	then	nightly	daily

Adverb Position An adverb can appear almost anywhere in a sentence.

Monthly Abraham Baldwin talked to constituents.

Abraham Baldwin talked *monthly* to constituents.

Abraham Baldwin talked to constituents *monthly*.

Even though the adverb *monthly* modifies the verb *talked* in each of the sentences above, it is not necessarily placed near the verb. Since the placement of the adverb can vary, we must learn to identify adverbs even when they are separated from the verbs they modify.

Example 1 For each sentence, write the adverb that tells "when" and the verb or verb phrase it modifies.

(a) Abraham Baldwin is now remembered as an outstanding teacher at Yale University.

(b) Baldwin had served as chaplain in the American army before.

(c) Later, he effected the compromises on slavery and equal representation in the Senate.

(d) He finally embraced Southern attitudes and political beliefs.

Solution (a) The adverb **now** tells "when" Abraham Baldwin **is remembered** as an outstanding teacher. *Now* modifies the verb is remembered.

(b) The adverb **before** modifies the verb **had served.**

(c) The adverb **later** modifies the verb **effected.**

(d) The adverb **finally** modifies the verb **embraced.**

Example 2 Diagram this sentence: Shall we discuss politics today?

Solution We place the adverb *today* under the verb shall discuss:

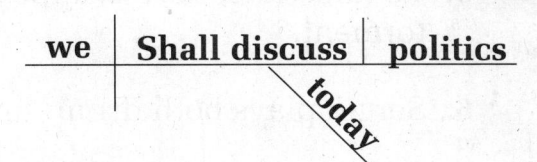

we | Shall discuss | politics
          \today

Practice For sentences a–d, write the adverb that tells "when" and the verb or verb phrase it modifies.

a. Earlier, Abraham Baldwin had favored a division of the Senate based on property.

b. He eventually became one of the South's most trusted figures.

c. He cautioned daily, "Hold the wagon back."

d. We will resolve this dispute tomorrow.

Diagram sentences e and f.

e. Mom quotes Ben Franklin daily.

f. He always loathed laziness.

For g–i, replace each blank with the correct vocabulary word.

g. The _____ was steep, so we hikers were out of breath.

h. Clotilda gave her _____ to marry Clyde.

i. Will he _____ to her proposals?

Review set 85

Choose the correct word(s) to complete sentences 1–15.

1. (Procrustes, Proteus, Mercury) was a robber who stretched or mutilated his victims to make them fit the length of his bed.
(84)

2. The Federal government may exercise its right of (modus vivendi, primogeniture, eminent domain) to purchase all property needed to built the railway.
(83)

3. (Later, Latter) refers to the second of the two mentioned.
(82)

4. To filibuster is to obstruct (presidential, judicial, legislative) action by long speeches or debate.
(29)

5. To (alleviate, hector, apportion) is to bully, intimidate, or torment.
(28)

6. Sergio plays both drums and flute (well, good).
(81)

7. Can you and (he, him) sit with (me and her, she and I, her and me) at the concert?
(50, 51)

8. The young campers were impressed with (me, my) playing taps at sundown.
(53)

9. Tui will sing with either Judy or (me, myself, I).
(28, 51)

10. The clippers (isn't, ain't, aren't) sharp enough to shear all those sheep.
(78)

11. Since Nora (don't, doesn't) have a toothbrush, she would like to borrow (your's, yours).
(53, 78)

12. The classmate from (who, whom) she borrowed the toothbrush doesn't want it back.

13. The toothbrush (that, which) Nora borrowed now belongs to her.

14. Yesterday, the geese (flew, flown) south.

15. Today Dunky seems the (less, least) ambitious of my two brothers.

16. Rewrite the following letter, adding capital letters and punctuation marks as needed:

dear mr steinbeck

the grapes of wrath is an unforgettable story thank you for encouraging us to be more responsible and compassionate

                with appreciation

                stacey

17. For a–c, write whether the *-ing* word in each sentence is a verb, participle, or gerund.

(a) After the accident, the beagle was limping.

(b) The beagle's limping concerned me.

(c) Was the limping beagle all right?

18. In the following sentence, write the verb phrase and name its tense: Well-informed citizens have been scrutinizing newspaper articles about the coming election.

19. In the following sentence, write each dependent clause and label it essential or nonessential: That mercurial candidate, who is running for the senate, now favors legislation that he opposed yesterday.

20. From this sentence, write the dependent clause, circling the subordinating conjunction: That portrait is actually called *La Giaconda* although we know it as *Mona Lisa*.

21. From this sentence, write the indefinite pronoun and label it singular or plural: Was either of the batters ambidextrous?

22. Write the possessive case, first person, singular personal pronoun.
₍₅₂₎

23. For a–c, write the question answered by the italicized adverb. The first one is done for you.
_(83, 85)
(a) Suzette slept *peacefully*.   (How?)
(b) She had finished her homework *early*.
(c) Were her friends waiting *there*?

24. Write seven common coordinating conjunctions. Then write four pairs of correlative conjunctions.
₍₃₃₎

25. Write the four principal parts of the irregular verb *stand*.
_(13, 77)

26. Rewrite the following as it is. Then add proofreading symbols to indicate corrections:
₍₃₂₎

Last Week end Annie read a book by Rudyard Kipling she she doesn't remember its title.

27. For a–c, hyphenate each word correctly.
_(10, 11)
(a) smashed   (b) brother-in-law (c) toothbrushes

28. Write and underline each word that should be italicized in this sentence: A recent volume of the Smithsonian magazine featured an article about Cambodia's magnificent, ancient temples.
₍₆₉₎

Diagram sentences 29 and 30.

29. Jeb wants to play a game of table tennis, but he needs to practice playing the trumpet.
_(56, 59)

30. Having apportioned the funds from the estate, the executor of the trust left her office hastily.
_(56, 85)

LESSON 86 — Adverbs that Tell "How Much"

> **Dictation or Journal Entry**
>
> **Vocabulary:** Let's learn the difference between a *warrant* and a *writ*.
>
> A *warrant* is an authorization, justification, or sanction. His word is our *warrant*. A *warrant* is needed to spend public funds. *Warrant* can also be a verb meaning "to approve officially; authorize; sanction" or "to provide sufficient grounds for." Will the committee *warrant* the spending of this money? The facts did not *warrant* his conclusion.
>
> A *writ* is a legal document ordering the person or persons named in it to do or refrain from doing a specific act. A *writ* from the Pope prevented the priest from marrying.

"How Much" or "To What Extent"

Some adverbs tell "how much" or "to what extent." These adverbs are sometimes called **intensifiers** because they add intensity (either positive or negative) to the words they modify.

Notice how the "intensifiers" in the sentences below add intensity to the words they modify:

William Few was *very* insistent.

She arrived *really* early.

We came *too* late.

You have been *most* kind.

William Few was *terribly* outraged.

Some adverbs that tell "how much" or "to what extent" are easy to identify because they end in *-ly*. However, many others do not. Here are some common intensifiers:

absolutely	*almost*	*altogether*
awfully	*barely*	*completely*
especially	*even*	*extremely*
fully	*hardly*	*highly*
incredibly	*just*	*least*
less	*most*	*not*
partly	*quite*	*rather*
really	*so*	*somewhat*
terribly	*thoroughly*	*too*
totally	*vastly*	*very*

An adverb that tells "how much" or "to what extent" usually modifies an adjective or another adverb. However, it occasionally modifies a verb.

MODIFYING AN ADJECTIVE

He was *extremely* helpful.

The adverb *extremely* modifies the adjective *helpful* and tells "how helpful" he was.

MODIFYING ANOTHER ADVERB

William Few spoke *quite* frequently.

The adverb *quite* modifies the adverb *frequently* and tells "how frequently" William Few spoke.

MODIFYING A VERB

William Few *mildly* supported the Federalists.

The adverb *mildly* modifies the verb *supported* and tells "to what extent" William Few supported the Federalists.

Example 1 For each sentence, write the adverb that tells "how much" or "to what extent" and give the word it modifies.

(a) Did William Few totally commit to the patriot cause?

(b) He became quite interested in politics and law.

(c) Mr. Few most carefully defended the Georgia frontier.

Solution (a) The adverb **totally** modifies the verb **"did commit."**

(b) The adverb **quite** modifies the predicate adjective **"interested."**

(c) The adverb **most** modifies the adverb **"carefully."**

not Notice that the word *not* is an adverb. In contractions like could*n't*, *n't* is an adverb. When we diagram contractions, we show *not* as an adverb as in the example below:

Doesn't this warrant concern?

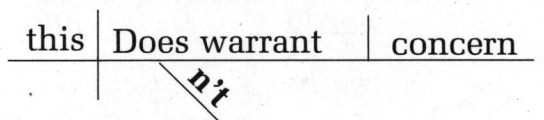

```
  this | Does warrant | concern
            \n't
```

Example 2 Diagram this sentence:

Didn't he deliver the writ hastily?

Solution We place the adverbs *hastily* and *n't* underneath the verb "did deliver."

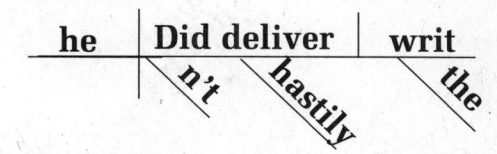

```
     he  |  Did deliver  |  writ
            \n't \hastily    \the
```

Diagramming Adverbs that Modify Adjectives or Other Adverbs

We have diagrammed adverbs that modify verbs. Now we will diagram adverbs that modify adjectives or other adverbs. As shown in the examples below, we place the adverb on a line underneath the adjective or other adverb which is modified:

Didn't he deliver the writ rather hastily?

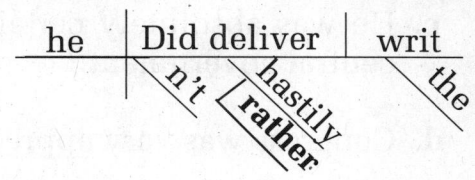

```
     he  |  Did deliver  |  writ
            \n't \hastily    \the
                  \rather
```

An adverb may be a part of a prepositional phrase as in the sentence below:

William Few is one of the most admirable American success stories.

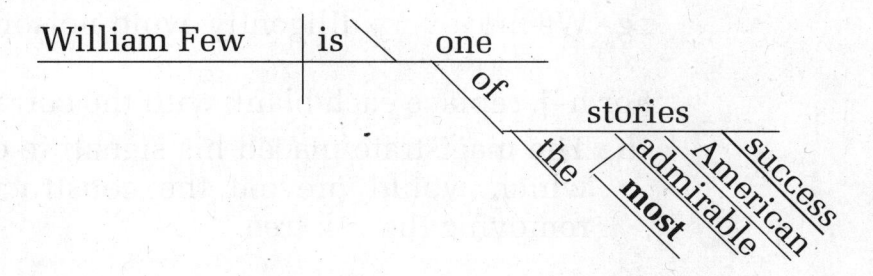

```
William Few | is \ one
                    \of
                      \stories
                       \the \admirable \American \success
                             \most
```

In the sentence above, notice that the adverb *most* modifies the adjective "admirable" which modifies "stories" which is the object of the preposition "of."

Example 3 Diagram this sentence:

Slightly immoral politicians aren't guaranteed long political careers.

Solution We place the adverb *slightly* underneath the adjective it modifies, *immoral*, which describes "politicians."

Remembering that *not* is an adverb, we place *n't*, under the verb "are guaranteed."

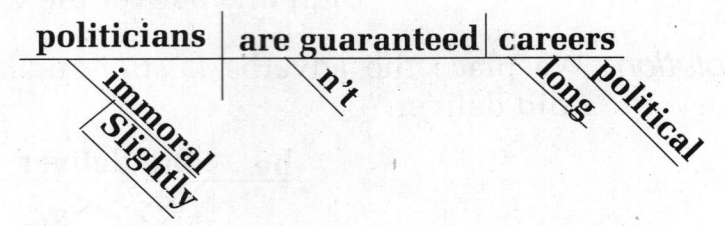

```
    politicians | are guaranteed \ careers
       \immoral        \n't        \long  \political
       \Slightly
```

Practice For sentences a–e, write each adverb that tells "how much" or "to what extent" and the word it modifies.

a. We remember William Leigh Pierce for his extremely incisive literary sketches of his colleagues.

b. Pierce rather poignantly described the "military Federalists."

c. He was absolutely certain about the need for a stronger central government.

d. Congress was very appreciative of his military service.

e. Didn't he receive an award for his valor?

Diagram sentences f and g.

f. Aren't parrots really noisy?

g. We must very diligently avoid noisome fumes.

For h–j, replace each blank with the correct vocabulary word.

h. The magistrate placed his signature on the _____, which would prevent the construction company from removing the oak tree.

i. The police need a _____ in order to search someone's home.

j. Does this crime _____ dire punishment?

More Practice See Master Worksheets.

Review set 86 Choose the correct word(s) to complete sentences 1–14.

1. (Ascent, Assent, Accent) is upward movement.

2. Procrustean means forcing (laughter, conformity, smiles).

3. An (eminent domain, enacting clause) by the Senate and House of Representatives makes a bill become a law.

4. A phase is a (bully, period, hung jury).

5. (Cicero, Caesar, Nestor) was the oldest and wisest of the Greek warriors at Troy.

6. Dr. Corndog (doesn't, don't) make (no, any) mistakes.

7. (Ain't, Aren't, Isn't) your hair-cutting scissors too dull?

8. A jar of homemade pickles (make, makes) a practical gift.

9. (Us, We) engineers shall design a quake-proof structure.

10. Noah and (him, he) speak Hebrew more fluently than (we, us) beginners.

11. None of the swimmers (know, knows) when (their, his or her) race will begin.

12. We (saw, seen) (them, those) swimmers warming up before the race.

13. Using pen and ink, the artist (drew, drawed, drawn) a horned toad with its mouth open.

14. My sister thinks the horned toad resembles Dr. Corndog or (me, myself, I).

15. Write whether the following sentence is declarative, imperative, interrogative, or exclamatory: Franklin D. Roosevelt said, "The only limit to our realization of tomorrow will be our doubts of today."

16. Rewrite the following, adding capital letters and punctuation marks as needed: on july 17 2004 a team of twenty six swimmers met in ocean grove new jersey for a relaxing refreshing revitalizing weekend

17. For a–c, write whether the *-ing* word in each sentence is a verb, participle, or gerund.
(a) The sneezing passenger had used her last tissue.
(b) Had she been sneezing all day long?
(c) Her excessive sneezing might indicate an allergy.

18. Rewrite the following as it is. Then add proofreading symbols to indicate corrections:

Spunk seemed rude and un educated because of his poor tablemanners did you notice?

19. In the following sentence, write the dependent clause, label it essential or nonessential, and circle the subordinating conjunction: The procrustean policy, which leaves no room for creativity, requires uniforms for all employees.

20. Rewrite the following sentence so that it is in active voice: Unfortunately, the whole pumpkin pie was consumed by my dog Spunk.

21. Write the comparative form of the adjective *protean*.

22. Write the possessive case, first person, plural personal pronoun.

23. For a and b, write the adjective and adverb forms of each noun.
(a) rest   (b) care

24. Write whether this sentence is simple or compound: Spunk ate the dessert, yet he did not touch the vegetable dish.

25. Write the four principal parts of the irregular verb *sit*.

26. Use an appositive to make one sentence from these two sentences: Peter Ilyich Tchaikovsky was a great Russian musician. Peter Ilyich Tchaikovsky composed a famous ballet called *The Nutcracker*.

27. Write the plural of each noun.
(a) ox   (b) pocketful   (c) calf

28. Write and underline each word that should be italicized
(69) in this sentence: The Peaceable Kingdom, a three-dimensional painting by a Quaker named Edward Hicks, portrays a peaceful world in which all people and animals live in harmony.

Diagram sentences 29 and 30.

29. We mustn't walk so slowly, or we might miss Ms.
(59, 86) Burkey's lecture on the rainforests.

30. The mischievous crow that stole my cheese sandwich has
(61, 80) already flown away.

LESSON 87 — Comparison Adverbs

> **Dictation or Journal Entry**
>
> **Vocabulary:** The Eighteenth Amendment made it illegal to manufacture, transport, or sell alcoholic beverages in the United States during the period of Prohibition (1920–33). Two words associated with this period are *prohibition* and *bootleg*.
>
> *Prohibition* is the legal restriction of the manufacture and sale of alcoholic drinks for common consumption. The Eighteenth Amendment instated *prohibition*.
>
> *Bootleg* is a verb meaning to make, sell, or transport (liquor or other goods) illegally. Sometimes thieves *bootleg* music or movies from the internet. *Bootleg* is also an adjective meaning made, sold, or transported illegally. In 1921, the old farmer hid his *bootleg* whisky under a pile of hay in his barn.

Like adjectives, some adverbs can express the three degrees of comparison: positive, comparative, and superlative. Below are examples of the positive, comparative, and superlative forms of some adverbs:

POSITIVE	COMPARATIVE	SUPERLATIVE
fast	*faster*	*fastest*
bright	*brighter*	*brightest*
soon	*sooner*	*soonest*

Positive — The positive form describes an action without comparing it to anything.

> William Houstoun died *early*.

Comparative — The comparative form compares the action of **two** people, places, or things.

> Mr. Houstoun died *earlier* than Mr. Few.

Superlative — The superlative form compares the action of **three or more** people, places, or things.

> Of the three, Houstoun died *earliest*.

Example 1 Choose the correct adverb form for each sentence.

(a) Of the two delegates, William Houstoun served (long, longer, longest).

(b) Of all the Georgian delegates, William Leigh Pierce fought (hard, harder, hardest) for a stronger central government.

Solution (a) Of the two delegates, William Houstoun served **longer**. (We use the comparative form since there are two delegates.)

(b) Of all the Georgian delegates, William Leigh Pierce fought **hardest** for a stronger central government. (We use the superlative form since we are comparing more than two delegates.)

Forming Comparison Adverbs

We form comparison adverbs the same way we form comparison adjectives. How we create the comparative and superlative forms of an adverb depends on how the adverb appears in its positive form. There are two main categories to remember.

One-Syllable Adverbs

We create the comparative form of most one-syllable adverbs by adding *er* to the end of the word. We create the superlative form by adding *est*.

POSITIVE	COMPARATIVE	SUPERLATIVE
late	later	latest
close	closer	closest
high	higher	highest

Two or More Syllables

Most two-syllable adverbs do not have comparative or superlative forms. Instead, we put the word "more" (or "less") in front of the adverb to form the comparative, and the word "most" (or "least") to form the superlative.

POSITIVE	COMPARATIVE	SUPERLATIVE
elegantly	more elegantly less elegantly	most elegantly least elegantly
arrogantly	more arrogantly less arrogantly	most arrogantly least arrogantly

Since most adverbs are formed by adding the suffix *-ly* to an adjective, the rule above applies to most adverbs.

Irregular Comparison Adverbs

Some adverbs have irregular comparative and superlative forms. We must learn these if we haven't already.

POSITIVE	COMPARATIVE	SUPERLATIVE
well	better	best
badly	worse	worst
far	farther	farthest

little	*less*	*least*
much	*more*	*most*

We check the dictionary if we are unsure how to create the comparative or superlative form of a two-syllable adverb.

Example 2 Complete the comparison chart by adding the comparative and superlative forms of each adverb.

POSITIVE	COMPARATIVE	SUPERLATIVE
(a) far	_____	_____
(b) honestly	_____	_____
(c) badly	_____	_____
(d) kindly	_____	_____

Solution

POSITIVE	COMPARATIVE	SUPERLATIVE
(a) far	**farther**	**farthest**
(b) honestly	**more honestly**	**most honestly**
(c) badly	**worse**	**worst**
(d) kindly	**more kindly**	**most kindly**

Practice Write the correct adverb form for sentences a–e.

a. Of the four men, Abraham Baldwin rose (high, higher, highest) in the public's trust.

b. William Houstoun spoke (vehemently, more vehemently, most vehemently) than William Few.

c. In his later years, William Houstoun liked the state of New York (well, better, best) than Georgia.

d. Of all the cellists, Lucita plays (skillfully, more skillfully, most skillfully) in concerts.

e. Pancho paints (badly, worse, worst) than Penelope, but I paint (badly, worse, worst) of all.

For f and g, replace each blank with the correct vocabulary word.

f. "Hide the _____ liquor before the sheriff comes!" shouted Hiram.

g. Most citizens supported _____ during the 1920s.

More Practice Write the correct comparison adverb for each sentence.

1. Of the three First Ladies, Abigail Adams wrote (faithfully, more faithfully, most faithfully) to the leaders of the Revolution.

2. *Marine One*, the President's helicopter, cost (little, less, least) than *Air Force One*.

3. Of the four senators, Nelson Aldrich fought (hard, harder, hardest) against the policies of President Theodore Roosevelt.

4. Of the two legislative bodies, the U.S. Senate compares (better, best) to the House of Lords.

5. The Constitution of the United States took (long, longer, longest) to be adopted than the Articles of Confederation.

6. Senator Dubois feels (badly, worse, worst) than Senator Nelson about the unavailability of bean soup.

7. Of all the bean soups, the House version appeals (well, better, best) to most representatives of Congress.

8. *Air Force One* flies (fast, faster, fastest) than *Marine One*.

9. Do members of the House eat (little, less, least) than members of the Senate?

10. Of all the justices, that one raps his gavel (much, more, most).

Review set 87 Choose the correct word to complete sentences 1–15.

1. A(n) (warrant, ascent, odyssey) is an authorization, justification, or sanction.
(86)

2. (Ascent, Assent, Accent) is agreement, or concurrence.
(85)

3. (Protean, Procrustean, Spartan) means forcing conformity.
(84)

4. Conscious means (guilty, aware, innocent).
(32)

5. A spartan lifestyle allows for (many, few, rich) luxuries.
(33)

6. We use (*good, well*) when talking about one's health or
(81) how one feels.

7. The inspector and (them, they) intend to discover the
(50) source of the noisome fumes.

8. Inspector Sniff is (well-prepared, well prepared) for the
(82) task.

9. The (well-prepared, well prepared) inspector appears
(82) infallible.

10. The neighbor lady has complained about (us, our)
(53, 63) collecting compost for our garden.

11. She (doesn't, don't) realize that the fumes (aren't, ain't)
(78) (ours, our's).

12. The inspector (who, whom) examined our compost
(61, 78) didn't smell (any, no) fumes.

13. Noisome fumes, (that, which) sometimes emanate from
(62) the sewer, have dispersed.

14. Have you ever (beat, beaten) the computer at a game of
(49, 70) chess?

15. Of all the cattle on the ranch, Geraldine moos (louder,
(87) loudest).

16. Rewrite the following, adding capital letters and correct
(9, 41) punctuation marks: wait shouted inspector sniff i am not
finished i shall inspect the sewer test the gas line and
examine the soil after lunch

17. In this sentence, write the participial phrase followed by
(45, 56) the word it modifies: Having ruled out our compost pile,
Inspector Sniff departed.

18. In the following sentence, write the verb phrase, name its
(26) tense, and label it transitive or intransitive: Locked in a

dungeon, the prisoner dreamed of freedom, blue sky, and sunshine.

19. Write whether the following sentence is simple or compound: In the 1740s, widespread revivals known as the "Great Awakening" stimulated one of the most productive periods for Jonathan Edwards's writings.
(1, 59)

20. Write whether the following is a complete sentence, sentence fragment, or run-on sentence: Born into a Puritan, evangelical household in East Windsor, Connecticut Colony.
(2)

21. Write the relative pronoun in the following sentence: Jonathan Edwards was the American theologian who wrote the famous sermon "Sinners in the Hands of an Angry God."
(61)

22. Write the objective case, first person, plural personal pronoun.
(51, 52)

23. For a and b, write the adjective and adverb forms of each noun.
(80)

(a) joy (b) truth

24. In this sentence, write the infinitive and label it an adjective or a noun: I have noticed that my siblings like to exaggerate.
(19, 45)

25. Write the four principal parts of the irregular verb *write*.
(13, 72)

26. In this sentence, write the indefinite pronoun and label it singular or plural: Does everyone agree that an inspection is warranted?
(68)

27. Write and hyphenate each part as needed in this sentence: Does channel fifty five offer up to the minute news covering world events?
(79, 82)

28. Rewrite the following as it is. Then add proofreading symbols to indicate corrections:
(32)

In 1757, Jonathan Edwards accepted the presidency of the Colledge of New jersey, Which latter became Princeton University.

Diagram sentences 29 and 30.

29. Having sold her home, she left rather abruptly.
(56, 86)

30. Gladys, a mercurial constituent, frequently loses her temper.
(42, 86)

LESSON 88 — The Semicolon

> **Dictation or Journal Entry**
>
> **Vocabulary:** Let's examine the meanings of the similar-looking words *premier* and *premiere*.
>
> A *premier* is a prime minister in certain European countries. The *premier* of France leads the cabinet in their decision-making. *Premier* can also be an adjective meaning "first in position, rank, or authority" or "first in order of time; earliest." With his extensive knowledge, the philatelist Mr. Steve was the *premier* philatelic authority on Icelandic postage stamps.
>
> A *premiere* is the first public showing of a movie, drama, opera, etc. The *premiere* of *Pilgrim* may occur on Broadway in the near future.

The **semicolon** (;), sometimes called a "mild period," is used as a connector. It indicates a pause longer than a comma yet shorter than a colon. In this lesson we will learn how to use the semicolon correctly.

Related Thoughts In a compound sentence, we can use a semicolon instead of a coordinating conjunction (*and, but, or, for, nor, yet, so*) between the two independent clauses. However, these clauses must contain related thoughts.

> YES: During Ronald Reagan's presidency, a group of conservative Democratic representatives arose in the South and West; they became known as the Boll Weevils. (related thoughts)

> NO: Southern cotton experienced the serious effects of boll weevils; Boll Weevils voted with the Republicans to enact Reagan's economic program. (not related thoughts)

Example 1 Use a semicolon instead of the coordinating conjunction in this sentence:

> The original Brains Trust advised President Franklin D. Roosevelt, and they helped him develop his New Deal.

Solution We replace the coordinating conjunction with a semicolon:

> The original Brains Trust advised President Franklin D. Roosevelt; they helped him develop his New Deal.

With Other Commas If an independent clause contains other commas, we use a semicolon to show where one independent clause ends and where another one begins.

UNCLEAR: Lydia grows figs, peaches, and pomegranates, and Lola grows apricots, oranges, and lemons. (ending of the first clause is unclear)

CLEAR: Lydia grows figs, peaches, and pomegranates; and Lola grows apricots, oranges, and lemons. (clear)

Semicolons can also be used to separate phrases or dependent clauses that contain commas.

The Brains Trust included Adolph A. Berle, professor of law; Rexford G. Tugwell, professor of economics; and Samuel Rosenman, a speech writer.

She promised that she would plant some carrots, tomatoes, and zucchini; sweep the porch, sidewalk, and driveway; and write her brother a long letter.

Example 2 Place semicolons where they are needed in sentences a and b.

(a) Does this train stop in San Francisco, California, Portland, Oregon, and Seattle, Washington?

(b) You can bring the paper, scissors, and tape, and I'll bring the paint, brushes, and glue.

Solution (a) We separate each "city, state" pair of words with a semicolon for clarity.

Does this train stop in San Francisco, California; Portland, Oregon; and Seattle, Washington?

(b) Because the independent clauses in this sentence already contain commas, we separate the two clauses with a semicolon.

You can bring the paper, scissors, and tape; and I'll bring the paint, brushes, and glue.

Conjunctive Adverbs An adverb used as a conjunction is called a **conjunctive adverb**. Below are some examples.

however	*therefore*	*consequently*
accordingly	*for this reason*	*for example*
on the other hand	*furthermore*	*besides*
moreover	*still*	*likewise*
in addition	*at the same time*	*nevertheless*
otherwise	*thus*	*hence*

We place a semicolon before a conjunctive adverb.

> YES: Senator John Bricker proposed a constitutional amendment to limit the President's power in foreign affairs; however, the Bricker Amendment failed by one vote.

Using a comma where a semicolon is needed results in a run-on sentence:

> NO: Senator John Bricker proposed a constitutional amendment to limit the President's power in foreign affairs, however, the Bricker Amendment failed by one vote.

Example 3 Place a semicolon where it is needed in this sentence:

> Historians record the engagement of James Buchanan to Anne Caroline Coleman, however, her family's objections resulted in a broken engagement and his distinction as the only bachelor President.

Solution A semicolon is necessary before the conjunctive adverb, *however*. So we write,

> Historians record the engagement of James Buchanan to Anne Caroline Coleman; however, her family's objections resulted in a broken engagement and his distinction as the only bachelor President.

Practice Rewrite sentences a–c, and replace commas with semicolons where they are needed.

a. The list of Presidents of the United States begins with George Washington, first, John Adams, second, and Thomas Jefferson, third.

b. Briefs submitted to the Supreme Court must be free from burdensome, irrelevant, and scandalous matter, they are limited to fifty pages.

c. The Congresswoman's speech was designed to promote her chances of re-election, therefore, it was labeled "bunk."

For d–f, replace each blank with the correct vocabulary word.

d. The _____ of the musical will take place in New York City.

e. The _____ of Italy hosted a dinner in honor of the world's leaders.

f. The management considers my grandmother the _____ cook in the restaurant.

More Practice See Master Worksheets.

Review set 88 Choose the correct word(s) to complete sentences 1–14.

1. (Hedonism, Prohibition, Filibuster) restricted the manufacture and sale of alcoholic drinks in the 1920s.

2. A warrant is a(n) (nestor, conscience, authorization).

3. Ascent is (upward, downward, sideways) movement.

4. (Procrustes, Proteus, Mercury) had the ability to change himself into any shape he chose.

5. At the hardware store, I purchased nails, wood glue, plywood, (*etc., et al.*).

6. A bushel of oranges (feed, feeds) a cageful of monkeys.

7. Lacy and (me, myself, I) (isn't, ain't, aren't) interested in camping in the forest.

8. We (can, can't) see no reason to endanger ourselves.

9. "Please wake (us, we) campers if you see a bear," said Amelia.

10. Maria and (her, she) have seen more bears than than (me, I).

11. Previously, a mother bear had (lead, leaded, led) her cub into Maria's tent!

12. Each of the campers (promise, promises) to take (their, his or her) turn watching for bears.

13. (Good, Well) is a descriptive adjective or predicate adjective that describes a noun or pronoun.

14. (Good, Well) is usually an adverb that modifies an action
(81) verb and explains "how."

15. In the following sentence, write each infinitive and label
(19, 45) it an adjective or a noun: Please give me a chance to
prove my ability to protect you from the bears.

16. Rewrite the following, adding capital letters and
(43, 65) punctuation marks as needed: no said amelia to the
sleepy camper you might fall asleep therefore i shall
guard the campsite tonight

17. In the following sentence, write the gerund phrase:
(55) Everyone should thank Amelia for guarding the campsite.

18. In this sentence, write the verb phrase, name its tense,
(3, 18) and label it action or linking: Ishmael is thinking about
going to sea.

19. In the following sentence, write the dependent clause,
(54) circling the subordinating conjunction: Ishmael, a
schoolmaster, travels to New Bedford where he finds a
job on a whaling ship.

20. Write whether the following is a phrase or a clause:
(20) although the harpooner Queequeg appears hardened and
savage

21. Write whether the underlined part in this sentence is
(62) essential or nonessential: My friend <u>Amelia</u> heard a
scratching sound near her tent.

22. Write the seven common coordinating conjunctions.
(33)

23. Write the comparative form of the adverb *well*.
(87)

24. Use an appositive to make one sentence from the
(42) following two sentences:
Ishmael and Queequeg board the *Pequod*.
The *Pequod* is a whaling ship in the wind-swept Atlantic.

25. Write the four principal parts of the irregular verb *swing*.
(72)

26. Rewrite the following sentence so that it is in active
(27) voice: Moby Dick, a larger-than-usual sperm whale with

a white forehead and a malicious temper, is spotted by the crew.

27. Rewrite the following as it is. Then add proofreading symbols to indicate corrections:
(32)

A feerce typhoon descends upon the *Pequod*, and raging winds rip the sails still Captain Ahab urges the vessel for ward to hunt down Moby Dick.

28. Write and underline each part that should be italicized in this sentence: Do I use the adjectives good and nice too frequently in my writing?
(23, 69)

Diagram sentences 29 and 30.

29. Knowing the tremendous strength of the black bear increases my anxiety about camping.
(21, 56)

30. The pictures in that book about grizzlies look awfully scary.
(36, 86)

LESSON 89

Descriptive Adverbs
• Adverb Usage

> **Dictation or Journal Entry**
>
> **Vocabulary:** In your study of government, you will find the words *repeal* and *appeal*.
>
> To *repeal* a law or a tax is to revoke or withdraw it by a formal legislative act. In 1933, Congress *repealed* the Eighteenth Amendment and replaced it with the Twenty-first Amendment, which allowed the transport and sale of alcoholic beverages in the United States once again.
>
> An *appeal* is a formal request made by a person or institution regarding the correctness of a judgment or ruling. The Bricker Amendment was a Senator's *appeal* to Congress to restrict the decision-making power of the President. An *appeal* is also the procedure by which a legal case is taken to a higher court for the possible reversal of the lower court's decision. The losing party might make an *appeal* to the U. S. Supreme Court.

Improving Our Writing Without adverbs, our sentences would be dull. This sentence has no adverbs:

Congress argues.

In order to express ourselves in a vivid and colorful manner, we can use **descriptive adverbs.** The sentence above is more interesting when we add adverbs to describe how the Congress argues:

Congress argues *vehemently*.

Congress might also argue *futilely, effectively, heatedly, furiously, weakly, productively, continually,* or *seldom*.

Example 1 Replace each blank with at least one adverb to make the sentence more descriptive.

(a) Carpetbaggers _____ governed the South after the Civil War.

(b) Opportunists profited _____ during the reorganization of the South after the Civil War.

Solution Our answers will vary. Here are some examples.

(a) Carpetbaggers **conspicuously, opportunistically, unfairly, frantically, gallantly, greedily, selfishly** governed the South after the Civil War.

(b) Opportunists profited **greatly, significantly, exceedingly, dishonestly, illegally, avariciously** during the reorganization of the South after the Civil War.

Sure or Surely? People often use the word *sure* incorrectly. It is an adjective and not an adverb. *Sure* should not take the place of the adverbs *surely, certainly,* or *really.*

    NO: Henry Clay *sure* puzzles historians.
    YES: Clay *surely* puzzles historians. (modifies verb "puzzles")

    NO: Carpetbaggers are *sure* culpable.
    YES: Carpetbaggers are *certainly* (or *surely*) culpable.
        (modifies predicate adjective "culpable")

    NO: Some were *sure* corrupt.
    YES: Some were *really* (or *surely*) corrupt.
        (modifies predicate adjective "corrupt")

We remember that *sure* is an adjective, and we use it only as an adjective or predicate adjective as in the sentences below:

    Henry Clay was *sure* of himself. (predicate adjective)

    Was abolition a *sure* cure for the South? (adjective)

Example 2 Replace each blank with *sure* or *surely*.

    (a) Are historians _____ about Aaron Burr's military intentions?

    (b) One can _____ understand why Henry Clay was both loved and hated.

Solution (a) Are historians **sure** about Aaron Burr's military intentions? The predicate adjective "sure" modifies the noun "historians."

    (b) One can **surely** understand why Henry Clay was both loved and hated. The adverb "surely" modifies the verb "can understand."

Real or Really? Like *sure,* the word *real* is an adjective and should not take the place of the adverb *really*. *Real* modifies a noun or pronoun, while *really* modifies a verb, adjective, or adverb.

    NO: I'm *real* interested in your comments.
    YES: I'm *really* interested in your comments.
        (modifies the predicate adjective "interested")

    NO: That was a *real* good suggestion.
    YES: That was a *really* good suggestion.
        (modifies adjective "good")

NO: You write *real* effectively.
YES: You write *really* effectively. (modifies adverb "effectively")

We remember that *real* is an adjective, and we use it only as an adjective or predicate adjective, as in the sentences below:

That looks like a *real* diamond.
(adjective modifying the noun "diamond")

That diamond looks *real*. (predicate adjective)

Example 3 Replace each blank with *real* or *really*.

(a) She tried (real, really) hard to promote peace.

(b) The thief's penitence appears (real, really).

Solution (a) She tried **really** hard to promote peace. (*Really* is an adverb that modifies another adverb, "hard."

(b) The thief's penitence appears **real**. (*Real* is a predicate adjective that follows the linking verb "appears" and describes the subject "penitence.")

Bad or Badly? The word *bad* is an adjective. It describes a noun or pronoun, and often follows linking verbs like *feel, look, seem, taste, smell,* and *is*. The word *badly* is an adverb that tells "how." We do not use *bad* as an adverb.

NO: I debate *bad* in public.
YES: I debate *badly* in public. (adverb that tells "how")

NO: They speak *bad* about it.
YES: They speak *badly* about it. (adverb that tells "how")

We remember that "bad" is an adjective, and we use it only as an adjective or predicate adjective as in these sentences:

Some felt *bad* about the election. (predicate adjective)

The weather looks *bad*. (predicate adjective)

Did Henry Clay's *bad* temper repulse other politicians? (adjective that describes "temper")

Example 4 Replace each blank with *bad* or *badly*.

(a) Was the politician's reputation damaged _____ by the scandal?

(b) After the scandal, the politician looked _____ in the eyes of the public.

Solution (a) Was the politician's reputation damaged **badly** by the scandal? ("Badly" is an adverb that tells "to what extent" the reputation "was damaged.")

(c) After the scandal, the politician looked **bad** in the eyes of the public. ("Bad" is a predicate adjective that follows the linking verb "looked" and describes the subject, "politician."

Practice For a–c, replace each blank with the correct vocabulary word.

a. Adopting the Twenty-first Amendment made possible the _____ of the Eighteenth Amendment.

b. The governor rejected the convicted criminal's _____ for pardon.

c. One who loses a case in a lower court may _____ to a higher court.

For d and e, replace each blank with at least one adverb to make the sentence more descriptive.

d. The meteorologist _____ predicted good weather.

e. We laughed _____.

Choose the correct word to complete sentences f–k.

f. The four clerks are (sure, surely) helpful to the Supreme Court.

g. Law clerks work (real, really) hard.

h. People felt (real, really) excited about President Grover Cleveland's White House wedding.

i. The opponents of the bill responded (bad, badly) to the supporters' appeal for cloture.

j. The costumed man possessed a (real, really) likeness to George Washington.

k. Did President Grover Cleveland feel (bad, badly) about his performance in foreign affairs?

More Practice Choose the correct word to complete each sentence.

1. That orchestra (sure, surely) performs well.
2. They're (sure, really) talented.
3. The musicians (sure, certainly) give generously of their time.
4. I'm not (real, really) sure who played the drums.
5. Our vacuum cleaner works (real, really) well.
6. Did Heather break her ankle (bad, badly)?
7. A toothache is a (bad, badly) ailment.
8. Liezl's tooth hurts (bad, badly).
9. Unfortunately, we raced (bad, badly) in the mile relay.
10. It was a (bad, badly) event for our track team.

Review set 89 Choose the correct word(s) to complete sentences 1–15.

1. A (retraction, premier, premiere) is a prime minister in certain European countries.
   (88)

2. Prohibition (allowed, encouraged, restricted) the manufacture and sale of alcoholic drinks during the 1920s.
   (87)

3. A (plutocrat, writ, finale) is a legal document ordering the person or persons named in it to do or refrain from doing a specific act.
   (86)

4. A (bureaucrat, Spartan, plutocrat) has power because of his or her wealth.
   (35)

5. (Sybaritic, Spartan, Stoic) means extravagant and sensual.
   (36)

6. Amelia and (she, her) saddled the elephants (theirselves, themselves).
   (50, 57)

7. I haven't (never, ever) (rode, ridden) an elephant with Amelia and (they, them).
   (71, 78)

8. Of the two elephants, Taj dances (more, most) gracefully.
   (87)

9. Does Doris have an (out-of-town, out of town) guest?
(23, 82)

10. Obviously, the guest is from (out-of-town, out of town).
(28, 82)

11. Doris is in agreement with (me, my) asking her guest to silence his noisy rooster.
(28, 53)

12. Mr. Li (doesn't, don't) know that the noisy rooster (isn't, ain't, aren't) (our's, ours).
(53, 78)

13. The guest (who, whom) Doris invited brought his prized white rooster.
(61, 64)

14. Does Doris feel (good, well) today?
(81)

15. Has the rooster (flew, flown) over the fence?
(13, 70)

16. Rewrite the following, adding capital letters and punctuation marks as needed: stop screamed doris to the rooster do you realize that vicious animals live beyond the fence they might harm you but i shall protect you
(9, 65)

17. Rewrite the following as it is. Then add proofreading symbols to indicate corrections.
(32)

One-legged Captian Ahab has sworn death for for the gigantic whitewhale that cripled him.

18. In this sentence, write the verb phrase, name its tense, and label it transitive or intransitive: Will that noisy rooster crow again tomorrow morning?
(26)

19. In the following sentence, write the dependent clause and circle the subordinating conjunction: Please silence your rooster so that I can sleep!
(54)

20. For a–c, write whether the *-ing* word is a gerund, participle, or verb.
(55)

(a) Crowing at dawn comes naturally for a rooster.

(b) Crowing at dawn, the rooster woke Mr. Li.

(c) The rooster has been crowing since dawn.

21. Write whether the underlined part in this sentence is essential or nonessential: Our geometry teacher, <u>Mr. Martinez</u>, taught us the Pythagorean theorem.
(62)

22. Write the nominative case, first person plural personal pronoun.
(48)

23. Write the superlative form of the adverb *well*.
(87)

24. Write whether the following sentence is simple or compound: In Herman Melville's novel *Moby Dick*, Ahab is the captain, and Starbuck and Stubb are Ahab's first and second mates.
(59)

25. Write the four principal parts of the irregular verb *teach*.
(13, 72)

26. Write the conjunctive adverb in this sentence: Mr. Li doesn't like roosters; nevertheless, he won't complain.
(88)

27. Rewrite the following sentence, adding a dash where it is appropriate: Samara brought my three favorite ice cream flavors strawberry, French vanilla, and chocolate chip.
(73)

28. Rewrite the following so that it is in active voice: The story of *Moby Dick* is narrated by Ishmael, a simple seaman.
(27)

Diagram sentences 29 and 30.

29. Has your friend Amelia ridden an elephant before?
(21, 42)

30. Saddling an elephant must be really difficult, for these animals are so large.
(16, 59)

LESSON 90 — The Colon

> **Dictation or Journal Entry**
>
> **Vocabulary:** Writers use *alliteration*, *assonance*, and *consonance* to highlight certain sounds in phrases for a poetic effect.
>
> *Alliteration* is the repetition of the same initial letter, sound, or group of sounds in a series of words. "Prickly, parched, and pale pair" is an example of *alliteration*.
>
> *Assonance* is the repetition of same vowel sounds in a series of words. The phrase "Icy, shining, and climbing knight" contains *assonance*.
>
> *Consonance* is the repetition of consonants anywhere in a word. "Hissing a mist of spit" demonstrates *consonance*.

The **colon** (:) signals to the reader that more information is to come. In this lesson we will learn to use the colon correctly.

Between Independent Clauses

We have learned that a semicolon can join two independent clauses that contain related thoughts. A colon can join two independent clauses when the first clause introduces the second or the second clause illustrates the first.

> Remember the most important rule: be on time.
>
> The team was jubilant: they had won their game and were tied for the championship.

Example 1 Insert colons where they are needed in these sentences.

(a) I knew I had forgotten something my keys were at home on my desk.

(b) His bicycle was not fit to ride its tires were flat; its brakes were worn out; and its handle bars were bent.

Solution (a) The first independent clause introduces the second, so we place a colon between them:

> I knew I had forgotten something: my keys were at home on my desk.

(b) The second independent clause illustrates the first. We place a colon between them:

> His bicycle was not fit to ride: its tires were flat; its brakes were worn out; and its handle bars were bent.

Salutation of a Business Letter

We use a colon after a salutation in a business letter.

> Fellow Americans:
>
> Dear Mayor Yoshima:

Time When we write the time of day with digits, we use a colon to separate the hours and minutes.

> The tour of the Capitol Building begins at 11:00 a.m.

Example 2 Insert colons where they are needed in these sentences.

(a) Lunch will be served at 1200 p.m.

(b) Dear President
Please consider Colonel Poteet for a Medal ...

Solution (a) We place a colon between the hours and minutes when we write about time, so we write **12:00** p.m.

(b) We use a colon after the salutation in a business letter, so we write **Dear President:**

Introducing a List We use a colon at the end of a sentence to introduce a list.

> Here are some famous Supreme Court Justices: Henry Baldwin, Philip Barbour, Hugo Black, and John Blair.

> These Supreme Court cases are noteworthy: *Abrams vs. United States, Barron vs. Baltimore, Benton vs. Maryland, Betts vs. Brady,* and *Brown vs. Board of Education.*

We do not use a colon if the sentence is grammatically correct without it.

> No: You should bring: a pencil, a book, and an eraser.

> Yes: You should bring these things: a pencil, a book and an eraser.

The Following, As Follows We often use a colon after the words *the following* or *as follows* when they introduce a list. Sometimes the list will begin on a separate line.

> The "Brains Trust" included *the following* Columbia University professors: Adolph A. Berle, Jr., Rexford G. Tugwell, and Raymond Moley.

> We refinish the surface *as follows*:
> With a damp rag, remove all dust and dirt.
> Lightly sand the edges.
> Apply a thin coat...

Introducing a Quotation We can use a colon to introduce a quotation.

Many of us can recite the Preamble to the Constitution of the United States:

> We the people of the United States, in order to form a more perfect union, establish justice, insure domestic tranquility, provide for the common defense, promote the general welfare…

Grandpa continued to reminisce: "I remember the first time I saw your Grandma…

Bible References We use a colon between the chapter and verse in a Bible reference.

A good life verse might be Jeremiah 29:11.

Let us read John 3:16.

Psalm 16:8 gives me confidence.

Example 3 Insert colons where they are needed in these sentences.

(a) For the Bible class, each student memorized I John 5 14–15.

(b) To make banana bread, you will need the following ingredients flour, sugar, oil, vanilla, salt, soda, eggs, and bananas.

(c) President Eisenhower commented on the Bricker Amendment "If it's true that when you die the things that bothered you most are engraved on your skull, I am sure I'll have there…the name of Senator Bricker."

Solution (a) We use a colon between the chapter and verse in a Bible reference, so we write **I John 5:14–15**.

(b) We use a colon to introduce a list, so we write the sentence like this:

To make banana bread, you will need the following ingredients: flour, sugar, oil, vanilla, salt, soda, eggs, and bananas.

(c) We can use a colon to introduce a quotation.

President Eisenhower commented on the Bricker Amendment: "If it's true that when you die the things that bothered you most are engraved on your skull, I am sure I'll have there...the name of Senator Bricker."

Practice Rewrite a–e and insert colons where they are needed

a. The Washington Monument opens at 9 00 a.m. daily.

b. Hebrews 12 14–15 offers God's instruction on peaceful living.

c. The Presidential weekend retreat at Camp David has the following amenities one hundred eighty forested acres, many residence cabins, a heated pool, a skeet range, some tennis courts, and a horseshoe pit.

d. Dear President Lincoln
Thank you for issuing the Proclamation of...

e. John C. Calhoun said this about Henry Clay "I don't like Clay. He is a bad man...but, by God, I love him."

For f–h, replace each blank with the correct vocabulary word.

f. "Blind mice might deny my rights" uses a poetic device called _____.

g. "Happy Pepper raps properly" contains _____.

h. "Fanny found a friend" is an example of _____.

More Practice See "Hysterical Fiction #5" in Master Worksheets.

Review set 90 Choose the correct word to complete sentences 1–17.

1. To revoke or withdraw a law or a tax is to (appeal, repeal, conceal) it.
(89)

2. (Premier, Appellate, Judicial) means "first in position, rank, or authority."
(88)

3. The Eighteenth Amendment brought about a period of (deduction, conjecture, prohibition) in the United States.
(87)

4. Sybaritic means (frugal, simple, extravagant).
(36)

5. Fortuitous means (lucky, appropriate, extravagant).
(37)

6. Doris and her guest (wasn't, weren't) (ever, never) in agreement.
(78)

7. (Those, Them) incompetent hoodlums didn't manage to pilfer (anything, nothing). Ha!
(67)

8. (Do, Does) a large bag of peanuts feed ten squirrels for a month?
(12)

9. If (we, us) campers see a bear, we shall flee.
(50, 63)

10. Amelia and (they, them) are braver than (me, I).
(50, 63)

11. *Well* is usually an (adjective, adverb) modifying an action verb and explaining "how."
(81)

12. I slept (real, really) (good, well) last night.
(81, 89)

13. Each of those hoodlums (have, has) (their, his or her) hat on backwards.
(76, 77)

14. Have you (strove, striven) for excellence in writing?
(72)

15. Jared baked Melody and (me, myself, I) a peach pie.
(30, 51)

16. There are three types of verbals: the gerund, the participle, and the (appositive, infinitive, antecedent).
(16)

17. A(n) (antecedent, gerund, infinitive) ends in *-ing* and functions as a noun.
(16)

18. Rewrite the following, adding capital letters and correct punctuation marks: come back here you silly rooster yelled doris you do not belong to me nevertheless i feel responsible for you since you are my guest
(65, 88)

19. Write whether the following is a phrase or a clause: viewing the White Whale as the symbol of all the evil of the universe
(20)

20. In the following sentence, write the verb phrase, name its tense, and label it action or linking: Looking for a place to eat and sleep, Ishmael enters the Spouter Inn.

21. In this sentence, write the dependent clause, circling the subordinating conjunction: Father Mapple waves a benediction as he ends his sermon about Jonah and the whale.

22. In this sentence, write the indefinite pronoun and label it singular or plural: Was either of the hoodlums wearing a mask?

23. Write the comparative form of the adverb *carefully*.

24. Write the four principal parts of the irregular verb *think*.

25. Write whether the following is a complete sentence, sentence fragment, or run-on sentence: Doris carries a handful of corn kernels this will lure the rooster.

26. Write the conjunctive adverb in this sentence: Ishmael and Queequeg heartily accept Ahab's challenge to find Moby Dick; on the other hand, Starbuck and Stubb doubt Ahab's sense of reason.

27. For a and b, write the word from each pair that is divided correctly.
(a) shouldn't, should-n't (b) north-eastern, northeas-tern

28. Rewrite this sentence, replacing a comma with a semicolon as needed: Jen brought lettuce, tomatoes, and cheese, and Rob brought chips, salsa, and tortillas.

Diagram sentences 29 and 30.

29. Don't give that lazy Mr. Do-it-later an excuse to procrastinate.

30. Carrying a handful of corn, Doris lures the rooster and gingerly leads him home.

LESSON 91

Proofreading Symbols, Part 2

> **Dictation or Journal Entry**
>
> **Vocabulary:** The prefix *mal-*, meaning "bad" or "badly," appears in the familiar words *mal*practice and *mal*nourished. Let's learn the definitions of *malodorous* and *malevolent*.
>
> *Malodorous* means "having an unpleasant or offensive odor." The *malodorous* air suggested a rotting carcass in the vicinity.
>
> *Malevolent* means doing or desiring to do evil or harm to others. Uriah Heep, a *malevolent* clerk at Mr. Wickfield's law office, hates David Copperfield with a passion.

In order to apply the standards of written English to our writing, we proofread our work to find and correct errors in grammar, usage, spelling, and punctuation. In an earlier lesson, we learned to use some standard **proofreading symbols** that all writers understand. The chart below shows additional proofreading symbols.

Symbol	Example	Meaning
⟋—	under / ~~over~~ the log	Replace a word.
⌒	mal/evolent	Delete letter and close space.
tr	the traitor / most malicious	Transfer the circled words. (Write *tr* in margin)
¶	¶ "No," he said.	Begin a new paragraph.
⋏ or ⋏;	cold⋏dry toast	Add a comma or a semicolon.
⊙	the following⊙	Add a colon.
=	sky=high price	Add a hyphen.
⋎ or ⋎⋎	Jan⋎s shop	Add an apostrophe or a quotation mark.
stet.....	a ~~very~~ hot day	Keep the crossed-out part. (Write *stet* in margin)

Example 1 Carefully read the pledge below. Then use proofreading symbols to replace a word, transfer word(s), or delete a letter and close up the space.

I pledge allegiance of the flag of the United States of America and to the Republic for which it stands, one

Nation under God, indivissible, with liberty and for all justice.

Solution

I pledge allegiance to~~of~~ the flag of the United States of America and to the Republic for which it stands, one Nation under God, indivissible, with liberty and for all justice.

Example 2 In the story below, use proofreading symbols to begin a new paragraph or to add a comma, semicolon, or colon.

Pablo's last words were these "You will find the key the map and the money under the tree." "Which tree?" asked Poncho.
Pablo didn't answer he was gone.

Solution

Pablo's last words were these: "You will find the key, the map, and the money under the tree."
¶ "Which tree?" asked Poncho.
Pablo didn't answer; he was gone.

Example 3 In the following paragraph, use proofreading symbols to keep crossed-out material or to add a hyphen, an apostrophe, or a quotation mark.

The well known frontiersman Davy Crockett remains one of the ~~most~~ colorful personalities ever elected to Congress. One day, Davys frustration led him to say, We generally lounge and squabble the greater part of the session...."

Solution

The well-known frontiersman Davy Crockett stet remains one of the most colorful personalities ever elected to Congress. One day, Davy's frustration led him to say, "We generally lounge and squabble the greater part of the session...."

Practice For a–k, write the correct proofreading symbol.

    a. Add a quotation mark.   **b.** Add a colon.

    c. Add an apostrophe   **d.** Add a semicolon.

    e. Begin a new paragraph.   **f.** Replace a word.

    g. Add a comma.   **h.** Add a hyphen.

    i. Keep crossed out part.   **j.** Transfer circled words.

    k. Delete letter and close the space.

    l. Rewrite this dialogue exactly as it is written. Then add proofreading symbols to indicate corrections.

        This was my aunts sugarcoated plea My dearest niece will you please feed my gila monster while Im away?" "Oh, anything but that!" I replied, for those monsters gila really frighten me.

For m and n, replace each blank with the correct vocabulary word.

    m. A skunk is notorious for its _____ scent.

    n. The _____ sword fighter hissed venomous threats at his opponent.

More Practice See Master Worksheets.

Review set 91 Choose the correct word to complete sentences 1–13.

    1. Alliteration, assonance, and (consciousness, conjecture, consonance) highlight certain sounds in phrases for poetic effect.
(90)

    2. In 1933, Congress (appealed, enveloped, repealed) the Eighteenth Amendment and replaced it with the Twenty-first Amendment.
(89)

    3. A (premier, premiere, appropriation) is the first public showing of a movie, drama, opera, or show.
(88)

4. It was (gravid, fortuitous, contemptible) that my friend happened to drive down Hickory Lane and find me with a flat tire.
(37)

5. The Latin word *venire* means (love, come, guest).
(38)

6. (Do Does) either of the mechanics have a wrench?
(12, 76)

7. Daisy and (her, she) play basketball (real, really) (good, well).
(50, 89)

8. Have you ever (growed, grew, grown) zucchini?
(49)

9. It (began, begun) to rain while we (was, were) gardening.
(12, 49)

10. (You're, Your) rake is over (they're, there, their).
(53, 67)

11. Will (him, he, his) leaving the lecture early offend the speaker?
(53, 63)

12. The young man (who, whom) left early distracted several listeners.
(61, 64)

13. Of the two speakers, Dr. Droner gave the (more, most) boring lecture.
(40)

14. Rewrite the following so that it is in active voice: Ahab's leg was bitten off by Moby Dick.
(27)

15. Rewrite the following as it is. Then add proofreading symbols to indicate corrections.
(32)

"Only Ishmael lives too tell the tail of Moby Dick Ahab, and the *Pequod,* said Mr Vega.

16. In the following sentence, write the participle phrase and the word it modifies: Having taken part of Heaven with him, Moby Dick sunk deep into hell.
(45, 56)

17. Rewrite the following, adding capital letters and punctuation marks as needed: If you search deeply commented mrs pencall you will see that herman melville's novel reveals the struggle between good and evil.
(9, 65)

18. Rewrite the following interrogative sentence, making it declarative: Did Herman Melville recognize the power of both God and the devil?
(1)

19. Rewrite the following, adding a colon where it is needed: *Moby Dick* has captured the interest of many people young readers, naturalists, historians, and literary scholars.
(90)

20. In the following sentence, write the verb phrase, name its tense, and label it action or linking: Hanging on one wall at the Spouter Inn, a large oil painting of a sinking ship looked ominous.
(3, 18)

21. In the following sentence, write the dependent clause and circle the subordinating conjunction: From the beginning of the story, we are reminded frequently that the ship and its crew will eventually meet catastrophe.
(54)

22. In the following sentence, write whether the underlined part is essential or nonessential: The giant squid <u>that caught the crew's attention</u> had long tentacles twisting around like huge snakes.
(61, 62)

23. Write the nominative case, third person, singular, feminine gender personal pronoun.
(50, 52)

24. Write the four principle parts of the verb *snap*.
(5, 13)

25. Write whether the following is a complete sentence, a sentence fragment, or a run-on sentence: In the Spouter Inn, Ishmael sleeps peacefully he realizes that it is better to be with a sober cannibal than with a drunken Christian.
(2)

26. Write whether the following sentence is simple or compound: Starbuck goes to sea only to make money, but Stubb goes for the excitement of the whale hunt.
(59)

27. Write the conjunctive adverb in this sentence: The great white whale symbolizes evil; however, Ahab's obsession to destroy the whale becomes an even darker symbol of evil.
(88)

28. From this list, write the word that is divided correctly:
(84)
mal-o-dor-ous   ma-levo-lent   rep-eal

Diagram sentences 29 and 30.

29. Yesterday, Ed skillfully videotaped the two eaglets flapping their wings.
(56, 85)

30. Didn't Ed's videotaping disturb the two eaglets?
(16, 21)

LESSON 92

The Prepositional Phrase as an Adverb • Diagramming

> **Dictation or Journal Entry**
>
> **Vocabulary:** Both *like* and *as* can function as prepositions, but they do not both function as subordinating conjunctions.
>
> *Like* and *as* are used as prepositions in these two sentences: Sansloy acts *like* a lawless guy. The reader views Fidess *as* a faithful young woman.
>
> While *as* can be used as a subordinating conjunction (introducing a dependent clause), *like* cannot. The characters of Strength and Guile confronted each other in battle, just *as* (not *like*) the writer said they would.

Adverb Phrase We have learned that a prepositional phrase can function as an adjective by modifying a noun or a pronoun. A prepositional phrase can also function as an adverb. A prepositional phrase that modifies a verb, an adjective, or another adverb is called an **adverb phrase.** It answers the questions "how," "when," "where," "why," and "to what extent." The italicized adverb phrases below modify the verb "objected."

> How
> The President objected *with a loud voice.*
>
> When
> The President objected *during the meeting.*
>
> Where
> The President objected *behind closed doors.*
>
> Why
> The President objected *for the citizens' sake.*
>
> To What Extent
> The President objected *to every foolish suggestion.*

Most adverb phrases modify verbs. However, an adverb phrase can also modify an adjective or another adverb as in the examples below.

> The President is ready *for their criticism.* (modifies predicate adjective "ready")
>
> The President looks far *beyond the present.* (modifies the adverb "far")

Example 1 Write the adverb prepositional phrase, and tell which word it modifies.

(a) Jefferson Davis is remembered for his passion.

(b) He was inconsistent at controlling his temper.

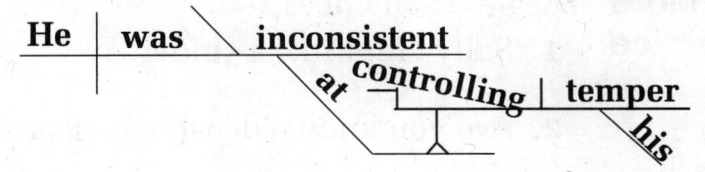

(c) He revealed his feelings there in the meeting hall.

Solution (a) The adverb phrase **for his passion** modifies the verb **is remembered**. It tells "why."

(b) The adverb phrase **at controlling his temper** modifies the adjective **inconsistent.**

(c) The adverb phrase **in the meeting hall** modifies the adverb **there.**

Diagramming We diagram a prepositional phrase under the word it modifies. Therefore, we place an adverb phrase under a verb, adjective, or other adverb. Let us diagram this sentence:

Jefferson Davis fought for a compromise.

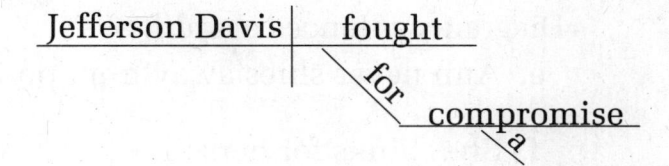

In the sentence above, the adverb phrase *for a compromise* modifies the verb, telling why Jefferson Davis fought.

Example 2 Diagram the three sentences from Example 1.

Solution (a) Jefferson Davis is remembered for his passion.

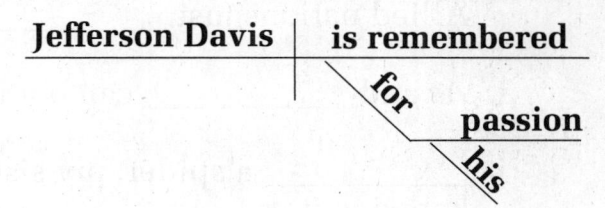

(b) He was inconsistent at controlling his temper.

(c) He revealed his feelings there in the meeting hall.

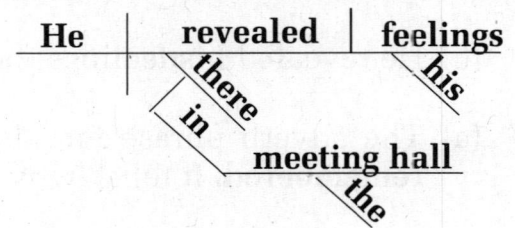

```
         He  |  revealed  |  feelings
                \there        \his
                 \in
                  \meeting hall
                            \the
```

Practice For a–d, write each adverb phrase and tell which word or phrase it modifies.

    a. Vice President Charles Dawes behaved like a gentleman.

    b. Charles Dawes served as a brigadier general.

    c. He was watchful over the troops.

    d. He rose high in public opinion.

Diagram sentences e and f.
    e. Ann never shies away from politics.

    f. She thinks for herself.

For g–j, replace each blank with *like* or *as*.
    g. In a sentence, _____ can serve as a subordinating conjunction or as a preposition.

    h. The Dawes Plan provided for payments to the victorious Allied nations just _____ they expected.

    i. *As* and _____ can both function as prepositions.

    j. _____ a spider, my sister can creep in without my knowing it.

More Practice Diagram sentences 1–3.

    1. Sally crept like a spider.

    2. Are you knowledgeable concerning politics?

    3. Wait here at the library.

Write each prepositional phrase from sentences 4 and 5, and star the object of each preposition.

4. Stephen A. Douglas was popularly known as the "Little Giant."

5. In 1854, Douglas's bill raised a storm of protest from the Northern opposition.

Review set 92

Choose the correct word to complete sentences 1–14.

1. The prefix (*ambi-*, *epi-*, *mal-*) means "bad" or "badly."
   (91)

2. (Alliteration, Assonance, Consonance) is the repetition of consonants anywhere in a word.
   (90)

3. To repeal a law or a tax is to (appeal, lobby, revoke) it.
   (89)

4. An advent is a(n) (departure, arrival, chimney).
   (38)

5. (Explicit, Appellate, Stoic) is an antonym of implicit.
   (39)

6. Ed hasn't (ever, never) (ate, eaten) an artichoke.
   (70, 78)

7. Peggy and (him, he) are (sure, really) enthusiastic bird watchers.
   (50, 89)

8. The (conscience stricken, conscience-stricken) hoodlums knew their fun was over.
   (82)

9. The hoodlums were (conscience stricken, conscience-stricken).
   (82)

10. Would they prefer (me, my) contacting the newspaper about their outrageous activities?
    (53, 55)

11. Juanita (doesn't, don't) know how to groom a horse or clean (its, it's) stall.
    (53, 78)

12. (Who, Whom) did you see at the fair?
    (64)

13. Allison works (harder, hardest) of all the nurses in the clinic.
    (87)

14. Has the hero (slew, slain) the dragon yet?
    (72)

15. Rewrite the following sentence so that it is in active voice: *Prometheus Bound*, a classical tragic drama, was written by Aeschylus.
(27)

16. In the following sentence, write the infinitive and label it a noun or an adjective: Prometheus defected to the Olympian gods because of his determination to avoid violence.
(19, 45)

17. In this sentence, write and underline each part that should be italicized: Violeta makes delicious sopa con frijoles every Friday night.
(69)

18. Rewrite the following letter, adding capital letters and punctuation marks as needed:
(25, 47)

dear zeus

i cannot support your edict to destroy all mankind for it seems too violent

your subject

prometheus

19. Rewrite the following declarative sentence, making it an interrogative sentence: Zeus usurps the throne from the old Titan King Chronus.
(1)

20. In this sentence, write the verb phrase, name its tense, and label it transitive or intransitive: Zeus hopes to replace mankind with a more noble, servile race.
(26)

21. In this sentence, write the dependent clause, circling the subordinating conjunction: Even though mankind appears flawed, Prometheus sees a spark of divine promise.
(54)

22. In this sentence, write whether the underlined clause is essential or nonessential: Prometheus willingly and courageously commits a crime <u>that saves mankind from extinction</u>.
(62)

23. Write the objective case, third person, singular, masculine gender personal pronoun.
(51, 52)

24. Write the four principal parts of the irregular verb *buy*.
(13, 70)

25. Rewrite the following as it is. Then add proofreading symbols to indicate corrections.

Pro metheus gived people fire and teached them howtoo use it.

26. Write the conjunctive adverb in this sentence: Prometheus tutored mankind in practical arts; in addition, he schooled the human race in science and philosophy.

27. From this list, write the word that is divided correctly: o-bedient, ob-edient, obe-dient

28. Rewrite the following, adding a colon where it is needed: Ian purchased these camping supplies lanterns, tarps, propane, and marshmallows.

Diagram sentences 29 and 30.

29. Thoroughly studying the material should give you enough confidence for passing the test.

30 A magnanimous player wins without gloating and loses without complaining.

LESSON 93

Preposition or Adverb?
• Preposition Usage

> **Dictation or Journal Entry**
>
> **Vocabulary:** *Cataclysm,* *catapult,* and *catacomb* contain the prefix *cata-*, which comes from the Greek *kata,* meaning "down" or "against."
>
> A *cataclysm* is a violent change or sudden upheaval. The bombing of Pearl Harbor was a great *cataclysm* in modern history.
>
> A *catapult* is an ancient military weapon for hurling stones, arrows, or other missiles. The invaders used *catapults* to throw rocks over the walls of the fort.
>
> A *catacomb* is an underground cemetery. The archaeologist discovered a *catacomb* where Christians were buried near Rome, Italy.

Preposition or Adverb?

Most prepositions can be used as adverbs as well. We remember that an adverb stands alone, but a preposition always has an object.

ADVERB: The senator strolled *through.*

PREPOSITION: The senator strolled *through the *room.*

ADVERB: The senator hurried *out.*

PREPOSITION: The senator hurried *out the *door.*

ADVERB: The senator gazed *around.*

PREPOSITION: The senator gazed *around the *courtyard.*

Diagramming can help us determine whether a word is being used as an adverb or a preposition. Look at the word "off" in these two sentences:

ADVERB: Mario took *off* his hat.

(We can see that "hat" is a direct object telling what Mario took. It is not an object of a preposition. "Off" is an adverb telling where.)

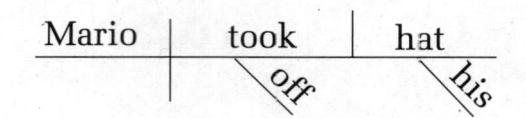

```
Mario  |  took  |  hat
           \off     \his
```

PREPOSITION: Then he stepped *off the train.*

(In this sentence, "train" is the object of the preposition "off.")

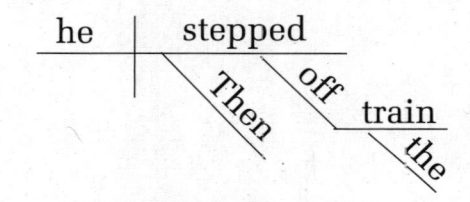

```
he  |  stepped
        \Then  \off
                  \train
                    \the
```

Example 1 Tell whether the italicized word in each sentence is an adverb or a preposition.

(a) Will Congress vote *down* this bill?

(b) Would you vote *against* this bill?

(c) Lobbyists are gathering *inside* the Capitol.

(d) My favorite candidate is lagging *behind*.

Solution (a) *Down* is an **adverb** telling how Congress "will vote." The word *bill* is not an object of the preposition; it is the direct object.

(b) We see that *against* is a **preposition** because it has an object—"bill."

(c) We see that *inside* is a **preposition** because it has an object—"Capitol."

(d) *Behind* is an **adverb** telling where the candidate "is lagging."

Preposition Usage Certain pairs of prepositions are frequently misused. In this lesson, we will learn to use these prepositions correctly:

in and *into*

between and *among*

beside and *besides*

In or into? The preposition *in* means you are already there.

The President is *in* the Oval Office.

We were *in* the White House.

The preposition *into* refers to moving from the outside to the inside.

The President is walking *into* the Oval Office.

We stepped *into* the White House.

Between or Among? We use *between* when referring to two people, places, or things.

> The two candidates divided the votes *between* them.
>
> In 1952, the public chose *between* Eisenhower and Stevenson.

We use *among* when referring to three or more people, places, or things.

> Canada is *among* the several nations belonging to the North Atlantic Treaty Organization.
>
> The Emancipation Proclamation is *among* the many political triumphs of President Abraham Lincoln.

Beside or Besides? The preposition *beside* means "at the side of."

> The First Lady stood *beside* the President.
>
> I placed your luggage *beside* mine.

Besides means "in addition to" or "as well as."

> *Besides* the Potomac River, I'd like to see the Delaware.
>
> Which state *besides* Maryland borders Washington, D.C.?

Example 2 Choose the correct preposition for each sentence.

(a) Which amendment forbids government officials from going (in, into) someone's home without a warrant?

(b) Harry Truman is (between, among) the most successful campaigners for the Presidency.

(c) Who (beside, besides) Alexander Hamilton wrote *The Federalist*?

Solution (a) Which amendment forbids government officials from going **into** someone's home without a warrant?

(b) Harry Truman is **among** the most successful campaigners for the Presidency.

(c) Who **besides** Alexander Hamilton wrote *The Federalist*?

Practice For sentences a–d, tell whether the italicized word is an adverb or a preposition.

   a. The time zoomed *by*.

   b. They waited *aboard* the plane.

   c. Air Force One flew *over* the White House.

   d. We picked *up* our lunches.

For e–g, choose the correct preposition.

   e. Has anyone (beside, besides) Rebecca Latimer Felton served in the Senate for only one day?

   f. She walked (in, into) the Senate and delivered a speech in defense of women.

   g. She is (between, among) the most determined women in American history.

For sentences h–k, replace each blank with the correct vocabulary word or definition.

   h. By searching the _____ of Rome, Italy, archeologists have increased understanding of ancient civilizations.

   i. To defend themselves, warriors used a _____ to fire arrows.

   j. The earthquake was a _____ for the city.

   k. The Greek root *kata* means _____ or _____.

Review set 93 Choose the best word to complete sentences 1–15.

   1. The Smith Family painted their house green (like, as) I had suggested.
   (92)

   2. Malodorous means having a (pleasant, bad, sweet) odor.
   (91)

   3. (Alliteration, Assonance, Consonance) is the repetition of same vowel sounds in a series of words.
   (90)

   4. A flare is a (natural talent, blaze of light).
   (56)

5. Perceptible means (lucky, noticeable, appropriate).
(40)

6. Neither the hens nor the rooster (is, are) in the coop.
(35)

7. Neither the rooster nor the hens (is, are) in the coop.
(35)

8. (Does, Do) this stack of newspapers belong in the trash?
(12, 77)

9. The band director gave (we, us) flute players some new music.
(51, 63)

10. The trumpet players and (them, they) play more wrong notes than (us, we).
(50, 63)

11. A(n) (gerund, participle, infinitive) is a verbal that is the basic form of the verb, usually preceded by the preposition "to."
(16, 19)

12. Emma is (sure, surely) fatigued, for she hasn't been sleeping (good, well).
(81, 89)

13. Neither of the drummers (keep, keeps) time with the music.
(13, 76)

14. How many songs has the choir (sang, sung)?
(49)

15. The Broadway show, (that, which) will be here for at least ten months, opens next Saturday.
(62)

16. Write the plural of each noun.
(10, 11)
(a) Chris (b) Danny (c) beach

17. In the following sentence, write and underline each part that should be italicized: Timmy and Tucker named their two pet pigs Sus and Scrofa after the scientific name for a domestic hog, Sus scrofa.
(69)

18. Rewrite the following as it is. Then add proofreading symbols to indicate corrections.
(32, 91)

In Greek myth ology, Prometheus a Titan god, bestows upon humanity tha gift of fire this angers Zeus.

19. Use an appositive to make one sentence from the following two sentences: Wilhelm Konrad Roentgen was a great German physicist. He discovered X rays in 1895.
(42)

20. Rewrite the following sentence so that it is in active
(27) voice: Revenge for Prometheus's treasonous crimes is
demanded by Zeus.

21. In this sentence, write the dependent clause, circling the
(54) subordinating conjunction: Hephaestus halfheartedly
shackles Prometheus to the side of a cliff where an eagle
preys on him.

22. In this sentence, write whether the underlined part is
(62) essential or nonessential: The rings that surround Saturn
are made of ice, rocks, and moons.

23. Write the superlative form of the adverb *carefully*.
(87)

24. Write the four principal parts of the irregular verb *sell*.
(13, 71)

25. In the following sentence, write the indefinite pronoun
(68) and label it singular or plural: We must patch up that
chicken coop, for one of the hens has escaped!

26. Write the conjunctive adverb in the following sentence:
(88) Kratos taunts Prometheus; at the same time, Hephaestus
pities him.

27. Rewrite the following sentence, adding dashes where
(73) they are appropriate: A man with red hair and a mustache
I don't remember his eye color tip-toed past the security
guard and into the museum after hours.

28. Rewrite the following sentence, placing a semicolon
(88) where it is needed: The museum has been robbed several
ancient artifacts have disappeared.

Diagram sentences 29 and 30.

29. Does Mr. Prickle, the curator, specialize in old roses from
(28, 42) ancient times?

30. Having planted the antique rose in its new garden, Mr.
(38, 56) Prickle is ready for his next project.

LESSON 94

The Infinitive as an Adverb • The Infinitive Phrase • Diagramming

> **Dictation or Journal Entry**
>
> **Vocabulary:** The words *incumbent, recumbent*, and *succumb*, contain the Latin root *cub-*, meaning "to lie down."
>
> *Incumbent* means "imposed as a duty of obligation." Obeying traffic laws is *incumbent* upon drivers. *Incumbent* also means "holding an office." Will the *incumbent* president win the next election?
>
> *Recumbent* means "leaning, reclining, or lying down." After the basketball game, the fatigued players assumed *recumbent* postures.
>
> To *succumb* is to give in to a greater power; to submit, or yield. I finally *succumbed* to the temptation of a second slice of pie. *Succumb* can also mean "to die." Unfortunately, the animal *succumbed* to the disease.

The Infinitive as an Adverb

We remember that the infinitive is the basic form of the verb, usually preceded by the preposition "to." Thus far, we have examined infinitives that function as nouns or adjectives in a sentence. In this lesson, we will see that the infinitive can also function as an adverb. Infinitives that function as adverbs are italicized in the sentences below.

To filibuster, talk continuously. (modifies the verb; tells "how" talk)

They were eager *to filibuster*. (modifies the adjective "eager")

He's talkative enough *to filibuster*. (modifies the adverb "enough")

Example 1 Write the infinitive from each sentence and tell whether it functions as a noun, an adjective, or an adverb.

(a) Do you have the ability to filibuster?

(b) The Senate is reluctant to ban the filibuster.

(c) To filibuster requires imagination, charisma, and energy.

Solution (a) **To filibuster** functions as an **adjective** modifying the noun "ability."

(b) **To ban** functions as an **adverb** modifying the adjective "reluctant."

(c) **To filibuster** is a **noun.** It is the subject of the sentence.

Example 2 The sentences below contain infinitives that function as adverbs. For each sentence, write the infinitive and tell whether it modifies a verb, an adjective, or another adverb.

(a) To adjourn, we must win the vote.

(b) During a filibuster, Shakespeare and the Bible were acceptable to be read.

(c) Are you patient enough to endure?

Solution (a) "To adjourn" modifies the verb "must win."

(b) "To read" modifies the adjective "acceptable."

(c) "To endure" modifies the adverb "enough."

The Infinitive Phrase An **infinitive phrase** is an infinitive along with its objects and modifiers. The phrase may contain adverbs, adjectives, predicate nominatives, direct objects, indirect objects, and prepositional phrases.

The infinitive phrase may function as a noun, an adjective, or an adverb.

INFINITIVE PHRASE AS A NOUN:

To speak to the nation was the purpose of President Franklin D. Roosevelt's "fireside chats." (subject)

President Franklin D. Roosevelt began *to build public confidence in his policies*. (direct object)

His goal was *to connect warmly and informally with the people*. (predicate nominative)

INFINITIVE PHRASE AS AN ADJECTIVE:

It's his hope *to divert a banking crisis*. (modifies the noun "hope")

People need someone *to assure them*. (modifies the pronoun)

INFINITIVE PHRASE AS AN ADVERB:

He speaks *to educate the public*. (modifies the verb; tells "why")

Are they courageous enough *to try something new*? (modifies the adverb "enough")

Diagramming We remember that we place the infinitive on stilts. We diagram the infinitive along with its objects and modifiers in the location that shows how the infinitive phrase functions in the sentence. The sentence below contains an infinitive phrase that functions as an adverb.

To explain more fully, Naomi outlined the plan.
(modifies the verb "outlined")

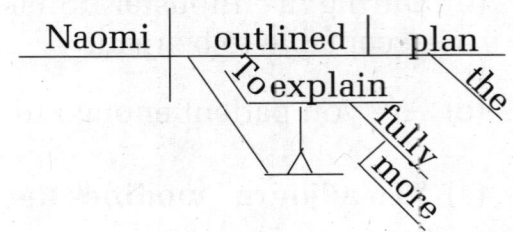

Example 3 Diagram each sentence.
(a) To communicate effectively requires patience.

(b) Rosita is patient enough to listen to others.

(c) Now is the time to lay aside our differences.

Solution (a) The infinitive phrase, "to communicate effectively," is the subject of the sentence.

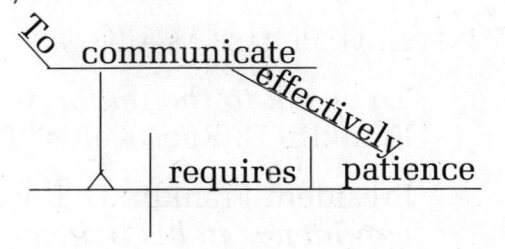

(b) The infinitive phrase, "to listen to others," functions as an adverb, for it modifies another adverb, "enough."

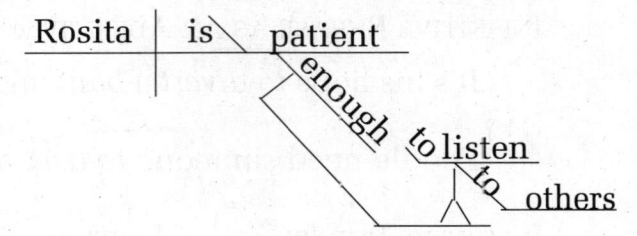

(c) The infinitive phrase, "to lay aside our differences" functions as an adjective, for it modifies the noun "time."

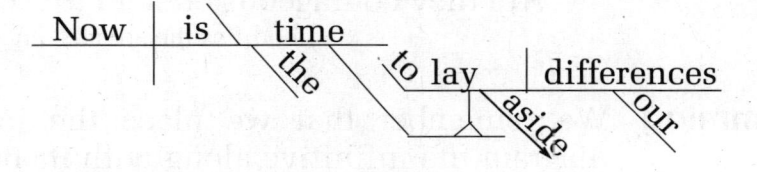

Practice For a–e, replace each blank with the correct vocabulary word.

a. The Latin root _____ means "to lie down."

b. It is _____ upon Congress to vote on the bill.

c. I did not _____ to the temptation to say, "I told you so."

d. Does the _____ officer have an advantage over others who are running in this election?

e. While recovering from a broken leg, Heather did her homework in a _____ position.

For f–h, write whether the infinitive phrase functions as a noun, an adjective, or an adverb.

f. Quan loves *to hike in the foothills.*

g. *To join Quan on the hike,* call him for directions.

h. Juanita chose someone *to take her place.*

For i–k, write the infinitive phrase that functions as an adverb. Then, write the word it modifies.

i. Is Quan fit enough to hike Mount Whitney?

j. Lizel is hopeful to join the hikers.

k. To reach the summit tomorrow, you must start early in the morning.

l. Diagram this sentence: To condition herself, Vivian rows her canoe daily.

More Practice Diagram each sentence.

1. Ann is eager to hike down.

2. I came to listen to your story.

3. To open the lid, press here.

4. She claps to catch flies.

5. We are happy to help you.

6. To write well, practice often.

Review Set 94

Choose the correct word to complete sentences 1–16.

1. The prefix (mal-, epi-, cata-) means "down" or "against."
(93)

2. The swimmers found the strong current dangerous (like, as) the lifeguard had warned them.
(92)

3. (Malodorous, Bicameral, Contemptible) means "having an unpleasant or offensive odor."
(91)

4. Susceptible means (vulnerable, noticeable, implied).
(40)

5. (Altogether, All together), how many sculptures has Thelma created this year?
(41)

6. I promised Blanca and (she, her) that I would try (real, really) hard to catch that gopher.
(89)

7. Blanca (doesn't, don't) have (nobody, anybody) else to help her catch gophers.
(12, 78)

8. A (fast-moving, fast moving) critter just burrowed beneath the lawn.
(82)

9. That critter was (fast-moving, fast moving).
(82)

10. Do you remember (our, us) telling you about Blanca's gopher problem?
(53, 55)

11. (There's, There are) enough homeowner complaints without (her's, hers).
(53, 93)

12. The homeowner (who, whom) called pest control could not be reached for comment.
(61, 64)

13. Mr. Prickle (sure, surely) prunes roses (good, well).
(81, 89)

14. The sun had (rose, risen) over the sleepy village.
(15, 72)

15. Of the two pilots, Kim had (flew, flown) (farther, farthest) that day.
(70, 87)

16. The pesky gopher plunged headfirst (in, into) the hole and hid (between, among) his seven cousins.
(28, 93)

17. Write the six adverbs from this list that tell "how much" or "to what extent": two, to, too, not, quite, quiet, very, writ, rather, somewhat, something

18. Rewrite the dialogue below as it is. Then add proofreading symbols to indicate corrections.

    Oceanus says to Prometheus "Please ask forgiveness frum Zeus.

    No, answers Prometheus, "I would rather suffre."

19. Write the plural of each noun.
(a) rose bush   (b) truckload   (c) goose

20. In this sentence, write the verb phrase, name its tense, and label it action or linking: Tomorrow my grandparents will have been married for fifty years.

21. Write whether this sentence is simple or compound: Oceanus and his daughters beg Prometheus to seek forgiveness from Zeus, and Hermes rebukes Prometheus for his refusal.

22. Write the seven common coordinating conjunctions.

23. Write the objective case, third person, plural personal pronoun.

24. Write the four principal parts of the irregular verb *make*.

25. Write the word from this list that is divided correctly: a-ssonance, asso-nance, assonan-ce

26. Write the conjunctive adverb in this sentence: Gophers are killing the vegetation in Blanca's yard; for this reason, she has called an exterminator.

27. Write and underline each part that should be italicized in the following sentence: The Confederate vessel Merrimack fought the Union vessel Monitor in an important American Civil War battle.

28. Rewrite the following, adding a colon where it is needed: I have memorized the eight parts of speech adjectives, adverbs, conjunctions, interjections, nouns, prepositions, pronouns, and verbs.

Diagram sentences 29 and 30.

29. The guard and I apprehended and questioned a man carrying an unusually large briefcase.
(34, 56)

30. Nervously twisting his bright red mustache, he tried to avoid answering our questions.
(55, 56)

LESSON 95 — The Apostrophe: Possessives

> **Dictation or Journal Entry**
> **Vocabulary:** The Greek prefix *proto-*, meaning "first in time" or "first formed," appears in the words *prototype*, *protocol*, and *protoplasm*.
>
> A *prototype* is the original model on which something is patterned. The engineers have developed a *prototype* for the new lampposts that will line the streets of the future.
>
> *Protocol* is a set of rules for diplomatic conduct. The ambassador dressed appropriately, according to *protocol*.
>
> *Protoplasm* is the jellylike substance that is the living matter of every plant and animal cell. Under the microscope, we could see the *protoplasm* of the skin cells.

We use the apostrophe to show possession.

Singular Possessive   To give a singular noun ownership, we add an apostrophe and an s (*'s*). The noun then becomes a **singular possessive noun** as in the examples below.

SINGULAR NOUN	POSSESSIVE NOUN
justice	*justice's* decision
manager	*manager's* choice
flag	*flag's* emblem
citizen	*citizen's* rights

In a compound noun, possession is formed by adding *'s* to the last word.

next-of-kin	next-of-kin's address
rabble rouser	rabble rouser's clamor
busybody	busybody's offense

Shared or Separate Possession   When more than one noun shares possession, we add *'s* to the last noun as in the example below.

　　Maristela, Opal, and Sybil's drama presentation

When the nouns each possess something separately, we add *'s* to each noun.

　　Christie's and Bob's jackets

Example 1   Use the apostrophe to make each singular noun possessive.

(a) Polly

(b) Silas

(c) sister-in-law

(d) albatross

(e) Lum, Levi, and Tim (jazz band)

Solution (a) **Polly's** (b) **Silas's**

(c) **sister-in-law's** (d) **albatross's**

(e) **Lum, Levi, and Tim's** jazz band

Plural Possessive To give a regular plural noun ownership, we add only an apostrophe. The noun then becomes a **plural possessive noun,** as in the examples below.

PLURAL NOUN	PLURAL POSSESSIVE
sparrows	*sparrows'* nests
turkeys	*turkeys'* feathers
tree trimmers	*tree trimmers'* tools

Irregular Plurals To give an irregular plural noun ownership, add *'s.*

PLURAL NOUN	PLURAL POSSESSIVE
women	*women's* ideas
sheep	*sheep's* pasture
gentlemen	*gentlemen's* manners
geese	*geese's* destination

Many people make errors when forming plural possessive nouns. To avoid this, form the plural noun first. Then apply the guidelines above to make it possessive.

Remember that in a compound word, possession is formed by adding *'s* to the last word.

physicians-on-call's calendar

Example 2 Use the apostrophe to form a plural possessive noun from each plural noun.

(a) lice (b) children

(c) earthworms (d) grandparents

(e) earth-dwellers (f) brothers-in-law

Solution (a) **lice's** (b) **children's**

(c) **earthworms'** (d) **grandparents'**

(e) **earth-dwellers'** (f) **brothers-in-law's**

Practice For a–d, replace each blank with the correct vocabulary word.

    a. Spectators froze in amazement as the _____ of the stealth aircraft flew overhead.

    b. The Greek prefix _____ means "first formed."

    c. Good _____ includes written responses of thanks for most gifts.

    d. The _____ of a cell consists of water, proteins, sugars, fats, acids, and salts.

For e–j, write the possessive form of each italicized noun.

    e. The two *sisters-in-law* babies wiggled noisily in the pew.

    f. John, Robert, and *James* jokes always make me laugh.

    g. Is the *mice* favorite cheese cheddar or Swiss?

    h. Some of the *ex-Presidents* wives wrote stories about their own lives in the White House.

    i. I saw the *deer* eyes shining in the headlights.

    j. Betsy *Ross* first flag displayed fewer stripes and stars than the current United States flag.

More Practice For 1–8, write the possessive form of each singular noun.

    1. gallery   **2.** chief   **3.** bus   **4.** slave

    5. prototype   **6.** boss   **7.** puppy   **8.** baboon

For 9–16, write the possessive form of each plural noun.

    9. trout   **10.** flies   **11.** Democrats   **12.** nuclei

    13. societies   **14.** men   **15.** cattle   **16.** radii

Review Set 95 Choose the correct word(s) to complete sentences 1–15.

    1. The Latin root (*pac-, plas-, cub-*) means "to lie down."
    (94)

    2. A (cataclysm, catapult, catacomb) is a violent change or sudden upheaval.
    (93)

3. Shall we eat at this restaurant (like, as) the newspaper
(92) recommends?

4. Thelma gathered her sculptures (altogether, all together)
(41) in the exhibition hall.

5. To agitate is to (stir, delude, gravitate).
(42)

6. I didn't have (nothing, anything) to do with making that
(78) mess.

7. Either the cats or the dog (is, are) responsible for those
(12, 76) torn pillows.

8. (Isn't, Aren't, Ain't) that a gigantic pile of pillow feathers?
(76)

9. (Us, We) pet owners are accustomed to this.
(50, 63)

10. Ruth and (we, us) (laughs, laugh) more than (they, them).
(50, 63)

11. The word *not* is an (adverb, adjective, preposition).
(86)

12. They were (sure, surely) overwhelmed by the mess.
(89)

13. Only one of the pillows (remain, remains) intact.
(76)

14. Yesterday, I (lay, lain) in the hammock, for I didn't feel
(71, 81) (good, well).

15. The moose (which, that) I photographed in Alaska had
(53, 62) already shed (it's, its) antlers.

16. Rewrite the following as it is. Then add proofreading
(32, 91) symbols to indicate corrections.

Oneday prometheus wood be freed from bon dage an Zeus would be defeated.

17. Write the five adverbs from this list:
(80, 89)
friendly, lovely, here, still, almost, lonely, now, quite

18. Rewrite the following letter, adding capital letters and punctuation marks as needed:
(25, 47)

dear io

    i am so sorry that zeus turned you into a cow someday you will be restored to your true form

       with compassion

       prometheus

19. In the following sentence, write the infinitive phrase and label it a noun, adjective, or adverb: Isn't she too young to drive a car?
(45, 94)

20. In the sentence below, write the verb phrase, name its tense, and label it transitive or intransitive. Then write whether it is in active or passive voice.
(17, 27)

Have those pets been ripping apart pillows from the sofa?

21. In this sentence, write each dependent clause, circling each subordinating conjunction: I'll take you wherever you want if you'll help me to clean up the feathers.
(54)

22. In this sentence, write whether the underlined part is essential or nonessential: The vacuum cleaner <u>that I used</u> is now clogged with feathers.
(62)

23. In the following sentence, write the indefinite pronoun and label it singular or plural:
(68)

Has anyone volunteered to repair the damage?

24. Write the four principal parts of the irregular verb *hold*.
(13, 71)

25. Write the comparative form of the adverb *gently*.
(87)

26. Write the conjunctive adverb in the following sentence:
(88)

Prometheus openly denounces Zeus; consequently, the enraged Zeus sends Prometheus to hell.

27. Rewrite the following, adding a dash where it is needed:
(73)

Miss Beagle, Buttercup, and Fluffy had littered the floor with their toys catnip-filled balls, rawhide bones, and stuffed animals.

28. Rewrite the following, replacing a comma with a semicolon where it is needed:
(88)

The drama *Prometheus Bound* seized Elle's imagination, moreover, it caused her to reflect on some philosophical ideas.

Diagram sentences 29 and 30.

29. Breathing feathers, they stormed into the living room and chased their mischievous pets outside.
(34, 56)

30. Had they come home early enough to save any pillows from destruction?
(92, 94)

LESSON 96

The Apostrophe: Contractions, Omitting Digits and Letters

> **Dictation or Journal Entry**
> **Vocabulary:** *Aid, aide,* and *-ade* are homophones.
>
> As a noun, *aid* is assistance or help. The United States sends *aid* to hungry people around the world. As a verb, *aid* means to help or assist. We shall *aid* the starving.
>
> An *aide* is an assistant or a helper. The nurse's *aide* recorded my weight and blood pressure.
>
> The suffix *-ade* is attached to certain fruits indicating fruit drinks. Lemon*ade* and lime*ade* are refreshing on a hot day.

Contractions When we combine two words and shorten one of them, we form a **contraction.** We insert an apostrophe to take the place of the letter or letters taken out.

Sometimes a verb is shortened as in the examples below.

you have	→	you've
we would	→	we'd
he will	→	he'll
that is	→	that's

Other times we combine the verb and the word *not*. We shorten the word *not*, and use an apostrophe where the letter *o* is missing.

do not	→	don't
was not	→	wasn't
is not	→	isn't
are not	→	aren't
cannot	→	can't
should not	→	shouldn't
were not	→	weren't
have not	→	haven't
does not	→	doesn't
has not	→	hasn't

Note: the contraction *won't* (will not) is spelled irregularly.

Example 1 Use an apostrophe to write the contractions of a–d.

(a) she is   (b) they are

(c) could not   (d) did not

Solution   (a) **she's**   (b) **they're**

(c) **couldn't**   (d) **didn't**

Omitted Digits   We use an apostrophe when the first two digits are omitted from the year.

     2004 → **'04**
     1997 → **'97**
     1965 → **'65**
     1920 → **'20**

Omitted Letters   We use an apostrophe to show that we have taken letters out of a word. In informal writing, we can leave out letters to indicate the way we imagine the words being spoken.

     you all → y'all
     baking, cooking → bakin', cookin'
     good morning → g'mornin'
     until later → 'til later

Plurals of Lowercase Letters and Words Used as Nouns   For clarity, we use an apostrophe to form the plurals of lowercase letters and words used as nouns. The letters or words may be italicized or underlined.

Be sure that your handwritten *a*'s do not look like *o*'s.

The Senator used too many *and uh*'s in his speech.

Wearing *pj*'s to a meeting is against protocol.

This is one of the few times when an apostrophe is used to form a plural. Be especially careful not to form regular plurals with apostrophes.

We usually form the plural of a capital letter, number, or sign with an *s* alone.

     four *B*s   two 7s   several +s

Example 2   Write the expression that needs an apostrophe in each sentence.

(a) Was Ceci born in 01 or 02?

(b) Twas many months ago that the story began.

(c) The braggart's self-centered letter was full of *I*s and *me*s.

Solution (a) Was Ceci born in **'01** or **'02**?

(b) **'Twas** many months ago that the story began.

(c) The braggart's self-centered letter was full of ***I*'s** and ***me*'s**.

Practice For sentences a–d, write each expression that needs an apostrophe.

a. "I havent finished studyin for the test," said Arnold.

b. "Wasnt Grandfather livin here in 46?" asked Sid.

c. Shes going to call us when its time to go.

d. The Secretary of Treasury paid a stack of c.o.d.s.

Make contractions for e and f.
e. had not
f. we are

For g–j, replace each blank with the correct vocabulary word.

g. Lime juice and sugar makes lime_____.

h. Will the United States _____ a country that doesn't respect human rights?

i. An _____ handed each fourth grader his or her art project.

j. The poor country requested _____ in the form of food and medical supplies.

More Practice See Master Worksheets.

Review set 96 Choose the best word(s) to complete sentences 1–16.

1. The Greek prefix (*epi-*, *ambi-*, *proto-*) means "first in time" or "first formed."
(95)

2. (Recumbent, Incumbent, Ambient) means "imposed as a duty or obligation."
(94)

3. A (cataclysm, catapult, catacomb) is an ancient military weapon.
(93)

4. An agenda is a list of things to (discover, do, hide).
(42)

5. Finite means having (luck, boundaries, peace).
(43)

6. Juan and (he, him) were (real, really) thirsty.
(50, 89)

7. *Really* is an (adjective, adverb).
(89)

8. Mariah has a (full-time, full time) job.
(82)

9. She works (full-time, full time).
(82)

10. Have you forgotten (us, our) signing the peace treaty?
(50, 53)

11. (Ours, Our's) is here, but they can't find (their's, theirs) (anywhere, nowhere).
(53, 78)

12. The ambassador (who, whom) the President just appointed (doesn't, don't) speak German.
(61, 96)

13. (Bad, Badly) is an adverb.
(89)

14. Dozens of goldfinches (flew, flown) out of the eucalyptus tree.
(70)

15. I think Nien is the (more, most) talkative of the two.
(40)

16. Who (beside, besides) Kurt likes parking his bicycle (between, among) the two school buses?
(93)

17. For a–c, write the possessive form of each noun.
(95)   (a) The Rivases   (b) Larry   (c) brother-in-law

Rewrite 18 and 19, adding capital letters and punctuation marks as needed.

18. the blue socks a womens softball team from azusa city have had bad luck said lorna they havent won a single game
(9, 65)

19. bob replied theyd do better if they practiced the essential skills batting throwing catching and running
(41, 65)

20. Use an appositive to make one sentence from the following two sentences:

Daniel Defoe was an English novelist and journalist.

In 1719, Daniel Defoe wrote *The Life and Adventures of Robinson Crusoe,* a tale about a shipwrecked sailor marooned on an island.

21. Write whether the following sentence is simple or compound:

Young Robinson Crusoe wished to go to sea, but he had little knowledge about the perils of a sailor's life.

22. In the following sentence, write the three dependent clauses, circling each subordinating conjunction:

If you cut Samson's hair while he is sleeping, will he be powerless when he awakes?

23. Write the nominative case, third person, singular, feminine gender, personal pronoun.

24. Write the antecedent of the italicized pronoun in the following sentence:

A Portuguese ship rescues Robinson Crusoe, and *he* sails to Brazil.

25. Write whether the following is a phrase or a clause: even though Robinson Crusoe establishes a prosperous sugar plantation

26. Write the word from this list that is divided correctly:

malo-dorous, mal-odorous, malodo-rous

27. Write the conjunctive adverb in this sentence:

Robinson Crusoe vows never to sail again; nevertheless, he joins a slave ship bound for Africa.

28. Rewrite the following sentence so that it is in active voice:

Goats were domesticated by Robinson Crusoe for their milk, butter, and meat.

Diagram sentences 29 and 30.

29. Attempting to reverse their losing streak, the Blue Socks consumed twelve boxes of fortune cookies before the game.
(92, 94)

30. To win a game, the team needs to practice more diligently.
(21, 94)

LESSON 97

The Adjective Clause •
The Adverb Clause •
The Noun Clause

> **Dictation or Journal Entry**
>
> **Vocabulary:** The Latin root *rectus*, meaning "right" or "straight," appears in the familiar word *rectangle* and also in the words *rectify* and *rectitude*.
>
> To *rectify* means "to set right, correct, or adjust." We hope to *rectify* our errors.
>
> *Rectitude* is moral integrity; uprightness of moral character. We can trust people whose *rectitude* is obvious.

A dependent clause is also called a *subordinate clause*. Like a phrase, a subordinate clause acts as a single part of speech—as an adjective, an adverb, or a noun. In this lesson we will learn to identify the adjective clause, the adverb clause, and the noun clause.

The Adjective Clause

An **adjective clause** is a subordinate clause that, like an adjective, modifies a noun or pronoun. We have italicized adjective clauses in the sentences below. An arrow points to the word that the clause modifies. We have underlined the relative pronouns, which connect the clause with the rest of the sentence.

Benjamin Harrison, *who is the topic of my book report,* was the twenty-third President.

People vote for someone *whom they can trust.*

Benjamin Harrison had a grandfather *that he admired and respected.*

Here are the qualities *for which he is remembered.*

The Adverb Clause

An **adverb clause** is a subordinate clause that, like an adverb, modifies a verb, an adjective, or an adverb. We have italicized adverb clauses in the sentences below. We see that the first four adverb clauses below modify the verb "debates" and tell *how, when, where,* and *why*. The last clause modifies the adverb "more" and tells *how much* more.

> She debates *as though her life depends on it.* [how]
>
> She debates *whenever a controversy arises.* [when]
>
> She debates *wherever listeners gather.* [where]
>
> She debates *because she has strong opinions.* [why]
>
> She debates more *than I do.* [how much "more"]

We remember that adverb clauses may modify adjectives as well as verbs and other adverbs. See the examples below.

> Julia feels confident *that she will win.* [modifies the adjective "confident"]
>
> José is taller *than she is.* [modifies the adjective "taller"]

The Noun Clause A **noun clause** is a subordinate clause used as a noun. It may function as a subject, object, or predicate nominative. We have italicized noun clauses in the sentences below, and we explain how the clause functions in the sentence.

> *Whoever challenges her* is in for a battle. [sentence subject]
>
> We discovered *that she is a Senator.* [direct object]
>
> Here is a summary of *what she proposes.* [object of the preposition "of"]
>
> This is *what she hopes to achieve.* [predicate nominative]

Example Write whether the italicized clause is an adjective clause, an adverb clause, or a noun clause.

(a) The senator was uncertain *that he could sway the vote.*

(b) He recognized *whose ideas were most popular.*

(c) People *who talk the most* listen the least.

Solution (a) "That he could sway the vote" is an **adverb clause** that modifies the adjective "uncertain."

(b) "Whose ideas were most popular" is a **noun clause** that functions as the direct object of the sentence.

(c) "Who talk the most" is an **adjective clause** that modifies the noun "people."

Practice For a–c, replace each blank with the correct vocabulary word.

a. The Latin root _____ means "right" or "straight."

b. Will an apology _____ the offense?

c. Honesty and _____ are essential qualities for an elected official.

For d–h, write whether the italicized clause is an adjective clause, an adverb clause, or a noun clause.

d. *Whoever labeled Dennis J. Hastert a "stealth Speaker"* recognized his ability to work behind the scenes in Congress.

e. Hastert replaced the Speaker *who unexpectedly resigned*.

f. I forgot *what day it was*.

g. She laughs *whenever I lose my keys*.

h. Laughing is *what she likes most*.

Review Set 97 Choose the correct word(s) to complete sentences 1–15.

1. (Aid, Aide, Ade) is assistance or help.
(96)

2. A (catacomb, warrant, prototype) is an original model.
(95)

3. (Implicit, Incumbent, Recumbent) means "holding an office."
(94)

4. The root (ven-, ced-, fin-) means "end".
(43)

5. He felt discouraged, but he smiled (any way, anyways, anyway).
(44)

6. The Blue Socks haven't won (no, any) games yet.
(78)

7. Neither the players nor the coach (believe, believes) they can win the next game.
(76)

8. Even (those, them) positive thinkers have (there, their) doubts.
(53, 63)

9. (Is, Are) physics essential for all baseball players to comprehend?
(77)

10. (We, Us) Blue Socks have had fewer base hits than (they, them).
(50, 63)

11. A(n) (transitive, intransitive) verb has a direct object.
(26)

12. Hilda tries (real, really) hard to pitch strikes.
(89)

13. Each of the women (promises, promise) (their, her) best effort.
(76)

14. Have all the players (strove, striven) for excellence throughout the season?
(72)

15. The Grand Slam Stadium, (that, which) holds a thousand fans, will be full next Saturday.
(62)

16. Rewrite the following sentence so that it is in active voice: A raft had been constructed by Robinson Crusoe.
(27)

17. For a–c, write the possessive form of each noun.
(95)   (a) sisters-in-law   (b) Chris   (c) The Cruzes

18. Rewrite the following, adding capital letters and punctuation marks as needed: phooey yelled the coach after another dismal loss my team lost again nevertheless we shall not give up
(65, 73)

19. Rewrite the following as it is. Then add proofreading symbols to indicate corrections.
(32, 91)

Do everyone Drown accept RobinsonCrusoe?

20. Write the superlative form of the adverb *loudly*.
(87)

21. In the following sentence, write the indefinite pronoun and label it singular or plural: No one thinks the Blue Socks have a chance against the Pink Petunias.
(68)

22. In the following sentence, write each dependent clause, circling each subordinating conjunction:
(54, 61)

Since all other crewmen perish, Robinson Crusoe makes his home on an island where no one else lives.

23. Write the seven common coordinating conjunctions.
(33)

24. Write the four principal parts of the irregular verb *wake*.
(13, 72)

25. In this sentence, write the participial phrase and the word it modifies: The young woman putting on her batting gloves plans to hit a home run.
(45, 56)

26. Write the word from this list that is divided correctly: pro-toplasm, prot-oplasm, proto-plasm
(84)

27. Write the conjunctive adverb in this sentence: Unfortunately, we found that trail rocky and steep; hence, we shall choose a different route.
(88)

28. In the following sentence, write the verb phrase, name its tense, and label it action or linking: Had Robinson Crusoe been keeping a calendar and a journal?
(17, 18)

Diagram sentences 29 and 30.

29. Having hit a high fly ball to center field, Tamara gleefully ran the bases.
(56, 80)

30. Does the center fielder have a reputation for catching high fly balls?
(21, 56)

LESSON 98

Diagramming the Noun Clause

> **Dictation or Journal Entry**
>
> **Vocabulary:** The Greek prefix *eu-* means "well" or "good."
>
> A *eulogy* is strong praise or commendation either spoken or written. At the retirement dinner, friends gave *eulogies* about those who were retiring.
>
> *Euthanasia* is painless death for a hopeless, suffering patient; mercy killing. Most states regard *euthanasia* as an illegal solution for the terminally ill.
>
> *Euphoria* is feeling of well-being and happiness. Athletes often experience *euphoria* at the end of a challenging workout.

We have learned to diagram a dependent clause that functions as an adjective. In this lesson, we will learn to diagram a dependent clause that functions as a noun—a **noun clause.** We remember that a noun clause may serve as a subject, direct object, object of a preposition, or predicate nominative in a sentence.

SENTENCE SUBJECT

The sentence below contains a noun clause that serves as the subject of the sentence. Notice that we place the entire clause on stilts that sit on the base line where the sentence subject belongs.

Whoever examines Kim's life finds a woman of integrity.

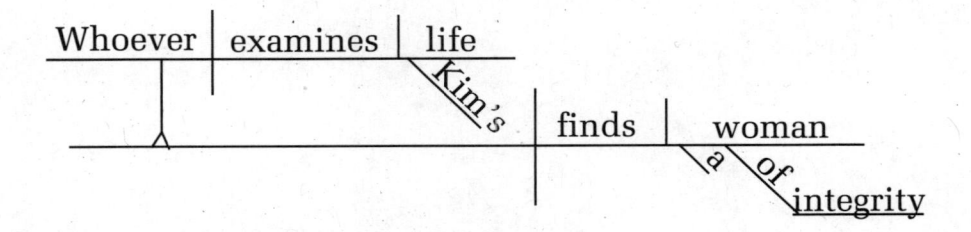

DIRECT OBJECT

The sentence below contains a noun clause that functions as the direct object. We set the clause on the base line where the direct object belongs.

We know *whom we can trust*.

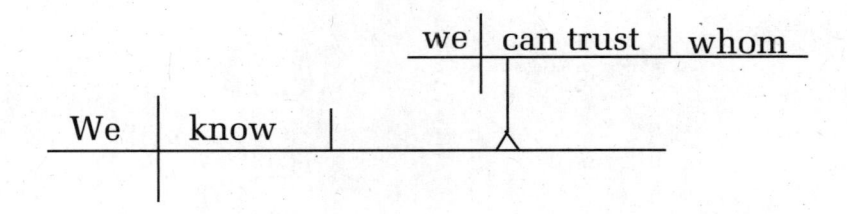

604

OBJECT OF A PREPOSITION

This sentence contains a noun clause that serves as the object of a preposition.

This is a picture of *what I am building.*

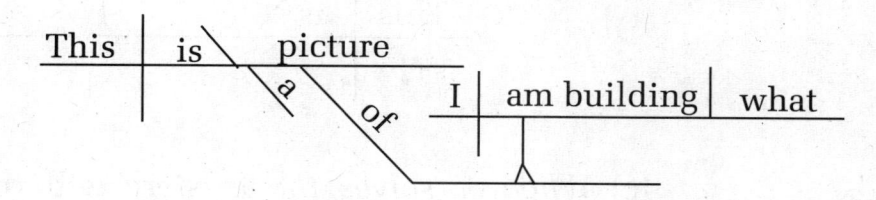

```
This | is \ picture
          \a  \of    I | am building \ what
```

PREDICATE NOMINATIVE

This sentence contains a noun clause that serves as a predicate nominative.

That is *where we are going.*

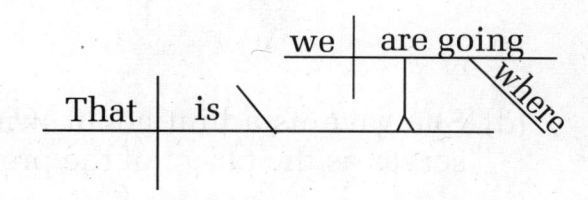

```
                      we | are going \where
That | is \
```

Example Diagram each sentence.

(a) I discovered where she hid the document.

(b) This is what I found.

(c) Whoever solves the mystery will receive a prize.

(d) She gave us a hint about where it was.

Solution (a) I discovered *where she hid the document.* The noun clause functions as a direct object.

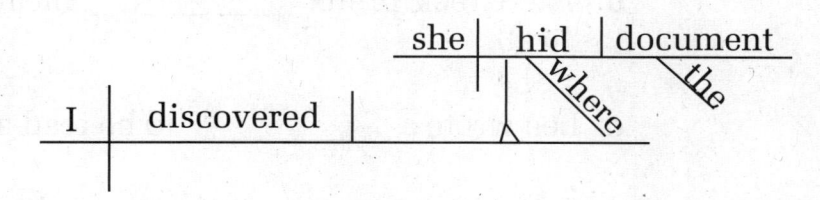

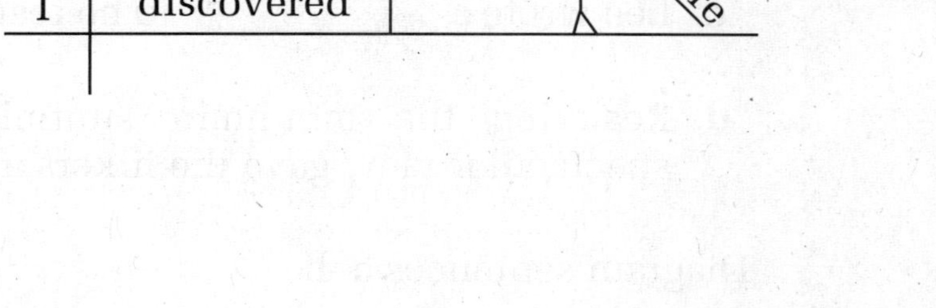

```
                    she | hid | document
                              \where  \the
I | discovered |
```

(b) This is *what I found*. The noun clause serves as a predicate nominative.

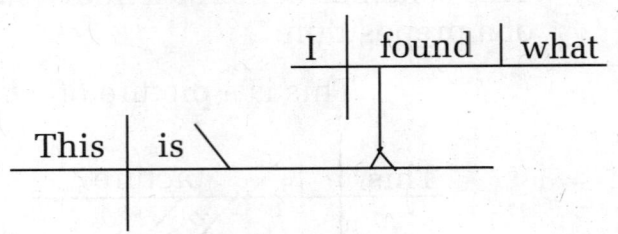

```
                        I │ found │ what
          This │ is  \           △
```

(c) *Whoever solves the mystery* will receive a prize. The noun clause functions as the subject of the sentence.

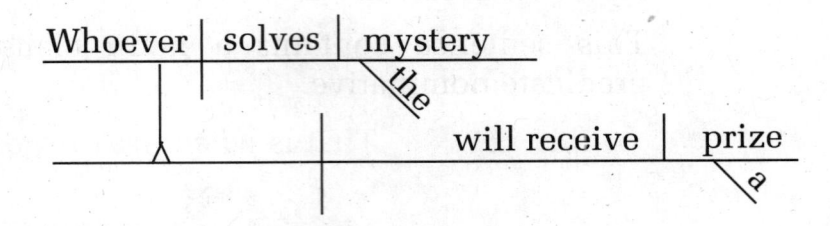

```
     Whoever │ solves │ mystery
                       \the
             △
                    will receive │ prize
                                   \a
```

(d) She gave us a hint about *where it was*. The noun clause serves as the object of the preposition.

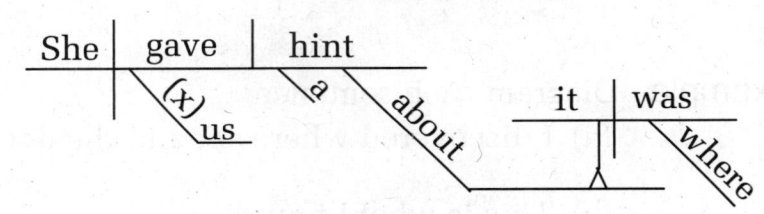

```
    She │ gave │ hint
         \(x)   \a
          \us       \about    it │ was
                                    \where
                              △
```

Practice For a–d, replace each blank with the correct vocabulary word.

    a. Those opposing _____ believe that life and death should lie in God's hands.

    b. The Greek prefix _____ means "good," "true," or "well."

    c. Lee wrote a _____ to be read at his father's funeral.

    d. Reaching the mountain summit and gazing at the spectacular view gave the hikers a sense of _____.

Diagram sentences e–h.

    e. Whatever happens is fine with me.

f. I like what you cook.

g. That is why I am smiling.

h. I wrote a poem about why I like snow.

Review Set 98 Choose the correct word(s) to complete sentences 1–14.

1. The Latin root (*crim-, prob-, rectus*) means "right" or
(97) "straight."

2. An (aid, aide, ade) is an assistant, or helper.
(96)

3. (Primogeniture, Protocol, Suffrage) is a set of rules for
(95) diplomatic conduct.

4. You may repair the roof (any way, anyways, anyway) you
(44) want.

5. A (filibuster, hospice, trajectory) is the curved path taken
(45) by a projectile such as a missile, meteor, or bullet.

6. In a sentence, a(n) (adjective, adverb, noun) clause may
(97, 98) function as a subject, direct object, object of a preposition, or predicate nominative.

7. A (phrase, clause) has both a subject and a predicate.
(20)

8. I found my (long lost, long-lost) history book at the
(82) bottom of my backpack.

9. Please give Scot and (me, myself, I) the combination to
(51, 53) (your, you're) lock.

10. (Brian, Brian's) repairing the tractor allowed me to
(53, 95) harvest the wheat.

11. Does the man (who, whom) coaches the Blue Socks have
(61, 64) a prickly temperament?

12. He (don't, doesn't) have (no, any) patience for
(78) foolishness.

13. Yesterday's fiasco was the (worse, worst) of the two home
(40) games.

14. In fact, it was the (worse, worst) game of the entire season.
₍₄₀₎

15. Rewrite the following sentence so that it is in active voice: Robinson Crusoe's supplies are damaged by a hurricane and an earthquake.
₍₂₇₎

16. Rewrite the following as it is. Then add proofreading symbols to indicate corrections.
_(32, 91)

Crusoe begins too read the bible and seke for giveness.

17. Write the *plural possessive* form of each singular noun.
₍₉₅₎
(a) fox   (b) lady   (c) father-in-law

18. Rewrite the following, adding capital letters and punctuation marks as needed:
_(65, 73)

robinson crusoe comments fear of danger is ten thousand times more terrifying than danger itself

19. Write the four common pairs of correlative conjunctions.
₍₃₅₎

20. Write the superlative form of the adverb *malevolently*.
₍₈₇₎

21. In the following sentence, write whether the underlined part is essential or nonessential: Debby's dog <u>Whipper</u> is a goofy, overweight black Labrador.
_(42, 62)

22. In the following sentence, write each dependent clause, circling each subordinating conjunction: I will call you when I arrive in Palm Beach if the phones are working.
₍₅₄₎

23. Write the objective case, first person, plural personal pronoun.
_(51, 52)

24. Write whether the following is a complete sentence, sentence fragment, or run-on sentence:
₍₂₎

Although Robinson Crusoe has believed himself alone on the island, he spies a human footprint after fifteen years of solitude.

25. In the following sentence, write whether the italicized clause is a noun clause, an adjective clause, or an adverb clause: Crusoe discovers *that cannibals inhabit the island*.
₍₉₇₎

26. Write the conjunctive adverb in the following sentence: Robinson Crusoe captures a cannibal named Friday; consequently, Friday learns a different way of living.
(88)

27. Write and underline each word that should be underlined in the following sentence: Grandpa Walter decided to name his new seafaring vessel Wally's Whaler II.
(69)

28. In the following sentence, write the verb phrase, name its tense, and label it action or linking: Will Crusoe feel safe with Friday?
(3, 18)

Diagram sentences 29 and 30.

29. Did eating fortune cookies bring the Blue Socks amazingly good luck?
(30, 56)

30. Both the coach and the players expect to win their game against the Green Screamers.
(33, 94)

LESSON 99

The Complex Sentence • The Compound-complex Sentence • Diagramming the Adverb Clause

> **Dictation or Journal Entry**
>
> **Vocabulary:** In Greek, *dys-* means "bad" or "difficult." It is the opposite of the Greek prefix *eu-*.
>
> A *dysfunction* is abnormal or impaired functioning. Unfortunately, the mechanic found a *dysfunction* in my car's alternator. *Dysfunctional* means operating in an impaired or abnormal manner. Psychologists label families *dysfunctional* when the needs of its members are not met.
>
> *Dyslexia* is the inability to process words, letters, and numbers in order to read and write effectively. People with *dyslexia* often read or write letters in reverse order.
>
> *Dyspepsia* is indigestion. After eating a jar of chiles, I suffered from *dyspepsia*. *Dyspeptic* means "suffering from *dyspepsia*." It also means "gloomy, despondent, or irritable." The *dyspeptic* librarian muttered to himself as he examined a long list of overdue books.

We have learned how to join two simple sentences, or independent clauses, with a coordinating conjunction to form a compound sentence.

The President smiled, **for** his ratings were good.

↑ independent clause   coordinating conjunction   ↑ independent clause

In a compound sentence, each of the independent clauses can stand alone. They are equal grammatical parts.

The President smiled. = His ratings were good.

Subordinate Clauses   Not all sentences are composed of equal parts. Sometimes a dependent clause is connected to an independent clause. We remember that we can turn an independent clause into a dependent clause, or **subordinate clause**, by adding a subordinating conjunction such as *after*, *although*, *because*, *even though*, *if*, *since*, or *unless*.

The President smiled **because** his ratings were good.

↑ independent clause   subordinating conjunction   ↑ dependent clause

The subordinate clause "because his ratings were good" cannot stand alone; it is dependent on the main clause, "The President smiled."

Complex Sentence A **complex sentence** contains one independent clause and one or more dependent, or subordinate, clauses. In the sentence below we have underlined the independent (main) clause and italicized the subordinating conjunction which introduces the dependent clause.

> <u>The President enjoyed good ratings</u> *even though* some people criticized his foreign policy.

Notice that the subordinate clause above is an *adverb clause* modifying the verb "enjoyed." A complex sentence might also contain a dependent *adjective* or *noun clause.* In the complex sentences below, we have underlined the main clauses and italicized the dependent clauses.

> ADJECTIVE CLAUSE:
> <u>Herbert C. Hoover was the first President</u> *who was born on the west side of the Mississippi.*

> NOUN CLAUSE:
> <u>Grandma says</u> *that Hoover had a slogan, "a chicken in every pot and a car in every garage."*

Compound-complex Sentence A **compound-complex sentence** contains two or more independent clauses and one or more dependent or subordinate clauses. In the compound-complex sentence below, we have underlined the two independent clauses and italicized the subordinating conjunction which introduces the dependent clause.

> <u>Politicians can be impeached</u>, but <u>they may remain in office</u> *if* they are declared "not guilty."

Example 1 For a–d, tell whether each sentence is simple, compound, complex, or compound-complex.

(a) To American politics, Andrew Jackson brought the ways of the West and a whole new generation of leaders.

(b) Andrew Jackson was an extraordinary President since he was born of immigrant parents.

(c) Jackson was a dominant political figure, and he created the Democratic Party even though there was a party-less Era of Good Feelings.

(d) His ascension to power in Washington represented a political, social, and economic revolution; for he was a man of the people.

Solution (a) This is a **simple** sentence—one independent clause.

(b) This sentence is **complex.** It has one independent clause ("Andrew Jackson was an extraordinary President") and one dependent clause ("*since* he was born of immigrant parents").

(c) This is a **compound-complex** sentence. It has two independent clauses ("Jackson was a dominant political figure" and "he created the Democratic Party") and one dependent clause ("*even though* there was a party-less Era of Good Feelings").

(d) This is a **compound** sentence—two independent clauses ("His ascension to power in Washington represented a political, social, and economic revolution" and "he was a man of the people") joined by the coordinating conjunction "for."

Diagramming the Adverb Clause Notice that we diagram the subordinating conjunction on a dotted vertical line connecting the dependent clause (subordinate clause) to the independent clause (main clause). We place the adverb clause below the word that it modifies in the main clause, and diagram it as if it were a separate sentence. The dotted line connects the verb in the dependent clause with the word that the clause modifies.

While the senator presented the plan, we listened carefully.

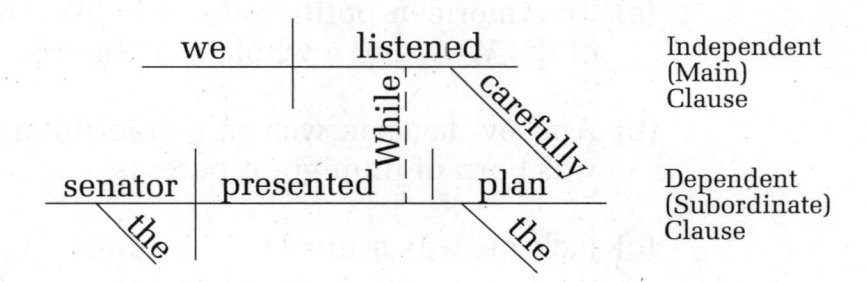

Example 2 Diagram this sentence:

Since the President desires peace, he speaks often to foreign leaders.

Solution We connect the dependent clause to the independent clause with a dotted vertical line upon which we place the subordinating conjunction, "since."

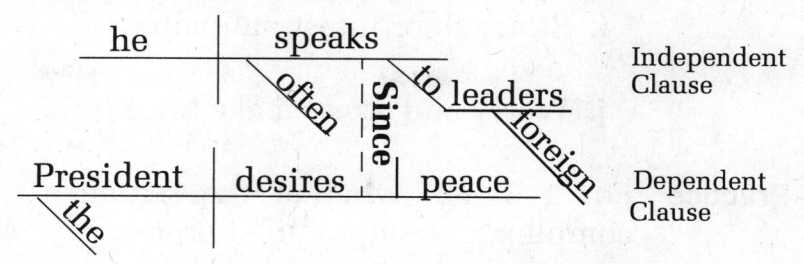

```
           he  |  speaks                    Independent
              \ | /\                        Clause
          often\|  \ to\ leaders
               Since    foreign
      President | desires | peace           Dependent
             \the                           Clause
```

Practice For a–c, tell whether each sentence is simple, compound, complex, or compound-complex.

    a. Do you remember John Jay, a great founder of the United States?

    b. Although Alexander Hamilton and James Madison were the primary authors of *The Federalist Papers*, John Jay wrote five of those articles.

    c. Though President John Adams desired to reappoint John Jay as Chief Justice, Jay refused, for he believed that the Court lacked energy.

    d. Diagram this sentence: After I read the book, I wanted to see the movie. Hint:

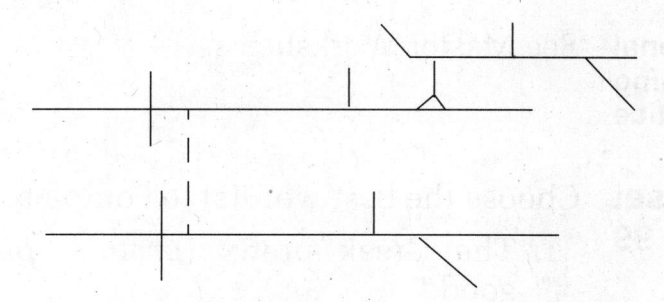

For e–j, replace each blank with the correct vocabulary word.

    e. A person who frequently reverses letters, numbers, or words might have _____.

    f. In the Greek language, _____ means "bad" or "difficult."

    g. My lawn mower doesn't work because of a _____ in its starter.

h. The psychologist says the couple's relationship is _____ since they refuse to speak to one another.

i. Stomach or intestinal pain might indicate _____.

j. Worry and stress make Miss Julia _____.

More Practice For 1–5, tell whether the sentence is simple, compound, complex, or compound-complex.

1. Jonathan's well-constructed bike helmet would keep him safe unless an asteroid hit him.

2. Andy Benito took the road less traveled, for he wasn't afraid to stand alone.

3. The coach urges her players to iron out their differences, to forgive one another, and to enjoy their games.

4. When the leopard escaped, trouble began, and we fled.

5. The dyspeptic treasurer grumbled as he tried to rectify his mathematical error.

6. Diagram this compound-complex sentence: As we sang, Jim fiddled, and people clapped.

Additional Diagramming Practice See Master Worksheets.

Review set 99 Choose the best word(s) to complete sentences 1–16

1. The Greek prefix (*proto-, epi-, eu-*) means "well or good."
(98)

2. To (succumb, comprise, rectify) means "to set right, correct, or adjust."
(97)

3. (Lemonaid, Lemonaide, Lemonade) is a fruit drink.
(96)

4. The root *ject-* means (guest, love, throw).
(45)

5. Fifty states (compose, comprise) the United States of America.
(46)

6. The two sisters, Ann and (her, she), play tennis every weekend.
^(42, 63)

7. Rosa was exhausted last weekend, but now she is feeling (real, really) (good, well).
^(81, 87)

8. From Walter's boat, we spotted a (sixty ton, sixty-ton) blue whale.
^(79, 82)

9. The four types of sentences include declarative, interrogative, imperative, and (transitive, exclamatory, important).
⁽¹⁾

10. Tom would appreciate (you, your) guarding his luggage.
^(50, 53)

11. They hadn't (no, a) choice but to put out the fire (theirselves, themselves).
^(57, 78)

12. The acrimonious remark (that, which) Claudia made in her speech will only exacerbate quarrels in this election.
^(61, 62)

13. The candidate (who, whom) is running against Claudia (don't, doesn't) make acrimonious remarks.
^(61, 64)

14. Crickets chirped, and a full moon (shined, shone) overhead.
^(71, 72)

15. Of the two candidates, which do you like (better, best)?
^(86, 87)

16. We use (*between, among*) when referring to two people, places, or things.
⁽⁹³⁾

17. For a–c, write the possessive form of each noun.
⁽⁹⁵⁾ (a) Ms. Cox   (b) pilgrims   (c) Jonathan Edwards

18. Rewrite the following. Then add proofreading symbols to indicate corrections:
^(32, 91)

Friday an Robin son Crusoe resceu two man from a boiling pot.

19. Rewrite the following, adding capital letters and punctuation marks as needed: Allison's gentle words ameliorate strained relations moreover her magnanimous acts of kindness bring peace
^(47, 88)

20. Write the comparative form of the adverb *loudly*.
(87)

21. In this sentence, write whether the underlined part is essential or nonessential: Jacqueline Kennedy, <u>John F. Kennedy's wife</u>, received wide-spread acclaim for restoring the White House.
(62)

22. In this sentence, write the dependent clause, circling the subordinating conjunction: Questioning Friday, Crusoe learns that his island is near Trinidad.
(54)

23. Write the nominative case, first person, singular personal pronoun.
(50, 52)

24. Write whether the following sentence is simple or compound: Just in time, Robinson Crusoe rescues Friday's father and a Spaniard from the cannibals.
(1, 59)

25. Write whether the italicized clause is a noun clause, an adjective clause, or an adverb clause: I need to clean my room *before company comes.*
(97, 98)

26. Write and underline each word that should be italicized in this sentence: The abbreviation e.g. stands for the Latin words exempli gratia, meaning "for example."
(69)

27. Write the conjunctive adverb in this sentence: Some of the children wore costumes to the harvest festival; for example, Elle came as a duckling.
(88)

28. In this sentence, write the verb phrase, name its tense, and label it transitive or intransitive: Have Crusoe's friends been managing his Brazilian plantation quite well?
(26)

Diagram sentences 29 and 30.

29. I wouldn't have dropped the carton of fresh eggs if you hadn't startled me!
(97, 99)

30. Neither Earl nor Pearl noticed when the eggs began to hatch.
(35, 98)

LESSON 100 — Parallel Structure

> **Dictation or Journal Entry**
>
> **Vocabulary:** The English language borrows many Latin words, such as *bona fide*, *caveat emptor*, and *carpe diem*.
>
> *Bona fide* means "in good faith;" genuine; authentic. She made a *bona fide* promise to return the book within a week.
>
> *Caveat emptor* means "let the buyer beware." A *caveat emptor* philosophy governs the local swap meet.
>
> *Carpe diem* means "seize the day," or "take advantage of the present; enjoy today." Refusing to worry about the future, Kay adopted a *carpe diem* slogan for her life.

Similar Parts   When ideas are similar, they should be expressed in similar form. Parts of sentences that are similar in function should also be expressed in similar form. The balance, consistency, and symmetry resulting from **parallel structure** produces simplicity, elegance, and logic in our writing. Important words strike the eye at once. The second paragraph of the Declaration of Independence provides a perfect example of parallel structure:

> We hold these truths to be self-evident,
> <u>that</u> all men are created equal,
> <u>that</u> they are endowed by their Creator with certain unalienable Rights,
> <u>that</u> among these are Life, Liberty and the pursuit of Happiness.

Notice that the Declaration of Independence uses a series of similarly constructed dependent clauses beginning with the subordinating conjunction *that*. Since the sentence parts in the series are equal in form and function, we call them **parallel**.

Examine the structure of these sentences:

NON-PARALLEL

Thomas Jefferson <u>practiced</u> law, <u>founded</u> the Democratic-Republican party, and <u>serves</u> as President of the American Philosophical Society.
(mixes past and present verb tenses)

PARALLEL

Thomas Jefferson <u>practiced</u> law, <u>founded</u> the Democratic-Republican party, and <u>served</u> as President of the American Philosophical Society.
(series of past tense verbs)

NON-PARALLEL

He likes <u>reading</u>, <u>singing</u>, and <u>to paint</u>. (two gerunds and an infinitive)

PARALLEL

He likes <u>reading</u>, <u>singing</u>, and <u>painting</u>. (series of gerunds)

or

He likes <u>to read</u>, <u>to sing</u>, and <u>to paint</u>. (series of infinitives)

or

He likes to <u>read</u>, <u>sing</u>, and <u>paint</u>. (It is acceptable to drop the *to* in the second and third parts because it is "understood.")

Example 1 Write which sentence has parallel structure. Choose A or B.

A. He tried inventing new things, playing the violin, and to practice law.

B. He tried inventing new things, playing the violin, and practicing law.

Solution Sentence **B** has parallel structure; it contains a series of gerund phrases—"inventing...," "playing...," "practicing...." Sentence *A* is not parallel because it mixes two gerund phrases with the infinitive phrase "to practice law."

Articles and Prepositions We apply an article (definite or indefinite) or a preposition to *all* the parts in the sentence or *only to the first part*.

PARALLEL

Jefferson was the author <u>of</u> "A Summary View of the Rights of British America", <u>of</u> "Causes for Taking Up Arms", and <u>of</u> the Declaration of Independence. (The preposition is applied to *all* the parts.)

or

Jefferson was the author <u>of</u> "A Summary View of the Rights of British America", "Causes for Taking Up Arms", and the Declaration of Independence. (The preposition is applied *only to the first part*.)

PARALLEL

Amelia Earhart flew over <u>the</u> deserts, <u>the</u> mountains, and <u>the</u> farmlands. (The article is applied to *all* the parts.)

or

Amelia Earhart flew over <u>the</u> deserts, mountains, and farmlands. (The article is applied *only to the first part*.)

NON-PARALLEL

> Amelia Earhart flew over <u>the</u> deserts, mountains, and <u>the</u> farmlands. (To make a sentence parallel, we apply the article to *all* the parts or *only to the first part*.)

Example 2 Rewrite each sentence so that it has parallel structure:

(a) Thomas Jefferson was an author, inventor, and a statesman.

(b) Jefferson overthrew Federalist policies by abolishing federal judgeships, by reducing the national debt, and eliminating domestic taxes.

Solution (a) **Thomas Jefferson was <u>an</u> author, <u>an</u> inventor, and <u>a</u> statesman.** We apply the article to *all* the parts.

or

Thomas Jefferson was <u>an</u> author, inventor, and statesman. We apply the preposition *only to the first part*.

(b) **Jefferson overthrew Federalist policies <u>by</u> abolishing federal judgeships, <u>by</u> reducing the national debt, and <u>by</u> eliminating domestic taxes.** We apply the preposition to *all* the parts.

or

Jefferson overthrew Federalist policies <u>by</u> abolishing federal judgeships, reducing the national debt, and eliminating domestic taxes. We apply the preposition *only to the first part*.

Correlative Conjunctions If we write a sentence using a pair of correlative conjunctions (either/or, neither/nor, not only/but also, both/and, whether/or), we must match the parts after each conjunction. Each member of the conjunction pair must be followed by the same kind of construction. For example, if a prepositional phrase follows one correlative conjunction, a prepositional phrase should follow the other.

NON-PARALLEL

> Jefferson *not only* <u>designed the buildings of the University of Virginia</u> *but also* <u>the state capitol building</u>. (The first conjunction is followed by a verb and a noun phrase, the second by a noun phrase but no verb.)

PARALLEL

Jefferson designed *not only* the buildings of the University of Virginia *but also* the state capitol building. (Both conjunctions are followed by noun phrases only.)

NON-PARALLEL

Jefferson was *both* stubborn *and* he was brilliant. (The first conjunction is followed by only a predicate adjective; the second by a subject, a verb, and a predicate adjective.)

PARALLEL

Jefferson was *both* stubborn *and* brilliant. (Each conjunction is followed by a predicate adjective only.)

Example 3 Write which sentence has parallel structure. Choose A or B.

A. We will either visit the Jefferson Memorial or climb the Washington Monument.

B. We will either visit the Jefferson Memorial or the Washington Monument.

Solution Sentence **A** has parallel structure. Both conjunctions are followed by a verb and direct object. Sentence B is not parallel because the parts following the conjunctions are not similar. The first conjunction is followed by a verb and direct object; but the second is followed by only a direct object. We could make Sentence B parallel this way: "We will visit *either* the Jefferson Memorial *or* the Washington Monument."

Practice For a–c, write which sentence has parallel structure. Choose A or B.

a. A. Iona is always hiking, skiing, or she'll play tennis.

B. Iona is always hiking, skiing, or playing tennis.

b. A. She leafed through the books, magazines, and newspapers in search of a recipe.

B. She leafed through the books, magazines, and the newspapers in search of a recipe.

c. A. She desires neither to cook the squash nor eat it.

B. She desires neither to cook the squash nor to eat it.

Rewrite sentences d and e so that they have parallel structure.

d. At the zoo, Gladys photographed a leopard, an elephant, and python.

e. On our voyage, we fought against hunger, thirst, and against fear.

For f–h, replace each blank with the correct vocabulary word.

f. Has that painter signed a _____ contract to create the mural?

g. Hoping to purchase a car, I have a _____ attitude as I wander through the used car lot.

h. Making the most of today, Polly has a _____ philosophy of life.

More Practice With a teacher or friend, read each sentence and note its non-parallel structure. Then reword the sentence so that its structure is parallel. (There is more than one correct answer.) This may be either an oral or a written exercise.

1. Maribel placed her friends' pictures around her room inside her wallet, and put them on her refrigerator.

2. I will leave the key either outside the door or put it inside the house.

3. Hans has neither the time nor does he have the money to take a vacation.

4. Mia studied her Mandarin, called her friend, and walks her dog.

5. This afternoon, she will begin organizing, cleaning, and to pack for the trip.

6. Rawlin has the strength of an ox, the speed of a cheetah, and is wise as an owl.

7. Some people lack the desire, energy, and the conviction to recycle things.

8. While camping she learned that she could survive without computer games, without fast-food restaurants, and her television set.

9. During the summer Mario likes to read historical novels, to play chess, and working jigsaw puzzles.

10. Mr. Li not only grows delicious plums but also large, juicy apricots.

Review Set 100 Choose the correct word(s) to complete sentences 1–16.

1. (99) The Greek prefix (*dys-, cata-, proto-*) means "bad" or "difficult."

2. (97) To rectify is to set (apart, right, down).

3. (98) A eulogy gives (good, bad, questionable) information about a person.

4. (46) The United States of America (composes, comprises) fifty states.

5. (47) Intractable means (noble, stubborn, extravagant).

6. (78) Robinson Crusoe (don't, doesn't) have (no, any) desire to remain in Brazil.

7. (74) Either the Spaniards or Friday's father (return, returns) to the island.

8. (76) Tweezers (was, were) unknown to the natives.

9. (51, 63) Sirob has read several of (them, those) classic books.

10. (50, 63) Daniel Defoe's *Robinson Crusoe* remains a favorite a choice for (us, we) readers.

11. (26) A(n) (transitive, intransitive) verb has no direct object.

12. (87) Robinson Crusoe was (sure, surely) relieved to see England's soil.

13. (53, 76) One of the boys (has, have) the responsibility of feeding (their, his) whole family.

14. (72) The sun (shone, shined) brightly as Tom Canty, a pauper boy, journeyed to the King's palace.

15. The portrait (that, which) hangs above the fireplace might be a hundred years old.

16. From out of nowhere (come, comes) a soldier to arrest Tom Canty.

17. For a–c, write the possessive form of each noun.
(a) people   (b) seamstress   (c) matron of honor

Rewrite 18 and 19, adding capital letters and punctuation marks as needed.

18. dear mr canty

ive wonderful news for you your son tom has switched places with the prince of wales

truly

miles hendon

19. will tom canty find a monk named father andrew at the monastery

20. Write the word from this list that is divided correctly:

dysfunc-tion   dy-sfunc-tion   dys-function

21. In the following sentence, write the personal pronoun and its antecedent: When a soldier snatches up Tom Canty, Prince Edward Tudor comes to his rescue.

22. Write the four principal parts of the verb *eat*.

23. Write the four common pairs of correlative conjunctions.

24. Write whether the sentence below is simple, compound, complex, or compound-complex.

The story begins on a January morning in sixteenth century London, England, as Tom Canty journeys to Charing Village.

25. In the sentence below, write whether the italicized clause is a noun clause, an adjective clause, or an adverb clause.

Mark Twain wrote about an age controlled by nobility and royalty, *which he enjoyed deriding*.

26. In the following sentence, write the participial phrase and the word it modifies: Wearing the Prince's clothes, Tom switches places with the Prince.
(55, 56)

27. Write the conjunctive adverb in the following sentence: Edward experiences the life of a commoner; moreover, he gains insight to the injustices and hardships surrounding the poor.
(88)

28. In the sentence below, write the verb phrase, name its tense, and label it action or linking:
(15, 18)

Miles Hendon, a gentleman, has observed Edward claiming to be Prince.

Diagram sentences 29 and 30.

29. Is Edward's story believable enough to convince Miles?
(28, 86)

30. Will Miles continue protecting Edward from the commoners until Edward returns to the throne?
(55, 56)

LESSON 101

Sentence Conciseness

Dictation or Journal Entry

Vocabulary: *Rog-*, as in *inter__rog__ate*, *ab__rog__ate*, and *ar__rog__ate*, comes from the Latin verb *rogare*, meaning "to ask" or "to propose."

To *interrogate* is to examine by questioning methodically. The police will *interrogate* the suspect.

The Latin prefix *ab-* as in *abrogate* means "from, away," and therefore to *abrogate* means to "propose away," "repeal or annul." The Senate considered *abrogating* the Jay Treaty.

To *arrogate* is to claim or seize without justification. Some senators believed that Andrew Johnson tried to *arrogate* powers that were not his.

Conciseness is the expression of much in few words. Effective writing is concise and clear; it is not cluttered with unnecessary words. In this lesson, we will learn to avoid superfluous words and to reduce wordy clauses and phrases.

Avoiding Superfluous Words

Superfluous words are needless. They do not add to the meaning of the sentence. We can avoid wordiness by eliminating superfluous words and the unnecessary repetition of ideas. Notice the difference between the first and second sentences in the following pairs.

    WORDY: Lilibet has six baby puppies.

    CONCISE: Lilibet has six puppies.

    (*Baby puppies* is redundant, or needlessly repetitive.)

    WORDY: Lilibet's collar is red in color.

    CONCISE: Lilibet's collar is red.

    (The words *in color* are unnecessary because red is a color.)

    WORDY: We have a weekly spelling test every Friday.

    CONCISE: We have a weekly spelling test.

             or

    We have a spelling test every Friday.

    (*Weekly* and *every Friday* are redundant.)

    WORDY: I did well on the test owing to the fact that I had studied.

    CONCISE: I did well on the test because I had studied.

    (The phrase *owing to the fact that* is wordy.)

    WORDY: The list is entirely complete.

    CONCISE: The list is complete.

    (The word *complete* cannot be modified. A thing is either complete, or it isn't.)

Other examples of wordiness include the expressions *very unique* and *slightly impossible.* The words *unique* and *impossible,* like the word *complete,* cannot be modified.

Example 1 Rewrite the following sentences making them more concise.

(a) My train leaves at eight a.m. in the morning.

(b) The big giant fell with a thump.

(c) The noise was barely audible to my ears.

(d) We planted some tiny miniature roses.

(e) In my opinion, I think skydiving is scary.

Solution (a) **My train leaves at eight a.m.** (or) **My train leaves in the morning.** The expressions *a.m.* and *in the morning* are redundant.

(b) **The giant fell with a thump.** The word *big* is unnecessary.

(c) **The noise was barely audible.** *To my ears* is unnecessary since *audible* refers only to the sense of hearing and not to seeing, smelling, tasting, or touching.

(d) **We planted some miniature roses.** (or) **We planted some tiny roses.** *Tiny* and *miniature* are redundant.

(e) **In my opinion, skydiving is scary.** (or) **I think skydiving is scary.** *In my opinion* and *I think* are redundant.

Reducing Wordy Clauses and Phrases

Sometimes we can make our sentences more concise by reducing clauses to phrases, or phrases to single words. Notice how clauses are reduced to phrases or appositives in the sentence pairs below.

CLAUSE: *When I was stuck in traffic,* I listened to the radio.

PARTICIPIAL PHRASE: *Stuck in traffic,* I listened to the radio.

CLAUSE: They decided *that they would take the train.*

INFINITIVE PHRASE: They decided *to take the train.*

CLAUSE: *When the sun rises,* the birds begin to sing.

PREPOSITIONAL
PHRASE: *At sunrise,* the birds begin to sing.

CLAUSE: Mr. Chen, *who is the department head,* wrote the test.

APPOSITIVE: Mr. Chen, *the department head,* wrote the test.

Example 2 Revise the following sentences by reducing the italicized clauses to phrases or appositives.

(a) We will wait for a sale *so that we can save money.*

(b) I am learning a piano piece *that was composed by Mozart.*

(c) I invited Miss Lopez, *who is my English teacher,* to join us.

Solution (a) **To save money, we will wait for a sale.** We reduce the adverb clause to an infinitive phrase.

(b) **I am learning a piano piece *composed by Mozart*.** We reduce the adjective clause to a participial phrase.

(c) **I invited Miss Lopez, *my English teacher*, to join us.** We reduce the adjective clause to an appositive.

Notice how clauses and phrases are reduced to single words in the sentences below.

CLAUSE: We will prune the branches *that have been broken.*
WORD: We will prune the *broken* branches.

PHRASE: His career *in the field of photography* was challenging.
WORD: His *photography* career was challenging.

PHRASE: Let us write *in a concise manner.*
WORD: Let us write *concisely.*

Example 3 Revise the following sentences by reducing the italicized clauses or phrases to single words.

(a) I saw a spider *that was enormous.*

(b) Do you enjoy the music *of Mozart*?

(c) Sally sings *in a harmonious way.*

Solution (a) I saw an *enormous* spider.

(b) Do you enjoy *Mozart's* music?

(c) Sally sings *harmoniously*.

Practice Rewrite sentences a–d, making them more concise.

a. Combine together the sugar, flour, and spices.

b. Should we vote to reelect him again for President?

c. We shall study anthropology for a period of a month.

d. Your writing style is very unique.

Revise sentences e and f by reducing the italicized clauses to phrases of appositives.

e. The rancher *who had come from Iowa* had never seen the ocean.

f. The monument, *which is situated in Colorado*, marks the continental divide.

Revise sentences g and h by reducing the italicized phrases or clauses to single words.

g. We have been reading poetry *that was written by Longfellow*.

h. Hepzy listened *in an attentive manner*.

For i–l, replace each blank with the correct vocabulary word.

i. _____ is a Latin verb meaning "to ask" or "to propose."

j. Authorities plan to _____ that prisoner.

k. The city council voted to _____ the law that banned motor vehicles in the park.

l. The Federal Government will not _____ citizens' lawful possessions.

Review set 101 Choose the correct word(s) to complete sentences 1–16.

1. (*Bona fide, Caveat Emptor, Carpe diem*) means "in good faith."

2. The Greek prefix *dys-* means (true, first, bad).

3. (*Modus operandi,* Gerrymandering, Euthanasia) is mercy killing.

4. The root *tract-* means (power, end, draw).

5. (Any one, Anyone) of the candidates might win the election.

6. The two travelers, Miles and (he, him), received word that King Henry VIII had died.

7. Annalie (sure, surely) outlines her history chapters (good, well).

8. A (compound, simple, complex) sentence contains one independent clause and one or more dependent clauses.

9. Dependent clauses are sometimes called (independent, subordinate) clauses.

10. Julianne says she (don't, doesn't) remember (nothing, anything) about Igor Stravinsky.

11. Jonathan recalls (us, our) discussing Stravinsky's ballet music.

12. Trevor, (who, whom) I reminded about the pizza party, arrived on time.

13. Two simple sentences joined with a (preposition, adverb, coordinating conjunction) form a compound sentence.

14. Of the two volleyball players, who runs (faster, fastest)?

15. Stephanie (shined, shone) her violin before playing it in the concert.

16. Jade sees kindness and loyalty (between, among) Ivana, Kathryn, and Zachary.

17. For a–c, write the possessive form of each plural noun.
(a) stallions (b) apprentices (c) men

Rewrite 18 and 19, adding capital letters and punctuation marks as needed.

18. molly if you wish to avoid dads displeasure warned kurt you will wash the dirty plates cups and spoons

19. johnnys employer mrs lapham gives madge dorcas and cilla permission to marry mr tweedie however the three girls have their own preferences

20. For a–c, write the plural of each singular noun.
(a) calamity (b) Ashley (c) Max

21. Write whether the underlined part of the following sentence is essential or nonessential.
Tomorrow two exceptional students, *Christine and Steven*, will lay a wreath on the Tomb of the Unknown Soldier.

22. Write the superlative form of the adverb *notoriously*.

23. Write the objective case, first person, singular personal pronoun.

24. Write whether the following sentence is simple, compound, complex, or compound-complex: With consistent effort and discipline, Matt will achieve his goals.

25. In the sentence below, write the dependent clause, circling the subordinating conjunction. Then write whether the clause functions as a noun, adjective, or adverb.
Kyle will repair his dune buggy as soon as the engine parts arrive.

26. Write and underline each word that should be italicized in this sentence: Racial discrimination and growth to maturity are two main themes in To Kill a Mockingbird.

27. Write the conjunctive adverb in this sentence: Michael and Domini have not yet completed their persuasive essays; consequently, they will not be watching TV tonight.

28. Rewrite the following sentence so that it has parallel structure: While on vacation, Kalvin plans to stay in a luxurious hotel, eat delicious food, and swimming in a heated pool.
(100, 101)

Diagram sentences 29 and 30.

29. Aaron, who sits in front of the teacher, displays self-control and attentiveness during English class.
(61, 85)

30. After Jeff recovers from the flu, Mrs. Curtis will allow him to take the test on *Johnny Tremain*.
(30, 99)

LESSON 102

Dangling or Misplaced Modifiers

Dictation or Journal Entry

Vocabulary: The word *quis* is related to the Latin verb *quaerere* which means "to seek." We see this meaning in such words as *inquisition*, *acquisitive*, and *requisition*.

An *inquisition* is strict, thorough inquiry or questioning. The Spanish *Inquisition* was a Roman Catholic tribunal established in the thirteenth century for the trial of heretics.

Acquisitive is an adjective meaning greedy or eager to acquire. The *acquisitive* nation invaded neighboring countries and governed them by force.

A *requisition* is an official written request. The teachers filled out *requisitions* for classroom supplies needed for the school year. A *requisition* can also be the act of taking. The army's *requisition* of vehicles left few for civilians to drive.

Dangling Modifiers

A **dangling modifier** is a participle, infinitive, or gerund that has no clear subject to modify. Consider the sentence pairs below. Modifiers are underlined.

UNCLEAR—DANGLING MODIFIER

<u>Having achieved emancipation for slaves</u>, it was time to reconcile with the South. (Which word does the phrase modify?)

CLEAR

<u>Having achieved emancipation for slaves</u>, *the North* needed to reconcile with the South. (The phrase modifies the subject, "the North.")

UNCLEAR—DANGLING MODIFIER

The assassination occurred while <u>watching a play</u>. (Was the *assassination* watching a play?)

CLEAR

The assassination occurred while *President Lincoln* <u>was watching a play</u>. (The phrase now has a subject, "President Lincoln.")

Misplaced Modifiers

Some modifiers cause confusion when they are out of place. We place modifiers as close as possible to the words or phrases they modify. Examine the **misplaced modifiers** in the sentences below.

Participle Phrases

We are especially careful to place participle phrases near the words they modify.

MISPLACED MODIFIER

I saw a picture of Abraham Lincoln <u>walking through a museum</u>. (Was a *picture of Lincoln* walking through a museum?)

CORRECTED SENTENCE

<u>Walking through a museum</u>, I saw a picture of Abraham Lincoln. (We move the participle phrase closer to the subject, "I.")

MISPLACED MODIFIER

<u>Written harshly</u>, Abraham Lincoln vetoed the Wade-Davis Reconstruction Bill. (Was *Abraham Lincoln* written harshly?)

CORRECTED SENTENCE

Abraham Lincoln vetoed the <u>harshly written</u> Wade-Davis Reconstruction Bill. (Yes, the *bill* was harshly written.)

Prepositional Phrases We also place prepositional phrases close to the words they modify.

MISPLACED MODIFIER

The lobbyists attempted to explain <u>before lunch</u> what Congress had accomplished. (Does *before lunch* tell when the lobbyists attempted to explain, or does it tell when Congress had accomplished something?)

CORRECTED SENTENCE

<u>Before lunch</u>, the lobbyists attempted to explain what Congress had accomplished. (Now it is clear that the lobbyists attempted to explain *before lunch*.)

or

The lobbyists attempted to explain what Congress had accomplished <u>before lunch</u>. (Now it is clear that Congress had accomplished something *before lunch*.)

MISPLACED MODIFIER

<u>Without insight</u>, the tasks overwhelmed the new Senator. (Were the *tasks* without insight?)

CORRECTED SENTENCE

The tasks overwhelmed the new Senator without insight. (Clearly, *the new Senator* lacked insight.)

Example For each pair of sentences, tell which is more clear. Choose A or B.

(a) A. Henry Cabot Lodge pondered the Treaty of Versailles rocking in a chair.

B. Rocking in a chair, Henry Cabot Lodge pondered the Treaty of Versailles.

(b) A. With help from fellow leaders, the idea seemed plausible.

B. With help from fellow leaders, he found the idea plausible.

(c) A. Objecting to the treaty, Henry Cabot Lodge led the United States into isolationism.

B. Objecting to the treaty, isolationism began in the United States.

Solution (a) Sentence **B** is more clear. The participal phrase, "rocking in a chair," is close to the subject, "Henry Cabot Lodge," the person doing the rocking. Sentence *A* says that *the Treaty of Versailles* was rocking in a chair. The sentence has a misplaced modifier.

(b) Sentence **B** is more clear. The prepositional phrase, "with help from fellow leaders," modifies the subject, "he." In sentence *A*, the prepositional phrase is dangling; it has no subject to modify. It sounds like the *idea* had help from fellow leaders.

(c) Sentence **A** is more clear. The participal phrase, "objecting to the treaty" is near the subject, "Henry Cabot Lodge." In sentence *B*, the participal phrase is dangling; it has no subject to modify. It sounds like *isolationism* was objecting to the treaty.

Practice For a–d, tell which sentence is more clear. Choose A or B.

a. A. Acting like a gadfly, his strong political base made Huey Long influential in Congress.

B. Acting like a gadfly, Huey Long became influential through his strong political base.

b. A. At the meeting, Wang realized what had happened.

B. Wang realized at the meeting what had happened.

c. A. Historians discovered a "dandy" researching Nicholas Longworth.

B. Researching Nicholas Longworth, historians discovered a "dandy."

d. A. Popular and fair, one of the House buildings is named after Nicholas Longworth.

B. The House named one of its buildings after the popular and fair Nicholas Longworth.

For e–h, replace each blank with the correct vocabulary word.

e. We remember King Midas's _____, greedy behavior in legends written by Greek and Roman authors.

f. Please fill out a _____ for any equipment that you will need for your job.

g. The Latin verb _____ means "to seek."

h. The _____ by the authorities was justified by the seriousness of the crime.

More Practice With your teacher or with a friend, read each sentence and answer these questions orally for each sentence: (1) What is wrong with this sentence? (2) What do you think the writer meant to say?

1. Eating dinner, my fork flipped off the table.

2. Having been written and revised, France was ready to accept the document of the Louisiana Purchase.

3. Yin saw an orangutan on the way to school.

4. Doubling its size, France agreed to sell the Louisiana Territory to the United States.

5. Tying my shoe, the bus left without me.

6. Leaving the Old Senate Chamber, the seats were empty.

7. Thomas Jefferson found a loophole examining the Constitution.

8. Attempting to act quickly, the law passed in Congress.

9. Being cold and windy, Mom recommended we come inside.

10. Tui wanted to know after class what the teacher said to her friend.

11. Boiling potatoes, a fly landed in the pot.

12. Blocking traffic, I could hardly wait till the road construction was finished.

Review Set 102

Choose the correct word(s) to complete sentences 1–15.

1. The Latin verb (*currere, rogare, flectere*) means "to ask" or "to propose."
   (101)

2. (*Bona fide, Caveat emptor, Carpe diem*) means "let the buyer beware."
   (100)

3. A dysfunction is (proper, excellent, impaired) functioning.
   (99)

4. Have you painted (every one, everyone) of the windows?
   (48)

5. (Every one, Everyone) in my family has brown eyes.
   (48)

6. There (ain't, aren't) (no, any) young people named Lisa or Allan in this room.
   (78)

7. Everyone in the classroom (enjoy, enjoys) socializing with (their, his or her) neighbor.
   (75, 76)

8. Derek presented me with a (hand-drawn, hand drawn) portrait of Darlene.
   (82)

9. Sirob has more homework than (her, she).
   (63)

10. (Us, We) contestants hope to be selected for this season's game show.
    (50, 63)

11. A sentence containing two or more independent clauses and one or more dependent clauses is called a (simple, compound, complex, compound-complex) sentence.
    (99)

12. Darron was (real, really) prepared for the class discussion of the San Andreas fault.
    (89)

13. Both the boys and Megan (attend, attends) the weight lifting classes.
(75, 76)

14. Before the alarm sounded, Tan had already (rose, risen) for his morning walk.
(71, 72)

15. Long, silky black hair, (that, which) shone in the sunlight, fell softly around Jaimie's face.
(62)

16. Rewrite this sentence to make it more concise: The baby kittens were meowing in a soft manner.
(101)

17. For a–c, write the possessive form of each noun.
(95) (a) Andy   (b) The Yans   (c) Mr. Kruis

Rewrite 18 and 19, adding capital letters and punctuation marks, and making necessary changes to abbreviations for formal writing.

18. dr breanna walker i hope will perform mrs buxtons kidney transplant scheduled for thurs oct 26 at 9 am
(31, 47)

19.   where is your assignment asked professor chen
(9, 65)   it is finished whispered jon but i left it at home

20. Write the four principal parts of the irregular verb *teach*.
(13, 72)

21. Use an appositive to make one sentence from these two sentences: Louisa May Alcott was a nurse during the American Civil War. She wrote classic novels such as *Little Women* and *Little Men*, which depict a deep sense of family loyalty and intimacy.
(42, 43)

22. Write the word from this list that is divided correctly: pro-totype, proto-type, protot-ype
(84)

23. In this sentence, write each personal pronoun and its antecedent: Denver forgot to retrieve his grammar book from the playground, and it was ruined by the rain.
(46)

24. Write whether the following sentence is simple, compound, complex, or compound-complex: Yesterday, Brian's head throbbed intensely, but today he feels fine.
(99)

25. In the sentence below, write the dependent clause, circling the subordinating conjunction. Then write
(54, 99)

whether the clause functions as a noun, adjective, or adverb.

Ruben's suggestion that we postpone the math test elicited a laugh from Mr. Green.

26. In this sentence, write whether the verb is in the active or passive voice: Danielle was thrilled by her perfect score on the grammar test.
(27)

27. Write the conjunctive adverb in this sentence: Michael Hsu responded intelligently to the question about Norman Rockwell's painting; moreover, he gave insightful information about Rockwell's life and times.
(88)

28. Rewrite this sentence so that it has parallel structure: Ashley's chores include washing the dishes, mopping the floor, and to feed the dog.
(100)

Diagram sentences 29 and 30.

29. Describing the funny incident to Sam sent Derek into fits of laughter.
(36, 56)

30. Mr. Lopez instantly grew silent when the masked bandit asked for the attention of the group.
(61, 85)

LESSON 103

Parentheses • Brackets

> **Dictation or Journal Entry**
>
> **Vocabulary:** The *ple-* found in words such as *complete*, *complement*, *deplete*, and *replete* comes from a Latin word meaning "to fill."
>
> A *complement* is that which completes or makes perfect. Some say that salt is the *complement* of pepper.
>
> To *deplete* is to reduce considerably; to use up, or exhaust. Notice that the *de* in this word undoes the *ple-*. After a long drought, our water supply was *depleted*.
>
> *Replete* means filled; abundantly supplied; overflowing. I laughed till tears streamed down my face, for the movie was *replete* with silliness and slapstick humor.

Parentheses We use **parentheses** to enclose a thought only loosely related to the main idea of the sentence. Parentheses can enclose additional or explanatory information, personal commentary, figures, or examples that are not essential to the sentence and are not intended to be a part of it grammatically. A single word or figure, a phrase, or an entire sentence can be enclosed in parentheses. (The singular form of *parentheses* is *parenthesis*. Remember, however, that parentheses are always used in pairs.)

Additional Information In the sentences below, the information enclosed in parentheses is additional, but nonessential, information.

On the New England tour, we visited Boston and Cape Cod (in addition to other places).

William Maclay (although an Antifederalist) described in detail the first Senate Committees and the early lobbyists.

Clarifying Meaning or Figures We use parentheses around words or figures that are included to explain or clarify meaning.

Faneuil Hall (Boston) served as a meeting place for the Revolutionaries.

Minutemen (civilians who were prepared to fight at a moment's notice) fought the British at Lexington Green.

There were five (5) casualties in the Boston Massacre.

Personal Commentary In informal writing, we can use parentheses around words that express our personal thoughts about something in the sentence.

www.saxonhomeschool.com
©Houghton Mifflin Harcourt Publishers, Inc.

639

Grammar and Writing 8
Student Edition, 9781419098581

The Boston Tea Party (it's always made me chuckle) involved colonists who dumped three hundred forty-two chests of tea, valued at more than ten thousand pounds, into the harbor.

Boston and the rest of New England (have you ever been there?) is beautiful in the fall.

Punctuation with Parentheses

All of the *sentence's* punctuation marks are placed outside the parentheses.

YES: If you have questions, ask Jenny (my cousin).

NO: If you have questions, ask Jenny (my cousin.)

If the *words in parentheses* require a question mark or exclamation mark, we place it inside the parentheses. However, we never include a period if the parentheses are within a sentence.

YES: Our camp counselor (he's a clown!) fixes our meals.

NO: Andy (you'll remember him from camp.) will inspect the cabins.

If parentheses are inserted into a sentence where a comma, colon, or semicolon would normally occur, the punctuation is placed after the parentheses.

YES: If Dalia is elected mayor (please vote for her), crime will decrease.

YES: We could not sail yesterday (Monday); the wind was too strong.

Example 1 Rewrite sentences a and b below and add parentheses where they are needed.

(a) We saw a portrait of James Madison now called the Father of the Constitution in the art gallery.

(b) The Boston Tea Party involved colonists who dumped three hundred forty-two 342 chests of tea, valued at more than ten thousand pounds 10,000 £, into the harbor.

(c) I had three incorrect answers on the test phooey!, but I remembered that Francis Scott Key wrote the national anthem.

Solution   (a) The words "now called the Father of the Constitution" provide additional but nonessential information, so we enclose them in parentheses.

We saw a portrait of James Madison (now called the Father of the Constitution) in the art gallery.

(b) We enclose 342 and 10,000 £ in parentheses to confirm the numbers.

The Boston Tea Party involved colonists who dumped three hundred forty-two (342) chests of tea, valued at more than ten thousand pounds (10,000 £), into the harbor.

(c) We enclose the personal commentary in parentheses. The comma goes after the parentheses.

I had three incorrect answers on the test (phooey!), but I remembered that Francis Scott Key wrote the national anthem.

Brackets   We use **brackets** to insert our own words (additions, explanations, comments, etc.) into quoted material.

The Marine explained, "The U.S. Marine Band [known as the President's own] is a unit of the U.S. Marine Corps."

"In addition," said the Marine, "the Marine Band [established on July 11, 1798] is the oldest musical organization in the U.S. armed forces."

"I [Martin Luther King, Jr.] have a dream…"

Professor Gladly taught, "John Philip Sousa's new marches ["Semper Fidelis" and "The Washington Post"] inspired a dance craze in the United States and Europe."

Example 2   In the sentence below, use brackets to enclose words that are not a part of the direct quotation.

The historian shared, "Recordings of his John Sousa's marches were made for Thomas Edison's phonograph."

Solution   **[John Sousa's]** is not a part of the direct quotation. These words were inserted by the writer to make clear who "his" refers to.

Practice For sentences a–d, insert parentheses or brackets as needed.

a. The lecturer said, "He Thurgood Marshall was the first African-American justice of the Supreme Court."

b. When he presented a list of two hundred five 205 known communists, Joseph R. McCarthy became a household name.

c. Mavericks disruptive people in Congress slowed down action on the bill.

d. My friend earned a hundred dollars wow! mowing people's lawns.

For e–h, replace each blank with the correct vocabulary word.

e. Jelly may be the _____ of peanut butter on a sandwich.

f. The word part _____ comes from the Latin word meaning "to fill."

g. Vigorous exercise in warm weather can _____ the body of water and minerals.

h. Their garden is _____ with flowering bushes and singing birds.

Review Set 103 Choose the best word(s) to complete sentences 1–15.

1. The root (*vor-, curr-, quis*) comes from a Latin word meaning "to seek."
   (102)

2. The Latin verb *rogare* means to (run, bend, ask).
   (101)

3. (*Bona fide, Caveat emptor, Carpe diem*) means "seize the day."
   (100)

4. A (retraction, plutocrat, deduction) is a conclusion made by reasoning.
   (49)

5. You might place a letter in an (envelope, envelop).
   (50)

6. Tomorrow, Chris and (her, she) will present their pumpkins at the carving contest.
   (50, 52)

7. Kim played soccer (real, really) (good, well) today.

8. We try to use (passive, active) voice whenever possible.

9. Verb phrases in the (passive, active) voice contain a form of "to be."

10. Patil didn't know (anything, nothing) about Jonathan Edwards prior to her history class.

11. Did Dustin anticipate (us, our) reading the essays aloud?

12. The contestant (who, whom) wins the grand prize will accompany Ms. Roberts to the country fair.

13. The verb *apologize* is (transitive, intransitive).

14. Of all Dean's friends, who works (harder, hardest)?

15. A car's headlights (shined, shone) from afar.

16. Rewrite this sentence to make it more concise: Skylar, Brycen, and Madeline have written a story that is superb.

17. For a–c, write the possessive form of each noun.
(a) Ms. Vargas   (b) The Vargases   (c) Wednesday

18. Rewrite the following sentence, adding the necessary punctuation marks and underlining each word that should be italicized: Adelina tried to reassure the worried Nicaraguan sisters with the following words Para Dios no hay nada imposible.

19. Rewrite this sentence, adding capital letters and punctuation marks as needed: i cycle every day to keep in shape and i havent had a flat tire yet declared mr sousa

20. For a–c, write the plural form of each noun.
(a) Rufus   (b) gratuity   (c) lady-in-waiting

21. Which sentence is clearer? Choose A or B.

A. Jan photographed a pelican using her digital camera.

B. Using her digital camera, Jan photographed a pelican.

22. Write the comparative form of the adverb *succinctly*.
(87)

23. Write the possessive case, first person, plural personal pronoun.
(52)

24. Write whether the following sentence is simple, compound, complex, or compound-complex: Since Corey received one low test score, he has studied harder and raised his grades.
(99)

25. In the sentence below, write the dependent clause, circling the subordinating conjunction. Then write whether the clause functions as a noun, adjective, or adverb.
(54, 97)

People smiled as Samantha guided the Shetland pony through the market place.

26. In this sentence, write whether the verb is in the active or passive voice: Jade's unfortunate accident at the volleyball game has ended her playing season.
(27)

27. Write the conjunctive adverb in this sentence: On the basketball court, my brother lacks experience and maturity; on the other hand, he has speed, agility, and intelligence.
(88)

28. Rewrite this sentence so that it has parallel structure: Sam says he bought a bike, helmet, and a tire pump.
(100)

Diagram sentences 29 and 30.

29. Sprinting magnificently, Robert shows his determination to win the race.
(56, 97)

30. Not only Mrs. Cho but also Mr. Atwater had urged students to study for the science exam.
(35, 100)

LESSON 104 — Interjections

> **Dictation or Journal Entry**
>
> **Vocabulary:** The Latin root *son-* means "sound."
>
> A *sonata* is a type of music written for one or two instruments. The student composed a *sonata* for the piano.
>
> *Sonorous* means producing a deep, full, or rich sound. The *sonorous* echo could be heard five miles away.
>
> *Dissonant* means harsh, clashing, or unpleasant in sound. *Dissonant* musical compositions disturb my dog Ruff and cause him to howl.

Interjections   A word or short phrase used to show strong emotion is called an **interjection**. An interjection is one of the eight parts of speech. It can express excitement, happiness, joy, rage, surprise, pain, or relief. Interjections are italicized below.

Hey! Where are you going?

Yikes! The ice is slippery.

Aha, I found the missing puzzle piece.

Oh dear, this is an important election.

An interjection is not a sentence and has no relationship with the words around it. For this reason, it is usually set apart from the rest of the sentence by some sort of punctuation. Generally, an exclamation point follows an interjection, but, if the emotion is not very intense, a comma follows the interjection.

INTENSE: *Bravo!* You passed the test.

NOT INTENSE: *Oh yes*, I recall Harry Truman.

Below is a list of common interjections. Notice that sounds can be interjections too.

ah	oh dear	ugh	man
aha	oh my	uh oh	drat
bam	oh yes	well	oops
boy	far out	yippee	bravo
oh no	whee	good grief	okay
whoops	goodness	ouch	wow
hey	ow	yikes	hooray
phew	yuck	hurrah	pow
boo	oh	shh	whew

We must not overuse interjections. They lose their effectiveness when used too frequently.

Example 1 Write each interjection that you find in a–d.

(a) I made it in time for the Morning Hour. Phew!

(b) The morning announcements have begun. Shh!

(c) Good grief! I forgot who originated the New Deal.

(d) Oh yes, it was Franklin D. Roosevelt.

Solution (a) **Phew** (b) **Shh**

(c) **Good grief** (d) **Oh yes**

Diagramming We diagram interjections like this:

Hurrah! We've almost finished this book.

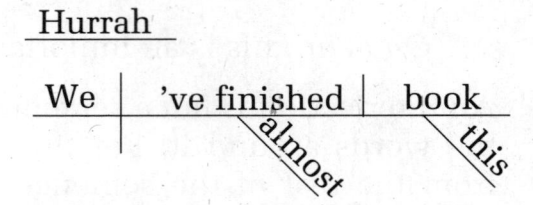

Example 2 Diagram this sentence:

Drat, I forgot to turn off the water.

Solution We place the interjection on a line apart from the rest of the sentence.

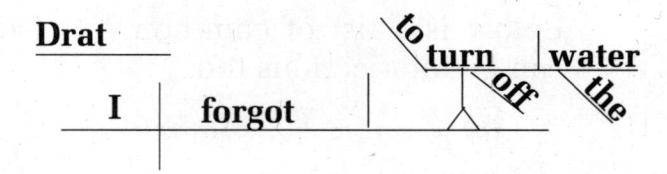

Practice Write the interjection that you find in a–d.

a. Ah, John F. Kennedy coined the New Frontier.

b. During President Kennedy's term the country faced many challenges. Goodness!

c. Well, Richard M. Nixon was a very young Vice President.

d. Maybe we can tour the Capitol. Cool!

Diagram e and f.

e. Uh oh, we missed the bus.

f. Oops, that note sounds dissonant.

For g–j, replace each blank with the correct vocabulary word.

g. Some people enjoy _____ music, but most people prefer harmonious music.

h. _____ is the Latin root meaning "sound."

i. The composer wrote a _____ for the violin and flute.

j. The baritone was heard throughout the auditorium, for he had a _____ voice.

Review set 104

Choose the best word(s) to complete sentences 1–14.

1. The word part *ple-* comes from a Latin word meaning to (seek, run, fill).
(103)

2. The word *quis* comes from a Latin word meaning to (run, lead, seek).
(102)

3. To (flare, repeal, interrogate) is to examine by questioning.
(101)

4. A deduction is a (problem, conclusion, crime).
(49)

5. A (bureaucrat, sequence, deduction) is a fixed order of one thing following after another.
(51)

6. There (isn't, ain't, aren't) (anyone, no one) in the gym on Sunday mornings.
(78)

7. One of the perfidious pirates (leave, leaves) (their, his) footprints in the sand.
(75)

8. Perhaps Mrs. Zertuche has read more Shakespeare than (me, I).
(63)

9. The mousse that Christie made was (chocolate-covered, chocolate covered).
(79, 82)

10. At the Globe Theater, Shakespeare's *The Tempest*
(50, 63) provided (us, we) spectators many laughs.

11. The actors (sure, surely) performed (well, good).
(81, 89)

12. A phrase that does not clearly modify a certain word is
(65, 102) called a (direct quotation, dangling modifier, passive voice).

13. Either the courtiers or Ariel (has, have) the best part in
(35, 76) the play.

14. Antonio, the character (that, which) Prospero tolerates,
(62) fails to usurp Prospero's power.

15. Rewrite this sentence to make it more concise: Using
(101) scraps of wood, Maggie made a birdhouse that was very unique.

16. In the following sentence, write the verb phrase, name its
(17, 18) tense, and label it action or linking:

For how many years has *The Tempest* been bringing laughter to theaters?

17. For a–c, write the possessive form of each noun.
(95) (a) island   (b) Laertes   (c) philosophers

18. Rewrite the following, underlining each word that should
(47, 103) be italicized and adding punctuation marks (including brackets or parentheses) as needed:

Reading the Global Review Mrs Sykes discovered that tickets for balcony seats cost two hundred fifty dollars $250 each but she and Lauren are still going to see The Tempest.

19. Rewrite the following, adding capital letters and
(60, 65) punctuation marks as needed:

i think said mrs sykes to her daughter that experiencing a live play will change your opinion of william shakespeare

20. Use an appositive to make one sentence from these two
(42, 43) sentences: Prospero is the rightful Duke of Milan. Prospero is the main character in *The Tempest*.

21. Which sentence is clearer? Choose A or B.
(101)

    A. Mrs. Sykes looked under her theater seat and saw a little mouse holding the stub of her expensive ticket.

    B. Holding the stub of her expensive ticket, Mrs. Sykes looked under her theater seat and saw a little mouse.

22. In the following sentence write whether the underlined part is an essential or nonessential part:
(42, 43)

My friend <u>Susan</u> will interrogate the masked bandit.

23. Write the four principal parts of the irregular verb *drive*.
(70)

24. Write whether the following sentence is simple, compound, complex, or compound-complex:
(59, 99)

Food and drink from Gonzalo, a counselor on ship, save Prospero.

25. In the sentence below, write the dependent clause, circling the subordinating conjunction. Then write whether the clause functions as a noun, adjective, or adverb.
(54, 97)

Caliban, a deformed savage, does not appreciate that Prospero treats him kindly.

26. Rewrite this sentence using active voice: A storm is called up by Prospero.
(27)

27. Rewrite the following sentence, adding punctuation as needed and circling the conjunctive adverb:
(88)

Prospero gives his governmental power to Antonio however Prospero does not approve of Antonio's seizure of the throne

28. Rewrite the following sentence so that it has parallel structure:
(100)

Antonio takes the reins of government, captured Prospero and Miranda, and sets them adrift at sea.

Diagram sentences 29 and 30.

29. Mrs. Sykes, whom we talked about, drives great distances
(21, 61) to see Shakespeare plays.

30. Both Trinculo and Stephano are drunken courtiers, but
(35, 59) Gonzalo is a kind philosopher.

LESSON 105 Dictionary Information about a Word

> **Dictation or Journal Entry**
>
> **Vocabulary:** The root *err-* from the Latin word *errare,* meaning "to wander" or "to stray," appears in the words <u>*aberr*</u>*ant,* <u>*err*</u>*atic,* and <u>*err*</u>*oneous.*
>
> *Aberrant* means straying from that which is usual, normal, or correct. The horse's *aberrant* behavior indicated that something was wrong with it.
>
> *Erratic* means having no fixed course; inconsistent or irregular. The patient's EKG revealed an *erratic* heartbeat.
>
> *Erroneous* means mistaken or incorrect. First impressions may give us *erroneous* opinions of people.

Definitions A dictionary's main function is to provide word meanings. Since a single word may have many meanings, we carefully read all its definitions.

Parts of Speech Usually, an italicized abbreviation indicates the part of speech of the word being defined. A dictionary's front or back matter explains its abbreviations, like the ones below.

n.	noun	*v.*	verb
adj.	adjective	*adv.*	adverb
pron.	pronoun	*prep.*	preposition
conj.	conjunction	*interj.*	interjection
vt.	transitive verb	*vi.*	intransitive verb

Spelling The boldfaced word that begins a dictionary entry gives the accepted spelling. If there are two or more accepted spellings, these are given as well. The dictionary also provides the spelling of irregular plurals, principal parts of verbs, comparative or superlative forms of adjectives, and other grammatical changes in word forms.

Syllable Division We have learned to divide a word between its syllables when the word must be divided at the end of a line. The boldfaced dictionary entry shows syllable division by a dot or by a space.

con·gress   con gress

Pronunciation Using a fixed symbol for each of the common English sounds, the pronunciation guide respells the entry word with accent marks to show which syllables are spoken with more stress than the others. A heavier mark indicates the heaviest accent, or stress on the syllable; a lighter mark indicates a lighter accent.

tech·ni·cal·ity   tek´ ni kal´ ə tē

Etymologies   **Etymologies** are word histories showing the word's original language and meaning. Usually, the dictionary's front matter explains abbreviations used to indicate the languages from which words come. The symbol < or the abbreviation *fr.* may mean "from." See examples below.

DICTIONARY ABBREVIATION	MEANING
< F	from French
< Heb-Aram	from Hebrew-Aramaic
fr. OE	from Old English
< Gr	from Classical Greek
< Heb	from Hebrew
fr. L	from Latin

Field Labels   Some dictionary words are not part of our general vocabulary but have to do with a special subject, area, or usage. These words may have **field labels** such as the ones below.

SUBJECT LABELS

Med. (medicine)   *Chem.* (chemistry)
Zool. (zoology)   *Music*
Baseball   *Comput.* (Computer Science)

AREA LABELS

Netherl. (Netherlandic)   *Scotland*
Northwest U.S.   *NGmc* (North Germanic)

USAGE LABELS

Dialect   *Slang*   *Rare*
Informal   *Old-fashioned*   *Literary*
Archaic   *Obsolete*   *Vulgar*

Synonyms and Antonyms   At the end of an entry, a dictionary may list **synonyms** (SYN, words of similar meaning) and/or **antonyms** (ANT, words of opposite meaning).

Example Use a dictionary to complete the following.

(a) Write two different definitions for the word *etiology*.

(b) Write the part of speech indicated by the dictionary for the word *eucalyptus*.

(c) Write two accepted spellings for the plural of *eucalyptus*.

(d) Rewrite the word *opportunistic* showing its syllable division.

(e) Rewrite the word *opaque* showing its pronunciation, including accent marks.

(f) The word *resuscitate* comes from what language?

(g) Write the field label given to the word *pianissimo*.

Solution (a) Answers will vary. **1. the assignment of a cause. 2. the science of causes or origins.**

(b) **noun**   (c) **eucalyptuses, eucalypti**

(d) **op·por·tun·is·tic**   (e) **ō pāk´**

(f) **Latin**   (g) *Music*

Practice Use a dictionary to answer a–g.

a. Write two different meanings for the word *disregard*.

b. The word *dispersion* is what part of speech?

c. Write two accepted spellings for the plural of *effluvium*.

d. Rewrite the word *effervescent* showing its syllable division.

e. Rewrite the word *efficacious* showing its pronunciation.

f. Write the origin of the word *fricative*.

g. Write the field label given to the word *stapes*.

For h–k, replace each blank with the correct vocabulary word.

h. The bird's _____ flight made it difficult to keep the bird in the viewfinder of my camera.

i. The Latin word _____ means "to wander" or "to stray."

j. Joseph R. McCarthy's _____ behavior resulted in his censure by the Senate in 1954.

k. Unfortunately, my figures were _____; I do not have as much money in the bank as I thought.

Review set 105

Choose the correct word(s) to complete sentences 1–15.

1. The Latin root (*ple-, ven-, son-*) means "sound."
   (104)

2. A (jurisdiction, stoic, complement) is that which completes or makes perfect.
   (103)

3. The words inquisition and (dysfunction, interrogation, credence) have similar meanings.
   (102)

4. A sequence is a(n) (tax, order, gadget).
   (51)

5. Hans is disinterested; he is (neutral, indifferent, unconcerned).
   (52)

6. There (isn't, ain't, aren't) (anyone, no one) in the audience who likes Antonio.
   (78)

7. The following expression is a (phrase, clause): the storm called up by Prospero
   (20, 54)

8. The two usurpers, Alonso and Antonio, will (sure, surely) learn the consequences of bad choices on Prospero's island.
   (89, 93)

9. The survivors, Miranda and (him, he), meet Ariel and Caliban on the island.
   (50, 93)

10. (Beside, Besides) Antonio and Alonso, Gonzalo and Ferdinand are shipwrecked on Prospero's island.
    (92, 93)

11. Fortunately, Ferdinand, Alonso's son, does not support
(78) (none, any) of Alonso's treachery.

12. I missed some crucial lines in the play because of (you,
(23, 53) your) booing and hissing.

13. Ariel, the fairy spirit, (which, whom) Prospero frees from
(61, 64) a tree, becomes his servant.

14. The verb in the following sentence is (transitive,
(21, 26) intransitive): Sebastian and Antonio mock the other
castaways for their optimism.

15. Of the two brothers, Sebastian has the (least, lesser) right
(39, 40) to the Milan throne.

16. Write the following sentence to make it more concise: I
(101) slept well last night owing to the fact that I had finished
all my homework.

17. In the following sentence, write the verb phrase, name its
(15, 26) tense, and label it transitive or intransitive: Has Ariel cast
a spell on the castaways?

18. For a–c, write the possessive form of each noun.
(95) (a) Gonzalo and Sylvius   (b) play   (c) costumes

19. Rewrite the following as it is. Then add proofreading
(32, 91) symbols to indicate corrections.

Sebastian and antonios plot to kill Alonso Was downright
wicked" said Mrs Curtis.

20. Rewrite the sentence below, adding a colon where it is
(90) needed.

My favorite characters from *The Tempest* are these
Prospero, Miranda, Ariel, Caliban, and Gonzalo.

21. For a–c, write the plural of each noun.
(10, 11) (a) Marquez   (b) Emily   (c) thesis

22. Which sentence is clearer? Write A or B.
_(101, 102)

A. Half eaten, I threw away the bag of popcorn when the movie ended.

B. I threw away the half-eaten bag of popcorn when the movie ended.

23. Write the superlative form of the adjective *awkwardly*.
₍₈₇₎

24. Write the possessive case, third person, plural personal pronoun.
₍₅₂₎

25. Write whether the sentence below is simple, compound, complex, or compound-complex:
_(59, 99)

Alonso believes that Ferdinand, his son, has drowned, but Ferdinand has landed on another part of the island.

26. In the sentence below, write the dependent clause, circling the subordinating conjunction. Then write whether the clause functions as a noun, adjective, or adverb.
_(54, 99)

Ariel's music moves Ferdinand as he mourns his father.

27. Rewrite this sentence using active voice: Ferdinand was given menial work by Prospero.
₍₂₇₎

28. Rewrite the sentence below, adding a semicolon and a comma as needed and circling the conjunctive adverb.
₍₈₈₎

Prospero rejoices at the devotion between Miranda and Ferdinand nevertheless Prospero demands proof of Ferdinand's devotion.

29. Rewrite this sentence using parallel construction: Jesse prepared for the test by memorizing the prepositions, studying the vocabulary, and practiced sentence diagrams.
₍₁₀₀₎

30. Diagram this sentence: No, Jesse doesn't like to read Shakespeare, who wrote in old English.
_(61, 104)

LESSON 106 The Subjunctive Mood

> **Dictation or Journal Entry**
>
> **Vocabulary:** The roots *cess-* and *ced-* come from the Latin verb *cedere* meaning "to go" or "to proceed."
>
> A *procession* is a formal, orderly, forward movement. We watched the wedding *procession*. A *procession* can also be a group of persons or things moving in this way. The wedding *procession* moved slowly toward the altar.
>
> A *recession* is the act of moving back or withdrawing. It often refers to a period of decline in business activity, less severe than a depression. When a country's economy is slowing down, experts label the condition as a *recession*.
>
> A *precedent* is something that is said or done that serves as an example or rule to guide future actions. A ruling in a court case may serve as a *precedent* for future cases of similar nature.

Verbs may be in one of three moods: indicative, imperative, or **subjunctive.** Most of the verbs we use are in the indicative mood. We remember that the imperative mood expresses a command or request. In the English language, the subjunctive mood has two common uses: (1) to express a condition contrary to fact and (2) to express a wish. The chart below shows how the past subjunctive mood differs from the past indicative.

Past Subjunctive

PAST INDICATIVE		PAST SUBJUNCTIVE	
SINGULAR	PLURAL	SINGULAR	PLURAL
I was	we were	(if) I were	(if) we were
you were	you were	(if) you were	(if) you were
he was	they were	(if) he were	(if) they were

Contrary to Fact We usually use the subjunctive *were* in clauses that begin with *if, as if,* or *as though* when the clause states a condition that is doubtful, improbable, or contrary to fact.

<u>If</u> I were (not was) older, I could vote. (I am not older.)

Ann acts <u>as if</u> she were (not was) older. (Ann is not older.)

He gives orders <u>as though</u> he were (not was) the boss. (He is not the boss.)

Wish We usually use the subjunctive *were* in statements expressing a wish.

> I wish I were (not was) President.
>
> Mrs. Ng wishes she were (not was) here.
>
> We wish Lionel were (not was) on our team.

Example 1 Choose the correct verb form for each sentence.

(a) He wishes Maxine (was, were) there with him.

(b) If I (was, were) you, I would study hard.

(c) Dr. Corndog spoke as though he (was, were) an expert.

Solution (a) He wishes Maxine **were** there with him. (wish)

(b) If I **were** you, I would study hard. (I am not you.)

(c) Dr. Corndog spoke as though he **were** an expert. (Dr. Corndog is not an expert.)

Present Subjunctive The chart below shows how the present subjunctive differs from the present indicative.

Present Indicative		Present Subjunctive	
Singular	Plural	Singular	Plural
I am	we are	(that) I be	(that) we be
you are	you are	(that) you be	(that) you be
he is	they are	(that) he be	(that) they be

The present subjunctive form of verbs other than *be* is the same as the ordinary present tense. However, we do not add *s* for third person singular.

> (that) he, she, it *arrive* (not *arrives*)
>
> (that) he, she, it *wait* (not *waits*)
>
> (that) he, she, it *come* (not *comes*)
>
> (that) he, she, it *represent* (not *represents*)

The present subjunctive is used in somewhat formal statements to express necessity, demand, urging, strong request, or resolution as in the following sentences.

> It is important that you be (not are) on time. (necessity)
>
> I insist that she join (not joins) our group. (demand)
>
> The judge urged that the jury be (not is) fair. (urging)
>
> Mom asks that he wait (not waits) here. (strong request)
>
> The committee ruled that the game be (not is) official. (resolution)

Example 2 Choose the subjunctive verb form for each sentence.
   (a) Michael demands that she (write, writes) to him today.

   (b) It is essential that he (is, are, be) patient.

   (c) The teacher insists that he (takes, take) the test on Monday.

Solution (a) Michael demands that she **write** to him today. (demand)

   (b) It is essential that he **be** patient. (necessity)

   (c) The teacher insists that he **take** the test on Monday. (strong request)

Practice Choose the subjunctive verb form for sentences a–e.
   a. I wish I (was, were) as tall as he.

   b. She acts as if she (was, were) your sister.

   c. The teacher requests that he (stays, stay) after class.

   d. She would be here if she (was, were) able.

   e. It is important that she (call, calls) today.

   For f–i, replace each blank with the correct vocabulary word.
   f. Unfortunately, the _____ has lowered the profits of many businesses.

   g. The Latin verb _____ means "to go" or "to proceed."

h. The Presidential _____ moving slowly down the street received world-wide coverage on television.

i. The Supreme Court will rely on _____ to guide them on rulings of present and future cases.

Review Set 106 Choose the correct word(s) to complete sentences 1–16

1. The Latin word (*fides, flectere, errare*) means "to wander" or "to stray."
(105)

2. The Latin root *son-* means (fill, after, sound).
(104)

3. A complement is that which (flatters, completes, questions).
(103)

4. (Apollo, Bacchus, Stentor) was the Roman god of wine and frenzy.
(53)

5. The Romanized Greek god (Apollo, Bacchus, Stentor) is associated with calm rationality.
(53)

6. My friend Lisa has a small part in the play, but Gonzalo has fewer lines than (her, she).
(63)

7. Trinculo and Stephano's lines gave (us, we) spectators a laugh.
(54, 63)

8. A phrase that does not clearly modify a certain word is called a (direct quotation, dangling modifier, passive voice).
(102)

9. The following is a (phrase, clause): having read *Silas Marner* by George Eliot
(20, 54)

10. Do readers of *Silas Marner* understand (Eppie, Eppie's) needing a father?
(16, 53)

11. The reader wasn't familiar with (none, any) of George Eliot's works.
(78)

12. *Silas Marner*, (that, which) takes place in the nineteenth-century English village of Raveloe, talks about a reclusive weaver infatuated with money.
(61, 62)

13. In a dictionary entry, the abbreviation *vt.* means (vast, transitive verb, Vermont).
(105)

14. Of the two men, Silas responds (worse, worst) to conviction.
(87)

15. I requested that Elle (loans, loan) me her physics book.
(106)

16. If the weather (was, were) warmer, we'd go to the beach.
(106)

17. For a–c, write the possessive form of the noun.
(95) (a) lady   (b) Silas   (c) friends

18. Rewrite the sentence below, using brackets to enclose words that are probably not a part of the direct quotation.
(47, 103)

A witness said, "The shop owner Hargus Bigg threw a jar of pickles at the masked bandit."

19. Rewrite the following as it is. Then add proofreading symbols to indicate corrections.
(43, 65)

"Did the jar of pikkles actually hit the masked bandit? asked the the reporter. "No" replied Mr Bigg.

20. Use an appositive to make one sentence from these two sentences: Silas Marner was once a respected elder in a small fundamental sect. Silas Marner is now a lonely, bitter man.
(42, 43)

21. Which sentence is clearer? Choose A or B.
(101, 102)

A. Whistling as he worked, Hargus swept up a large cockroach.

B. Hargus swept up a large cockroach whistling as he worked.

22. In the following sentence, write whether the underlined part is essential or nonessential: Yes, my brother <u>Bob</u> is an incumbent in this school board election.
(62)

23. Write the four principal parts of the verb *sell*.
(74, 75)

24. Write whether the sentence below is simple, compound, or compound-complex.
(59, 99)

With his faith shattered and his trust in man destroyed, Silas Marner, the eccentric visionary, becomes a lone alien in the village of Raveloe.

25. In the sentence below, write the dependent clause, circling the subordinating conjunction. Then write whether the clause functions as a noun, adjective, or adverb.
(97, 98)

Silas Marner knew that his life was growing more and more empty.

26. Rewrite this sentence using active voice: The nightly parties in Raveloe were thrown by Squire Cass.
(27)

27. Rewrite the sentence below, adding punctuation as needed and circling the conjunctive adverb.
(88)

Silas Marner acknowledged his obsession with money nevertheless he continued to accumulate gold and caress his coins.

28. Rewrite this sentence so that it has parallel structure: Rita raised her grades by doing her homework, by watching less TV, and asking for help with difficult concepts.
(100)

Diagram sentences 28 and 29.

29. Dunstan, whom the author describes as opportunistic, keeps the money for Godfrey's horse.
(61)

30. Both the devil and gypsy peddlers were blamed for the robbery, but Dunstan stole Marner's gold.
(34, 59)

LESSON 107

Spelling Rules: Silent Letters *k, g, w, t, d,* and *c*

> **Dictation or Journal Entry**
>
> **Vocabulary:** The Latin noun *verbum* means "word."
>
> *Verbatim* is to write or say something word for word. Madeline repeated the Shakespeare passage *verbatim*.
>
> *Verbose* means using or having an excessive number of words; wordy. I fidgeted as my neighbor gave me a *verbose* description of her physical ailments.
>
> *Verbiage*, a noun, is the use of more words than necessary; wordiness. Some senators criticized the long document for its *verbiage*.

Why Are Some Letters Silent? The English language contains many words that are spelled differently than they are pronounced. There are several reasons for this.

As the language changed and grew through the centuries, the way people pronounced a word often changed, yet the way the word was spelled remained the same.

Some early scholars insisted on applying Latin rules of spelling to English words. (Since English borrowed the Latin alphabet, this idea wasn't illogical.)

More words were borrowed from other languages, and their foreign spellings were kept.

In the midst of this, the printing press appeared. It helped to "freeze" the spelling of all these words, no matter how irregular. Most English words are spelled today just as they were in the 1500s. As a result, there are many words that contain letters we no longer (or never did) pronounce.

The Letter *k* A silent *k* at the beginning of a word is always followed by an *n*.

*k*nack   *k*neel   *k*now   *k*nuckle

The Letter *g* A silent *g* may also be followed by an *n* at the beginning or the end of a word.

*g*nat   *g*naw   si*g*n   fei*g*n

The Letter *w* A silent *w* can come before the letter *r*.

*w*rath   *w*rong   *w*rote   *w*rinkle

Sometimes the silent *w* comes before *h*:

*w*ho   *w*hole   *w*hose   *w*holesome

Other silent *w*'s appear in the words *answer*, *sword*, and *two*.

The Letter *t* A silent *t* can follow the letter *s*.

    ne*st*le   bri*st*le   jo*st*le   ca*st*le

A silent *t* can also come before the letters *ch*.

    no*tch*   ca*tch*   bu*tch*er   fe*tch*   wa*tch*

Not all words that end with the "ch" sound have a silent *t* (touch, which, rich, attack, detach, such, much, sandwich, etc.). When in doubt, check the dictionary.

Other silent *t*'s appear in words borrowed from the French such as *ballet, depot, debut, gourmet,* and *mortgage*.

The Letter *d* The letters *ge* usually follow a silent *d*.

    bu*dge*   he*dge*   ri*dge*   lo*dge*   ba*dge*

We also find silent *d*'s in these words:

    a*dj*ective   a*dj*acent   a*dj*ust   We*dn*esday

The Letter *c* A silent *c* can follow the letter *s*.

    *sc*issors   *sc*ene   *sc*ience   *sc*ent   *sc*epter

Example Rewrite these words and circle each silent letter.

(a) glitch   (b) gnarl   (c) dredge

(d) wrist   (e) sword   (f) knead

Solution (a) gli(t)ch   (b) (g)narl   (c) dre(d)ge

(d) (w)rist   (e) s(w)ord   (f) (k)nead

Practice For a–h, rewrite the words and circle each silent letter.

a. wrestle   **b.** who   **c.** gnu   **d.** know

e. knit   **f.** knelt   **g.** Gnostic   **h.** wrangler

For i–l, replace each blank with the correct vocabulary word.

i. The Latin word _____ means "word."

j. If someone talks too much, we might say that he or she is _____.

k. I wrote the doctor's instructions _____, or word for word.

l. The paragraph was not concise; it was too long because of _____.

Review set 107 Choose the correct word(s) to complete sentences 1–14.

1. The Latin verb (*errare, flectere, cedere*) means "to go" or "to proceed."
⁽¹⁰⁶⁾

2. (Replete, Sonorous, Aberrant) means straying from that which is usual or correct.
⁽¹⁰⁵⁾

3. A sonata is a type of (monkey, music, fruit).
⁽¹⁰⁴⁾

4. Dionysian and (Apollonian, Delphic, Bacchanalian) have similar meanings.
⁽⁵⁵⁾

5. A flair is a (natural talent, blaze of light).
⁽⁵⁶⁾

6. Please let me know when (us, we) siblings can get together for lunch.
⁽⁶³⁾

7. Squire Cass's rage (sure, surely) surprised people who knew him.
^(86, 87)

8. The following is a (phrase, clause): when Dunstan doesn't return
^(20, 54)

9. (Beside, Besides) Dolly Winthrop and her little son, few neighbors remember Silas's problem.
⁽⁹³⁾

10. If I (was, were) you, I'd study the vocabulary.
⁽¹⁰⁶⁾

11. I don't understand (Thurvis, Thurvis's) complaining about the noise.
⁽⁹⁵⁾

12. Molly's little girl, (which, who) wanders into Silas's home, becomes the delight of his life.
^(61, 62)

13. There was never (any, no) hard feelings (between, among) the two aunts.
^(78, 93)

14. Of the two characters, Godfrey grows (more, most) disgruntled and sullen.
⁽⁸⁷⁾

15. Rewrite the following sentence to make it more concise:
(101) Through the fog, the stop sign was barely visible to my eyes.

16. In this sentence, write the verb phrase, name its tense,
(15, 26) and label it transitive or intransitive: For sixteen years, Godfrey had been hiding his daughter from his wife.

17. For a–c, write the possessive form of each noun.
(95) (a) Eppie and Cass   (b) squires   (c) citizens

18. Rewrite the following as it is. Then add proofreading
(27, 47) symbols to indicate corrections.

"If Jasper was malevolent, I wouldn't trust him" said Ann. "What makes you think he's trust worthy? aksed Kim.

19. Rewrite the following, adding a colon where it is needed:
(90) Some significant characters in *Silas Marner* have uncommon names Silas, Godfrey, Dunstan, and Eppie.

20. For a–c, write the plural of each noun.
(10, 11) (a) Marquez   (b) Godfrey   (c) analysis

21. Which sentence is clearer? Choose A or B.
(101, 102)
A. Sue Ellen asked me what I was going to do at two p.m.

B. Sue Ellen asked me at two p.m. what I was going to do.

22. Write the superlative form of the adverb *serenely*.
(87)

23. Write the possessive case, third person, singular,
(52) feminine gender personal pronoun.

24. Write whether the following sentence is simple,
(54, 99) compound, complex, or compound-complex: Silas loves his gold, but he treasures Eppie even more.

25. In the sentence below, write the dependent clause,
(54, 97) circling the subordinating conjunction. Then write whether the clause functions as a noun, adjective, or adverb.

Eppie prefers to remain with Silas even though Godfrey is her father.

26. Rewrite this sentence using active voice: Godfrey is rejected by Eppie.
(27)

27. Rewrite this sentence, adding a semicolon and a comma as needed and circling the conjunctive adverb: Mr. Blab's speeches are usually verbose on the other hand his written reports are succinct.
(88)

28. Rewrite this sentence using parallel structure: Godfrey is thankful for his wife, life, and his daughter.
(100)

29. Which sentence is correctly written using the subjunctive mood? Choose A or B.
(106)

   A. Law requires that Noel recites the creed verbatim.

   B. Law requires that Noel recite the creed verbatim.

30. Diagram this sentence: No, Eppie doesn't want to live with Godfrey.
(85, 104)

LESSON 108

Spelling Rules: Silent Letters *p, b, l, u, h, n* and *gh*

> **Dictation or Journal Entry**
>
> **Vocabulary:** The Latin root *ped-*, meaning "foot," forms the base of the familiar words *ped*al and *ped*estrian.
>
> A *centipede* is a wormlike invertebrate with many legs (*centi-* hundred + *ped-* foot). Crawling across a leaf, the *centipede* had legs too numerous to count.
>
> To *impede* is to retard or hinder the progress of. Literally, it means to "entangle the feet." I hope bad weather will not *impede* our travel tomorrow.
>
> A *pedometer* is an instrument that measures the distance covered in walking. A *pedometer* counts the number of steps taken and multiplies by the length of a single step.
>
> A *pedicure* is the cosmetic treatment of the feet. Grandma's weekly *pedicure* included trimming and polishing her toenails.

The Letter *p*   The Greek language is a source of many words that contain a silent *p*. The silent *p* occurs only before the letters *s*, *t*, and *n*.

     pseudonym   **p**salm   **p**tomaine   **p**neumonia

The Letter *b*   Many words contain the letter *m* followed by a silent *b*.

     nu**m**b   li**m**b   succu**m**b   la**m**b

Other silent *b*'s are found in the words *debt, doubt,* and *subtle.*

The Letter *l*   Many words that contain a silent *l* follow a similar pattern: an *l* followed by a consonant that makes the *l* difficult to pronounce.

     ta*l*k   cau*l*k   wa*l*k   yo*l*k   fo*l*k

     ba*l*m   psa*l*m   wou*l*d   shou*l*d

     ca*l*ves   ha*l*f

The Letter *u*   A silent *u* usually follows the letter *g*. It reminds us to pronounce the *g* with a "hard" sound (g) rather than a "soft" sound (j), at either the beginning or the end of a word.

     g**u**ilt   g**u**est   g**u**arantee   dialog**u**e   vag**u**e

The Letter *h*   A silent *h* usually follows *c, r,* or *g,* as in these words:

     ac**h**e   sc**h**eme   r**h**yme

     ag**h**ast   g**h**etto   r**h**apsody

An initial *h* can also be silent, as in the words *honest, hour, herb* and *heir.*

The Letter *n* Sometimes the letter *m* is followed by a silent *n*, as in these words:

        colu**mn**   conde**mn**   hy**mn**   sole**mn**

The Letters *gh* The letter combination *gh* is always silent when it comes before the letter *t*.

    strai**gh**t   brou**gh**t   ei**gh**t   fou**gh**t
    mi**gh**t   ou**gh**t   kni**gh**t   sou**gh**t

A *gh* at the end of a word can be silent as well:

    nei**gh**   thorou**gh**   wei**gh**   si**gh**
    slei**gh**   dou**gh**   bou**gh**   hi**gh**

Example Rewrite each word and circle each silent letter.

(a) freight   (b) calf   (c) balk   (d) psalm

(e) earache   (f) climb   (g) through   (h) thumb

(i) should   (j) rhythm   (k) pterodactyl   (l) guild

Solution (a) frei(gh)t   (b) ca(l)f   (c) ba(l)k   (d) psa(l)m

(e) earac(h)e   (f) clim(b)   (g) throu(gh)   (h) thum(b)

(i) shou(l)d   (j) r(h)ythm   (k) (p)terodactyl   (l) g(u)ild

Practice Rewrite words a–l, and circle each silent letter.

  a. guillotine   **b.** thorough   **c.** charisma   **d.** rhinoceros

  e. solder   **f.** ghost   **g.** could   **h.** chalk

  i. debt   **j.** pneumatic   **k.** bomb   **l.** yolk

For m–q, replace each blank with the correct vocabulary word.

m. The Latin root _____ means "foot."

n. In addition to a manicure, I shall have a _____, for my toenails need trimming.

o. Melinda squealed when a _____ with its many tiny legs crawled across her bare foot.

p. I used a _____ to measure how far I hiked along the trail.

q. Poor study habits may _____ academic progress.

Review set 108

Choose the correct word to complete sentences 1–14.

1. (Protocol, Rectitude, Verbiage) is wordiness.
(107)

2. Aaron and Eppie led the marriage (recession, inquisition, procession) to the feast.
(106)

3. Silas Marner's (verbose, aberrant, sonorous) behavior of hoarding gold ceases when Eppie restores his faith in mankind.
(105)

4. (Sonorous, Replete, Dissonant) means "filled."
(103)

5. Notice the (requisition, sequence, protoplasm) of events leading to the climax of the story.
(51)

6. In a dictionary entry, the abbreviation *vi.* means (intransitive verb, violent, Victorian).
(105)

7. Each of the young fishermen (have, has) (their, his) eyes on the new girl in town.
(68)

8. Shinji fishes as expertly as (they, them).
(63)

9. The (self-conscious, self conscious) Shinji admires Hatsue from afar.
(79, 82)

10. (Us, We) readers are wondering if Shinji will marry Hatsue.
(52)

11. A (phrase, clause) may contain nouns and verbs, but it does not have both a subject and a predicate.
(20)

12. Shinji treats the master and the mistress of the lighthouse very (good, well).
(81)

13. We usually place punctuation marks (before, after) parentheses.
(103)

14. Shinji and Hatsue try to keep a secret (between, among)
(93) themselves.

15. Rewrite this sentence, adding parentheses as needed:
(103) Richard also called Doc, Monty, and Orthocratus straightens people's teeth beautifully.

16. For a–c, rewrite each word, circling the silent letters.
(107, 108) (a) whack   (b) hedge   (c) knowledge

17. For a–c, write the possessive form of each noun.
(95) (a) mistress   (b) Shinji and the master   (c) shadows

18. Rewrite the following, adding punctuation marks and
(69) underlining each word that should be italicized:

In November 2004 ZooLogical Digest magazine featured an article titled The Heavy Elephant

19. Rewrite the following as it is. Then add proofreading
(32, 91) symbols to indicate corrections.

"Whats the title of that modern japanese novel by Yukio Mishima? asked Phil. "I dont remember" replied Jenny.

20. Use an appositive to make one sentence from these two
(42, 43) sentences: Yukio Mishima was a Japanese novelist. Yukio Mishima wrote during the 1950s and '60s about the dichotomy between traditional Japanese values and the spiritual barrenness of contemporary life.

21. Which sentence is clearer? Choose A or B.
(101, 102) A. While spying on Hatsue, a hornet stung Yasuo.

B. A hornet stung Yasuo while he was spying on Hatsue.

22. In this sentence, write whether the underlined part is an
(62) essential or nonessential part: I think my friend <u>Mildred</u> still has two iguanas.

23. Write the four principal parts of the irregular verb *slay*.
(74, 75)

24. Write whether the following sentence is simple,
(59, 99) compound, complex, or compound-complex: Shinji works hard on Hatsue's father's ship while Yasuo hides from his tasks.

25. In the sentence below, write the dependent clause, circling the subordinating conjunction. Then write whether the clause functions as a noun, adjective, or adverb.
(20, 97)

Because of the thick fog, we couldn't see where we were going.

26. Rewrite this sentence using active voice: Sybil and Lilibet were driven to the airport by Scot.
(27)

27. Rewrite this sentence, adding a semicolon and a comma as needed and circling the conjunctive adverb: *The Sound of Waves* portrays the triumph of good over evil in addition it gives us a simple picture of island life.
(88)

28. Rewrite this sentence using parallel structure: In *Their Eyes Were Watching God*, Zora Neale writes to relieve her frustrations, for striking out for equality, and to find her identity.
(100)

29. Which sentence is correctly written using the subjunctive mood? Choose A or B.
(106)

A. If I were taller, I could reach that jar of pickles.

B. If I was taller, I could reach that jar of pickles.

30. Diagram this sentence: Would you like to sample my pickle sandwich with mayonnaise and anchovies while I pour the iced tea?
(97, 99)

LESSON 109

Spelling Rules: Suffixes, Part 1

Dictation or Journal Entry

Vocabulary: The Latin root *dole-* means "to grieve."

Dolorous means expressing or causing pain or sorrow. Having lost his best friend, the man gave a *dolorous* cry. The train wreck was a *dolorous* tragedy.

Doleful means full of or expressing grief or sorrow. The convict threw the jury a *doleful* glance as the judge read the verdict.

Condolence is sympathy with someone suffering grief or sorrow. I sent him my *condolences* when his dog died.

Words Ending in y A final *y* usually changes to *i* when suffixes (except for the suffix *-ing*) are added:

deny + ed = denied
modify + er = modifier
exemplify + ed = exemplified
pity + ful = pitiful
pry + s = pries
worry + some = worrisome
cloudy + ness = cloudiness
foggy + er = foggier
ready + ly = readily
sporty + est = sportiest
glory + ous = glorious
plenty + ful = plentiful

but: *denying, modifying, exemplifying, pitying, prying, worrying, glorying*

When preceded by a vowel, the final *y* does not change to *i*.

enjoy + able = enjoyable
play + er = player
annoy + ed = annoyed
ray + s = rays
gray + est = grayest

Exceptions Important exceptions include the following:

lay + ed = laid
pay + ed = paid
say + ed = said
day + ly = daily

www.saxonhomeschool.com
©Houghton Mifflin Harcourt Publishers, Inc.
673
Grammar and Writing 8
Student Edition, 9781419098581

Example 1 Add suffixes to these words ending in *y*.

(a) toy + ed = _____

(b) shiny + er = _____

(c) tardy + ness = _____

(d) mercy + less = _____

(e) happy + ly = _____

Solution (a) toy + ed = **toyed** (The *y* is preceded by a vowel, so it does not change to an *i*.

(b) shiny + er = **shinier** (The final *y* usually changes to *i* when suffixes are added.)

(c) tardy + ness = **tardiness**

(d) mercy + less = **merciless**

(e) happy + ly = **happily**

Words Ending in a Silent *e* We generally drop the silent *e* before adding a suffix beginning with a vowel (including the suffix -*y*).

nerve + ous = nervous
rose + y = rosy
wire + y = wiry
blame + ing = blaming
explore + ation = exploration
love + able = lovable
achieve + able = achievable

However, we keep the final *e* when we add a suffix beginning with a consonant.

arrange + ment = arrangement
like + ness = likeness
care + less = careless
sure + ly = surely
grace + ful = graceful

Exceptions Exceptions to the rules above include the following words:

judge + ment = judgment

argue + ment = argument
wise + dom = wisdom
gentle + ly = gently
true + ly = truly

Also, when adding *ous* or *able* to a word ending in *ge* or *ce*, we keep the final *e* to indicate the soft sound of the *c* (as in *celery*) or *g* (as in *giant*).

manage + able = manageable
trace + able = traceable
change + able = changeable
outrage + ous = outrageous
courage + ous = courageous

Example 2 Add suffixes to these words ending in a silent *e*.

(a) conceive + able = _____

(b) shave + ing = _____

(c) glare + ing = _____

(d) live + ly = _____

(e) lame + ly = _____

(f) trace + able = _____

(g) true + ly = _____

Solution (a) conceive + able = **conceivable** (We usually drop the silent *e* when the suffix begins with a vowel.)

(b) shave + ing = **shaving**

(c) glare + ing = **glaring**

(d) live + ly = **lively** (We usually keep the final *e* when the suffix begins with a consonant.)

(e) lame + ly = **lamely**

(f) trace + able = **traceable** (We keep the silent *e* after the *c* to retain the soft *c* ("*s*") sound.

(g) True + ly = **truly** (This is an exception to the rule.)

Practice Add suffixes to words a-k.

a. shame + less = _____

b. drowsy + ly = _____

c. weary + ness = _____

d. steady + est = _____

e. force + ful = _____

f. slave + ing = _____

g. late + ly = _____

h. tame + er = _____

i. fame + ous = _____

j. skate + ing = _____

k. plenty + ful = _____

For l–o, replace each blank with the correct vocabulary word.

l. The Latin root _____ means grieve.

m. If your friend loses a loved one, you might send him or her _____.

n. Sadly, two people lost their lives in that _____ car accident.

o. Dolorous and _____ are both adjectives meaning "expressing sorrow."

Review set 109

Choose the correct word(s) to complete sentences 1–13.

1. The Latin word (amare, verbum, ad hominem) means "word."
(107)

2. The Latin root (*ped-, rog-, ced-*) means foot.
(108)

3. Unfortunately, Max had the (sonorous, erroneous, replete) belief that adjectives modify verbs.
(105)

4. The Latin root (*err-, ced-, son-*) means "sound."
(104)

5. A (sonata, procession, complement) is that which completes or makes perfect.
(103)

6. Margaret bought new dictionaries for Christie and (I, me).
(21, 51)

7. Debby and (her, she) were (real, really) pleased with the textbook revision.
(50, 89)

8. The following is a (phrase, clause): when Janie plunges into the raging waters
(20, 54)

9. Tea Cake runs (beside, besides) the floating cow until he can rescue Janie.
(93)

10. There were hardly (any, no) survivors from the hurricane.
(78)

11. (Tea Cup, Tea Cup's) grasping the dog results in a bite and rabies.
(53, 95)

12. What happened to the cow (which, that) saved Janie's life?
(62)

13. Sheilah has not (forsook, forsaken) her Scottish heritage.
(70, 71)

14. Rewrite the following sentence to make it more concise: In my opinion, I think anchovies taste terrible in flavor.
(101)

15. Rewrite this sentence, adding parentheses as needed: Tea Cup spent more than fifty dollars $50 on a party for his railroad friends.
(103)

16. For a–c, rewrite each word, circling the silent letters.
(107, 108)
    (a) lamb   (b) gnome   (c) psyche

17. For a–c, write the possessive form of each noun.
(95)
    (a) refugees   (b) lice   (c) chicken

18. Rewrite the following, adding punctuation marks and underlining each word that should be italicized: C'est la vie a French phrase meaning "that's life" sums up my attitude after my flight to Europe was cancelled.
(65, 69)

19. Rewrite the following as it is. Then add proofreading symbols to indicate corrections.
(32, 91)

"Im sorry" said the doctor "but Tea Cup has con tracted rabies from the the dog bite.

20. For a–c, write the plural of each noun.
(10, 11)
(a) groomsman   (b) alumnus   (c) rally

21. Which sentence is clearer? Choose A or B.
(102)
A. I tripped over a big stick trembling and frightened in the dark forest.

B. Trembling and frightened in the dark forest, I tripped over a big stick.

22. Write the comparative form of the adverb *hastily*.
(87)

23. Write the possessive case, third person, plural personal pronoun.
(48, 52)

24. Write whether the following sentence is simple, compound, complex, or compound-complex: Elle plays the piano, and Allison runs the vacuum cleaner while Monty snoozes.
(59, 99)

25. In the sentence below, write the dependent clause, circling the subordinating conjunction or relative pronoun. Then write whether the clause functions as a noun, adjective, or adverb.
(54, 99)

As we watched the sad movie together, my sister gave me doleful looks.

26. Rewrite this sentence using active voice: Our journey across the country was impeded by tornadoes and dust storms.
(27)

27. Rewrite this sentence, adding a semicolon and a comma as needed and circling the conjunctive adverb: We should break for lunch because it's after one o'clock besides I'm hungry.
(88)

28. Rewrite this sentence using parallel structure: Because of his eye injury, Reuven remains in the hospital, receives visitors, and listened to the radio.
(100)

29. Which sentence is correctly written using the subjunctive mood? Choose A or B.
(106)

A. It is essential that Reuven forgives Danny.

B. It is essential that Reuven forgive Danny.

30. Diagram this sentence: Oops, Reuven made a big mistake in taunting Danny's team.
(56, 104)

LESSON 110

Spelling Rules: Suffixes, Part 2

> **Dictation or Journal Entry**
>
> **Vocabulary:** The Latin prefix *retro-* means "back," "behind," or "backward."
>
> To *retrogress* is to move backward. Without electricity, Meg had to *retrogress* to more primitive methods of cooking and cleaning.
>
> *Retrospect* is a contemplative view of past events. In *retrospect*, I think I made a mistake.
>
> *Retrograde* means moving backward; reversed. Countdown numbers are given in *retrograde* order. *Retrograde* also means becoming worse; deteriorating. The *retrograde* condition of the old bridge makes it unsafe.

Doubling Final Consonants

When a one-syllable word ends with a single consonant preceded by a single vowel, we double the final consonant before adding a suffix that begins with a vowel.

chop + ed = chopped
plan + er = planner
drip + ing = dripping
wrap + ing = wrapping
split + ing = splitting
big + est = biggest
run + y = runny

Exceptions include the words *bus* (bused), *sew* (sewing), *bow* (bowed), and *tax* (taxing).

When a word of two or more syllables ends with a single consonant preceded by a single vowel, we double the final consonant if the word is accented (stressed) on the last syllable.

begin + ing = beginning
confer + ed = conferred
submit + ed = submitted

Do Not Double

We **do not** double the final consonant of any of the words described above (words ending with a single consonant preceded by a single vowel) when adding a suffix that begins with a consonant.

mad + ly = madly
sad + ly = sadly
glad + ness = gladness

We **do not** double the final consonant if it is preceded by two vowels or another consonant:

rain + ed = rained
great + ly = greatly
cold + est = coldest
bash + ful = bashful

Words Ending in *ful* All words ending in *ful* have only one *l*.

successful	beautiful	cupful
cheerful	bountiful	handful
graceful	hopeful	spoonful

Example Add suffixes to these words.

(a) wrap + ing = _____

(b) tan + er = _____

(c) submit + ed = _____

(d) hot + ly = _____

(e) ear + full = _____

Solution (a) wrap + ing = **wrapping** (In most one-syllable words, we double the final consonant when we add a suffix beginning with a vowel.)

(b) tan + er = **tanner**

(c) submit + ed = **submitted**

(d) hot + ly = **hotly** (When the suffix begins with a consonant, we do not double the final consonant before adding the suffix.)

(e) ear + full = **earful** (Words ending in *ful* have only one *l*.)

Practice Add suffixes to words a–e.

a. chip + ed = _____

b. flop + ing = _____

c. bad + ly = _____

d. eye + full = _____

e. sad + ness = _____

For f–j, replace each blank with the correct vocabulary word.

f. The Latin prefix _____ means "back," "behind," or "backward."

g. A _____ sequence of assembly instructions will help me to take apart the appliance.

h. In _____ I am glad I made that long journey to China, for I learned a great deal.

i. Poor nutrition may lead to _____ health.

j. Your fitness may _____ if you do not exercise.

Review set 110

Choose the correct word(s) to complete sentences 1–14.

1. The Latin root (*dole-, ped-, quis*) means "grieve."
   (109)

2. To *impede* is to (speed, hinder, encourage) progress.
   (108)

3. The Eatonsville townspeople ask Phoeby to relate Janie's tale (verbatim, sonorous, replete).
   (107)

4. A (sonata, precedent, pedicure) serves as an example or rule to guide future actions.
   (106)

5. The Latin word *errare* means to (stray, fill, giggle).
   (105)

6. There wasn't (anyone, no one) in the office today.
   (78)

7. Each of the incumbents (promise, promises) us (their, his/her) loyalty and support.
   (53, 76)

8. Molly is talkative, but Kurt is more verbose than (her, she).
   (63)

9. A (fast-moving, fast moving) baseball hit Reuven in the eye.
   (79, 82)

10. The incident gave (us, we) boys a chance to develop a friendship.
    (51, 63)

11. Within a quotation, we use (brackets, semicolons) to insert our own explanations.
(103)

12. I didn't feel (good, well) after four hours in a rocking boat.
(81)

13. Danny was (real, really) angry with Reuven for laughing at the baseball team.
(89)

14. Have you noticed a friendship developing (between, among) Reuven and Danny?
(93)

15. For a–c, combine each word and suffix to make one word.
(109, 110) (a) lecture + ing   (b) blame + less   (c) rectify + ed

16. For a–c, rewrite each word, circling the silent letters.
(107, 108) (a) knickers   (b) neighbor   (c) patch

17. For a–c, write the possessive form of each noun.
(95) (a) Mr. Saunders   (b) The Adamses   (c) Danny

18. Rewrite the following, adding punctuation marks and underlining each word that should be italicized: Procyon lotor is the scientific name for raccoon a black-masked mammal that lives in trees in North and Central America.
(69)

19. Rewrite the following as it is. Then add proofreading symbols to indicate corrections.
(32, 91)

My brothers left there muddy socks on the porch Thay should toss them into the washingmachine.

20. Use an appositive to make one sentence from these two sentences: Reuven and Danny are Jewish teenagers. They play on opposing baseball teams.
(43)

21. Which sentence is clearer? Choose A or B.
(101, 102)
A. Driving slowly through the neighborhood in Dad's old pick-up truck, Mom finally found my run-away guinea pig.

B. Mom finally found my run-away guinea pig driving slowly through the neighborhood in Dad's old pick-up truck.

22. In this sentence, write whether the underlined part is essential or nonessential: Reuven's father, <u>Mr. Malter</u>, allows Danny to read forbidden books.
(42, 62)

23. Rewrite the following sentence to make it more concise: All the walls that have been painted look fresh and clean.
(101)

24. Write whether the following sentence is simple, compound, complex, or compound-complex: Stomping on the brakes in Dad's old pick-up truck, Mom came to a sudden stop in front of Hatteras Pinochle, my run-away guinea pig.
(59, 99)

25. In the sentence below, write the dependent clause, circling the subordinating conjunction or relative pronoun. Then write whether the clause functions as a noun, adjective, or adverb.
(54, 97)
The centipede that inched across my burrito appeared oblivious to my displeasure.

26. Rewrite this sentence using active voice: Hatteras Pinochle was frightened by the screeching brakes.
(27)

27. Rewrite this sentence, adding a semicolon and a comma as needed and circling the conjunctive adverb: John has backed up his computer files and installed new software in addition he has scanned the computer for viruses.
(88)

28. Rewrite this sentence using parallel structure: Cats generally don't like swimming for recreation, riding in cars, or to share their food.
(100)

29. Which sentence is correctly written using the subjunctive mood? Choose A or B.
(106)
   A. If Mr. Saunders was more honest, he would tell Danny his fears.
   B. If Mr. Saunders were more honest, he would tell Danny his fears.

30. Diagram this sentence: The skillful plumber replacing faucets asked me to turn off the main valve.
(56, 94)

LESSON 111

Spelling Rules: *ie* or *ei*

> **Dictation or Journal Entry**
>
> **Vocabulary:** The Latin root *loqu-* means "speak."
>
> *Soli<u>loqu</u>y* is the act of talking to oneself. During the second act of the drama, the main character appears on stage alone and gives a long *soliloquy* revealing his thoughts and feelings.
>
> A *col<u>loqu</u>y* is a formal conversation, discussion, or conference. Next week the county commissioners will meet for a *colloquy* concerning traffic problems in the valley.
>
> <u>*Loqu*</u>*acious* means excessively talkative. One *loquacious* committee member monopolized the conversation.

To determine whether to use *ie* or *ei* to make the long *e* sound in a word, we recall this rhyme:

<p align="center">Use i before e
Except <i>after</i> c
Or when sounded like <i>ay</i>
As in <i>neighbor</i> and <i>weigh</i>.</p>

USE *i* BEFORE *e*:

| ach*ie*ve | w*ie*ld | sh*ie*ld |
| th*ie*f | pr*ie*st | p*ie*ce |

EXCEPT AFTER *c*:

| c*ei*ling | dec*ei*ve | conc*ei*t |
| conc*ei*ve | rec*ei*pt | perc*ei*ve |

OR WHEN SOUNDED LIKE *ay*:

| n*ei*ghbor | v*ei*n | *ei*ght | r*ei*gn |

Exceptions The following words are exceptions to the rule. We must memorize them.

either	leisure	neither	seize
conscience	height	forfeit	weird
sovereign	omniscient	counterfeit	feisty

Example Write the words that are spelled correctly.

(a) feild, field   (b) beleif, belief

(c) recieve, receive   (d) acheive, achieve

(e) freight, frieght (f) niether, neither

Solution (a) **field** (Use *i* before *e*.) (b) **belief** (Use *i* before *e*.)

(c) **receive** (Except after *c*.) (d) **achieve** (Use *i* before *e*.)

(e) **freight** (Or when sounded as *ay*.)

(f) **neither** (exception)

Practice For a–f, write the words that are spelled correctly.
- **a.** neice, niece
- **b.** sieze, seize
- **c.** reprieve, repreive
- **d.** reciept, receipt
- **e.** weight, wieght
- **f.** sliegh, sleigh

For g–j, replace each blank with the correct vocabulary word.
- **g.** The Latin root _____ means "speak."
- **h.** Will you arrange a _____ for students on the subject of bicycle safety?
- **i.** I can hardly get a word in edgewise, for my golf partner is so _____.
- **j.** The character was speaking to no one in particular; she was giving a _____.

More Practice See Master Worksheets for a fun "Spell Czech" poem.

Review set 111 Choose the correct word(s) to complete sentences 1–14.

1. A pedometer measures the distance one (flies, drives, walks).
(108)

2. Old fashioned, or (acquisitive, dissonant, retrograde), styles may become popular again someday.
(110)

3. The widow's (aberrant, doleful, malevolent) expression revealed her deep sense of loss.
(109)

4. The Latin root *loqu-* means (foot, backward, speak).
(111)

5. Aberrant behavior is (normal, correct, unusual).
(105)

6. Shant asked Sirob and (they, them) to read *Henderson the*
(51) *Rain King* by Saul Bellow.

7. Sirob and (they, them) read for a (real, really) long time
(50, 89) this afternoon.

8. The following is a (phrase, clause): replete with
(20) successions of dissonant chords

9. Is Henderson strong, dependable, and (fast-thinking, fast
(82) thinking)?

10. If I (was, were) Henderson, I wouldn't try to rid the river
(106) of frogs.

11. Henderson embarks on one of (those, them) safaris to
(53, 67) Africa.

12. The snow drifts, (that, which) have been accumulating
(62) for three days, will impede our plowing the fields.

13. Mankind has (strove, striven) to learn the secrets of the
(72) universe.

14. Did you (recieve, receive) my letter?
(111)

15. Rewrite this sentence to make it more concise: Along the
(101) shore, I found a five-dollar bill and a rock that was shaped like a heart.

16. For a–c, rewrite each word, circling the silent letters.
(107, 108) (a) guardian (b) plumber (c) folk

17. For a–c, write the possessive form of each plural noun.
(95) (a) Chris (b) dogs (c) sheep

18. Rewrite the following, adding punctuation marks and
(69, 95) underlining each word that should be italicized: Harper Lees most famous novel To Kill a Mockingbird illustrates the maturing of a young girl named Scout.

19. Rewrite the following as it is. Then add proofreading symbols to indicate corrections.
(32, 91)

The meadowlark is a very unique North american songbird that sings a exuberant flute-like bubbling song from a a conspicuous perch.

20. For a–c, write the plural of each noun.
(10, 11)

(a) prefix   (b) oxeye daisy   (c) Thomas

21. For a–c, combine each word and suffix to make one word.
(109, 110)

(a) hop + ing   (b) glad + ly   (c) plot + ed

22. Write the superlative form of the adverb *succinctly*.
(87)

23. Write the objective case, third person, plural personal pronoun.
(52)

24. Write whether the following sentence is simple, compound, complex, or compound-complex: Jacob needed information on the Tower of London, so he went to the public library.
(59, 99)

25. In the sentence below, write the dependent clause, circling the subordinating conjunction or relative pronoun. Then write whether the clause functions as a noun, adjective, or adverb.
(54, 97)

Does Henderson realize that he is lost in Africa?

26. Rewrite this sentence using active voice: This three-story mansion was built by Dale and his brothers-in-law.
(27)

27. Write whether this sentence is true or false: When we write, we should try to use as many interjections as we possibly can.
(104)

28. Which sentence has parallel structure? Choose A or B.
(100)

A. Henderson lacked not only humility but also didn't have wisdom.

B. Henderson lacked not only humility but also wisdom.

29. Rewrite the following sentence to make it more clear: I always enjoy catching crawdads like my uncle.
(102)

30. Diagram this sentence: Because Henderson threw
(54, 99) explosives into the river, the retaining wall collapsed and
flooded the village

Appendix

Dictations

At the beginning of class each Monday, students will copy their dictation to study and prepare for a test on Friday.

Week 1   Geoffrey Chaucer, the author of *Canterbury Tales*, lived in England six hundred years ago. At that time, people believed that divine providence gave a reason to everything even though that reason wasn't always obvious. The satire and social put-downs presented in *Canterbury Tales* relied on an unshaken belief in a divine order. Chaucer's contemporaries knew that underneath his fun and ridicule existed the same belief system that they embraced. Yesterday's readers enjoyed the chaotic, ridiculous portraits of Chaucer's pilgrims; yet, they realized that God's truth prevailed in the midst of confusion and unexplained circumstances.

Week 2   The General Prologue to the *Canterbury Tales* opens with wonderful descriptions of spring, for this is the time "to go on pilgrimages." On a sunny April day, the narrator, Chaucer, joins twenty-nine other pilgrims at the Tabard Inn in Southwark. The next morning, the group leaves for Canterbury, and Chaucer chats with them along the way. The reader learns all about the group: who they are, what their station in life is, and even what clothing they are wearing. Beginning with the knight, the highest-ranking member of the group, Chaucer describes in detail each of the pilgrims.

Week 3   Before the pilgrims leave Tabard Inn, the host proposes that each pilgrim tell two tales on the way to Canterbury and two more on the way back. Whoever tells the most morally instructive as well as the most amusing tales will be treated to dinner by the other pilgrims on the return trip. Everyone draws straws to see who will tell the first tale, and the knight picks the shortest straw. It is fitting that the pilgrim with the highest position in the social hierarchy should go first. Although Chaucer never completed all the stories, *Canterbury Tales* entertains us with twenty-four tales.

Week 4 Carefully written by thoughtful and virtuous people who were strongly dedicated to principle, the Declaration of Independence opens with these words:

> When, in the course of human events, it becomes necessary for one people to dissolve the political bands which have connected them with another, and to assume, among the powers of the earth, the separate and equal station to which the laws of nature and of nature's God entitle them, a decent respect to the opinions of mankind requires that they should declare the causes which impel them to the separation.

Week 5 The authors of the Declaration of Independence stood firmly on principle when they wrote these words:

> We hold these truths to be self-evident: that all men are created equal; that they are endowed by their Creator with certain inalienable rights; that among thses are life, liberty, and the pursuit of happiness. That to secure these rights, governments are instituted among men, deriving their just powers from the consent of the governed.

Week 6 One of the most honored and versatile of America's founders, Benjamin Franklin invented the lightning rod, the Franklin stove, and bifocal glasses. He helped organize a library, a school, and one of the first fire departments. In 1775, he was a delegate to the Second Continental Congress, where he spoke these famous words:

I have lived a long time, and the longer I live the more convincing proofs I see of the truth: that God governs in the affairs of men. And if a sparrow cannot fall to the ground without His notice, is it possible that an empire [a great nation] can rise without His aid?

Week 7   The Preamble, an introductory paragraph for the U.S. Constitution, is made up of one single sentence explaining what our forefathers hoped to achieve by creating this document. Here is the Preamble:

> We the people of the United States, in order to form a more perfect Union, establish justice, insure domestic tranquility, provide for the common defense, promote the general welfare, and secure the blessings of liberty to ourselves and our posterity, do ordain and establish this Constitution of the United States of America.

Week 8   We find the inaugural oath of the President of the United States in Article II, Section 1, of the Constitution of the United States of America. It reads: "I do solemnly swear (or affirm) that I will faithfully execute the Office of President of the United States, and will to the best of my ability, preserve, protect, and defend the Constitution of the United States." George Washington added the following statement in his 1789 inauguration, "So help me, God." Every subsequent President has followed Washington's example and added this phrase at the end of his oath.

Week 9   The Constitution of the United States remains one of the most respected documents in the world. Articles I, II, and III outline the limitations and powers of the legislative, executive, and judicial departments, respectively. Article IV delineates the rights and responsibilities of the states. Article V discusses the lengthy process of amending the Constitution. According to Article VI, the United States must conduct itself honorably. Article VII lists the nine states that ratified the Constitution on September 17, 1787. The Constitution has been amended twenty-seven times; the first ten are titled the Bill of Rights.

Week 10 We use the friendly letter style when we write to people with whom we are well aquainted. This informal type of letter strengthens friendships. A standard friendly letter consists of five parts: the heading, the salutation, the body, the closing, and the signature. The heading includes the date and the writer's address. The salutation includes the word "Dear" and the recipient's name. The body is the main part containing information and ideas. The closing has words like "Your friend" or "With love." We sign our first name at the end of the letter.

Week 11 Below is an example of a social note, one type of friendly letter.

217 Magnolia Drive
Burbank, WI 53405
November 19, 2003

Dear Dr. Lu,

On Monday, October 13, you rushed over to Mount Sinai Hospital to make sure that my mother was receiving proper treatment. On behalf of my family, I want to thank you for your professionalism and commitment.

Gratefully,
Eli Wilson

Week 12 When Serpents Bargain for the Right to Squirm
By E. E. Cummings

when serpents bargain for the right to squirm
and the sun strikes to gain a living wage—
when thorns regard their roses with alarm
and rainbows are insured against old age

when every thrush may sing no new moon in
if all screech-owls have not okayed his voice
—and any wave signs on the dotted line

or else an ocean is compelled to close

when the oak begs permission of the birch
to make an acorn—valleys accuse their
mountains of having altitude—and march
denounces april as a saboteur

then we'll believe in that incredible
unanimal mankind (and not until)

Week 13   Writing a business letter is a practical skill we should all acquire. A business letter either gives or requests information and is written differently from a friendly letter. More formal than a friendly letter, the business letter is always written according to a standard form on appropriate stationery—plain white paper that is eight and a half by eleven inches in size. The six basic parts of the business letter are the heading, inside address, salutation, body, closing, and signature.

Week 14   The six parts of a business letter conform to standard practice. The heading includes the sender's full address and the date. The inside address gives the receiver's name and address. Below this, we place the salutation, or greeting. Next comes the body written in simple, courteous language. The standard form for the closing is "Yours truly" or "Very truly yours" followed by a comma. We write the signature immediately below the closing and type the sender's name below the signature.

Week 15   A business letter should be easy to read and attractive to the reader at first glance. To frame a letter attractively, we center the letter on the page, leaving equal margins on the sides, top, and bottom. We consistently follow a standard pattern for indentation and punctuation. There are two popular syles: the block style, without paragraph indentations, and the semiblock style, with paragraph indentations. We write a business letter as clearly and concisely as possible without being abrupt.

Week 16   There are four different types of business letters: a letter of inquiry, a letter to an editor or official, a letter of complaint, and a letter of application. We will discuss the first three types in this dictation. A letter of inquiry asks for information or answers to questions. A letter to an editor or official gives critical opinions supported by facts and coupled with suggested changes or improvements. It may also offer objective and sincere compliments. A letter of complaint addresses problems with a product and includes a careful description of the product, its problems, and the buyer's expectations of the company.

Week 17   The fourth type of business letter, the letter of application, makes a request for employment. A well-written letter with a clear and direct approach will give a good impression. The first paragraph identifies the desired job and explains how it was publicized. The second paragraph gives personal information such as age, gender, schooling, and reasons for seeking employment. The third paragraph explains personal qualifications for the job and previous work experience. An optional paragraph might provide the names of people who would be willing to speak with an employer about the applicant. The letter ends with contact information and a request for an interview at the employer's convenience.

Week 18   Below is a sample business letter of inquiry.

124 Magnolia Street
Rancho Bernardo, CO 80532
January 17, 2003

Publications Director
American Council on Exercise
4851 Paramount Drive

San Diego, CA 92123

Dear Director:

I am an eighth-grade student writing a health report latest nutrition pyramid.

I would appreciate any up-to-date information you have on the newest guidelines. I am especially interested in answers to the following questions:

1. What percentage of one's diet should be carbohydrates?
2. What are the best types of cooking oils?
3. How much protein is needed daily?
4. Should one take a multivitamin?
5. How much water should one drink?

Thank you for your assistance.

Sincerely,

Jessica Wu

Week 19   Art, letters, science, and philosophy flourished during the sixteenth century. The Age of Renaissance, as it came to be called, produced such great names as Da Vinci, Michelangelo, Montaigne, Cervantes, Sir Thomas More, Shakespeare, and Spenser. One literary masterpiece from this time period, Spenser's *The Faerie Queene,* is an epic poem featuring fantastic adventures of knights and dragons in Fairy Land. At first glance, *The Faerie Queene* appears difficult to read because of its vocabulary and archaic system of spelling. However, taking the time to become accustomed to Spenser's style proves worthwhile, for it enables one to enjoy the colorful and romantic action, creative imagery, delightful verse, and allegorical undercurrents of the poem.

Week 20   Spenser wrote to Sir Walter Raleigh, explaining his general plan for *The Faerie Queene*. To present a perfect gentleman, Spenser intended to create a historical poem composed of twelve books, each having a hero to demonstrate one of the twelve private virtues. King Arthur, who possesses all of these virtues, adds unity by his presence in each book.

The Fairy Queen, Gloriana, also serves as a unifying element, for she commissions each of the heroes for his particular adventure. Unfortunately, Spenser completed only six books of his grandiose plan. Each book presents one of the following virtues: holiness, temperance, chastity, friendship, justice, and courtesy.

Week 21   Spenser employs a literary device known as allegory to give double meanings to his poem. The plain meaning is clearly expressed, but the second meaning is only subtly suggested. A simple way to create an allegory is to tell a story in which the characters' names are abstract, human qualities. Spenser uses this strategy, although he adds a twist by translating some of the character names into a foreign language. *The Faerie Queene* includes characters named Despair and Penance but also Sansloy (Lawless), Fidess (Faithful), Kirkrapine (Church Robber), and Speranza (Hope). Paying close attention to the meaning of names enables the reader to grasp a deeper, allegorical meaning of the story.

Week 22   The reader must pay close attention to Spenser's literary techniques, for comprehension goes much deeper than the moral allegory. Not only do the characters represent human qualities, but also their adventures reveal the history of mankind. Spenser's characters depict man's conquest and enthrallment by Satan in the Garden of Eden. Their adventures portray Christ's encounter with and defeat of Satan, the purpose of which is to deliver humanity. Biblical scholars recognize the scriptural references and allusions throughout *The Faerie Queene* and have suggested that alternative titles could be "Adam and Eve" or "The History of Man Allegory."

Week 23   In addition to an allegory of human history, Spenser's poem is also an allegory of English history. *The Faerie*

Queene reflects people and events connected with the church in England during the sixteenth century. Catholic leaders such as the Pope, Queen Mary, Mary Queen of Scots, and King Philip II of Spain appear as villains representing deceit, propaganda, falsehood, and pride. Spenser and his contemporary readers viewed the Church of England as the only true church and other religions, especially Roman Catholicism, as heresy. A basic knowledge of history helps the reader to more fully understand Spenser's work.

Week 24 First Part of the Inaugural Address
of President John F. Kennedy
Washington, D.C., January 20, 1961

We observe today not a victory of party but a celebration of freedom—symbolizing an end as well as a beginning—signifying renewal as well as change. For I have sworn before you and Almighty God the same solemn oath our forbears prescribed nearly a century and three-quarters ago.

The world is very different now. For man holds in his mortal hands the power to abolish all forms of human poverty and all forms of human life. And yet the same revolutionary beliefs for which our forebears fought are still at issue around the globe—the belief that the rights of man come not from the generosity of the state but from the hand of God.

Week 25 John F. Kennedy's Inaugural Address ends with these words:

And so, my fellow Americans: ask not what your country can do for you—ask what you can do for your country.

My fellow citizens of the world: ask not what America will do for you, but what together we can do for the freedom of man.

Finally, whether you are citizens of America or citizens of the world, ask of us here the same high standards of strength and sacrifice which we ask of you. With a good conscience our only sure reward, with history the final judge of our deeds, let us go forth to lead the land we love, asking His blessing and His help, but knowing that here on earth God's work must truly be our own.

Week 26

The Road Not Taken
(Robert Frost, 1874–1963)

Two roads diverged in a yellow wood,
And sorry I could not travel both
And be one traveler, long I stood
And looked down one as far as I could
To where it bent in the undergrowth;
Then took the other, as just as fair,
And having perhaps the better claim,
Because it was grassy and wanted wear;
Though as for that the passing there
Had worn them really about the same,
And both that morning equally lay
In leaves no step had trodden black.
Oh, I kept the first for another day!
Yet knowing how way leads on to way,
I doubted if I should ever come back.
I shall be telling this with a sigh
Somewhere ages and ages hence:
Two roads diverged in a wood, and I—
I took the one less traveled by,
And that has made all the difference.

Week 27

The Gettysburg Address
Delivered by Abraham Lincoln
November 19, 1863

Four score and seven years ago our fathers brought forth on this continent, a new nation, conceived in Liberty, and dedicated to the proposition that all men are created equal.

Now we are engaged in a great civil war, testing whether that nation, or any nation so conceived and so dedicated, can long endure. We are met on a great battle-field of that war. We have come to dedicate a portion of that field, as a final resting place for those who here gave their lives that that nation might live. It is altogether fitting and proper that we should do this.

Week 28 (Gettysburg Address continued)

But, in a larger sense, we can not dedicate—we can not consecrate—we can not hallow—this ground. The brave men, living and dead, who struggled here, have consecrated it, far above our poor power to add or detract. The world will little note, not long remember what we say here, but it can never forget what they did here. It is for us the living, rather, to be dedicated here to the unfinished work which they who fought here have thus far so nobly advanced. It is rather for us to be here dedicated to the great task remaining before us—that from these honored dead we take increased devotion to that cause for which they gave the last full measure of devotion—that we here highly resolve that these dead shall not have died in vain—that this nation, under God, shall have a new birth of freedom—and that government of the people, by the people, for the people, shall not perish from the earth.

Week 29

Journal Topics

At the beginning of class on Tuesday, Wednesday, and Thursday, students will spend five minutes writing in their journals. Each entry should be at least three sentences long. The following are suggested topics.

Topic # 1. Write about your favorite vacation, holiday, or trip.

2. Write about a time when you had to compromise on an issue.

3. If you were President of the United States, what changes would you try to make in our country or in the world?

4. Write about two personal liberties that are important to you.

5. Give reasons why people might be afraid of a strong central government.

6. Do you think that politicians should be paid for their service to the people? Explain why or why not.

7. Write about something that you do well.

8. Describe the area where you live. Is it urban? Rural? Mountainous? Desert?

9. Write about a kitchen skill that you would like to acquire.

10. How can you show your gratitude to your parent(s) or guardian for the food and shelter they provide you?

11. Write about a place you would like to explore.

12. Have you ever thought about running for office? Would you like to be a member of Congress? Why or why not?

13. Write about how you can practice hospitality in your home or in your school.

14. Describe a pet that belongs to you or to someone else.

15. Write about the kinds of books that you like to read.

16. Describe someone you know who would make a good Senator or Representative someday.

17. Describe someone you know who would make a good President of the United States.

18. Write about what you like to do in your free time.

19. In your opinion, what is the most difficult job of the President? Why?

20. After learning the many responsibilities of the President, would you like the job? Why or why not?

21. Write about an existing law that you'd like to change or a new law that you'd like to create.

22. In *Poor Richard's Almanac*, Benjamin Franklin wrote, "Love your neighbor; yet don't pull down your hedge." What do you think he meant? Do you agree or disagree? Explain.

23. In *Poor Richard's Almanac*, Benjamin Franklin wrote, "One today is worth two tomorrows." Do you agree? Why or why not?

24. In *Poor Richard's Almanac*, Benjamin Franklin wrote, "Glass, china, and reputation are easily cracked and never well mended." What do you think he meant?

25. Write about the kind(s) of music that you enjoy; explain what makes it enjoyable.

26. Would you like to serve on a jury? Why or why not?

27. Write about a time when you lost or misplaced something.

28. Which season of the year do you enjoy most? Explain.

29. Write about ways in which you could help the elderly or the ill.

30. Write about things you can do to preserve our natural resources and our environment.

31. Write about a national monument you have visited or one you would like to visit.

32. If you were living in America during colonial times, how would your life be different from what it is today?

33. Write about a friend whom you admire.

34. Have you ever planted something and watched it grow? If not, would you like to? Explain.

35. Some colonists wanted the president of the United States to serve for life. What do you think about that?

36. Write about an outdoor activity that you enjoy.

37. Robert Morris was once the wealthiest man in North America, but he sacrificed his entire fortune for the Patriot cause. Write about how you or someone you know has sacrificed something for the sake of others.

38. Write about things you can do to help people who are less fortunate than you.

39. Describe a kind of animal that interests you.

40. Write about a gift you would like to receive.

41. Imagine that you are a sculptor. What kind of sculpture would you like to create? Why?

42. If you had an opportunity to paint a billboard, what would you paint on it? Why?

43. We usually gain wisdom from our life experiences. What have you learned that you could share with someone younger or less experienced than you?

44. Write about a game that you enjoy playing or watching.

45. Describe a potato.

46. Write about how you can improve your physical fitness or your health.

47. From whom would you like to receive a friendly letter? Why?

48. To whom could you write a friendly letter? What might you say in the letter?

49. The founders of our country disagreed on many issues. Yet, they created a government that has withstood the test of time. Write about a time when you disagreed with someone.

50. Can we disagree and still respect one another? Explain why or why not.

51. James Thomas Flexner said, "Washington was more than a military leader; he was the eagle, the standard, the flag, the

living symbol of the cause." Write your own description of George Washington.

52. How do you feel about slavery?

53. Write about how your life would be different if you lived during the time of the Revolutionary War.

54. Have you ever trusted or believed in something without evidence? Write about it.

55. Write about a friendship that you value.

56. Write about a decision that you will have to make in the future.

57. Write about a disagreement that you have had with someone.

58. Alexander Hamilton was mortally wounded in a duel against Aaron Burr. What do you think about dueling?

59. Do you like snow? Explain why or why not.

60. Write a physical description of a friend or relative.

61. Describe your home.

62. How would your life be different if the United States were ruled by a dictator?

63. How would your life be different if you lived in a communist country?

64. It has been said that Charles Cotesworth Pinckney grew to manhood in an atmosphere where privilege was balanced by duty. Write about how your privileges are balanced by duty, or responsibility.

65. The Federalists nicknamed Charles Pinckney "Blackguard Charlie." Have you ever had a nickname? Write about nicknames that you or someone you know has had. Explain, if you can, why these names were used.

66. Have you ever experienced very hot sun, strong wind, heavy rain, snow, or sleet? Write about how weather has affected you or someone you know.

67. Describe the place(s) where you usually do your homework.

68. Write about something funny that makes you laugh.

69. If you could improve the structure of your home or the home of someone you know, explain what you would do to it.

70. Write about a neighbor or someone who lives nearby.

71. Write about your favorite holiday of the year.

72. Describe the perfect vacation.

73. Do you eat healthful foods? Explain how you could improve your nutrition.

74. Do you ever dream at night? Do you ever daydream? Describe a memorable dream.

75. Write about a book you've read that you think others ought to read also.

76. Write about a musical or artistic talent that you would like to acquire someday.

77. Some bugs are pests. Have you ever been bothered by a pesky bug? Explain.

78. Exercise is important for a healthy body. How do you exercise?

79. Some people like spinach; others don't. Everyone has different tastes in food. Write about a food that you dislike.

80. Some people like to camp outdoors; others don't. How do you feel about camping?

81. Would you like to walk on the moon someday? Explain why or why not.

82. Have you ever taken a sea voyage? Write about it. If you have never taken a sea voyage, would you like to someday? Explain why or why not.

83. Describe a tomato.

84. Some people like snakes; others don't. How do you feel about snakes?

85. Write about your favorite school subject.

86. Write about your least favorite school subject.

87. Cicero once said, "Friendship can exist only where men harmonize in their views of things human and divine." Do you agree? Explain.

88. James M. Barrie said, "Life is a long lesson in humility." What do you think he meant? Do you agree? Why or why not?

89. In a speech before the Senate on June 3, 1834, Daniel Webster said, "God grants liberty only to those who love it, and are always ready to guard and defend it." Write about what you can do to guard and defend liberty in your country.

90. Ralph Waldo Emerson said, "Life is a series of surprises." Do you agree? Explain.

91. An Irish proverb says, "A little nest is warmer than a big nest." What does this proverb mean to you? Do you agree?

92. A Latin proverb says, "The patient conquer." Write about a time when you or someone you know exercised patience.

93. In *The Faerie Queene*, Edmund Spenser wrote, "The noblest mind the best contentment has." Why is contentment important? Do you have contentment? Explain.

94. Abraham Lincoln said, "The only assurance of our Nation's safety is to lay our foundation in morality and religion." Do you agree? Why or why not?

95. Naomi has a pet rock. Write about some advantages of having a pet rock.

96. Write about some disadvantages of having a pet rock.

97. If you could plant a tree today, what kind would you plant? Why?

98. If you could plant a garden today, what would you plant in it? Why?

99. Some people prefer to wake up early in the morning; others prefer to sleep late. Which do you prefer? Why?

100. If you were to paint a picture today, what would you paint? Describe it.

Index

A

A, an, the (articles), 140
Abbreviations, 182
Aberrant, 652
Abrogate, 626
Acquisitive, 633
Action verb, 16–18
Active voice, 158
Addresses, 244–247
-ade, 594
Ad hoc, 411
Ad hominem, 411
Adjective(s), defined, 134
   a, an, the, 140
   adverb, confusion with, 496
   clarity, 263
   comparison, 231–233
      irregular, 238–240
   compound adjective, 134
      with hyphens, 507
   demonstrative, 140
   descriptive, 134–136
   diagramming, 140, 171, 226, 269, 326, 345
   indefinite, 141
   modified by adverb, 532
   over-used, 263
   possessive noun or pronoun, as, 326
   predicate adjective, 226–229
   prepositional phrase, as, 170–172
   pronoun, confusion with, 324
   proper, 134–137
   superlative, 231–233
      irregular, 248–240
Advent, 226
Adverb(s), defined, 495–498
   adding suffixes to form, 495, 496
   comparison, 537–540
   conjunctive, 545
   descriptive, 550
   diagramming, 570–574, 581–587, 600
   distinguished from adjectives, 496
   double negatives, 482–486
   negatives, 482
   position of, 525
   preposition or adverb, 575
   superlative, 537–540
   telling how, 495
      how much, 530
      when, 525
      where, 514
   usage, 550–555
   using *well*, 501–503
Advert, 9
Affectation, 29
Affection, 29
Affidavit, 450
Agenda, 521
Agitate, 521
Agreement, subject-verb, 457–480
Aid, 594
Aide, 594
Alleviate, 140
Alliteration, 557
All ready, 244
All right, 244
Allusion, 153
Already, 244
Altogether, 244
Amare, 70
Ambi-, 363
Ambidextrous, 363
Ambient, 363
Ambiguous, 63
Ambivalent, 63. 363
Amendment, 146
Amiable, 70
Amicable, 70
Among, 576
Amphi-, 363
And (conjunction), 196, 363
Antebellum, 16
Antecedent, defined, 276
   agreement with pronoun, 276, 392
Any one, 292
Anyone, 292
Any way, 263
Anyway, 263
Apollonian, 324
Apostrophe, 588–592, 594–598
   contractions, 594
   omitted digits or letters, 594–598

plurals of letters, numbers, and words, 594–598
possessives, 588–592
Appeal, 550
Appease, 36
Appelate, 134
Apportion, 134
Appositive, 256–259
Approbation, 112
Appropriation, 134
Aristocracy, 207
Arrogate, 626
Articles (*a, an, the*), 140, 263
As, 569
Ascent, 525
Assent, 525
Assonance, 557
Auxiliary verb, 36–38
Avert, 9

B
Bacchanalian, 324
Bad or *Badly*, 550
Be, 70
Being verb, defined, 70
Bell-, 16
Bellicose, 16
Between, 575
Biannual, 331
Bicameral, 22
Biennial, 331
Bona fide, 618
Bootleg, 537
Both—and (correlative conjunctions), 207
Brackets, 640–644
Bureaucrat, 207
But (conjunction), 196, 363

C
Can, 80
Capitalization, 51–56, 129–133, 146–150
abbreviations and initials, 182
areas of country, 146
family words, 129
first words of direct quotation, 51
first word of sentence, 9, 51
first word in line of poetry, 51
greetings and closings, 146
hyphenated words, 489
I, 51
literary and music titles, 51
outlines, 51
proper adjectives 134

proper nouns, 22
religions, Bible, deity, 146
rules for, 22, 51, 129, 146
seasons of the year, 146
school subjects, 129
titles of persons (family words), 129
Carnivorous, 422
Carpe diem, 618
Case, 219, 305, 311, 324
nominative, 219, 305
nominative pronoun, 305
objective, 219, 311
objective pronoun, 311
personal pronoun, 318
possessive, 318
Cataclysm, 575
Catacomb, 575
Catapult, 575
Caucus, 58
Caveat emptor, 618
Ced, cess, 658
Censor, 106
Censure, 106
Census, 75
Centipede, 669
Certain or *certainly*, 550
Cicerone, 164
Clarity, 283–289
Clause, 117, 331, 357, 376, 385
dependent, 331, 357, 376, 385
independent, 331
subordinate, 331
Collective noun, 22–24
Colloquy, 686
Colon, 557–561
Comma, 244–248, 256–260, 283–291, 357–361, 370–374, 385–390
after introductory words, 283–291
after dependent clauses, 357–361
and appositives, 256–260
and interjections, 283–291
before conjunction, 370–374
in compound sentence, 370–374
in dates, 244–248
in direct address, 256–260
in direct quotation, 370–374
in letter, 283
in series, 244
in titles or academic degrees, 256
reversed names, 283
separating descriptive adjectives, 357
words in a series, 244
words out of natural order, 283

Common, 45
Common noun, 22, 40
Comparative degree, 231, 537
Comparison adjectives, 231, 537
Comparison adverbs, 537
Comparisons using pronouns, 392–396
Complement, 640
Complete sentence, 9
Complex sentence, 611
Compose, 276
Compound adjective, 507
Compound forms, hyphen in, 489–509
Compound nouns, forming plurals, 63
Compound parts of sentence, 201
    diagramming, 201–205
    subject and verbs, 201–205
Compound personal pronouns, 392
Compound relative pronouns, 376
Compound sentence, 363, 370
    diagramming, 363
Compound subject, with singular or plural verb, 457
Compound word, division of, 489
Comprise, 276
Conciseness, sentence, 626
Concrete noun, 22
Concurrent, 457
Condolence, 674
Conducive, 299
Conjecture, 269
Conjunction(s), defined, 196, 207
    coordinating, 196
    correlative, 207
    in compound parts of a sentence, 201
    in compound sentence, 363
    subordinating, 331
        list of, 331, 544–548
Conjunctive adverb, 544
Connote, 476
Conscience, 190
Conscientious, 190
Conscious, 190
Consciousness, 190
Consequential, 311
Consonance, 557
Constituent, 501
Consul, 99
Contemptible, 88
Contemptuous, 88
Contraction(s), 594
    apostrophe in, 594
    list of common, 594
    subject-verb agreement with, 476

    verb, a part of, 594
Coordinating conjunction(s), 196, 363
    list of, 196
Correlative conjunction(s), 207–210
    list of, 207
Credere, 435
Credence, 435
Credulity, 435
Crim-, 93
Currere, 457
Cursory, 457

D

Dangling Modifier, 633–638
Dash, 450
Dates, punctuation in, 244
Declarative sentence, 2
Deduction, 299
Delphic, 337
Delusion, 153
Democracy, 207
Demonstrative adjective, 417
Demonstrative pronoun, 417
Denote, 476
Dependent clause, 331, 357
Deplete, 640
Descriptive adjective, 134
Descriptive adverb, 550
Diagramming
    adjective phrases, 170
    adjectives, 140
    adverb phrases, 569
    adverbs, 514
    appositives, 251
    compound parts of a sentence, 201–205
    compound sentence, 363–366
    conjunctions, 363, 611
    dependent clauses, 376
    direct objects, 123
    gerund phrases, 349
    indirect objects, 176
    infinitive phrases, 581
    objects of prepositions, 164
    participle phrases, 344
    predicate adjectives, 226
    predicate nominatives, 212
    prepositional phrases, 164
    pronouns, 324
    steps in, 16, 123, 176, 201, 212, 226, 324, 344, 363, 376, 569, 581, 605, 611
    verbs and subjects, 16
    you understood, 16
Dictionary information, 652

Dionysian, 337
Direct address, 256
Direct democracy, 2
Direct object, 123
    defined, 123
        diagramming, 123
        pronoun as, 311, 392
Direct Quotation, 370
Disinterested, 318
Dissonant, 646
Dole, 674
Doleful, 674
Dollars and cents, decimal in, 182
Dolorous, 674
Double comparisons (avoiding), 238
Double negatives (avoiding), 482
Dys-, 611
Dysfunction, 611
Dyslexia, 611
Dyspepsia, 611

E
e.g., 123
Either—or (correlative conjunction), 207, 618
Eminent domain, 514
Emphasis (dash), 450
Enacting clause, 514
End punctuation, 2, 182, 450
Envelop, 305
Envelope, 305
Ep-, 376
Ephemeral, 376
Epi-, 376
Epidermis, 376
Err, 652
Errare, 652
Erratic, 652
Erroneous, 652
Essential appositives, 256
et al., 201
etc., 201
Eu-, 605
Eulogy, 605
Euphoria, 605
Euthanasia, 605
Every one, 292
Everyone, 292
Exclamation mark, 2, 450
Exclamatory sentence, 2, 450
Explicit, 231
Ex post facto, 117

F
Family words, 129
Faze, 176
Felicitous, 219
Fides, 450
Fiduciary, 450
Figuratively, 445
Filibuster, 170
Finale, 256
Finite, 256
Flair, 344
Flare, 344
Flaunt, 489
Flectere, 469
Flexor, 469
Flout, 489
Foreign words and phrases, 429
Fortuitous, 219
Fractions, hyphens in, 489
Fragment, sentence, 9
    defined, 9
    correcting, 9
Future perfect tense, 88
Future perfect progressive tense, 99
Future progressive tense, 99
Future tense, 45

G
Genuflect, 469
Gerrymandering, 501
Gerund(s), 93, 337, 344
Good or *well*, 501
Gravid, 158
Gravitate, 158
Gravity, 158
Greeting, in a letter, 283
Grisly, 417
Grizzly, 417

H
Hector, 164
Hedonism, 182
Helping verb(s), 36
Herbivorous, 422
Hospice, 51
Hung jury, 170
Hyphen(s), 489, 507, 519
    in compound nouns, 489
    in fractions, 507
    in numbers, 507
    in word division, 519

I
i.e., 123

I, me, 292, 305, 311
Illusion, 153
Impeachment, 22
Impede, 669
Imperative Sentence, 2
Implicit, 231
Improving our writing, 16, 134, 263
Incriminate, 93
Incumbent, 581
Indefinite adjective, 140
Indefinite pronoun, 422
Independent clause, 331
Indirect democracy, 2
Indirect object 176
    defined, 176
        diagramming, 176–180
        recognizing, 176–180
Indirect quotation, 406
Infinitive(s), 112, 269, 581
Inhospitable, 51
Initials, 146, 182
Inquisition, 633
Intensive pronoun, 350
Interjection, 646
Interrogate, 626
Interrogative pronoun, 398
Interrogative sentence, 2, 398, 450
Interrupting elements, 283
Interruptions (dash), 450
Intervene, 226
Intractable, 283
Intransitive verb, 153
Introductory elements, 283
Introductory *there*, 476
    subject-verb agreement with, 476
Irregular plural noun(s), 58, 63
    defined, 58
    forms, 58, 63
    rules for forming, 58, 63
Irregular verbs, 70, 299, 435, 440, 445
    be, have, do, 70
    defined, 70, 299
Italics, 429

J
Jovial, 350
Judicial, 129
Judicious, 129
Jurisdiction, 129

L
Last name first, 283
Later, 507

Latter, 507
Levity, 140
Libel, 357
Lightening, 429
Lightning, 429
Like, 569
Limp, 463
Limpid, 463
Linking verb(s), 106, 212, 226
Literally, 445
Lobby, 75
Loath, 406
Loathe, 406
Loqu, 686
Loquacious, 686

M
Malevolent, 563
Malodorous, 563
May, 80
Mercurial, 350
Misplaced modifiers, 633
Modifier(s), defined, 134, 495
    adjective as, 134, 140, 170, 226, 231, 238
    adverb as, 482, 495, 501, 514, 528, 530,
        537, 550, 569, 581, 600
Modus operandi, 398
Modus vivendi, 398
Mood, subjunctive, 658
Mutual, 45

N
Negatives, 482
    avoiding double, 482
    in contractions, 482
Neither (conjunction), 207
Neither—nor (correlative conjunction), 207
Nestor, 182
No and *yes*, comma after, 283
Noisome, 440
Noisy, 440
Nominative case, 219, 305, 318
Nominative of address (direct address), 256
Nominative pronoun, 305, 318
Nor (conjunction), 207
Not (adverb), 482, 495
Not only—but also (correlative conjunction),
    207
Noun(s), defined, 22
    abstract, 22
    adding suffixes to form, 58, 63
    as antecedents, 276
    as appositives, 256

clause, 605
collective, 22
common, 22
compound, 40
concrete, 22
diagramming, 16, 123, 164, 170, 176, 201, 219, 250, 324, 344, 363, 376, 600, 605
direct address, 256
direct object, 123
forming plurals of, 58–61, 63–68
gender, 40–43
indirect object, 176
kinds of, 22–27, 40–44
modifiers, 134, 140, 170, 226, 238
neuter gender, 40–44
number, 318
object of preposition, 164
possessive, 40
as adjective, 140
predicate nominative, 212
proper, 22
singular, 40
special, 476

O
Object(s), 123, 164, 176, 311
compound, 201
diagramming, 201
direct, 123
diagramming, 123–127
indirect, 176–180
of preposition, 164–168
correct use of pronouns as, 311
diagramming, 324–329
Objective case, 219, 311, 318
pronouns in, 311, 318
Odyssey, 495
Or, (conjunction), 196, 363
Outline, 51, 182
Capitalization in, 51
Punctuation in, 182
Over-used adjectives, 263

P
Pac-, 36
Pacifist, 36
Parallel structure, 618
Parentheses, 640–644
Participle(s), 269, 344
Passive voice, 158
Past participle, 75, 299, 435, 440, 445
Past tense, 29, 75, 299, 435, 440, 445

Pause (comma), 244, 256, 283, 357, 370, 385
Peas-, 36
Ped, 669
Pedicure, 669
Pedometer, 669
Penelope, 495
Perceptible, 238
Perfect tense, 88–91
Period, 182–188
in outlines, 182
rules for use of, 192–188
Person, 292, 318
Personal pronoun case forms, 318
singular, 318
list of, 318
plural, 318
Phase, 176
Phrase, 117, 164, 170, 337, 344, 569, 581
diagramming, 170, 344, 569, 581
Ple, 640
Plural(s), formation of, 58–61, 63–68
Plutocrat, 207
Pocket veto, 117
Point of view, 457
Positive degree, 231, 537
Possessive adjective, 324
Possessive noun, 40
diagramming, 140
Possessive pronoun, 324
distinguishing from contractions, 324
Post-, 482
Posterior, 482
Posthumus, 482
Precedent, 658
Predicate, 2, 16, 201, 363
compound, 201
diagramming, 16, 201, 363
simple, 2
split, 2, 16, 457
Predicate adjective, 226
compound, 226
diagramming, 226
Predicate nominative, 212
compound, 212
diagramming, 212
noun as, 212
pronoun as, 305
Premier, 544
Premiere, 544
Preposition(s), 80–86, 164, 170, 569
list of, 80
simple, 80
object of, 164

(understood) with indirect object, 176
Prepositional phrase, 164
   as an adjective, 170
   as an adverb, 569
   between subject and verb, 463
   diagramming, 170, 569
   indirect object, 176
Present participle, 75
Present tense, 29
Prim-, 385
Primal, 385
Primogeniture, 385
Principal parts of verbs, 75
   list of troublesome, 70, 299, 435, 440, 445
Prob-, 112
Probity, 112
Procession, 658
Procrustean, 519
Progressive tense, 99
Prohibition, 537
Prone, 392
Pronoun(s), defined, 276, 292
   antecedent of, 276
   apposition, 392–396
   as a subject, 305
   as an adjective, 324
   as an object, 311
   case, 318
   compound personal, 392
   demonstrative, 417
   diagramming, 324–329
   I, 51–56, 292, 305, 318
   indefinite, 422–427
   intensive, 350–355
   interrogative, 398–404
   nominative case, 305–309
   number, 292, 318
   objective case, 311
   person, 292, 318
   personal, 292
   possessive, 324
   reflexive, 350
   relative, 376
   use of *who* and *whom*, 376–383
Proofreading, 190, 563
Proper adjective, 134–138
   capitalization of, 134–138
Proper noun(s), 22
   abstract, 22
   capitalization of, 22
Protean, 519
Pro tempore, 40
Proto-, 588

Protocol, 588
Protoplasm, 588
Prototype, 588
Punctuation
   apostrophe, 588–592, 594–598
   brackets, 640–644
   colon, 557–561
   comma, 244, 256, 283, 357, 370, 385
   dash, 450
   exclamation mark, 450
   hyphen, 489–493, 519–521
   italics or underline, 429–433
   parentheses, 640–644
   period, 182–188
   of appositives, 256–261
   of dialogue, 370–374
   of letters, 283–290
   of outlines, 182
   of sentence, 2, 9, 182, 244, 256, 357, 370, 385, 406, 411, 429, 450, 544, 557, 640
   question mark, 450
   quotation mark, 406, 411
   semi-colon, 544
   underline or italics, 429

Q
Question mark, 450–455
Quis, 633
Quorum, 58
Quotation, direct, 51, 370–374
Quotation, indirect, 370–374
Quotation marks, 406–409, 411–414

R
Real or *really*, 550
Recession, 658
Recrimination, 93
Rectify, 600
Rectitude, 600
Rectus, 600
Recumbent, 581
Reflexive pronoun, 350–355
Relative pronoun, 376–383
Regular verb, 29–34, 75
Religions, capitalization of, 146, 147
Renames the subject, 212
Repeal, 550
Replete, 640
Requisition, 633
Retraction, 283
Retro-, 681
Retrograde, 681

Retrogress, 681
Retrospect, 681
Rog, 626
Run-on sentence, 9–14
    correcting, 9–14

S
Salutation of letter (colon after), 557–561
Seasons of the year, 146
Semi-colon, 544–548
Sentence, defined, 2, 9
    capitalization of first word of, 51
    complex, 376, 611–616
    compound, 370
    declarative, 2
    diagramming, 16–20, 123–127, 140–144, 170–174, 176, 201, 226, 324, 344, 376
    exclamatory, 2–7
    fragment, 9–14
    imperative, 2–7
    interrogative, 2–7
    punctuation of, 2–7, 9–14, 182–188, 190, 244, 256, 283, 357, 370, 385, 450, 544, 557, 563, 640
    run-on, 9–14
    simple, 363
Sequence, 311
Series, commas in, 244–248
Silent letters, 664–667, 669–672
Simple predicate, 2–7
Simple sentence, 363
Simple preposition, 80
Simple subject, 2–7
Singular, 40, 292, 318
Slander, 357
Soliloquy, 686
Sonata, 646
Sonorous, 646
Spartan, 196
Spelling 58–61, 63–68, 664–668, 669–672
    adding suffixes, 674, 681
        to words ending in consonants, 681
        to words ending in silent *e*, 674
        to words ending in *y*, 674
    adjectives and adverbs, 495, 496
    guidelines, 58–61, 63–68, 664–689
    plural forms, 58–61, 63–68
    possessives, 588–592
    words with *ie* and *ei*, 686–690
    words with silent letters, 664–668, 669–672
Split predicate, 2–7

State of the Union Message, 99
Stentorian, 196
Stoic, 212
Subject of a sentence, 2–7, 93–97, 112–115, 305
    agreement with verb, 457–461, 463–467
    complete, 9–14
    compound, 201–205
    diagramming, 16–20, 93–97, 112–115, 201–205
    of imperative and interrogative sentences, 2, 9
    pronoun as, 305–309
    simple, 2
    understood, 16–20
Subject-verb agreement, 457–461, 463–467
Subjunctive, 658
Subordinating conjunction, 331–335
Succumb, 581
Suffixes, 674–684
Suffrage, 146
Superlative degree, 231–236, 537–542
Supine, 392
Sure and *surely*, 550–556
Susceptible, 238
Sybaritic, 212
Symbols, proofreading, 190–194, 563–567

T
That or *which*, 385–390
Titles, 51, 129, 411
Tortuous, 370
Torturous, 370
Trajectory, 269
Transitive verb, 153–156
Troublesome verbs, 70, 299, 435, 440, 445

U
Underline or italics, 429–433
Uninterested, 318

V
Verb(s), defined, 16, 29, 36, 75, 88, 99
    action, 16–20
    active voice, 158–162
    agreement with subject, 457–467
    being, 36, 70, 99
    compound, 201–205
    diagramming, 16–20, 201–205
    helping (auxiliary), 36–39
        list of, 36
    in contractions, 594–598
    irregular, 70, 299, 435, 440, 445
    linking, 106–110

    passive voice, 158–162
    principal parts of, 75–78
    regular, 29–34, 75–78
    tense, 29, 45, 88, 99
    transitive, 153–156
Verbal(s), 93, 112, 269, 337, 344
Verbatim, 664
Verbiage, 664
Verbose, 664
Verbum, 664
Vivid words, 16–20, 134–138, 269–274
Vorare, 422

W
Warrant, 530
Well and *good*, 501–505
Which or *that*, 385–390
Who and *whom*, 376–383
Writ, 530
Writ of habeas corpus, 40

Y
Yes and *no*, comma after, 283–290
You understood, 16–20